CRAFTING AND EXECUTING STRATEGY

The Quest for Competitive Advantage

Concepts | 23RD EDITION

Arthur A. Thompson
The University of Alabama

Margaret A. Peteraf
Dartmouth College

John E. Gamble
Texas A&M University—Corpus Christi

A.J. Strickland III
The University of Alabama

McGraw Hill

CRAFTING & EXECUTING STRATEGY: CONCEPTS

1 2 3 4 5 6 7 8 9 LWI 24 23 22 21

ISBN 978-1-264-37059-7
MHID 1-264-37059-8

Cover Image: *Image Source/Getty Images*

mheducation.com/highered

To our families and especially our spouses:
Hasseline, Paul, Heather, and Kitty.

About the Authors

Courtesy of Arthur A. Thompson, Jr.

Arthur A. Thompson, Jr., earned his BS and PhD degrees in economics from The University of Tennessee, spent three years on the economics faculty at Virginia Tech, and served on the faculty of The University of Alabama's College of Commerce and Business Administration for 24 years. In 1974 and again in 1982, Dr. Thompson spent semester-long sabbaticals as a visiting scholar at the Harvard Business School.

His areas of specialization are business strategy, competition and market analysis, and the economics of business enterprises. In addition to publishing over 30 articles in some 25 different professional and trade publications, he has authored or co-authored five textbooks and six computer-based simulation exercises. His textbooks and strategy simulations have been used at well over 1,000 college and university campuses worldwide.

Dr. Thompson and his wife of 58 years have two daughters, two grandchildren, and a Yorkshire Terrier.

Courtesy of Margaret A. Peteraf

Margaret A. Peteraf is the Leon E. Williams Professor of Management Emerita at the Tuck School of Business at Dartmouth College. She is an internationally recognized scholar of strategic management, with a long list of publications in top management journals. She has earned myriad honors and prizes for her contributions, including the 1999 Strategic Management Society Best Paper Award recognizing the deep influence of her work on the field of Strategic Management. Professor Peteraf is a fellow of the Strategic Management Society and the Academy of Management. She served previously as a member of the Board of Governors of both the Society and the Academy of Management and as Chair of the Business Policy and Strategy Division of the Academy. She has also served in various editorial roles and on numerous editorial boards, including the *Strategic Management Journal,* the *Academy of Management Review,* and *Organization Science.* She has taught in Executive Education programs in various programs around the world and has won teaching awards at the MBA and Executive level.

Professor Peteraf earned her PhD, MA, and MPhil at Yale University and held previous faculty appointments at Northwestern University's Kellogg Graduate School of Management and at the University of Minnesota's Carlson School of Management.

John E. Gamble is a Professor of Management and Dean of the College of Business at Texas A&M University–Corpus Christi. His teaching and research for 25 years has focused on strategic management at the undergraduate and graduate levels. He has conducted courses in strategic management in Germany since 2001, which have been sponsored by the University of Applied Sciences in Worms.

Courtesy of Richard's Photography, LLC.

Dr. Gamble's research has been published in various scholarly journals and he is the author or co-author of more than 75 case studies published in an assortment of strategic management and strategic marketing texts. He has done consulting on industry and market analysis for clients in a diverse mix of industries.

Professor Gamble received his PhD, MA, and BS degrees from The University of Alabama and was a faculty member in the Mitchell College of Business at the University of South Alabama before his appointment to the faculty at Texas A&M University–Corpus Christi.

Dr. A. J. (Lonnie) Strickland is the Thomas R. Miller Professor of Strategic Management at the Culverhouse School of Business at The University of Alabama. He is a native of north Georgia, and attended the University of Georgia, where he received a BS degree in math and physics; Georgia Institute of Technology, where he received an MS in industrial management; and Georgia State University, where he received his PhD in business administration.

Courtesy of Dr. A. J. (Lonnie) Strickland

Lonnie's experience in consulting and executive development is in the strategic management arena, with a concentration in industry and competitive analysis. He has developed strategic planning systems for numerous firms all over the world. He served as Director of Marketing and Strategy at BellSouth, has taken two companies to the New York Stock Exchange, is one of the founders and directors of American Equity Investment Life Holding (AEL), and serves on numerous boards of directors. He is a very popular speaker in the area of strategic management.

Lonnie and his wife, Kitty, have been married for over 49 years. They have two children and two grandchildren. Each summer, Lonnie and his wife live on their private game reserve in South Africa where they enjoy taking their friends on safaris.

Preface

By offering the most engaging, clearly articulated, and conceptually sound text on strategic management, *Crafting and Executing Strategy* has been able to maintain its position as the leading textbook in strategic management for over 35 years. With this latest edition, we build on this strong foundation, maintaining the attributes of the book that have long made it the most teachable text on the market, while updating the content, sharpening its presentation, and providing enlightening new illustrations and examples.

The distinguishing mark of the 23rd edition is its enriched and enlivened presentation of the material in each of the 12 chapters, providing an as up-to-date and engrossing discussion of the core concepts and analytical tools as you will find anywhere.

While this 23rd edition retains the 12-chapter structure of the prior edition, every chapter—indeed every paragraph and every line—has been reexamined, refined, and refreshed. New content has been added to keep the material in line with the latest developments in the theory and practice of strategic management. In other areas, coverage has been trimmed to keep the book at a more manageable size. Scores of new examples have been added, along with many new Illustration Capsules, to enrich understanding of the content and to provide students with a ringside view of strategy in action. The result is a text that cuts straight to the chase in terms of what students really need to know and gives instructors a leg up on teaching that material effectively. It remains, as always, solidly mainstream and balanced, mirroring *both* the penetrating insight of academic thought and the pragmatism of real-world strategic management.

For some years now, growing numbers of strategy instructors at business schools worldwide have been transitioning from a purely text-case course structure to a more robust and energizing text-case-simulation course structure. Incorporating a competition-based strategy simulation has the strong appeal of providing class members with *an immediate and engaging opportunity to apply the concepts and analytical tools covered in the chapters and to become personally involved in crafting and executing a strategy for a virtual company that they have been assigned to manage and that competes head-to-head with companies run by other class members.* Two widely used and pedagogically effective online strategy simulations, *The Business Strategy Game* and *GLO-BUS,* are optional companions for this text. Both simulations were created by Arthur Thompson, one of the text authors, and are closely linked to the content of each chapter in the text. The Exercises for Simulation Participants, found at the end of each chapter and integrated into the Connect package for the text, provide clear guidance to class members in applying the concepts and analytical tools covered in the chapters to the issues and decisions that they have to wrestle with in managing their simulation company.

To assist instructors in assessing student achievement of program learning objectives, in line with AACSB requirements, the 23rd edition includes a set of Assurance of Learning Exercises at the end of each chapter that link to the specific learning objectives appearing at the beginning of each chapter and highlighted throughout the text. An important instructional feature of the 23rd edition is its more closely *integrated* linkage of selected chapter-end Assurance of Learning Exercises and cases to Connect™. Your students will be able to use Connect™ to (1) complete chapter-specific activities, including selected Assurance of Learning Exercises appearing at the end of each of the 12 chapters, as well as video and comprehension cases, (2) complete chapter-end quizzes, (3) complete suggested assignment questions for 14 of the 27 cases in this edition and (4) complete assignment questions for simulation users. All Connect exercises are automatically graded, (with the exception of select Exercises for Simulation Participants) thereby enabling you to easily assess the learning that has occurred.

In addition, both of the companion strategy simulations have a built-in Learning Assurance Report that quantifies how well each member of your class performed on nine skills/learning measures *versus tens of thousands of other students worldwide* who completed the simulation in the past 12 months. We believe the chapter-end Assurance of Learning Exercises, the all-new online and automatically graded Connect™ exercises, and the Learning Assurance Report generated at the conclusion of *The Business Strategy Game* and *GLO-BUS* simulations provide you with easy-to-use, empirical measures of student learning in your course. All can be used in conjunction with other instructor-developed or school-developed scoring rubrics and assessment tools to comprehensively evaluate course or program learning outcomes and measure compliance with AACSB accreditation standards.

Taken together, the various components of the 23rd edition package and the supporting set of instructor resources provide you with enormous course design flexibility and a powerful kit of teaching/learning tools. We've done our very best to ensure that the elements constituting the 23rd edition will work well for you in the classroom, help you economize on the time needed to be well prepared for each class, and cause students to conclude that your course is one of the very best they have ever taken—from the standpoint of both enjoyment and learning.

DIFFERENTIATING FEATURES OF THE 23RD EDITION

Eight standout features strongly differentiate this text and the accompanying instructional package from others in the field:

1. *We provide the clearest discussion of business models to be found anywhere.* By introducing this often-misunderstood concept right in the first chapter and defining it precisely, we give students a leg up on grasping this important concept. Follow-on discussions in the next eight chapters drive the concept home. Illustration capsules show how a new business model can enable a company to compete successfully even against well-established rivals. In some cases, a new business model can even be the agent for disrupting an existing industry.

2. *Our integrated coverage of the two most popular perspectives on strategic management— positioning theory and resource-based theory—is unsurpassed by any other leading strategy text.* Principles and concepts from both the positioning perspective and the resource-based perspective are prominently and comprehensively integrated into our coverage of crafting both single-business and multibusiness strategies. By highlighting the relationship between a firm's resources and capabilities to the activities it conducts along its value chain, we show explicitly how these two perspectives relate to one another. Moreover, in Chapters 3 through 8 it is emphasized repeatedly that a company's strategy must be matched *not only* to its external market circumstances *but also* to its internal resources and competitive capabilities.

3. *With this new edition, we provide the clearest, easiest to understand presentation of the value-price-cost framework.* In recent years, this framework has become an essential

aid to teaching students how companies create economic value in the course of conducting business. We show how this simple framework informs the concept of the business model as well as the all-important concept of competitive advantage. In Chapter 5, we add further clarity by showing in pictorial fashion how the value-price-cost framework relates to the different sources of competitive advantage that underlie the five generic strategies.

4. *Our coverage of cooperative strategies and the role that interorganizational activity can play in the pursuit of competitive advantage is similarly distinguished.* The topics of the value net, ecosystems, strategic alliances, licensing, joint ventures, and other types of collaborative relationships are featured prominently in a number of chapters and are integrated into other material throughout the text. We show how strategies of this nature can contribute to the success of single-business companies as well as multibusiness enterprises, whether with respect to firms operating in domestic markets or those operating in the international realm.

5. *The attention we give to international strategies, in all their dimensions, make this textbook an indispensable aid to understanding strategy formulation and execution in an increasingly connected, global world.* Our treatment of this topic as one of the most critical elements of the *scope* of a company's activities brings home to students the connection between the topic of international strategy with other topics concerning firm scope, such as multibusiness (or corporate) strategy, outsourcing, insourcing, and vertical integration.

6. *With a standalone chapter devoted to these topics, our coverage of business ethics, corporate social responsibility, and environmental sustainability goes well beyond that offered by any other leading strategy text.* Chapter 9, "Ethics, Corporate Social Responsibility, Environmental Sustainability, and Strategy," fulfills the important functions of (1) alerting students to the role and importance of ethical and socially responsible decision making and (2) addressing the accreditation requirement of the AACSB International that business ethics be visibly and thoroughly embedded in the core curriculum. Moreover, discussions of the roles of values and ethics are integrated into portions of other chapters, beginning with the first chapter, to further reinforce why and how considerations relating to ethics, values, social responsibility, and sustainability should figure prominently into the managerial task of crafting and executing company strategies.

7. *The text is now optimized for hybrid and online delivery through robust assignment and assessment content integrated into Connect™.* This will enable professors to gauge class members' prowess in accurately completing (a) additional exercises and selected chapter-end exercises, (b) chapter-end quizzes, (c) exercises for simulation participants, and (d) exercises for 14 of the cases in this edition.

8. *Two cutting-edge and widely used strategy simulations—The Business Strategy Game and GLO-BUS—are optional companions to the 23rd edition.* These give you an unmatched capability to employ a text-case-simulation model of course delivery.

ORGANIZATION, CONTENT, AND FEATURES OF THE 23RD-EDITION TEXT CHAPTERS

- Chapter 1 serves as a brief, general introduction to the topic of strategy, focusing on the central questions of *"What is strategy?"* and *"Why is it important?"* As such, it serves as the perfect accompaniment for your opening-day lecture on what the course is all about and why it matters. Using the example of Apple, Inc., to drive home the concepts in this chapter, we introduce students to what we mean by "competitive advantage" and the key features of business-level strategy. Describing strategy making as a process, we explain why a company's strategy is partly planned and partly reactive and why a strategy tends to co-evolve with its environment over time. As part of this strategy making process, we discuss the importance of ethics in choosing among strategic alternatives. We introduce the concept of a business model and offer a clear definition along with an illustration capsule that provides examples from the real world of business. We explain why a viable business model must provide both an attractive value proposition for the company's customers and a formula for making profits for the company. A key feature of this chapter is a depiction of how the value-price-cost framework can be used to frame this discussion. We show how the mark of a winning strategy is its ability to pass three tests: (1) the *fit test* (for internal and external fit), (2) the *competitive advantage test,* and (3) the *performance test.* And we explain why good company performance depends not only upon a sound strategy but upon solid strategy execution as well.

- Chapter 2 presents a more complete overview of the strategic management process, covering topics ranging from the role of vision, mission, and values to what constitutes good corporate governance. It makes a great assignment for the second day of class and provides a smooth transition into the heart of the course. It introduces students to such core concepts as strategic versus financial objectives, the balanced scorecard, strategic intent, and business-level versus corporate-level strategies. It explains why *all managers are on a company's strategy-making, strategy-executing team* and why a company's strategic plan is a collection of strategies devised by different managers at different levels in the organizational hierarchy. The chapter concludes with a section on the role of the board of directors in the strategy-making, strategy-executing process and examines the conditions that have led to recent high-profile corporate governance failures. The illustration capsule on Volkswagen's emissions scandal brings this section to life.

- The next two chapters introduce students to the two most fundamental perspectives on strategy making: the positioning view, exemplified by Michael Porter's classic "five forces model of competition," and the resource-based view. Chapter 3 provides *what has long been the clearest, most straightforward discussion of the five forces framework to be found in any text on strategic management.* It also offers a set of complementary analytical tools for conducting competitor analysis, identifying strategic groups along with the mobility barriers that limit movement among them, and demonstrates the importance of tailoring strategy to fit the circumstances of a company's industry and competitive environment. The chapter includes a discussion of the value net framework, which is useful for conducting analysis of how cooperative as well as competitive moves by various parties contribute to the creation and capture of value in an industry.

- Chapter 4 presents the resource-based view of the firm, showing why resource and capability analysis is such a powerful tool for sizing up a company's competitive assets. It offers a simple framework for identifying a company's resources and capabilities and explains how the VRIN framework can be used to determine whether they can provide the company with a sustainable competitive advantage over its competitors. Other topics covered in this chapter include dynamic capabilities, SWOT analysis, value chain analysis, benchmarking, and competitive strength assessments, thus enabling a solid appraisal of a company's cost position and customer value proposition vis-á-vis its rivals. *An important feature of this chapter is a table showing how key financial and operating ratios are calculated and how to interpret them.* Students will find this table handy in doing the number crunching needed to evaluate whether a company's strategy is delivering good financial performance.

- Chapter 5 sets forth the basic approaches available for competing and winning in the marketplace in terms of the five generic competitive strategies— broad low-cost, broad differentiation, best-cost, focused differentiation, and focused low cost. It demonstrates pictorially the link between generic strategies, the value-price-cost framework, and competitive advantage. The chapter also describes when each of the five approaches works best and what pitfalls to avoid. Additionally, it explains the role of *cost drivers* and *uniqueness drivers* in reducing a company's costs and enhancing its differentiation, respectively.

- Chapter 6 focuses on *other strategic actions* a company can take to complement its competitive approach and maximize the power of its overall strategy. These include a variety of offensive or defensive competitive moves, and their timing, such as blue-ocean strategies and first-mover advantages and disadvantages. It also includes choices concerning the breadth of a company's activities (or its *scope* of operations along an industry's entire value chain), ranging from horizontal mergers and acquisitions, to vertical integration, outsourcing, and strategic alliances. This material serves to segue into the scope issues covered in the next two chapters on international and diversification strategies.

- Chapter 7 takes up the topic of how to compete in international markets. It begins with a discussion of why differing market conditions across countries must necessarily influence a company's strategic choices about how to enter and compete in foreign markets. It presents five major strategic options for expanding a company's geographic scope and competing in foreign markets: export strategies, licensing, franchising, establishing a wholly owned subsidiary via acquisition or "greenfield" venture, and alliance strategies. It includes coverage of topics such as Porter's Diamond of National Competitive Advantage, multi-market competition, and the choice between multidomestic, global, and transnational strategies. This chapter explains the impetus for sharing, transferring, or accessing valuable resources and capabilities across national borders in the quest for competitive advantage, connecting the material to that on the resource-based view from Chapter 4. The chapter concludes with a discussion of the unique characteristics of competing in developing-country markets.

- Chapter 8 concerns strategy making in the multibusiness company, introducing the topic of corporate-level strategy with its special focus on diversification. The first portion of this chapter describes when and why diversification makes good strategic sense, the different means of diversifying a company's business lineup, and the pros and cons of related versus unrelated diversification strategies. The second part of the chapter looks at how to evaluate the attractiveness of a diversified company's business lineup, how to decide whether it has a good diversification strategy, and what strategic options are available for improving a diversified company's future performance. The evaluative technique integrates material concerning both industry analysis and the resource-based view, in that it considers the relative attractiveness of the various industries the company has diversified into, the company's competitive strength in each of its lines of business, and the extent to which its different businesses exhibit both *strategic fit* and *resource fit*.

- Although the topic of ethics and values comes up at various points in this textbook, Chapter 9 brings more direct attention to such issues and may be used as a stand-alone assignment in either the early, middle, or late part of a course. It concerns the themes of ethical standards in business, approaches to ensuring consistent ethical standards for companies with international operations, corporate social responsibility, and environmental sustainability. The contents of this chapter are sure to give students some things to ponder, rouse lively discussion, and help to make students more *ethically aware* and conscious of *why all companies should conduct their business in a socially responsible and sustainable manner.*

- The next three chapters (Chapters 10, 11, and 12) comprise a module on strategy execution that is presented in terms of a 10-step action framework. Chapter 10 provides an overview of this framework and then explores the first three of these tasks: (1) *staffing the organization* with people capable of executing the strategy well, (2) *building the organizational capabilities* needed for successful strategy execution, and (3) *creating an organizational structure* supportive of the strategy execution process.

- Chapter 11 discusses five additional managerial actions that advance the cause of good strategy execution: (1) *allocating resources* to enable the strategy execution process, (2) ensuring that *policies and procedures* facilitate rather than impede strategy execution, (3) using *process management tools* and *best practices* to drive continuous improvement in the performance of value chain activities, (4) installing *information and operating systems* that help company personnel carry out their strategic roles, and (5) using *rewards and incentives* to encourage good strategy execution and the achievement of performance targets.

- Chapter 12 completes the 10-step framework with a consideration of the importance of *creating a healthy* corporate *culture* and *exercising effective leadership* in promoting good strategy execution. The recurring theme throughout the final three chapters is that executing strategy involves deciding on the specific actions, behaviors, and conditions needed for a smooth strategy-supportive operation and then following through to get things done and deliver results. The goal here is to ensure that students understand that the strategy-executing phase is a *make-things-happen and make-them-happen-right* kind of managerial exercise—one that is critical for achieving operating excellence and reaching the goal of strong company performance.

In this latest edition, we have put our utmost effort into ensuring that the 12 chapters are consistent with the latest and best thinking of academics and practitioners in the field of strategic management and provide the topical coverage required for both undergraduate and MBA-level strategy courses. The ultimate test of the text, of course, is the positive pedagogical impact it has in the classroom. If this edition sets a more effective stage for your lectures and does a better job of helping you persuade students that the discipline of strategy merits their rapt attention, then it will have fulfilled its purpose.

THE TWO STRATEGY SIMULATION SUPPLEMENTS: *THE BUSINESS STRATEGY GAME* AND *GLO-BUS*

The Business Strategy Game and *GLO-BUS: Developing Winning Competitive Strategies*—two competition-based strategy simulations that are delivered online and that feature automated processing and grading of performance—are being marketed by the publisher as companion supplements for use with the 23rd edition (and other texts in the field).

- *The Business Strategy Game* is the world's most popular strategy simulation, having been used by nearly 3,600 different instructors for courses involving close to one million students at 1,300 university campuses in 76 countries. It features global competition in the athletic footwear industry, a product/market setting familiar to students everywhere and one whose managerial challenges are easily grasped. A freshly updated and much-enhanced version of *The Business Strategy Game* was introduced in August 2018.

- *GLO-BUS,* a newer and somewhat simpler strategy simulation first introduced in 2004 and freshly revamped in 2016 to center on competition in two exciting product categories—wearable miniature action cameras and unmanned camera-equipped drones suitable for multiple commercial purposes, has been used by 2,100 different instructors for courses involving nearly 360,000 students at 800+ university campuses in 53 countries.

How the Strategy Simulations Work

In both *The Business Strategy Game (BSG)* and *GLO-BUS,* class members are divided into teams of one to five persons and assigned to run a company that competes head-to-head against companies run by other class members. In both simulations, companies compete in a global market arena, selling their products in four geographic regions—Europe-Africa, North America, Asia-Pacific, and Latin America. Each management team is called upon to craft a strategy for their company and make decisions relating to production operations, workforce compensation, pricing and marketing, social responsibility/citizenship, and finance.

Company co-managers are held accountable for their decision making. Each company's performance is scored on the basis of earnings per share, return-on-equity investment, stock price, credit rating, and image rating. Rankings of company performance, along with a wealth of industry and company statistics, are available to company co-managers after each decision round to use in making strategy adjustments and operating decisions for the next competitive round. You can be certain that the market environment, strategic issues, and operating challenges that company co-managers must contend with are *very tightly linked* to what your class members will be reading about in the text chapters. The circumstances that co-managers face in running their simulation company embrace the very concepts, analytical tools, and strategy options they encounter in the text chapters (this is something you can quickly confirm by skimming through some of the Exercises for Simulation Participants that appear at the end of each chapter).

We suggest that you schedule one or two practice rounds and anywhere from four to 10 regular (scored) decision rounds (more rounds are better than fewer rounds). Each decision round represents a year of company operations and will entail roughly two hours of time for company co-managers to complete. In traditional 13-week, semester-long courses, there is merit in scheduling one decision round per week. In courses that run five to 10 weeks, it is wise to schedule two decision rounds per week for the last several weeks of the term (sample course schedules are provided for courses of varying length and varying numbers of class meetings).

When the instructor-specified deadline for a decision round arrives, the simulation server automatically accesses the saved decision entries of each company, determines the competitiveness and buyer appeal of each company's product offering relative to the other companies being run by students in your class, and then awards sales and market shares to the competing companies, geographic region by geographic region. The unit sales volumes awarded to each company *are totally governed by*

- How its prices compare against the prices of rival brands.
- How its product quality compares against the quality of rival brands.

- How its product line breadth and selection compare.
- How its advertising effort compares.
- And so on, for a total of 11 competitive factors that determine unit sales and market shares.

The competitiveness and overall buyer appeal of each company's product offering *in comparison to the product offerings of rival companies* is all-decisive—this algorithmic feature is what makes *BSG* and *GLO-BUS* "competition-based" strategy simulations. Once each company's sales and market shares are awarded based on the competitiveness and buyer appeal of its respective overall product offering vis-à-vis those of rival companies, the various company and industry reports detailing the outcomes of the decision round are then generated. Company co-managers can access the results of the decision round 15 to 20 minutes after the decision deadline.

The Compelling Case for Incorporating Use of a Strategy Simulation

There are *three exceptionally important benefits* associated with using a competition-based simulation in strategy courses taken by seniors and MBA students:

- *A three-pronged text-case-simulation course model delivers significantly more teaching-learning power than the traditional text-case model.* Using *both* cases and a strategy simulation to drill students in thinking strategically and applying what they read in the text chapters is a stronger, more effective means of helping them connect theory with practice and develop better business judgment. What cases do that a simulation cannot is give class members broad exposure to a variety of companies and industry situations and insight into the kinds of strategy-related problems managers face. But what a competition-based strategy simulation does far better than case analysis is thrust class members squarely into *an active, hands-on managerial role* where they are totally responsible for assessing market conditions, determining how to respond to the actions of competitors, forging a long-term direction and strategy for their company, and making all kinds of operating decisions. Because they are held fully accountable for their decisions and their company's performance, *co-managers are strongly motivated* to dig deeply into company operations, probe for ways to be more cost-efficient and competitive, and ferret out strategic moves and decisions calculated to boost company performance. *Consequently, incorporating both case assignments and a strategy simulation to develop the skills of class members in thinking strategically and applying the concepts and tools of strategic analysis turns out to be more pedagogically powerful than relying solely on case assignments—there's stronger retention of the lessons learned and better achievement of course learning objectives.*

    To provide you with quantitative evidence of the learning that occurs with using *The Business Strategy Game* or *GLO-BUS,* there is a built-in Learning Assurance Report showing how well each class member performs on nine skills/learning measures versus tens of thousands of students worldwide who have completed the simulation in the past 12 months.

- *The competitive nature of a strategy simulation arouses positive energy and steps up the whole tempo of the course by a notch or two.* Nothing sparks class excitement quicker or better than the concerted efforts on the part of class members at each decision round to achieve a high industry ranking and avoid the perilous consequences of being outcompeted by other class members. Students really enjoy taking on the role of a manager, running their own company, crafting strategies, making all kinds of operating decisions, trying to outcompete rival companies, and getting immediate feedback on the resulting company performance. Lots of back-and-forth chatter occurs when the results of the latest simulation round become available and co-managers renew their quest for strategic moves and actions that will strengthen company performance. Co-managers become *emotionally invested* in running their company and figuring out what strategic moves to make to boost their company's performance. Interest levels climb. All this stimulates learning and causes students to see the practical relevance of the subject matter and the benefits of taking your course.

As soon as your students start to say, "Wow! Not only is this fun but I am learning a lot," *which they will,* you have won the battle of engaging students in the subject matter and moved the value of taking your course to a much higher plateau in the business school curriculum. This translates into *a livelier, richer learning experience from a student perspective and better instructor-course evaluations.*

- *Use of a fully automated online simulation reduces the time instructors spend on course preparation, course administration, and grading.* Since the simulation exercise involves a 20- to 30-hour workload for student teams (roughly two hours per decision round times 10 to 12 rounds, plus optional assignments), simulation adopters often compensate by trimming the number of assigned cases from, say, 10 to 12 to perhaps 4 to 6. This significantly reduces the time instructors spend reading cases, studying teaching notes, and otherwise getting ready to lead class discussion of a case or grade oral team presentations. Course preparation time is further cut because you can use several class days to have students bring their laptops to class or meet in a computer lab to work on upcoming decision rounds or a three-year strategic plan (in lieu of lecturing on a chapter or covering an additional assigned case). Not only does use of a simulation permit assigning fewer cases, but it also permits you to eliminate at least one assignment that entails considerable grading on your part. Grading one less written case or essay exam or other written assignment saves enormous time. With *BSG* and *GLO-BUS,* grading is effortless and takes only minutes; once you enter percentage weights for each assignment in your online grade book, a suggested overall grade is calculated for you. You'll be pleasantly surprised—and quite pleased—at how little time it takes to gear up for and administer *The Business Strategy Game* or *GLO-BUS.*

In sum, incorporating use of a strategy simulation turns out to be *a win-win proposition for both students and instructors.* Moreover, a very convincing argument can be made that a competition-based strategy simulation is *the single most effective teaching/learning tool that instructors can employ to teach the discipline of business and competitive strategy, to make learning more enjoyable, and to promote better achievement of course learning objectives.*

A Bird's-Eye View of *The Business Strategy Game*

The setting for *The Business Strategy Game (BSG)* is the global athletic footwear industry (there can be little doubt in today's world that a globally competitive strategy simulation is *vastly superior* to a simulation with a domestic-only setting). Global market demand for footwear grows at the rate of seven to nine percent annually for the first five years and five to seven percent annually for the second five years. However, market growth rates vary by geographic region—North America, Latin America, Europe-Africa, and Asia-Pacific.

Companies begin the simulation producing branded and private-label footwear in two plants, one in North America and one in Asia. They have the option to establish production facilities in Latin America and Europe-Africa. Company co-managers exercise control over production costs on the basis of the styling and quality they opt to manufacture, plant location (wages and incentive compensation vary from region to region), the use of best practices and Six Sigma programs to reduce the production of defective footwear and to boost worker productivity, and compensation practices.

All newly produced footwear is shipped in bulk containers to one of four geographic distribution centers. All sales in a geographic region are made from footwear inventories in that region's distribution center. Costs at the four regional distribution centers are a function of inventory storage costs, packing and shipping fees, import tariffs paid on incoming pairs shipped from foreign plants, and exchange rate impacts. At the start of the simulation, import tariffs average $4 per pair in North America, $6 in Europe-Africa, $8 per pair in Latin America, and $10 in the Asia-Pacific region. Instructors have the option to alter tariffs as the game progresses.

Companies market their brand of athletic footwear to footwear retailers worldwide and to individuals buying online at the company's website. Each company's sales and market share in the branded footwear segments hinge on its competitiveness on 13 factors: attractive pricing, footwear styling and quality, product line breadth, advertising, use of mail-in rebates, appeal of celebrities endorsing a company's brand, success in convincing footwear retailers to carry its brand, number of weeks it takes to fill retailer orders, effectiveness of a company's online sales effort at its website, and brand reputation. Sales of private-label footwear hinge solely on being the low-price bidder.

All told, company co-managers make as many as 57 types of decisions each period that cut across production operations (up to 11 decisions per plant, with a maximum of four plants), the addition of facility space, equipment, and production improvement options (up to eight decisions per plant), worker compensation and training (up to six decisions per plant), shipping and distribution center operations (five decisions per geographic region), pricing and marketing (up to nine decisions in four geographic regions), bids to sign celebrities (two decision entries per bid), financing of company operations (up to eight decisions), and corporate social responsibility and environmental sustainability (up to eight decisions). Plus, there are 10 entries for each region pertaining to assumptions about the upcoming-year actions and competitive efforts of rival companies that factor directly into the forecasts of a company's unit sales, revenues, and market share in each of the four geographic regions.

Each time company co-managers make a decision entry, an assortment of on-screen calculations instantly shows the projected effects on unit sales, revenues, market shares, unit costs, profit, earnings per share, ROE, and other operating statistics. The on-screen calculations help team members evaluate the relative merits of one decision entry versus another and put together a promising strategy.

Companies can employ any of the five generic competitive strategy options in selling branded footwear—low-cost leadership, differentiation, best-cost provider, focused low cost, and focused differentiation. They can pursue essentially the same strategy worldwide or craft slightly or very different strategies for the Europe-Africa, Asia-Pacific, Latin America, and North America markets. They can strive for competitive advantage based on more advertising, a wider selection of models, more appealing styling/quality, bigger rebates, and so on.

Any well-conceived, well-executed competitive approach is capable of succeeding, provided it is not overpowered by the strategies of competitors or defeated by the presence of too many copycat strategies that dilute its effectiveness. The challenge for each company's management team is to craft and execute a competitive strategy that produces good performance on five measures: earnings per share, return on equity investment, stock price appreciation, credit rating, and brand image.

All activity for *The Business Strategy Game* takes place at **www.bsg-online.com**.

A Bird's-Eye View of *GLO-BUS*

In *GLO-BUS,* class members run companies that are in a neck-and-neck race for global market leadership in two product categories: (1) wearable video cameras smaller than a teacup that deliver stunning video quality and have powerful photo capture capabilities (comparable to those designed and marketed by global industry leader GoPro and numerous others) and (2) sophisticated camera-equipped copter drones that incorporate a company designed and assembled action-capture camera and that are sold to commercial enterprises for prices in the $850 to 2,000+ range. Global market demand for action cameras grows at the rate of six to eight percent annually for the first five years and four to six percent annually for the second five years. Global market demand for commercial drones grows briskly at rates averaging 18 percent for the first two years, then gradually slows over eight years to a rate of four to six percent.

Companies assemble action cameras and drones of varying designs and performance capabilities at a Taiwan facility and ship finished goods directly to buyers in North America, Asia-Pacific, Europe-Africa, and Latin America. Both products are assembled usually within two weeks of being received and are then shipped to buyers no later than two to three days after assembly. Companies maintain no finished goods inventories and all parts and components are delivered by suppliers on a just-in-time basis (which eliminates the need to track inventories and simplifies the accounting for plant operations and costs).

Company co-managers determine the quality and performance features of the cameras and drones being assembled. They impact production costs by raising/lowering specifications for parts/components and expenditures for product R&D, adjusting work force compensation, spending more/less on worker training and productivity improvement, lengthening/shortening warranties offered (which affects warranty costs), and how cost-efficiently they manage assembly operations. They have options to manage/control selling and certain other costs as well.

Each decision round, company co-managers make some 50 types of decisions relating to the design and performance of the company's two products (21 decisions, 10 for cameras and 11 for drones), assembly operations and workforce compensation (up to eight decision entries for each product), pricing and marketing (seven decisions for cameras and five for drones), corporate social responsibility and citizenship (up to six decisions), and the financing of company operations (up to eight decisions). In addition, there are 10 entries for cameras and seven entries for drones involving assumptions about the competitive actions of rivals; these entries help company co-managers to make more accurate forecasts of their company's unit sales (so they have a good idea of how many cameras and drones will need to be assembled each year to fill customer orders). Each time co-managers make a decision entry, an assortment of on-screen calculations instantly shows the projected effects on unit sales, revenues, market shares, total profit, earnings per share, ROE, costs, and other operating outcomes. All of these on-screen calculations help co-managers evaluate the relative merits of one decision entry versus another. Company managers can try out as many different decision combinations as they wish in stitching the separate decision entries into a cohesive whole that is projected to produce good company performance.

Competition in action cameras revolves around 11 factors that determine each company's unit sales/market share:

1. How each company's average wholesale price to retailers compares against the all-company average wholesale prices being charged in each geographic region.

2. How each company's camera performance and quality compares against industry-wide camera performance/quality.

3. How the number of week-long sales promotion campaigns a company has in each region compares against the regional average number of weekly promotions.

4. How the size of each company's discounts off the regular wholesale prices during sales promotion campaigns compares against the regional average promotional discount.

5. How each company's annual advertising expenditures compare against regional average advertising expenditures.

6. How the number of models in each company's camera line compares against the industry-wide average number of models.

7. The number of retailers stocking and merchandising a company's brand in each region.

8. Annual expenditures to support the merchandising efforts of retailers stocking a company's brand in each region.

9. The amount by which a company's expenditures for ongoing improvement and updating of its company's website in a region is above/below the all-company regional average expenditure.

10. How the length of each company's camera warranties compare against the warranty periods of rival companies.

11. How well a company's brand image/reputation compares against the brand images/reputations of rival companies.

Competition among rival makers of commercial copter drones is more narrowly focused on just nine sales-determining factors:

1. How a company's average retail price for drones at the company's website in each region compares against the all-company regional average website price.

2. How each company's drone performance and quality compares against the all-company average drone performance/quality.

3. How the number of models in each company's drone line compares against the industry-wide average number of models.

4. How each company's annual expenditures to recruit/support third-party online electronics retailers in merchandising its brand of drones in each region compares against the regional average.

5. The amount by which a company's price discount to third-party online retailers is above/below the regional average discounted price.

6. How well a company's expenditures for search engine advertising in a region compares against the regional average.

7. How well a company's expenditures for ongoing improvement and updating of its website in a region compares against the regional average.

8. How the length of each company's drone warranties in a region compares against the regional average warranty period.

9. How well a company's brand image/reputation compares against the brand images/reputations of rival companies.

Each company typically seeks to enhance its performance and build competitive advantage via its own custom-tailored competitive strategy based on more attractive pricing, greater advertising, a wider selection of models, more appealing performance/quality, longer warranties, a better image/reputation, and so on. The greater the differences in the overall competitiveness of the product offerings of rival companies, the bigger the differences in their resulting sales volumes and market shares. Conversely, the smaller the overall competitive differences in the product offerings of rival companies, the smaller the differences in sales volumes and market shares. This algorithmic approach is what makes *GLO-BUS* a "competition-based" strategy simulation and accounts for why *the sales and market share outcomes for each decision round are always unique to the particular strategies and decision combinations employed by the competing companies.*

As with *BSG, all the various generic competitive strategy options*—low-cost leadership, differentiation, best-cost provider, focused low-cost, and focused differentiation—*are viable choices for pursuing competitive advantage and good company performance.* A company can have a strategy aimed at being the clear market leader in either action cameras or drones or both. It can focus its competitive efforts on one or two or three geographic regions or strive to build strong market positions in all four geographic regions. It can pursue essentially the same strategy worldwide or craft customized strategies for the Europe-Africa, Asia-Pacific, Latin America, and North America markets. Just as with *The Business Strategy Game, most any well-conceived, well-executed competitive approach is capable of succeeding, provided it is not overpowered by the strategies of competitors or defeated by the presence of too many copycat strategies that dilute its effectiveness.*

The challenge for each company's management team is to craft and execute a competitive strategy that produces good performance on five measures: earnings per share, return on equity investment, stock price appreciation, credit rating, and brand image.

All activity for *GLO-BUS* occurs at **www.glo-bus.com**.

Special Note: The time required of company co-managers to complete each decision round in *GLO-BUS* is typically about 15 to 30 minutes less than for *The Business Strategy Game* because

(a) there are only 8 market segments (versus 12 in *BSG*),

(b) co-managers have only one assembly site to operate (versus potentially as many as four plants in *BSG,* one in each geographic region), and

(c) newly assembled cameras and drones are shipped directly to buyers, eliminating the need to manage finished goods inventories and operate distribution centers.

Administration and Operating Features of the Two Simulations

The Internet delivery and user-friendly designs of both *BSG* and *GLO-BUS* make them incredibly easy to administer, even for first-time users. And the menus and controls are so similar that you can readily switch between the two simulations or use one in your undergraduate class and the other in a graduate class. If you have not yet used either of the two simulations, you may find the following of particular interest:

• Setting up the simulation for your course is done online and takes about 10 to 15 minutes. Once setup is completed, no other administrative actions are required beyond those of moving participants to a different team (should the need arise) and monitoring the progress of the simulation (to whatever extent desired).

- Participant's Guides are delivered electronically to class members at the website—students can read the guide on their monitors or print out a copy, as they prefer.

- There are two to four minute Video Tutorials scattered throughout the software (including each decision screen and each page of each report) that provide on-demand guidance to class members who may be uncertain about how to proceed.

- Complementing the Video Tutorials are detailed and clearly written Help sections explaining "all there is to know" about (a) each decision entry and the relevant cause-effect relationships, (b) the information on each page of the Industry Reports, and (c) the numbers presented in the Company Reports. *The Video Tutorials and the Help screens allow company co-managers to figure things out for themselves, thereby curbing the need for students to ask the instructor "how things work."*

- Team members running the same company who are logged in simultaneously on different computers at different locations can click a button to enter Collaboration Mode, enabling them to work collaboratively from the same screen in viewing reports and making decision entries, and click a second button to enter Audio Mode, letting them talk to one another and hold an online meeting.

  ○ When in "Collaboration Mode," each team member sees the same screen at the same time as all other team members who are logged in and have joined Collaboration Mode. If one team member chooses to view a particular decision screen, that same screen appears on the monitors for all team members in Collaboration Mode.

  ○ Each team member controls their own color-coded mouse pointer (with their first-name appearing in a color-coded box linked to their mouse pointer) and can make a decision entry or move the mouse to point to particular on-screen items.

  ○ A decision entry change made by one team member is seen by all, in real time, and all team members can immediately view the on-screen calculations that result from the new decision entry.

  ○ If one team member wishes to view a report page and clicks on the menu link to the desired report, that same report page will immediately appear for the other team members engaged in collaboration.

  ○ Use of Audio Mode capability requires that each team member work from a computer with a built-in microphone (if they want to be heard by their team members) and speakers (so they may hear their teammates) or else have a headset with a microphone that they can plug into their desktop or laptop. A headset is recommended for best results, but most laptops now are equipped with a built-in microphone and speakers that will support use of our new voice chat feature.

  ○ Real-time VoIP audio chat capability among team members who have entered both the Audio Mode and the Collaboration Mode is a tremendous boost in functionality that enables team members to go online simultaneously on computers at different locations and conveniently and effectively collaborate in running their simulation company.

  ○ In addition, instructors have the capability to join the online session of any company and speak with team members, thus circumventing the need for team members to arrange for and attend a meeting in the instructor's office. Using the standard menu for administering a particular industry, instructors can connect with the company desirous of assistance. Instructors who wish not only to talk but also to enter Collaboration (highly recommended because all attendees are then viewing the same screen) have a red-colored mouse pointer linked to a red box labeled Instructor.

Without a doubt, the Collaboration and Voice-Chat capabilities are hugely valuable for students enrolled in online and distance-learning courses where meeting face-to-face is impractical or time-consuming. Likewise, the instructors of online and distance-learning courses will appreciate having the capability to join the online meetings of particular company teams when their advice or assistance is requested.

- Both simulations work equally well for online courses and in-person classes.
- Participants and instructors are notified via e-mail when the results are ready (usually about 15 to 20 minutes after the decision round deadline specified by the instructor/game administrator).
- Following each decision round, participants are provided with a complete set of reports—a six-page Industry Report, a Competitive Intelligence report for each geographic region that includes strategic group maps and a set of Company Reports (income statement, balance sheet, cash flow statement, and assorted production, marketing, and cost statistics).
- Two "open-book" multiple-choice tests of 20 questions are built into each simulation. The quizzes, which you can require or not as you see fit, are taken online and automatically graded, with scores reported instantaneously to participants and automatically recorded in the instructor's electronic grade book. Students are automatically provided with three sample questions for each test.
- Both simulations contain a three-year strategic plan option that you can assign. Scores on the plan are automatically recorded in the instructor's online grade book.
- At the end of the simulation, you can have students complete online peer evaluations (again, the scores are automatically recorded in your online grade book).
- Both simulations have a Company Presentation feature that enables each team of company co-managers to easily prepare PowerPoint slides for use in describing their strategy and summarizing their company's performance in a presentation to either the class, the instructor, or an "outside" board of directors.
- *A Learning Assurance Report provides you with hard data concerning how well your students performed vis-à-vis students playing the simulation worldwide over the past 12 months.* The report is based on nine measures of student proficiency, business know-how, and decision-making skill and can also be used in evaluating the extent to which your school's academic curriculum produces the desired degree of student learning insofar as accreditation standards are concerned.

For more details on either simulation, please consult Section 2 of the Instructor's Manual accompanying this text or register as an instructor at the simulation websites (www.bsg-online.com and www.glo-bus.com) to access even more comprehensive information. You should also consider signing up for one of the webinars that the simulation authors conduct several times each month (sometimes several times weekly) to demonstrate how the software works, walk you through the various features and menu options, and answer any questions. You have an open invitation to call the senior author of this text at (205) 722-9145 to arrange a personal demonstration or talk about how one of the simulations might work in one of your courses. We think you'll be quite impressed with the cutting-edge capabilities that have been programmed into *The Business Strategy Game* and *GLO-BUS,* the simplicity with which both simulations can be administered, and their exceptionally tight connection to the text chapters, core concepts, and standard analytical tools.

RESOURCES AND SUPPORT MATERIALS FOR THE 23RD EDITION

For Students

Key Points Summaries   At the end of each chapter is a synopsis of the core concepts, analytical tools, and other key points discussed in the chapter. These chapter-end synopses, along with the core concept definitions and margin notes scattered throughout each chapter, help students focus on basic strategy principles, digest the messages of each chapter, and prepare for tests.

Two Sets of Chapter-End Exercises   Each chapter concludes with two sets of exercises. The *Assurance of Learning Exercises* are useful for helping students prepare for class discussion and to gauge their understanding of the material. The *Exercises for Simulation Participants* are designed expressly for use in class which incorporate the use of a simulation. These exercises explicitly connect the chapter content to the simulation company the students are running. Even if they are not assigned by the instructor, they can provide helpful practice for students as a study aid.

Connect™   The 23rd edition takes full advantage of Connect™, a personalized teaching and learning tool. The Connect™ package for this edition includes several robust and valuable features that simplify the task of assigning and grading three types of exercises for students:

- Autograded chapter quizzes that students can take to measure their grasp of the material presented in each of the 12 chapters.
- A variety of interactive exercises for each of the 12 chapters that drill students in the use and application of the concepts and tools of strategic analysis, including selected Assurance of Learning Exercises and newly integrated Exercises for Simulation Participants.
- Case Exercises for 14 of the 27 cases in this edition that require students to work through answers to a select number of the assignment questions for the case. These exercises have multiple components and are tailored to match the circumstances presented in each case, calling upon students to do whatever strategic thinking and strategic analysis are called for to arrive at pragmatic, analysis-based action recommendations for improving company performance.

All Connect™ exercises are automatically graded, (with the exception of a few select Exercises for Simulation Participants that entail answers in the form of short essays) thereby simplifying the task of evaluating each class member's performance and monitoring the learning outcomes. The progress-tracking function built into Connect™ enables you to

- View scored work immediately and track individual or group performance with assignment and grade reports.
- Access an instant view of student or class performance relative to learning objectives.
- Collect data and generate reports required by many accreditation organizations, such as AACSB International.

SmartBook 2.0®   SmartBook 2.0 is the first and only adaptive reading experience designed to change the way students read and learn. It creates a personalized reading experience by highlighting the most impactful concepts a student needs to learn at that moment in time. As a student engages with SmartBook, the reading experience continuously adapts by highlighting content based on what the student knows and doesn't know. This ensures that the focus is on the content he or she needs to learn, while simultaneously promoting long-term retention of material. Use SmartBook's real-time reports to quickly identify the concepts that require more attention from individual students–or the entire class. The end result? Students are more engaged with course content, can better prioritize their time, and come to class ready to participate.

For Instructors

Assurance of Learning Aids   Each chapter begins with a set of Learning Objectives, which are tied directly to the material in the text meant to address these objectives with helpful signposts. At the conclusion of each chapter, there is a set of *Assurance of Learning Exercises* that can be used as the basis for class discussion, oral presentation assignments, short written reports, and substitutes for case assignments. Similarly, there is a set of *Exercises for Simulation Participants* that are designed expressly for use by adopters who have incorporated use of a simulation and want to go a step further in tightly and explicitly connecting the chapter content to the simulation company their students are running. New to this edition is the incorporation of these assignable Exercises for Simulation Participants within Connect. The questions in both sets of exercises (along with those Illustration Capsules that qualify as "mini-cases") can be used to round out the rest of a 75-minute class period should your lecture on a chapter last for only 50 minutes.

Instructor Library   The Connect Instructor Library is your repository for additional resources to improve student engagement in and out of class. You can select and use any asset that enhances your lecture.

Instructor's Manual   The accompanying IM contains:

- A section on suggestions for organizing and structuring your course.
- Sample syllabi and course outlines.
- A set of lecture notes on each chapter.
- Answers to the chapter-end Assurance of Learning Exercises.
- A test bank for all 12 chapters.
- A comprehensive case teaching note for each of the 27 cases. These teaching notes are filled with suggestions for using the case effectively, have very thorough, analysis-based answers to the suggested assignment questions for the case, and contain an epilogue detailing any important developments since the case was written.

Test Builder   The accompanying Test Bank, which contains over 900 multiple choice and short answer/essay questions, is available in Connect™ via Test Builder.

Test Builder is a cloud-based tool that enables instructors to format tests that can be printed or administered within an LMS. Test Builder offers a modern, streamlined interface for easy content configuration that matches course needs, without requiring a download. Test Builder provides a secure interface for better protection of content and allows for just-in-time updates to flow directly into assessments.

PowerPoint Slides   To facilitate delivery preparation of your lectures and to serve as chapter outlines, you'll have access to approximately 500 colorful and professional-looking slides displaying core concepts, analytical procedures, key points, and all the figures in the text chapters.

CREATE™   is McGraw-Hill's custom-publishing program where you can access full-length readings and cases that accompany *Crafting and Executing Strategy: The Quest for a Competitive Advantage* (http://create.mheducation.com/thompson). Through Create™, you will be able to select from 30 readings that go specifically with this text-book. These include cases and readings from Harvard, MIT, and much more! You can assemble your own course and select the chapters, cases, and readings that work best for you. Also, you can choose from several ready-to-go, author-recommended complete course solutions. Among the pre-loaded solutions, you'll find options for undergrad, MBA, accelerated, and other strategy courses.

The Business Strategy Game and *GLO-BUS Online Simulations*   Using one of the two companion simulations is a powerful and constructive way of emotionally connecting students to the subject matter of the course. We know of no more effective way to arouse the competitive energy of students and prepare them for the challenges of real-world business decision making than to have them match strategic wits with class-mates in running a company in head-to-head competition for global market leadership.

ACKNOWLEDGMENTS

We heartily acknowledge the contributions of the case researchers whose case-writing efforts appear herein and the companies whose cooperation made the cases possible. To each one goes a very special thank-you. We cannot overstate the importance of timely, carefully researched cases in contributing to a substantive study of strategic management issues and practices.

A great number of colleagues and students at various universities, business acquaintances, and people at McGraw-Hill provided inspiration, encouragement, and counsel during the course of this project. Like all text authors in the strategy field, we are intellectually indebted to the many academics whose research and writing have blazed new trails and advanced the discipline of strategic management. In addition, we'd like to thank the following reviewers who provided seasoned advice and splendid suggestions over the years for improving the chapters:

Robert B. Baden, Edward Desmarais, Stephen F. Hallam, Joy Karriker, Wendell Seaborne, Joan H. Bailar, David Blair, Jane Boyland, William J. Donoher, Stephen A. Drew, Jo Anne Duffy, Alan Ellstrand, Susan Fox-Wolfgramm, Rebecca M. Guidice, Mark Hoelscher, Sean D. Jasso, Xin Liang, Paul Mallette, Dan Marlin, Raza Mir, Mansour Moussavi, James D. Spina, Monica A. Zimmerman, Dennis R. Balch, Jeffrey R. Bruehl, Edith C. Busija, Donald A. Drost, Randall Harris, Mark Lewis Hoelscher, Phyllis Holland, James W. Kroeger, Sal Kukalis, Brian W. Kulik, Paul Mallette, Anthony U. Martinez, Lee Pickler, Sabine Reddy, Thomas D. Schramko, V. Seshan, Charles Strain, Sabine Turnley, S. Stephen Vitucci, Andrew Ward, Sibin Wu, Lynne Patten, Nancy E. Landrum, Jim Goes, Jon Kalinowski, Rodney M. Walter, Judith D. Powell, Seyda Deligonul, David

Flanagan, Esmerlda Garbi, Mohsin Habib, Kim Hester, Jeffrey E. McGee, Diana J. Wong, F. William Brown, Anthony F. Chelte, Gregory G. Dess, Alan B. Eisner, John George, Carle M. Hunt, Theresa Marron-Grodsky, Sarah Marsh, Joshua D. Martin, William L. Moore, Donald Neubaum, George M. Puia, Amit Shah, Lois M. Shelton, Mark Weber, Steve Barndt, J. Michael Geringer, Ming-Fang Li, Richard Stackman, Stephen Tallman, Gerardo R. Ungson, James Boulgarides, Betty Diener, Daniel F. Jennings, David Kuhn, Kathryn Martell, Wilbur Mouton, Bobby Vaught, Tuck Bounds, Lee Burk, Ralph Catalanello, William Crittenden, Vince Luchsinger, Stan Mendenhall, John Moore, Will Mulvaney, Sandra Richard, Ralph Roberts, Thomas Turk, Gordon Von Stroh, Fred Zimmerman, S. A. Billion, Charles Byles, Gerald L. Geisler, Rose Knotts, Joseph Rosenstein, James B. Thurman, Ivan Able, W. Harvey Hegarty, Roger Evered, Charles B. Saunders, Rhae M. Swisher, Claude I. Shell, R. Thomas Lenz, Michael C. White, Dennis Callahan, R. Duane Ireland, William E. Burr II, C. W. Millard, Richard Mann, Kurt Christensen, Neil W. Jacobs, Louis W. Fry, D. Robley Wood, George J. Gore, and William R. Soukup.

We owe a debt of gratitude to Professors Catherine A. Maritan, Jeffrey A. Martin, Richard S. Shreve, and Anant K. Sundaram for their helpful comments on various chapters. We'd also like to thank the following students of the Tuck School of Business for their assistance with the revisions: Alen A. Ameni, Dipti Badrinath, Stephanie K. Berger, Courtney D. Bragg, Katie Coster, Jacob Crandall, Robin Daley, Kathleen T. Durante, Shawnda Lee Duvigneaud, Isaac E. Freeman, Vedrana B. Greatorex, Brittany J. Hattingh, Sadé M. Lawrence, Heather Levy, Margaret W. Macauley, Ken Martin, Brian R. McKenzie, Mathew O'Sullivan, Sara Paccamonti, Byron Peyster, Jeremy Reich, Carry S. Resor, Edward J. Silberman, David Washer, and Lindsey Wilcox. And we'd like to acknowledge the help of Dartmouth students Avantika Agarwal, Charles K. Anumonwo, Maria Hart, Meaghan I. Haugh, Artie Santry, as well as Tuck staff member Doreen Aher.

As always, we value your recommendations and thoughts about the book. Your comments regarding coverage and contents will be taken to heart, and we always are grateful for the time you take to call our attention to printing errors, deficiencies, and other shortcomings. Please e-mail us at **athompso@cba.ua.edu**, **margaret.a.peteraf@ tuck.dartmouth.edu**, **john.gamble@tamucc.edu**, or **astrickl@cba.ua.edu**.

Arthur A. Thompson

Margaret A. Peteraf

John E. Gamble

A. J. Strickland

The Business Strategy Game or *GLO-BUS* Simulation Exercises

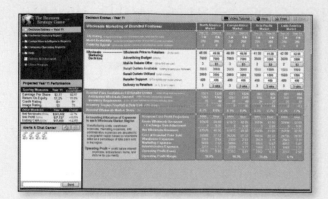 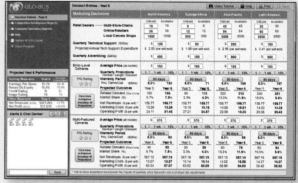

***The Business Strategy Game* or *GLO-BUS* Simulation Exercises**

Either one of these text supplements involves teams of students managing companies in a head-to-head contest for global market leadership. Company co-managers have to make decisions relating to product quality, production, workforce compensation and training, pricing and marketing, and financing of company operations. The challenge is to craft and execute a strategy that is powerful enough to deliver good financial performance despite the competitive efforts of rival companies. Each company competes in North America, Latin America, Europe-Africa, and Asia-Pacific.

Instructors: Student Success Starts with You

Tools to enhance your unique voice

Want to build your own course? No problem. Prefer to use our turnkey, prebuilt course? Easy. Want to make changes throughout the semester? Sure. And you'll save time with Connect's auto-grading too.

65%
Less Time Grading

Laptop: McGraw Hill; Woman/dog: George Doyle/Getty Images

Study made personal

Incorporate adaptive study resources like SmartBook® 2.0 into your course and help your students be better prepared in less time. Learn more about the powerful personalized learning experience available in SmartBook 2.0 at **www.mheducation.com/highered/connect/smartbook**

Affordable solutions, added value

Make technology work for you with LMS integration for single sign-on access, mobile access to the digital textbook, and reports to quickly show you how each of your students is doing. And with our Inclusive Access program you can provide all these tools at a discount to your students. Ask your McGraw Hill representative for more information.

Padlock: Jobalou/Getty Images

Solutions for your challenges

A product isn't a solution. Real solutions are affordable, reliable, and come with training and ongoing support when you need it and how you want it. Visit **www.supportateverystep.com** for videos and resources both you and your students can use throughout the semester.

Checkmark: Jobalou/Getty Images

Students: Get Learning that Fits You

Effective tools for efficient studying

Connect is designed to make you more productive with simple, flexible, intuitive tools that maximize your study time and meet your individual learning needs. Get learning that works for you with Connect.

Study anytime, anywhere

Download the free ReadAnywhere app and access your online eBook or SmartBook 2.0 assignments when it's convenient, even if you're offline. And since the app automatically syncs with your eBook and SmartBook 2.0 assignments in Connect, all of your work is available every time you open it. Find out more at **www.mheducation.com/readanywhere**

> *"I really liked this app—it made it easy to study when you don't have your text-book in front of you."*
>
> - Jordan Cunningham, Eastern Washington University

Calendar: owattaphotos/Getty Images

Everything you need in one place

Your Connect course has everything you need—whether reading on your digital eBook or completing assignments for class, Connect makes it easy to get your work done.

Learning for everyone

McGraw Hill works directly with Accessibility Services Departments and faculty to meet the learning needs of all students. Please contact your Accessibility Services Office and ask them to email accessibility@mheducation.com, or visit **www.mheducation.com/about/accessibility** for more information.

Top: Jenner Images/Getty Images, Left: Hero Images/Getty Images, Right: Hero Images/Getty Images

Brief Contents

Contents

8 Corporate Strategy   222

9 Ethics, Corporate Social Responsibility, Environmental Sustainability, and Strategy   266

PART 1

Concepts and Techniques for Crafting and Executing Strategy

chapter 1

What Is Strategy and Why Is It Important?

Learning Objectives

After reading this chapter, you should be able to:

LO 1-1 Understand what is meant by a company's *strategy* and why it needs to differ from competitors' strategies.

LO 1-2 Grasp the concept of a *sustainable competitive advantage*.

LO 1-3 Identify the five most basic strategic approaches for setting a company apart from its rivals.

LO 1-4 Understand why a company's strategy tends to evolve.

LO 1-5 Identify what constitutes a viable business model.

LO 1-6 Identify the three tests of a winning strategy.

Gary Waters/Ikon Images/Superstock

Strategy is about setting yourself apart from the competition.

Michael Porter—*Professor and consultant*

Strategy means making clear-cut choices about how to compete.

Jack Welch—*Former CEO of General Electric*

I believe that people make their own luck by great preparation and good strategy.

Jack Canfield—*Corporate trainer and entrepreneur*

According to *The Economist,* a leading publication on business, economics, and international affairs, "In business, strategy is king. Leadership and hard work are all very well and luck is mighty useful, but it is strategy that makes or breaks a firm."[1] Luck and circumstance can explain why some companies are blessed with initial, short-lived success. But only a well-crafted, well-executed, constantly evolving strategy can explain why an elite set of companies somehow manage to rise to the top and stay there, year after year, pleasing their customers, shareholders, and other stakeholders alike in the process. Companies such as Apple, Disney, Starbucks, Alphabet (parent company of Google), Berkshire Hathaway, General Electric, and Amazon come to mind—but long-lived success is not just the province of U.S. companies. Diverse kinds of companies, both large and small, from many different countries have been able to sustain strong performance records, including Denmark's Lego Group, the United Kingdom's HSBC (in banking), Dubai's Emirates Airlines, Switzerland's Rolex China Mobile (in telecommunications), and India's Tata Steel.

In this opening chapter, we define the concept of strategy and describe its many facets. We introduce you to the concept of competitive advantage and explore the tight linkage between a company's strategy and its quest for competitive advantage. We will also explain why company strategies are partly proactive and partly reactive, why they evolve over time, and the relationship between a company's strategy and its business model. We conclude the chapter with a discussion of what sets a winning strategy apart from others and why that strategy should also pass the test of moral scrutiny. By the end of this chapter, you will have a clear idea of why the tasks of crafting and executing strategy are core management functions and why excellent execution of an excellent strategy is the most reliable recipe for turning a company into a standout performer over the long term.

WHAT DO WE MEAN BY *STRATEGY*?

A company's **strategy** is the set of coordinated actions that its managers take in order to outperform the company's competitors and achieve superior profitability. The objective of a well-crafted strategy is not merely temporary competitive success and profits in the short run, but rather the sort of lasting success that can support growth and secure the company's future over the long term. Achieving this entails making a managerial commitment to a coherent array of well-considered choices about how to compete.[2] These include

- *How* to position the company in the marketplace.
- *How* to attract customers.
- *How* to compete against rivals.
- *How* to achieve the company's performance targets.
- *How* to capitalize on opportunities to grow the business.
- *How* to respond to changing economic and market conditions.

In most industries, companies have considerable freedom in choosing the *hows* of strategy.[3] Some companies strive to achieve lower costs than rivals, while others aim for product superiority or more personalized customer service dimensions that rivals cannot match. Some companies opt for wide product lines, while others concentrate their energies on a narrow product lineup. Some deliberately confine their operations to local or regional markets; others opt to compete nationally, internationally (several countries), or globally (all or most of the major country markets worldwide). Choices of how best to compete against rivals have to be made in light of the firm's resources and capabilities and in light of the competitive approaches rival companies are employing.

Strategy Is about Competing Differently

Mimicking the strategies of successful industry rivals—with either copycat product offerings or maneuvers to stake out the same market position—rarely works. Rather, every company's strategy needs to have some distinctive element that draws in customers and provides a competitive edge. Strategy, at its essence, is about competing differently—doing what rival firms *don't* do or what rival firms *can't* do.[4] This does not mean that the key elements of a company's strategy have to be 100 percent different, but rather that they must differ in at least *some important respects*. A strategy stands a better chance of succeeding when it is predicated on actions, business approaches, and competitive moves aimed at (1) appealing to buyers in ways that *set a company apart from its rivals* and (2) staking out a market position that is not crowded with strong competitors.

A company's strategy provides direction and guidance, in terms of not only what the company *should* do but also what it *should not* do. Knowing what not to do can be as important as knowing what to do, strategically. At best, making the wrong strategic moves will prove a distraction and a waste of company resources. At worst, it can bring about unintended long-term consequences that put the company's very survival at risk.

Figure 1.1 illustrates the broad types of actions and approaches that often characterize a company's strategy in a particular business or industry. For a more concrete example, see Illustration Capsule 1.1 describing the elements of Apple, Inc.'s successful strategy.

FIGURE 1.1   Identifying a Company's Strategy—What to Look For

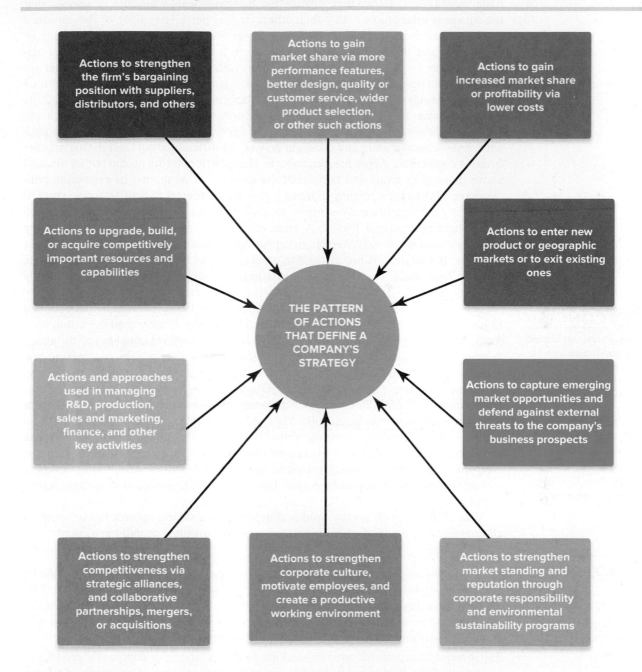

Strategy and the Quest for Competitive Advantage

The heart and soul of any strategy are the actions in the marketplace that managers take to gain a competitive advantage over rivals. A company has a **competitive advantage** whenever it has some type of edge over rivals in attracting buyers and coping with competitive forces. A competitive advantage is essential for realizing greater marketplace success and higher profitability over the long term.

● **LO 1-2**

Grasp the concept of a *sustainable competitive advantage.*

There are many routes to competitive advantage, but they all involve one of two basic mechanisms. Either they provide the customer with a product or service that the customer values more highly than others (higher perceived value), or they produce their product or service more efficiently (lower costs). Delivering superior value or delivering value more efficiently—whatever form it takes—nearly always requires performing value chain activities differently than rivals and building capabilities that are not readily matched. In Illustration Capsule 1.1, it is evident that Apple, Inc. has gained a competitive advantage over its rivals in the technological device industry through its efforts to create "must-have," exciting new products, that are beautifully designed, technologically advanced, easy to use, and sold in appealing stores that offer a fun experience, knowledgeable staff, and excellent service. By differentiating itself in this manner from its competitors Apple has been able to charge prices for its products that are well above those of its rivals and far exceed the low cost of its inputs. Its expansion policies have allowed the company to make it easy for customers to find an Apple store in almost any high-quality mall or urban shopping district, further enhancing the brand and cementing customer loyalty. A creative *distinctive* strategy such as that used by Apple is a company's most reliable ticket for developing a competitive advantage over its rivals. If a strategy is not distinctive, then there can be no competitive advantage, since no firm would be meeting customer needs better or operating more efficiently than any other.

If a company's competitive edge holds promise for being *sustainable* (as opposed to just temporary), then so much the better for both the strategy and the company's future profitability. What makes a competitive advantage **sustainable** (or durable), as opposed to temporary, are elements of the strategy that give buyers lasting reasons to prefer a company's products or services over those of competitors—*reasons that competitors are unable to nullify, duplicate, or overcome despite their best efforts.* In the case of Apple, the company's unparalleled name recognition, its reputation for technically superior, beautifully designed, "must-have" products, and the accessibility of the appealing, consumer-friendly stores with knowledgeable staff, make it difficult for competitors to weaken or overcome Apple's competitive advantage. Not only has Apple's strategy provided the company with a sustainable competitive advantage, but it has made Apple, Inc. one of the most admired companies on the planet.

Five of the most frequently used and dependable strategic approaches to setting a company apart from rivals, building strong customer loyalty, and gaining a competitive advantage are

1. *A low-cost provider strategy*—achieving a cost-based advantage over rivals. Walmart and Southwest Airlines have earned strong market positions because of the low-cost advantages they have achieved over their rivals. Low-cost provider strategies can produce a durable competitive edge when rivals find it hard to match the low-cost leader's approach to driving costs out of the business.

2. *A broad differentiation strategy*—seeking to differentiate the company's product or service from that of rivals in ways that will appeal to a broad spectrum of buyers. Successful adopters of differentiation strategies include Apple (innovative products), Johnson & Johnson in baby products (product reliability), Rolex (luxury and prestige), and BMW (engineering design and performance). One way to sustain this type of competitive advantage is to be sufficiently innovative to thwart the efforts of clever rivals to copy or closely imitate the product offering.

Apple Inc. is one of the most profitable companies in the world, with revenues of more than $265 billion. For more than 10 consecutive years, it has ranked number one on Fortune's list of the "World's Most Admired Companies." Given the worldwide popularity of its products and services, along with its reputation for superior technological innovation and design capabilities, this is not surprising. The key elements of Apple's successful strategy include:

PUGUN SJ/Shutterstock

- *Designing and developing its own operating systems, hardware, application software, and services.* This allows Apple to bring the best user experience to its customers through products and solutions with innovative design, superior ease-of-use, and seamless integration across platforms. The ability to use services like iCloud across devices incentivizes users to join Apple's technological ecosystem and has been critical to fostering brand loyalty.

- *Continuously investing in research and development (R&D) and frequently introducing products.* Apple has invested heavily in R&D, spending upwards of $11 billion a year, to ensure a continual and timely injection of competitive products, services, and technologies into the marketplace. Its successful products and services include the Mac, iPod, iPhone, iPad, Apple Watch, Apple TV, and Apple Music. It is currently investing in an Apple electric car and Apple solar energy.

- *Strategically locating its stores and staffing them with knowledgeable personnel.* By operating its own Apple stores and positioning them in high-traffic locations, Apple is better equipped to provide its customers with the optimal buying experience. The stores' employees are well versed in the value of the hardware and software integration and demonstrate the unique solutions available on its products. This high-quality sale and after-sale supports allows Apple to continuously attract new and retain existing customers.

- *Expanding Apple's reach domestically and internationally.* Apple operates more than 500 retail stores across 24 countries. During fiscal year 2019, 60 percent of Apple's revenue came from international sales.

- *Maintaining a quality brand image, supported by premium pricing.* Although the computer industry is incredibly price competitive, Apple has managed to sustain a competitive edge by focusing on its inimitable value proposition and deliberately keeping a price premium—thus creating an aura of prestige around its products.

- *Committing to corporate social responsibility and sustainability through supplier relations.* Apple's strict Code of Conduct requires its suppliers to comply with several standards regarding safe working conditions, fair treatment of workers, and environmentally safe manufacturing.

- *Cultivating a diverse workforce rooted in transparency.* Apple believes that diverse teams make innovation possible and is dedicated to incorporating a broad range of perspectives in its workforce. Every year, Apple publishes data showing the representation of women and different race and ethnicity groups across functions.

Note: Developed with Shawnda Lee Duvigneaud
Sources: Apple 10-K, Company website.

3. *A focused low-cost strategy*—concentrating on a narrow buyer segment (or market niche) and outcompeting rivals by having lower costs and thus being able to serve niche members at a lower price. Private-label manufacturers of food, health and beauty products, and nutritional supplements use their low-cost advantage to offer supermarket buyers lower prices than those demanded by producers of branded

products. IKEA's emphasis on modular furniture, ready for assembly, makes it a focused low-cost player in the furniture market.

4. *A focused differentiation strategy*—concentrating on a narrow buyer segment (or market niche) and outcompeting rivals by offering buyers customized attributes that meet their specialized needs and tastes better than rivals' products. Lululemon, for example, specializes in high-quality yoga clothing and the like, attracting a devoted set of buyers in the process. Tesla, Inc., with its electric cars, LinkedIn specializing in the business and employment aspects of social networking, and Goya Foods in Hispanic specialty food products provide some other examples of this strategy.

5. *A best-cost provider strategy*—giving customers more value for the money by satisfying their expectations on key quality features, performance, and/or service attributes while beating their price expectations. This approach is a hybrid strategy that blends elements of low-cost provider and differentiation strategies; the aim is to have lower costs than rivals while simultaneously offering better differentiating attributes. Target is an example of a company that is known for its hip product design (a reputation it built by featuring limited edition lines by designers such as Rodarte, Victoria Beckham, and Jason Wu), as well as a more appealing shopping ambience for discount store shoppers. Its dual focus on low costs as well as differentiation shows how a best-cost provider strategy can offer customers great value for the money.

Winning a *sustainable* competitive edge over rivals with any of the preceding five strategies generally hinges as much on building competitively valuable expertise and capabilities that rivals cannot readily match as it does on having a distinctive product offering. Clever rivals can nearly always copy the attributes of a popular product or service, but for rivals to match the experience, know-how, and specialized capabilities that a company has developed and perfected over a long period of time is substantially harder to do and takes much longer. The success of the Swatch in watches, for example, was driven by impressive design, marketing, and engineering capabilities, while Apple has demonstrated outstanding product innovation capabilities in digital music players, smartphones, and e-readers. Hyundai has become the world's fastest-growing automaker as a result of its advanced manufacturing processes and unparalleled quality control systems. Capabilities such as these have been hard for competitors to imitate or best.

Why a Company's Strategy Evolves over Time

● **LO 1-4**

Understand why a company's strategy tends to evolve.

The appeal of a strategy that yields a sustainable competitive advantage is that it offers the potential for a more enduring edge than a temporary advantage over rivals. But sustainability is a relative term, with some advantages lasting longer than others. And regardless of how sustainable a competitive advantage may appear to be at a given point in time, conditions change. Even a substantial competitive advantage over rivals may crumble in the face of drastic shifts in market conditions or disruptive innovations. Therefore, managers of every company must be willing and ready to modify the strategy in response to changing market conditions, advancing technology, unexpected moves by competitors, shifting buyer needs, emerging market opportunities, and new ideas for improving the strategy. Most of the time, a company's strategy evolves incrementally as management fine-tunes various pieces of the strategy and adjusts the strategy in response to unfolding events.[5] However, on occasion, major strategy shifts are called for, such as when the strategy is clearly failing or when industry conditions change in dramatic ways. Industry environments characterized by high-velocity change require companies to repeatedly adapt their strategies.[6] For example, companies in industries with rapid-fire advances in technology like 3-D printing, shale fracking, and genetic engineering often find it essential to adjust key elements of their strategies several times a year. When the technological change is drastic enough to "disrupt" the entire industry, displacing market leaders and altering market boundaries, companies may find it necessary to "reinvent" entirely their approach to providing value to their customers.

Regardless of whether a company's strategy changes gradually or swiftly, the important point is that the task of crafting strategy is not a one-time event but always a work in progress. Adapting to new conditions and constantly evaluating what is working well enough to continue and what needs to be improved are normal parts of the strategy-making process, resulting in an *evolving strategy*.[7]

A Company's Strategy Is Partly Proactive and Partly Reactive

The evolving nature of a company's strategy means that the typical company strategy is a blend of (1) *proactive,* planned initiatives to improve the company's financial performance and secure a competitive edge and (2) *reactive* responses to unanticipated developments and fresh market conditions. The biggest portion of a company's current strategy flows from previously initiated actions that have proven themselves in the marketplace and newly launched initiatives aimed at edging out rivals and boosting financial performance. This part of management's action plan for running the company is its **deliberate strategy,** consisting of proactive strategy elements that are both planned and realized as planned (while other planned strategy elements may not work out and are abandoned in consequence)—see Figure 1.2.[8]

But managers must always be willing to supplement or modify the proactive strategy elements with as-needed reactions to unanticipated conditions. Inevitably, there will be occasions when market and competitive conditions take an unexpected turn that calls for some kind of strategic reaction. Hence, *a portion of a company's strategy is always developed on the fly,* coming as a response to fresh strategic maneuvers on the part of rival firms, unexpected shifts in customer requirements, fast-changing technological developments, newly appearing market opportunities, a changing political or economic climate, or other unanticipated happenings in the surrounding environment. These adaptive strategy adjustments make up the firm's **emergent strategy.** A company's strategy *in toto* (its **realized strategy**) thus tends to be a *combination* of proactive and reactive elements, with certain strategy elements being *abandoned* because they have become obsolete or ineffective. A company's realized strategy can be observed in the pattern of its actions over time, which is a far better indicator than any of its strategic plans on paper or any public pronouncements about its strategy.

Strategy and Ethics: Passing the Test of Moral Scrutiny

In choosing among strategic alternatives, company managers are well advised to embrace actions that can pass the test of moral scrutiny. Just keeping a company's strategic actions within the bounds of what is legal does not mean the strategy is

Changing circumstances and ongoing management efforts to improve the strategy cause a company's strategy to evolve over time—a condition that makes the task of crafting strategy a *work in progress,* not a one-time event.

A company's strategy is shaped partly by management analysis and choice and partly by the necessity of adapting and learning by doing.

CORE CONCEPT

A company's **deliberate strategy** consists of *proactive* strategy elements that are planned; its **emergent strategy** consists of *reactive* strategy elements that emerge as changing conditions warrant.

A strategy cannot be considered ethical just because it involves actions that are legal. To meet the standard of being ethical, a strategy must entail actions and behavior that can pass moral scrutiny in the sense of *not being* deceitful, unfair or harmful to others, disreputable, or unreasonably damaging to the environment.

FIGURE 1.2   A Company's Strategy Is a Blend of Proactive Initiatives and Reactive Adjustments

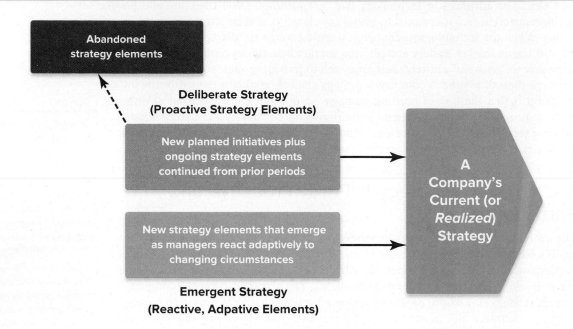

ethical. Ethical and moral standards are not fully governed by what is legal. Rather, they involve issues of "right" versus "wrong" and duty—what one should do. A strategy is ethical only if it does not entail actions that cross the moral line from "can do" to "should not do." For example, a company's strategy *definitely* crosses into the "should not do" zone and cannot pass moral scrutiny if it entails actions and behaviors that are deceitful, unfair or harmful to others, disreputable, or unreasonably damaging to the environment. A company's strategic actions cross over into the "should not do" zone and are likely to be deemed unethical when (1) they reflect badly on the company or (2) they adversely impact the legitimate interests and well-being of shareholders, customers, employees, suppliers, the communities where it operates, and society at large or (3) they provoke public outcries about inappropriate or "irresponsible" actions, behavior, or outcomes.

Admittedly, it is not always easy to categorize a given strategic behavior as ethical or unethical. Many strategic actions fall in a gray zone and can be deemed ethical or unethical depending on how high one sets the bar for what qualifies as ethical behavior. For example, is it ethical for advertisers of alcoholic products to place ads in media having an audience of as much as 50 percent underage viewers? Is it ethical for companies to employ undocumented workers who may have been brought to the United States as children? Is it ethical for Nike, Under Armour, and other makers of athletic wear to pay a university athletic department large sums of money as an "inducement" for the university's athletic teams to use their brand of products? Is it ethical for pharmaceutical manufacturers to charge higher prices for life-saving drugs in some countries than they charge in others? Is it ethical for a company to ignore the damage done to the environment by its operations in a particular country, even though they are in compliance with current environmental regulations in that country?

Senior executives with strong ethical convictions are generally proactive in linking strategic action and ethics; they forbid the pursuit of ethically questionable business opportunities and insist that all aspects of company strategy are in accord with high ethical standards. They make it clear that all company personnel are expected to act with integrity, and they put organizational checks and balances into place to monitor behavior, enforce ethical codes of conduct, and provide guidance to employees regarding any gray areas. Their commitment to ethical business conduct is genuine, not hypocritical lip service.

The reputational and financial damage that unethical strategies and behavior can do is substantial. When a company is put in the public spotlight because certain personnel are alleged to have engaged in misdeeds, unethical behavior, fraudulent accounting, or criminal behavior, its revenues and stock price are usually hammered hard. Many customers and suppliers shy away from doing business with a company that engages in sleazy practices or turns a blind eye to its employees' illegal or unethical behavior. Repulsed by unethical strategies or behavior, wary customers take their business elsewhere and wary suppliers tread carefully. Moreover, employees with character and integrity do not want to work for a company whose strategies are shady or whose executives lack character and integrity. Consequently, solid business reasons exist for companies to shun the use of unethical strategy elements. Besides, immoral or unethical actions are just plain wrong.

A COMPANY'S STRATEGY AND ITS BUSINESS MODEL

At the core of every sound strategy is the company's **business model.** A business model is management's blueprint for delivering a valuable product or service to customers in a manner that will generate revenues sufficient to cover costs and yield an attractive profit.[9] The two elements of a company's business model are (1) its *customer value proposition* and (2) its *profit formula*. The customer value proposition lays out the company's approach to satisfying buyer wants and needs at a price customers will consider a good value. The profit formula describes the company's approach to determining a cost structure that will allow for acceptable profits, given the pricing tied to its customer value proposition. Figure 1.3 illustrates the elements of the business model in terms of what is known as the *value-price-cost framework*.[10] As the framework indicates,

LO 1-5

Identify what constitutes a viable business model.

FIGURE 1.3   The Business Model and the Value-Price-Cost Framework

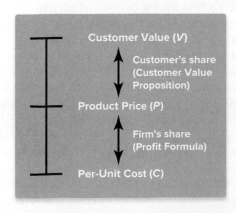

> **CORE CONCEPT**
>
> A company's **business model** sets forth the logic for how its strategy will create value for customers and at the same time generate revenues sufficient to cover costs and realize a profit.

the customer value proposition can be expressed as $V - P$, which is essentially the customers' perception of how much value they are getting for the money. The profit formula, on a per-unit basis, can be expressed as $P - C$. Plainly, from a customer perspective, the greater the value delivered (V) and the lower the price (P), the more attractive is the company's value proposition. On the other hand, the lower the costs (C), given the customer value proposition ($V - P$), the greater the ability of the business model to be a moneymaker. Thus, the profit formula reveals how efficiently a company can meet customer wants and needs and deliver on the value proposition. The nitty-gritty issue surrounding a company's business model is whether it can execute its customer value proposition profitably. Just because company managers have crafted a strategy for competing and running the business does not automatically mean that the strategy will lead to profitability—it may or it may not.

Aircraft engine manufacturer Rolls-Royce employs an innovative "power-by-the-hour" business model that charges airlines leasing fees for engine use, maintenance, and repairs based on actual hours flown. The company retains ownership of the engines and is able to minimize engine maintenance costs through the use of sophisticated sensors that optimize maintenance and repair schedules. Gillette's business model in razor blades involves selling a "master product"—the razor—at an attractively low price and then making money on repeat purchases of razor blades that can be produced cheaply and sold at high profit margins. Printer manufacturers like Hewlett-Packard, Canon, and Epson pursue much the same business model as Gillette—selling printers at a low (virtually break-even) price and making large profit margins on the repeat purchases of ink cartridges and other printer supplies. McDonald's invented the business model for fast food—providing value to customers in the form of economical quick-service meals at clean, convenient locations. Its profit formula involves such elements as standardized cost-efficient store design, stringent specifications for ingredients, detailed operating procedures for each unit, sizable investment in human resources and training, and heavy reliance on advertising and in-store promotions to drive volume. Illustration Capsule 1.2 describes three contrasting business models in radio broadcasting.

WHAT MAKES A STRATEGY A WINNER?

> **LO 1-6**
>
> Identify the three tests of a winning strategy.

Three tests can be applied to determine whether a strategy is a *winning strategy:*

1. ***The Fit Test:*** *How well does the strategy fit the company's situation?* To qualify as a winner, a strategy has to be well matched to industry and competitive conditions, a company's best market opportunities, and other pertinent aspects of the business environment in which the company operates. No strategy can work well unless it exhibits good *external fit* with respect to prevailing market conditions. At the same time, a winning strategy must be tailored to the company's resources and competitive capabilities and be supported by a complementary set of functional activities (i.e., activities in the realms of supply chain management, operations, sales and marketing, and so on). That is, it must also exhibit *internal fit* and be compatible with a company's ability to execute the strategy in a competent manner. Unless a strategy exhibits good fit with both the external and internal aspects of a company's overall situation, it is likely to be an underperformer and fall short of producing winning results. Winning strategies also exhibit *dynamic fit* in the sense that they evolve over time in a manner that maintains close and effective alignment with the company's situation even as external and internal conditions change.[11]

> To pass the *fit test,* a strategy must exhibit fit along three dimensions: (1) external, (2) internal, and (3) dynamic.

Pandora, SiriusXM, and Over-the-Air Broadcast Radio: Three Contrasting Business Models

Vivien Killilea/Stringer/Getty Images

	Pandora	SiriusXM	Over-the-Air Radio Broadcasters
Customer value proposition	• Through free-of-charge Internet radio service, allowed PC, tablet computer, and smartphone users to create up to 100 personalized music and comedy stations. • Utilized algorithms to generate playlists based on users' predicted music preferences. • Offered programming interrupted by brief, occasional ads; eliminated advertising for Pandora One subscribers.	• For a monthly subscription fee, provided satellite-based music, news, sports, national and regional weather, traffic reports in limited areas, and talk radio programming. • Also offered subscribers streaming Internet channels and the ability to create personalized commercial-free stations for online and mobile listening. • Offered programming interrupted only by brief, occasional ads.	• Provided free-of-charge music, national and local news, local traffic reports, national and local weather, and talk radio programming. • Included frequent programming interruption for ads.
Profit formula	*Revenue generation:* Display, audio, and video ads targeted to different audiences and sold to local and national buyers; subscription revenues generated from an advertising-free option called Pandora One. *Cost structure:* Fixed costs associated with developing software for computers, tablets, and smartphones. Fixed and variable costs related to operating data centers to support streaming network, content royalties, marketing, and support activities.	*Revenue generation:* Monthly subscription fees, sales of satellite radio equipment, and advertising revenues. *Cost structure:* Fixed costs associated with operating a satellite-based music delivery service and streaming Internet service. Fixed and variable costs related to programming and content royalties, marketing, and support activities.	*Revenue generation:* Advertising sales to national and local businesses. *Cost structure:* Fixed costs associated with terrestrial broadcasting operations. Fixed and variable costs related to local news reporting, advertising sales operations, network affiliate fees, programming and content royalties, commercial production activities, and support activities.

(Continued)

Pandora	SiriusXM	Over-the-Air Radio Broadcasters
Profit margin: Profitability dependent on generating sufficient advertising revenues and subscription revenues to cover costs and provide attractive profits.	*Profit margin:* Profitability dependent on attracting a sufficiently large number of subscribers to cover costs and provide attractive profits.	*Profit margin:* Profitability dependent on generating sufficient advertising revenues to cover costs and provide attractive profits.

A **winning strategy** must pass three tests:
1. The fit test
2. The competitive advantage test
3. The performance test

2. *The Competitive Advantage Test: Is the strategy helping the company achieve a competitive advantage? Is the competitive advantage likely to be sustainable?* Strategies that fail to achieve a competitive advantage over rivals are unlikely to produce superior performance. And unless the competitive advantage is sustainable, superior performance is unlikely to last for more than a brief period of time. Winning strategies enable a company to achieve a competitive advantage over key rivals that is long-lasting. The bigger and more durable the competitive advantage, the more powerful it is.

3. *The Performance Test: Is the strategy producing superior company performance?* The mark of a winning strategy is strong company performance. Two kinds of performance indicators tell the most about the caliber of a company's strategy: (1) competitive strength and market standing and (2) profitability and financial strength. Above-average financial performance or gains in market share, competitive position, or profitability are signs of a winning strategy.

Strategies—either existing or proposed—that come up short on one or more of the preceding tests are plainly less desirable than strategies passing all three tests with flying colors. New initiatives that don't seem to match the company's internal and external situations should be scrapped before they come to fruition, while existing strategies must be scrutinized on a regular basis to ensure they have good fit, offer a competitive advantage, and are contributing to above-average performance or performance improvements. Failure to pass one or more of the three tests should prompt managers to make immediate changes in an existing strategy.

WHY CRAFTING AND EXECUTING STRATEGY ARE IMPORTANT TASKS

Crafting and executing strategy are top-priority managerial tasks for two big reasons. First, a clear and reasoned strategy is management's prescription for doing business, its road map to competitive advantage, its game plan for pleasing customers, and its formula for improving performance. High-performing enterprises are nearly always the product of astute, creative, and proactive strategy making. Companies don't get to the top of the industry rankings or stay there with flawed strategies, copycat strategies, or timid attempts to try to do better. Only a handful of companies can boast of hitting home runs in the marketplace due to lucky breaks or the good fortune of having stumbled into the right market at the right time with the right product. Even if this is the case, success will not be lasting unless the companies subsequently craft a strategy that capitalizes on their luck, builds on what is working, and discards the rest. So there can be little argument that the process of crafting a company's strategy matters—and matters a lot.

Second, even the best-conceived strategies will result in performance shortfalls if they are not executed proficiently. The processes of crafting and executing strategies must go hand in hand if a company is to be successful in the long term. The chief executive officer of one successful company put it well when he said

> In the main, our competitors are acquainted with the same fundamental concepts and techniques and approaches that we follow, and they are as free to pursue them as we are. More often than not, the difference between their level of success and ours lies in the relative thoroughness and self-discipline with which we and they develop and execute our strategies for the future.

Good Strategy + Good Strategy Execution = Good Management

Crafting and executing strategy are thus core management tasks. Among all the things managers do, nothing affects a company's ultimate success or failure more fundamentally than how well its management team charts the company's direction, develops competitively effective strategic moves, and pursues what needs to be done internally to produce good day-in, day-out strategy execution and operating excellence. Indeed, *good strategy and good strategy execution are the most telling and trustworthy signs of good management.* The rationale for using the twin standards of good strategy making and good strategy execution to determine whether a company is well managed is therefore compelling: *The better conceived a company's strategy and the more competently it is executed, the more likely the company will be a standout performer in the marketplace.* In stark contrast, a company that lacks clear-cut direction, has a flawed strategy, or can't execute its strategy competently is a company whose financial performance is probably suffering, whose business is at long-term risk, and whose management is sorely lacking.

THE ROAD AHEAD

Throughout the chapters to come and in Part 2 of this text, the spotlight is on the foremost question in running a business enterprise: *What must managers do, and do well, to make a company successful in the marketplace?* The answer that emerges is that doing a good job of managing inherently requires good strategic thinking and good management of the strategy-making, strategy-executing process.

The mission of this book is to provide a solid overview of what every business student and aspiring manager needs to know about crafting and executing strategy. We will explore what good strategic thinking entails, describe the core concepts and tools of strategic analysis, and examine the ins and outs of crafting and executing strategy. The accompanying cases will help build your skills in both diagnosing how well the strategy-making, strategy-executing task is being performed

> How well a company performs is directly attributable to the caliber of its strategy and the proficiency with which the strategy is executed.

and prescribing actions for how the strategy in question or its execution can be improved. The strategic management course that you are enrolled in may also include a strategy simulation exercise in which you will run a company in head-to-head competition with companies run by your classmates. Your mastery of the strategic management concepts presented in the following chapters will put you in a strong position to craft a winning strategy for your company and figure out how to execute it in a cost-effective and profitable manner. As you progress through the chapters of the text and the activities assigned during the term, we hope to convince you that first-rate capabilities in crafting and executing strategy are essential to good management.

As you tackle the content and accompanying activities of this book, ponder the following observation by the essayist and poet Ralph Waldo Emerson: "Commerce is a game of skill which many people play, but which few play well." If your efforts help you become a savvy player and better equip you to succeed in business, the time and energy you spend here will indeed prove worthwhile.

KEY POINTS

1. A company's strategy is the set of coordinated actions that its managers take in order to outperform its competitors and achieve superior profitability.

2. The success of a company's strategy depends upon *competing differently* from rivals and gaining a competitive advantage over them.

3. A company achieves a *competitive advantage* when it provides buyers with superior value compared to rival sellers or produces its products or services more efficiently. The advantage is *sustainable* if it persists despite the best efforts of competitors to match or surpass this advantage.

4. A company's strategy typically evolves over time, emerging from a blend of (1) proactive deliberate actions on the part of company managers to improve the strategy and (2) reactive emergent responses to unanticipated developments and fresh market conditions.

5. A company's business model sets forth the logic for how its strategy will create value for customers and at the same time generate revenues sufficient to cover costs and realize a profit. Thus, it contains two crucial elements: (1) the *customer value proposition*—a plan for satisfying customer wants and needs at a price customers will consider good value, and (2) the *profit formula*—a plan for a cost structure that will enable the company to deliver the customer value proposition profitably. These elements are illustrated by the value-price-cost framework.

6. A winning strategy will pass three tests: (1) *fit* (external, internal, and dynamic consistency), (2) *competitive advantage* (durable competitive advantage), and (3) *performance* (outstanding financial and market performance).

7. Ethical strategies must entail actions and behavior that can pass the test of moral scrutiny in the sense of *not being* deceitful, unfair or harmful to others, disreputable, or unreasonably damaging to the environment.

8. Crafting and executing strategy are core management functions. How well a company performs and the degree of market success it enjoys are directly attributable to the caliber of its strategy and the proficiency with which the strategy is executed.

ASSURANCE OF LEARNING EXERCISES

1. Based on your experiences and/or knowledge of Apple's current products and services, does Apple's strategy (as described in Illustration Capsule 1.1) seem to set it apart from rivals? Does the strategy seem to be keyed to a cost-based advantage, differentiating features, serving the unique needs of a niche, or some combination of these? What is there about Apple's strategy that can lead to sustainable competitive advantage?

LO 1-1, LO 1-2, LO 1-3

2. Elements of Amazon's strategy have evolved in meaningful ways since the company's founding in 1994. After reviewing the company's history and all of the links at the company's investor relations site **ir.aboutamazon.com** prepare a one- to two-page report that discusses how its strategy has evolved. Your report should also assess how well Amazon's strategy passes the three tests of a winning strategy.

LO 1-4, LO 1-6

3. Go to **investor.siriusxm.com** and check whether Sirius XM's recent financial reports indicate that its business model is working. Are its subscription fees increasing or declining? Are its revenue stream advertising and equipment sales growing or declining? Does its cost structure allow for acceptable profit margins?

LO 1-5

EXERCISES FOR SIMULATION PARTICIPANTS

Three basic questions must be answered by managers of organizations of all sizes as they begin the process of crafting strategy:

- What is our present situation?
- Where do we want to go from here?
- How are we going to get there?

After you have read the Participant's Guide or Player's Manual for the strategy simulation exercise that you will participate in during this academic term, you and your co-managers should come up with brief one- or two-paragraph answers to these three questions *prior to* entering your first set of decisions. While your answer to the first of the six questions can be developed from your reading of the manual, the remaining questions will require a collaborative discussion among the members of your company's management team about how you intend to manage the company you have been assigned to run.

1. Your company's strategy in the business simulation for this course should include choices about what types of issues?

LO 1-1

2. What is your company's current situation? A substantive answer to this question should cover the following issues:

LO 1-6

- Does your company appear to be in sound financial condition?
- What problems does your company have that need to be addressed?

3. Why will your company matter to customers? A complete answer to this question should say something about each of the following: How will you goals or aspirations do you have for your company?

LO 1-3

- How will you create customer value?
- What will be distinctive about the company's products or services?
- How will capabilities and resources be deployed to deliver customer value?

LO 1-5 4. What are the primary elements of your company's business model?
- Describe your customer value proposition.
- Discuss the profit formula tied to your business model.
- What level of revenues is required for your company's business model to become a moneymaker?

LO 1-6 5. How will you build and sustain competitive advantage?
- Which of the basic strategic and competitive approaches discussed in this chapter do you think makes the most sense to pursue?
- What kind of competitive advantage over rivals will you try to achieve?
- How do you envision that your strategy might evolve as you react to the competitive moves of rival firms?
- Does your strategy have the ability to pass the three tests of a winning strategy? Explain.

LO 1-1, 1-2, 1-6 6. Why will strategy execution be important to your company's success?

ENDNOTES

[1] B. R, "Strategy," *The Economist,* October 19, 2012, www.economist.com/blogs/schumpeter/2012/10/z-business-quotations-1 (accessed January 4, 2014).

[2] Jan Rivkin, "An Alternative Approach to Making Strategic Choices," Harvard Business School case 9-702-433, 2001.

[3] Michael E. Porter, "What Is Strategy?" *Harvard Business Review* 74, no. 6 (November–December 1996), pp. 65–67.

[4] Ibid.

[5] Eric T. Anderson and Duncan Simester, "A Step-by-Step Guide to Smart Business Experiments," *Harvard Business Review* 89, no. 3 (March 2011).

[6] Shona L. Brown and Kathleen M. Eisenhardt, *Competing on the Edge: Strategy as Structured Chaos* (Boston, MA: Harvard Business School Press, 1998).

[7] Cynthia A. Montgomery, "Putting Leadership Back into Strategy," *Harvard Business Review* 86, no. 1 (January 2008).

[8] Henry Mintzberg and J. A. Waters, "Of Strategies, Deliberate and Emergent," *Strategic Management Journal* 6 (1985); Costas Markides, "Strategy as Balance: From 'Either-Or' to 'And,' " *Business Strategy Review* 12, no. 3 (September 2001).

[9] Mark W. Johnson, Clayton M. Christensen, and Henning Kagermann, "Reinventing Your Business Model," *Harvard Business Review* 86, no. 12 (December 2008); Joan Magretta, "Why Business Models Matter," *Harvard Business Review* 80, no. 5 (May 2002).

[10] A. Brandenburger and H. Stuart, "Value-Based Strategy," *Journal of Economics and Management Strategy* 5 (1996), pp. 5–24; D. Hoopes, T. Madsen, and G. Walker, "Guest Editors' Introduction to the Special Issue: Why Is There a Resource-Based View? Toward a Theory of Competitive Heterogeneity," *Strategic Management Journal* 24 (2003), pp. 889–992; M. Peteraf and J. Barney, "Unravelling the Resource-Based Tangle," *Managerial and Decision Economics* 24 (2003), pp. 309–323.

[11] Rivkin, "An Alternative Approach to Making Strategic Choices."

chapter 2

Charting a Company's Direction

Its Vision, Mission, Objectives, and Strategy

Learning Objectives

After reading this chapter, you should be able to:

LO 2-1 Understand why it is critical for managers to have a clear strategic vision of where the company needs to head.

LO 2-2 Explain the importance of setting both strategic and financial objectives.

LO 2-3 Explain why the strategic initiatives taken at various organizational levels must be tightly coordinated.

LO 2-4 Recognize what a company must do to execute its strategy proficiently.

LO 2-5 Comprehend the role and responsibility of a company's board of directors in overseeing the strategic management process.

Pamela Hamilton/Getty Images

Sound strategy starts with having the right goal.

Michael Porter—*Professor and consultant*

Purpose must be deliberately conceived and chosen, and
then pursued.

Clayton Christensen—*Professor and consultant*

A vision without a strategy remains an illusion.

Lee Bolman—*Author and leadership consultant*

Crafting and executing strategy are the heart and soul of managing a business enterprise. But exactly what is involved in developing a strategy and executing it proficiently? What goes into charting a company's strategic course and long-term direction? Is any analysis required? Does a company need a strategic plan? What are the various components of the strategy-making, strategy-executing process and to what extent are company personnel—aside from senior management—involved in the process?

This chapter presents an overview of the ins and outs of crafting and executing company strategies. The focus is on management's direction-setting responsibilities—charting a strategic course, setting performance targets, and choosing a strategy capable of producing the desired outcomes. We explain why strategy-making is a task for a company's entire management team and which kinds of strategic decisions tend to be made at which levels of management. The chapter concludes with a look at the roles and responsibilities of a company's board of directors and how good corporate governance protects shareholder interests and promotes good management.

WHAT DOES THE STRATEGY-MAKING, STRATEGY-EXECUTING PROCESS ENTAIL?

Crafting and executing a company's strategy is an ongoing process that consists of five interrelated stages:

1. *Developing a strategic vision* that charts the company's long-term direction, a *mission statement* that describes the company's purpose, and a set of *core values* to guide the pursuit of the vision and mission.
2. *Setting objectives* for measuring the company's performance and tracking its progress in moving in the intended long-term direction.
3. *Crafting a strategy* for advancing the company along the path management has charted and achieving its performance objectives.
4. *Executing the chosen strategy* efficiently and effectively.
5. *Monitoring developments, evaluating performance, and initiating corrective adjustments* in the company's vision and mission statement, objectives, strategy, or approach to strategy execution in light of actual experience, changing conditions, new ideas, and new opportunities.

> **CORE CONCEPT**
>
> A **strategic inflection point** is the point at which the extent of industry change requires management to consider changing the company's strategic vision.

Figure 2.1 displays this five-stage process, which we examine next in some detail. The first three stages of the strategic management process involve making a strategic plan. A **strategic plan** maps out where a company is headed, establishes strategic and financial targets, and outlines the basic business model, competitive moves, and approaches to be used in achieving the desired business results.[1] We explain this more fully at the conclusion of our discussion of stage 3, later in this chapter.

The five-stage process model illustrates the need for management to evaluate a number of external and internal factors in deciding upon a strategic direction, appropriate objectives, and approaches to crafting and executing strategy (see Table 2.1). Management's decisions that are made in the strategic management process must be shaped by the prevailing economic conditions and competitive environment and the company's own internal resources and competitive capabilities. These strategy-shaping conditions will be the focus of Chapters 3 and 4.

The model shown in Figure 2.1 also illustrates the need for management to evaluate the company's performance on an ongoing basis. Any indication that the company is failing to achieve its objectives calls for corrective adjustments in one of the first four stages of the process. The company's implementation efforts might have fallen short, and new tactics must be devised to fully exploit the potential of the company's strategy. If management determines that the company's execution efforts are sufficient, it should challenge the assumptions underlying the company's business model and strategy, and make alterations to better fit competitive conditions and the company's internal capabilities. If the company's strategic approach to competition is rated as sound, then perhaps management set overly ambitious targets for the company's performance.

The evaluation stage of the strategic management process shown in Figure 2.1 also allows for a change in the company's vision, but this should be necessary only when it becomes evident to management that the industry has changed in a significant way that renders the vision obsolete. Such occasions can be referred to as strategic inflection points. When a company reaches a strategic inflection point, management has tough decisions to make about the company's direction because abandoning an established

FIGURE 2.1   The Strategy-Making, Strategy-Executing Process

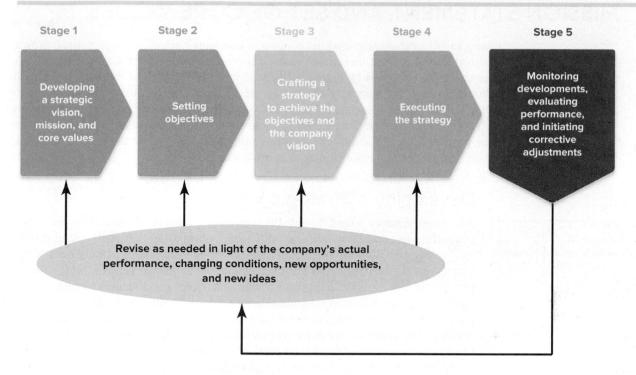

Stage 1	Stage 2	Stage 3	Stage 4	Stage 5
Developing a strategic vision, mission, and core values	Setting objectives	Crafting a strategy to achieve the objectives and the company vision	Executing the strategy	Monitoring developments, evaluating performance, and initiating corrective adjustments

Revise as needed in light of the company's actual performance, changing conditions, new opportunities, and new ideas

TABLE 2.1   Factors Shaping Decisions in the Strategy-Making, Strategy-Execution Process

External Considerations
- Does sticking with the company's present strategic course present attractive opportunities for growth and profitability?
- What kind of competitive forces are industry members facing, and are they acting to enhance or weaken the company's prospects for growth and profitability?
- What factors are driving industry change, and what impact on the company's prospects will they have?
- How are industry rivals positioned, and what strategic moves are they likely to make next?
- What are the key factors of future competitive success, and does the industry offer good prospects for attractive profits for companies possessing those capabilities?

Internal Considerations
- Does the company have an appealing customer value proposition?
- What are the company's competitively important resources and capabilities, and are they potent enough to produce a sustainable competitive advantage?
- Does the company have sufficient business and competitive strength to seize market opportunities and nullify external threats?
- Are the company's costs competitive with those of key rivals?
- Is the company competitively stronger or weaker than key rivals?

course carries considerable risk. However, responding to unfolding changes in the marketplace in a timely fashion lessens a company's chances of becoming trapped in a stagnant or declining business or letting attractive new growth opportunities slip away.

STAGE 1: DEVELOPING A STRATEGIC VISION, MISSION STATEMENT, AND SET OF CORE VALUES • • • •

Very early in the strategy-making process, a company's senior managers must wrestle with the issue of what directional path the company should take. Can the company's prospects be improved by changing its product offerings, or the markets in which it participates, or the customers it aims to serve? Deciding to commit the company to one path versus another pushes managers to draw some carefully reasoned conclusions about whether the company's present strategic course offers attractive opportunities for growth and profitability or whether changes of one kind or another in the company's strategy and long-term direction are needed.

Developing a Strategic Vision

Top management's views about the company's long-term direction and what product-market-customer business mix seems optimal for the road ahead constitute a **strategic vision** for the company. A strategic vision delineates management's aspirations for the company's future, providing a panoramic view of "where we are going" and a convincing rationale for why this makes good business sense. A strategic vision thus points an organization in a particular direction, charts a strategic path for it to follow, builds commitment to the future course of action, and molds organizational identity. A clearly articulated strategic vision communicates management's aspirations to stakeholders (customers, employees, stockholders, suppliers, etc.) and helps steer the energies of company personnel in a common direction. The vision of Google's cofounders Larry Page and Sergey Brin "to organize the world's information and make it universally accessible and useful" provides a good example. In serving as the company's guiding light, it has captured the imagination of stakeholders and the public at large, served as the basis for crafting the company's strategic actions, and aided internal efforts to mobilize and direct the company's resources.

Well-conceived visions are *distinctive* and *specific* to a particular organization; they avoid generic, feel-good statements like "We will become a global leader and the first choice of customers in every market we serve."[2] Likewise, a strategic vision proclaiming management's quest "to be the most innovative" or "to be recognized as the best company in the industry" offers scant guidance about a company's long-term direction or the kind of company that management is striving to build.

A surprising number of the vision statements found on company websites and in annual reports are vague and unrevealing, saying very little about the company's future direction. Some could apply to almost any company in any industry. Many read like a public relations statement—high-sounding words that someone came up with because it is fashionable for companies to have an official vision statement.[3] An example is Hilton Hotel's vision "to fill the earth with light and the warmth of hospitality," which simply borders on the incredulous. The real purpose of a vision statement is to serve as a management tool for giving the organization a sense of direction.

For a strategic vision to function as a valuable management tool, it must convey what top executives want the business to look like and provide managers at all organizational levels with a reference point in making strategic decisions and preparing the company for the future. It must say something definitive about how the company's leaders intend to position the company beyond where it is today.

TABLE 2.2   Wording a Vision Statement—the Dos and Don'ts

The Dos	The Don'ts
Be graphic. Paint a clear picture of where the company is headed and the market position(s) the company is striving to stake out.	**Don't be vague or incomplete.** Never skimp on specifics about where the company is headed or how the company intends to prepare for the future.
Be forward-looking and directional. Describe the strategic course that will help the company prepare for the future.	**Don't dwell on the present.** A vision is not about what a company once did or does now; it's about "where we are going."
Keep it focused. Focus on providing managers with guidance in making decisions and allocating resources.	**Don't use overly broad language.** Avoid all-inclusive language that gives the company license to pursue any opportunity.
Have some wiggle room. Language that allows some flexibility allows the directional course to be adjusted as market, customer, and technology circumstances change.	**Don't state the vision in bland or uninspiring terms.** The best vision statements have the power to motivate company personnel and inspire shareholder confidence about the company's future.
Be sure the journey is feasible. The path and direction should be within the realm of what the company can accomplish; over time, a company should be able to demonstrate measurable progress in achieving the vision.	**Don't be generic.** A vision statement that could apply to companies in any of several industries (or to any of several companies in the same industry) is not specific enough to provide any guidance.
Indicate why the directional path makes good business sense. The directional path should be in the long-term interests of stakeholders (especially shareholders, employees, and suppliers).	**Don't rely on superlatives.** Visions that claim the company's strategic course is the "best" or "most successful" usually lack specifics about the path the company is taking to get there.
Make it memorable. A well-stated vision is short, easily communicated, and memorable. Ideally, it should be reducible to a few choice lines or a one-phrase slogan.	**Don't run on and on.** A vision statement that is not concise and to the point will tend to lose its audience.

Sources: John P. Kotter, *Leading Change* (Boston: Harvard Business School Press, 1996); Hugh Davidson, *The Committed Enterprise* (Oxford: Butterworth Heinemann, 2002); Michel Robert, *Strategy Pure and Simple II* (New York: McGraw-Hill, 1992).

Table 2.2 provides some dos and don'ts in composing an effectively worded vision statement. Illustration Capsule 2.1 provides a critique of the strategic visions of several prominent companies.

Communicating the Strategic Vision

A strategic vision offers little value to the organization unless it's effectively communicated down the line to lower-level managers and employees. A vision cannot provide direction for middle managers or inspire and energize employees unless everyone in the company is familiar with it and can observe senior management's commitment to the vision. It is particularly important for executives to provide a compelling rationale for a dramatically *new* strategic vision and company direction. When company

Examples of Strategic Visions—How Well Do They Measure Up?

Philip Arno Photography/Shutterstock

Vision Statement	Effective Elements	Shortcomings
Whole Foods Whole Foods Market is a dynamic leader in the quality food business. We are a mission-driven company that aims to set the standards of excellence for food retailers. We are building a business in which high standards permeate all aspects of our company. Quality is a state of mind at Whole Foods Market. Our motto—Whole Foods, Whole People, Whole Planet—emphasizes that our vision reaches far beyond just being a food retailer. Our success in fulfilling our vision is measured by customer satisfaction, team member happiness and excellence, return on capital investment, improvement in the state of the environment and local and larger community support. Our ability to instill a clear sense of interdependence among our various stakeholders (the people who are interested and benefit from the success of our company) is contingent upon our efforts to communicate more often, more openly, and more compassionately. Better communication equals better understanding and more trust.	• Forward-looking • Graphic • Focused • Makes good business sense	• Long • Not memorable
Keurig Dr. Pepper A leading producer and distributor of hot and cold beverages to satisfy every consumer need, anytime and anywhere.	• Easy to communicate • Focused	• Not distinctive • Not forward-looking
Nike NIKE, Inc. fosters a culture of invention. We create products, services and experiences for today's athlete* while solving problems for the next generation. *If you have a body, you are an athlete.	• Forward-looking • Flexible	• Vague • Not focused

Note: Developed with Frances C. Thunder.

Source: Company websites (accessed online February 12, 2016).

personnel don't understand or accept the need for redirecting organizational efforts, they are prone to resist change. Hence, explaining the basis for the new direction, addressing employee concerns head-on, calming fears, lifting spirits, and providing updates and progress reports as events unfold all become part of the task in mobilizing support for the vision and winning commitment to needed actions.

Winning the support of organization members for the vision nearly always requires putting "where we are going and why" in writing, distributing the statement organization-wide, and having top executives personally explain the vision and its rationale to as many people as feasible. Ideally, executives should present their vision for the company in a manner that reaches out and grabs people. An engaging and convincing strategic vision has enormous motivational value—for the same reason that a stonemason is more inspired by the opportunity to build a great cathedral for the ages than a house. Thus, executive ability to paint a convincing and inspiring picture of a company's journey to a future destination is an important element of effective strategic leadership.

Expressing the Essence of the Vision in a Slogan The task of effectively conveying the vision to company personnel is assisted when management can capture the vision of where to head in a catchy or easily remembered slogan. A number of organizations have summed up their vision in a brief phrase. Instagram's vision is "Capture and share the world's moments," while Charles Schwab's is simply "Helping investors help themselves." Habitat for Humanity's aspirational vision is "A world where everyone has a decent place to live." Even Scotland Yard has a catchy vision, which is to "make London the safest major city in the world." Creating a short slogan to illuminate an organization's direction and using it repeatedly as a reminder of "where we are headed and why" helps rally organization members to maintain their focus and hurdle whatever obstacles lie in the company's path.

Why a Sound, Well-Communicated Strategic Vision Matters A well-thought-out, forcefully communicated strategic vision pays off in several respects: (1) It crystallizes senior executives' own views about the firm's long-term direction; (2) it reduces the risk of rudderless decision making; (3) it is a tool for winning the support of organization members to help make the vision a reality; (4) it provides a beacon for lower-level managers in setting departmental objectives and crafting departmental strategies that are in sync with the company's overall strategy; and (5) it helps an organization prepare for the future. When top executives are able to demonstrate significant progress in achieving these five benefits, the first step in organizational direction setting has been successfully completed.

Developing a Company Mission Statement

The defining characteristic of a strategic vision is what it says about the company's *future strategic course*—"the direction we are headed and the shape of our business in the future." It is aspirational. In contrast, a **mission statement** describes the enterprise's *present business and purpose*—"who we are, what we do, and why we are here." It is purely descriptive. Ideally, a company mission statement (1) identifies the company's products and/or services, (2) specifies the buyer needs that the company seeks to satisfy and the customer groups or markets that it serves, and (3) gives the company its own identity. The mission statements that one finds in company annual reports or posted on company websites are typically quite brief; some do a better job than others of conveying what the enterprise's current business operations and purpose are all about.

> The distinction between a strategic vision and a mission statement is fairly clear-cut: A **strategic vision** portrays a company's aspirations for its *future* ("where we are going"), whereas a company's **mission** describes the scope and purpose of its *present* business ("who we are, what we do, and why we are here").

Consider, for example, the mission statement of FedEx Corporation, which has long been known for its overnight shipping service, but also for pioneering the package tracking system now in general use:

> The FedEx Corporation offers express and fast delivery transportation services, delivering an estimated 3 million packages daily all around the globe. Its services include overnight courier, ground, heavy freight, document copying, and logistics services.

Note that FedEx's mission statement does a good job of conveying "who we are, what we do, and why we are here," but it provides no sense of "where we are headed." This is as it should be, since a company's vision statement is that which speaks to the future.

Another example of a well-stated mission statement with ample specifics about what the organization does is that of St. Jude Children's Research Hospital: "to advance cures, and means of prevention, for pediatric catastrophic diseases through research and treatment. Consistent with the vision of our founder Danny Thomas, no child is denied treatment based on race, religion or a family's ability to pay." Twitter's mission statement, while short, still captures the essence of what the company is about: "To give everyone the power to create and share ideas and information instantly, without barriers." An example of a not-so-revealing mission statement is that of JetBlue: "To inspire humanity—both in the air and on the ground." It says nothing about the company's activities or business makeup and could apply to many companies in many different industries. A person unfamiliar with JetBlue could not even discern from its mission statement that it is an airline, without reading between the lines. Coca-Cola, which markets more than 500 beverage brands in over 200 countries, also has an uninformative mission statement: "to refresh the world; to inspire moments of optimism and happiness; to create value and make a difference." The usefulness of a mission statement that cannot convey the essence of a company's business activities and purpose is unclear.

All too often, companies couch their mission in terms of making a profit, like Dean Foods with its mission "To maximize long-term stockholder value." This, too, is flawed.

> To be well worded, a company mission statement must employ language specific enough to distinguish its business makeup and purpose from those of other enterprises and give the company its own identity.

Profit is more correctly an *objective* and a *result* of what a company does. Moreover, earning a profit is the obvious intent of every commercial enterprise. Companies such as Gap, Inc., Edward Jones, Honda, The Boston Consulting Group, Citigroup, DreamWorks Animation, and Intuit are all striving to earn a profit for shareholders; but plainly the fundamentals of their businesses are substantially different when it comes to "who we are and what we do." It is management's answer to "make a profit doing what and for whom?" that reveals the substance of a company's true mission and business purpose.

Linking the Vision and Mission with Company Values

Companies commonly develop a set of values to guide the actions and behavior of company personnel in conducting the company's business and pursuing its strategic vision and mission. By **values** (or **core values,** as they are often called) we mean certain designated beliefs, traits, and behavioral norms that management has determined should guide the pursuit of its vision and mission. Values relate to such things as fair treatment, honor and integrity, ethical behavior, innovativeness, teamwork, a passion for top-notch quality or superior customer service, social responsibility, and community citizenship.

> **CORE CONCEPT**
>
> A company's **values** are the beliefs, traits, and behavioral norms that company personnel are expected to display in conducting the company's business and pursuing its strategic vision and mission.

Most companies articulate four to eight core values that company personnel are expected to display and that are supposed to be mirrored in how the company conducts its business. Build-A-Bear Workshop, with its cuddly Teddy bears and stuffed animals, credits six core values with creating its highly acclaimed working environment: (1) Reach, (2) Learn, (3) Di-bear-sity (4) Colla-bear-ate, (5) Give, and (6) Cele-bear-ate. Zappos prides itself on its 10 core values, which employees are expected to embody:

1. Deliver WOW Through Service
2. Embrace and Drive Change
3. Create Fun and a Little Weirdness
4. Be Adventurous, Creative, and Open-Minded
5. Pursue Growth and Learning
6. Build Open and Honest Relationships with Communication
7. Build a Positive Team and Family Spirit
8. Do More with Less
9. Be Passionate and Determined
10. Be Humble

Do companies practice what they preach when it comes to their professed values? Sometimes no, sometimes yes—it runs the gamut. At one extreme are companies with window-dressing values; the values are given lip service by top executives but have little discernible impact on either how company personnel behave or how the company operates. Such companies have value statements because they are in vogue and make the company look good. The limitation of these value statements becomes apparent whenever corporate misdeeds come to light. Prime examples include Volkswagen, with its emissions scandal, and Uber, facing multiple allegations of misbehavior and a criminal probe of illegal operations. At the other extreme are companies whose executives are committed to grounding company operations on sound values and principled ways of doing business. Executives at these companies deliberately seek to ingrain the designated core values into the corporate culture—the core values thus become an integral part of the company's DNA and what makes the company tick. At such values-driven companies, executives "walk the talk" and company personnel are held accountable for embodying the stated values in their behavior.

At companies where the stated values are real rather than cosmetic, managers connect values to the pursuit of the strategic vision and mission in one of two ways. In companies with long-standing values that are deeply entrenched in the corporate culture, senior managers are careful to craft a vision, mission, strategy, and set of operating practices that match established values; moreover, they repeatedly emphasize how the value-based behavioral norms contribute to the company's business success. If the company changes to a different vision or strategy, executives make a point of explaining how and why the core values continue to be relevant. Few companies with sincere commitment to established core values ever undertake strategic moves that conflict with ingrained values. In new companies, top management has to consider what values and business conduct should characterize the company and then draft a value statement that is circulated among managers and employees for discussion and possible modification. A final value statement that incorporates the desired behaviors and that connects to the vision and mission is then officially adopted. Some companies combine their vision, mission, and values into a single statement or document, circulate it to all organization members, and in many instances post the vision, mission, and value statement on the company's website. Illustration Capsule 2.2 describes how the success of TOMS Shoes has been largely driven by the nature of its mission, linked to the vision and core values of its founder.

TOMS Shoes was founded in 2006 by Blake Mycoskie after a trip to Argentina where he witnessed many children with no access to shoes in areas of extreme poverty. Mycoskie returned to the United States and founded TOMS Shoes with the purpose of matching every pair of shoes purchased by customers with a new pair of shoes to give to a child in need, a model he called One for One®. In contrast to many companies that begin with a product and then articulate a mission, Mycoskie started with the mission and then built a company around it. Although the company has since expanded their product portfolio, its mission remains essentially the same:

With every product you purchase, TOMS will help a person in need. One for One.®

TOMS's mission is ingrained in their business model. While Mycoskie could have set up a nonprofit organization to address the problem he witnessed, he was certain he didn't want to rely on donors to fund giving to the poor; he wanted to create a business that would fund the giving itself. With the one-for-one model, TOMS built the cost of giving away a pair of shoes into the price of each pair they sold, enabling the company to make a profit while still giving away shoes to the needy.

Much of TOMS's success (and ability to differentiate itself in a competitive marketplace) is attributable to the appeal of its mission and origin story. Mycoskie first got TOMS shoes into a trendy store in LA because he told them the story of why he founded the company, which got picked up by the LA Times and quickly spread. As the company has expanded communication channels, they continue to focus on leading with the story of their mission to ensure that customers know they are doing more than just buying a product.

As TOMS expanded to other products, they stayed true to the one-for-one business model, adapting it

Shutterstock/Teresa Schaeffer

to each new product category. In 2011, the company launched TOMS Eyewear, where every purchase of glasses helps restore sight to an individual. They've since launched TOMS Roasting Co. that helps support access to safe water with every purchase of coffee, TOMS Bags where purchases fund resources for safe birth, and TOMS High Road Backpack Collection where purchases provide training for bullying prevention.

By ingraining the mission in the company's business model, TOMS has been able to truly live up to Mycoskie's aspiration of a mission with a company, funding giving through a for-profit business. TOMS even ensured that the business model will never change; when Mycoskie sold 50 percent of the company to Bain Capital in 2014, part of the transaction protected the one-for-one business model forever. TOMS is a successful example of a company that proves a commitment to core values can spur both revenue growth and giving back.

Note: Developed with Carry S. Resor

Sources: TOMS Shoes website, accessed February 2018, http://www.toms.com/about-toms; Lebowitz, Shana, *Business Insider,* "TOMS Blake Mycoskie Talks Growing a Business While Balancing Profit with Purpose," June 15, 2016, http://www.businessinsider.com/toms-blake-mycoskie-talks-growing-a-business-while-balancing-profit-with-purpose-2016-6; Mycoskie, Blake, *Harvard Business Review,* "The Founder of TOMS on Reimaging the Company's Mission," from January-February 2016 issue, https://hbr.org/2016/01/the-founder-of-toms-on-reimagining-the-companys-mission.

STAGE 2: SETTING OBJECTIVES

The managerial purpose of setting **objectives** is to convert the vision and mission into specific performance targets. Objectives reflect management's aspirations for company performance in light of the industry's prevailing economic and competitive conditions and the company's internal capabilities. Well-stated objectives must be *specific,* as well as *quantifiable* or *measurable.* As Bill Hewlett, cofounder of Hewlett-Packard, shrewdly observed, "You cannot manage what you cannot measure. . . . And what gets measured gets done."[4] Concrete, measurable objectives are managerially valuable for three reasons: (1) They focus organizational attention and align actions throughout the organization, (2) they serve as *yardsticks* for tracking a company's performance and progress, and (3) they motivate employees to expend greater effort and perform at a high level. For company objectives to serve their purpose well, they must also meet three other criteria: they must contain a deadline for achievement and they must be challenging, yet achievable.

● LO 2-2

Explain the importance of setting both strategic and financial objectives.

CORE CONCEPT

Objectives are an organization's performance targets—the specific results management wants to achieve.

Setting Stretch Objectives

The experiences of countless companies teach that one of the best ways to promote outstanding company performance is for managers to set performance targets high enough to *stretch an organization to perform at its full potential and deliver the best possible results.* Challenging company personnel to go all out and deliver "stretch" gains in performance pushes an enterprise to be more inventive, to exhibit more urgency in improving both its financial performance and its business position, and to be more intentional and focused in its actions. Employing stretch goals can help create an exciting work environment and attract the best people. In many cases, stretch objectives spur exceptional performance and help build a firewall against contentment with modest gains in organizational performance.

There is a difference, however, between stretch goals that are clearly reachable with enough effort, and those that are well beyond the organization's current capabilities, regardless of the level of effort. Extreme stretch goals, involving radical expectations, fail more often than not. And failure to meet such goals can kill motivation, erode employee confidence, and damage both worker and company performance. CEO Marissa Mayer's inability to return Yahoo to greatness is a case in point.

Extreme stretch goals can work as envisioned under certain circumstances. High profile success stories at companies such as Southwest Airlines, 3M, SpaceX, and General Electric provide evidence. But research suggests that success of this sort depends upon two conditions being met: (1) the company must have ample resources available, and (2) its recent performance must be strong. Under any other circumstances, managers would be well advised not to pursue overly ambitious stretch goals.[5]

Well-chosen **objectives** are:
- specific
- measurable
- time-limited
- challenging
- achievable

CORE CONCEPT

Stretch objectives set performance targets high enough to *stretch* an organization to perform at its full potential and deliver the best possible results. **Extreme stretch goals** are warranted only under certain conditions.

What Kinds of Objectives to Set

Two distinct types of performance targets are required: those relating to financial performance and those relating to strategic performance. **Financial objectives** communicate management's goals for financial performance. **Strategic objectives** are goals concerning a company's marketing standing and competitive position. A company's set of financial and strategic objectives should include both near-term and longer-term performance targets. Short-term (quarterly or annual) objectives focus

CORE CONCEPT

Financial objectives communicate management's goals for financial performance. **Strategic objectives** lay out target outcomes concerning a company's market standing, competitive position, and future business prospects.

attention on delivering performance improvements in the current period and satisfy shareholder expectations for near-term progress. Longer-term targets (three to five years off) force managers to consider what to do *now* to put the company in position to perform better later. Long-term objectives are critical for achieving optimal long-term performance and stand as a barrier to a nearsighted management philosophy and an undue focus on short-term results. When trade-offs have to be made between achieving long-term objectives and achieving short-term objectives, long-term objectives should take precedence (unless the achievement of one or more short-term performance targets has unique importance). Examples of commonly used financial and strategic objectives are listed in Table 2.3. Illustration Capsule 2.3 provides selected financial and strategic objectives of three prominent companies.

The Need for a Balanced Approach to Objective Setting

The importance of setting and attaining financial objectives is obvious. Without adequate profitability and financial strength, a company's long-term health and ultimate survival are jeopardized. Furthermore, subpar earnings and a weak balance sheet alarm shareholders and creditors and put the jobs of senior executives at risk. In consequence, companies often focus most of their attention on financial outcomes. However, good financial performance, by itself, is not enough. Of equal or greater importance is a company's strategic performance—outcomes that indicate whether a company's market position and competitiveness are deteriorating, holding steady, or improving. *A stronger market standing and greater competitive vitality—especially when accompanied by competitive advantage—is what enables a company to improve its financial performance.*

Moreover, financial performance measures are really *lagging indicators* that reflect the results of past decisions and organizational activities.[6] But a company's past or current financial performance is not a reliable indicator of its future prospects—poor financial performers often turn things around and do better, while good financial

TABLE 2.3   Common Financial and Strategic Objectives

Financial Objectives	Strategic Objectives
• An *x* percent increase in annual revenues	• Winning an *x* percent market share
• Annual increases in after-tax profits *of x* percent	• Achieving lower overall costs than rivals
• Annual increases in earnings per share of *x* percent	• Overtaking key competitors on product performance, quality, or customer service
• Annual dividend increases of *x* percent	• Deriving *x* percent of revenues from the sale of new products introduced within the past five years
• Profit margins of *x* percent	• Having broader or deeper technological capabilities than rivals
• An *x* percent return on capital employed (ROCE) or return on shareholders' equity (ROE) investment	• Having a wider product line than rivals
• Increased shareholder value in the form of an upward-trending stock price	• Having a better-known or more powerful brand name than rivals
• Bond and credit ratings of *x*	• Having stronger national or global sales and distribution capabilities than rivals
• Internal cash flows of *x* dollars to fund new capital investment	• Consistently getting new or improved products to market ahead of rivals

JETBLUE

Produce above average industry margins by offering a quality product at a competitive price; generate revenues of over $6.6 billion, up 3.4 percent year over year; earn a net income of $759 million, an annual increase of 12.0 percent; further develop fare options, a co-branded credit card, and the Mint franchise; commit to achieving total cost savings of $250 to $300 million by 2020; kickoff multi-year cabin restyling program; convert all core A321 aircraft from 190 to 200 seats; target growth in key cities like Boston, plan to grow 150 flights a day to 200 over the coming years; grow toward becoming the carrier of choice in South Florida; organically grow west coast presence by expanding Mint offering to more transcontinental routes; optimize fare mix to increase overall average fare.

LULULEMON ATHLETICA, INC.

Optimize and strategically grow square footage in North America; explore new concepts such as stores that are tailored to each community; build a robust digital ecosystem with key investments in customer relationship management, analytics, and capabilities to elevate guest experience across all touch points; continue to expand the brand globally through international expansion, open 11 new stores in Asia and Europe, which include the first stores in China, South Korea, and Switzerland—operating a total of 50+ stores across nine countries outside of North America; increase revenue $4 billion by 2020; increase total comparable sales, which includes comparable store sales and direct to consumer, by 6 percent increase gross profit as a percentage of net revenue, or gross margin, by 51.2 percent; increase income from operations for fiscal 2016 by 14 percent.

Eric Broder Van Dyke/Shutterstock

GENERAL MILLS

Generate low single-digit organic net sales growth and high single-digit growth in earnings per share. Deliver double-digit returns to shareholders over the long term. To drive future growth, focus on Consumer First strategy to gain a deep understanding of consumer needs and respond quickly to give them what they want; more specifically: (1) grow cereal globally with a strong line-up of new products, including new flavors of iconic Cheerios, (2) innovate in fast growing segments of the yogurt category to improve performance and expand the yogurt platform into new cities in China; (3) expand distribution and advertising for high performing brands, such as Häagen-Dazs and Old El Paso; (4) build a more agile organization by streamlining support functions, allowing for more fluid use of resources and idea sharing around the world; enhancing e-commerce know-how to capture more growth in this emerging channel; and investing in strategic revenue management tools to optimize promotions, prices and mix of products to drive sales growth.

Note: Developed with Kathleen T. Durante

Sources: Information posted on company websites.

---

performers can fall upon hard times. The best and most reliable *leading indicators* of a company's future financial performance and business prospects are strategic outcomes that indicate whether the company's competitiveness and market position are stronger or weaker. The accomplishment of strategic objectives signals that the company is well positioned to sustain or improve its performance. For instance, if a company is achieving ambitious strategic objectives such that its competitive strength and market position are on the rise, then there's reason to expect that its *future* financial performance will be better than its current or past performance. If a company is losing ground to competitors and its market position is slipping—outcomes that reflect weak strategic performance—then its ability to maintain its present profitability is highly suspect.

Consequently, it is important to use a performance measurement system that strikes a *balance* between financial and strategic objectives.[7] The most widely used framework of this sort is known as the **Balanced Scorecard.**[8] This is a method for linking financial performance objectives to specific strategic objectives that derive from a company's business model. It maps out the key objectives of a company, with performance indicators, along four dimensions:

- Financial: listing financial objectives
- Customer: objectives relating to customers and the market
- Internal process: objectives relating to productivity and quality
- Organizational: objectives concerning human capital, culture, infrastructure, and innovation

Done well, this can provide a company's employees with clear guidelines about how their jobs are linked to the overall objectives of the organization, so they can contribute most productively and collaboratively to the achievement of these goals. The balanced scorecard methodology continues to be ranked as one of the most popular management tools.[9] Over 50 percent of companies in the United States, Europe, and Asia report using a balanced scorecard approach to measuring strategic and financial performance.[10] Organizations that have adopted the balanced scorecard approach include 7-Eleven, Ann Taylor Stores, Allianz Italy, Wells Fargo Bank, Ford Motor Company, Verizon, ExxonMobil, Pfizer, DuPont, Royal Canadian Mounted Police, U.S. Army Medical Command, and over 30 colleges and universities.[11] Despite its popularity, the balanced scorecard is not without limitations. Importantly, it may not capture some of the most important priorities of a particular organization, such as resource acquisition or partnering with other organizations. Further, as with most strategy tools, its value depends on implementation and follow through as much as on substance.

Setting Objectives for Every Organizational Level

Objective setting should not stop with top management's establishing companywide performance targets. Company objectives need to be broken down into performance targets for each of the organization's separate businesses, product lines, functional departments, and individual work units. Employees within various functional areas and operating levels will be guided much better by specific objectives relating directly to their departmental activities than broad organizational-level goals. Objective setting is thus a *top-down process* that must extend to the lowest organizational levels. This means that each organizational unit must take care to set performance targets that support—rather than conflict with or negate—the achievement of companywide strategic and financial objectives.

The ideal situation is a team effort in which each organizational unit strives to produce results that contribute to the achievement of the company's performance targets and strategic vision. Such consistency signals that organizational units know their strategic role and are on board in helping the company move down the chosen strategic path and produce the desired results.

STAGE 3: CRAFTING A STRATEGY

As indicated in Chapter 1, the task of stitching a strategy together entails addressing a series of "hows": *how* to attract and please customers, *how* to compete against rivals, *how* to position the company in the marketplace, *how* to respond to changing market conditions, *how* to capitalize on attractive opportunities to grow the business, and *how* to achieve strategic and financial objectives. Choosing among the alternatives available in a way that coheres into a viable business model requires an understanding of the basic principles of strategic management. Fast-changing business environments demand astute entrepreneurship searching for opportunities to do new things or to do existing things in new or better ways.

● **LO 2-3**

Explain why the strategic initiatives taken at various organizational levels must be tightly coordinated.

In choosing among opportunities and addressing the hows of strategy, strategists must embrace the risks of uncertainty and the discomfort that naturally accompanies such risks. Bold strategies involve making difficult choices and placing bets on the future. Good strategic planning is not about eliminating risks, but increasing the odds of success.

This places a premium on astute entrepreneurship searching for opportunities to do new things or to do existing things in new or better ways.[12] The faster a company's business environment is changing, the more critical it becomes for its managers to be good entrepreneurs in diagnosing the direction and force of the changes underway and in responding with timely adjustments in strategy. Strategy makers have to pay attention to early warnings of future change and be willing to experiment with dare-to-be-different ways to establish a market position in that future. When obstacles appear unexpectedly in a company's path, it is up to management to adapt rapidly and innovatively. *Masterful strategies come from doing things differently from competitors where it counts—out-innovating them, being more efficient, being more imaginative, adapting faster—rather than running with the herd.* Good strategy making is therefore inseparable from good business entrepreneurship. One cannot exist without the other.

Strategy Making Involves Managers at All Organizational Levels

A company's senior executives obviously have lead strategy-making roles and responsibilities. The chief executive officer (CEO), as captain of the ship, carries the mantles of chief direction setter, chief objective setter, chief strategy maker, and chief strategy implementer for the total enterprise. Ultimate responsibility for *leading* the strategy-making, strategy-executing process rests with the CEO. And the CEO is always fully accountable for the results the strategy produces, whether good or bad. In some enterprises, the CEO or owner functions as chief architect of the strategy, personally deciding what the key elements of the company's strategy will be, although he or she may seek the advice of key subordinates and board members. A CEO-centered approach to strategy development is characteristic of small owner-managed companies and some large corporations that were founded by the present CEO or that have a CEO with strong strategic leadership skills. Elon Musk at Tesla Motors and SpaceX, Mark Zuckerberg at Facebook, Jeff Bezos at Amazon, Jack Ma of Alibaba, Warren Buffett at Berkshire Hathaway, and Marillyn Hewson at Lockheed Martin are examples of high-profile corporate CEOs who have wielded a heavy hand in shaping their company's strategy.

In most corporations, however, strategy is the product of more than just the CEO's handiwork. Typically, other senior executives—business unit heads, the chief financial officer, and vice presidents for production, marketing, and other functional departments—have influential strategy-making roles and help fashion the chief strategy components. Normally, a company's chief financial officer is in charge of devising and implementing an appropriate financial strategy; the production vice president takes the lead in developing the company's production strategy; the marketing vice president orchestrates sales and marketing strategy; a brand manager is in charge of the strategy for a particular brand in the company's product lineup; and so on. Moreover, the strategy-making efforts of top managers are complemented by advice and counsel from the company's board of directors; normally, all major strategic decisions are submitted to the board of directors for review, discussion, perhaps modification, and official approval.

> In most companies, crafting and executing strategy is a *collaborative team effort* in which every manager has a role for the area he or she heads; it is rarely something that only high-level managers do.

But strategy making is by no means solely a *top* management function, the exclusive province of owner-entrepreneurs, CEOs, high-ranking executives, and board members. The more a company's operations cut across different products, industries, and geographic areas, the more that headquarters executives have little option but to delegate considerable strategy-making authority to down-the-line managers in charge of particular subsidiaries, divisions, product lines, geographic sales offices, distribution centers, and plants. On-the-scene managers who oversee specific operating units can be reliably counted on to have more detailed command of the strategic issues for the particular operating unit under their supervision since they have more intimate knowledge of the prevailing market and competitive conditions, customer requirements and expectations, and all the other relevant aspects affecting the several strategic options available. Managers with day-to-day familiarity of, and authority over, a specific operating unit thus have a big edge over headquarters executives in making wise strategic choices for their unit. The result is that, in most of today's companies, crafting and executing strategy is a *collaborative team effort* in which *every company manager plays a strategy-making role*—ranging from minor to major—for the area he or she heads.

> The larger and more diverse the operations of an enterprise, the more points of strategic initiative it has and the more levels of management that have a significant strategy-making role.

Take, for example, a company like General Electric, a $213 billion global corporation with nearly 300,000 employees, operations in over 180 countries, and businesses that include jet engines, lighting, power generation, medical imaging and diagnostic equipment, locomotives, industrial automation, aviation services, and financial services. While top-level headquarters executives may well be personally involved in shaping GE's *overall* strategy and fashioning *important* strategic moves, they simply cannot know enough about the situation in every GE organizational unit to direct every strategic move made in GE's worldwide organization. Rather, it takes involvement on the part of GE's whole management team—top executives, business group heads, the heads of specific business units and product categories, and key managers in plants, sales offices, and distribution centers—to craft the thousands of strategic initiatives that end up composing the whole of GE's strategy.

A Company's Strategy-Making Hierarchy

In diversified companies like GE, where multiple and sometimes strikingly different businesses have to be managed, crafting a full-fledged strategy involves four distinct types of strategic actions and initiatives. Each of these involves different facets of the company's overall strategy and calls for the participation of different types of managers, as shown in Figure 2.2.

FIGURE 2.2   A Company's Strategy-Making Hierarchy

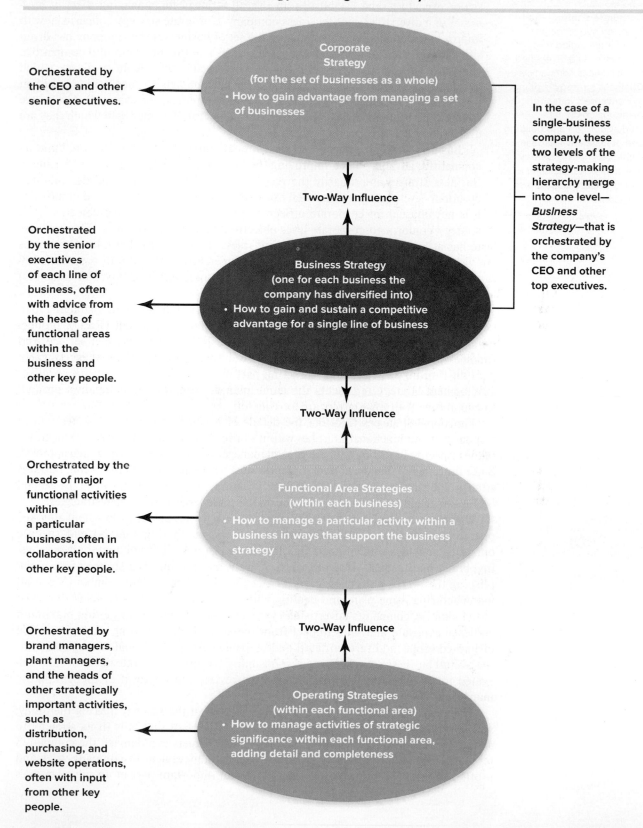

Orchestrated by the CEO and other senior executives.

Corporate Strategy
(for the set of businesses as a whole)
• How to gain advantage from managing a set of businesses

In the case of a single-business company, these two levels of the strategy-making hierarchy merge into one level—*Business Strategy*—that is orchestrated by the company's CEO and other top executives.

Two-Way Influence

Orchestrated by the senior executives of each line of business, often with advice from the heads of functional areas within the business and other key people.

Business Strategy
(one for each business the company has diversified into)
• How to gain and sustain a competitive advantage for a single line of business

Two-Way Influence

Orchestrated by the heads of major functional activities within a particular business, often in collaboration with other key people.

Functional Area Strategies
(within each business)
• How to manage a particular activity within a business in ways that support the business strategy

Two-Way Influence

Orchestrated by brand managers, plant managers, and the heads of other strategically important activities, such as distribution, purchasing, and website operations, often with input from other key people.

Operating Strategies
(within each functional area)
• How to manage activities of strategic significance within each functional area, adding detail and completeness

As shown in Figure 2.2, **corporate strategy** is orchestrated by the CEO and other senior executives and establishes an overall strategy for managing a *set of businesses* in a diversified, multibusiness company. Corporate strategy concerns how to improve the combined performance of the set of businesses the company has diversified into by capturing cross-business synergies and turning them into competitive advantage. It addresses the questions of what businesses to hold or divest, which new markets to enter, and how to best enter new markets (by acquisition, creation of a strategic alliance, or through internal development, for example). Corporate strategy and business diversification are the subjects of Chapter 8, in which they are discussed in detail.

Business strategy is concerned with strengthening the market position, building competitive advantage, and improving the performance of a single line of business. Business strategy is primarily the responsibility of business unit heads, although corporate-level executives may well exert strong influence; in diversified companies it is not unusual for corporate officers to insist that business-level objectives and strategy conform to corporate-level objectives and strategy themes. The business head has at least two other strategy-related roles: (1) seeing that lower-level strategies are well conceived, consistent, and adequately matched to the overall business strategy; and (2) keeping corporate-level officers (and sometimes the board of directors) informed of emerging strategic issues.

Functional-area strategies concern the approaches employed in managing particular functions within a business—like research and development (R&D), production, procurement of inputs, sales and marketing, distribution, customer service, and finance. A company's marketing strategy, for example, represents the managerial game plan for running the sales and marketing part of the business. A company's product development strategy represents the game plan for keeping the company's product lineup in tune with what buyers are looking for.

Functional strategies flesh out the details of a company's business strategy. Lead responsibility for functional strategies within a business is normally delegated to the heads of the respective functions, with the general manager of the business having final approval. Since the different functional-level strategies must be compatible with the overall business strategy and with one another to have beneficial impact, there are times when the general business manager exerts strong influence on the content of the functional strategies.

Operating strategies concern the relatively narrow approaches for managing key operating units (e.g., plants, distribution centers, purchasing centers) and specific operating activities with strategic significance (e.g., quality control, materials purchasing, brand management, Internet sales). A plant manager needs a strategy for accomplishing the plant's objectives, carrying out the plant's part of the company's overall manufacturing game plan, and dealing with any strategy-related problems that exist at the plant. A company's advertising manager needs a strategy for getting maximum audience exposure and sales impact from the ad budget. Operating strategies, while of limited scope, add further detail and completeness to functional strategies and to the overall business strategy. Lead responsibility for operating strategies is usually delegated to frontline managers, subject to the review and approval of higher-ranking managers.

Even though operating strategy is at the bottom of the strategy-making hierarchy, its importance should not be downplayed. A major plant that fails in its strategy to achieve production volume, unit cost, and quality targets can damage the company's reputation for quality products and undercut the achievement of company sales and profit objectives. Frontline managers are thus an important part of an organization's strategy-making team. One cannot reliably judge the strategic importance of a given action simply by the strategy level or location within the managerial hierarchy where it is initiated.

In single-business companies, the uppermost level of the strategy-making hierarchy is the business strategy, so a single-business company has three levels of strategy: business strategy, functional-area strategies, and operating strategies. Proprietorships, partnerships, and owner-managed enterprises may have only one or two strategy-making levels since it takes only a few key people to craft and oversee the firm's strategy. The larger and more diverse the operations of an enterprise, the more points of strategic initiative it has and the more levels of management that have a significant strategy-making role.

> A company's strategy is at full power only when its many pieces are united.

Uniting the Strategy-Making Hierarchy

The components of a company's strategy up and down the strategy hierarchy should be cohesive and mutually reinforcing, fitting together like a jigsaw puzzle. *Anything less than a unified collection of strategies weakens the overall strategy and is likely to impair company performance.*[13] It is the responsibility of top executives to achieve this unity by clearly communicating the company's vision, mission, objectives, and major strategy components to down-the-line managers and key personnel. Midlevel and frontline managers cannot craft unified strategic moves without first understanding the company's long-term direction and knowing the major components of the corporate and/or business strategies that their strategy-making efforts are supposed to support and enhance. Thus, as a general rule, strategy making must start at the top of the organization, then proceed downward from the corporate level to the business level, and then from the business level to the associated functional and operating levels. Once strategies up and down the hierarchy have been created, lower-level strategies must be scrutinized for consistency with and support of higher-level strategies. Any strategy conflicts must be addressed and resolved, either by modifying the lower-level strategies with conflicting elements or by adapting the higher-level strategy to accommodate what may be more appealing strategy ideas and initiatives bubbling up from below.

A Strategic Vision + Mission + Objectives + Strategy = A Strategic Plan

Developing a strategic vision and mission, setting objectives, and crafting a strategy are basic direction-setting tasks. They map out where a company is headed, delineate its strategic and financial targets, articulate the basic business model, and outline the competitive moves and operating approaches to be used in achieving the desired business results. Together, these elements constitute a **strategic plan** for coping with industry conditions, competing against rivals, meeting objectives, and making progress along the chosen strategic course.[14] Typically, a strategic plan includes a commitment to allocate resources to carrying out the plan and specifies a time period for achieving goals.

CORE CONCEPT

A company's **strategic plan** lays out its direction, business model, competitive strategy, and performance targets for some specified period of time.

In companies that do regular strategy reviews and develop explicit strategic plans, the strategic plan usually ends up as a written document that is circulated to most managers. Near-term performance targets are the part of the strategic plan most often communicated to employees more generally and spelled out explicitly. A number of companies summarize key elements of their strategic plans in the company's annual report to shareholders, in postings on their websites, or in statements provided to the business media; others, perhaps for reasons of competitive sensitivity, make only vague, general statements about their strategic plans.[15] In small, privately owned companies it is rare for strategic plans to exist in written form. Small-company strategic plans tend to reside in the thinking and directives of owner-executives; aspects of the plan are revealed in conversations with company personnel about where to head, what to accomplish, and how to proceed.

STAGE 4: EXECUTING THE STRATEGY

● ● ● ●

● LO 2-4

Recognize what a company must do to achieve operating excellence and to execute its strategy proficiently.

Managing the implementation of a strategy is easily the most demanding and time-consuming part of the strategic management process. Converting strategic plans into actions and results tests a manager's ability to direct organizational change, motivate company personnel, build and strengthen competitive capabilities, create and nurture a strategy-supportive work climate, and meet or beat performance targets. Initiatives to put the strategy in place and execute it proficiently must be launched and managed on many organizational fronts.

Management's action agenda for executing the chosen strategy emerges from assessing what the company will have to do to achieve the financial and strategic performance targets. Each company manager has to think through the answer to the question "What needs to be done in my area to execute my piece of the strategic plan, and what actions should I take to get the process under way?" How much internal change is needed depends on how much of the strategy is new, how far internal practices and competencies deviate from what the strategy requires, and how well the present work culture supports good strategy execution. Depending on the amount of internal change involved, full implementation and proficient execution of the company strategy (or important new pieces thereof) can take several months to several years.

In most situations, managing the strategy execution process includes the following principal aspects:

- Creating a strategy-supporting structure.
- Staffing the organization to obtain needed skills and expertise.
- Developing and strengthening strategy-supporting resources and capabilities.
- Allocating ample resources to the activities critical to strategic success.
- Ensuring that policies and procedures facilitate effective strategy execution.
- Organizing the work effort along the lines of best practice.
- Installing information and operating systems that enable company personnel to perform essential activities.
- Motivating people and tying rewards directly to the achievement of performance objectives.
- Creating a company culture conducive to successful strategy execution.
- Exerting the internal leadership needed to propel implementation forward.

Good strategy execution requires diligent pursuit of operating excellence. It is a job for a company's whole management team. Success hinges on the skills and cooperation of operating managers who can push for needed changes in their organizational units and consistently deliver good results. Management's handling of the strategy implementation process can be considered successful if things go smoothly enough that the company meets or beats its strategic and financial performance targets and shows good progress in achieving management's strategic vision. In Chapters 10, 11, and 12, we discuss the various aspects of the strategy implementation process more fully.

STAGE 5: EVALUATING PERFORMANCE AND INITIATING CORRECTIVE ADJUSTMENTS

The fifth component of the strategy management process—monitoring new external developments, evaluating the company's progress, and making corrective adjustments—is the trigger point for deciding whether to continue or change the company's vision and mission, objectives, strategy, business model and/or strategy execution methods.[16] As long as the company's strategy continues to pass the three tests of a winning strategy discussed in Chapter 1 (good fit, competitive advantage, strong performance), company executives may decide to stay the course. Simply fine-tuning the strategic plan and continuing with efforts to improve strategy execution are sufficient.

But whenever a company encounters disruptive changes in its environment, questions need to be raised about the appropriateness of its direction and strategy. If a company experiences a downturn in its market position or persistent shortfalls in performance, then company managers are obligated to ferret out the causes—do they relate to poor strategy, poor strategy execution, or both?—and take timely corrective action. A company's direction, objectives, business model, and strategy have to be revisited anytime external or internal conditions warrant.

Likewise, managers are obligated to assess which of the company's operating methods and approaches to strategy execution merit continuation and which need improvement. Proficient strategy execution is always the product of much organizational learning. It is achieved unevenly—coming quickly in some areas and proving troublesome in others. Consequently, top-notch strategy execution entails vigilantly searching for ways to improve and then making corrective adjustments whenever and wherever it is useful to do so.

> A company's vision, mission, objectives, strategy, and approach to strategy execution are never final; reviewing whether and when to make revisions is an ongoing process.

CORPORATE GOVERNANCE: THE ROLE OF THE BOARD OF DIRECTORS IN THE STRATEGY-CRAFTING, STRATEGY-EXECUTING PROCESS

Although senior managers have the *lead responsibility* for crafting and executing a company's strategy, it is the duty of a company's board of directors to exercise strong oversight and see that management performs the various tasks involved in each of the five stages of the strategy-making, strategy-executing process in a manner that best serves the interests of shareholders and other stakeholders, including the company's customers, employees, and the communities in which the company operates.[17] A company's board of directors has four important obligations to fulfill:

> ● **LO 2-5**
>
> Comprehend the role and responsibility of a company's board of directors in overseeing the strategic management process.

1. *Oversee the company's financial accounting and financial reporting practices.* While top executives, particularly the company's CEO and CFO (chief financial

officer), are primarily responsible for seeing that the company's financial statements fairly and accurately report the results of the company's operations, board members have a *legal obligation* to warrant the accuracy of the company's financial reports and protect shareholders. It is their job to ensure that generally accepted accounting principles (GAAP) are used properly in preparing the company's financial statements and that proper financial controls are in place to prevent fraud and misuse of funds. Virtually all boards of directors have an audit committee, always composed entirely of *outside directors* (*inside directors* hold management positions in the company and either directly or indirectly report to the CEO). The members of the audit committee have the lead responsibility for overseeing the decisions of the company's financial officers and consulting with both internal and external auditors to ensure accurate financial reporting and adequate financial controls.

2. *Critically appraise the company's direction, strategy, and business approaches.* Board members are also expected to guide management in choosing a strategic direction and to make independent judgments about the validity and wisdom of management's proposed strategic actions. This aspect of their duties takes on heightened importance when the company's strategy is failing or is plagued with faulty execution, and certainly when there is a precipitous collapse in profitability. But under more normal circumstances, many boards have found that meeting agendas become consumed by compliance matters with little time left to discuss matters of strategic importance. The board of directors and management at Philips Electronics hold annual two- to three-day retreats devoted exclusively to evaluating the company's long-term direction and various strategic proposals. The company's exit from the semiconductor business and its increased focus on medical technology and home health care resulted from management-board discussions during such retreats.[18]

3. *Evaluate the caliber of senior executives' strategic leadership skills.* The board is always responsible for determining whether the current CEO is doing a good job of strategic leadership (as a basis for awarding salary increases and bonuses and deciding on retention or removal).[19] Boards must also exercise due diligence in evaluating the strategic leadership skills of other senior executives in line to succeed the CEO. When the incumbent CEO steps down or leaves for a position elsewhere, the board must elect a successor, either going with an insider or deciding that an outsider is needed to perhaps radically change the company's strategic course. Often, the outside directors on a board visit company facilities and talk with company personnel personally to evaluate whether the strategy is on track, how well the strategy is being executed, and how well issues and problems are being addressed by various managers. For example, independent board members at GE visit operating executives at each major business unit once a year to assess the company's talent pool and stay abreast of emerging strategic and operating issues affecting the company's divisions. Home Depot board members visit a store once per quarter to determine the health of the company's operations.[20]

4. *Institute a compensation plan for top executives that rewards them for actions and results that serve stakeholder interests, and most especially those of shareholders.* A basic principle of corporate governance is that the owners of a corporation (the shareholders) delegate operating authority and managerial control to top management in return for compensation. In their role as *agents* of shareholders, top executives have a clear and unequivocal duty to make decisions and operate the

company in accord with shareholder interests. (This does not mean disregarding the interests of other stakeholders—employees, suppliers, the communities in which the company operates, and society at large.) Most boards of directors have a compensation committee, composed entirely of directors from *outside* the company, to develop a salary and incentive compensation plan that rewards senior executives for boosting the company's *long-term* performance on behalf of shareholders. The compensation committee's recommendations are presented to the full board for approval. But during the past 10 years, many boards of directors have done a poor job of ensuring that executive salary increases, bonuses, and stock option awards are tied tightly to performance measures that are truly in the long-term interests of shareholders. Rather, compensation packages at many companies have increasingly rewarded executives for short-term performance improvements—most notably, for achieving quarterly and annual earnings targets and boosting the stock price by specified percentages. This has had the perverse effect of causing company managers to become preoccupied with actions to improve a company's near-term performance, often motivating them to take unwise business risks to boost short-term earnings by amounts sufficient to qualify for multimillion-dollar compensation packages (that many see as obscenely large). The focus on short-term performance has proved damaging to long-term company performance and shareholder interests— witness the huge loss of shareholder wealth that occurred at many financial institutions during the banking crisis of 2008–2009 because of executive risk-taking in subprime loans, credit default swaps, and collateralized mortgage securities. As a consequence, the need to overhaul and reform executive compensation has become a hot topic in both public circles and corporate boardrooms. Illustration Capsule 2.4 discusses how weak governance at Volkswagen contributed to the 2015 emissions cheating scandal, which cost the company billions of dollars and the trust of its stakeholders.

> **CORE CONCEPT**
>
> A company's **stakeholders** include its stockholders, employees, suppliers, the communities in which the company operates, and society at large.

Every corporation should have a strong independent board of directors that (1) is well informed about the company's performance, (2) guides and judges the CEO and other top executives, (3) has the courage to curb management actions the board believes are inappropriate or unduly risky, (4) certifies to shareholders that the CEO is doing what the board expects, (5) provides insight and advice to management, and (6) is intensely involved in debating the pros and cons of key decisions and actions.[21] Boards of directors that lack the backbone to challenge a strong-willed or "imperial" CEO or that rubber-stamp almost anything the CEO recommends without probing inquiry and debate abdicate their fiduciary duty to represent and protect shareholder interests.

> Effective corporate governance requires the board of directors to oversee the company's strategic direction, evaluate its senior executives, handle executive compensation, and oversee financial reporting practices.

In 2015, Volkswagen admitted to installing "defeat devices" on at least 11 million vehicles with diesel engines. These devices enabled the cars to pass emission tests, even though the engines actually emitted pollutants up to 40 times above what is allowed in the United States. Current estimates are that it will cost the company at least €7 billion to cover the cost of repairs and lawsuits. Although management must have been involved in approving the use of cheating devices, the Volkswagen supervisory board has been unwilling to accept any responsibility. Some board members even questioned whether it was the board's responsibility to be aware of such problems, stating "matters of technical expertise were not for us" and "the scandal had nothing, not one iota, to do with the advisory board." Yet governing boards do have a responsibility to be well informed, to provide oversight, and to become involved in key decisions and actions. So what caused this corporate governance failure? Why is this the third time in the past 20 years that Volkswagen has been embroiled in scandal?

The key feature of Volkswagen's board that appears to have led to these issues is a lack of independent directors. However, before explaining this in more detail it is important to understand the German governance model. German corporations operate two-tier governance structures, with a management board, and a separate supervisory board that does not contain any current executives. In addition, German law requires large companies to have at least 50 percent supervisory board representation from workers. This structure is meant to provide more oversight by independent board members and greater involvement by a wider set of stakeholders.

In Volkswagen's case, these objectives have been effectively circumvented. Although Volkswagen's supervisory board does not include any current management, the chairmanship appears to be a revolving door of former senior executives. Ferdinand Piëch, the chair during the scandal, was CEO for 9 years prior to becoming

Vytautas Kielaitis/Shutterstock

chair in 2002. Martin Winterkorn, the recently ousted CEO, was expected to become supervisory board chair prior to the scandal. The company continues to elevate management to the supervisory board even though they have presided over past scandals. Hans Dieter Poetsch, the newly appointed chair, was part of the management team that did not inform the supervisory board of the EPA investigation for two weeks.

VW also has a unique ownership structure where a single family, Porsche, controls more than 50 percent of voting shares. Piëch, a family member and chair until 2015, forced out CEOs and installed unqualified family members on the board, such as his former nanny and current wife. He also pushed out independent-minded board members, such as Gerhard Cromme, author of Germany's corporate governance code. The company has lost numerous independent directors over the past 10 years, leaving it with only one non-shareholder, non-labor representative. Although Piëch has now been removed, it is unclear that Volkswagen's board has solved the underlying problem. Shareholders have seen billions of dollars wiped away and the Volkswagen brand tarnished. As long as the board continues to lack independent directors, change will likely be slow.

Note: Developed with Jacob M. Crandall.

Sources: "Piëch under Fire," *The Economist,* December 8, 2005; Chris Bryant and Richard Milne, "Boardroom Politics at Heart of VW Scandal," *Financial Times,* October 4, 2015; Andreas Cremer and Jan Schwartz, "Volkswagen Mired in Crisis as Board Members Criticize Piech," Reuters, April 24, 2015; Richard Milne, "Volkswagen: System Failure," *Financial Times,* November 4, 2015.

KEY POINTS

The strategic management process consists of five interrelated and integrated stages:

1. *Developing a strategic vision* of the company's future, a *mission statement* that defines the company's current purpose, and a set of *core values* to guide the pursuit of the vision and mission. This stage of strategy making provides direction for the company, motivates and inspires company personnel, aligns and guides actions throughout the organization, and communicates to stakeholders management's aspirations for the company's future.

2. *Setting objectives* to convert the vision and mission into performance targets that can be used as yardsticks for measuring the company's performance. Objectives need to spell out *how much* of *what kind* of performance *by when.* Two broad types of objectives are required: *financial objectives* and *strategic objectives.* A *balanced scorecard* approach for measuring company performance entails setting both financial objectives and strategic objectives. *Stretch objectives* can spur exceptional performance and help build a firewall against complacency and mediocre performance. Extreme stretch objectives, however, are only warranted in limited circumstances.

3. *Crafting a strategy* to achieve the objectives and move the company along the strategic course that management has charted. A single business enterprise has three levels of strategy—business strategy for the company as a whole, functional-area strategies (e.g., marketing, R&D, logistics), and operating strategies (for key operating units, such as manufacturing plants). In diversified, multibusiness companies, the strategy-making task involves four distinct types or levels of strategy: corporate strategy for the company as a whole, business strategy (one for each business the company has diversified into), functional-area strategies within each business, and operating strategies. Thus, strategy making is an inclusive collaborative activity involving not only senior company executives but also the heads of major business divisions, functional-area managers, and operating managers on the frontlines.

4. *Executing the chosen strategy* and converting the strategic plan into action. Management's agenda for executing the chosen strategy emerges from assessing what the company will have to do to achieve the targeted financial and strategic performance. Management's handling of the strategy implementation process can be considered successful if things go smoothly enough that the company meets or beats its strategic and financial performance targets and shows good progress in achieving management's strategic vision.

5. *Monitoring developments, evaluating performance, and initiating corrective adjustments* in light of actual experience, changing conditions, new ideas, and new opportunities. This stage of the strategy management process is the trigger point for deciding whether to continue or change the company's vision and mission, objectives, business model strategy, and/or strategy execution methods.

The sum of a company's strategic vision, mission, objectives, and strategy constitutes a *strategic plan* for coping with industry conditions, outcompeting rivals, meeting objectives, and making progress toward aspirational goals.

Boards of directors have a duty to shareholders as well as other stakeholders to play a vigilant role in overseeing management's handling of a company's strategy-making, strategy-executing process. This entails four important obligations: (1) Ensure that the company issues accurate financial reports and has adequate financial controls; (2) critically appraise the company's direction, strategy, and strategy execution; (3) evaluate the caliber of senior executives' strategic leadership skills; and (4) institute a compensation plan for top executives that rewards them for actions and results that serve stakeholder interests, most especially those of shareholders.

ASSURANCE OF LEARNING EXERCISES

LO 2-1

1. Using the information in Table 2.2, critique the adequacy and merit of the following vision statements, listing effective elements and shortcomings. Rank the vision statements from best to worst once you complete your evaluation.

Vision Statement	Effective Elements	Shortcomings
American Express • We work hard every day to make American Express the world's most respected service brand.		
Hilton Hotels Corporation Our vision is to be the first choice of the world's travelers. Hilton intends to build on the rich heritage and strength of our brands by: • Consistently delighting our customers • Investing in our team members • Delivering innovative products and services • Continuously improving performance • Increasing shareholder value • Creating a culture of pride • Strengthening the loyalty of our constituents		
MasterCard • A world beyond cash.		
BASF We are "The Chemical Company" successfully operating in all major markets. • Our customers view BASF as their partner of choice. • Our innovative products, intelligent solutions and services make us the most competent worldwide supplier in the chemical industry. • We generate a high return on assets. • We strive for sustainable development. • We welcome change as an opportunity. • We, the employees of BASF, together ensure our success.		

Sources: Company websites and annual reports.

2. Go to the company investor relations websites for Starbucks (**investor.starbucks.com**), Pfizer (**www.pfizer.com/investors**), and Salesforce (**investor.salesforce.com**) to find examples of strategic and financial objectives. List four objectives for each company, and indicate which of these are strategic and which are financial. **LO 2-2**

3. Go to the investor relations website for Walmart (**investors.walmartstores.com**) and review past presentations Walmart has made during various investor conferences by clicking on the Events option in the navigation bar. Prepare a one- to two-page report that outlines what Walmart has said to investors about its approach to strategy execution. Specifically, what has management discussed concerning staffing, resource allocation, policies and procedures, information and operating systems, continuous improvement, rewards and incentives, corporate culture, and internal leadership at the company? **LO 2-4**

4. Based on the information provided in Illustration Capsule 2.4, describe the ways in which Volkswagen did not fulfill the requirements of effective corporate governance. In what ways did the board of directors sidestep its obligations to protect shareholder interests? How could Volkswagen better select its board of directors to avoid mistakes such as the emissions scandal in 2015? **connect LO 2-5**

EXERCISES FOR SIMULATION PARTICIPANTS **connect**

1. Which of the five stages of the strategy formulation, strategy execution process apply to your company in the simulation? **LO 2-5**

2. Meet with your co-managers and prepare a strategic vision statement for your company. It should be at least one sentence long and no longer than a brief paragraph. When you are finished, check to see if your vision statement meets the conditions for an effectively worded strategic vision set forth in Table 2.2. If not, then revise it accordingly. What would be a good slogan that captures the essence of your strategic vision and that could be used to help communicate the vision to company personnel, shareholders, and other stakeholders? **LO 2-1**

3. What are your company's financial objectives? What are your company's strategic objectives? **LO 2-2**

4. What are the three to four key elements of your company's strategy? **LO 2-3**

5. The strategy execution process for your company in the business simulation includes which principle aspects? **LO 2-4**

ENDNOTES

[1] Gordon Shaw, Robert Brown, and Philip Bromiley, "Strategic Stories: How 3M Is Rewriting Business Planning," *Harvard Business Review* 76, no. 3 (May–June 1998); David J. Collis and Michael G. Rukstad, "Can You Say What Your Strategy Is?" *Harvard Business Review* 86, no. 4 (April 2008) pp. 82–90.
[2] Hugh Davidson, *The Committed Enterprise: How to Make Vision and Values Work*

(Oxford: Butterworth Heinemann, 2002); W. Chan Kim and Renée Mauborgne, "Charting Your Company's Future," *Harvard Business Review* 80, no. 6 (June 2002), pp. 77–83; James C. Collins and Jerry I. Porras, "Building Your Company's Vision," *Harvard Business Review* 74, no. 5 (September–October 1996), pp. 65–77; Jim Collins and Jerry Porras, *Built to Last: Successful Habits of Visionary Companies*

(New York: HarperCollins, 1994); Michel Robert, *Strategy Pure and Simple II: How Winning Companies Dominate Their Competitors* (New York: McGraw-Hill, 1998).
[3] Davidson, *The Committed Enterprise*, pp. 20 and 54.
[4] As quoted in Charles H. House and Raymond L. Price, "The Return Map: Tracking Product Teams," *Harvard Business Review* 60, no. 1 (January–February 1991), p. 93.

[5] Sitkin, S., Miller, C. and See, K., "The Stretch Goal Paradox", *Harvard Business Review*, 95, no. 1 (January–February, 2017, pp. 92–99.

[6] Robert S. Kaplan and David P. Norton, *The Strategy-Focused Organization* (Boston: Harvard Business School Press, 2001); Robert S. Kaplan and David P. Norton, *The Balanced Scorecard: Translating Strategy into Action* (Boston: Harvard Business School Press, 1996).

[7] Kaplan and Norton, *The Strategy-Focused Organization;* Kaplan and Norton, *The Balanced Scorecard;* Kevin B. Hendricks, Larry Menor, and Christine Wiedman, "The Balanced Scorecard: To Adopt or Not to Adopt," *Ivey Business Journal* 69, no. 2 (November–December 2004), pp. 1–7; Sandy Richardson, "The Key Elements of Balanced Scorecard Success," *Ivey Business Journal* 69, no. 2 (November–December 2004), pp. 7–9.

[8] Kaplan and Norton, *The Balanced Scorecard.*

[9] Ibid.

[10] Ibid.

[11] Information posted on the website of the Balanced Scorecard Institute, **balancedscorecard .org** (accessed October, 2015).

[12] Henry Mintzberg, Bruce Ahlstrand, and Joseph Lampel, *Strategy Safari: A Guided Tour through the Wilds of Strategic Management* (New York: Free Press, 1998); Bruce Barringer and Allen C. Bluedorn, "The Relationship between Corporate Entrepreneurship and Strategic Management," *Strategic Management Journal* 20 (1999), pp. 421–444; Jeffrey G. Covin and Morgan P. Miles, "Corporate Entrepreneurship and the Pursuit of Competitive Advantage," *Entrepreneurship: Theory and Practice* 23, no. 3 (Spring 1999), pp. 47–63; David A. Garvin and Lynne C. Levesque, "Meeting the Challenge of Corporate Entrepreneurship," *Harvard Business Review* 84, no. 10 (October 2006), pp. 102–112.

[13] Joseph L. Bower and Clark G. Gilbert, "How Managers' Everyday Decisions Create or Destroy Your Company's Strategy," *Harvard Business Review* 85, no. 2 (February 2007), pp. 72–79.

[14] Gordon Shaw, Robert Brown, and Philip Bromiley, "Strategic Stories: How 3M Is Rewriting Business Planning," *Harvard Business Review* 76, no. 3 (May–June 1998), pp. 41–50.

[15] David Collis and Michael Rukstad, "Can You Say What Your Stratgey Is?" *Harvard Business Review*, May 2008, pp. 82–90.

[16] Cynthia A. Montgomery, "Putting Leadership Back into Strategy," *Harvard Business Review* 86, no. 1 (January 2008), pp. 54–60.

[17] Jay W. Lorsch and Robert C. Clark, "Leading from the Boardroom," *Harvard Business Review* 86, no. 4 (April 2008), pp. 105–111.

[18] Ibid.

[19] Stephen P. Kaufman, "Evaluating the CEO," *Harvard Business Review* 86, no. 10 (October 2008), pp. 53–57.

[20] Ibid.

[21] David A. Nadler, "Building Better Boards," *Harvard Business Review* 82, no. 5 (May 2004), pp. 102–105; Cynthia A. Montgomery and Rhonda Kaufman, "The Board's Missing Link," *Harvard Business Review* 81, no. 3 (March 2003), pp. 86–93; John Carver, "What Continues to Be Wrong with Corporate Governance and How to Fix It," *Ivey Business Journal* 68, no. 1 (September–October 2003), pp. 1–5. See also Gordon Donaldson, "A New Tool for Boards: The Strategic Audit," *Harvard Business Review* 73, no. 4 (July–August 1995), pp. 99–107.

chapter 3

Evaluating a Company's External Environment

Learning Objectives

After reading this chapter, you should be able to:

LO 3-1 Recognize the factors in a company's broad macro-environment that may have strategic significance.

LO 3-2 Use analytic tools to diagnose the competitive conditions in a company's industry.

LO 3-3 Map the market positions of key groups of industry rivals.

LO 3-4 Determine whether an industry's outlook presents a company with sufficiently attractive opportunities for growth and profitability.

Fanatic Studio/Getty Images

No matter what it takes, the goal of *strategy* is to beat the competition.

    Kenichi Ohmae—*Consultant and author*

Companies that solely focus on competition will die. Those that focus on value creation will thrive.

    Edward de Bono—*Author and consultant*

Continued innovation is the best way to beat the competition.

    Thomas A Edison—*Inventor and Businessman*

In Chapter 2, we learned that the strategy formulation, strategy execution process begins with an appraisal of the company's present situation. Two facets of a company's situation are especially pertinent: (1) its external environment—most notably, the competitive conditions of the industry in which the company operates; and (2) its internal environment—particularly the company's resources and organizational capabilities.

Insightful diagnosis of a company's external and internal environments is a prerequisite for managers to succeed in crafting a strategy that is an excellent *fit* with the company's situation—the first test of a winning strategy. As depicted in Figure 3.1, strategic thinking begins with an appraisal of the company's external and internal environments (as a basis for deciding on a long-term direction and developing a strategic vision). It then moves toward an evaluation of the most promising alternative business models, and strategies and finally culminates in choosing a specific strategy.

This chapter presents the concepts and analytic tools for zeroing in on those aspects of a company's external environment that should be considered in making strategic choices. Attention centers on the broad environmental context, the specific market arena in which a company operates, the drivers of change, the positions and likely actions of rival companies, and key success factors. In Chapter 4, we explore the methods of evaluating a company's internal circumstances and competitive capabilities.

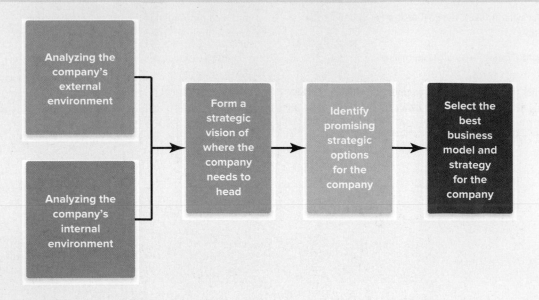

ASSESSING THE COMPANY'S INDUSTRY AND COMPETITIVE ENVIRONMENT

Thinking strategically about a company's industry and competitive environment entails using some well-validated concepts and analytical tools to get clear answers to seven questions:

1. Do macro-environmental factors and industry characteristics offer sellers opportunities for growth and attractive profits?
2. What kinds of competitive forces are industry members facing, and how strong is each force?
3. What forces are driving industry change, and what impact will these changes have on competitive intensity and industry profitability?
4. What market positions do industry rivals occupy—who is strongly positioned and who is not?
5. What strategic moves are rivals likely to make next?
6. What are the key factors of competitive success?
7. Does the industry outlook offer good prospects for profitability?

Analysis-based answers to these questions are prerequisites for a strategy offering good fit with the external situation. The remainder of this chapter is devoted to describing the methods of obtaining solid answers to these seven questions.

ANALYZING THE COMPANY'S MACRO-ENVIRONMENT

A company's external environment includes the immediate industry and competitive environment and a broader "macro-environment" (see Figure 3.2). This macro-environment comprises six principal components: political factors; economic conditions in the firm's general environment (local, country, regional, worldwide); sociocultural forces; technological factors; environmental factors (concerning the natural environment); and legal/regulatory conditions. Each of these components has the potential to affect the firm's more immediate industry and competitive environment, although some are likely to have a more important effect than others. An analysis of the impact of these factors is often referred to as **PESTEL analysis,** an acronym that

● **LO 3-1**

Recognize the factors in a company's broad macro-environment that may have strategic significance.

FIGURE 3.2   The Components of a Company's Macro-Environment

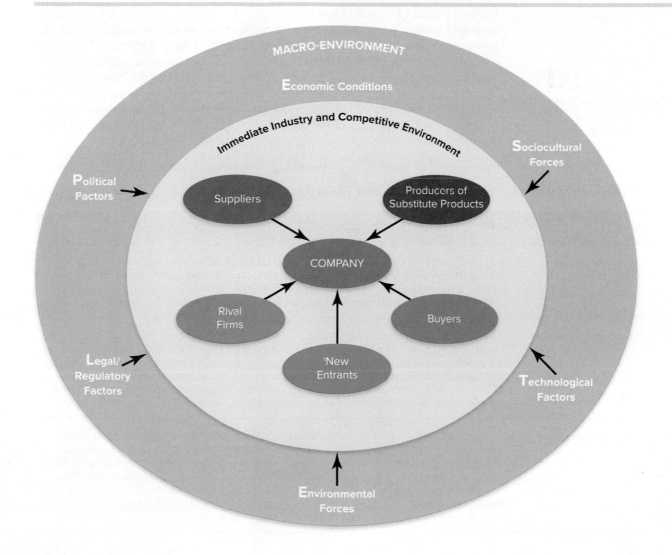

serves as a reminder of the six components involved (Political, Economic, Sociocultural, Technological, Environmental, Legal/regulatory).

Since macro-economic factors affect different industries in different ways and to different degrees, it is important for managers to determine which of these represent the most *strategically relevant factors* outside the firm's industry boundaries. By *strategically relevant,* we mean important enough to have a bearing on the decisions the company ultimately makes about its long-term direction, objectives, strategy, and business model. The impact of the outer-ring factors depicted in Figure 3.2 on a company's choice of strategy can range from big to small. Those factors that are likely to a bigger impact deserve the closest attention. But even factors that have a low impact on the company's business situation merit a watchful eye since their level of impact may change.

For example, when stringent new federal banking regulations are announced, banks must rapidly adapt their strategies and lending practices to be in compliance. Cigarette producers must adapt to new antismoking ordinances, the decisions of governments to impose higher cigarette taxes, the growing cultural stigma attached to smoking and newly emerging e-cigarette technology. The homebuilding industry is affected by such macro-influences as trends in household incomes and buying power, rules and regulations that make it easier or harder for homebuyers to obtain mortgages, changes in mortgage interest rates, shifting preferences of families for renting versus owning a home, and shifts in buyer preferences for homes of various sizes, styles, and price ranges. Companies in the food processing, restaurant, sports, and fitness industries have to pay special attention to changes in lifestyles, eating habits, leisure-time preferences, and attitudes toward nutrition and fitness in fashioning their strategies. Table 3.1 provides a brief description of the components of the macro-environment and some examples of the industries or business situations that they might affect.

TABLE 3.1   The Six Components of the Macro-Environment

Component	Description
Political factors	Pertinent political factors include matters such as tax policy, fiscal policy, tariffs, the political climate, and the strength of institutions such as the federal banking system. Some political policies affect certain types of industries more than others. An example is energy policy, which clearly affects energy producers and heavy users of energy more than other types of businesses.
Economic conditions	Economic conditions include the general economic climate and specific factors such as interest rates, exchange rates, the inflation rate, the unemployment rate, the rate of economic growth, trade deficits or surpluses, savings rates, and per-capita domestic product. Some industries, such as construction, are particularly vulnerable to economic downturns but are positively affected by factors such as low interest rates. Others, such as discount retailing, benefit when general economic conditions weaken, as consumers become more price-conscious.
Sociocultural forces	Sociocultural forces include the societal values, attitudes, cultural influences, and lifestyles that impact demand for particular goods and services, as well as demographic factors such as the population size, growth rate, and age distribution. Sociocultural forces vary by locale and change over time. An example is the trend toward healthier lifestyles, which can shift spending toward exercise equipment and health clubs and away from alcohol and snack foods. The demographic effect of people living longer is having a huge impact on the health care, nursing homes, travel, hospitality, and entertainment industries.

(continued)

TABLE 3.1   *(continued)*

Component	Description
Technological factors	Technological factors include the pace of technological change and technical developments that have the potential for wide-ranging effects on society, such as genetic engineering, nanotechnology, and solar energy technology. They include institutions involved in creating new knowledge and controlling the use of technology, such as R&D consortia, university-sponsored technology incubators, patent and copyright laws, and government control over the Internet. Technological change can encourage the birth of new industries, such as drones, virtual reality technology, and connected wearable devices. They can disrupt others, as cloud computing, 3-D printing, and big data solution have done, and they can render other industries obsolete (film cameras, music CDs).
Environmental forces	These include ecological and environmental forces such as weather, climate, climate change, and associated factors like flooding, fire, and water shortages. These factors can directly impact industries such as insurance, farming, energy production, and tourism. They may have an indirect but substantial effect on other industries such as transportation and utilities. The relevance of environmental considerations stems from the fact that some industries contribute more significantly than others to air and water pollution or to the depletion of irreplaceable natural resources, or to inefficient energy/resource usage, or are closely associated with other types of environmentally damaging activities (unsustainable agricultural practices, the creation of waste products that are not recyclable or biodegradable). Growing numbers of companies worldwide, in response to stricter environmental regulations and also to mounting public concerns about the environment, are implementing actions to operate in a more environmentally and ecologically responsible manner.
Legal and regulatory factors	These factors include the regulations and laws with which companies must comply, such as consumer laws, labor laws, antitrust laws, and occupational health and safety regulation. Some factors, such as financial services regulation, are industry-specific. Others affect certain types of industries more than others. For example, minimum wage legislation largely impacts low-wage industries (such as nursing homes and fast food restaurants) that employ substantial numbers of relatively unskilled workers. Companies in coal-mining, meat-packing, and steel-making, where many jobs are hazardous or carry high risk of injury, are much more impacted by occupational safety regulations than are companies in industries such as retailing or software programming.

As the events surrounding the coronavirus pandemic of 2020 made abundantly clear, there is a class of macro-level external factors that is not included as part of PESTEL analysis. This is the set of factors that occurs more irregularly and unpredictably, unlike the categories within PESTEL that can be expected to affect firms in an ongoing and more foreseeable manner. This additional set of factors can be thought of as **societal shocks** to the macro-environment; they include terrorism (whether by domestic or foreign agents), civil war, foreign invasion or occupation, and epidemics and pandemics. Societal shocks such as these also affect different industries and companies to varying degrees, but they are much harder for companies to anticipate and prepare for since they often begin with little warning. The coordinated terrorist attacks by al-Qaeda against the United States now referred to as 9/11 (since they occurred on September 11, 2001) offer an example. These attacks had a significant economic impact, not only within the United States, but on world markets as well. New York City's businesses suffered enormously, particularly those located

The Differential Effects of the Coronavirus Pandemic of 2020

While the world had suffered through a number of other pandemics, including the Spanish Flu (which caused somewhere between 20 to 50 million deaths in 1918–1919), the Coronavirus pandemic of 2020 was predicted to be even more devastating. Not only was the world now more interconnected due to globalization, but the disease causing the pandemic, known as Covid-19, was easily transmissible. By April 1, 2020, there were already more than 31,000 deaths worldwide, despite the fact that the disease had not yet peaked in some of the world's most populous countries.

The virus was new to the world and identified as such in early January, 2020. First appearing in Wuhan, a Chinese city of 11 million, it spread around the globe rapidly, reaching at least 170 countries by the end of March. Different countries were affected by the pandemic at different rates and handled the crisis in different ways. Nations that were particularly hard hit by Covid-19 include China, Italy (with 1/3 of the deaths as of April 1, 2020), Spain, France, Iran, and the United States. Italy's high death rate may be explained in part due to demographics, since its much older population was more susceptible to the disease. But in contrast to South Korea, which utilized extensive testing to identify and control the spread of the disease, Italy failed to test widely. The United States also found itself with insufficient test kits to implement South Korea's strategy, a situation exacerbated by the Trump administration's downplaying the seriousness of the threat until March.

The economic impact of the pandemic was catastrophic, despite a $2 trillion U.S. fiscal stimulus package and similar measures elsewhere designed to combat its economic consequences. Emerging markets seemed destined to absorb much of the hit, as international investment dried up, tourism collapsed, and demand for commodities fell. But even wealthy nations were not immune from dire consequences, although different sectors and industries were affected to varying degrees. In the United States, the hospitality and transportation industries were hard hit, along with retail, oil and gas,

Shutterstock / theskaman306

live sports and other forms of entertainment. Small businesses and low-margin industries, with little ability to weather a significant downturn, were particularly vulnerable. Some industries, such as health care, online retail, and delivery services found themselves facing demand in excess of their capabilities, especially in light of supply chain breakdowns. A number of large companies responded to the crisis by switching to the production of supplies needed for managing the crisis. GM, Ford, and other automakers aided the efforts to produce critically needed ventilators, while distilleries such as Tito's Handmade Vodka and Dillon's Distillery began making hand sanitizers. Fashion companies, such as Inditex (with its Zara brand) and Los Angeles Apparel, turned their production capabilities toward making hospital gowns and face masks. Virtually no company was unaffected by the pandemic, but those which quickly adopted practices to remain nimble, control costs, minimize job losses, support their workers and suppliers, and join in the effort to combat the crisis were best positioned to weather it.

Sources: "Timeline: How the new coronavirus spread, Aljazeera news, March 29, 2020; "These companies are switching gears to help address coronavirus shortages", by Chloe Hadavas, Slate, March 23, 2020; SlateStatista.com (accessed April 1, 2020).

within and nearby the World Trade Center complex. Industries suffering an outsized effect include the airline industry, which had to cut back travel capacity by nearly 20%, and the export industry. Illustration Capsule 3.1 illustrates how another such societal shock—the coronavirus pandemic of 2020—affected industries, businesses, geographies, and countries differentially.

As company managers scan the external environment, they must be alert for potentially important outer-ring developments (whether in the form of societal shocks or among the components of PESTEL analysis), assess their impact and influence, and adapt the company's direction and strategy as needed. However, the factors in a company's environment having the *greatest* strategy-shaping impact typically pertain to the company's immediate industry and competitive environment. Consequently, it is on a company's industry and competitive environment (depicted in the center of Figure 3.2) that we concentrate the bulk of our attention in this chapter.

ASSESSING THE COMPANY'S INDUSTRY AND COMPETITIVE ENVIRONMENT

After gaining an understanding of the industry's general economic characteristics, attention should be focused on the competitive dynamics of the industry. This entails using some well-validated concepts and analytic tools. These include the five forces framework, the value net, driving forces, strategic groups, competitor analysis, and key success factors. Proper use of these analytic tools can provide managers with the understanding needed to craft a strategy that fits the company's situation within their industry environment. The remainder of this chapter is devoted to describing how managers can use these tools to inform and improve their strategic choices.

● ● ● ●

● **LO 3-2**

Use analytic tools to diagnose the competitive conditions in a company's industry.

The Five Forces Framework

The character and strength of the competitive forces operating in an industry are never the same from one industry to another. The most powerful and widely used tool for diagnosing the principal competitive pressures in a market is the *five forces framework*.[1] This framework, depicted in Figure 3.3, holds that competitive pressures on companies within an industry come from five sources. These include (1) competition from *rival sellers,* (2) competition from *potential new entrants* to the industry, (3) competition from producers of *substitute products,* (4) *supplier* bargaining power, and (5) *customer* bargaining power.

   Using the five forces model to determine the nature and strength of competitive pressures in a given industry involves three steps:

- *Step 1:* For each of the five forces, identify the different parties involved, along with the specific factors that bring about competitive pressures.
- *Step 2:* Evaluate how strong the pressures stemming from each of the five forces are (strong, moderate, or weak).
- *Step 3:* Determine whether the five forces, overall, are supportive of high industry profitability.

Competitive Pressures Created by the Rivalry among Competing Sellers

The strongest of the five competitive forces is often the rivalry for buyer patronage among competing sellers of a product or service. The intensity of rivalry among competing sellers within an industry depends on a number of identifiable factors. Figure 3.4 summarizes these factors, identifying those that intensify or weaken rivalry among direct competitors in an industry. A brief explanation of why these factors affect the degree of rivalry is in order:

FIGURE 3.3   The Five Forces Model of Competition: A Key Analytic Tool

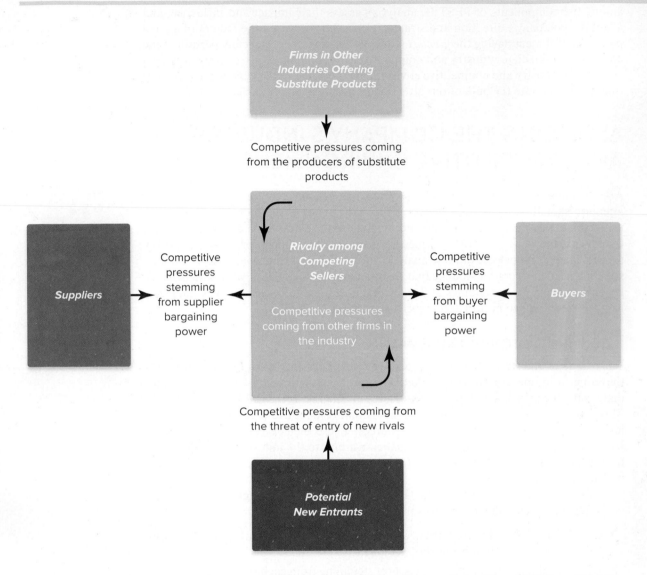

Sources: Adapted from M. E. Porter, "How Competitive Forces Shape Strategy," *Harvard Business Review* 57, no. 2 (1979), pp. 137–145; M. E. Porter, "The Five Competitive Forces That Shape Strategy," *Harvard Business Review* 86, no. 1 (2008), pp. 80–86.

- *Rivalry increases when buyer demand is growing slowly or declining.* Rapidly expanding buyer demand produces enough new business for all industry members to grow without having to draw customers away from rival enterprises. But in markets where buyer demand is slow-growing or shrinking, companies eager to gain more business are likely to engage in aggressive price discounting, sales promotions, and other tactics to increase their sales volumes at the expense of rivals, sometimes to the point of igniting a fierce battle for market share.

- *Rivalry increases as it becomes less costly for buyers to switch brands.* The less costly (or easier) it is for buyers to switch their purchases from one seller to another, the easier it is for sellers to steal customers away from rivals. When the cost of

FIGURE 3.4   Factors Affecting the Strength of Rivalry

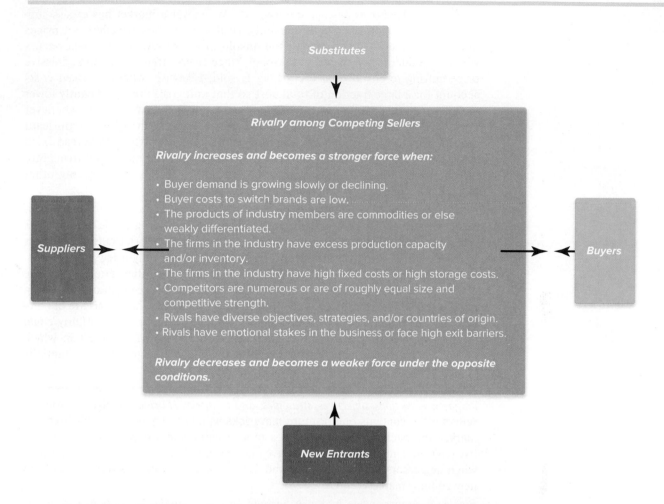

switching brands is higher, buyers are less prone to brand switching and sellers have protection from rivalrous moves. Switching costs include not only monetary costs but also the time, inconvenience, and psychological costs involved in switching brands. For example, retailers may not switch to the brands of rival manufacturers because they are hesitant to sever long-standing supplier relationships or incur the additional expense of retraining employees, accessing technical support, or testing the quality and reliability of the new brand. Consumers may not switch brands because they become emotionally attached to a particular brand (e.g. if you identify with the Harley motorcycle brand and lifestyle).

- *Rivalry increases as the products of rival sellers become less strongly differentiated.* When the offerings of rivals are identical or weakly differentiated, buyers have less reason to be brand-loyal—a condition that makes it easier for rivals to convince buyers to switch to their offerings. Moreover, when the products of different sellers are virtually identical, shoppers will choose on the basis of price, which can result in fierce price competition among sellers. On the other hand, strongly differentiated product offerings among rivals breed high brand loyalty on the part of buyers who view the attributes of certain brands as more appealing or better suited to their needs.

- *Rivalry is more intense when industry members have too much inventory or significant amounts of idle production capacity, especially if the industry's product entails high fixed costs or high storage costs.* Whenever a market has excess supply (overproduction relative to demand), rivalry intensifies as sellers cut prices in a desperate effort to cope with the unsold inventory. A similar effect occurs when a product is perishable or seasonal, since firms often engage in aggressive price cutting to ensure that everything is sold. Likewise, whenever fixed costs account for a large fraction of total cost so that unit costs are significantly lower at full capacity, firms come under significant pressure to cut prices whenever they are operating below full capacity. Unused capacity imposes a significant cost-increasing penalty because there are fewer units over which to spread fixed costs. The pressure of high fixed or high storage costs can push rival firms into offering price concessions, special discounts, and rebates and employing other volume-boosting competitive tactics.

- *Rivalry intensifies as the number of competitors increases and they become more equal in size and capability.* When there are many competitors in a market, companies eager to increase their meager market share often engage in price-cutting activities to drive sales, leading to intense rivalry. When there are only a few competitors, companies are more wary of how their rivals may react to their attempts to take market share away from them. Fear of retaliation and a descent into a damaging price war leads to restrained competitive moves. Moreover, when rivals are of comparable size and competitive strength, they can usually compete on a fairly equal footing—an evenly matched contest tends to be fiercer than a contest in which one or more industry members have commanding market shares and substantially greater resources than their much smaller rivals.

- *Rivalry becomes more intense as the diversity of competitors increases in terms of long-term directions, objectives, strategies, and countries of origin.* A diverse group of sellers often contains one or more mavericks willing to try novel or rule-breaking market approaches, thus generating a more volatile and less predictable competitive environment. Globally competitive markets are often more rivalrous, especially when aggressors have lower costs and are intent on gaining a strong foothold in new country markets.

- *Rivalry is stronger when high exit barriers keep unprofitable firms from leaving the industry.* In industries where the assets cannot easily be sold or transferred to other uses, where workers are entitled to job protection, or where owners are committed to remaining in business for personal reasons, failing firms tend to hold on longer than they might otherwise—even when they are bleeding red ink. Deep price discounting typically ensues, in a desperate effort to cover costs and remain in business. This sort of rivalry can destabilize an otherwise attractive industry.

The previous factors, taken as whole, determine whether the rivalry in an industry is relatively strong, moderate, or weak. When rivalry is *strong,* the battle for market share is generally so vigorous that the profit margins of most industry members are squeezed to bare-bones levels. When rivalry is *moderate,* a more normal state, the maneuvering among industry members, while lively and healthy, still allows most industry members to earn acceptable profits. When rivalry is *weak,* most companies in the industry are relatively well satisfied with their sales growth and market shares and rarely undertake offensives to steal customers away from one another. Weak rivalry means that there is no downward pressure on industry profitability due to this particular competitive force.

The Choice of Competitive Weapons

Competitive battles among rival sellers can assume many forms that extend well beyond lively price competition. For example, competitors may resort to such marketing tactics as special sales promotions, heavy advertising, rebates, or low-interest-rate financing to drum up additional sales. Rivals may race one another to differentiate their products by offering better performance features or higher quality or improved customer service or a wider product selection. They may also compete through the rapid introduction of next-generation products, the frequent introduction of new or improved products, and efforts to build stronger dealer networks, establish positions in foreign markets, or otherwise expand distribution capabilities and market presence. Table 3.2 displays the competitive weapons that firms often employ in battling rivals, along with their primary effects with respect to price (P), cost (C), and value (V)—the elements of an effective business model and the value-price-cost framework, discussed in Chapter 1.

Competitive Pressures Associated with the Threat of New Entrants

New entrants into an industry threaten the position of rival firms since they will compete fiercely for market share, add to the number of industry rivals, and add to the industry's production capacity in the process. But even the *threat* of new entry puts added competitive pressure on current industry members and thus functions as an important competitive force. This is because credible threat of entry often prompts industry members to lower their prices and initiate defensive actions in an attempt

TABLE 3.2   Common "Weapons" for Competing with Rivals

Types of Competitive Weapons	Primary Effects
Discounting prices, holding clearance sales	Lowers price (P), increases total sales volume and market share, lowers profits if price cuts are not offset by large increases in sales volume
Offering coupons, advertising items on sale	Increases sales volume and total revenues, lowers price (P), increases unit costs (C), may lower profit margins per unit sold ($P - C$)
Advertising product or service characteristics, using ads to enhance a company's image	Boosts buyer demand, increases product differentiation and perceived value (V), increases total sales volume and market share, but may increase unit costs (C) and lower profit margins per unit sold
Innovating to improve product performance and quality	Increases product differentiation and value (V), boosts buyer demand, boosts total sales volume, likely to increase unit costs (C)
Introducing new or improved features, increasing the number of styles to provide greater product selection	Increases product differentiation and value (V), strengthens buyer demand, boosts total sales volume and market share, likely to increase unit costs (C)
Increasing customization of product or service	Increases product differentiation and value (V), increases buyer switching costs, boosts total sales volume, often increases unit costs (C)
Building a bigger, better dealer network	Broadens access to buyers, boosts total sales volume and market share, may increase unit costs (C)
Improving warranties, offering low-interest financing	Increases product differentiation and value (V), increases unit costs (C), increases buyer switching costs, boosts total sales volume and market share

to deter new entrants. Just how serious the threat of entry is in a particular market depends on (1) whether entry barriers are high or low, and (2) the expected reaction of existing industry members to the entry of newcomers.

Whether Entry Barriers Are High or Low   The strength of the threat of entry is governed to a large degree by the height of the industry's entry barriers. High barriers reduce the threat of potential entry, whereas low barriers enable easier entry. Entry barriers are high under the following conditions:[2]

- *There are sizable economies of scale in production, distribution, advertising, or other activities.* When incumbent companies enjoy cost advantages associated with large-scale operations, outsiders must either enter on a large scale (a costly and perhaps risky move) or accept a cost disadvantage and consequently lower profitability.

- *Incumbents have other hard to replicate cost advantages over new entrants.* Aside from enjoying economies of scale, industry incumbents can have cost advantages that stem from the possession of patents or proprietary technology, exclusive partnerships with the best and cheapest suppliers, favorable locations, and low fixed costs (because they have older facilities that have been mostly depreciated). Learning-based cost savings can also accrue from experience in performing certain activities such as manufacturing or new product development or inventory management. The extent of such savings can be measured with learning/experience curves. The steeper the learning/experience curve, the bigger the cost advantage of the company with the largest *cumulative* production volume. The microprocessor industry provides an excellent example of this:

    > *Manufacturing unit costs for microprocessors tend to decline about 20 percent each time cumulative production volume doubles. With a 20 percent experience curve effect, if the first 1 million chips cost $100 each, once production volume reaches 2 million, the unit cost would fall to $80 (80 percent of $100), and by a production volume of 4 million, the unit cost would be $64 (80 percent of $80).*[3]

- *Customers have strong brand preferences and high degrees of loyalty to seller.* The stronger the attachment of buyers to established brands, the harder it is for a newcomer to break into the marketplace. In such cases, a new entrant must have the financial resources to spend enough on advertising and sales promotion to overcome customer loyalties and build its own clientele. Establishing brand recognition and building customer loyalty can be a slow and costly process. In addition, if it is difficult or costly for a customer to switch to a new brand, a new entrant may have to offer a discounted price or otherwise persuade buyers that its brand is worth the switching costs. Such barriers discourage new entry because they act to boost financial requirements and lower expected profit margins for new entrants.

- *Patents and other forms of intellectual property protection are in place.* In a number of industries, entry is prevented due to the existence of intellectual property protection laws that remain in place for a given number of years. Often, companies have a "wall of patents" in place to prevent other companies from entering with a "me too" strategy that replicates a key piece of technology.

- *There are strong "network effects" in customer demand.* In industries where buyers are more attracted to a product when there are many other users of the product, there are said to be "network effects," since demand is higher the larger the network of users. Video game systems are an example because users prefer to have the same systems as their friends so that they can play together on systems they all know and can share games. When incumbents have a large existing base of users, new entrants with otherwise comparable products face a serious disadvantage in attracting buyers.

- *Capital requirements are high.* The larger the total dollar investment needed to enter the market successfully, the more limited the pool of potential entrants. The most obvious capital requirements for new entrants relate to manufacturing facilities and equipment, introductory advertising and sales promotion campaigns, working capital to finance inventories and customer credit, and sufficient cash to cover startup costs.

- *There are difficulties in building a network of distributors/dealers or in securing adequate space on retailers' shelves.* A potential entrant can face numerous distribution-channel challenges. Wholesale distributors may be reluctant to take on a product that lacks buyer recognition. Retailers must be recruited and convinced to give a new brand ample display space and an adequate trial period. When existing sellers have strong, well-functioning distributor–dealer networks, a newcomer has an uphill struggle in squeezing its way into existing distribution channels. Potential entrants sometimes have to "buy" their way into wholesale or retail channels by cutting their prices to provide dealers and distributors with higher markups and profit margins or by giving them big advertising and promotional allowances. As a consequence, a potential entrant's own profits may be squeezed unless and until its product gains enough consumer acceptance that distributors and retailers are willing to carry it.

- *There are restrictive regulatory policies.* Regulated industries like cable TV, telecommunications, electric and gas utilities, radio and television broadcasting, liquor retailing, nuclear power, and railroads entail government-controlled entry. Government agencies can also limit or even bar entry by requiring licenses and permits, such as the medallion required to drive a taxicab in New York City. Government-mandated safety regulations and environmental pollution standards also create entry barriers because they raise entry costs. Recently enacted banking regulations in many countries have made entry particularly difficult for small new bank startups—complying with all the new regulations along with the rigors of competing against existing banks requires very deep pockets.

- *There are restrictive trade policies.* In international markets, host governments commonly limit foreign entry and must approve all foreign investment applications. National governments commonly use tariffs and trade restrictions (antidumping rules, local content requirements, quotas, etc.) to raise entry barriers for foreign firms and protect domestic producers from outside competition.

The Expected Reaction of Industry Members in Defending against New Entry

A second factor affecting the threat of entry relates to the ability and willingness of industry incumbents to launch strong defensive maneuvers to maintain their positions and make it harder for a newcomer to compete successfully and profitably. Entry candidates may have second thoughts about attempting entry if they conclude that existing firms will mount well-funded campaigns to hamper (or even defeat) a newcomer's attempt to gain a market foothold big enough to compete successfully. Such campaigns can include any of the "competitive weapons" listed in Table 3.2, such as ramping up advertising expenditures, offering special price discounts to the very customers a newcomer is seeking to attract, or adding attractive new product features (to match or beat the newcomer's product offering). Such actions can raise a newcomer's cost of entry along with the risk of failing, making the prospect of entry less appealing. The result is that even the expectation on the part of new entrants that industry incumbents will contest a newcomer's entry may be enough to dissuade entry candidates from going forward. Microsoft can be counted on to fiercely defend the position that Windows enjoys in computer operating systems and that Microsoft Office has in office productivity software. This may well have contributed to Microsoft's ability to continuously dominate this market space.

However, there are occasions when industry incumbents have nothing in their competitive arsenal that is formidable enough to either discourage entry or put obstacles in a newcomer's path that will defeat its strategic efforts to become a viable competitor. In the restaurant industry, for example, existing restaurants in a given geographic market have few actions they can take to discourage a new restaurant from opening or to block it from attracting enough patrons to be profitable. A fierce competitor like Nike was unable to prevent newcomer Under Armour from rapidly growing its sales and market share in sports apparel. Furthermore, there are occasions when industry incumbents can be expected to refrain from taking or initiating any actions specifically aimed at contesting a newcomer's entry. In large industries, entry by small startup enterprises normally poses no immediate or direct competitive threat to industry incumbents and their entry is not likely to provoke defensive actions. For instance, a new online retailer with sales prospects of maybe $5 to $10 million annually can reasonably expect to escape competitive retaliation from much larger online retailers selling similar goods. The less that a newcomer's entry will adversely impact the sales and profitability of industry incumbents, the more reasonable it is for potential entrants to expect industry incumbents to refrain from reacting defensively.

Even high entry barriers may not suffice to keep out certain kinds of entrants: those with resources and capabilities that enable them to leap over or bypass the barriers.

Figure 3.5 summarizes the factors that cause the overall competitive pressure from potential entrants to be strong or weak. An analysis of these factors can help managers determine whether the threat of entry into their industry is high or low, *in general.* But certain kinds of companies—those with sizable financial resources, proven competitive capabilities, and a respected brand name—may be able to hurdle an industry's entry barriers even when they are high.[4] For example, when Honda opted to enter the U.S. lawn-mower market in competition against Toro, Snapper, Craftsman, John Deere, and others, it was easily able to hurdle entry barriers that would have been formidable to other newcomers because it had long-standing expertise in gasoline engines and a reputation for quality and durability in automobiles that gave it instant credibility with homeowners. As a result, Honda had to spend relatively little on inducing dealers to handle the Honda lawn-mower line or attracting customers. Similarly, Samsung's brand reputation in televisions, DVD players, and other electronics products gave it strong credibility in entering the market for smartphones—Samsung's Galaxy smartphones are now a formidable rival of Apple's iPhone.

High entry barriers and weak entry threats today do not always translate into high entry barriers and weak entry threats tomorrow.

It is also important to recognize that the barriers to entering an industry can become stronger or weaker over time. For example, once key patents preventing new entry in the market for functional 3-D printers expired, the way was open for new competition to enter this industry. On the other hand, new strategic actions by incumbent firms to increase advertising, strengthen distributor–dealer relations, step up R&D, or improve product quality can erect higher roadblocks to entry.

Competitive Pressures from the Sellers of Substitute Products

Companies in one industry are vulnerable to competitive pressure from the actions of companies in a closely adjoining industry whenever buyers view the products of the two industries as good substitutes. Substitutes do *not* include other brands within your

FIGURE 3.5   Factors Affecting the Threat of Entry

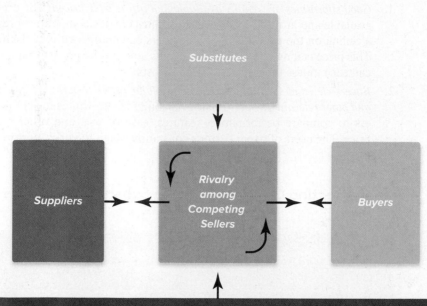

Substitutes

Suppliers

Rivalry among Competing Sellers

Buyers

Competitive Pressures from Potential Entrants

Threat of entry is a stronger force when (1) incumbents are unlikely to make retaliatory moves against new entrants and (2) entry barriers are low. Entry barriers are high (and threat of entry is low) when

- Incumbents have large cost advantages over potential entrants due to
  - High economies of scale
  - Significant experience-based cost advantages or learning curve effects
  - Other cost advantages (e.g., favorable access to inputs, technology, location, or low fixed costs)
- Customers with strong brand preferences and/or loyalty to incumbent sellers
- Patents and other forms of intellectual property protection
- Strong network effects
- High capital requirements
- Limited new access to distribution channels and shelf space
- Restrictive government policies
- Restrictive trade policies

industry; this type of pressure comes from *outside* the industry. Substitute products from outside the industry are those that can perform the same or similar functions for the consumer as products within your industry. For instance, the producers of eyeglasses and contact lenses face competitive pressures from the doctors who do corrective laser surgery. Similarly, the producers of sugar experience competitive pressures from the producers of sugar substitutes (high-fructose corn syrup, agave syrup, and artificial sweeteners). Internet providers of news-related information have put brutal competitive pressure on the publishers of newspapers. The makers of smartphones, by building ever better cameras into their cell phones, have cut deeply into the sales of producers of handheld digital cameras—most smartphone owners now use their phone to take pictures rather than carrying a digital camera for picture-taking purposes.

As depicted in Figure 3.6, three factors determine whether the competitive pressures from substitute products are strong or weak. Competitive pressures are stronger when

1. *Good substitutes are readily available and attractively priced.* The presence of readily available and attractively priced substitutes creates competitive pressure by placing a ceiling on the prices industry members can charge without risking sales erosion. This price ceiling, at the same time, puts a lid on the profits that industry members can earn unless they find ways to cut costs.

2. *Buyers view the substitutes as comparable or better in terms of quality, performance, and other relevant attributes.* The availability of substitutes inevitably invites customers to compare performance, features, ease of use, and other attributes besides price. The users of paper cartons constantly weigh the price-performance trade-offs

FIGURE 3.6   Factors Affecting Competition from Substitute Products

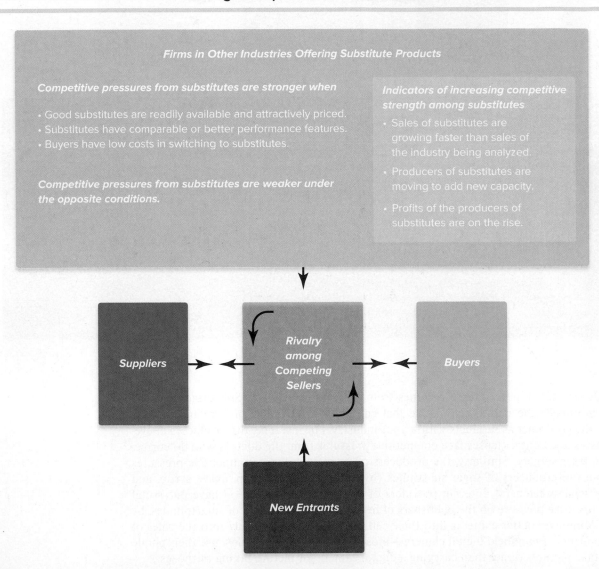

Firms in Other Industries Offering Substitute Products

Competitive pressures from substitutes are stronger when

- Good substitutes are readily available and attractively priced.
- Substitutes have comparable or better performance features.
- Buyers have low costs in switching to substitutes.

Competitive pressures from substitutes are weaker under the opposite conditions.

Indicators of increasing competitive strength among substitutes

- Sales of substitutes are growing faster than sales of the industry being analyzed.
- Producers of substitutes are moving to add new capacity.
- Profits of the producers of substitutes are on the rise.

Suppliers

Rivalry among Competing Sellers

Buyers

New Entrants

with plastic containers and metal cans, for example. Movie enthusiasts are increasingly weighing whether to go to movie theaters to watch newly released movies or wait until they can watch the same movies streamed to their home TV by Netflix, Amazon Prime, cable providers, and other on-demand sources.

3. *The costs that buyers incur in switching to the substitutes are low.* Low switching costs make it easier for the sellers of attractive substitutes to lure buyers to their offerings; high switching costs deter buyers from purchasing substitute products.

Some signs that the competitive strength of substitute products is increasing include (1) whether the sales of substitutes are growing faster than the sales of the industry being analyzed, (2) whether the producers of substitutes are investing in added capacity, and (3) whether the producers of substitutes are earning progressively higher profits.

But before assessing the competitive pressures coming from substitutes, company managers must identify the substitutes, which is less easy than it sounds since it involves (1) determining where the industry boundaries lie and (2) figuring out which other products or services can address the same basic customer needs as those produced by industry members. Deciding on the industry boundaries is necessary for determining which firms are direct rivals and which produce substitutes. This is a matter of perspective—there are no hard-and-fast rules, other than to say that other brands of the same basic product constitute rival products and not substitutes. Ultimately, it's simply the buyer who decides what can serve as a good substitute.

Competitive Pressures Stemming from Supplier Bargaining Power

Whether the suppliers of industry members represent a weak or strong competitive force depends on the degree to which suppliers have sufficient *bargaining power* to influence the terms and conditions of supply in their favor. Suppliers with strong bargaining power are a source of competitive pressure because of their ability to charge industry members higher prices, pass costs on to them, and limit their opportunities to find better deals. For instance, Microsoft and Intel, both of which supply PC makers with essential components, have been known to use their dominant market status not only to charge PC makers premium prices but also to leverage their power over PC makers in other ways. The bargaining power of these two companies over their customers is so great that both companies have faced antitrust charges on numerous occasions. Prior to a legal agreement ending the practice, Microsoft pressured PC makers to load only Microsoft products on the PCs they shipped. Intel has defended itself against similar antitrust charges, but in filling orders for newly introduced Intel chips, it continues to give top priority to PC makers that use the biggest percentages of Intel chips in their PC models. Being on Intel's list of preferred customers helps a PC maker get an early allocation of Intel's latest chips and thus allows the PC maker to get new models to market ahead of rivals.

Small-scale retailers often must contend with the power of manufacturers whose products enjoy well-known brand names, since consumers expect to find these products on the shelves of the retail stores where they shop. This provides the manufacturer with a degree of pricing power and often the ability to push hard for favorable shelf displays. Supplier bargaining power is also a competitive factor in industries where unions have been able to organize the workforce (which supplies labor). Air pilot unions, for example, have employed their bargaining power to increase pilots' wages and benefits in the air transport industry. The growing clout of the largest healthcare union in the United States has led to better wages and working conditions in nursing homes.

As shown in Figure 3.7, a variety of factors determine the strength of suppliers' bargaining power. Supplier power is stronger when

- *Demand for suppliers' products is high and the products are in short supply.* A surge in the demand for particular items shifts the bargaining power to the suppliers of those products; suppliers of items in short supply have pricing power.

- *Suppliers provide differentiated inputs that enhance the performance of the industry's product.* The more valuable a particular input is in terms of enhancing the performance or quality of the products of industry members, the more bargaining leverage suppliers have. In contrast, the suppliers of commodities are in a weak bargaining position, since industry members have no reason other than price to prefer one supplier over another.

- *It is difficult or costly for industry members to switch their purchases from one supplier to another.* Low switching costs limit supplier bargaining power by enabling industry members to change suppliers if any one supplier attempts to raise prices by more than the costs of switching. Thus, the higher the switching costs of industry members, the stronger the bargaining power of their suppliers.

- *The supplier industry is dominated by a few large companies and it is more concentrated than the industry it sells to.* Suppliers with sizable market shares and strong demand for the items they supply generally have sufficient bargaining power to charge high prices and deny requests from industry members for lower prices or other concessions.

FIGURE 3.7   Factors Affecting the Bargaining Power of Suppliers

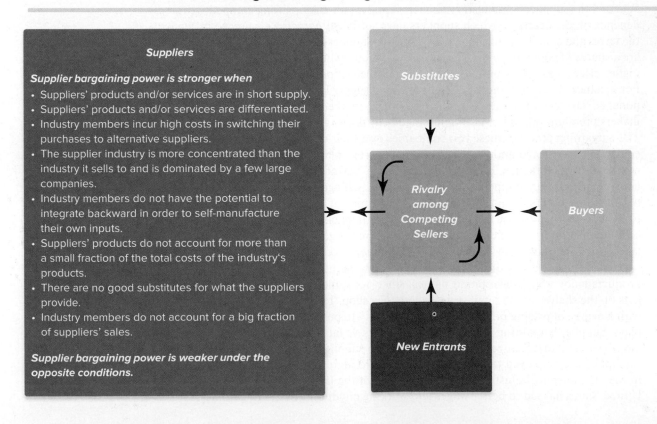

Suppliers

Supplier bargaining power is stronger when
- Suppliers' products and/or services are in short supply.
- Suppliers' products and/or services are differentiated.
- Industry members incur high costs in switching their purchases to alternative suppliers.
- The supplier industry is more concentrated than the industry it sells to and is dominated by a few large companies.
- Industry members do not have the potential to integrate backward in order to self-manufacture their own inputs.
- Suppliers' products do not account for more than a small fraction of the total costs of the industry's products.
- There are no good substitutes for what the suppliers provide.
- Industry members do not account for a big fraction of suppliers' sales.

Supplier bargaining power is weaker under the opposite conditions.

Substitutes

Rivalry among Competing Sellers

Buyers

New Entrants

- *Industry members are incapable of integrating backward to self-manufacture items they have been buying from suppliers.* As a rule, suppliers are safe from the threat of self-manufacture by their customers until the volume of parts a customer needs becomes large enough for the customer to justify backward integration into self-manufacture of the component. When industry members can threaten credibly to self-manufacture suppliers' goods, their bargaining power over suppliers increases proportionately.

- *Suppliers provide an item that accounts for no more than a small fraction of the costs of the industry's product.* The more that the cost of a particular part or component affects the final product's cost, the more that industry members will be sensitive to the actions of suppliers to raise or lower their prices. When an input accounts for only a small proportion of total input costs, buyers will be less sensitive to price increases. Thus, suppliers' power increases when the inputs they provide do *not* make up a large proportion of the cost of the final product.

- *Good substitutes are not available for the suppliers' products.* The lack of readily available substitute inputs increases the bargaining power of suppliers by increasing the dependence of industry members on the suppliers.

- *Industry members are not major customers of suppliers.* As a rule, suppliers have less bargaining leverage when their sales to members of the industry constitute a big percentage of their total sales. In such cases, the well-being of suppliers is closely tied to the well-being of their major customers, and their dependence upon them increases. The bargaining power of suppliers is stronger, then, when they are *not* bargaining with major customers.

In identifying the degree of supplier power in an industry, it is important to recognize that different types of suppliers are likely to have different amounts of bargaining power. Thus, the first step is for managers to identify the different types of suppliers, paying particular attention to those that provide the industry with important inputs. The next step is to assess the bargaining power of each type of supplier separately.

Competitive Pressures Stemming from Buyer Bargaining Power and Price Sensitivity

Whether buyers are able to exert strong competitive pressures on industry members depends on (1) the degree to which buyers have bargaining power and (2) the extent to which buyers are price-sensitive. Buyers with strong bargaining power can limit industry profitability by demanding price concessions, better payment terms, or additional features and services that increase industry members' costs. Buyer price sensitivity limits the profit potential of industry members by restricting the ability of sellers to raise prices without losing revenue due to lost sales.

As with suppliers, the leverage that buyers have in negotiating favorable terms of sale can range from weak to strong. Individual consumers seldom have much bargaining power in negotiating price concessions or other favorable terms with sellers. However, their price sensitivity varies by individual and by the type of product they are buying (whether it's a necessity or a discretionary purchase, for example). Similarly, small businesses usually have weak bargaining power because of the small-size orders they place with sellers. Many relatively small wholesalers and retailers join buying groups to pool their purchasing power and approach manufacturers for better terms than could be gotten individually. Large business buyers, in contrast, can have considerable bargaining power. For example, large retail chains like

Walmart, Best Buy, Staples, and Home Depot typically have considerable bargaining power in purchasing products from manufacturers, not only because they buy in large quantities, but also because of manufacturers' need for access to their broad base of customers. Major supermarket chains like Kroger, Albertsons, Hannaford, and Aldi have sufficient bargaining power to demand promotional allowances and lump-sum payments (called *slotting fees*) from food products manufacturers in return for stocking certain brands or putting them in the best shelf locations. Motor vehicle manufacturers have strong bargaining power in negotiating to buy original-equipment tires from tire makers such as Bridgestone, Goodyear, Michelin, Continental, and Pirelli, partly because they buy in large quantities and partly because consumers are more likely to buy replacement tires that match the tire brand on their vehicle at the time of its purchase. The starting point for the analysis of buyers as a competitive force is to identify the different types of buyers along the value chain—then proceed to analyzing the bargaining power and price sensitivity of each type separately. It is important to recognize that *not all buyers of an industry's product have equal degrees of bargaining power with sellers, and some may be less sensitive than others to price, quality, or service differences.*

Figure 3.8 summarizes the factors determining the strength of buyer power in an industry. The top of this chart lists the factors that increase buyers' bargaining power,

FIGURE 3.8   Factors Affecting the Power of Buyers

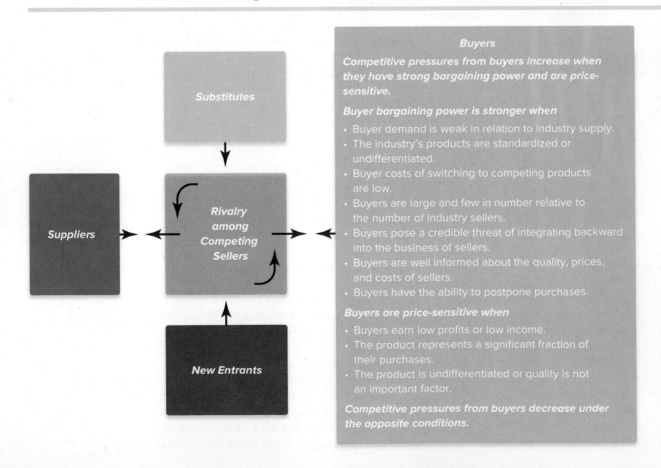

Buyers

Competitive pressures from buyers increase when they have strong bargaining power and are price-sensitive.

Buyer bargaining power is stronger when
- Buyer demand is weak in relation to industry supply.
- The industry's products are standardized or undifferentiated.
- Buyer costs of switching to competing products are low.
- Buyers are large and few in number relative to the number of industry sellers.
- Buyers pose a credible threat of integrating backward into the business of sellers.
- Buyers are well informed about the quality, prices, and costs of sellers.
- Buyers have the ability to postpone purchases.

Buyers are price-sensitive when
- Buyers earn low profits or low income.
- The product represents a significant fraction of their purchases.
- The product is undifferentiated or quality is not an important factor.

Competitive pressures from buyers decrease under the opposite conditions.

Substitutes

Suppliers

Rivalry among Competing Sellers

New Entrants

which we discuss next. Note that the first five factors are the mirror image of those determining the bargaining power of suppliers.

Buyer bargaining power is stronger when

- *Buyer demand is weak in relation to the available supply.* Weak or declining demand and the resulting excess supply create a "buyers' market," in which bargain-hunting buyers have leverage in pressing industry members for better deals and special treatment. Conversely, strong or rapidly growing market demand creates a "sellers' market" characterized by tight supplies or shortages—conditions that put buyers in a weak position to wring concessions from industry members.

- *Industry goods are standardized or differentiation is weak.* In such circumstances, buyers make their selections on the basis of price, which increases price competition among vendors.

- *Buyers' costs of switching to competing brands or substitutes are relatively low.* Switching costs put a cap on how much industry producers can raise prices or reduce quality before they will lose the buyer's business.

- *Buyers are large and few in number relative to the number of sellers.* The larger the buyers, the more important their business is to the seller and the more sellers will be willing to grant concessions.

- *Buyers pose a credible threat of integrating backward into the business of sellers.* Beer producers like Anheuser Busch InBev SA/NV (whose brands include Budweiser, Molson Coors, and Heineken) have partially integrated backward into metal-can manufacturing to gain bargaining power in obtaining the balance of their can requirements from otherwise powerful metal-can manufacturers.

- *Buyers are well informed about the product offerings of sellers (product features and quality, prices, buyer reviews) and the cost of production (an indicator of markup).* The more information buyers have, the better bargaining position they are in. The mushrooming availability of product information on the Internet (and its ready access on smartphones) is giving added bargaining power to consumers, since they can use this to find or negotiate better deals. Apps such as ShopSavvy and BuyVia are now making comparison shopping even easier.

- *Buyers have discretion to delay their purchases or perhaps even not make a purchase at all.* Consumers often have the option to delay purchases of durable goods (cars, major appliances), or decline to buy discretionary goods (massages, concert tickets) if they are not happy with the prices offered. Business customers may also be able to defer their purchases of certain items, such as plant equipment or maintenance services. This puts pressure on sellers to provide concessions to buyers so that the sellers can keep their sales numbers from dropping off.

Whether Buyers Are More or Less Price-Sensitive   Low-income and budget-constrained consumers are almost always price-sensitive; bargain-hunting consumers are highly price-sensitive by nature. Most consumers grow more price-sensitive as the price tag of an item becomes a bigger fraction of their spending budget. Similarly, business buyers besieged by weak sales, intense competition, and other factors squeezing their profit margins are price-sensitive. Price sensitivity also grows among businesses as the cost of an item becomes a bigger fraction of their cost structure. Rising prices of frequently purchased items heighten the price sensitivity of all types of buyers. On the other hand, the price sensitivity of all types of buyers decreases the more that the quality of the product matters.

The following factors increase buyer price sensitivity and result in greater competitive pressures on the industry as a result:

- *Buyer price sensitivity increases when buyers are earning low profits or have low income.* Price is a critical factor in the purchase decisions of low-income consumers and companies that are barely scraping by. In such cases, their high price sensitivity limits the ability of sellers to charge high prices.

- *Buyers are more price-sensitive if the product represents a large fraction of their total purchases.* When a purchase eats up a large portion of a buyer's budget or represents a significant part of his or her cost structure, the buyer cares more about price than might otherwise be the case.

- *Buyers are more price-sensitive when the quality of the product is not uppermost in their considerations.* Quality matters little when products are relatively undifferentiated, leading buyers to focus more on price. But when quality affects performance, or can reduce a business buyer's other costs (by saving on labor, materials, etc.), price will matter less.

Is the Collective Strength of the Five Competitive Forces Conducive to Good Profitability?

Assessing whether each of the five competitive forces gives rise to strong, moderate, or weak competitive pressures sets the stage for evaluating whether, overall, the strength of the five forces is conducive to good profitability. Is any of the competitive forces sufficiently powerful to undermine industry profitability? Can companies in this industry reasonably expect to earn decent profits in light of the prevailing competitive forces?

The most extreme case of a "competitively unattractive" industry occurs when all five forces are producing strong competitive pressures: Rivalry among sellers is vigorous, low entry barriers allow new rivals to gain a market foothold, competition from substitutes is intense, and both suppliers and buyers are able to exercise considerable leverage. Strong competitive pressures coming from all five directions drive industry profitability to unacceptably low levels, frequently producing losses for many industry members and forcing some out of business. But an industry can be competitively unattractive without all five competitive forces being strong. In fact, *intense competitive pressures from just one of the five forces may suffice to destroy the conditions for good profitability and prompt some companies to exit the business.*

CORE CONCEPT

The strongest of the five forces determines the extent of the downward pressure on an industry's profitability.

As a rule, *the strongest competitive forces determine the extent of the competitive pressure on industry profitability.* Thus, in evaluating the strength of the five forces overall and their effect on industry profitability, managers should look to the strongest forces. Having more than one strong force will not worsen the effect on industry profitability, but it does mean that the industry has multiple competitive challenges with which to cope. In that sense, an industry with three to five strong forces is even more "unattractive" as a place to compete. Especially intense competitive conditions due to multiple strong forces seem to be the norm in tire manufacturing, apparel, and commercial airlines, three industries where profit margins have historically been thin.

In contrast, when the overall impact of the five competitive forces is moderate to weak, an industry is "attractive" in the sense that the *average* industry member can reasonably expect to earn good profits and a nice return on investment. The ideal competitive environment for earning superior profits is one in which both suppliers and customers have limited power, there are no good substitutes, high barriers block further entry, and rivalry among present sellers is muted. Weak competition is the best of all possible worlds for also-ran companies because even they can usually eke out a decent profit—if a company can't make a decent profit when competition is weak, then its business outlook is indeed grim.

Matching Company Strategy to Competitive Conditions

Working through the five forces model step by step not only aids strategy makers in assessing whether the intensity of competition allows good profitability but also promotes sound strategic thinking about how to better match company strategy to the specific competitive character of the marketplace. Effectively matching a company's business strategy to prevailing competitive conditions has two aspects:

> A company's strategy is strengthened the more it provides insulation from competitive pressures, shifts the competitive battle in the company's favor, and positions the firm to take advantage of attractive growth opportunities.

1. Pursuing avenues that shield the firm from as many of the different competitive pressures as possible.

2. Initiating actions calculated to shift the competitive forces in the company's favor by altering the underlying factors driving the five forces.

But making headway on these two fronts first requires identifying competitive pressures, gauging the relative strength of each of the five competitive forces, and gaining a deep enough understanding of the state of competition in the industry to know which strategy buttons to push.

COMPLEMENTORS AND THE VALUE NET

Not all interactions among industry participants are necessarily competitive in nature. Some have the potential to be cooperative, as the value net framework demonstrates. Like the five forces framework, the value net includes an analysis of buyers, suppliers, and substitutors (see Figure 3.9). But it differs from the five forces framework in several important ways.

First, the analysis focuses on the interactions of industry participants with a particular company. Thus, it places that firm in the center of the framework, as Figure 3.9 shows. Second, the category of "competitors" is defined to include not only the focal firm's direct competitors or industry rivals but also the sellers of substitute products and potential entrants. Third, the value net framework introduces a new category of industry participant that is not found in the five forces framework—that of "complementors." **Complementors** are the producers of complementary products, which are products that enhance the value of the focal firm's products when they are used together. Some examples include snorkels and swim fins or shoes and shoelaces.

> **CORE CONCEPT**
>
> **Complementors** are the producers of complementary products, which are products that enhance the value of the focal firm's products when they are used together.

The inclusion of complementors draws particular attention to the fact that success in the marketplace need not come at the expense of other industry participants. Interactions among industry participants may be cooperative in nature rather than competitive. In the case of complementors, an increase in sales for them is likely to increase the sales of the focal firm as well. But the value net framework also encourages managers to consider other forms of cooperative interactions and realize that value is created jointly by all industry participants. For example, a company's success in the marketplace depends on establishing a reliable supply chain for its inputs, which implies the need for cooperative relations with its suppliers. Often a firm works

FIGURE 3.9   The Value Net

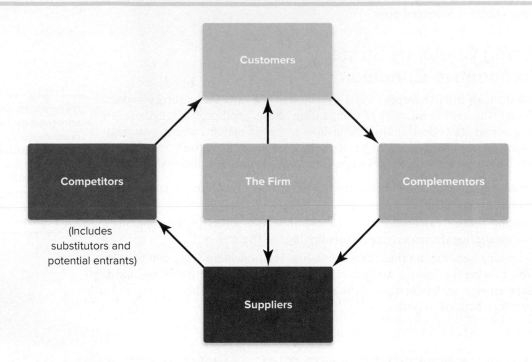

hand in hand with its suppliers to ensure a smoother, more efficient operation for both parties. Newell-Rubbermaid, and Procter & Gamble for example, work cooperatively as suppliers to companies such as Walmart, Target, and Kohl's. Even direct rivals may work cooperatively if they participate in industry trade associations or engage in joint lobbying efforts. Value net analysis can help managers discover the potential to improve their position through cooperative as well as competitive interactions.

INDUSTRY DYNAMICS AND THE FORCES DRIVING CHANGE

While it is critical to understand the nature and intensity of competitive and cooperative forces in an industry, it is equally critical to understand that the intensity of these forces is fluid and subject to change. All industries are affected by new developments and ongoing trends that alter industry conditions, some more speedily than others. The popular hypothesis that industries go through a life cycle of takeoff, rapid growth, maturity, market saturation and slowing growth, followed by stagnation or decline is but one aspect of industry change—many other new developments and emerging trends cause industry change.[5] Any strategies devised by management will therefore play out in a dynamic industry environment, so it's imperative that managers consider the factors driving industry change and how they might affect the industry environment. Moreover, with early notice, managers may be able to influence the direction or scope of environmental change and improve the outlook.

Industry and competitive conditions change because forces are enticing or pressuring certain industry participants (competitors, customers, suppliers, complementors) to alter their actions in important ways. The most powerful of the change agents are called **driving forces** because they have the biggest influences in reshaping the industry landscape and altering competitive conditions. Some driving forces originate in the outer ring of the company's macro-environment (see Figure 3.2), but most originate in the company's more immediate industry and competitive environment.

> **CORE CONCEPT**
>
> **Driving forces** are the major underlying causes of change in industry and competitive conditions.

Driving-forces analysis has three steps: (1) identifying what the driving forces are; (2) assessing whether the drivers of change are, on the whole, acting to make the industry more or less attractive; and (3) determining what strategy changes are needed to prepare for the impact of the driving forces. All three steps merit further discussion.

Identifying the Forces Driving Industry Change

Many developments can affect an industry powerfully enough to qualify as driving forces. Some drivers of change are unique and specific to a particular industry situation, but most drivers of industry and competitive change fall into one of the following categories:

- *Changes in an industry's long-term growth rate.* Shifts in industry growth up or down have the potential to affect the balance between industry supply and buyer demand, entry and exit, and the character and strength of competition. Whether demand is growing or declining is one of the key factors influencing the intensity of rivalry in an industry, as explained earlier. But the strength of this effect will depend on how changes in the industry growth rate affect entry and exit in the industry. If entry barriers are low, then growth in demand will attract new entrants, increasing the number of industry rivals and changing the competitive landscape.

- *Increasing globalization.* Globalization can be precipitated by such factors as the blossoming of consumer demand in developing countries, the availability of lower-cost foreign inputs, and the reduction of trade barriers, as has occurred recently in many parts of Latin America and Asia. Significant differences in labor costs among countries give manufacturers a strong incentive to locate plants for labor-intensive products in low-wage countries and use these plants to supply market demand across the world. Wages in China, India, Vietnam, Mexico, and Brazil, for example, are much lower than those in the United States, Germany, and Japan. The forces of globalization are sometimes such a strong driver that companies find it highly advantageous, if not necessary, to spread their operating reach into more and more country markets. Globalization is very much a driver of industry change in such industries as energy, mobile phones, steel, social media, public accounting, commercial aircraft, electric power generation equipment, and pharmaceuticals.

- *Emerging new Internet capabilities and applications.* Mushrooming use of high-speed Internet service and Voice-over-Internet-Protocol (VoIP) technology, growing acceptance of online shopping, and the exploding popularity of Internet applications ("apps") have been major drivers of change in industry after industry. The Internet has allowed online discount stock brokers, such as E*TRADE, and TD Ameritrade to mount a strong challenge against full-service firms such as Edward Jones and Merrill Lynch. The newspaper industry has yet to figure out a strategy for surviving the advent of online news.

Massive open online courses (MOOCs) facilitated by organizations such as Coursera, edX, and Udacity are profoundly affecting higher education. The "Internet of things" will feature faster speeds, dazzling applications, and billions of connected gadgets performing an array of functions, thus driving further industry and competitive changes. But Internet-related impacts vary from industry to industry. The challenges are to assess precisely how emerging Internet developments are altering a particular industry's landscape and to factor these impacts into the strategy-making equation.

- *Shifts in who buys the products and how the products are used.* Shifts in buyer demographics and the ways products are used can greatly alter competitive conditions. Longer life expectancies and growing percentages of relatively well-to-do retirees, for example, are driving demand growth in such industries as cosmetic surgery, assisted living residences, and vacation travel. The burgeoning popularity of streaming video has affected broadband providers, wireless phone carriers, and television broadcasters, and created opportunities for such new entertainment businesses as Hulu and Netflix.

- *Technological change and manufacturing process innovation.* Advances in technology can cause disruptive change in an industry by introducing substitutes or can alter the industry landscape by opening up whole new industry frontiers. For instance, revolutionary change in autonomous system technology has put Google, Tesla, Apple, and every major automobile manufacturer into a race to develop viable self-driving vehicles.

- *Product innovation.* An ongoing stream of product innovations tends to alter the pattern of competition in an industry by attracting more first-time buyers, rejuvenating industry growth, and/or increasing product differentiation, with concomitant effects on rivalry, entry threat, and buyer power. Product innovation has been a key driving force in the smartphone industry, which in an ever more connected world is driving change in other industries. Philips Lighting Hue bulbs now allow homeowners to use a smartphone app to remotely turn lights on and off, blink if an intruder is detected, and create a wide range of white and color ambiances. Wearable action-capture cameras and unmanned aerial view drones are rapidly becoming a disruptive force in the digital camera industry by enabling photography shots and videos not feasible with handheld digital cameras.

- *Marketing innovation.* When firms are successful in introducing new ways to market their products, they can spark a burst of buyer interest, widen industry demand, increase product differentiation, and lower unit costs—any or all of which can alter the competitive positions of rival firms and force strategy revisions. Consider, for example, the growing propensity of advertisers to place a bigger percentage of their ads on social media sites like Facebook and Twitter.

- *Entry or exit of major firms.* Entry by a major firm thus often produces a new ball game, not only with new key players but also with new rules for competing. Similarly, exit of a major firm changes the competitive structure by reducing the number of market leaders and increasing the dominance of the leaders who remain.

- *Diffusion of technical know-how across companies and countries.* As knowledge about how to perform a particular activity or execute a particular manufacturing technology spreads, products tend to become more commodity-like. Knowledge diffusion can occur through scientific journals, trade publications, onsite plant tours, word of mouth among suppliers and customers, employee migration, and Internet sources.

- *Changes in cost and efficiency.* Widening or shrinking differences in the costs among key competitors tend to dramatically alter the state of competition. Declining costs of producing tablets have enabled price cuts and spurred tablet sales (especially lower-priced models) by making them more affordable to lower-income households worldwide. Lower cost e-books are cutting into sales of costlier hardcover books as increasing numbers of consumers have laptops, iPads, Kindles, and other brands of tablets.

- *Reductions in uncertainty and business risk.* Many companies are hesitant to enter industries with uncertain futures or high levels of business risk because it is unclear how much time and money it will take to overcome various technological hurdles and achieve acceptable production costs (as is the case in the solar power industry). Over time, however, diminishing risk levels and uncertainty tend to stimulate new entry and capital investments on the part of growth-minded companies seeking new opportunities, thus dramatically altering industry and competitive conditions.

- *Regulatory influences and government policy changes.* Government regulatory actions can often mandate significant changes in industry practices and strategic approaches—as has recently occurred in the world's banking industry. New rules and regulations pertaining to government-sponsored health insurance programs are driving changes in the health care industry. In international markets, host governments can drive competitive changes by opening their domestic markets to foreign participation or closing them to protect domestic companies.

- *Changing societal concerns, attitudes, and lifestyles.* Emerging social issues as well as changing attitudes and lifestyles can be powerful instigators of industry change. Growing concern about the effects of climate change has emerged as a major driver of change in the energy industry. Concerns about the use of chemical additives and the nutritional content of food products have been driving changes in the restaurant and food industries. Shifting societal concerns, attitudes, and lifestyles alter the pattern of competition, favoring those players that respond with products targeted to the new trends and conditions.

The most important part of driving-forces analysis is to determine whether the collective impact of the driving forces will increase or decrease market demand, make competition more or less intense, and lead to higher or lower industry profitability.

While many forces of change may be at work in a given industry, *no more than three or four* are likely to be true driving forces powerful enough to qualify as the *major determinants* of why and how the industry is changing. Thus, company strategists must resist the temptation to label every change they see as a driving force. Table 3.3 lists the most common driving forces.

TABLE 3.3 The Most Common Drivers of Industry Change

- Changes in the long-term industry growth rate
- Increasing globalization
- Emerging new Internet capabilities and applications
- Shifts in buyer demographics
- Technological change and manufacturing process innovation
- Product and marketing innovation
- Entry or exit of major firms
- Diffusion of technical know-how across companies and countries
- Changes in cost and efficiency
- Reductions in uncertainty and business risk
- Regulatory influences and government policy changes
- Changing societal concerns, attitudes, and lifestyles

Assessing the Impact of the Forces Driving Industry Change

The second step in driving-forces analysis is to determine whether the prevailing change drivers, on the whole, are acting to make the industry environment more or less attractive. Three questions need to be answered:

1. Are the driving forces, on balance, acting to cause demand for the industry's product to increase or decrease?
2. Is the collective impact of the driving forces making competition more or less intense?
3. Will the combined impacts of the driving forces lead to higher or lower industry profitability?

Getting a handle on the collective impact of the driving forces requires looking at the likely effects of each factor separately, since the driving forces may not all be pushing change in the same direction. For example, one driving force may be acting to spur demand for the industry's product while another is working to curtail demand. Whether the net effect on industry demand is up or down hinges on which change driver is the most powerful.

> The real payoff of driving-forces analysis is to help managers understand what strategy changes are needed to prepare for the impacts of the driving forces.

Adjusting the Strategy to Prepare for the Impacts of Driving Forces

The third step in the strategic analysis of industry dynamics—where the real payoff for strategy making comes—is for managers to draw some conclusions about *what strategy adjustments will be needed to deal with the impacts of the driving forces.* But taking the "right" kinds of actions to prepare for the industry and competitive changes being wrought by the driving forces first requires accurate diagnosis of the forces driving industry change and the impacts these forces will have on both the industry environment and the company's business. To the extent that managers are unclear about the drivers of industry change and their impacts, or if their views are off-base, the chances of making astute and timely strategy adjustments are slim. So driving-forces analysis is not something to take lightly; it has practical value and is basic to the task of thinking strategically about where the industry is headed and how to prepare for the changes ahead.

STRATEGIC GROUP ANALYSIS

● LO 3-3

Map the market positions of key groups of industry rivals.

Within an industry, companies commonly sell in different price/quality ranges, appeal to different types of buyers, have different geographic coverage, and so on. Some are more attractively positioned than others. Understanding which companies are strongly positioned and which are weakly positioned is an integral part of analyzing an industry's competitive structure. The best technique for revealing the market positions of industry competitors is **strategic group mapping.**

Using Strategic Group Maps to Assess the Market Positions of Key Competitors

A **strategic group** consists of those industry members with similar competitive approaches and positions in the market. Companies in the same strategic group can resemble one another in a variety of ways. They may have comparable product-line breadth, sell in the same price/quality range, employ the same distribution channels, depend on identical technological approaches, compete in much the same geographic areas, or offer buyers essentially the same product attributes or similar services and technical assistance.[6] Evaluating strategy options entails examining what strategic groups exist, identifying the companies within each group, and determining if a competitive "white space" exists where industry competitors are able to create and capture altogether new demand. As part of this process, the number of strategic groups in an industry and their respective market positions can be displayed on a strategic group map.

The procedure for constructing a *strategic group map* is straightforward:

- Identify the competitive characteristics that delineate strategic approaches used in the industry. Typical variables used in creating strategic group maps are price/quality range (high, medium, low), geographic coverage (local, regional, national, global), product-line breadth (wide, narrow), degree of service offered (no frills, limited, full), use of distribution channels (retail, wholesale, Internet, multiple), degree of vertical integration (none, partial, full), and degree of diversification into other industries (none, some, considerable).

- Plot the firms on a two-variable map using pairs of these variables.

- Assign firms occupying about the same map location to the same strategic group.

- Draw circles around each strategic group, making the circles proportional to the size of the group's share of total industry sales revenues.

This produces a two-dimensional diagram like the one for the U.S. pizza chain industry in Illustration Capsule 3.2.

Several guidelines need to be observed in creating strategic group maps. First, the two variables selected as axes for the map should *not* be highly correlated; if they are, the circles on the map will fall along a diagonal and reveal nothing more about the relative positions of competitors than would be revealed by comparing the rivals on just one of the variables. For instance, if companies with broad product lines use multiple distribution channels while companies with narrow lines use a single distribution channel, then looking at the differences in distribution-channel approaches adds no new information about positioning.

Second, the variables chosen as axes for the map should reflect important differences among rival approaches—when rivals differ on both variables, the locations of the rivals will be scattered, thus showing how they are positioned differently. Third, the variables used as axes don't have to be either quantitative or continuous; rather, they can be discrete variables, defined in terms of distinct classes and combinations. Fourth, drawing the sizes of the circles on the map proportional to the combined sales of the firms in each strategic group allows the map to reflect the relative sizes of each strategic group. Fifth, if more than two good variables can be used as axes for the map, then it is wise to draw several maps to give different exposures to the competitive positioning relationships present in the industry's structure—there is not necessarily one best map for portraying how competing firms are positioned.

The Value of Strategic Group Maps

Strategic group maps are revealing in several respects. The most important has to do with identifying which industry members are close rivals and which are distant rivals. Firms in the same strategic group are the closest rivals; the next closest rivals

CORE CONCEPT

Strategic group mapping is a technique for displaying the different market or competitive positions that rival firms occupy in the industry.

CORE CONCEPT

A **strategic group** is a cluster of industry rivals that have similar competitive approaches and market positions.

Strategic group maps reveal which companies are close competitors and which are distant competitors.

Comparative Market Positions of Selected Companies in the Pizza Chain Industry: A Strategic Group Map Example

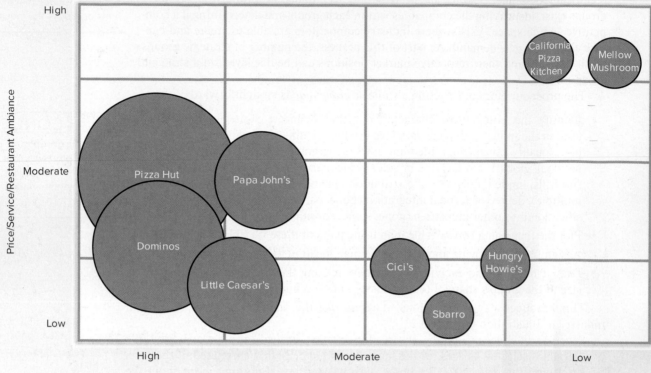

Note: Circles are drawn roughly proportional to the sizes of the chains, based on revenues.

are in the immediately adjacent groups. Often, firms in strategic groups that are far apart on the map hardly compete at all. For instance, Walmart's clientele, merchandise selection, and pricing points are much too different to justify calling Walmart a close competitor of Neiman Marcus or Saks Fifth Avenue. For the same reason, the beers produced by Yuengling are really not in competition with the beers produced by Pabst.

The second thing to be gleaned from strategic group mapping is that *not all positions on the map are equally attractive.*[7] Two reasons account for why some positions can be more attractive than others:

1. *Prevailing competitive pressures from the industry's five forces may cause the profit potential of different strategic groups to vary.* The profit prospects of firms in different strategic groups can vary from good to poor because of differing degrees of competitive rivalry within strategic groups, differing pressures from potential entrants to each group, differing degrees of exposure to competition from substitute products outside the industry, and differing degrees of supplier or customer bargaining power from group to group. For instance, in the ready-to-eat cereal industry, there are significantly higher entry barriers (capital requirements, brand loyalty, etc.) for

the strategic group comprising the large branded-cereal makers than for the group of generic-cereal makers or the group of small natural-cereal producers. Differences among the branded rivals versus the generic cereal makers make rivalry stronger within the generic-cereal strategic group. Among apparel retailers, the competitive battle between Marshall's and TJ MAXX is more intense (with consequently smaller profit margins) than the rivalry among Prada, Burberry, Gucci, Armani, and other high-end fashion retailers.

2. *Industry driving forces may favor some strategic groups and hurt others.* Likewise, industry driving forces can boost the business outlook for some strategic groups and adversely impact the business prospects of others. In the energy industry, producers of renewable energy, such as solar and wind power, are gaining ground over fossil fuel-based producers due to improvements in technology and increased concern over climate change. Firms in strategic groups that are being adversely impacted by driving forces may try to shift to a more favorably situated position. If certain firms are known to be trying to change their competitive positions on the map, then attaching arrows to the circles showing the targeted direction helps clarify the picture of competitive maneuvering among rivals.

> Some strategic groups are more favorably positioned than others because they confront weaker competitive forces and/or because they are more favorably impacted by industry driving forces.

Thus, part of strategic group map analysis always entails drawing conclusions about where on the map is the "best" place to be and why. Which companies/strategic groups are destined to prosper because of their positions? Which companies/strategic groups seem destined to struggle? What accounts for why some parts of the map are better than others? Since some strategic groups are more attractive than others, one might ask why less well-positioned firms do not simply migrate to the more attractive position. The answer is that **mobility barriers** restrict movement between groups in the same way that entry barriers prevent easy entry into attractive industries. The most profitable strategic groups may be protected from entry by high mobility barriers.

> **CORE CONCEPT**
>
> **Mobility barriers** restrict firms in one strategic group from entering another more attractive strategic group in the same industry.

COMPETITOR ANALYSIS AND THE SOAR FRAMEWORK

Unless a company pays attention to the strategies and situations of competitors and has some inkling of what moves they will be making, it ends up flying blind into competitive battle. As in sports, scouting the opposition is an essential part of game plan development. Gathering competitive intelligence about the strategic direction and likely moves of key competitors allows a company to prepare defensive countermoves, to craft its own strategic moves with some confidence about what market maneuvers to expect from rivals in response, and to exploit any openings that arise from competitors' missteps. The question is where to look for such information, since rivals rarely reveal their strategic intentions openly. If information is not directly available, what are the best indicators?

> Studying competitors' past behavior and preferences provides a valuable assist in anticipating what moves rivals are likely to make next and outmaneuvering them in the marketplace.

Michael Porter's **SOAR Framework for Competitor Analysis** points to four indicators of a rival's likely strategic moves and countermoves. These include a rival's *Strategy, Objectives, Assumptions* about itself and the industry, and *Resources and capabilities,* as shown in Figure 3.10. A strategic profile of a competitor that provides good clues to its behavioral proclivities can be constructed by characterizing the rival along these four dimensions. By "behavioral proclivities," we mean what competitive moves a rival is likely to make and how they are likely to react to the competitive moves of your company—its

FIGURE 3.10   The SOAR Framework for Competitor Analysis

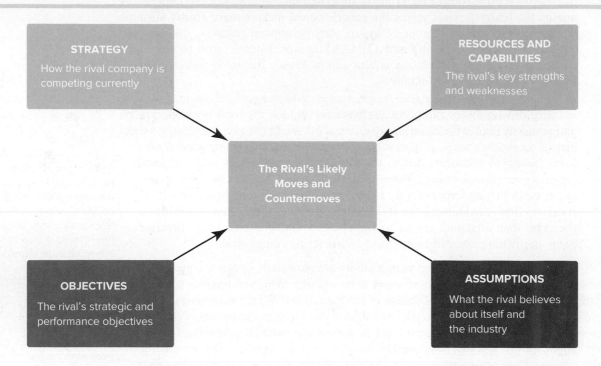

probable actions and reactions. By listing all that you know about a competitor (or a set of competitors) with respect to each of the four elements of the SOAR framework, you are likely to gain some insight about how the rival will behave in the near term. And knowledge of this sort can help you to predict how this will affect you, and how you should position yourself to respond. That is, what should you do to protect yourself or gain advantage now (in advance); and what should you do in response to your rivals next moves?

Current Strategy   To succeed in predicting a competitor's next moves, company strategists need to have a good understanding of each rival's current strategy, as an indicator of its pattern of behavior and best strategic options. Questions to consider include: How is the competitor positioned in the market? What is the basis for its competitive advantage (if any)? What kinds of investments is it making (as an indicator of its growth trajectory)?

Objectives   An appraisal of a rival's objectives should include not only its financial performance objectives but strategic ones as well (such as those concerning market share). What is even more important is to consider the extent to which the rival is meeting these objectives and whether it is under pressure to improve. Rivals with good financial performance are likely to continue their present strategy with only minor fine-tuning. Poorly performing rivals are virtually certain to make fresh strategic moves.

Resources and Capabilities   A rival's strategic moves and countermoves are both enabled and constrained by the set of resources and capabilities the rival has at hand. Thus, a rival's resources and capabilities (and efforts to acquire new resources and capabilities) serve as a strong signal of future strategic actions (and reactions to your company's moves). Assessing a rival's resources and capabilities involves sizing up not only its strengths in this respect but its weaknesses as well.

Assumptions   How a rival's top managers think about their strategic situation can have a big impact on how the rival behaves. Banks that believe they are "too big to fail," for example, may take on more risk than is financially prudent. Assessing a rival's assumptions entails considering its assumptions about itself as well as about the industry it participates in.

Information regarding these four analytic components can often be gleaned from company press releases, information posted on the company's website (especially the presentations management has recently made to securities analysts), and such public documents as annual reports and 10-K filings. Many companies also have a competitive intelligence unit that sifts through the available information to construct up-to-date strategic profiles of rivals.[8]

Doing the necessary detective work can be time-consuming, but scouting competitors well enough to anticipate their next moves allows managers to prepare effective countermoves (perhaps even beat a rival to the punch) and to take rivals' probable actions into account in crafting their own best course of action. Despite the importance of gathering such information, these activities should never cross the bounds of ethical impropriety (see Illustration Capsule 3.3).

KEY SUCCESS FACTORS

An industry's **key success factors (KSFs)** are those competitive factors that most affect industry members' ability to survive and prosper in the marketplace: the particular strategy elements, product attributes, operational approaches, resources, and competitive capabilities that spell the difference between being a strong competitor and a weak competitor—and between profit and loss. KSFs by their very nature are so important to competitive success that *all firms* in the industry must pay close attention to them or risk becoming an industry laggard or failure. To indicate the significance of KSFs another way, how well the elements of a company's strategy measure up against an industry's KSFs determines whether the company can meet the basic criteria for surviving and thriving in the industry. Identifying KSFs, in light of the prevailing and anticipated industry and competitive conditions, is therefore always a top priority in analytic and strategy-making considerations. Company strategists need to understand the industry landscape well enough to separate the factors most important to competitive success from those that are less important.

> **CORE CONCEPT**
>
> **Key success factors** are the strategy elements, product and service attributes, operational approaches, resources, and competitive capabilities that are essential to surviving and thriving in the industry.

Key success factors vary from industry to industry, and even from time to time within the same industry, as change drivers and competitive conditions change. But regardless of the circumstances, an industry's key success factors can always be deduced by asking the same three questions:

1. On what basis do buyers of the industry's product choose between the competing brands of sellers? That is, what product attributes and service characteristics are crucial?

2. Given the nature of competitive rivalry prevailing in the marketplace, what resources and competitive capabilities must a company have to be competitively successful?

3. What shortcomings are almost certain to put a company at a significant competitive disadvantage?

Only rarely are there more than five key factors for competitive success. And even among these, two or three usually outrank the others in importance. Managers should therefore bear in mind the purpose of identifying key success factors—to determine which factors are most important to competitive success—and resist the temptation to label a factor that has only minor importance as a KSF.

In the beer industry, for example, although there are many types of buyers (wholesale, retail, end consumer), it is most important to understand the preferences and buying behavior of the beer drinkers. Their purchase decisions are driven by price, taste, convenient access, and marketing. Thus, the KSFs include a *strong network of wholesale distributors* (to get the company's brand stocked and favorably displayed in retail outlets, bars, restaurants, and stadiums, where beer is sold) and *clever advertising* (to induce beer drinkers to buy the company's brand and thereby pull beer sales through the established wholesale and retail channels). Because there is a potential for strong buyer power on the part of large distributors and retail chains, competitive success depends on some mechanism to offset that power, of which advertising (to create demand pull) is one. Thus, the KSFs also include *superior product differentiation* (as in microbrews) or *superior firm size and branding capabilities* (as in national brands). The KSFs also include *full utilization of brewing capacity* (to keep manufacturing costs low and offset the high costs of advertising, branding, and product differentiation).

Correctly diagnosing an industry's KSFs also raises a company's chances of crafting a sound strategy. The key success factors of an industry point to those things that every firm in the industry needs to attend to in order to retain customers and weather the competition. If the company's strategy cannot deliver on the key success factors of its industry, it is unlikely to earn enough profits to remain a viable business.

THE INDUSTRY OUTLOOK FOR PROFITABILITY ●●●●

Each of the frameworks presented in this chapter—PESTEL, five forces analysis, driving forces, strategy groups, competitor analysis, and key success factors—provides a useful perspective on an industry's outlook for future profitability. Putting them all together provides an even richer and more nuanced picture. Thus, the final step in evaluating the industry and competitive environment is to use the results of each of the analyses performed to determine whether the industry presents the company with strong prospects for competitive success and attractive profits. The important factors on which to base a conclusion include

- How the company is being impacted by the state of the macro-environment.
- Whether strong competitive forces are squeezing industry profitability to subpar levels.
- Whether the presence of complementors and the possibility of cooperative actions improve the company's prospects.
- Whether industry profitability will be favorably or unfavorably affected by the prevailing driving forces.
- Whether the company occupies a stronger market position than rivals.
- Whether this is likely to change in the course of competitive interactions.
- How well the company's strategy delivers on the industry key success factors.

As a general proposition, *the anticipated industry environment is fundamentally attractive if it presents a company with good opportunity for above-average profitability; the industry outlook is fundamentally unattractive if a company's profit prospects are unappealingly low.*

However, it is a mistake to think of a particular industry as being equally attractive or unattractive to all industry participants and all potential entrants.[9] Attractiveness is relative, not absolute, and conclusions one way or the other have to be drawn from the perspective of a particular company. For instance, a favorably positioned competitor may see ample opportunity to capitalize on the vulnerabilities of weaker rivals even though industry conditions are otherwise somewhat dismal. At the same time, industries attractive to insiders may be unattractive to outsiders because of the difficulty of challenging current market leaders or because they have more attractive opportunities elsewhere.

> The degree to which an industry is attractive or unattractive is not the same for all industry participants and all potential entrants.

When a company decides an industry is fundamentally attractive and presents good opportunities, a strong case can be made that it should invest aggressively to capture the opportunities it sees and to improve its long-term competitive position in the business. When a strong competitor concludes an industry is becoming less attractive, it may elect to simply protect its present position, investing cautiously—if at all—and looking for opportunities in other industries. A competitively weak company in an unattractive industry may see its best option as finding a buyer, perhaps a rival, to acquire its business.

KEY POINTS
● ● ● ●

Thinking strategically about a company's external situation involves probing for answers to the following questions:

1. *What are the strategically relevant factors in the macro-environment, and how do they impact an industry and its members?* Industries differ significantly as to how they are affected by conditions and developments in the broad macro-environment. Using PESTEL analysis to identify which of these factors is strategically relevant is the first step to understanding how a company is situated in its external environment.

2. *What kinds of competitive forces are industry members facing, and how strong is each force?* The strength of competition is a composite of five forces: (1) rivalry within

the industry, (2) the threat of new entry into the market, (3) inroads being made by the sellers of substitutes, (4) supplier bargaining power, and (5) buyer power. All five must be examined force by force, and their collective strength evaluated. One strong force, however, can be sufficient to keep average industry profitability low. Working through the five forces model aids strategy makers in assessing how to insulate the company from the strongest forces, identify attractive arenas for expansion, or alter the competitive conditions so that they offer more favorable prospects for profitability.

3. *What cooperative forces are present in the industry, and how can a company harness them to its advantage?* Interactions among industry participants are not only competitive in nature but cooperative as well. This is particularly the case when complements to the products or services of an industry are important. The Value Net framework assists managers in sizing up the impact of cooperative as well as competitive interactions on their firm.

4. *What factors are driving changes in the industry, and what impact will they have on competitive intensity and industry profitability?* Industry and competitive conditions change because certain forces are acting to create incentives or pressures for change. The first step is to identify the three or four most important drivers of change affecting the industry being analyzed (out of a much longer list of potential drivers). Once an industry's change drivers have been identified, the analytic task becomes one of determining whether they are acting, individually and collectively, to make the industry environment more or less attractive.

5. *What market positions do industry rivals occupy—who is strongly positioned and who is not?* Strategic group mapping is a valuable tool for understanding the similarities, differences, strengths, and weaknesses inherent in the market positions of rival companies. Rivals in the same or nearby strategic groups are close competitors, whereas companies in distant strategic groups usually pose little or no immediate threat. The lesson of strategic group mapping is that some positions on the map are more favorable than others. The profit potential of different strategic groups may not be the same because industry driving forces and competitive forces likely have varying effects on the industry's distinct strategic groups. Moreover, mobility barriers restrict movement between groups in the same way that entry barriers prevent easy entry into attractive industries.

6. *What strategic moves are rivals likely to make next?* Anticipating the actions of rivals can help a company prepare effective countermoves. Using the SOAR Framework for Competitor Analysis is helpful in this regard.

7. *What are the key factors for competitive success?* An industry's key success factors (KSFs) are the particular strategy elements, product attributes, operational approaches, resources, and competitive capabilities that all industry members must have in order to survive and prosper in the industry. For any industry, they can be deduced by answering three basic questions: (1) On what basis do buyers of the industry's product choose between the competing brands of sellers, (2) what resources and competitive capabilities must a company have to be competitively successful, and (3) what shortcomings are almost certain to put a company at a significant competitive disadvantage?

8. *Is the industry outlook conducive to good profitability?* The last step in industry analysis is summing up the results from applying each of the frameworks employed in answering questions 1 to 7: PESTEL, five forces analysis, Value Net, driving forces, strategic group mapping, competitor analysis, and key success factors.

Applying multiple lenses to the question of what the industry outlook looks like offers a more robust and nuanced answer. If the answers from each framework, seen as a whole, reveal that a company's profit prospects in that industry are above-average, then the industry environment is basically attractive *for that company.* What may look like an attractive environment for one company may appear to be unattractive from the perspective of a different company.

Clear, insightful diagnosis of a company's external situation is an essential first step in crafting strategies that are well matched to industry and competitive conditions. To do cutting-edge strategic thinking about the external environment, managers must know what questions to pose and what analytic tools to use in answering these questions. This is why this chapter has concentrated on suggesting the right questions to ask, explaining concepts and analytic approaches, and indicating the kinds of things to look for.

ASSURANCE OF LEARNING EXERCISES

1. Prepare a brief analysis of the organic food industry using the information provided by the Organic Trade Association at **www.ota.com** and the ***Organic Report*** magazine at **theorganicreport.com.** That is, based on the information provided on these websites, draw a five forces diagram for the organic food industry and briefly discuss the nature and strength of each of the five competitive forces.   **LO 3-2**

2. Based on the strategic group map in Illustration Capsule 3.2, which pizza chains are Hungry Howie's closest competitors? With which strategic group does California Pizza Kitchen compete the least, according to this map? Why do you think no Pizza chains are positioned in the area above the Pizza Hut's strategic group?   **LO 3-3**

3. The National Restaurant Association publishes an annual industry fact book that can be found at **www.restaurant.org.** Based on information in the latest report, does it appear that macro-environmental factors and the economic characteristics of the industry will present industry participants with attractive opportunities for growth and profitability? Explain.   **LO 3-1, LO 3-4**

EXERCISES FOR SIMULATION PARTICIPANTS

1. Which of the factors listed in Table 3.1 might have the most strategic relevance for your industry?   **LO 3-1**

2. Which of the five competitive forces is creating the strongest competitive pressures for your company?   **LO 3-2**

3. What are the "weapons of competition" that rival companies in your industry can use to gain sales and market share? See Table 3.2 to help you identify the various competitive factors.   **LO 3-3**

4. What are the factors affecting the intensity of rivalry in the industry in which your company is competing? Use Figure 3.4 and the accompanying discussion to help you in pinpointing the specific factors most affecting competitive intensity. Would you characterize the rivalry and jockeying for better market position, increased sales, and market share among the companies in your industry as fierce, very strong, strong, moderate, or relatively weak? Why?   **LO 3-4**

LO 3-2   **5.**   Are there any driving forces in the industry in which your company is competing? If so, what impact will these driving forces have? Will they cause competition to be more or less intense? Will they act to boost or squeeze profit margins? List at least two actions your company should consider taking in order to combat any negative impacts of the driving forces.

LO 3-3   **6.**   Draw a strategic group map showing the market positions of the companies in your industry. Which companies do you believe are in the most attractive position on the map? Which companies are the most weakly positioned? Which companies do you believe are likely to try to move to a different position on the strategic group map?

LO 3-4   **7.**   What do you see as the key factors for being a successful competitor in your industry? List at least three.

LO 3-4   **8.**   Does your overall assessment of the industry suggest that industry rivals have sufficiently attractive opportunities for growth and profitability? Explain.

ENDNOTES

[1] Michael E. Porter, *Competitive Strategy* (New York: Free Press, 1980); Michael E. Porter, "The Five Competitive Forces That Shape Strategy," *Harvard Business Review* 86, no. 1 (January 2008), pp. 78–93.

[2] J. S. Bain, *Barriers to New Competition* (Cambridge, MA: Harvard University Press, 1956); F. M. Scherer, *Industrial Market Structure and Economic Performance* (Chicago: Rand McNally, 1971).

[3] Ibid.

[4] C. A. Montgomery and S. Hariharan, "Diversified Expansion by Large Established Firms," *Journal of Economic Behavior & Organization* 15, no. 1 (January 1991).

[5] For a more extended discussion of the problems with the life-cycle hypothesis, see Porter, *Competitive Strategy,* pp. 157–162.

[6] Mary Ellen Gordon and George R. Milne, "Selecting the Dimensions That Define Strategic Groups: A Novel Market-Driven Approach," *Journal of Managerial Issues* 11, no. 2 (Summer 1999), pp. 213–233.

[7] Avi Fiegenbaum and Howard Thomas, "Strategic Groups as Reference Groups: Theory, Modeling and Empirical Examination of Industry and Competitive Strategy," *Strategic Management Journal* 16 (1995), pp. 461–476; S. Ade Olusoga, Michael P. Mokwa, and Charles H. Noble, "Strategic Groups, Mobility Barriers, and Competitive Advantage," *Journal of Business Research* 33 (1995), pp. 153–164.

[8] Larry Kahaner, *Competitive Intelligence* (New York: Simon & Schuster, 1996).

[9] B. Wernerfelt and C. Montgomery, "What Is an Attractive Industry?" *Management Science* 32, no. 10 (October 1986), pp. 1223–1230.

chapter 4

Evaluating a Company's Resources, Capabilities, and Competitiveness

Learning Objectives

After reading this chapter, you should be able to:

LO 4-1 Evaluate how well a company's strategy is working.

LO 4-2 Assess the company's strengths and weaknesses in light of market opportunities and external threats.

LO 4-3 Explain why a company's resources and capabilities are critical for gaining a competitive edge over rivals.

LO 4-4 Understand how value chain activities affect a company's cost structure and customer value proposition.

LO 4-5 Explain how a comprehensive evaluation of a company's competitive situation can assist managers in making critical decisions about their next strategic moves.

PhotoDisc Imaging/Getty Images

Crucial, of course, is having a difference that matters in the industry.

Cynthia Montgomery—*Professor and author*

If you don't have a competitive advantage, don't compete.

Jack Welch—*Former CEO of General Electric*

Organizations succeed in a competitive marketplace over the long run because they can do certain things their customers value better than can their competitors.

Robert Hayes, Gary Pisano, and David Upton—
Professors and consultants

Chapter 3 described how to use the tools of industry and competitor analysis to assess a company's external environment and lay the groundwork for matching a company's strategy to its external situation. This chapter discusses techniques for evaluating a company's internal situation, including its collection of resources and capabilities and the activities it performs along its value chain. Internal analysis enables managers to determine whether their strategy is likely to give the company a significant competitive edge over rival firms (given external conditions). Combined with external analysis, it facilitates an understanding of how to reposition a firm to take advantage of new opportunities and to cope with emerging competitive threats. The analytic spotlight will be trained on six questions:

1. How well is the company's present strategy working?

2. What are the company's strengths and weaknesses in relation to the market opportunities and external threats?

3. What are the company's most important resources and capabilities, and will they give the company a lasting competitive advantage over rival companies?

4. How do a company's value chain activities impact its cost structure and customer value proposition?

5. Is the company competitively stronger or weaker than key rivals?

6. What strategic issues and problems merit front-burner managerial attention?

In probing for answers to these questions, five analytic tools—resource and capability analysis, SWOT analysis, value chain analysis, benchmarking, and competitive strength assessment—will be used. All five are valuable techniques for revealing a company's competitiveness and for helping company managers match their strategy to the company's particular circumstances. Accordingly, this will enable the company to pass the first of the three tests of a *winning strategy* (the Fit Test), as discussed in Chapter 1.

QUESTION 1: HOW WELL IS THE COMPANY'S PRESENT STRATEGY WORKING?

● LO 4-1

Evaluate how well a company's strategy is working.

Before evaluating how well a company's present strategy is working, it is best to start with a clear view of what the strategy entails. The first thing to examine is the company's competitive approach. What moves has the company made recently to attract customers and improve its market position—for instance, has it cut prices, improved the design of its product, added new features, stepped up advertising, entered a new geographic market, or merged with a competitor? Is it striving for a competitive advantage based on low costs or a better product offering? Is it concentrating on serving a broad spectrum of customers or a narrow market niche? The company's functional strategies in R&D, production, marketing, finance, human resources, information technology, and so on further characterize company strategy, as do any efforts to establish alliances with other enterprises. Figure 4.1 shows the key components of a single-business company's strategy.

A determination of the effectiveness of this strategy requires a more in-depth type of analysis. The two best indicators of how well a company's strategy is working are (1) whether the company is recording gains in financial strength and profitability, and (2) whether the company's competitive strength and market standing are improving. Persistent shortfalls in meeting company performance targets and weak marketplace performance relative to rivals are reliable warning signs that the company has a weak

FIGURE 4.1   Identifying the Components of a Single-Business Company's Strategy

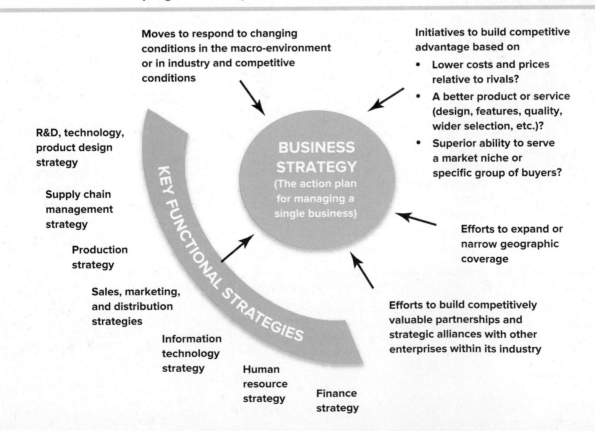

strategy, suffers from poor strategy execution, or both. Specific indicators of how well a company's strategy is working include

- Trends in the company's sales and earnings growth.
- Trends in the company's stock price.
- The company's overall financial strength.
- The company's customer retention rate.
- The rate at which new customers are acquired.
- Evidence of improvement in internal processes such as defect rate, order fulfill-ment, delivery times, days of inventory, and employee productivity.

The stronger a company's current overall performance, the more likely it has a well-conceived, well-executed strategy. The weaker a company's financial perfor-mance and market standing, the more its current strategy must be questioned and the more likely the need for radical changes. Table 4.1 provides a compilation of the financial ratios most commonly used to evaluate a company's financial perfor-mance and balance sheet strength.

> Sluggish financial perfor-mance and second-rate market accomplishments almost always signal weak strategy, weak execution, or both.

TABLE 4.1   Key Financial Ratios: How to Calculate Them and What They Mean

Ratio	How Calculated	What It Shows
Profitability ratios		
1. Gross profit margin	$\dfrac{\text{Sales revenues} - \text{Cost of goods sold}}{\text{Sales revenues}}$	Shows the percentage of revenues available to cover operating expenses and yield a profit.
2. Operating profit margin (or return on sales)	$\dfrac{\text{Sales revenues} - \text{Operating expenses}}{\text{Sales revenues}}$ or $\dfrac{\text{Operating income}}{\text{Sales revenues}}$	Shows the profitability of current operations without regard to interest charges and income taxes. Earnings before interest and taxes is known as *EBIT* in financial and business accounting.
3. Net profit margin (or net return on sales)	$\dfrac{\text{Profits after taxes}}{\text{Sales revenues}}$	Shows after-tax profits per dollar of sales.
4. Total return on assets	$\dfrac{\text{Profits after taxes} + \text{Interest}}{\text{Total assets}}$	A measure of the return on total investment in the enterprise. Interest is added to after-tax profits to form the numerator, since total assets are financed by creditors as well as by stockholders.
5. Net return on total assets (ROA)	$\dfrac{\text{Profits after taxes}}{\text{Total assets}}$	A measure of the return earned by stockholders on the firm's total assets.
6. Return on stockholders' equity (ROE)	$\dfrac{\text{Profits after taxes}}{\text{Total stockholders' equity}}$	The return stockholders are earning on their capital investment in the enterprise. A return in the 12% to 15% range is average.
7. Return on invested capital (ROIC)—sometimes referred to as return on capital employed (ROCE)	$\dfrac{\text{Profits after taxes}}{\text{Long-term debt} + \text{Total stockholders' equity}}$	A measure of the return that shareholders are earning on the monetary capital invested in the enterprise. A higher return reflects greater bottom-line effectiveness in the use of long-term capital.

(continued)

TABLE 4.1   *(continued)*

Ratio	How Calculated	What It Shows
Liquidity ratios		
1. Current ratio	$$\dfrac{\text{Current assets}}{\text{Current liabilities}}$$	Shows a firm's ability to pay current liabilities using assets that can be converted to cash in the near term. Ratio should be higher than 1.0.
2. Working capital	Current assets − Current liabilities	The cash available for a firm's day-to-day operations. Larger amounts mean the company has more internal funds to (1) pay its current liabilities on a timely basis and (2) finance inventory expansion, additional accounts receivable, and a larger base of operations without resorting to borrowing or raising more equity capital.
Leverage ratios		
1. Total debt-to-assets ratio	$$\dfrac{\text{Total debt}}{\text{Total assets}}$$	Measures the extent to which borrowed funds (both short-term loans and long-term debt) have been used to finance the firm's operations. A low ratio is better—a high fraction indicates overuse of debt and greater risk of bankruptcy.
2. Long-term debt-to-capital ratio	$$\dfrac{\text{Long-term debt}}{\text{Long-term debt} + \text{Total stockholders' equity}}$$	A measure of creditworthiness and balance sheet strength. It indicates the percentage of capital investment that has been financed by both long-term lenders and stockholders. A ratio below 0.25 is preferable since the lower the ratio, the greater the capacity to borrow additional funds. Debt-to-capital ratios above 0.50 indicate an excessive reliance on long-term borrowing, lower creditworthiness, and weak balance sheet strength.
3. Debt-to-equity ratio	$$\dfrac{\text{Total debt}}{\text{Total stockholders' equity}}$$	Shows the balance between debt (funds borrowed both short term and long term) and the amount that stockholders have invested in the enterprise. The further the ratio is below 1.0, the greater the firm's ability to borrow additional funds. Ratios above 1.0 put creditors at greater risk, signal weaker balance sheet strength, and often result in lower credit ratings.
4. Long-term debt-to-equity ratio	$$\dfrac{\text{Long-term debt}}{\text{Total stockholders' equity}}$$	Shows the balance between long-term debt and stockholders' equity in the firm's *long-term* capital structure. Low ratios indicate a greater capacity to borrow additional funds if needed.
5. Times-interest-earned (or coverage) ratio	$$\dfrac{\text{Operating income}}{\text{Interest expenses}}$$	Measures the ability to pay annual interest charges. Lenders usually insist on a minimum ratio of 2.0, but ratios above 3.0 signal progressively better creditworthiness.
Activity ratios		
1. Days of inventory	$$\dfrac{\text{Inventory}}{\text{Cost of goods sold} \div 365}$$	Measures inventory management efficiency. Fewer days of inventory are better.

(continued)

TABLE 4.1   *(continued)*

Ratio	How Calculated	What It Shows
2. Inventory turnover	$\dfrac{\text{Cost of goods sold}}{\text{Inventory}}$	Measures the number of inventory turns per year. Higher is better.
3. Average collection period	$\dfrac{\text{Accounts receivable}}{\text{Total sales} \div 365}$ *or* $\dfrac{\text{Accounts receivable}}{\text{Average daily sales}}$	Indicates the average length of time the firm must wait after making a sale to receive cash payment. A shorter collection time is better.

Other important measures of financial performance

1. Dividend yield on common stock	$\dfrac{\text{Annual dividends per share}}{\text{Current market price per share}}$	A measure of the return that shareholders receive in the form of dividends. A "typical" dividend yield is 2% to 3%. The dividend yield for fast-growth companies is often below 1%; the dividend yield for slow-growth companies can run 4% to 5%.
2. Price-to-earnings (P/E) ratio	$\dfrac{\text{Current market price per share}}{\text{Earnings per share}}$	P/E ratios above 20 indicate strong investor confidence in a firm's outlook and earnings growth; firms whose future earnings are at risk or likely to grow slowly typically have ratios below 12.
3. Dividend payout ratio	$\dfrac{\text{Annual dividends per share}}{\text{Earnings per share}}$	Indicates the percentage of after-tax profits paid out as dividends.
4. Internal cash flow	After-tax profits + Depreciation	A rough estimate of the cash a company's business is generating after payment of operating expenses, interest, and taxes. Such amounts can be used for dividend payments or funding capital expenditures.
5. Free cash flow	After-tax profits + Depreciation − Capital expenditures − Dividends	A rough estimate of the cash a company's business is generating after payment of operating expenses, interest, taxes, dividends, and desirable reinvestments in the business. The larger a company's free cash flow, the greater its ability to internally fund new strategic initiatives, repay debt, make new acquisitions, repurchase shares of stock, or increase dividend payments.

QUESTION 2: WHAT ARE THE COMPANY'S STRENGTHS AND WEAKNESSES IN RELATION TO THE MARKET OPPORTUNITIES AND EXTERNAL THREATS?

An examination of the financial and other indicators discussed previously can tell you how well a strategy is working, but they tell you little about the underlying reasons—*why* it's working or not. The simplest and most easily applied tool for gaining some insight into the reasons for the success of a strategy or lack thereof is known as

SWOT analysis. SWOT is an acronym that stands for a company's internal **S**trengths and **W**eaknesses, market **O**pportunities, and external **T**hreats. Another name for SWOT analysis is Situational Analysis. A first-rate SWOT analysis can help explain why a strategy is working well (or not) by taking a good hard look a company's strengths in relation to its weaknesses and in relation to the strengths and weaknesses of competitors. Are the company's strengths great enough to make up for its weaknesses? Has the company's strategy built on these strengths and shielded the company from its weaknesses? Do the company's strengths exceed those of its rivals or have they been overpowered? Similarly, a SWOT analysis can help determine whether a strategy has been effective in fending off external threats and positioning the firm to take advantage of market opportunities.

SWOT analysis has long been one of the most popular and widely used diagnostic tools for strategists. It is used fruitfully by organizations that range in type from large corporations to small businesses, to government agencies to non-profits such as churches and schools. Its popularity stems in part from its ease of use, but also because it can be used not only to evaluate the efficacy of a strategy, but also as the basis for crafting a strategy from the outset that capitalizes on the company's strengths, overcomes its weaknesses, aims squarely at capturing the company's best opportunities, and defends against competitive and macro-environmental threats. Moreover, a SWOT analysis can help a company with a strategy that is working well in the present determine whether the company is in a position to pursue new market opportunities and defend against emerging threats to its future well-being.

Identifying a Company's Internal Strengths

An internal **strength** is something a company is good at doing or an attribute that enhances its competitiveness in the marketplace.

One way to appraise a company's strengths is to ask: What activities does the company perform well? This question directs attention to the company's skill level in performing key pieces of its business—such as supply chain management, R&D, production, distribution, sales and marketing, and customer service. A company's skill or proficiency in performing different facets of its operations can range from the extreme of having minimal ability to perform an activity (perhaps having just struggled to do it the first time) to the other extreme of being able to perform the activity better than any other company in the industry.

When a company's proficiency rises from that of mere ability to perform an activity to the point of being able to perform it consistently well and at acceptable cost, it is said to have a **competence**—a true *capability,* in other words. If a company's competence level in some activity domain is superior to that of its rivals it is known as a **distinctive competence. A core competence** is a proficiently performed internal activity that is *central* to a company's strategy and is typically distinctive as well. A core competence is a more competitively valuable strength than a competence because of the activity's key role in the company's strategy and the contribution it makes to the company's market success and profitability. Often, core competencies can be leveraged to create new markets or new product demand, as the engine behind a company's growth. Procter and Gamble has a core competence in brand management, which has led to an ever-increasing portfolio of market-leading consumer products, including Charmin, Tide, Crest, Tampax, Olay, Febreze, Luvs, Pampers, and Swiffer. Nike has a core competence in designing and marketing innovative athletic footwear and sports apparel. Kellogg has a core competence in developing, producing, and marketing breakfast cereals.

Identifying Company Internal Weaknesses

An internal **weakness** is something a company lacks or does poorly (in comparison to others) or a condition that puts it at a disadvantage in the marketplace. It can be thought of as a competitive deficiency. A company's internal weaknesses can relate to (1) inferior or unproven skills, expertise, or intellectual capital in competitively important areas of the business, or (2) deficiencies in competitively important physical, organizational, or intangible assets. Nearly all companies have competitive deficiencies of one kind or another. Whether a company's internal weaknesses make it competitively vulnerable depends on how much they matter in the marketplace and whether they are offset by the company's strengths.

Table 4.2 lists many of the things to consider in compiling a company's strengths and weaknesses. Sizing up a company's complement of strengths and deficiencies is akin to constructing a *strategic balance sheet,* where strengths represent *competitive assets* and weaknesses represent *competitive liabilities.* Obviously, the ideal condition is for the company's competitive assets to outweigh its competitive liabilities by an ample margin!

Identifying a Company's Market Opportunities

Market opportunity is a big factor in shaping a company's strategy. Indeed, managers can't properly tailor strategy to the company's situation without first identifying its market opportunities and appraising the growth and profit potential each one holds. Depending on the prevailing circumstances, a company's opportunities can be plentiful or scarce, fleeting or lasting, and can range from wildly attractive to marginally interesting or unsuitable.

Newly emerging and fast-changing markets sometimes present stunningly big or "golden" opportunities, but it is typically hard for managers at one company to peer into "the fog of the future" and spot them far ahead of managers at other companies.[1] But as the fog begins to clear, golden opportunities are nearly always seized rapidly— and the companies that seize them are usually those that have been staying alert with diligent market reconnaissance and preparing themselves to capitalize on shifting market conditions swiftly. Table 4.2 displays a sampling of potential market opportunities.

Identifying External Threats

Often, certain factors in a company's external environment pose *threats* to its profitability and competitive well-being. Threats can stem from such factors as the emergence of cheaper or better technologies, the entry of lower-cost competitors into a company's market stronghold, new regulations that are more burdensome to a company than to its competitors, unfavorable demographic shifts, and political upheaval in a foreign country where the company has facilities.

External threats may pose no more than a moderate degree of adversity (all companies confront some threatening elements in the course of doing business), or they may be imposing enough to make a company's situation look tenuous. On rare occasions, market shocks can give birth to a *sudden-death* threat that throws a

> **CORE CONCEPT**
>
> A **core competence** is an activity that a company performs proficiently and that is also central to its strategy and competitive success.

> **CORE CONCEPT**
>
> A company's **strengths** represent its competitive assets; its **weaknesses** are shortcomings that constitute competitive liabilities.

> Simply making lists of a company's strengths, weaknesses, opportunities, and threats is not enough; the payoff from SWOT analysis comes from the conclusions about a company's situation and the implications for strategy improvement that flow from the four lists.

TABLE 4.2   What to Look for in Identifying a Company's Strengths, Weaknesses, Opportunities, and Threats

Strengths and Competitive Assets	Weaknesses and Competitive Deficiencies
• Ample financial resources to grow the business • Strong brand-name image or reputation • Distinctive core competencies • Cost advantages over rivals • Attractive customer base • Proprietary technology, superior technological skills, important patents • Strong bargaining power over suppliers or buyers • Superior product quality • Wide geographic coverage and/or strong global distribution capability • Alliances and/or joint ventures that provide access to valuable technology, competencies, and/or attractive geographic markets	• No distinctive core competencies • Lack of attention to customer needs • Inferior product quality • Weak balance sheet, too much debt • Higher costs than competitors • Too narrow a product line relative to rivals • Weak brand image or reputation • Lack of adequate distribution capability • Lack of management depth • A plague of internal operating problems or obsolete facilities • Too much underutilized plant capacity
Market Opportunities	**External Threats**
• Meet sharply rising buyer demand for the industry's product • Serve additional customer groups or market segments • Expand into new geographic markets • Expand the company's product line to meet a broader range of customer needs • Enter new product lines or new businesses • Take advantage of falling trade barriers in attractive foreign markets • Take advantage of an adverse change in the fortunes of rival firms • Acquire rival firms or companies with attractive technological expertise or competencies • Take advantage of emerging technological developments to innovate • Enter into alliances or other cooperative ventures	• Increased intensity of competition • Slowdowns in market growth • Likely entry of potent new competitors • Growing bargaining power of customers or suppliers • A shift in buyer needs and tastes away from the industry's product • Adverse demographic changes that threaten to curtail demand for the industry's product • Adverse economic conditions that threaten critical suppliers or distributors • Changes in technology—particularly disruptive technology that can undermine the company's distinctive competencies • Restrictive foreign trade policies • Costly new regulatory requirements • Tight credit conditions • Rising prices on energy or other key inputs

company into an immediate crisis and a battle to survive. Many of the world's major financial institutions were plunged into unprecedented crisis in 2008–2009 by the after-effects of high-risk mortgage lending, inflated credit ratings on subprime mortgage securities, the collapse of housing prices, and a market flooded with mortgage-related investments (collateralized debt obligations) whose values suddenly evaporated. It is management's job to identify the threats to the company's future prospects and to evaluate what strategic actions can be taken to neutralize or lessen their impact.

What Do the SWOT Listings Reveal?

SWOT analysis involves more than making four lists. In crafting a new strategy, it offers a strong foundation for understanding how to position the company to build on its strengths in seizing new business opportunities and how to mitigate external threats by shoring up its competitive deficiencies. In assessing the effectiveness of an existing strategy, it can be used to glean insights regarding the company's overall business situation (thus the name Situational Analysis); and it can help translate these insights into recommended strategic actions. Figure 4.2 shows the steps involved in gleaning insights from SWOT analysis.

The beauty of SWOT analysis is its simplicity; but this is also its primary limitation. For a deeper and more accurate understanding of a company's situation, more sophisticated tools are required. Chapter 3 introduced you to a set of tools for analyzing a company's external situation. In the rest of this chapter, we look more deeply at a company's internal situation, beginning with the company's resources and capabilities.

FIGURE 4.2   The Steps Involved in SWOT Analysis: Identify the Four Components of SWOT, Draw Conclusions, Translate Implications into Strategic Actions

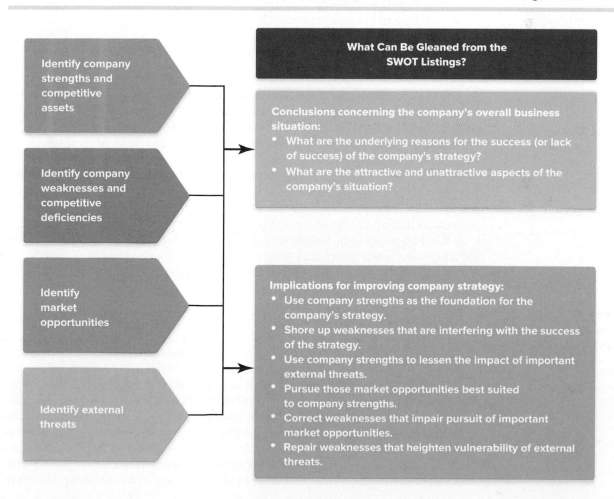

QUESTION 3: WHAT ARE THE COMPANY'S MOST IMPORTANT RESOURCES AND CAPABILITIES, AND WILL THEY GIVE THE COMPANY A LASTING COMPETITIVE ADVANTAGE?

● ● ● ●

CORE CONCEPT

A company's resources and capabilities represent its **competitive assets** and are determinants of its competitiveness and ability to succeed in the marketplace.

An essential element of a company's internal environment is the nature of resources and capabilities. A company's resources and capabilities are its **competitive assets** and determine whether its competitive power in the marketplace will be impressively strong or disappointingly weak. Companies with second-rate competitive assets nearly always are relegated to a trailing position in the industry.

Resource and capability analysis provides managers with a powerful tool for sizing up the company's competitive assets and determining whether they can provide the foundation necessary for competitive success in the marketplace. This is a two-step process. The first step is to identify the company's resources and capabilities. The second step is to examine them more closely to ascertain which are the most competitively important and whether they can support a sustainable competitive advantage over rival firms.[2] This second step involves applying the *four tests of a resource's competitive power.*

Resource and capability analysis is a powerful tool for sizing up a company's competitive assets and determining whether the assets can support a sustainable competitive advantage over market rivals.

Identifying the Company's Resources and Capabilities

A firm's resources and capabilities are the fundamental building blocks of its competitive strategy. In crafting strategy, it is essential for managers to know how to take stock of the company's full complement of resources and capabilities. But before they can do so, managers and strategists need a more precise definition of these terms.

In brief, a **resource** is a productive input or competitive asset that is owned or controlled by the firm. Firms have many different types of resources at their disposal that vary not only in kind but in quality as well. Some are of a higher quality than others, and some are more competitively valuable, having greater potential to give a firm a competitive advantage over its rivals. For example, a company's brand is a resource, as is an R&D team—yet some brands such as Coca-Cola and Xerox are well known, with enduring value, while others have little more name recognition than generic products. In similar fashion, some R&D teams are far more innovative and productive than others due to the outstanding talents of the individual team members, the team's composition, its experience, and its chemistry.

● **LO 4-3**

Explain why a company's resources and capabilities are critical for gaining a competitive edge over rivals.

A **capability** (or **competence**) is the capacity of a firm to perform some internal activity competently. Capabilities or competences also vary in form, quality, and competitive importance, with some being more competitively valuable than others. American Express displays superior capabilities in brand management and marketing; Starbucks's employee management, training, and real estate capabilities are the drivers behind its rapid growth; Microsoft's competences are in developing operating systems for computers and user software like Microsoft Office®. *Organizational capabilities are developed and enabled through the deployment of a company's resources.*[3] For example, Nestlé's brand management capabilities for its 2,000 + food, beverage, and pet care brands draw on the knowledge of the company's brand managers, the expertise of its marketing department, and the company's relationships with retailers in nearly

CORE CONCEPT

A **resource** is a competitive asset that is owned or controlled by a company; a **capability** (or **competence**) is the capacity of a firm to perform some internal activity competently. Capabilities are developed and enabled through the deployment of a company's resources.

200 countries. W. L. Gore's product innovation capabilities in its fabrics and medical and industrial product businesses result from the personal initiative, creative talents, and technological expertise of its associates and the company's culture that encourages accountability and creative thinking.

Types of Company Resources   A useful way to identify a company's resources is to look for them within categories, as shown in Table 4.3. Broadly speaking, resources can be divided into two main categories: **tangible** and **intangible** resources. Although *human resources* make up one of the most important parts of a company's resource base, we include them in the intangible category to emphasize the role played by the skills, talents, and knowledge of a company's human resources.

Tangible resources are the most easily identified, since tangible resources are those that can be *touched* or *quantified* readily. Obviously, they include various types of *physical resources* such as manufacturing facilities and mineral resources, but they also include a company's *financial resources, technological resources,* and *organizational resources* such as the company's communication and control systems. Note that technological resources are included among tangible resources, *by convention,* even though some types, such as copyrights and trade secrets, might be more logically categorized as intangible.

Intangible resources are harder to discern, but they are often among the most important of a firm's competitive assets. They include various sorts of *human assets and intellectual capital,* as well as a company's *brands, image, and reputational assets.*

TABLE 4.3   Types of Company Resources

Tangible resources

- *Physical resources:* land and real estate; manufacturing plants, equipment, and/or distribution facilities; the locations of stores, plants, or distribution centers, including the overall pattern of their physical locations; ownership of or access rights to natural resources (such as mineral deposits)
- *Financial resources:* cash and cash equivalents; marketable securities; other financial assets such as a company's credit rating and borrowing capacity
- *Technological assets:* patents, copyrights, production technology, innovation technologies, technological processes
- *Organizational resources:* IT and communication systems (satellites, servers, workstations, etc.); other planning, coordination, and control systems; the company's organizational design and reporting structure

Intangible resources

- *Human assets and intellectual capital:* the education, experience, knowledge, and talent of the workforce, cumulative learning, and tacit knowledge of employees; collective learning embedded in the organization, the intellectual capital and know-how of specialized teams and work groups; the knowledge of key personnel concerning important business functions; managerial talent and leadership skill; the creativity and innovativeness of certain personnel
- *Brands, company image, and reputational assets:* brand names, trademarks, product or company image, buyer loyalty and goodwill; company reputation for quality, service, and reliability; reputation with suppliers and partners for fair dealing
- *Relationships:* alliances, joint ventures, or partnerships that provide access to technologies, specialized know-how, or geographic markets; networks of dealers or distributors; the trust established with various partners
- *Company culture and incentive system:* the norms of behavior, business principles, and ingrained beliefs within the company; the attachment of personnel to the company's ideals; the compensation system and the motivation level of company personnel

While intangible resources have no material existence on their own, they are often embodied in something material. Thus, the skills and knowledge resources of a firm are embodied in its managers and employees; a company's brand name is embodied in the company logo or product labels. Other important kinds of intangible resources include a company's *relationships* with suppliers, buyers, or partners of various sorts, and the *company's culture and incentive system.*

Listing a company's resources category by category can prevent managers from inadvertently overlooking some company resources that might be competitively important. At times, it can be difficult to decide exactly how to categorize certain types of resources. For example, resources such as a work group's specialized expertise in developing innovative products can be considered to be technological assets or human assets or intellectual capital and knowledge assets; the work ethic and drive of a company's workforce could be included under the company's human assets or its culture and incentive system. In this regard, it is important to remember that *it is not exactly how a resource is categorized that matters but, rather, that all of the company's different types of resources are included in the inventory.* The real purpose of using categories in identifying a company's resources is *to ensure that none of a company's resources go unnoticed when sizing up the company's competitive assets.*

Identifying Organizational Capabilities   Organizational capabilities are more complex entities than resources; indeed, they are built up through the use of resources and draw on some combination of the firm's resources as they are exercised. Virtually all organizational capabilities are *knowledge-based, residing in people and in a company's intellectual capital, or in organizational processes and systems, which embody tacit knowledge.* For example, Amazon's speedy delivery capabilities rely on the knowledge of its fulfillment center managers, its relationship with the United Parcel Service, and the experience of its merchandisers to correctly predict inventory flow. Bose's capabilities in auditory system design arise from the talented engineers that form the R&D team as well as the company's strong culture, which celebrates innovation and beautiful design.

Because of their complexity, organizational capabilities are harder to categorize than resources and more challenging to search for as a result. There are, however, two approaches that can make the process of uncovering and identifying a firm's capabilities more systematic. The first method takes the completed listing of a firm's resources as its starting point. Since organizational capabilities are built from resources and utilize resources as they are exercised, a firm's resources can provide a strong set of clues about the types of capabilities the firm is likely to have accumulated. This approach simply involves looking over the firm's resources and considering whether (and to what extent) the firm has built up any related capabilities. So, for example, a fleet of trucks, the latest RFID tracking technology, and a set of large automated distribution centers may be indicative of sophisticated capabilities in logistics and distribution. R&D teams composed of top scientists with expertise in genomics may suggest organizational capabilities in developing new gene therapies or in biotechnology more generally.

The second method of identifying a firm's capabilities takes a functional approach. Many organizational capabilities relate to fairly specific functions; these draw on a limited set of resources and typically involve a single department or organizational unit. Capabilities in injection molding or continuous casting or metal stamping are manufacturing-related; capabilities in direct selling, promotional pricing, or database marketing all connect to the sales and marketing functions; capabilities in basic research, strategic innovation, or new product development link to a company's R&D

function. This approach requires managers to survey the various functions a firm performs to find the different capabilities associated with each function.

A problem with this second method is that many of the most important capabilities of firms are inherently *cross-functional*. Cross-functional capabilities draw on a number of different kinds of resources and are multidimensional in nature—they spring from the effective collaboration among people with different types of expertise working in different organizational units. Warby Parker draws from its cross-functional design process to create its popular eyewear. Its design capabilities are not just due to its creative designers, but are the product of their capabilities in market research and engineering as well as their relations with suppliers and manufacturing companies. Cross-functional capabilities and other complex capabilities involving numerous linked and closely integrated competitive assets are sometimes referred to as **resource bundles.**

It is important not to miss identifying a company's resource bundles, since they can be the most competitively important of a firm's competitive assets. Resource bundles can sometimes pass the four tests of a resource's competitive power (described below) even when the individual components of the resource bundle cannot. Although PetSmart's supply chain and marketing capabilities are matched well by rival Petco, the company continues to outperform competitors through its customer service capabilities (including animal grooming and veterinary and day care services). Nike's bundle of styling expertise, marketing research skills, professional endorsements, brand name, and managerial know-how has allowed it to remain number one in the athletic footwear and apparel industry for more than 20 years.

> **CORE CONCEPT**
>
> A **resource bundle** is a linked and closely integrated set of competitive assets centered around one or more cross-functional capabilities.

Assessing the Competitive Power of a Company's Resources and Capabilities

To assess a company's competitive power, one must go beyond merely identifying its resources and capabilities to probe its *caliber*.[4] Thus, the second step in resource and capability analysis is designed to ascertain which of a company's resources and capabilities are competitively superior and to what extent they can support a company's quest for a sustainable competitive advantage over market rivals. When a company has competitive assets that are central to its strategy and superior to those of rival firms, they can support a competitive advantage, as defined in Chapter 1. If this advantage proves durable despite the best efforts of competitors to overcome it, then the company is said to have a *sustainable* **competitive advantage.** While it may be difficult for a company to achieve a sustainable competitive advantage, it is an important strategic objective because it imparts a potential for attractive and long-lived profitability.

> **CORE CONCEPT**
>
> Recall that a **competitive advantage** means that you can produce more value (V) for the customer than rivals can, or the same value at lower cost (C). In other words, your **V-C** is *greater than* the **V-C** of competitors. **V-C** is what we call the *Total Economic Value* produced by a company.

The Four Tests of a Resource's Competitive Power   The competitive power of a resource or capability is measured by how many of four specific tests it can pass.[5] These tests are referred to as the **VRIN tests for sustainable competitive advantage**—*VRIN* is a shorthand reminder standing for *Valuable, Rare, Inimitable,* and *Nonsubstitutable.* The first two tests determine whether a resource or capability can support a competitive advantage. The last two determine whether the competitive advantage can be sustained.

> **CORE CONCEPT**
>
> The **VRIN tests for sustainable competitive advantage** ask whether a resource is valuable, rare, inimitable, and nonsubstitutable.

1. *Is the resource or organizational capability competitively* ***Valuable?*** To be competitively valuable, a resource or capability must be directly relevant to the company's strategy, making the company a more effective competitor. Unless the resource or capability contributes to the effectiveness of the company's strategy, it cannot pass

this first test. An indicator of its effectiveness is whether the resource enables the company to strengthen its business model by improving its customer value proposition and/or profit formula (see Chapter 1). Google failed in converting its technological resources and software innovation capabilities into success for Google Wallet, which incurred losses of more than $300 million before being abandoned in 2016. While these resources and capabilities have made Google the world's number-one search engine, they proved to be less valuable in the mobile payments industry.

2. *Is the resource or capability **Rare**—is it something rivals lack?* Resources and capabilities that are common among firms and widely available cannot be a source of competitive advantage. All makers of branded cereals have valuable marketing capabilities and brands, since the key success factors in the ready-to-eat cereal industry demand this. They are not rare. However, the brand strength of Oreo cookies is uncommon and has provided Kraft Foods with greater market share as well as the opportunity to benefit from brand extensions such as Golden Oreos, Oreo Thins, and Mega Stuf Oreos. A resource or capability is considered rare if it is held by only a small percentage of firms in an industry or specific competitive domain. Thus, while general management capabilities are not rare in an absolute sense, they are relatively rare in some of the less developed regions of the world and in some business domains.

3. *Is the resource or capability **Inimitable**—is it hard to copy?* The more difficult and more costly it is for competitors to imitate a company's resource or capability, the more likely that it can also provide a *sustainable* competitive advantage. Resources and capabilities tend to be difficult to copy when they are unique (a fantastic real estate location, patent-protected technology, an unusually talented and motivated labor force), when they must be built over time in ways that are difficult to imitate (a well-known brand name, mastery of a complex process technology, years of cumulative experience and learning), and when they entail financial outlays or large-scale operations that few industry members can undertake (a global network of dealers and distributors). Imitation is also difficult for resources and capabilities that reflect a high level of *social complexity* (company culture, interpersonal relationships among the managers or R&D teams, trust-based relations with customers or suppliers) and *causal ambiguity,* a term that signifies the hard-to-disentangle nature of the complex resources, such as a web of intricate processes enabling new drug discovery. Hard-to-copy resources and capabilities are important competitive assets, contributing to the longevity of a company's market position and offering the potential for sustained profitability.

4. *Is the resource or capability **Nonsubstitutable**—is it invulnerable to the threat of substitution from different types of resources and capabilities?* Even resources that are competitively valuable, rare, and costly to imitate may lose much of their ability to offer competitive advantage if rivals possess equivalent substitute resources. For example, manufacturers relying on automation to gain a cost-based advantage in production activities may find their technology-based advantage nullified by rivals' use of low-wage offshore manufacturing. Resources can contribute to a sustainable competitive advantage only when resource substitutes aren't on the horizon.

The vast majority of companies are not well endowed with standout resources or capabilities, capable of passing all four tests with high marks. Most firms have a mixed bag of resources—one or two quite valuable, some good, many satisfactory to mediocre. Resources and capabilities that are valuable pass the first of the four tests. As key contributors to the effectiveness of the strategy, they are relevant to the firm's competitiveness but are no guarantee of competitive advantage. They may offer no more than competitive parity with competing firms.

Passing both of the first two tests requires more—it requires resources and capabilities that are not only valuable but also rare. This is a much higher hurdle that can be cleared only by resources and capabilities that are *competitively superior.* Resources and capabilities that are competitively superior are the company's true strategic assets. They provide the company with a competitive advantage over its competitors, if only in the short run.

To pass the last two tests, a resource must be able to maintain its competitive superiority in the face of competition. It must be resistant to imitative attempts and efforts by competitors to find equally valuable substitute resources. Assessing the availability of substitutes is the most difficult of all the tests since substitutes are harder to recognize, but the key is to look for resources or capabilities held by other firms or being developed that *can serve the same function* as the company's core resources and capabilities.[6]

Very few firms have resources and capabilities that can pass all four tests, but those that do enjoy a sustainable competitive advantage with far greater profit potential. Costco is a notable example, with strong employee incentive programs and capabilities in supply chain management that have surpassed those of its warehouse club rivals for over 35 years. Lincoln Electric Company, less well known but no less notable in its achievements, has been the world leader in welding products for over 100 years as a result of its unique piecework incentive system for compensating production workers and the unsurpassed worker productivity and product quality that this system has fostered.

A Company's Resources and Capabilities Must Be Managed Dynamically   Even companies like Costco and Lincoln Electric cannot afford to rest on their laurels. Rivals that are initially unable to replicate a key resource may develop better and better substitutes over time. Resources and capabilities can depreciate like other assets if they are managed with benign neglect. Disruptive changes in technology, customer preferences, distribution channels, or other competitive factors can also destroy the value of key strategic assets, turning resources and capabilities "from diamonds to rust."[7]

Resources and capabilities must be continually strengthened and nurtured to sustain their competitive power and, at times, may need to be broadened and deepened to allow the company to position itself to pursue emerging market opportunities.[8] Organizational resources and capabilities that grow stale can impair competitiveness unless they are refreshed, modified, or even phased out and replaced in response to ongoing market changes and shifts in company strategy. Management's challenge in managing the firm's resources and capabilities dynamically has two elements: (1) attending to the ongoing modification of existing competitive assets, and (2) casting a watchful eye for opportunities to develop totally new kinds of capabilities.

> A company requires a dynamically evolving portfolio of resources and capabilities to sustain its competitiveness and help drive improvements in its performance.

The Role of Dynamic Capabilities   Companies that know the importance of recalibrating and upgrading their most valuable resources and capabilities ensure that these activities are done on a continual basis. By incorporating these activities into their routine managerial functions, they gain the experience necessary to be able to do them consistently well. At that point, their ability to freshen and renew their competitive assets becomes a capability in itself—a **dynamic capability.** A dynamic capability is the ability to modify, deepen, or augment the company's existing resources and capabilities.[9] This includes the capacity to improve existing resources and capabilities incrementally, in the way that Toyota aggressively upgrades the company's capabilities in fuel-efficient hybrid engine technology and constantly fine-tunes its famed Toyota production system. Likewise, management at BMW developed new organizational capabilities in hybrid engine design that allowed the company to launch its highly touted i3 and i8 plug-in hybrids. A dynamic capability

> **CORE** CONCEPT
>
> A **dynamic capability** is an ongoing capacity of a company to modify its existing resources and capabilities or create new ones.

also includes the capacity to add new resources and capabilities to the company's competitive asset portfolio. One way to do this is through alliances and acquisitions. An example is General Motor's partnership with Korean electronics firm LG Corporation, which enabled GM to develop a manufacturing and engineering platform for producing electric vehicles. This enabled GM to beat the likes of Tesla and Nissan to market with the first affordable all-electric car with good driving range—the Chevy Bolt EV.

QUESTION 4: HOW DO VALUE CHAIN ACTIVITIES IMPACT A COMPANY'S COST STRUCTURE AND CUSTOMER VALUE PROPOSITION?

LO 4-4

Understand how value chain activities can affect a company's cost structure and customer value proposition.

Company managers are often stunned when a competitor cuts its prices to "unbelievably low" levels or when a new market entrant introduces a great new product at a surprisingly low price. While less common, new entrants can also storm the market with a product that ratchets the quality level up so high that customers will abandon competing sellers even if they have to pay more for the new product. This is what seems to have happened with Apple's iPhone 7 and iMac computers.

Regardless of where on the quality spectrum a company competes, it must remain competitive in terms of its customer value proposition in order to stay in the game. Patagonia's value proposition, for example, remains attractive to customers who value quality, wide selection, and corporate environmental responsibility over cheaper outerwear alternatives. Since its inception in 1925, the *New Yorker*'s customer value proposition has withstood the test of time by providing readers with an amalgam of well-crafted and topical writing.

> The greater the amount of customer value that a company can offer profitably relative to close rivals, the less competitively vulnerable the company becomes.

Recall from our discussion of the Customer Value Proposition in Chapter 1: The value (V) provided to the customer depends on how well a customer's needs are met for the price paid (V-P). How well customer needs are met depends on the perceived quality of a product or service as well as on other, more tangible attributes. The greater the amount of customer value that the company can offer profitably compared to its rivals, the less vulnerable it will be to competitive attack. For managers, the key is to keep close track of how *cost-effectively* the company can deliver value to customers relative to its competitors. If it can deliver the same amount of value with lower expenditures (or more value at the same cost), it will maintain a competitive edge.

> The higher a company's costs are above those of close rivals, the more competitively vulnerable the company becomes.

Two analytic tools are particularly useful in determining whether a company's costs and customer value proposition are competitive: value chain analysis and benchmarking.

The Concept of a Company Value Chain

CORE CONCEPT

A company's **value chain** identifies the primary activities and related support activities that create customer value.

Every company's business consists of a collection of activities undertaken in the course of producing, marketing, delivering, and supporting its product or service. All the various activities that a company performs internally combine to form a **value chain**—so called because the underlying intent of a company's activities is ultimately to *create value for buyers.*

As shown in Figure 4.3, a company's value chain consists of two broad categories of activities: the *primary activities* foremost in creating value for customers and the requisite *support activities* that facilitate and enhance the performance of the

FIGURE 4.3   A Representative Company Value Chain

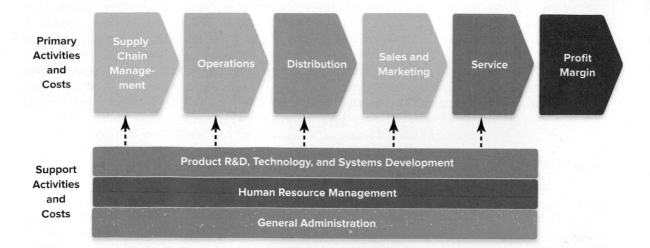

PRIMARY ACTIVITIES

- **Supply Chain Management**—Activities, costs, and assets associated with purchasing fuel, energy, raw materials, parts and components, merchandise, and consumable items from vendors; receiving, storing, and disseminating inputs from suppliers; inspection; and inventory management.

- **Operations**—Activities, costs, and assets associated with converting inputs into final product form (production, assembly, packaging, equipment maintenance, facilities, operations, quality assurance, environmental protection).

- **Distribution**—Activities, costs, and assets dealing with physically distributing the product to buyers (finished goods warehousing, order processing, order picking and packing, shipping, delivery vehicle operations, establishing and maintaining a network of dealers and distributors).

- **Sales and Marketing**—Activities, costs, and assets related to sales force efforts, advertising and promotion, market research and planning, and dealer/distributor support.

- **Service**—Activities, costs, and assets associated with providing assistance to buyers, such as installation, spare parts delivery, maintenance and repair, technical assistance, buyer inquiries, and complaints.

SUPPORT ACTIVITIES

- **Product R&D, Technology, and Systems Development**—Activities, costs, and assets relating to product R&D, process R&D, process design improvement, equipment design, computer software development, telecommunications systems, computer-assisted design and engineering, database capabilities, and development of computerized support systems.

- **Human Resource Management**—Activities, costs, and assets associated with the recruitment, hiring, training, development, and compensation of all types of personnel; labor relations activities; and development of knowledge-based skills and core competencies.

- **General Administration**—Activities, costs, and assets relating to general management, accounting and finance, legal and regulatory affairs, safety and security, management information systems, forming strategic alliances and collaborating with strategic partners, and other "overhead" functions.

Source: Based on the discussion in Michael E. Porter, *Competitive Advantage* (New York: Free Press, 1985), pp. 37–43.

primary activities.[10] The kinds of primary and secondary activities that constitute a company's value chain vary according to the specifics of a company's business; hence, the listing of the primary and support activities in Figure 4.3 is illustrative rather than definitive. For example, the primary activities at a hotel operator like Starwood Hotels and Resorts mainly consist of site selection and construction, reservations, and hotel operations (check-in and check-out, maintenance and housekeeping, dining and room service, and conventions and meetings); principal support activities that drive costs and impact customer value include hiring and training hotel staff and handling general administration. Supply chain management is a crucial activity for Boeing and Amazon but is not a value chain component at Facebook, WhatsApp, or Goldman Sachs. Sales and marketing are dominant activities at GAP and Match.com but have only minor roles at oil-drilling companies and natural gas pipeline companies. Customer delivery is a crucial activity at Domino's Pizza and Blue Apron but insignificant at Starbucks and Dunkin Donuts.

With its focus on value-creating activities, the value chain is an ideal tool for examining the workings of a company's customer value proposition and business model. It permits a deep look at the company's cost structure and ability to offer low prices. It reveals the emphasis that a company places on activities that enhance differentiation and support higher prices, such as service and marketing. It also includes a profit margin component (P-C), since profits are necessary to compensate the company's owners and investors, who bear risks and provide capital. Tracking the profit margin along with the value-creating activities is critical because unless an enterprise succeeds in delivering customer value profitably (with a sufficient return on invested capital), it can't survive for long. Attention to a company's profit formula in addition to its customer value proposition is the essence of a sound business model, as described in Chapter 1.

Illustration Capsule 4.1 shows representative costs for various value chain activities performed by Everlane, Inc., an American clothing retailer that sells primarily online.

Comparing the Value Chains of Rival Companies   Value chain analysis facilitates a comparison of how rivals, activity by activity, deliver value to customers. Even rivals in the same industry may differ significantly in terms of the activities they perform. For instance, the "operations" component of the value chain for a manufacturer that makes all of its own parts and components and assembles them into a finished product differs from the "operations" of a rival producer that buys the needed parts and components from outside suppliers and performs only assembly operations. How each activity is performed may affect a company's relative cost position as well as its capacity for differentiation. Thus, even a simple comparison of how the activities of rivals' value chains differ can reveal competitive differences.

A Company's Primary and Secondary Activities Identify the Major Components of Its Internal Cost Structure   The combined costs of all the various primary and support activities constituting a company's value chain define its internal cost structure. Further, the cost of each activity contributes to whether the company's overall cost position relative to rivals is favorable or unfavorable. The roles of value chain analysis and benchmarking are to develop the data for comparing a company's costs activity by activity against the costs of key rivals and to learn which internal activities are a source of cost advantage or disadvantage.

Evaluating a company's cost-competitiveness involves using what accountants call *activity-based costing* to determine the costs of performing each value chain activity.[11] The degree to which a company's total costs should be broken down into costs for

Everlane, Inc. prides itself on producing casual clothing, designed to last, in ethically managed factories, under a policy of what they call "radical transparency". From the start, they have made their cost and margin breakdowns readily available on their website. Below is such a break-down for a pair of their slim-fit denim jeans:

M4OS Photos/Alamy Stock Photo

Materials (11 oz. denim - 98% cotton; 2% elastane	$12.78
Hardware (metal fasteners, trim)	2.15
Labor	7.50
Cost of Goods	**22.43**
Shipping	1.90
Import Duties	3.70
Total Cost	**28.03**
Everlane Retail Price	**68.00**
Everlane Profit Margin (Retail Price – Total Cost)	**39.97**
Average Traditional Retailer's Price	**140.00**

Source: Everlane.com/about (accessed 2/08/20).

specific activities depends on how valuable it is to know the costs of specific activities versus broadly defined activities. At the very least, cost estimates are needed for each broad category of primary and support activities, but cost estimates for more specific activities within each broad category may be needed if a company discovers that it has a cost disadvantage vis-à-vis rivals and wants to pin down the exact source or activity causing the cost disadvantage. However, a company's own *internal costs* may be insufficient to assess whether its product offering and customer value proposition are competitive with those of rivals. Cost and price differences among competing companies can have their origins in activities performed by suppliers or by distribution allies involved in getting the product to the final customers or end users of the product, in which case the company's entire *value chain system* becomes relevant.

> A company's cost-competitiveness depends not only on the costs of internally performed activities (its own value chain) but also on costs in the value chains of its suppliers and distribution-channel allies.

The Value Chain System

A company's value chain is embedded in a larger system of activities that includes the value chains of its suppliers and the value chains of whatever wholesale distributors and retailers it utilizes in getting its product or service to end users. This *value chain system* (sometimes called a vertical chain) has implications that extend far beyond the company's costs. It can affect attributes like product quality that enhance differentiation and have importance for the company's customer value proposition, as well as its profitability.[12] Suppliers' value chains are relevant because suppliers perform activities and incur costs in creating and delivering the purchased inputs utilized in a company's own value-creating activities. The costs, performance features, and quality of these inputs influence a company's own costs and product differentiation capabilities.

Anything a company can do to help its suppliers drive down the costs of their value chain activities or improve the quality and performance of the items being supplied can enhance its own competitiveness—a powerful reason for working collaboratively with suppliers in managing supply chain activities.[13] For example, automakers have encouraged their automotive parts suppliers to build plants near the auto assembly plants to facilitate just-in-time deliveries, reduce warehousing and shipping costs, and promote close collaboration on parts design and production scheduling.

Similarly, the value chains of a company's distribution-channel partners are relevant because (1) the costs and margins of a company's distributors and retail dealers are part of the price the ultimate consumer pays and (2) the quality of the activities that such distribution allies perform affect sales volumes and customer satisfaction. For these reasons, companies that don't sell directly to the end consumer work closely with their distribution allies (including their direct customers) to perform value chain activities in mutually beneficial ways. For instance, motor vehicle manufacturers have a competitive interest in working closely with their automobile dealers to promote higher sales volumes and better customer satisfaction with dealers' repair and maintenance services. Producers of kitchen cabinets are heavily dependent on the sales and promotional activities of their distributors and building supply retailers and on whether distributors and retailers operate cost-effectively enough to be able to sell at prices that lead to attractive sales volumes.

As a consequence, *accurately assessing a company's competitiveness entails scrutinizing the nature and costs of value chain activities throughout the entire value chain system for delivering its products or services to end-use customers.* A typical value chain system that incorporates the value chains of suppliers, business buyers, and other forward-channel allies (if any) is shown in Figure 4.4. As was the case with company value chains, the specific activities constituting value chain systems vary significantly from industry to industry. The primary value chain system activities in the pulp and paper industry (timber farming, logging, pulp mills, and papermaking) differ from the primary value chain system activities in the home appliance industry (parts and components manufacture, assembly, wholesale distribution, retail sales) and yet again from the computer software industry (programming, disk loading, marketing, distribution). Some value chains may also include strategic partners whose activities may likewise affect both the value and cost of the end product.

FIGURE 4.4   A Representative Value Chain System

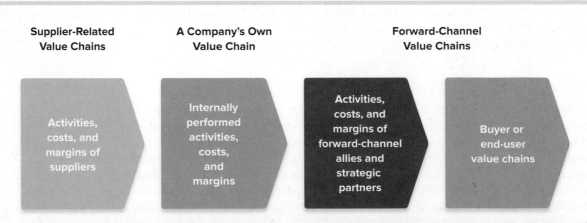

Source: Based in part on the single-industry value chain displayed in Michael E. Porter, *Competitive Advantage* (New York: Free Press, 1985), p. 35.

Benchmarking: A Tool for Assessing the Costs and Effectiveness of Value Chain Activities

Benchmarking entails comparing how different companies perform various value chain activities—how materials are purchased, how inventories are managed, how products are assembled, how fast the company can get new products to market, how customer orders are filled and shipped—and then making cross-company comparisons of the costs and effectiveness of these activities.[14] The comparison is often made between companies in the same industry, but benchmarking can also involve comparing how activities are done by companies in other industries. The objectives of benchmarking are simply to identify the best means of performing an activity and to emulate those best practices. It can be used to benchmark the activities of a company's internal value chain or the activities within an entire value chain system.

A **best practice** is a method of performing an activity or business process that consistently delivers superior results compared to other approaches.[15] To qualify as a legitimate best practice, the method must have been employed by at least one enterprise and shown to be *consistently more effective* in lowering costs, improving quality or performance, shortening time requirements, enhancing safety, or achieving some other highly positive operating outcome. Best practices thus identify a path to operating excellence with respect to value chain activities.

Xerox pioneered the use of benchmarking to become more cost-competitive, quickly deciding not to restrict its benchmarking efforts to its office equipment rivals but to extend them to *any company regarded as "world class"* in performing *any activity* relevant to Xerox's business. Other companies quickly picked up on Xerox's approach. Toyota managers got their idea for just-in-time inventory deliveries by studying how U.S. supermarkets replenished their shelves. Southwest Airlines reduced the turnaround time of its aircraft at each scheduled stop by studying pit crews on the auto racing circuit. More than 80 percent of Fortune 500 companies reportedly use benchmarking for comparing themselves against rivals on cost and other competitively important measures. Illustration Capsule 4.2 describes benchmarking practices in the solar industry.

The tough part of benchmarking is not whether to do it but, rather, how to gain access to information about other companies' practices and costs. Sometimes benchmarking can be accomplished by collecting information from published reports, trade groups, and industry research firms or by talking to knowledgeable industry analysts, customers, and suppliers. Sometimes field trips to the facilities of competing or noncompeting companies can be arranged to observe how things are done, compare practices and processes, and perhaps exchange data on productivity and other cost components. However, such companies, even if they agree to host facilities tours and answer questions, are unlikely to share competitively sensitive cost information. Furthermore, comparing two companies' costs may not involve comparing apples to apples if the two companies employ different cost accounting principles to calculate the costs of particular activities.

However, a third and fairly reliable source of benchmarking information has emerged. The explosive interest of companies in benchmarking costs and identifying best practices has prompted consulting organizations (e.g., Accenture, A. T. Kearney, Benchnet—The Benchmarking Exchange, and Best Practices, LLC) and several associations (e.g., the QualServe Benchmarking Clearinghouse, and the Strategic Planning Institute's Council on Benchmarking) to gather benchmarking data, distribute information about best practices, and provide comparative cost data without identifying the names of particular companies. Having an independent group gather the information and report it in a manner that disguises the names of

The cost of solar power production is dropping rapidly, leading to lower solar power prices for consumers and an expanding market for solar companies. According to the Solar Energy Industries Association, over 11 gigawatts (GW) of solar serving electric utilities were installed in 2016—enough to supply power for approximately 1.8 million households. Simultaneously, the solar landscape is becoming more competitive. As of 2017, 46 firms had installed a cumulative total of over 45 GW of solar serving electric utilities in the United States.

As competition grows, benchmarking plays an increasingly critical role in assessing a solar company's relative costs and price positioning compared to other firms. This is often measured using the all-in installation and production costs per kilowatt hour generated by a solar asset, called the "Levelized Cost of Energy" (LCOE). Kilowatt hours are the units of electricity that are sold to consumers.

In 2008, SunPower—one of the largest solar firms in the United States—used benchmarking to target a 50 percent decrease in its solar LCOE by 2012. This early benchmarking strategy helped the company to defend against new market entrants offering lower prices. But in the ensuing years, between 2009 and 2014, the overall industry solar LCOE fell by 78 percent, leading the company to conclude that an even more aggressive approach was needed to manage downward pricing pressure. Over the course of 2017, SunPower's quarterly earnings calls highlighted efforts to compete on benchmark prices by simplifying its company structure; divesting from non-core assets; and diversifying beyond the low-cost, large-scale utility solar market and into residential and commercial solar where it could compete more easily on price.

Geniusksy/Shutterstock

Continuing to anticipate and adapt to falling solar prices requires reliable industry data on benchmark costs. The National Renewable Energy Laboratory (NREL) Quarterly U.S. Solar Photovoltaic System Cost Benchmark breaks down industry solar costs by inputs, including solar modules, structural hardware, and electrical components, as well as soft costs like labor and land expenses. This enables firms like SunPower to assess how their component costs compare to benchmarks and informs SunPower's outlook for how solar prices will continue to fall over time.

For solar to play a major role in U.S. power generation, costs must keep decreasing. As solar companies race toward lower costs, benchmarking will continue to be a core strategic tool in determining pricing and market positioning.

Note: Developed with Mathew O'Sullivan.

Sources: Solar Power World, "Top 500 Solar Contractors" (2017); SunPower, "The Drivers of the Levelized Cost of Electricity for Utility-Scale Photovoltaics" (2008); Lazard, "Levelized Cost of Energy Analysis, Version 8.0" (2014).

individual companies protects competitively sensitive data and lessens the potential for unethical behavior on the part of company personnel in gathering their own data about competitors. The ethical dimension of benchmarking is discussed in Illustration Capsule 4.3.

Industry associations are another source of data that may be used for benchmarking purposes. In the cement industry, for example, the Portland Cement Association publishes key plant level data for the industry that enables companies to understand whether their own plants are cost leaders or laggards. Benchmarking data is also provided by some government agencies; data of this sort plays an important role in electricity pricing, for example.

Because discussions between benchmarking partners can involve competitively sensitive data, conceivably raising questions about possible restraint of trade or improper business conduct, the Strategic Planning Institute's Council on Benchmarking and the Global Benchmarking Network urge all individuals and organizations involved in benchmarking to abide by a code of conduct grounded in ethical business behavior. The code is based on the following principles:

- Principle of Legality. Avoid discussions or actions that might lead to or imply an interest in restraint of trade: market or customer allocation schemes, price fixing, dealing arrangements, bid rigging, bribery, or misappropriation. Do not discuss costs with competitors if costs are an element of pricing.

- Principle of Exchange. Be willing to provide the same level of information that you request, in any benchmarking exchange.

- Principle of Confidentiality. Treat benchmarking interchange as something confidential to the individuals and organizations involved. Information obtained must not be communicated outside the partnering organizations without prior consent of participating benchmarking partners.

An organization's participation in a study should not be communicated externally without their permission.

- Principle of Use. Use information obtained through benchmarking partnering only for the purpose of improvement of operations within the partnering companies themselves. External use or communication of a benchmarking partner's name with their data or observed practices requires permission of that partner. Do not, as a consultant or client, extend one company's benchmarking study findings to another without the first company's permission.

- Principle of First Party Contact. Initiate contacts, whenever possible, through a benchmarking contact designated by the partner company. Obtain mutual agreement with the contact on any hand off of communication or responsibility to other parties.

- Principle of Third Party Contact. Obtain an individual's permission before providing their name in response to a contact request.

- Principle of Preparation. Demonstrate commitment to the efficiency and effectiveness of the benchmarking process with adequate preparation at each process step; particularly, at initial partnering contact.

Source: BPIR.com (Business Performance Improvement Resource), https://www.bpir.com/benchmarking-code-of-conduct-bpir.com/menu-id-56.html (accessed 2/08/20).

Strategic Options for Remedying a Cost or Value Disadvantage

The results of value chain analysis and benchmarking may disclose cost or value disadvantages relative to key rivals. Such information is vital in crafting strategic actions to eliminate any such disadvantages and improve profitability. Information of this nature can also help a company find new avenues for enhancing its competitiveness through lower costs or a more attractive customer value proposition. There are three main areas in a company's total value chain system where company managers can try to improve its efficiency and effectiveness in delivering customer value: (1) a company's own internal activities, (2) suppliers' part of the value chain system, and (3) the forward-channel portion of the value chain system.

Improving Internally Performed Value Chain Activities   Managers can pursue any of several strategic approaches to reduce the costs of internally performed value chain activities and improve a company's cost-competitiveness. They can *implement best practices* throughout the company, particularly for high-cost activities. They can *redesign the product and/or some of its components* to eliminate high-cost components or facilitate speedier and more economical manufacture or assembly. They can *relocate* *high-cost activities* (such as manufacturing) to geographic areas where they can be performed more cheaply or *outsource activities* to lower-cost vendors or contractors.

To improve the effectiveness of the company's customer value proposition and enhance differentiation, managers can take several approaches. They can *adopt best practices for quality, marketing, and customer service.* They can *reallocate resources to activities that address buyers' most important purchase criteria,* which will have the biggest impact on the value delivered to the customer. They can *adopt new technologies that spur innovation, improve design, and enhance creativity.* Additional approaches to managing value chain activities to lower costs and/or enhance customer value are discussed in Chapter 5.

Improving Supplier-Related Value Chain Activities   Supplier-related cost disadvantages can be attacked by pressuring suppliers for lower prices, switching to lower-priced substitute inputs, and collaborating closely with suppliers to identify mutual cost-saving opportunities.[16] For example, just-in-time deliveries from suppliers can lower a company's inventory and internal logistics costs and may also allow suppliers to economize on their warehousing, shipping, and production scheduling costs—a win–win outcome for both. In a few instances, companies may find that it is cheaper to integrate backward into the business of high-cost suppliers and make the item in-house instead of buying it from outsiders.

Similarly, a company can enhance its customer value proposition through its supplier relationships. Some approaches include selecting and retaining suppliers that meet higher-quality standards, providing quality-based incentives to suppliers, and integrating suppliers into the design process. Fewer defects in parts from suppliers not only improve quality throughout the value chain system but can lower costs as well since less waste and disruption occur in the production processes.

Improving Value Chain Activities of Distribution Partners   Any of three means can be used to achieve better cost-competitiveness in the forward portion of the industry value chain:

1. Pressure distributors, dealers, and other forward-channel allies to reduce their costs and markups.
2. Collaborate with them to identify win–win opportunities to reduce costs—for example, a chocolate manufacturer learned that by shipping its bulk chocolate in liquid form in tank cars instead of as 10-pound molded bars, it could not only save its candy bar manufacturing customers the costs associated with unpacking and melting but also eliminate its own costs of molding bars and packing them.
3. Change to a more economical distribution strategy, including switching to cheaper distribution channels (selling direct via the Internet) or integrating forward into company-owned retail outlets.

The means to enhancing differentiation through activities at the forward end of the value chain system include (1) engaging in cooperative advertising and promotions with forward allies (dealers, distributors, retailers, etc.), (2) creating exclusive arrangements with downstream sellers or utilizing other mechanisms that increase their incentives to enhance delivered customer value, and (3) creating and enforcing standards for downstream activities and assisting in training channel partners in business practices. Harley-Davidson, for example, enhances the shopping experience and perceptions of buyers by selling through retailers that sell Harley-Davidson motorcycles exclusively and meet Harley-Davidson standards. The bottlers of Pepsi and Coca Cola engage in cooperative promotional activities with large grocery chains such as Kroger, Publix, and Safeway.

Translating Proficient Performance of Value Chain Activities into Competitive Advantage

A company that does a *first-rate job* of managing the activities of its value chain or value chain system *relative to competitors* stands a good chance of profiting from its competitive advantage. A company's value-creating activities can offer a competitive advantage in one of two ways (or both):

1. They can contribute to greater efficiency and lower costs relative to competitors.
2. They can provide a basis for differentiation, so customers are willing to pay relatively more for the company's goods and services.

Achieving a cost-based competitive advantage requires determined management efforts to be cost-efficient in performing value chain activities. Such efforts have to be ongoing and persistent, and they have to involve each and every value chain activity. The goal must be continuous cost reduction, not a one-time or on-again–off-again effort. Companies like Dollar General, Nucor Steel, Irish airline Ryanair, T.J.Maxx, and French discount retailer Carrefour have been highly successful in managing their value chains in a low-cost manner.

Ongoing and persistent efforts are also required for a competitive advantage based on differentiation. Superior reputations and brands are built up slowly over time, through continuous investment and activities that deliver consistent, reinforcing messages. Differentiation based on quality requires vigilant management of activities for quality assurance throughout the value chain. While the basis for differentiation (e.g., status, design, innovation, customer service, reliability, image) may vary widely among companies pursuing a differentiation advantage, companies that succeed do so on the basis of a commitment to coordinated value chain activities aimed purposefully at this objective. Examples include Rolex (status), Braun (design), Room and Board (craftsmanship), Zappos and L.L. Bean (customer service), Salesforce.com and Tesla (innovation), and FedEx (reliability).

How Value Chain Activities Relate to Resources and Capabilities   There is a close relationship between the value-creating activities that a company performs and its resources and capabilities. An organizational capability or competence implies a *capacity* for action; in contrast, a value-creating activity *initiates* the action. With respect to resources and capabilities, activities are "where the rubber hits the road." When companies engage in a value-creating activity, they do so by drawing on specific company resources and capabilities that underlie and enable the activity. For example, brand-building activities depend on human resources, such as experienced brand managers (including their knowledge and expertise in this arena), as well as organizational capabilities in advertising and marketing. Cost-cutting activities may derive from organizational capabilities in inventory management, for example, and resources such as inventory tracking systems.

Because of this correspondence between activities and supporting resources and capabilities, value chain analysis can complement resource and capability analysis as another tool for assessing a company's competitive advantage. Resources and capabilities that are *both valuable and rare* provide a company with *what it takes* for competitive advantage. For a company with competitive assets of this sort, the potential is there. When these assets are deployed in the form of a value-creating activity, that potential is realized due to their competitive superiority. Resource analysis is one tool for identifying competitively superior resources and capabilities. But their value and the competitive superiority of that value can be assessed

> Value chain analysis and benchmarking provide the type of data needed to assess objectively whether a company's resources and capabilities are competitively superior.

objectively only *after* they are deployed. Value chain analysis and benchmarking provide the type of data needed to make that objective assessment.

There is also a dynamic relationship between a company's activities and its resources and capabilities. Value-creating activities are more than just the embodiment of a resource's or capability's potential. They also contribute to the formation and development of organizational capabilities. The road to competitive advantage begins with management efforts to build organizational expertise in performing certain competitively important value chain activities. With consistent practice and continuous investment of company resources, these activities rise to the level of a reliable organizational capability or a competence. To the extent that top management makes the growing capability a cornerstone of the company's strategy, this capability becomes a core competence for the company. Later, with further organizational learning and gains in proficiency, the core competence may evolve into a distinctive competence, giving the company superiority over rivals in performing an important value chain activity. Such superiority, if it gives the company significant competitive clout in the marketplace, can produce an attractive competitive edge over rivals. Whether the resulting competitive advantage is on the cost side or on the differentiation side (or both) will depend on the company's choice of which types of competence-building activities to engage in over this time period.

QUESTION 5: IS THE COMPANY COMPETITIVELY STRONGER OR WEAKER THAN KEY RIVALS?

Using resource analysis, value chain analysis, and benchmarking to determine a company's competitiveness on value and cost is necessary but not sufficient. A more comprehensive assessment needs to be made of the company's *overall* competitive strength. The answers to two questions are of particular interest: First, how does the company rank relative to competitors on each of the important factors that determine market success? Second, all things considered, does the company have a *net* competitive advantage or disadvantage versus major competitors?

An easy-to-use method for answering these two questions involves developing quantitative strength ratings for the company and its key competitors on each industry key success factor and each competitively pivotal resource, capability, and value chain activity. Much of the information needed for doing a competitive strength assessment comes from previous analyses. Industry and competitive analyses reveal the key success factors and competitive forces that separate industry winners from losers. Benchmarking data and scouting key competitors provide a basis for judging the competitive strength of rivals on such factors as cost, key product attributes, customer service, image and reputation, financial strength, technological skills, distribution capability, and other factors. Resource and capability analysis reveals which of these are competitively important, given the external situation, and whether the company's competitive advantages are sustainable. SWOT analysis provides a more general forward-looking picture of the company's overall situation.

Step 1 in doing a competitive strength assessment is to make a list of the industry's key success factors and other telling measures of competitive strength or weakness (6 to 10 measures usually suffice). Step 2 is to assign weights to each of the measures of competitive strength based on their perceived importance. (The sum of the weights for each measure must add up to 1.) Step 3 is to calculate weighted strength ratings by scoring each competitor on each strength measure (using a 1-to-10 rating scale, where 1 is very weak and 10 is very strong) and multiplying the assigned rating by the assigned weight. Step 4 is to sum the weighted strength ratings on each factor to get an overall measure of competitive strength for each company being rated. Step 5 is to use the overall strength ratings to draw conclusions about the size and extent of the company's net competitive advantage or disadvantage and to take specific note of areas of strength and weakness.

Table 4.4 provides an example of competitive strength assessment in which a hypothetical company (ABC Company) competes against two rivals. In the example,

TABLE 4.4   A Representative Weighted Competitive Strength Assessment

Key Success Factor/Strength Measure	Importance Weight	ABC Co. Strength Rating	ABC Co. Weighted Score	Rival 1 Strength Rating	Rival 1 Weighted Score	Rival 2 Strength Rating	Rival 2 Weighted Score
Quality/product performance	0.10	8	0.80	5	0.50	1	0.10
Reputation/image	0.10	8	0.80	7	0.70	1	0.10
Manufacturing capability	0.10	2	0.20	10	1.00	5	0.50
Technological skills	0.05	10	0.50	1	0.05	3	0.15
Dealer network/distribution capability	0.05	9	0.45	4	0.20	5	0.25
New product innovation capability	0.05	9	0.45	4	0.20	5	0.25
Financial resources	0.10	5	0.50	10	1.00	3	0.30
Relative cost position	0.30	5	1.50	10	3.00	1	0.30
Customer service capabilities	0.15	5	0.75	7	1.05	1	0.15
Sum of importance weights	**1.00**						
Overall weighted competitive strength rating			**5.95**		**7.70**		**2.10**

relative cost is the most telling measure of competitive strength, and the other strength measures are of lesser importance. The company with the highest rating on a given measure has an implied competitive edge on that measure, with the size of its edge reflected in the difference between its weighted rating and rivals' weighted ratings. For instance, Rival 1's 3.00 weighted strength rating on relative cost signals a considerable cost advantage over ABC Company (with a 1.50 weighted score on relative cost) and an even bigger cost advantage over Rival 2 (with a weighted score of 0.30). The measure-by-measure ratings reveal the competitive areas in which a company is strongest and weakest, and against whom.

The overall competitive strength scores indicate how all the different strength measures add up—whether the company is at a net overall competitive advantage or disadvantage against each rival. The higher a company's *overall weighted strength rating,* the stronger its *overall competitiveness* versus rivals. The bigger the difference between a company's overall weighted rating and the scores of *lower-rated* rivals, the greater is its implied *net competitive advantage.* Thus, Rival 1's overall weighted score of 7.70 indicates a greater net competitive advantage over Rival 2 (with a score of 2.10) than over ABC Company (with a score of 5.95). Conversely, the bigger the difference between a company's overall rating and the scores of *higher-rated* rivals, the greater its implied *net competitive disadvantage.* Rival 2's score of 2.10 gives it a smaller net competitive disadvantage against ABC Company (with an overall score of 5.95) than against Rival 1 (with an overall score of 7.70).

> High-weighted competitive strength ratings signal a strong competitive position and possession of competitive advantage; low ratings signal a weak position and competitive disadvantage.

Strategic Implications of Competitive Strength Assessments

In addition to showing how competitively strong or weak a company is relative to rivals, the strength ratings provide guidelines for designing wise offensive and defensive strategies. For example, if ABC Company wants to go on the offensive to win additional sales and market share, such an offensive probably needs to be aimed directly at winning customers away from Rival 2 (which has a lower overall strength score) rather than Rival 1 (which has a higher overall strength score). Moreover, while ABC has high ratings for technological skills (a 10 rating), dealer network/distribution capability (a 9 rating), new product innovation capability (a 9 rating), quality/product performance (an 8 rating), and reputation/image (an 8 rating), these strength measures have low importance weights—meaning that ABC has strengths in areas that don't translate into much competitive clout in the marketplace. Even so, it outclasses Rival 2 in all five areas, plus it enjoys substantially lower costs than Rival 2 (ABC has a 5 rating on relative cost position versus a 1 rating for Rival 2)—and relative cost position carries the highest importance weight of all the strength measures. ABC also has greater competitive strength than Rival 3 regarding customer service capabilities (which carries the second-highest importance weight). Hence, because ABC's strengths are in the very areas where Rival 2 is weak, ABC is in a good position to attack Rival 2. Indeed, ABC may well be able to persuade a number of Rival 2's customers to switch their purchases over to its product.

> A company's competitive strength scores pinpoint its strengths and weaknesses against rivals and point directly to the kinds of offensive and defensive actions it can use to exploit its competitive strengths and reduce its competitive vulnerabilities.

But ABC should be cautious about cutting price aggressively to win customers away from Rival 2, because Rival 1 could interpret that as an attack by ABC to win away Rival 1's customers as well. And Rival 1 is in far and away the best position to compete on the basis of low price, given its high rating on relative cost in an industry where low costs are competitively important (relative cost carries an importance weight of 0.30).

Rival 1's strong relative cost position vis-à-vis both ABC and Rival 2 arms it with the ability to use its lower-cost advantage to thwart any price cutting on ABC's part. Clearly ABC is vulnerable to any retaliatory price cuts by Rival 1—Rival 1 can easily defeat both ABC and Rival 2 in a price-based battle for sales and market share. If ABC wants to defend against its vulnerability to potential price cutting by Rival 1, then it needs to aim a portion of its strategy at lowering its costs.

The point here is that a competitively astute company should utilize the strength scores in deciding what strategic moves to make. When a company has important competitive strengths in areas where one or more rivals are weak, it makes sense to consider offensive moves to exploit rivals' competitive weaknesses. When a company has important competitive weaknesses in areas where one or more rivals are strong, it makes sense to consider defensive moves to curtail its vulnerability.

QUESTION 6: WHAT STRATEGIC ISSUES AND PROBLEMS MERIT FRONT-BURNER MANAGERIAL ATTENTION?

The final and most important analytic step is to zero in on exactly what strategic issues company managers need to address—and resolve—for the company to be more financially and competitively successful in the years ahead. This step involves drawing on the results of both industry analysis and the evaluations of the company's internal situation. The task here is to get a clear fix on exactly what strategic and competitive challenges confront the company, which of the company's competitive shortcomings need fixing, and what specific problems merit company managers' front-burner attention. *Pinpointing the specific issues that management needs to address sets the agenda for deciding what actions to take next to improve the company's performance and business outlook.*

The "priority list" of issues and problems that have to be wrestled with can include such things as *how* to stave off market challenges from new foreign competitors, *how* to combat the price discounting of rivals, *how* to reduce the company's high costs, *how* to sustain the company's present rate of growth in light of slowing buyer demand, *whether* to correct the company's competitive deficiencies by acquiring a rival company with the missing strengths, *whether* to expand into foreign markets, *whether* to reposition the company and move to a different strategic group, *what to do* about growing buyer interest in substitute products, and *what to do* to combat the aging demographics of the company's customer base. The priority list thus always centers on such concerns as "how to . . . ," "what to do about . . . ," and "whether to . . ." The purpose of the priority list is to identify the specific issues and problems that management needs to address, not to figure out what specific actions to take. Deciding what to do—which strategic actions to take and which strategic moves to make—comes later (when it is time to craft the strategy and choose among the various strategic alternatives).

> Compiling a "priority list" of problems creates an agenda of strategic issues that merit prompt managerial attention.

> A good strategy must contain ways to deal with all the strategic issues and obstacles that stand in the way of the company's financial and competitive success in the years ahead.

If the items on the priority list are relatively minor—which suggests that the company's strategy is mostly on track and reasonably well matched to the company's overall situation—company managers seldom need to go much beyond fine-tuning the present strategy. If, however, the problems confronting the company are serious and indicate the present strategy is not well suited for the road ahead, the task of crafting a better strategy needs to be at the top of management's action agenda.

KEY POINTS

There are six key questions to consider in evaluating a company's ability to compete successfully against market rivals:

1. *How well is the present strategy working?* This involves evaluating the strategy in terms of the company's financial performance and market standing. The stronger a company's current overall performance, the less likely the need for radical strategy changes. The weaker a company's performance, the more its current strategy must be questioned.

2. *What is the company's overall situation, in terms of its internal strengths and weaknesses in relation to its market opportunities and external threats?* The answer to this question comes from performing a SWOT analysis. A company's strengths and competitive assets are strategically relevant because they are the most logical and appealing building blocks for strategy; internal weaknesses are important because they may represent vulnerabilities that need correction. External opportunities and threats come into play because a good strategy necessarily aims at capturing a company's most attractive opportunities and at defending against threats to its well-being.

3. *What are the company's most important resources and capabilities and can they give the company a sustainable advantage?* A company's resources can be identified using the tangible/intangible typology presented in this chapter. Its capabilities can be identified either by starting with its resources to look for related capabilities or looking for them within the company's different functional domains.

   The answer to the second part of the question comes from conducting the four tests of a resource's competitive power—the VRIN tests. If a company has resources and capabilities that are competitively *valuable* and *rare,* the firm will have a competitive advantage over market rivals. If its resources and capabilities are also hard to copy *(inimitable),* with no good substitutes *(nonsubstitutable),* then the firm may be able to sustain this advantage even in the face of active efforts by rivals to overcome it.

4. *Are the company's cost structure and value proposition competitive?* One telling sign of whether a company's situation is strong or precarious is whether its costs are competitive with those of industry rivals. Another sign is how the company compares with rivals in terms of differentiation—how effectively it delivers on its customer value proposition. Value chain analysis and benchmarking are essential tools in determining whether the company is performing particular functions and activities well, whether its costs are in line with those of competitors, whether it is differentiating in ways that really enhance customer value, and whether particular internal activities and business processes need improvement. They complement resource and capability analysis by providing data at the level of individual activities that provide more objective evidence of whether individual resources and capabilities, or bundles of resources and linked activity sets, are competitively superior.

5. *On an overall basis, is the company competitively stronger or weaker than key rivals?* The key appraisals here involve how the company matches up against key rivals on industry key success factors and other chief determinants of competitive success and whether and why the company has a *net* competitive advantage or disadvantage. Quantitative competitive strength assessments, using the method presented in Table 4.4, indicate where a company is competitively strong and weak and provide insight into the company's ability to defend or enhance its market position. As a rule, a company's competitive strategy should be built around its competitive strengths and should aim at shoring up areas where it is competitively vulnerable.

When a company has important competitive strengths in areas where one or more rivals are weak, it makes sense to consider offensive moves to exploit rivals' competitive weaknesses. When a company has important competitive weaknesses in areas where one or more rivals are strong, it makes sense to consider defensive moves to curtail its vulnerability.

6. *What strategic issues and problems merit front-burner managerial attention?* This analytic step zeros in on the strategic issues and problems that stand in the way of the company's success. It involves using the results of industry analysis as well as resource and value chain analysis of the company's competitive situation to identify a "priority list" of issues to be resolved for the company to be financially and competitively successful in the years ahead. Actually deciding on a strategy and what specific actions to take is what comes after developing the list of strategic issues and problems that merit front-burner management attention.

Like good industry analysis, solid analysis of the company's competitive situation vis-à-vis its key rivals is a valuable precondition for good strategy making.

ASSURANCE OF LEARNING EXERCISES

LO 4-1

1. Using the financial ratios provided in Table 4.1 and following the financial statement information presented for Urban Outfitters, Inc., calculate the following ratios for Urban Outfitters for both 2018 and 2019:

   a. Gross profit margin
   b. Operating profit margin
   c. Net profit margin
   d. Times-interest-earned (or coverage) ratio
   e. Return on stockholders' equity
   f. Return on assets
   g. Debt-to-equity ratio
   h. Days of inventory
   i. Inventory turnover ratio
   j. Average collection period

   Based on these ratios, did Urban Outfitter's financial performance improve, weaken, or remain about the same from 2018 to 2019?

Consolidated Income Statements for Urban Outfitters, Inc., 2018–2019 (in thousands, except per share data)

	2018	2019
Net sales (total revenue)	$3,616,014	$3,950,623
Cost of sales	2,440,507	2,603,911
Selling, general, and administrative	915,615	965,399

(continued)

	2018	2019
Operating income	$259,892	$381,313
Other income (expense)		
Other expenses	(4,840)	(6,325)
Interest income and other, net	6,314	10,565
Income before income taxes	261,366	385,553
Provision for income taxes	153,103	87,550
Net income	$108,263	$298,003
Basic earnings per share	$ 0.97	$ 2.75
Diluted earnings per share	$ 0.96	$ 2.72

Source: Urban Outfitters, Inc., 2019.

Consolidated Balance Sheets for Urban Outfitters, Inc., 2018–2019 (in thousands, except per share data)

	January 31, 2018	January 31, 2019
Assets		
Current Assets		
Cash and cash equivalents	$ 282,220	$ 358,260
Short-term investments	165,125	279,232
Receivables, net	76,962	80,461
Merchandise inventories	351,395	370,507
Prepaid expenses and other current assets	103,055	114,296
Total current assets	978,757	1,202,756
Net property and equipment	813,768	796,029
Deferred income taxes and Other assets	160,255	161,730
Total assets	$1,952,780	$2,160,515
Liabilities and Shareholders' Equity		
Current Liabilities		
Accounts payable	$ 128,246	$ 144,414
Accrued salaries and benefits	36,058	54,799
Accrued expenses and Other current liabilities	195,910	187,431
Total current liabilities	360,214	$ 386,644

(continued)

	January 31, 2018	January 31, 2019
Long-term debt	0	0
Deferred rent and other liabilities	284,773	291,663
Total liabilities	671,417	651,877
Commitments and Contingencies		
Equity		
Preferred stock $.0001 par value; 10,000,000 shares authorized; no shares issued and outstanding	0	0
Common stock $.0001 par value; 200,000,000 shares authorized; 105,642,283 and 108,248,568 shares issued and outstanding	11	11
Additional paid-in capital	$ 0	$ 684
Retained earnings	1,489,087	1,300,208
Total stockholders' equity	1,489,098	1,300,90
Total Liabilities and Equity	$2,160,515	$1,952,780

Source: Urban Outfitters, Inc., 2019 10-K.

2. Cinnabon, famous for its cinnamon rolls, is an American chain commonly located in high traffic areas, such as airports and malls. They operate more than 1,200 bakeries in more than 48 countries. How many of the four tests of the competitive power of a resource does the store network pass? Using your general knowledge of this industry, perform a SWOT analysis. Explain your answers.   **LO 4-2, LO 4-3**

3. Review the information in Illustration Capsule 4.1 concerning Everlane's average costs of producing and selling a pair of denim jeans, and compare this with the representative value chain depicted in Figure 4.3. Then answer the following questions: **LO 4-4**

   a. Which of the company's costs correspond to the primary value chain activities depicted in Figure 4.3?

   b. Which of the company's costs correspond to the support activities described in Figure 4.3?

   c. What value chain activities might be important in securing or maintaining Everlane's advantage? Explain your answer.

4. Using the methodology illustrated in Table 4.3 and your knowledge as an automobile owner, prepare a competitive strength assessment for General Motors and its rivals Ford, Chrysler, Toyota, and Honda. Each of the five automobile manufacturers should be evaluated on the key success factors and strength measures of cost-competitiveness, product-line breadth, product quality and reliability, financial resources and profitability, and customer service. What does your competitive strength assessment disclose about the overall competitiveness of each automobile manufacturer? What factors account most for Toyota's competitive success? Does Toyota have competitive weaknesses that were disclosed by your analysis? Explain.   **LO 4-5**

EXERCISES FOR SIMULATION PARTICIPANTS

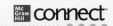

LO 4-1   **1.** Using the formulas in Table 4.1 and the data in your company's latest financial statements, calculate the following measures of financial performance for your company:

    a. Operating profit margin

    b. Total return on total assets

    c. Current ratio

    d. Working capital

    e. Long-term debt-to-capital ratio

    f. Price-to-earnings ratio

LO 4-1   **2.** On the basis of your company's latest financial statements and all the other available data regarding your company's performance that appear in the industry report, list the three measures of financial performance on which your company did best and the three measures on which your company's financial performance was worst.

LO 4-1   **3.** What hard evidence can you cite that indicates your company's strategy is working fairly well (or perhaps not working so well, if your company's performance is lagging that of rival companies)?

LO 4-2, LO 4-3   **4.** What internal strengths and weaknesses does your company have? What external market opportunities for growth and increased profitability exist for your company? What external threats to your company's future well-being and profitability do you and your co-managers see? What does the preceding SWOT analysis indicate about your company's present situation and future prospects—where on the scale from "exceptionally strong" to "alarmingly weak" does the attractiveness of your company's situation rank?

LO 4-2, LO 4-3   **5.** Does your company have any core competencies? If so, what are they?

LO 4-4   **6.** What are the key elements of your company's value chain? Refer to Figure 4.3 in developing your answer.

LO 4-5   **7.** Using the methodology presented in Table 4.4, do a weighted competitive strength assessment for your company and two other companies that you and your co-managers consider to be very close competitors.

ENDNOTES

[1] Donald Sull, "Strategy as Active Waiting," *Harvard Business Review* 83, no. 9 (September 2005), pp. 121–126.

[2] Birger Wernerfelt, "A Resource-Based View of the Firm," *Strategic Management Journal* 5, no. 5 (September–October 1984), pp. 171–180; Jay Barney, "Firm Resources and Sustained Competitive Advantage," *Journal of Management* 17, no. 1 (1991), pp. 99–120.

[3] R. Amit and P. Schoemaker, "Strategic Assets and Organizational Rent," *Strategic Management Journal* 14 (1993).

[4] Jay B. Barney, "Looking Inside for Competitive Advantage," *Academy of Management Executive* 9, no. 4 (November

1995), pp. 49–61; Christopher A. Bartlett and Sumantra Ghoshal, "Building Competitive Advantage through People," *MIT Sloan Management Review* 43, no. 2 (Winter 2002), pp. 34–41; Danny Miller, Russell Eisenstat, and Nathaniel Foote, "Strategy from the Inside Out: Building Capability-Creating Organizations," *California Management Review* 44, no. 3 (Spring 2002), pp. 37–54.

[5] M. Peteraf and J. Barney, "Unraveling the Resource-Based Tangle," *Managerial and Decision Economics* 24, no. 4 (June–July 2003), pp. 309–323.

[6] Margaret A. Peteraf and Mark E. Bergen, "Scanning Dynamic Competitive Landscapes: A Market-Based and Resource-Based

Framework," *Strategic Management Journal* 24 (2003), pp. 1027–1042.

[7] C. Montgomery, "Of Diamonds and Rust: A New Look at Resources," in C. Montgomery (ed.), *Resource-Based and Evolutionary Theories of the Firm* (Boston: Kluwer Academic, 1995), pp. 251–268.

[8] Constance E. Helfat and Margaret A. Peteraf, "The Dynamic Resource-Based View: Capability Lifecycles," *Strategic Management Journal* 24, no. 10 (2003).

[9] D. Teece, G. Pisano, and A. Shuen, "Dynamic Capabilities and Strategic Management," *Strategic Management Journal* 18, no. 7 (1997), pp. 509–533; K. Eisenhardt and J. Martin, "Dynamic Capabilities: What Are They?"

Strategic Management Journal 21, no. 10–11 (2000), pp. 1105–1121; M. Zollo and S. Winter, "Deliberate Learning and the Evolution of Dynamic Capabilities," *Organization Science* 13 (2002), pp. 339–351; C. Helfat et al., *Dynamic Capabilities: Understanding Strategic Change in Organizations* (Malden, MA: Blackwell, 2007).

[10] Michael Porter in his 1985 best seller *Competitive Advantage* (New York: Free Press).

[11] John K. Shank and Vijay Govindarajan, *Strategic Cost Management* (New York: Free Press, 1993), especially chaps. 2–6,

10, and 11; Robin Cooper and Robert S. Kaplan, "Measure Costs Right: Make the Right Decisions," *Harvard Business Review* 66, no. 5 (September–October, 1988), pp. 96–103; Joseph A. Ness and Thomas G. Cucuzza, "Tapping the Full Potential of ABC," *Harvard Business Review* 73, no. 4 (July–August 1995), pp. 130–138.

[12] Porter, *Competitive Advantage,* p. 34.

[13] Hau L. Lee, "The Triple-A Supply Chain," *Harvard Business Review* 82, no. 10 (October 2004), pp. 102–112.

[14] Gregory H. Watson, *Strategic Benchmarking: How to Rate Your Company's Performance*

against the World's Best (New York: Wiley, 1993); Robert C. Camp, *Benchmarking: The Search for Industry Best Practices That Lead to Superior Performance* (Milwaukee: ASQC Quality Press, 1989); Dawn Iacobucci and Christie Nordhielm, "Creative Benchmarking," *Harvard Business Review* 78 no. 6 (November–December 2000), pp. 24–25.

[15] www.businessdictionary.com/definition/best-practice.html (accessed December 2, 2009).

[16] Reuben E. Stone, "Leading a Supply Chain Turnaround," *Harvard Business Review* 82, no. 10 (October 2004), pp. 114–121.

chapter 5

The Five Generic Competitive Strategies

Learning Objectives

After reading this chapter, you should be able to:

LO 5-1 Understand what distinguishes each of the five generic strategies and explain why some of these strategies work better in certain kinds of competitive conditions than in others.

LO 5-2 Recognize the major avenues for achieving a competitive advantage based on lower costs.

LO 5-3 Identify the major avenues to a competitive advantage based on differentiating a company's product or service offering from the offerings of rivals.

LO 5-4 Explain the attributes of a best-cost strategy—a hybrid of low-cost and differentiation strategies.

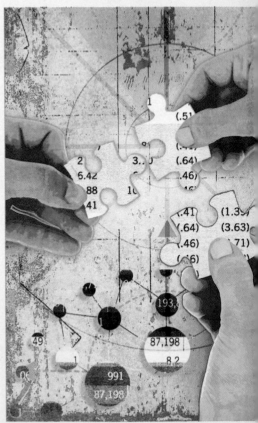

Roy Scott/Media Bakery

It's all about strategic positioning and competition.

Michele Hutchins—*Consultant*

Strategic positioning means performing different activities from rivals or performing similar activities in different ways.

Michael E. Porter—*Professor, author, and cofounder of Monitor Consulting*

I learnt the hard way about positioning in business, about catering to the right segments.

Shaffi Mather—*Social entrepreneur*

A company can employ any of several basic approaches to gaining a competitive advantage over rivals, but they all involve *delivering more value* to customers than rivals or *delivering value more efficiently* than rivals (or both). More value for customers can mean a good product at a lower price, a superior product worth paying more for, or a best-value offering that represents an attractive combination of price, features, service, and other appealing attributes. Greater efficiency means delivering a given level of value to customers at a lower cost to the company. But whatever approach to delivering value the company takes, it nearly always requires performing value chain activities differently than rivals and building competitively valuable resources and capabilities that rivals cannot readily match or outdo.

This chapter describes the five *generic competitive strategy options*. Each of the five generic strategies represents a distinctly different approach to competing in the marketplace. Which of the five to employ is a company's first and foremost choice in crafting an overall strategy and beginning its quest for competitive advantage.

TYPES OF GENERIC COMPETITIVE STRATEGIES

● **LO 5-1**

Understand what distinguishes each of the five generic strategies and explain why some of these strategies work better in certain kinds of competitive conditions than in others.

A company's competitive strategy lays out the specific efforts of the company to position itself in the marketplace, please customers, ward off competitive threats, and achieve a particular kind of competitive advantage. The chances are remote that any two companies—even companies in the same industry—will employ competitive strategies that are exactly alike in every detail. However, when one strips away the details to get at the real substance, the two biggest factors that distinguish one competitive strategy from another boil down to (1) whether a company's market target is broad or narrow and (2) whether the company is pursuing a competitive advantage linked to lower costs or differentiation. These two factors give rise to four distinct competitive strategy options, plus one hybrid option, as shown in Figure 5.1 and listed next.[1]

1. *A broad, low-cost strategy*—striving to achieve broad lower overall costs than rivals on comparable products that attract a broad spectrum of buyers, usually by underpricing rivals.

2. *A broad differentiation strategy*—seeking to differentiate the company's product offering from rivals' with attributes that will appeal to a broad spectrum of buyers.

3. *A focused low-cost strategy*—concentrating on the needs and requirements of a narrow buyer segment (or market niche) and striving to meet these needs at lower costs than rivals (thereby being able to serve niche members at a lower price).

4. *A focused differentiation strategy*—concentrating on a narrow buyer segment (or market niche) and offering niche members customized attributes that meet their tastes and requirements better than rivals' products.

FIGURE 5.1   The Five Generic Competitive Strategies

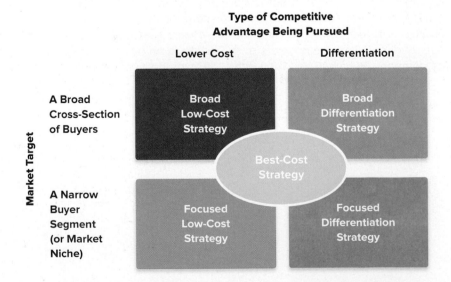

Source: This is an expanded version of a three-strategy classification discussed in Michael E. Porter, *Competitive Strategy* (New York: Free Press, 1980).

5. *A best-cost strategy*—striving to incorporate upscale product attributes at a lower cost than rivals. Being the "best-cost" producer of an upscale, multifeatured product allows a company to *give customers more value for their money* by underpricing rivals whose products have similar upscale, multifeatured attributes. This competitive approach is a *hybrid* strategy that *blends elements of the previous four options* in a unique and often effective way. It may be focused or broad in its appeal.

The remainder of this chapter explores the ins and outs of these five generic competitive strategies and how they differ.

BROAD LOW-COST STRATEGIES

Striving to achieve lower costs than rivals targeting a broad spectrum of buyers is an especially effective competitive approach in markets with many price-sensitive buyers. A company achieves **low-cost leadership** when it becomes the industry's lowest-cost producer rather than just being one of perhaps several competitors with comparatively low costs. But a low-cost producer's foremost strategic objective is *meaningfully* lower costs than rivals—*not necessarily the absolutely lowest possible cost.* In striving for a cost advantage over rivals, company managers must incorporate features and services that buyers consider essential. A product offering that is too frills-free can be viewed by consumers as offering little value regardless of its pricing.

A company has two options for translating a low-cost advantage over rivals into superior profit performance. Option 1 is to use the lower-cost edge to underprice competitors and attract price-sensitive buyers in great enough numbers to increase total profits. Option 2 is to maintain the present price, be content with the present market share, and use the lower-cost edge to raise total profits by earning a higher profit margin on each unit sold.

While many companies are inclined to exploit a low-cost advantage by using option 1 (attacking rivals with lower prices), this strategy can backfire if rivals respond with retaliatory price cuts (in order to protect their customer base and defend against a loss of sales). A rush to cut prices can often trigger a price war that lowers the profits of all price discounters. The bigger the risk that rivals will respond with matching price cuts, the more appealing it becomes to employ the second option for using a low-cost advantage to achieve higher profitability.

The Two Major Avenues for Achieving a Cost Advantage

To achieve a low-cost edge over rivals, a firm's cumulative costs across its overall value chain must be lower than competitors' cumulative costs. There are two major avenues for accomplishing this:[2]

1. Perform internal value chain activities and/or value chain system activities more cost-effectively than rivals.
2. Revamp the firm's overall value chain to eliminate or bypass some cost-producing activities.

Cost-Efficient Management of Value Chain Activities   For a company to do a more cost-effective job of managing its value chain than rivals, managers must diligently search out cost-saving opportunities in every part of the value chain.

> **LO 5-2**
>
> Recognize the major avenues for achieving a competitive advantage based on lower costs.

> **CORE** CONCEPT
>
> The essence of a **broad, low-cost strategy** is to produce goods or services for a broad base of buyers at a lower cost than rivals.

> A low-cost advantage over rivals can translate into superior profitability through lower price and higher market share or higher profit margins.

> **CORE** CONCEPT
>
> A **cost driver** is a factor that has a strong influence on a company's costs.

No activity can escape cost-saving scrutiny, and all company personnel must be expected to use their talents and ingenuity to come up with innovative and effective ways to keep down costs. Particular attention must be paid to a set of factors known as **cost drivers** that have a strong effect on a company's costs and can be used as levers to lower costs. Figure 5.2 shows the most important cost drivers. Cost-cutting approaches that demonstrate an effective use of the cost drivers include

1. *Capturing all available economies of scale.* Economies of scale stem from an ability to lower unit costs by increasing the scale of operation. Economies of scale may be available at different points along a company's value chain (both internally and elsewhere along its value chain system). Often, a large plant is more economical to operate than a small one, particularly if it can be operated round the clock roboti-cally. Economies of scale may be available due to a large warehouse operation on the input side or a large distribution center on the output side. In global industries, selling a mostly standard product worldwide tends to lower unit costs as opposed to making separate products (each at lower scale) for each country market. There are economies of scale in advertising as well. For example, Anheuser-Busch InBev SA/NV could afford to pay the $5.6 million cost of a 30-second Super Bowl ad in 2020 because the cost could be spread out over the hundreds of millions of units of Budweiser that the company sells.

FIGURE 5.2 Cost Drivers: The Keys to Driving Down Company Costs

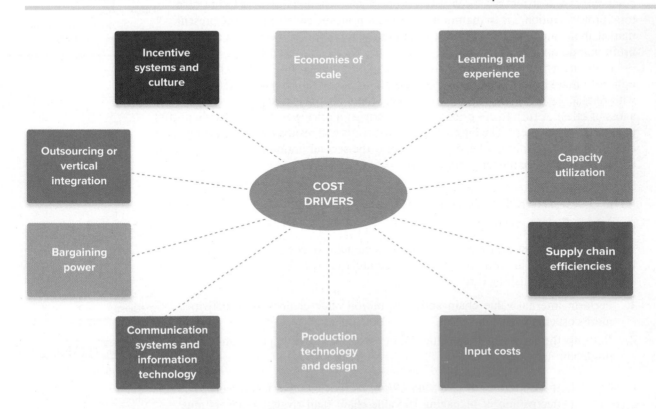

Source: Adapted from Michael E. Porter, *Competitive Advantage: Creating and Sustaining Superior Performance* (New York: Free Press, 1985).

2. *Taking full advantage of experience and learning-curve effects.* The cost of perform-ing an activity can decline over time as the learning and experience of company personnel build. Learning and experience economies can stem from debugging and mastering newly introduced technologies, using the experiences and suggestions of workers to install more efficient plant layouts and assembly procedures, and the added speed and effectiveness that accrues from repeatedly picking sites for and building new plants, distribution centers, or retail outlets.

3. *Operating facilities at full capacity.* Whether a company is able to operate at or near full capacity has a big impact on unit costs when its value chain contains activities associated with substantial fixed costs. Higher rates of capacity utilization allow depreciation and other fixed costs to be spread over a larger unit volume, thereby lowering fixed costs per unit. The more capital-intensive the business and the higher the fixed costs as a percentage of total costs, the greater the unit-cost penalty for operating at less than full capacity.

4. *Improving supply chain efficiency.* Partnering with suppliers to streamline the ordering and purchasing process, to reduce inventory carrying costs via just-in-time inventory practices, to economize on shipping and materials handling, and to ferret out other cost-saving opportunities is a much-used approach to cost reduction. A company with a distinctive competence in cost-efficient sup-ply chain management, such as Colgate-Palmolive or Unilever (leading consumer products companies), can sometimes achieve a sizable cost advantage over less adept rivals.

5. *Substituting lower-cost inputs wherever there is little or no sacrifice in product quality or performance.* If the costs of certain raw materials and parts are "too high," a company can switch to using lower-cost items or maybe even design the high-cost components out of the product altogether.

6. *Using the company's bargaining power vis-à-vis suppliers or others in the value chain system to gain concessions.* Home Depot, for example, has sufficient bargaining clout with suppliers to win price discounts on large-volume purchases.

7. *Using online systems and sophisticated software to achieve operating efficiencies.* For example, sharing data and production schedules with suppliers, coupled with the use of enterprise resource planning (ERP) and manufacturing execution system (MES) software, can reduce parts inventories, trim production times, and lower labor requirements.

8. *Improving process design and employing advanced production technology.* Often, pro-duction costs can be cut by (1) using design for manufacture (DFM) procedures and computer-assisted design (CAD) techniques that enable more integrated and efficient production methods, (2) investing in highly automated robotic production technology, and (3) shifting to a mass-customization production process. Dell's highly automated PC assembly plant in Austin, Texas, is a prime example of the use of advanced product and process technologies. Many companies are ardent users of total quality management (TQM) systems, business process reengineering, Six Sigma methodology, and other business process management techniques that aim at boosting efficiency and reducing costs.

9. *Being alert to the cost advantages of outsourcing or vertical integration.* Outsourcing the performance of certain value chain activities can be more economical than performing them in-house if outside specialists, by virtue of their expertise and vol-ume, can perform the activities at lower cost. On the other hand, there can be times when integrating into the activities of either suppliers or distribution-channel allies

can lower costs through greater production efficiencies, reduced transaction costs, or a better bargaining position.

10. *Motivating employees through incentives and company culture.* A company's incentive system can encourage not only greater worker productivity but also cost-saving innovations that come from worker suggestions. The culture of a company can also spur worker pride in productivity and continuous improvement. Companies that are well known for their cost-reducing incentive systems and culture include Nucor Steel, which characterizes itself as a company of "20,000 teammates," Southwest Airlines, and DHL Express (rival of FedEx).

Revamping of the Value Chain System to Lower Costs   Dramatic cost advantages can often emerge from redesigning the company's value chain system in ways that eliminate costly work steps and entirely bypass certain cost-producing value chain activities. Such value chain revamping can include

- *Selling direct to consumers and bypassing the activities and costs of distributors and dealers.* To circumvent the need for distributors and dealers, a company can create its own direct sales force, which adds the costs of maintaining and supporting a sales force but may be cheaper than using independent distributors and dealers to access buyers. Alternatively, they can conduct sales operations at the company's website, since the costs for website operations and shipping may be substantially cheaper than going through distributor-dealer channels). Costs in the wholesale and retail portions of the value chain frequently represent 35 to 50 percent of the final price consumers pay, so establishing a direct sales force or selling online may offer big cost savings.

- *Streamlining operations by eliminating low-value-added or unnecessary work steps and activities.* At Walmart, some items supplied by manufacturers are delivered directly to retail stores rather than being routed through Walmart's distribution centers and delivered by Walmart trucks. In other instances, Walmart unloads incoming shipments from manufacturers' trucks arriving at its distribution centers and loads them directly onto outgoing Walmart trucks headed to particular stores without ever moving the goods into the distribution center. Many supermarket chains have greatly reduced in-store meat butchering and cutting activities by shifting to meats that are cut and packaged at the meatpacking plant and then delivered to their stores in ready-to-sell form.

- *Reducing materials-handling and shipping costs by having suppliers locate their plants or warehouses close to the company's own facilities.* Having suppliers locate their plants or warehouses close to a company's own plant facilitates just-in-time deliveries of parts and components to the exact workstation where they will be used in assembling the company's product. This not only lowers incoming shipping costs but also curbs or eliminates the company's need to build and operate storerooms for incoming parts and to have plant personnel move the inventories to the workstations as needed for assembly.

Illustration Capsule 5.1 describes the path that Vanguard has followed in achieving its position as the low-cost leader of the investment management industry.

Examples of Companies That Revamped Their Value Chains to Reduce Costs
Nucor Corporation, the most profitable steel producer in the United States and one of the largest steel producers worldwide, drastically revamped the value chain process for

Vanguard's Path to Becoming the Low-Cost Leader in Investment Management

Vanguard is now one of the world's largest investment management companies. It became an industry giant by leading the way in low-cost passive index investing. In active trading, an investment manager is compensated for making an educated decision on which stocks to sell and which to buy. This incurs both transactional and management fees. In contrast, passive index portfolios aim to mirror the movements of a major market index like the S&P 500, Dow Jones Industrial Average, or NASDAQ. Passive portfolios incur fewer fees and can be managed with lower operating costs. A measure used to compare operating costs in this industry is known as the expense ratio, which is the percentage of an investment that goes toward expenses. In 2019, Vanguard's expense ratio was less than 14 percent of the industry's average expense ratio. Vanguard was the first to capitalize on what was at the time an underappreciated fact: over long horizons, well-managed index funds, with their lower costs and fees, typically outperform their actively trading competitors.

Vanguard provides low-cost investment options for its clients in several ways. By creating funds that track index(es) over a long horizon, the client does not incur transaction and management fees normally charged in actively managed funds. Possibly more important, Vanguard was created with a unique client-owner structure. When you invest with Vanguard you become an owner of Vanguard. This structure effectively cut out traditional shareholders who seek to share in profits. Under client ownership, any returns in excess of operating costs are returned to the clients/investors.

Vanguard keeps its costs low in several other ways. One notable one is its focus on its employees and organizational structure. The company prides itself on low turnover rates (8 percent) and very flat organizational

Keith Srakocic/AP Images

structure. In several instances Vanguard has been able to capitalize on being a fast follower. They launched several product lines after their competitors introduced those products. Being a fast follower allowed them to develop superior products and reach scale more quickly—both further lowering their cost structure.

The low-cost structure has not come at the expense of performance. Vanguard now has 410 funds, over 30 million investors, has surpassed $5.5 trillion in AUM (assets under management), and is growing faster than all its competitors combined. When *Money* published its January 2020 list of recommended investment funds, 44 percent of the funds listed were Vanguard funds.

Vanguard's low-cost strategy has been so successful that industry experts now refer to The Vanguard Effect. This refers to the pressure that this investment management giant has put on competitors to lower their fees in order to compete with Vanguard's low-cost value proposition.

Note: Developed with Vedrana B. Greatorex.

Sources: https://www.nytimes.com/2017/04/14/business/mutfund/vanguard-mutual-index-funds-growth.html; https://investor .vanguard.com; Sunderam, A., Viceira, L., & Ciechanover, A. (2016) *The Vanguard Group, Inc. in 2015: Celebrating 40.* HBS No. 9-216-026. Boston, MA: Harvard Business School Publishing; Money.com; About Vanguard.com/Fast Facts About Vanguard.

manufacturing steel products by using relatively inexpensive electric arc furnaces and continuous casting processes. Using electric arc furnaces to melt recycled scrap steel eliminated many of the steps used by traditional steel mills that made their steel products from iron ore, coke, limestone, and other ingredients using costly coke ovens, basic oxygen blast furnaces, ingot casters, and multiple types of finishing facilities—plus Nucor's value chain system required far fewer employees. As a consequence, Nucor produces steel with a far lower capital investment, a far smaller workforce, and far lower operating costs than traditional steel mills. Nucor's strategy to replace the

> Success in achieving a low-cost edge over rivals comes from out-managing rivals in finding ways to perform value chain activities faster, more accurately, and more cost-effectively.

traditional steelmaking value chain with its simpler, quicker value chain approach has made it one of the world's lowest-cost producers of steel, allowing it to take a huge amount of market share away from traditional steel companies and earn attractive profits. This approach has allowed the company to remain steadily profitable even as a flood of illegally subsidized imports wreaked havoc on the rest of the North American steel market.

Southwest Airlines has achieved considerable cost savings by reconfiguring the traditional value chain of commercial airlines, thereby permitting it to offer travelers lower fares. Its mastery of fast turnarounds at the gates (about 25 minutes versus 45 minutes for rivals) allows its planes to fly more hours per day. This translates into being able to schedule more flights per day with fewer aircraft, allowing Southwest to generate more revenue per plane on average than rivals. Southwest does not offer assigned seating, baggage transfer to connecting airlines, or first-class seating and service, thereby eliminating all the cost-producing activities associated with these features. The company's fast and user-friendly online reservation system facilitates e-ticketing and reduces staffing requirements at telephone reservation centers and airport counters. Its use of automated check-in equipment reduces staffing requirements for terminal check-in. The company's carefully designed point-to-point route system minimizes connections, delays, and total trip time for passengers, allowing about 75 percent of Southwest passengers to fly nonstop to their destinations and at the same time reducing Southwest's costs for flight operations.

The Keys to a Successful Broad Low-Cost Strategy

A low-cost producer is in the best position to win the business of price-sensitive buyers, set the floor on market price, and still earn a profit.

While broad, low-cost companies are champions of frugality, they seldom hesitate to spend aggressively on resources and capabilities *that promise to drive costs out of the business.* Indeed, having competitive assets of this type and ensuring that they remain competitively superior is essential for achieving competitive advantage as a broad, low-cost leader. Walmart, for example, has been an early adopter of state-of-the-art technology throughout its operations; however, the company *carefully estimates the cost savings of new technologies before it rushes to invest in them.* By continuously investing in complex, cost-saving technologies that are hard for rivals to match, Walmart has sustained its low-cost advantage for over 45 years.

Uber and Lyft, employing a formidable low-cost provider strategy and an innovative business model, have stormed their way into hundreds of locations across the world, totally disrupting and seemingly forever changing competition in the taxi markets where they have a presence. And, most significantly, the ultra-low fares charged by Uber and Lyft have resulted in dramatic increases in the demand for taxi services, particularly those provided by these two low-cost providers. Other companies noted for their successful use of broad low-cost strategies include Spirit Airlines, EasyJet, and Ryanair in airlines; Briggs & Stratton in small gasoline engines; Huawei in networking and telecommunications equipment; Bic in ballpoint pens; Stride Rite in footwear; and Poulan in chain saws.

When a Low-Cost Strategy Works Best

A low-cost strategy becomes increasingly appealing and competitively powerful when

1. *Price competition among rival sellers is vigorous.* Low-cost leaders are in the best position to compete offensively on the basis of price, to gain market share at the expense of rivals, to win the business of price-sensitive buyers, to remain profitable despite strong price competition, and to survive price wars.

2. *The products of rival sellers are essentially identical and readily available from many eager sellers.* Look-alike products and/or overabundant product supply set the stage for lively price competition; in such markets, it is the less efficient, higher-cost companies whose profits get squeezed the most.

3. *There are few ways to achieve product differentiation that have value to buyers.* When the differences between product attributes or brands do not matter much to buyers, buyers are nearly always sensitive to price differences, and industry-leading companies tend to be those with the lowest-priced brands.

4. *Buyers incur low costs in switching their purchases from one seller to another.* Low switching costs give buyers the flexibility to shift purchases to lower-priced sellers having equally good products or to attractively priced substitute products. A low-cost leader is well positioned to use low price to induce potential customers to switch to its brand.

5. *Buyers are price-sensitive or have the power to bargain down prices.* When buyers are focused primarily on price or have substantial bargaining power, then a low-cost strategy becomes something of a necessity!

Pitfalls to Avoid in Pursuing a Low-Cost Strategy

Perhaps the biggest mistake a low-cost producer can make is getting carried away with overly aggressive price cutting. *Higher unit sales and market shares do not automatically translate into higher profits.* Reducing price results in earning a lower profit margin on each unit sold. Thus, reducing price improves profitability *only if* the lower price increases unit sales enough to offset the loss in revenues due to the lower per unit profit margin. A simple numerical example tells the story: Suppose a firm selling 1,000 units at a price of $10, a cost of $9, and a profit margin of $1 opts to cut price 5 percent to $9.50—which reduces the firm's profit margin to $0.50 per unit sold. If unit costs remain at $9, then it takes a 100 percent sales increase to 2,000 units just to offset the narrower profit margin and get back to total profits of $1,000. Hence, whether a price cut will result in higher or lower profitability depends on how big the resulting sales gains will be and how much, if any, unit costs will fall as sales volumes increase.

A second pitfall is *relying on cost reduction approaches that can be easily copied by rivals.* If rivals find it relatively easy or inexpensive to imitate the leader's low-cost methods, then the leader's advantage will be too short-lived to yield a valuable edge in the marketplace.

A third pitfall is *becoming too fixated on cost reduction.* Low costs cannot be pursued so zealously that a firm's offering ends up being too feature-poor to generate buyer appeal. Furthermore, a company driving hard to push down its costs has to guard against ignoring declining buyer sensitivity to price, increased buyer interest in added features or service, or new developments that alter how buyers use the product. Otherwise, it risks losing market ground if buyers start opting for more upscale or feature-rich products.

Even if these mistakes are avoided, a low-cost strategy still entails risk. An innovative rival may discover an even lower-cost value chain approach. Important cost-saving technological breakthroughs may suddenly emerge. And if a low-cost producer has heavy investments in its present means of operating, then it can prove costly to quickly shift to the new value chain approach or a new technology.

Reducing price does not lead to higher total profits unless the added gains in unit sales are large enough to offset the loss in revenues due to lower margins per unit sold.

A low-cost producer's product offering must always contain enough attributes to be attractive to prospective buyers—low price, by itself, is not always appealing to buyers.

BROAD DIFFERENTIATION STRATEGIES

● **LO 5-3**

Identify the major avenues to a competitive advantage based on differentiating a company's product or service offering from the offerings of rivals.

CORE CONCEPT

The essence of a **broad differentiation strategy** is to offer unique product attributes that a wide range of buyers find appealing and worth paying more for.

Differentiation strategies are attractive whenever buyers' needs and preferences are too diverse to be fully satisfied by a standardized product offering. Successful product differentiation requires careful study to determine what attributes buyers will find appealing, valuable, and worth paying for.[3] Then the company must incorporate a combination of these desirable features into its product or service that will be different enough to stand apart from the product or service offerings of rivals. A broad differentiation strategy achieves its aim when a wide range of buyers find the company's offering more appealing than that of rivals and worth a somewhat higher price.

Successful differentiation allows a firm to do one or more of the following:

- Command a premium price for its product.
- Increase unit sales (because additional buyers are won over by the differentiating features).
- Gain buyer loyalty to its brand (because buyers are strongly attracted to the differentiating features and bond with the company and its products).

Differentiation enhances profitability whenever a company's product can command a sufficiently higher price or generate sufficiently bigger unit sales *to more than cover the added costs of achieving the differentiation.* Company differentiation strategies fail when buyers don't place much value on the brand's uniqueness and/ or when a company's differentiating features are easily matched by its rivals.

Companies can pursue differentiation from many angles: a unique taste (Red Bull, Listerine); multiple features (Microsoft Office, Apple Watch); wide selection and one-stop shopping (Home Depot, Alibaba.com); superior service (Ritz-Carlton, Nordstrom); spare parts availability (John Deere; Morgan Motors); engineering design and performance (Mercedes, BMW); high fashion design (Prada, Gucci); product reliability (Whirlpool, LG, and Bosch in large home appliances); quality manufacture (Michelin); technological leadership (3M Corporation in bonding and coating products); a full range of services (Charles Schwab in stock brokerage); and wide product selection (Campbell's soups; Frito-Lay snack foods.).

Managing the Value Chain in Ways that Enhance Differentiation

CORE CONCEPT

A **value driver** is a factor that is particularly effective in creating differentiation.

Differentiation is not something in marketing and advertising departments, nor is it limited to the catchalls of quality and service. Differentiation opportunities can exist in activities all along a company's value chain and value chain system. The most systematic approach that managers can take, however, involves focusing on the **value drivers,** a set of factors—analogous to cost drivers—that are particularly effective in creating differentiation. Figure 5.3 contains a list of important value drivers. Ways that managers can enhance differentiation based on value drivers include the following:

1. *Create product features and performance attributes that appeal to a wide range of buyers.* The physical and functional features of a product have a big influence on differentiation, including features such as added user safety or enhanced environmental protection. Styling and appearance are big differentiating factors in the apparel and motor vehicle industries. Size and weight matter in binoculars and mobile devices.

FIGURE 5.3   Value Drivers: The Keys to Creating a Differentiation Advantage

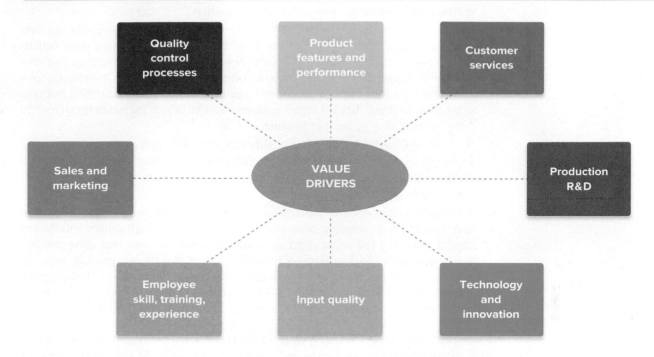

Source: Adapted from Michael E. Porter, *Competitive Advantage: Creating and Sustaining Superior Performance* (New York: Free Press, 1985).

Most companies employing broad differentiation strategies make a point of incorporating innovative and novel features in their product or service offering, especially those that improve performance and functionality.

2. *Improve customer service or add extra services.* Better customer services, in areas such as delivery, returns, and repair, can be as important in creating differentiation as superior product features. Examples include superior technical assistance to buyers, higher-quality maintenance services, more and better product information provided to customers, more and better training materials for end users, better credit terms, quicker order processing, and greater customer convenience.

3. *Invest in production-related R&D activities.* Engaging in production R&D may permit custom-order manufacture at an efficient cost, provide wider product variety and selection through product "versioning," or improve product quality. Many manufacturers have developed flexible manufacturing systems that allow different models and product versions to be made on the same assembly line. Being able to provide buyers with made-to-order products can be a potent differentiating capability.

4. *Strive for innovation and technological advances.* Successful innovation is the route to more frequent first-on-the-market victories and is a powerful differentiator. If the innovation proves hard to replicate, through patent protection or other means, it can provide a company with a first-mover advantage that is sustainable.

5. *Pursue continuous quality improvement.* Quality control processes reduce product defects, prevent premature product failure, extend product life, make it economical to offer longer warranty coverage, improve economy of use, result in more end-user

convenience, or enhance product appearance. Companies whose quality management systems meet certification standards, such as the ISO 9001 standards, can enhance their reputation for quality with customers.

6. *Increase marketing and brand-building activities.* Marketing and advertising can have a tremendous effect on the value perceived by buyers and therefore their willingness to pay more for the company's offerings. They can create differentiation even when little tangible differentiation exists otherwise. For example, blind taste tests show that even the most loyal Pepsi or Coke drinkers have trouble telling one cola drink from another.[4] Brands create customer loyalty, which increases the perceived "cost" of switching to another product.

7. *Seek out high-quality inputs.* Input quality can ultimately spill over to affect the performance or quality of the company's end product. Starbucks, for example, gets high ratings on its coffees partly because it has very strict specifications on the coffee beans purchased from suppliers.

8. *Emphasize human resource management activities that improve the skills, expertise, and knowledge of company personnel.* A company with high-caliber intellectual capital often has the capacity to generate the kinds of ideas that drive product innovation, technological advances, better product design and product performance, improved production techniques, and higher product quality. Well-designed incentive compensation systems can often unleash the efforts of talented personnel to develop and implement new and effective differentiating attributes.

Revamping the Value Chain System to Increase Differentiation   Just as pursuing a cost advantage can involve the entire value chain system, the same is true for a differentiation advantage. Activities performed upstream by suppliers or downstream by distributors and retailers can have a meaningful effect on customers' perceptions of a company's offerings and its value proposition. Approaches to enhancing differentiation through changes in the value chain system include

- *Coordinating with downstream channel allies to enhance customer value.* Coordinating with downstream partners such as distributors, dealers, brokers, and retailers can contribute to differentiation in a variety of ways. Methods that companies use to influence the value chain activities of their channel allies include setting standards for downstream partners to follow, providing them with templates to standardize the selling environment or practices, training channel personnel, or cosponsoring promotions and advertising campaigns. Coordinating with retailers is important for enhancing the buying experience and building a company's image. Coordinating with distributors or shippers can mean quicker delivery to customers, more accurate order filling, and/or lower shipping costs. The Coca-Cola Company considers coordination with its bottler-distributors so important that it has at times taken over a troubled bottler to improve its management and upgrade its plant and equipment before releasing it again.[5]

- *Coordinating with suppliers to better address customer needs.* Collaborating with suppliers can also be a powerful route to a more effective differentiation strategy. Coordinating and collaborating with suppliers can improve many dimensions affecting product features and quality. This is particularly true for companies that engage only in assembly operations, such as Dell in PCs and Ducati in motorcycles. Close coordination with suppliers can also enhance differentiation by speeding up new product development cycles or speeding delivery to end customers. Strong relationships with suppliers can also mean that the company's supply requirements are prioritized when industry supply is insufficient to meet overall demand.

Delivering Superior Value via a Broad Differentiation Strategy

Differentiation strategies depend on meeting customer needs in unique ways or creating new needs through activities such as innovation or persuasive advertising. The objective is to offer customers something that rivals can't—at least in terms of the level of satisfaction. There are four basic routes to achieving this aim:

The first route is to incorporate product attributes and user features that *lower the buyer's overall costs* of using the company's product. This is the least obvious and most overlooked route to a differentiation advantage. It is a differentiating factor since it can help *business buyers* be more competitive in their markets and more profitable. Producers of materials and components often win orders for their products by reducing a buyer's raw-material waste (providing cut-to-size components), reducing a buyer's inventory requirements (providing just-in-time deliveries), using online systems to reduce a buyer's procurement and order processing costs, and providing free technical support. This route to differentiation can also appeal to *individual consumers* who are looking to economize on their overall costs of consumption. Making a company's product more economical for a consumer to use can be done by incorporating energy-efficient features (energy-saving appliances and lightbulbs help cut buyers' utility bills; fuel-efficient vehicles cut buyer costs for gasoline) and/or by increasing maintenance intervals and product reliability to lower buyer costs for maintenance and repairs.

A second route is to incorporate *tangible* features that increase customer satisfaction with the product, such as product specifications, functions, and styling. This can be accomplished by including attributes that add functionality; enhance the design; save time for the user; are more reliable; or make the product cleaner, safer, quieter, simpler to use, more portable, more convenient, or longer-lasting than rival brands. Smartphone manufacturers are in a race to introduce next-generation devices capable of being used for more purposes and having simpler menu functionality.

A third route to a differentiation-based competitive advantage is to incorporate *intangible* features that enhance buyer satisfaction in noneconomic ways. Toyota's Prius and GM's Chevy Bolt appeal to environmentally conscious motorists not only because these drivers want to help reduce global carbon dioxide emissions but also because they identify with the image conveyed. Bentley, Ralph Lauren, Louis Vuitton, Burberry, Cartier, and Coach have differentiation-based competitive advantages linked to buyer desires for status, image, prestige, upscale fashion, superior craftsmanship, and the finer things in life. Intangibles that contribute to differentiation can extend beyond product attributes to the reputation of the company and to customer relations or trust.

> Differentiation can be based on *tangible* or *intangible* attributes.

The fourth route is to *signal the value* of the company's product offering to buyers. The value of certain differentiating features is rather easy for buyers to detect, but in some instances buyers may have trouble assessing what their experience with the product will be. Successful differentiators go to great lengths to make buyers knowledgeable about a product's value and employ various signals of value. Typical signals of value include a high price (in instances where high price implies high quality and performance), more appealing or fancier packaging than competing products, ad content that emphasizes a product's standout attributes, the quality of brochures and sales presentations, and the luxuriousness and ambience of a seller's facilities. The nature of a company's facilities are important for high-end retailers and other types of companies whose facilities are frequented by customers; they make potential buyers aware of the professionalism, appearance, and personalities of the seller's employees and/or make potential buyers realize that a company has prestigious customers. Signaling value is particularly important (1) when the nature of differentiation is based on intangible features and is therefore subjective or hard to quantify, (2) when buyers are making a first-time purchase and are unsure what their experience with the product will be, (3) when repurchase is infrequent, and (4) when buyers are unsophisticated.

Regardless of the approach taken, achieving a successful differentiation strategy requires, first, that the company have capabilities in areas such as customer service, marketing, brand management, and technology that can create and support differentiation. That is, the resources, competencies, and value chain activities of the company must be well matched to the requirements of the strategy. For the strategy to result in competitive advantage, the company's competencies must also be sufficiently unique in delivering value to buyers that they help set its product offering apart from those of rivals. They must be competitively superior. There are numerous examples of companies that have differentiated themselves on the basis of distinctive capabilities. Health care facilities like M.D. Anderson, Mayo Clinic, and Cleveland Clinic have specialized expertise and equipment for treating certain diseases that most hospitals and health care providers cannot afford to emulate. When a major news event occurs, many people turn to Fox News and CNN because they have the capabilities to get reporters on the scene quickly, break away from their regular programming (without suffering a loss of advertising revenues associated with regular programming), and devote extensive air time to newsworthy stories.

> Easy-to-copy differentiating features cannot produce sustainable competitive advantage.

The most successful approaches to differentiation are those that are difficult for rivals to duplicate. Indeed, this is the route to a sustainable competitive advantage based on differentiation. While resourceful competitors can, in time, clone almost any tangible product attribute, socially complex intangible attributes such as company reputation, long-standing relationships with buyers, and image are much harder to imitate. Differentiation that creates switching costs that lock in buyers also provides a route to sustainable advantage. For example, if a buyer makes a substantial investment in learning to use one type of system, that buyer is less likely to switch to a competitor's system. (This has kept many users from switching away from Microsoft Office products, despite the fact that there are other applications with superior features.) As a rule, differentiation yields a longer-lasting and more profitable competitive edge when it is based on a well-established brand image, patent-protected product innovation, complex technical superiority, a reputation for superior product quality and reliability, relationship-based customer service, and unique competitive capabilities.

When a Differentiation Strategy Works Best

Differentiation strategies tend to work best in market circumstances where

- *Buyer needs and uses of the product are diverse.* Diverse buyer preferences allow industry rivals to set themselves apart with product attributes that appeal to particular buyers. For instance, the diversity of consumer preferences for menu selection, ambience, pricing, and customer service gives restaurants exceptionally wide latitude in creating a differentiated product offering. Other industries with diverse buyer needs include magazine publishing, automobile manufacturing, footwear, and kitchen appliances.

- *There are many ways to differentiate the product or service that have value to buyers.* Industries in which competitors have opportunities to add features to products and services are well suited to differentiation strategies. For example, hotel chains can differentiate on such features as location, size of room, range of guest services, in-hotel dining, and the quality and luxuriousness of bedding and furnishings. Similarly, cosmetics producers are able to differentiate based on prestige and image, formulations that fight the signs of aging, UV light protection, exclusivity of retail locations, the inclusion of antioxidants and natural ingredients, or prohibitions against animal testing. Basic commodities, such as chemicals, mineral deposits, and agricultural products, provide few opportunities for differentiation.

- *Few rival firms are following a similar differentiation approach.* The best differentiation approaches involve trying to appeal to buyers on the basis of attributes that rivals are not emphasizing. A differentiator encounters less head-to-head rivalry when it goes its own separate way in creating value and does not try to out-differentiate rivals on the very same attributes. When many rivals base their differentiation efforts on the same attributes, the most likely result is weak brand differentiation and "strategy overcrowding"—competitors end up chasing much the same buyers with much the same product offerings.

- *Technological change is fast-paced and competition revolves around rapidly evolving product features.* Rapid product innovation and frequent introductions of next-version products heighten buyer interest and provide space for companies to pursue distinct differentiating paths. In smartphones and wearable Internet devices, drones for hobbyists and commercial use, automobile lane detection sensors, and battery-powered cars, rivals are locked into an ongoing battle to set themselves apart by introducing the best next-generation products. Companies that fail to come up with new and improved products and distinctive performance features quickly lose out in the marketplace.

Pitfalls to Avoid in Pursuing a Differentiation Strategy

Differentiation strategies can fail for any of several reasons. *A differentiation strategy keyed to product or service attributes that are easily and quickly copied is always suspect.* Rapid imitation means that no rival achieves differentiation, since whenever one firm introduces some value-creating aspect that strikes the fancy of buyers, fast-following copycats quickly reestablish parity. This is why a firm must seek out sources of value creation that are time-consuming or burdensome for rivals to match if it hopes to use differentiation to win a sustainable competitive edge.

| Any differentiating feature that works well is a magnet for imitators. |

 Differentiation strategies can also falter when buyers see little value in the unique attributes of a company's product. Thus, even if a company succeeds in setting its product apart from those of rivals, its strategy can result in disappointing sales and profits if the product does not deliver adequate perceived value to buyers. Anytime many potential buyers look at a company's differentiated product offering with indifference, the company's differentiation strategy is in deep trouble.

 The third big pitfall is overspending on efforts to differentiate the company's product offering, thus eroding profitability. Company efforts to achieve differentiation nearly always raise costs—often substantially, since marketing and R&D are expensive undertakings. The key to profitable differentiation is either to keep the unit cost of achieving differentiation below the price premium that the differentiating attributes can command (thus increasing the profit margin per unit sold) or to offset thinner profit margins per unit by selling enough additional units to increase total profits. If a company goes overboard in pursuing costly differentiation, it could be saddled with unacceptably low profits or even losses.

> *Over-differentiating and overcharging are fatal differentiation strategy mistakes. A low-cost strategy can defeat a differentiation strategy when buyers are satisfied with a basic product and don't think "extra" attributes are worth a higher price.*

Other common mistakes in crafting a differentiation strategy include

- *Offering only trivial improvements in quality, service, or performance features vis-à-vis rivals' products.* Trivial differences between rivals' product offerings may not be visible or important to buyers. If a company wants to generate the fiercely loyal customer following needed to earn superior profits and open up a differentiation-based competitive advantage over rivals, then its strategy must result in *strong rather than weak product differentiation*. In markets where differentiators do no better than achieve weak product differentiation, customer loyalty is weak, the costs of brand switching are low, and no one company has enough of a differentiation edge to command a price premium over rival brands.

- *Over-differentiating so that product quality, features, or service levels exceed the needs of most buyers.* A dazzling array of features and options not only drives up product price but also runs the risk that many buyers will conclude that a less deluxe and lower-priced brand is a better value since they have little occasion to use the deluxe attributes.

- *Charging too high a price premium.* While buyers may be intrigued by a product's deluxe features, they may nonetheless see it as being overpriced relative to the value delivered by the differentiating attributes. A company must guard against turning off would-be buyers with what is perceived as "price gouging." Normally, the bigger the price premium for the differentiating extras, the harder it is to keep buyers from switching to the lower-priced offerings of competitors.

FOCUSED (OR MARKET NICHE) STRATEGIES

What sets focused strategies apart from broad low-cost and broad differentiation strategies is concentrated attention on a narrow piece of the total market. The target segment, or niche, can be in the form of a geographic segment (such as New England), or a customer segment (such as young urban creatives or "yuccies"), or a product segment (such as a class of models or some version of the overall product type). Community Coffee, the largest family-owned specialty coffee retailer in the United States, has a geographic focus on the state of Louisiana and communities across the Gulf of Mexico. Community holds only a small share of the national coffee market but has recorded sales in excess of $100 million and has won a strong following in the Southeastern United States. Examples of firms that concentrate on a well-defined market niche keyed to a particular product or buyer segment include Zipcar (hourly and daily car rental in urban areas), Airbnb and HomeAway (owner of VRBO) (by-owner lodging rental), Fox News Channel and HGTV (cable TV), Blue Nile (online jewelry), Tesla Motors (electric cars), and CGA, Inc. (a specialist in providing insurance to cover the cost of lucrative hole-in-one prizes at golf tournaments). Microbreweries, local bakeries, bed-and-breakfast inns, and retail boutiques have also scaled their operations to serve narrow or local customer segments.

A Focused Low-Cost Strategy

A focused low-cost strategy aims at securing a competitive advantage by serving buyers in the target market niche at a lower cost (and usually lower price) than those of rival competitors. This strategy has considerable attraction when a firm can lower costs significantly by limiting its customer base to a well-defined buyer segment. The avenues to achieving a cost advantage over rivals also serving the target market niche are the same as those for broad low-cost leadership—use the cost drivers to perform value chain activities more

Though diabetes is a manageable condition, it is the leading cause of death in Mexico. Over 14 million adults (14 percent of all adults) suffer from diabetes, 3.5 million cases remain undiagnosed, and more than 80,000 die due to related complications each year. The key driver behind this public health crisis is limited access to affordable, high-quality care. Approximately 90 percent of the population cannot access diabetes care due to financial and time constraints; private care can cost upwards of $1,000 USD per year (approximately 45 percent of Mexico's population has an annual income less than $2,000 USD) while average wait times alone at public clinics surpass five hours. Clinícas del Azúcar (CDA), however, is quickly scaling a solution that uses a *focused low-cost strategy* to provide affordable and convenient care to low-income patients.

By relentlessly focusing only on the needs of its target population, CDA has reduced the cost of diabetes care by more than 70 percent and clinic visit times by over 80 percent. The key has been the use of proprietary technology and a streamlined care system. First, CDA leverages evidence-based algorithms to diagnose patients for a fraction of the costs of traditional diagnostic tests. Similarly, its mobile outreach significantly reduces the costs of supporting patients in managing their diabetes after leaving CDA facilities. Second, CDA has redesigned the care process to implement a streamlined "patient process flow" that eliminates the need for multiple referrals to other care providers and brings together the necessary professionals and equipment into one facility. Consequently, CDA has become a one-stop shop for diabetes care, providing every aspect of diabetes treatment under one roof.

Rob Marmion/Shutterstock

The bottom line: CDA's cost structure allows it to keep its prices for diabetes treatment very low, saving patients both time and money. Patients choose from three different care packages, ranging from preventive to comprehensive care, paying an annual fee that runs between approximately $70 and $200 USD. Given this increase in affordability and convenience, CDA estimates that it has saved its patients over $2 million USD in medical costs and will soon increase access to affordable, high-quality care for 10 to 80 percent of the population. These results have attracted investment from major funders including Endeavor, Echoing Green, and the Clinton Global Initiative. As a result, CDA and others expect CDA to grow from five clinics serving approximately 5,000 patients to more than 50 clinics serving over 100,000 patients throughout Mexico by 2020.

Note: Developed with David B. Washer.

Sources: www.clinicasdelazucar.com; "Funding Social Enterprises Report," *Echoing Green,* June 2014; Jude Webber, "Mexico Sees Poverty Climb Despite Rise in Incomes," *Financial Times* online, July 2015, www.ft.com/intl/cms/s/3/98460bbc-31e1-11e5-8873-775ba7c2ea3d.html#axzz3zz8grtec; "Javier Lozano," Schwab Foundation for Social Entrepreneurship online, 2016, www.schwabfound.org/content/javier-lozano.

efficiently than rivals and search for innovative ways to bypass nonessential value chain activities. The only real difference between a broad low-cost strategy and a focused low-cost strategy is the size of the buyer group to which a company is appealing—the former involves a product offering that appeals to almost all buyer groups and market segments, whereas the latter aims at just meeting the needs of buyers in a narrow market segment.

Budget motel chains, like Motel 6, Sleep Inn, and Super 8, cater to price-conscious travelers who just want to pay for a clean, no-frills place to spend the night. Illustration Capsule 5.2 describes how Clinícas del Azúcar's focus on lowering the costs of diabetes care is allowing it to address a major health issue in Mexico.

Focused low-cost strategies are fairly common. Costco, BJ's, and Sam's Club sell large lots of goods at wholesale prices to small businesses and bargain-hunters. Producers of private-label goods are able to achieve low costs in product development, marketing, distribution, and advertising by concentrating on making generic items imitative of name-brand merchandise and selling directly to retail chains wanting a low-priced store brand. The Perrigo Company Plc has become a leading manufacturer of over-the-counter health care products and self-care, with 2018 sales of nearly $5 billion, by focusing on producing private-label brands for retailers such as Walmart, CVS, Walgreens, Rite Aid, and Safeway.

A Focused Differentiation Strategy

Focused differentiation strategies involve offering superior products or services tailored to the unique preferences and needs of a narrow, well-defined group of buyers. Successful use of a focused differentiation strategy depends on (1) the existence of a buyer segment that is looking for special product or service attributes and (2) a firm's ability to create a product or service offering that stands apart from that of rivals competing in the same target market niche.

Companies like Molton Brown in bath, body, and beauty products, Bugatti in high-performance automobiles, and Four Seasons Hotels in lodging employ successful differentiation-based focused strategies targeted at upscale buyers wanting products and services with world-class attributes. Indeed, most markets contain a buyer segment willing to pay a big price premium for the very finest items available, thus opening the strategic window for some competitors to pursue differentiation-based focused strategies aimed at the very top of the market pyramid. Whole Foods Market, which was acquired by Amazon in 2017, became the largest organic and natural foods supermarket chain in the United States by catering to health-conscious consumers who prefer organic, natural, minimally processed, and locally grown foods. Whole Foods prides itself on stocking the highest-quality organic and natural foods it can find; the company defines quality by evaluating the ingredients, freshness, taste, nutritive value, appearance, and safety of the products it carries. Illustration Capsule 5.3 describes how Canada Goose has become a popular winter apparel brand with a focused differentiation strategy.

When a Focused Low-Cost or Focused Differentiation Strategy Is Attractive

A focused strategy aimed at securing a competitive edge based on either low costs or differentiation becomes increasingly attractive as more of the following conditions are met:

- The target market niche is big enough to be profitable and offers good growth potential.
- Industry leaders have chosen not to compete in the niche—in which case focusers can avoid battling head to head against the industry's biggest and strongest competitors.
- It is costly or difficult for multisegment competitors to meet the specialized needs of niche buyers and at the same time satisfy the expectations of their mainstream customers.
- The industry has many different niches and segments, thereby allowing a focuser to pick the niche best suited to its resources and capabilities. Also, with more niches there is room for focusers to concentrate on different market segments and avoid competing in the same niche for the same customers.
- Few if any rivals are attempting to specialize in the same target segment—a condition that reduces the risk of segment overcrowding.

ILLUSTRATION
CAPSULE 5.3   Canada Goose's Focused Differentiation Strategy

Open up a winter edition of *People* and you will probably see photos of a celebrity sporting a Canada Goose parka. Recognizable by a distinctive red, white, and blue arm patch, the brand's parkas have been spotted on movie stars like Emma Stone and Bradley Cooper, on New York City streets, and on the cover of *Sports Illustrated*. Lately, Canada Goose has become extremely successful thanks to a focused differentiation strategy that enables it to thrive within its niche in the $1.2 trillion fashion industry. By targeting upscale buyers and providing a uniquely functional and stylish jacket, Canada Goose can charge nearly $1,000 per jacket and never need to put its products on sale.

While Canada Goose was founded in 1957, its recent transition to a focused differentiation strategy allowed it to rise to the top of the luxury parka market. In 2001, CEO Dani Reiss took control of the company and made two key decisions. First, he cut private-label and non-outerwear production in order to focus on the branded outerwear portion of Canada Goose's business. Second, Reiss decided to remain in Canada despite many North American competitors moving production to Asia to increase profit margins. Fortunately for him, these two strategy decisions have led directly to the company's current success. While other luxury brands, like Moncler, are priced similarly, no competitor's products fulfill the promise of handling harsh winter weather quite like a Canada Goose "Made in Canada" parka. The Canadian heritage, use of down sourced from rural Canada, real coyote fur (humanely trapped), and promise to provide warmth in sub-25°F

Galit Rodan/Bloomberg/Getty Images

temperatures have let Canada Goose break away from the pack when it comes to selling parkas. The company's distinctly Canadian product has made it a hit among buyers, which is reflected in the willingness to pay a steep premium for extremely high-quality and warm winter outerwear.

Since Canada Goose's shift to a focused differentiation strategy, the company has seen a boom in revenue and appeal across the globe. Prior to Reiss's strategic decisions in 2001, Canada Goose had annual revenue of about $3 million. Within a decade, the company had experienced over 4,000 percent growth in annual revenue; by the end of 2019, revenues from purchases in more than 50 countries had exceeded $830 million. At this pace, it looks like Canada Goose will remain a hot commodity as long as winter temperatures remain cold.

Note: Developed with Arthur J. Santry.

Sources: Drake Bennett, "How Canada Goose Parkas Migrated South," *Bloomberg Businessweek,* March 13, 2015, www.bloomberg.com; Hollie Shaw, "Canada Goose's Made-in-Canada Marketing Strategy Translates into Success," *Financial Post,* May 18, 2012, www.financialpost.com; "The Economic Impact of the Fashion Industry," *The Economist,* June 13, 2015, www.maloney.house.gov; and company website (accessed January 26, 2020).

The advantages of focusing a company's entire competitive effort on a single market niche are considerable, especially for smaller and medium-sized companies that may lack the breadth and depth of resources to tackle going after a broader customer base with a more complex set of needs. YouTube became a household name by concentrating on short video clips posted online. Papa John's, Little Caesars, and Domino's Pizza have created impressive businesses by focusing on the home delivery segment.

The Risks of a Focused Low-Cost or Focused Differentiation Strategy

Focusing carries several risks. One is the chance that competitors outside the niche will find effective ways to match the focused firm's capabilities in serving the target niche—perhaps by coming up with products or brands specifically designed to appeal to buyers in the target niche or by developing expertise and capabilities that offset the focuser's strengths. In the lodging business, large chains like Marriott and Hilton have launched multibrand strategies that allow them to compete effectively in several lodging segments simultaneously. Hilton has flagship hotels with a full complement of services and amenities that allow it to attract travelers and vacationers going to major resorts; it has Waldorf Astoria, Conrad Hotels & Resorts, Hilton Hotels & Resorts, and DoubleTree hotels that provide deluxe comfort and service to business and leisure travelers; it has Homewood Suites, Embassy Suites, and Home2 Suites designed as a "home away from home" for travelers staying five or more nights; and it has nearly 700 Hilton Garden Inn and 2,100 Hampton by Hilton locations that cater to travelers looking for quality lodging at an "affordable" price. Tru by Hilton is the company's newly introduced brand focused on value-conscious travelers seeking basic accommodations. Hilton has also added Curio Collection, Tapestry Collection, and Canopy by Hilton hotels that offer stylish, distinctive decors and personalized services that appeal to young professionals seeking distinctive lodging alternatives. Multibrand strategies are attractive to large companies such as Hilton precisely because they enable a company to enter a market niche and siphon business away from companies that employ a focus strategy.

A second risk of employing a focused strategy is the potential for the preferences and needs of niche members to shift over time toward the product attributes desired by buyers in the mainstream portion of the market. An erosion of the differences across buyer segments lowers entry barriers into a focuser's market niche and provides an open invitation for rivals in adjacent segments to begin competing for the focuser's customers. A third risk is that the segment may become so attractive that it is soon inundated with competitors, intensifying rivalry and splintering segment profits. And there is always the risk for segment growth to slow to such a small rate that a focuser's prospects for future sales and profit gains become unacceptably dim.

BEST-COST (HYBRID) STRATEGIES

To profitably employ a best-cost strategy, a company *must have the capability to incorporate upscale attributes into its product offering at a lower cost than rivals.* When a company can incorporate more appealing features, good to excellent product performance or quality, or more satisfying customer service into its product offering *at a lower cost than rivals,* then it enjoys "best-cost" status—it is the low-cost provider of a product or service with *upscale attributes.* A best-cost producer can use its low-cost advantage to underprice rivals whose products or services have similarly upscale attributes and still earn attractive profits. As Figure 5.1 indicates, **best-cost strategies** are a hybrid of low-cost and differentiation strategies, incorporating features of both simultaneously. They may address either a broad or narrow (focused) customer base. This permits companies to aim squarely at the sometimes great mass of value-conscious buyers looking for a better product or service at a somewhat lower price. Value-conscious buyers frequently shy away from both cheap low-end products and expensive high-end products, but they are quite willing to pay a "fair" price for extra features and functionality they find appealing and useful. The essence of a best-cost strategy is giving customers *more value for the money* by satisfying buyer desires for appealing features and charging a lower price for these attributes compared to rivals with similar-caliber product offerings.[6]

A best-cost strategy is different from a low-cost strategy because the additional attractive attributes entail additional costs (which a low-cost producer can avoid by offering buyers a basic product with few frills). Moreover, the two strategies aim at a distinguishably different market target. *The target market for a best-cost producer is value-conscious buyers*—buyers who are looking for appealing extras and functionality at a comparatively low price, regardless of whether they represent a broad or more focused segment of the market. Value-hunting buyers (as distinct from *price-conscious buyers* looking for a basic product at a bargain-basement price) often constitute a very sizable part of the overall market for a product or service. A best-cost strategy differs from a differentiation strategy because it entails the ability to produce upscale features at a lower cost than other high-end producers. This implies the ability to profitably offer the buyer more value for the money.

Best-cost producers need not offer the highest end products and services (although they may); often the quality levels are simply better than average. Positioning of this sort permits companies to aim squarely at the sometimes great mass of value-conscious buyers looking for a better product or service at an economical price. Value-conscious buyers frequently shy away from both cheap low-end products and expensive high-end products, but they are quite willing to pay a "fair" price for extra features and functionality they find appealing and useful. The essence of a best-cost strategy is the ability to provide *more value for the money* by satisfying buyer desires for better quality while charging a lower price compared to rivals with similar-caliber product offerings.

Toyota has employed a classic best-cost strategy for its Lexus line of motor vehicles. It has designed an array of high-performance characteristics and upscale features into its Lexus models to make them comparable in performance and luxury to Mercedes, BMW, Audi, Jaguar, Cadillac, and Lincoln models. To signal its positioning in the luxury market segment, Toyota established a network of Lexus dealers, separate from Toyota dealers, dedicated to providing exceptional customer service. Most important, though, Toyota has drawn on its considerable know-how in making high-quality vehicles at low cost to produce its high-tech upscale-quality Lexus models at substantially lower costs than other luxury vehicle makers have been able to achieve in producing their models. To capitalize on its lower manufacturing costs, Toyota prices its Lexus models below those of comparable Mercedes, BMW, Audi, and Jaguar models to induce value-conscious luxury car buyers to purchase a Lexus instead. The price differential has typically been quite significant. For example, in 2017, a well-equipped Lexus RX 350 (a midsized SUV) had a sticker price of $54,370, whereas the sticker price of a comparably equipped Mercedes GLE-class SUV was $62,770 and the sticker price of a comparably equipped BMW X5 SUV was $66,670.

When a Best-Cost Strategy Works Best

A best-cost strategy works best in markets where product differentiation is the norm and an attractively large number of value-conscious buyers can be induced to purchase midrange products rather than cheap, basic products or expensive, top-of-the-line products. In markets such as these, a best-cost producer needs to position itself *near the*

● **LO 5-4**

Explain the attributes of a best-cost strategy—a hybrid of low-cost and differentiation strategies.

Trader Joe's Focused Best-Cost Strategy

Over the last 50 years, Trader Joe's has built a cult-like following by offering a limited selection of highly popular private-label products at great prices, under the Trader Joe's brand. By pursuing a *focused best-cost* strategy, Trader Joe's has been able to thrive in the notoriously low-margin grocery business. Today, Trader Joe's earns over $2,000 of annual sales per square foot—nearly double that of Whole Foods.

One key to Trader Joe's success, and a major part of its strategy, is its unique approach to product selection. By selling mainly private label goods under its own brand, Trader Joe's keeps its costs low, enabling it to offer lower prices. By being very selective about the particular products that it carries, it has also managed to ensure that its brand is associated with very high quality. The company's policy is to swiftly replace any product that does not prove popular with another more appealing product. This has paid off: when you ask U.S. consumers which grocery store represents quality, Trader Joe's tops the list. On a recent YouGov Brand Index poll, nearly 40 percent of consumers ranked Trader Joe's best for quality—the highest among its competitors. While Trader Joe's offers far fewer stock-keeping units (SKUs) than a typical grocery store—only 4,000 SKUs as compared to 50,000 + in a Kroger or Safeway—the upside for customers is that this also helps to keep costs and prices low. It results in higher inventory turns (a key measure of efficiency in retail), lower inventory costs, and lower rents since stores in any given location can be smaller.

Ken Wolter/Shutterstock

Trader Joe's also intentionally locates its stores in areas with value-focused customers who appreciate quality. Trader Joe's identifies potential sites for expansion by evaluating demographic information. This enables Trader Joe's to focus on serving young educated singles and couples who may not be able to afford more expensive groceries but prefer organics and ready-to-eat products. Given that it occupies smaller sized retail spaces, Trader Joe's can locate in walkable areas and urban centers, the very same neighborhoods in which its chosen customer base lives. Because of its focused best-cost strategy, it is unlikely that the company's loyal customers will quit lining up to buy its tasty corn salsa or organic cold brew coffee any time soon.

Note: Developed with Stephanie K. Berger.

Sources: Company website; Beth Kowitt, "Inside the Secret World of Trader Joe's," *Fortune* (August 2010); Elain Watson, "Quirky, Cult-life, Aspirational, but Affordable: The Rise and Rise of Trader Joes," Food Navigator USA (April 2014; Janie Ryan, "The Surprising Secrets Behind Trader Joe's Supply Chain", Elementum.com, (December 13, 2018).

middle of the market with either a medium-quality product at a below-average price or a high-quality product at an average or slightly higher price. But as the Lexus example shows, a firm with the capabilities to produce top-of-the-line products more efficiently than its rivals, would also do well to pursue a best-cost strategy. Best-cost strategies also work well in recessionary times, when masses of buyers become more value-conscious and are attracted to economically priced products and services with more appealing attributes. However, unless a company has the resources, know-how, and capabilities to incorporate upscale product or service attributes at a lower cost than rivals, adopting a best-cost strategy is ill-advised. Illustration Capsule 5.4 describes how Trader Joe's has applied the principles of a focused best-cost strategy to thrive in the competitive grocery store industry.

The Risk of a Best-Cost Strategy

A company's biggest vulnerability in employing a best-cost strategy is getting squeezed between the strategies of firms using low-cost and high-end differentiation strategies. Low-cost producers may be able to siphon customers away with the appeal of a lower price (despite less appealing product attributes). High-end differentiators may be able to steal customers away with the appeal of better product attributes (even though their products carry a higher price tag). Thus, to be successful, a firm employing a best-cost strategy must achieve significantly lower costs in providing upscale features so that it can outcompete high-end differentiators on the basis of a *significantly* lower price. Likewise, it must offer buyers *significantly* better product attributes to justify a price above what low-cost leaders are charging. In other words, it must offer buyers a more attractive customer value proposition.

THE CONTRASTING FEATURES OF THE GENERIC COMPETITIVE STRATEGIES

Deciding which generic competitive strategy should serve as the framework on which to hang the rest of the company's strategy is not a trivial matter. Each of the five generic competitive strategies *positions* the company differently in its market and competitive environment. Each establishes a *central theme* for how the company will endeavor to outcompete rivals. Each creates some boundaries or guidelines for maneuvering as market circumstances unfold and as ideas for improving the strategy are debated. Each entails differences in terms of product line, production emphasis, marketing emphasis, and means of maintaining the strategy, as shown in Table 5.1.

> A company's competitive strategy should be well matched to its internal situation and predicated on leveraging its collection of competitively valuable resources and capabilities.

Thus, a choice of which generic strategy to employ spills over to affect many aspects of how the business will be operated and the manner in which value chain activities must be managed. Deciding which generic strategy to employ is perhaps the most important strategic commitment a company makes—it tends to drive the rest of the strategic actions a company decides to undertake.

Successful Generic Strategies Are Resource-Based

For a company's competitive strategy to succeed in delivering good performance and gain a competitive edge over rivals, it has to be well matched to a company's internal situation and underpinned by an appropriate set of resources, know-how, and competitive capabilities. To succeed in employing a low-cost strategy, a company must have the resources and capabilities to keep its costs below those of its competitors. This means having the expertise to cost-effectively manage value chain activities better than rivals by leveraging the cost drivers more effectively, and/or having the innovative capability to bypass certain value chain activities being performed by rivals. To succeed in a differentiation strategy, a company must have the resources and capabilities to leverage value drivers more effectively than rivals and incorporate attributes into its product offering that a broad range of buyers will find appealing. Successful focus strategies (both low cost and differentiation) require the capability to do an outstanding job of satisfying the needs and expectations of niche buyers. Success in employing a best-cost strategy requires the resources and capabilities to incorporate upscale product or service attributes at a lower cost than rivals. *For all types of generic strategies, success in sustaining the competitive edge depends on having resources and capabilities that rivals have trouble duplicating and for which there are no good substitutes.*

TABLE 5.1 Distinguishing Features of the Five Generic Competitive Strategies

	Broad Low-Cost	Broad Differentiation	Focused Low-Cost	Focused Differentiation	Best-Cost
Strategic target	• A broad cross-section of the market.	• A broad cross-section of the market.	• A narrow market niche where buyer needs and preferences are distinctively different.	• A narrow market niche where buyer needs and preferences are distinctively different.	• A broad or narrow range of value-conscious buyers.
Basis of competitive strategy	• Lower overall costs than competitors.	• Ability to offer buyers something attractively different from competitors' offerings.	• Lower overall cost than rivals in serving niche members.	• Attributes that appeal specifically to niche members.	• Ability to incorporate upscale features and attributes at lower costs than rivals.
Product line	• A good basic product with few frills (acceptable quality and limited selection).	• Many product variations, wide selection; emphasis on differentiating features.	• Features and attributes tailored to the tastes and requirements of niche members.	• Features and attributes tailored to the tastes and requirements of niche members.	• Items with appealing attributes and assorted features; better quality, not necessarily best.
Production emphasis	• A continuous search for cost reduction without sacrificing acceptable quality and essential features.	• Build in whatever differentiating features buyers are willing to pay for; strive for product superiority.	• A continuous search for cost reduction for products that meet basic needs of niche members.	• Small-scale production or custom-made products that match the tastes and requirements of niche members.	• Build in appealing features and better quality at lower cost than rivals.
Marketing emphasis	• Low prices, good value. • Try to make a virtue out of product features that lead to low cost.	• Tout differentiating features. • Charge a premium price to cover the extra costs of differentiating features.	• Communicate attractive features of a budget-priced product offering that fits niche buyers' expectations.	• Communicate how product offering does the best job of meeting niche buyers' expectations.	• Emphasize delivery of best value for the money.
Keys to maintaining the strategy	• Strive to manage costs down, year after year, in every area of the business.	• Stress continuous improvement in products or services and constant innovation to stay ahead of imitative competitors.	• Stay committed to serving the niche at the lowest overall cost; don't blur the firm's image by entering other market segments or adding other products to widen market appeal.	• Stay committed to serving the niche better than rivals; don't blur the firm's image by entering other market segments or adding other products to widen market appeal.	• Stress continuous improvement in products or services and constant innovation, along with continuous efforts to improve efficiency.
Resources and capabilities required	• Capabilities for driving costs out of the value chain system. • *Examples:* large-scale automated plants, an efficiency-oriented culture, bargaining power.	• Capabilities concerning quality, design, intangibles, and innovation. • *Examples:* marketing capabilities, R&D teams, technology.	• Capabilities to lower costs on niche goods. • *Examples:* lower input costs for the specific product desired by the niche, batch production capabilities.	• Capabilities to meet the highly specific needs of niche members. • *Examples:* custom production, close customer relations.	• Capabilities to simultaneously deliver lower cost and higher-quality/differentiated features. • *Examples:* TQM practices, mass customization.

150

Generic Strategies and the Three Different Approaches to Competitive Advantage

Just as a company's resources and capabilities underlie its choice of generic strategy, its generic strategy determines its approach to gaining a competitive advantage. There are three such approaches. Clearly, low-cost strategies aim for a cost advantage over rivals, differentiation strategies strive to create relatively more perceived value for consumers, while best-cost strategies aim to do better than the average rival on both dimensions. Whether the strategy is broad based or focused makes no difference as to the basic approach employed (see Figure 5.1).

Exactly how this works is best understood with the use of the value-price-cost framework, first introduced in Chapter 1 in the context of different kinds of business models. Figure 5.4 illustrates the three basic approaches to competitive advantage in terms of the value-price-cost framework. The left figure in the diagram represents an average competitor's cost (C) of producing a good, how highly the customer values it (V), and its price (P). The difference between the good's value to the customer (V) and its cost (C) is the total economic value (V-C) produced by the average competitor. And as explained in Chapter 4, a company has a competitive advantage over another if its strategy generates *more total economic value.* It is this excess in total economic value over rivals that allows the company to offer customers a better value proposition or earn larger profits (or both). The dashed yellow lines facilitate a comparison of the average competitor's costs (C) and perceived value (V) with the costs and value produced by each of the three basic types of generic strategies (low cost, differentiation, best cost). In this way, it also facilitates a comparison of the total economic value generated by each of the three representative generic strategies in relation to the average competitor, thereby shedding light on the nature of each strategy's competitive advantage.

FIGURE 5.4   Three Approaches to Competitive Advantage and the Value-Price-Cost Framework

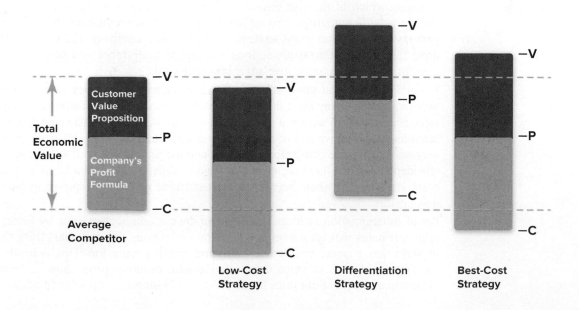

As Figure 5.4 shows, a low-cost generic strategy aims to achieve lower costs than an average competitor, at the sacrifice of some of the perceived value to the consumer. If the decrease in costs is less than the decrease in perceived value, then the total economic value (V-C) for the low-cost leader will be greater than the total economic value produced by its average rival and the low-cost leader will have a competitive advantage. This is clearly the case for the example of a low-cost strategy depicted in Figure 5.4. As is common with low-cost strategies, the example company has chosen to charge a lower price than its average rival. The result is that even with a lower V, the low-cost leader offers the consumer a more attractive (larger) consumer value proposition (depicted in mauve) and finds itself with a better profit formula (depicted in blue).

In contrast, the example of a differentiation strategy shows that costs might well exceed those of the average competitor. But with a successful differentiation strategy, that disadvantage is more than made up for by the rise in the perceived value (V) of the differentiated good, giving the differentiator a clear competitive advantage over the average rival (greater V-C). And while the price charged in this example is a good deal higher in comparison with the average rival's price, this differentiation strategy enables both a larger consumer value proposition (in mauve) as well as greater profits (in blue).

The depiction of a best-cost strategy shows a company pursuing the middle ground of offering neither the most highly valued goods in the market nor the lowest costs. But in comparison with the average rival, it does better on both scores, resulting in more total economic value (V-C) and a substantial competitive advantage. Once again, the example shows both a larger customer value proposition as well as a more attractive profit formula.

The last thing to note is that the generic strategies depicted in Figure 5.4 are examples of *successful* generic strategies. Being successful with a generic strategy depends on much more than positioning. It depends on the competitive context (the company's external situation) and on the company's internal situation, including its complement of resources and capabilities. Importantly, it also depends on how well the strategy is executed—the topic of this text's three concluding chapters.

KEY POINTS

1. Deciding which of the five generic competitive strategies to employ—broad low-cost, broad differentiation, focused low-cost, focused differentiation, or best-cost—is perhaps the most important strategic commitment a company makes. It tends to drive the remaining strategic actions a company undertakes and sets the whole tone for pursuing a competitive advantage over rivals.

2. In employing a broad low-cost strategy and trying to achieve a low-cost advantage over rivals, a company must do a better job than rivals of cost-effectively managing value chain activities and/or it must find innovative ways to eliminate cost-producing activities. An effective use of cost drivers is key. Low-cost strategies work particularly well when price competition is strong and the products of rival sellers are virtually identical, when there are not many ways to differentiate, when buyer switching costs are low, and when buyers are price-sensitive or have the power to bargain down prices.

3. Broad differentiation strategies seek to produce a competitive edge by incorporating attributes that set a company's product or service offering apart from rivals in ways that buyers consider valuable and worth paying for. This depends on the appropriate use of value drivers. Successful differentiation allows a firm to (1) command a premium price for its product, (2) increase unit sales (if additional

buyers are won over by the differentiating features), and/or (3) gain buyer loyalty to its brand (because some buyers are strongly attracted to the differentiating features and bond with the company and its products). Differentiation strategies work best when buyers have diverse product preferences, when few other rivals are pursuing a similar differentiation approach, and when technological change is fast-paced and competition centers on rapidly evolving product features. A differentiation strategy is doomed when competitors are able to quickly copy the appealing product attributes, when a company's differentiation efforts fail to interest many buyers, and when a company overspends on efforts to differentiate its product offering or tries to overcharge for its differentiating extras.

4. A focused strategy delivers competitive advantage either by achieving lower costs than rivals in serving buyers constituting the target market niche or by developing a specialized ability to offer niche buyers an appealingly differentiated offering that meets their needs better than rival brands do. A focused strategy based on either low cost or differentiation becomes increasingly attractive when the target market niche is big enough to be profitable and offers good growth potential, when it is costly or difficult for multisegment competitors to meet the specialized needs of the target market niche and at the same time satisfy the expectations of their mainstream customers, when there are one or more niches that present a good match for a focuser's resources and capabilities, and when few other rivals are attempting to specialize in the same target segment.

5. Best-cost strategies create competitive advantage on the basis of their capability to incorporate attractive or upscale attributes at a lower cost than rivals. Best-cost strategies can be either broad or focused. A best-cost strategy works best in broad or narrow market segments with value-conscious buyers desirous of purchasing better products and services for less money.

6. In all cases, competitive advantage depends on having competitively superior resources and capabilities that are a good fit for the chosen generic strategy. A sustainable advantage depends on maintaining that competitive superiority with resources, capabilities, and value chain activities that rivals have trouble matching and for which there are no good substitutes.

ASSURANCE OF LEARNING EXERCISES

1. Best Buy is the largest consumer electronics retailer in the United States, with fiscal 2019 sales of nearly $43 billion. The company competes aggressively on price with such rivals as Costco, Sam's Club, Walmart, and Target, but it is also known by consumers for its first-rate customer service. Best Buy customers have commented that the retailer's sales staff is exceptionally knowledgeable about the company's products and can direct them to the exact location of difficult-to-find items. Best Buy customers also appreciate that demonstration models of PC monitors, digital media players, and other electronics are fully powered and ready for in-store use. Best Buy's Geek Squad tech support and installation services are additional customer service features that are valued by many customers.

LO 5-1, LO 5-2, LO 5-3, LO 5-4

How would you characterize Best Buy's competitive strategy? Should it be classified as a low-cost strategy? A differentiation strategy? A best-cost strategy? Also, has the company chosen to focus on a narrow piece of the market, or does it appear to pursue a broad market approach? Explain your answer.

LO 5-2

2. Illustration Capsule 5.1 discusses Vanguard's position as the low-cost leader in the investment management industry. Based on information provided in the capsule, explain how Vanguard built its low-cost advantage in the industry and why a low-cost strategy can succeed in the industry.

LO 5-1, LO 5-2, LO 5-3, LO 5-4

3. USAA is a Fortune 500 insurance and financial services company with 2018 annual sales exceeding $30 billion. The company was founded in 1922 by 25 Army officers who decided to insure each other's vehicles and continues to limit its membership to active-duty and retired military members, officer candidates, and adult children and spouses of military-affiliated USAA members. The company has received countless awards, including being listed among *Fortune*'s World's Most Admired Companies in 2014 through 2019 and 100 Best Companies to Work For in 2010 through 2019. You can read more about the company's history and strategy at **www.usaa.com.**

   How would you characterize USAA's competitive strategy? Should it be classified as a low-cost strategy? A differentiation strategy? A best-cost strategy? Also, has the company chosen to focus on a narrow piece of the market, or does it appear to pursue a broad market approach? Explain your answer.

LO 5-3

4. Explore Kendra Scott's website at **www.kendrascott.com** and see if you can identify at least three ways in which the company seeks to differentiate itself from rival jewelry firms. Is there reason to believe that Kendra Scott's differentiation strategy has been successful in producing a competitive advantage? Why or why not?

EXERCISES FOR SIMULATION PARTICIPANTS

LO 5-1, LO 5-2, LO 5-3, LO 5-4

1. Which one of the five generic competitive strategies can best be utilized to compete successfully in the business simulation by your company?

2. Which rival companies appear to be employing a low-cost strategy?

3. Which rival companies appear to be employing a differentiation strategy?

4. Which rival companies appear to be employing a best-cost strategy?

5. Which cost drivers and/or value drivers are important for creating superior total economic value in the business simulation?

6. What is your company's action plan to achieve a sustainable competitive advantage over rival companies? List at least three (preferably more than three) specific kinds of decision entries on specific decision screens that your company has made or intends to make to win this kind of competitive edge over rivals.

ENDNOTES   ● ● ● ●

[1] Michael E. Porter, *Competitive Strategy: Techniques for Analyzing Industries and Competitors* (New York: Free Press, 1980), chap. 2; Michael E. Porter, "What Is Strategy?" *Harvard Business Review* 74, no. 6 (November–December 1996).
[2] Michael E. Porter, *Competitive Advantage: Creating and Sustaining Superior Performance* (New York: Free Press, 1985).

[3] Richard L. Priem, "A Consumer Perspective on Value Creation," *Academy of Management Review* 32, no. 1 (2007), pp. 219–235.
[4] **jrscience.wcp.muohio.edu/nsfall01/FinalArticles/Final-IsitWorthitBrandsan.html.**
[5] D. Yoffie, "Cola Wars Continue: Coke and Pepsi in 2006," Harvard Business School case 9-706-447.

[6] Peter J. Williamson and Ming Zeng, "Value-for-Money Strategies for Recessionary Times," *Harvard Business Review* 87, no. 3 (March 2009), pp. 66–74.

chapter 6

Strengthening a Company's Competitive Position

Strategic Moves, Timing, and Scope of Operations

Learning Objectives

After reading this chapter, you should be able to:

LO 6-1 Understand whether, how, and when to deploy offensive or defensive strategic moves.

LO 6-2 Identify when being a first mover, a fast follower, or a late mover is most advantageous.

LO 6-3 Explain the strategic benefits and risks of expanding a company's horizontal scope through mergers and acquisitions.

LO 6-4 Explain the advantages and disadvantages of extending the company's scope of operations via vertical integration.

LO 6-5 Recognize the conditions that favor farming out certain value chain activities to outside parties.

LO 6-6 Understand how to capture the benefits and minimize the drawbacks of strategic alliances and partnerships.

Fanatic Studio/Getty Images

Whenever you look at any potential merger or acquisition, you look at the potential to create value for your shareholders.

Dilip Shanghvi—*Founder and managing director of Sun Pharmaceuticals*

Alliances have become an integral part of contemporary strategic thinking.

Fortune Magazine

The important thing about outsourcing . . . is that it becomes a very powerful tool to leverage talent, improve productivity, and reduce work cycles.

Azim Premji—*Chairman of Wipro Limited (India's third-largest outsourcer)*

Once a company has settled on which of the five generic competitive strategies to employ, attention turns to what *other strategic actions* it can take to complement its competitive approach and maximize the power of its overall strategy. The first set of decisions concerns whether to undertake offensive or defensive competitive moves, and the timing of such moves. The second set concerns expanding or contracting the breadth of a company's activities (or its *scope* of operations along an industry's entire value chain). All in all, the following measures to strengthen a company's competitive position must be considered:

- Whether to go on the offensive and initiate aggressive strategic moves to improve the company's market position.
- Whether to employ defensive strategies to protect the company's market position.

- When to undertake new strategic initiatives—whether advantage or disadvantage lies in being a first mover, a fast follower, or a late mover.
- Whether to bolster the company's market position by merging with or acquiring another company in the same industry.
- Whether to integrate backward or forward into more stages of the industry value chain system.
- Which value chain activities, if any, should be outsourced.
- Whether to enter into strategic alliances or partnership arrangements with other enterprises.

This chapter presents the pros and cons of each of these strategy-enhancing measures.

LAUNCHING STRATEGIC OFFENSIVES TO IMPROVE A COMPANY'S MARKET POSITION

● ● ● ●

● **LO 6-1**

Understand whether, how, and when to deploy offensive or defensive strategic moves.

No matter which of the five generic competitive strategies a firm employs, there are times when a company should *go on the offensive* to improve its market position and performance. **Strategic offensives** are called for when a company spots opportunities to gain profitable market share at its rivals' expense or when a company has no choice but to try to whittle away at a strong rival's competitive advantage. Companies like Facebook, Amazon, Apple, and Google play hardball, aggressively pursuing competitive advantage and trying to reap the benefits a competitive edge offers—a leading market share, excellent profit margins, and rapid growth.[1] The best offensives tend to incorporate several principles: (1) focusing relentlessly on building competitive advantage and then striving to convert it into a sustainable advantage, (2) applying resources where rivals are least able to defend themselves, (3) employing the element of surprise as opposed to doing what rivals expect and are prepared for, and (4) displaying a capacity for swift and decisive actions to overwhelm rivals.[2]

Choosing the Basis for Competitive Attack

Sometimes a company's best strategic option is to seize the initiative, go on the attack, and launch a strategic offensive to improve its market position.

As a rule, challenging rivals on competitive grounds where they are strong is an uphill struggle.[3] Offensive initiatives that exploit competitor weaknesses stand a better chance of succeeding than do those that challenge competitor strengths, especially if the weaknesses represent important vulnerabilities and weak rivals can be caught by surprise with no ready defense.

Strategic offensives should exploit the power of a company's strongest competitive assets—its most valuable resources and capabilities such as a better-known brand name, a more efficient production or distribution system, greater technological capability, or a superior reputation for quality. But a consideration of the company's strengths should not be made without also considering the rival's strengths and weaknesses. A strategic offensive should be based on those areas of strength where the company has its greatest competitive advantage over the targeted rivals.

The best offensives use a company's most powerful resources and capabilities to attack rivals in the areas where they are competitively weakest.

If a company has especially good customer service capabilities, it can make special sales pitches to the customers of those rivals that provide subpar customer service. Likewise, it may be beneficial to pay special attention to buyer segments that a rival is neglecting or is weakly equipped to serve. The best offensives use a company's most powerful resources and capabilities to attack rivals in the areas where they are weakest.

Ignoring the need to tie a strategic offensive to a company's competitive strengths and what it does best is like going to war with a popgun—the prospects for success are dim. For instance, it is foolish for a company with relatively high costs to employ a price-cutting offensive. Likewise, it is ill-advised to pursue a product innovation offensive without having proven expertise in R&D and new product development.

The principal offensive strategy options include the following:

1. *Offering an equally good or better product at a lower price.* Lower prices can produce market share gains if competitors don't respond with price cuts of their own and if the challenger convinces buyers that its product is just as good or better. However, such a strategy increases total profits only if the gains in additional unit sales are enough to offset the impact of thinner margins per unit sold. Price-cutting offensives should be initiated only by companies that have *first achieved a cost advantage.*[4] British airline EasyJet used this strategy successfully against rivals such as

British Air, Alitalia, and Air France by first cutting costs to the bone and then targeting leisure passengers who care more about low price than in-flight amenities and service.[5] Spirit Airlines is using this strategy in the U.S. airline market.

2. *Leapfrogging competitors by being first to market with next-generation products.* In technology-based industries, the opportune time to overtake an entrenched competitor is when there is a shift to the next generation of the technology. Eero got its whole-home Wi-Fi system to market nearly one year before Linksys and Netgear developed competing systems, helping it build a sizable market share and develop a reputation for cutting-edge innovation in Wi-Fi systems.

3. *Pursuing continuous product innovation to draw sales and market share away from less innovative rivals.* Ongoing introductions of new and improved products can put rivals under tremendous competitive pressure, especially when rivals' new product development capabilities are weak. But such offensives can be sustained only if a company can keep its pipeline full with new product offerings that spark buyer enthusiasm.

4. *Pursuing disruptive product innovations to create new markets.* While this strategy can be riskier and more costly than a strategy of continuous innovation, it can be a game changer if successful. Disruptive innovation involves perfecting a new product with a few trial users and then quickly rolling it out to the whole market in an attempt to get many buyers to embrace an altogether new and better value proposition quickly. Examples include online universities, Twitter, Venmo, CampusBookRentals, and Waymo (Alphabet's self-driving tech company).

5. *Adopting and improving on the good ideas of other companies (rivals or otherwise).* The idea of warehouse-type home improvement centers did not originate with Home Depot cofounders Arthur Blank and Bernie Marcus; they got the "big-box" concept from their former employer, Handy Dan Home Improvement. But they were quick to improve on Handy Dan's business model and take Home Depot to the next plateau in terms of product-line breadth and customer service. Offensive-minded companies are often quick to adopt any good idea (not nailed down by a patent or other legal protection) and build on it to create competitive advantage for themselves.

6. *Using hit-and-run or guerrilla warfare tactics to grab market share from complacent or distracted rivals.* Options for "guerrilla offensives" include occasionally lowballing on price (to win a big order or steal a key account from a rival), surprising rivals with sporadic but intense bursts of promotional activity (offering a discounted trial offer to draw customers away from rival brands), or undertaking special campaigns to attract the customers of rivals plagued with a strike or problems in meeting buyer demand.[6] Guerrilla offensives are particularly well suited to small challengers that have neither the resources nor the market visibility to mount a full-fledged attack on industry leaders.

7. *Launching a preemptive strike to secure an industry's limited resources or capture a rare opportunity.*[7] What makes a move preemptive is its one-of-a-kind nature—whoever strikes first stands to acquire competitive assets that rivals can't readily match. Examples of preemptive moves include (1) securing the best distributors in a particular geographic region or country; (2) obtaining the most favorable site at a new interchange or intersection, in a new shopping mall, and so on; (3) tying up the most reliable, high-quality suppliers via exclusive partnerships, long-term contracts, or acquisition; and (4) moving swiftly to acquire the assets of distressed rivals at bargain prices. To be successful, a preemptive move doesn't have to totally block rivals from following; it merely needs to give a firm a prime position that is not easily circumvented.

How long it takes for an offensive action to yield good results varies with the competitive circumstances.[8] It can be short if buyers respond immediately (as can occur with a dramatic cost-based price cut, an imaginative ad campaign, or a disruptive innovation). Securing a competitive edge can take much longer if winning consumer acceptance of the company's product will take some time or if the firm may need several years to debug a new technology or put a new production capacity in place. But how long it takes for an offensive move to improve a company's market standing—and whether the move will prove successful—depends in part on whether market rivals recognize the threat and begin a counterresponse. Whether rivals will respond depends on whether they are capable of making an effective response and if they believe that a counterattack is worth the expense and the distraction.[9]

Choosing Which Rivals to Attack

Offensive-minded firms need to analyze which of their rivals to challenge as well as how to mount the challenge. The following are the best targets for offensive attacks:[10]

- *Market leaders that are vulnerable.* Offensive attacks make good sense when a company that leads in terms of market share is not a true leader in terms of serving the market well. Signs of leader vulnerability include unhappy buyers, an inferior product line, aging technology or outdated plants and equipment, a preoccupation with diversification into other industries, and financial problems. Caution is well advised in challenging strong market leaders—there's a significant risk of squandering valuable resources in a futile effort or precipitating a fierce and profitless industrywide battle for market share.

- *Runner-up firms with weaknesses in areas where the challenger is strong.* Runner-up firms are an especially attractive target when a challenger's resources and capabilities are well suited to exploiting their weaknesses.

- *Struggling enterprises that are on the verge of going under.* Challenging a hard-pressed rival in ways that further sap its financial strength and competitive position can weaken its resolve and hasten its exit from the market. In this type of situation, it makes sense to attack the rival in the market segments where it makes the most profits, since this will threaten its survival the most.

- *Small local and regional firms with limited capabilities.* Because small firms typically have limited expertise and resources, a challenger with broader and/or deeper capabilities is well positioned to raid their biggest and best customers—particularly those that are growing rapidly, have increasingly sophisticated requirements, and may already be thinking about switching to a supplier with a more full-service capability.

Blue-Ocean Strategy—a Special Kind of Offensive

CORE CONCEPT

A blue-ocean strategy offers growth in revenues and profits by discovering or inventing new industry segments that create altogether new demand.

A **blue-ocean strategy** seeks to gain a dramatic competitive advantage by abandoning efforts to beat out competitors in existing markets and, instead, *inventing a new market segment that allows a company to create and capture altogether new demand.*[11] This strategy views the business universe as consisting of two distinct types of market space. One is where industry boundaries are well defined, the competitive rules of the game are understood, and companies try to outperform rivals by capturing a bigger share of existing demand. In such markets, intense competition constrains a company's prospects for rapid growth and superior profitability since rivals move quickly to either imitate or counter the successes of competitors. The second type of market space is a "blue ocean," where the industry does not really exist yet, is untainted by competition, and offers wide-open opportunity for profitable and rapid growth if a company can create new demand with a new type of product offering. The "blue ocean" represents wide-open opportunity, offering smooth sailing in uncontested waters for the company first to venture out upon it.

A terrific example of such blue-ocean market space is the online auction industry that eBay created and now dominates. Other companies that have created blue-ocean market spaces include NetJets in fractional jet ownership, Drybar in hair blowouts, Tune Hotels in limited service "backpacker" hotels, Uber and Lyft in ride-sharing services, and Cirque du Soleil in live entertainment. Cirque du Soleil "reinvented the circus" by pulling in a whole new group of customers—adults and corporate clients—who not only were noncustomers of traditional circuses (like Ringling Brothers) but also were willing to pay several times more than the price of a conventional circus ticket to have a "sophisticated entertainment experience" featuring stunning visuals and star-quality acrobatic acts. Australian winemaker Casella Wines used a blue ocean strategy to find some uncontested market space for its Yellow Tail brand. By creating a product designed to appeal to wider market—one that also includes beer and spirit drinkers—Yellow Tail was able to unlock substantial new demand, becoming the fastest growing wine brand in U.S. history. Illustration Capsule 6.1 discusses the way that Etsy used a blue ocean strategy to open up new competitive space in online retailing.

Blue-ocean strategies provide a company with a great opportunity in the short run but they don't guarantee a company's long-term success, which depends more on whether a company can protect the market position it opened up and sustain its early advantage. Gilt Groupe serves as an example of a company that opened up new competitive space in online luxury retailing only to see its blue-ocean waters ultimately turn red. Its competitive success early on prompted an influx of fast followers into the luxury flash-sale industry, including HauteLook, RueLaLa, Lot18, and MyHabit.com. The new rivals not only competed for online customers, who could switch costlessly from site to site (since memberships were free), but also competed for unsold designer inventory. Once valued at over $1 billion, Gilt Groupe was finally sold to Hudson's Bay, the owner of Sak's Fifth Avenue, for just $250 million in 2016.

DEFENSIVE STRATEGIES—PROTECTING MARKET POSITION AND COMPETITIVE ADVANTAGE

In a competitive market, all firms are subject to offensive challenges from rivals. The purposes of defensive strategies are to lower the risk of being attacked, weaken the impact of any attack that occurs, and induce challengers to aim their efforts at other rivals. While defensive strategies usually don't enhance a firm's competitive advantage, they can definitely help fortify the firm's competitive position, protect its most valuable resources and capabilities from imitation, and defend whatever competitive advantage it might have. Defensive strategies can take either of two forms: actions to block challengers or actions to signal the likelihood of strong retaliation.

Etsy's Blue Ocean Strategy in Online Retailing of Handmade Crafts

Etsy, the online artisanal marketplace, was the inspirational idea of three New York entrepreneurs who saw that eBay had become too large and ineffective for craftsman and artisans who wished to sell their one-of-a-kind products online. While eBay's timed auction format made for an exciting experience for bargain-hunting consumers, Etsy in contrast promoted its ability to connect thoughtful consumers with artisans selling unique hand-crafted items. Typical Etsy buyers valued craftsmanship and wanted to know how items were made and who made them. The ability to develop a direct relationship with the seller was important to many Etsy buyers who enjoyed a personalized shopping experience. Purchases made by Etsy buyers ranged from $5 ornaments to $50 hand-made clothing items to $2,000 custom-made coffee tables.

Etsy thrived in what was initially uncontested competitive space. In 2015, to the surprise of many, theirs was the largest venture capital backed IPO (Initial Public Offering) to have come out of New York City. By 2018, they had 39 million active buyers and 2.1 million crafters and artisans offering their products. The company's gross merchandise sales totaled more than $3.9 billion that same year. Etsy charged sellers a 3.5 percent transaction fee and a 20-cent listing fee and generated additional revenue from payment processing fees and the sales of shipping labels. The company's revenues had grown from $74.6 million in 2012 to $603.7 million in 2018.

Piotr Swat/Shutterstock

The tremendous success of the company's Blue Ocean Strategy had not gone unnoticed. Amazon announced in May 2016 that it would launch a site featuring artisan goods named Handmade. Amazon believed that its free 2-day shipping to Prime members would give it an advantage over Etsy. Etsy's share price took a steep dive in 2016, but by late 2019, the company's stock was back up to nearly three times its IPO first-day closing price of $22.24. The strength of its strategy and the quality of its execution would determine if Etsy would be able to continue to thrive despite well-funded new entrants into its specialty online retailing sector.

Note: Developed with Rochelle R. Brunson and Marlene M. Reed.

Blocking the Avenues Open to Challengers

Good defensive strategies can help protect a competitive advantage but rarely are the basis for creating one.

The most frequently employed approach to defending a company's present position involves actions that restrict a challenger's options for initiating a competitive attack. There are any number of obstacles that can be put in the path of would-be challengers. A defender can introduce new features, add new models, or broaden its product line to close off gaps and vacant niches to opportunity-seeking challengers. It can thwart rivals' efforts to attack with a lower price by maintaining its own lineup of economy-priced options. It can discourage buyers from trying competitors' brands by lengthening warranties, making early announcements about impending new products or price changes, offering free training and support services, or providing coupons and sample giveaways to buyers most prone to experiment. It can induce potential buyers to reconsider switching. It can challenge the quality or safety of rivals' products. Finally, a defender can grant volume discounts or better financing terms to dealers and distributors to discourage them from experimenting with other suppliers, or it can convince them to handle its product line *exclusively* and force competitors to use other distribution outlets.

Signaling Challengers That Retaliation Is Likely

The goal of signaling challengers that strong retaliation is likely in the event of an attack is either to dissuade challengers from attacking at all or to divert them to less threatening options. Either goal can be achieved by letting challengers know the battle will cost more than it is worth. Signals to would-be challengers can be given by

- Publicly announcing management's commitment to maintaining the firm's present market share.
- Publicly committing the company to a policy of matching competitors' terms or prices.
- Maintaining a war chest of cash and marketable securities.
- Making an occasional strong counterresponse to the moves of weak competitors to enhance the firm's image as a tough defender.

> To be an effective defensive strategy signaling needs to be accompanied by a *credible commitment* to follow through.

To be an effective defensive strategy, however, signaling needs to be accompanied by a *credible commitment* to follow through.

TIMING A COMPANY'S STRATEGIC MOVES

When to make a strategic move is often as crucial as *what* move to make. Timing is especially important when **first-mover advantages and disadvantages** exist. Under certain conditions, being first to initiate a strategic move can have a high payoff in the form of a competitive advantage that later movers can't dislodge. Moving first is no guarantee of success, however, since first movers also face some significant disadvantages. Indeed, there are circumstances in which it is more advantageous to be a fast follower or even a late mover. Because the timing of strategic moves can be consequential, it is important for company strategists to be aware of the nature of first-mover advantages and disadvantages and the conditions favoring each type of move.[12]

> **CORE CONCEPT**
>
> Because of **first-mover advantages and disadvantages,** competitive advantage can spring from *when* a move is made as well as from what move is made.

The Potential for First-Mover Advantages

Market pioneers and other types of first movers typically bear greater risks and greater development costs than firms that move later. If the market responds well to its initial move, the pioneer will benefit from a monopoly position (by virtue of being first to market) that enables it to recover its investment costs and make an attractive profit. If the firm's pioneering move gives it a competitive advantage that can be sustained even after other firms enter the market space, its first-mover advantage will be greater still. The extent of this type of advantage, however, will depend on whether and how fast follower firms can piggyback on the pioneer's success and either imitate or improve on its move.

> **● LO 6-2**
>
> Identify when being a first mover, a fast follower, or a late mover is most advantageous.

There are six such conditions in which first-mover advantages are most likely to arise:

1. *When pioneering helps build a firm's reputation and creates strong brand loyalty.* Customer loyalty to an early mover's brand can create a tie that binds, limiting the success of later entrants' attempts to poach from the early mover's customer base and steal market share. For example, Open Table's early move as an online restaurant-reservation service built a strong brand that has since fueled its expansion worldwide.

2. *When a first mover's customers will thereafter face significant switching costs.* Switching costs can protect first movers when consumers make large investments in learning how to use a specific company's product or in purchasing complementary products that are also brand-specific. Switching costs can also arise from loyalty programs or long-term contracts that give customers incentives to remain with an initial provider. FreshDirect, for example, offers its grocery-delivery customers bigger savings, the longer they keep their service subscription.

3. *When property rights protections thwart rapid imitation of the initial move.* In certain types of industries, property rights protections in the form of patents, copyrights, and trademarks prevent the ready imitation of an early mover's initial moves. First-mover advantages in pharmaceuticals, for example, are heavily dependent on patent protections, and patent races in this industry are common. In other industries, however, patents provide limited protection and can frequently be circumvented. Property rights protections also vary among nations, since they are dependent on a country's legal institutions and enforcement mechanisms.

4. *When an early lead enables the first mover to reap scale economies or move down the learning curve ahead of rivals.* If significant scale-based advantages are available to an early mover, later entrants (with a smaller market share) will face relatively higher production costs. This disadvantage will make it even harder for later entrants to gain share and overcome the first-mover scale advantage. When there is a steep learning curve and when learning can be kept *proprietary,* a first mover can benefit from volume-based cost advantages that grow ever larger as its experience accumulates and its scale of operations increases. This type of first-mover advantage is self-reinforcing and, as such, can preserve a first mover's competitive advantage over long periods of time. Honda's advantage in small multiuse motorcycles has been attributed to such an effect.

5. *When a first mover can set the technical standard for the industry.* In many technology-based industries, the market will converge around a single technical standard. By establishing the industry standard, a first mover can gain a powerful advantage that, like experience-based advantages, builds over time. The lure of such an advantage, however, can result in standard wars among early movers, as each strives to set the industry standard. The key to winning such wars is to enter early on the basis of strong fast-cycle product development capabilities, gain the support of key customers and suppliers, employ penetration pricing, and make allies of the producers of complementary products.

6. *When strong network effects compel increasingly more consumers to choose the first mover's product or service.* As we described in Chapter 3, network effects are at work whenever consumers benefit from having other consumers use the same product or service that they use—a benefit that increases with the number of consumers using the product. An example is FaceTime. The more that people you know have FaceTime on their phones or devices, the more that you are able to have a video conversation with them if you also have FaceTime—a benefit that grows with the number of users in your circle. Network effects can also occur with respect to suppliers. eBay has enjoyed a considerable first-mover advantage for years, not just because of early brand name recognition but also because of powerful network

Tinder, a simple, swipe-based dating app, entered the market in 2012 with a bang, gaining over a million monthly active users in less than a year. While other dating apps were already in existence, Tinder started the swiping phenomenon, thereby easing the process of finding love online and making the use of dating apps commonplace. By 2014, Tinder was processing over a billion swipes daily and users were spending an average of an hour and a half on the app each day. (Today, the average user spends about an hour on Facebook, Instagram, Snapchat, and Twitter—combined.)

Tinder's fast start had much to do with the fact that it was easy-to-use, without the time-consuming questionnaires of other dating services, and fun, with a game-like aspect that many called addictive. In addition, Tinder was rolled out on college campuses using viral marketing techniques that helped it to quickly gain acceptance among social circles such as fraternities and sororities, in which "key influencers" boosted its popularity to the point where it reached a critical mass. But its sustained success has had more to do with the fact that it has been able to reap the benefits of a first mover advantage, as the first major entrant into the field of mobile dating.

In the dating service industry, efficacy is wholly dependent on network effects (where users of an app benefit increasingly as the number of users of that same app increases). By focusing first on ensuring high usage among local social domains, Tinder benefited from strong local network effects. As its popularity spread, users increasingly found Tinder to be the most attractive app to use, since so many others were using it—thereby strengthening the network effect advantage, and drawing ever more people to download the Tinder app. With increased volume, Tinder gained other classic

BigTunaOnline/Shutterstock

first mover advantages, such as enhanced reputational benefits, learning curve efficiencies, and increased interest from investors. By 2019, Tinder had nearly 8 million users, making the app the most popular online dating app in the United States.

Tinder's first mover advantage has not kept others from entering the mobile dating market. In fact, Tinder's phenomenal success has led to a surge in new entrants, with many imitating the Tinder's most popular features. Despite this, Tinder's first mover advantage has proven protective in many ways. Tinder's user base far outstrips the user base of rivals. And while other apps have been trying to play catch up, Tinder has been introducing new subscription products and other paid features to turn its market share advantage into a profitability advantage. As it stands, most analysts see Tinder as the mobile dating application with the highest commercial potential. And with a valuation of $3B and the distinction of Apple's *top-grossing* app in August 2017, it seems that Tinder is here to stay.

Note: Developed with Lindsey Wilcox and Charles K. Anumonwo.

Sources: https://www.inc.com/issie-lapowsky/how-tinder-is-winning-the-mobile-dating-wars.html; http://www.adweek.com/digital/mediakix-time-spent-social-media-infographic/; www.pewresearch.org/fact-tank/2016/02/29/5-facts-about-online-dating/; https://www.forbes.com/sites/stevenbertoni/2017/08/31/tinder-hits-3-billion-valuation-after-match-group-converts-options/#653a516f34f9; company website; J. Clement. Statista, November 22, 2019.

effects on the supply and demand side. The more suppliers choose to auction their items on eBay, the more attractive it is for others to do so as well, since the greater number of items being auctioned attracts more and more potential buyers, which in turn attracts more and more items being auctioned. Strong network effects are self-reinforcing and may lead to a winner-take-all situation for the first mover.

Illustration Capsule 6.2 describes how Tinder achieved a first-mover advantage in the field of mobile dating.

The Potential for Late-Mover Advantages or First-Mover Disadvantages

In some instances there are advantages *to being an adept follower* rather than a first mover. Late-mover advantages (or *first-mover disadvantages*) arise in four instances:

- When the costs of pioneering are high relative to the benefits accrued and imitative followers can achieve similar benefits with far lower costs. This is often the case when second movers can learn from a pioneer's experience and avoid making the same costly mistakes as the pioneer.
- When an innovator's products are somewhat primitive and do not live up to buyer expectations, thus allowing a follower with better-performing products to win disenchanted buyers away from the leader.
- When rapid market evolution (due to fast-paced changes in either technology or buyer needs) gives second movers the opening to leapfrog a first mover's products with more attractive next-version products.
- When market uncertainties make it difficult to ascertain what will eventually succeed, allowing late movers to wait until these needs are clarified.
- When customer loyalty to the pioneer is low and a first mover's skills, know-how, and actions are easily copied or even surpassed.
- When the first mover must make a risky investment in complementary assets or infrastructure (and these may be enjoyed at low cost or risk by followers).

To Be a First Mover or Not

In weighing the pros and cons of being a first mover versus a fast follower versus a late mover, it matters whether the race to market leadership in a particular industry is a 10-year marathon or a 2-year sprint. In marathons, a slow mover is not unduly penalized—first-mover advantages can be fleeting, and there's ample time for fast followers and sometimes even late movers to catch up.[13] Thus, the speed at which the pioneering innovation is likely to catch on matters considerably as companies struggle with whether to pursue an emerging market opportunity aggressively (as a first mover) or cautiously (as a late mover). For instance, it took 5.5 years for worldwide mobile phone use to grow from 10 million to 100 million, and it took close to 10 years for the number of at-home broadband subscribers to grow to 100 million worldwide. The lesson here is that there is a market penetration curve for every emerging opportunity. Typically, the curve has an inflection point at which all the pieces of the business model fall into place, buyer demand explodes, and the market takes off. The inflection point can come early on a fast-rising curve (like the use of e-mail and watching movies streamed over the Internet) or farther up on a slow-rising curve (as with battery-powered motor vehicles, solar and wind power, and textbook rental for college students). Any company that seeks competitive advantage by being a first mover thus needs to ask some hard questions:

- Does market takeoff depend on the development of complementary products or services that currently are not available?
- Is new infrastructure required before buyer demand can surge?
- Will buyers need to learn new skills or adopt new behaviors?
- Will buyers encounter high switching costs in moving to the newly introduced product or service?
- Are there influential competitors in a position to delay or derail the efforts of a first mover?

When the answers to any of these questions are yes, then a company must be careful not to pour too many resources into getting ahead of the market opportunity—the race is likely going to be closer to a 10-year marathon than a 2-year sprint.[14] On the other hand, if the market is a winner-take-all type of market, where powerful first-mover advantages insulate early entrants from competition and prevent later movers from making any headway, then it may be best to move quickly despite the risks.

STRENGTHENING A COMPANY'S MARKET POSITION VIA ITS SCOPE OF OPERATIONS

Apart from considerations of competitive moves and their timing, there is another set of managerial decisions that can affect the strength of a company's market position. These decisions concern the scope of a company's operations—the breadth of its activities and the extent of its market reach. Decisions regarding the **scope of the firm** focus on which activities a firm will perform internally and which it will not.

Consider, for example, Ralph Lauren Corporation. In contrast to Rambler's Way, a sustainable clothing company with a small chain of retail stores, Ralph Lauren designs, markets, and distributes fashionable apparel and other merchandise to approximately 13,000 major department stores and specialty retailers throughout the world. In addition, it operates nearly 500 retail stores, more than 650 concession-based shops within shops, and 10 e-commerce sites. Scope decisions also concern which segments of the market to serve—decisions that can include geographic market segments as well as product and service segments. Almost 50 percent of Ralph Lauren's sales are made outside North America, and its product line includes apparel, fragrances, home furnishings, eyewear, watches and jewelry, and handbags and other leather goods. Its lineup of brands includes Polo Ralph Lauren, Club Monaco, Chaps, and Double RL, as well as its Ralph Lauren Collection brands.

Decisions such as these, in essence, determine where the boundaries of a firm lie and the degree to which the operations within those boundaries cohere. They also have much to do with the direction and extent of a business's growth. In this chapter, we discuss different types of decisions regarding the scope of the company in relation to a company's business-level strategy. In the next two chapters, we develop two additional dimensions of a firm's scope; Chapter 7 focuses on international expansion—a matter of extending the company's geographic scope into foreign markets; Chapter 8 takes up the topic of corporate strategy, which concerns diversifying into a mix of different businesses. *Scope issues are at the very heart of corporate-level strategy.*

Several dimensions of firm scope have relevance for business-level strategy in terms of their capacity to strengthen a company's position in a given market. These include the firm's **horizontal scope,** which is the range of product and service segments that the firm serves within its product or service market. Mergers and acquisitions involving other market participants provide a means for a company to expand its horizontal scope. Expanding the firm's vertical scope by means of vertical integration can also affect the success of its market strategy. **Vertical scope** is the extent to which the firm engages in the various activities that make up the industry's entire value chain system, from initial activities such as raw-material production all the way to retailing and after-sale service activities. **Outsourcing** decisions concern another dimension of scope since they involve narrowing the firm's boundaries with respect to its participation in value chain activities. We discuss the pros and cons of each of

CORE CONCEPT

The **scope of the firm** refers to the range of activities that the firm performs internally, the breadth of its product and service offerings, the extent of its geographic market presence, and its mix of businesses.

CORE CONCEPT

Horizontal scope is the range of product and service segments that a firm serves within its focal market.

CORE CONCEPT

Vertical scope is the extent to which a firm's internal activities encompass the range of activities that make up an industry's entire value chain system, from raw-material production to final sales and service activities.

these options in the sections that follow. Because **strategic alliances and partnerships** provide an alternative to vertical integration and acquisition strategies and are sometimes used to facilitate outsourcing, we conclude this chapter with a discussion of the benefits and challenges associated with *cooperative arrangements* of this nature.

HORIZONTAL MERGER AND ACQUISITION STRATEGIES

● ● ● ●

● LO 6-3

Explain the strategic benefits and risks of expanding a company's horizontal scope through mergers and acquisitions.

Mergers and acquisitions are much-used strategic options to strengthen a company's market position. A *merger* is the combining of two or more companies into a single corporate entity, with the newly created company often taking on a new name. An *acquisition* is a combination in which one company, the acquirer, purchases and absorbs the operations of another, the acquired. The difference between a merger and an acquisition relates more to the details of ownership, management control, and financial arrangements than to strategy and competitive advantage. The resources and competitive capabilities of the newly created enterprise end up much the same whether the combination is the result of an acquisition or a merger.

Horizontal mergers and acquisitions, which involve combining the operations of firms *within the same product or service market,* provide an effective means for firms to rapidly increase the scale and horizontal scope of their core business. For example, the merger of AMR Corporation (parent of American Airlines) with US Airways has increased the airlines' scale of operations and extended their reach geographically to create the world's largest airline.

Merger and acquisition strategies typically set sights on achieving any of five objectives:[15]

1. *Creating a more cost-efficient operation out of the combined companies.* When a company acquires another company in the same industry, there's usually enough overlap in operations that less efficient plants can be closed or distribution and sales activities partly combined and downsized. Likewise, it is usually feasible to squeeze out cost savings in administrative activities, again by combining and downsizing such administrative activities as finance and accounting, information technology, human resources, and so on. The combined companies may also be able to reduce supply chain costs because of greater bargaining power over common suppliers and closer collaboration with supply chain partners. By helping consolidate the industry and remove excess capacity, such combinations can also reduce industry rivalry and improve industry profitability.

2. *Expanding a company's geographic coverage.* One of the best and quickest ways to expand a company's geographic coverage is to acquire rivals with operations in the desired locations. Since a company's size increases with its geographic scope, another benefit is increased bargaining power with the company's suppliers or buyers. Greater geographic coverage can also contribute to product differentiation by enhancing a company's name recognition and brand awareness. The vacation rental marketplace, HomeAway, Inc., relied on an aggressive horizontal acquisition strategy to expand internationally, as well as to extend its reach across the United States. It now offers vacation rentals in 190 countries through its 50 websites in 23 languages. Travel company Expedia has since acquired HomeAway, thus extending its reach horizontally into the vacation rental product category—an objective described in the next point.

3. *Extending the company's business into new product categories.* Many times a company has gaps in its product line that need to be filled in order to offer customers a more effective product bundle or the benefits of one-stop shopping. For example, customers might prefer to acquire a suite of software applications from a single vendor that can offer more integrated solutions to the company's problems. Acquisition can be a quicker and more potent way to broaden a company's product line than going through the exercise of introducing a company's own new product to fill the gap. In 2018, Keurig Green Mountain vastly expanded its range of beverage offerings by acquiring the Dr Pepper Snapple Group in an $18.7 billion deal.

4. *Gaining quick access to new technologies or other resources and capabilities.* Making acquisitions to bolster a company's technological know-how or to expand its skills and capabilities allows a company to bypass a time-consuming and expensive internal effort to build desirable new resources and capabilities. Over the course of its history, Cisco Systems has purchased over 200 companies to give it more technological reach and product breadth, thereby enhancing its standing as the world's largest provider of hardware, software, and services for creating and operating Internet networks.

5. *Leading the convergence of industries whose boundaries are being blurred by changing technologies and new market opportunities.* In fast-cycle industries or industries whose boundaries are changing, companies can use acquisition strategies to hedge their bets about the direction that an industry will take, to increase their capacity to meet changing demands, and to respond flexibly to changing buyer needs and technological demands. The convergence of the pharmacy industry with health insurers and the benefits management industry led to the merger between Cigna and Express Scripts as well as that between CVS and Aetna in 2018.

Illustration Capsule 6.3 describes how Walmart employed a horizontal acquisition strategy to expand into the e-commerce domain.

Why Mergers and Acquisitions Sometimes Fail to Produce Anticipated Results

Despite many successes, mergers and acquisitions do not always produce the hoped-for outcomes.[16] Cost savings may prove smaller than expected. Gains in competitive capabilities may take substantially longer to realize or, worse, may never materialize at all. Efforts to mesh the corporate cultures can stall due to formidable resistance from organization members. Key employees at the acquired company can quickly become disenchanted and leave; the morale of company personnel who remain can drop to disturbingly low levels because they disagree with newly instituted changes. Differences in management styles and operating procedures can prove hard to resolve. In addition, the managers appointed to oversee the integration of a newly acquired company can make mistakes in deciding which activities to leave alone and which activities to meld into their own operations and systems.

A number of mergers and acquisitions have been notably unsuccessful. Google's $12.5 billion acquisition of struggling smartphone manufacturer Motorola Mobility in 2012 turned out to be minimally beneficial in helping to "supercharge Google's Android ecosystem" (Google's stated reason for making the acquisition). When Google's attempts to rejuvenate Motorola's smartphone business by spending over $1.3 billion on new

Walmart's Expansion into E-Commerce via Horizontal Acquisition

As the boundaries between traditional retailing and online retailing have begun to blur, Walmart has responded by expanding its presence in e-commerce via horizontal acquisition. In 2016, Walmart acquired Jet.com, an innovative U.S. e-commerce start-up that was designed to compete with Amazon. Jet sells everything from household goods and electronics to beauty products, apparel, and toys from more than 2,400 retailer and brand partners. Jet.com rewards customers for ordering multiple items, using a debit card instead of a credit card, or choosing a no-returns option; it passes its cost savings on to customers in the form of lower prices. The low-price approach of Jet.com fit well with Walmart's low-price strategy. In addition, Walmart hoped that the acquisition would help it to accelerate its growth in e-commerce, provide quick access to some valuable e-commerce knowledge and capabilities, increase its breadth of online product offerings, and attract new customer segments.

Sundry Photography/Shutterstock

Walmart, like other brick and mortar retailers, was facing a myriad of issues caused by changing customer expectations. Consumers increasingly valued large assortments of products, a convenient shopping experience, and low prices. Price sensitivity was increasing due to the ease of comparing prices online. As a traditional retailer, Walmart was facing stiff competition from Amazon, the world's largest and fastest growing e-commerce company. Amazon's seemingly endless inventory of goods, excellent customer service, expertise in search engine marketing, and appeal to a wide consumer demographic added pressure on the overall global retail industry.

The acquisition of Jet built on the foundation already in place for Walmart to respond to the external pressure and continue growing as an omni-channel retailer (i.e., bricks and mortar, online, or mobile). After investing heavily in their own online channel,

Walmart.com, the company was looking for other ways to attract customers by lowering prices, broadening their product assortment, and offering the simplest, most convenient shopping experience. Jet's breadth of products, access to millennial and higher-income customer segments, and best in-class pricing algorithm would accelerate Walmart's progress across all of these priorities.

Since the acquisition, Jet has continued to expand its own offerings with private-label groceries, further increasing competition with Amazon's AmazonFresh grocery business. More recently, Walmart made several other acquisitions of online apparel companies, thereby strengthening Jet's apparel offerings and further expanding Walmart's presence in e-commerce. These include ShoeBuy (a competitor of Amazon-owned Zappos), Bonobos in menswear, Moosejaw in outdoor gear and apparel, and Modcloth in vintage and indie womenswear. While Walmart's e-commerce sales still pale in comparison to Amazon, this represents a promising start for Walmart, as the retail industry continues to transform.

Note: Developed with Dipti Badrinath.

Sources: http://www.businessinsider.com/jet-walmart-weapon-vs-amazon-2017-9; https://news.walmart.com/2016/08/08/walmart-agrees-to-acquire-jetcom-one-of-the-fastest-growing-e-commerce-companies-in-the-us; https://www.fool.com/investing/2017/10/03/1-year-later-wal-marts-jetcom-acquisition-is-an-un.aspx; https://blog.walmart.com/business/20160919/five-big-reasons-walmart-bought-jetcom.

product R&D and revamping Motorola's product line resulted in disappointing sales and huge operating losses, Google sold Motorola Mobility to China-based PC maker Lenovo for $2.9 billion in 2014 (however, Google retained ownership of Motorola's extensive patent portfolio). The jury is still out on whether Lenovo's acquisition of Motorola will prove to be a moneymaker.

VERTICAL INTEGRATION STRATEGIES

Expanding the firm's vertical scope by means of a vertical integration strategy provides another possible way to strengthen the company's position in its core market. A **vertically integrated firm** is one that participates in multiple stages of an industry's value chain system. Thus, if a manufacturer invests in facilities to produce component parts that it had formerly purchased from suppliers, or if it opens its own chain of retail stores to bypass its former distributors, it is engaging in vertical integration. A good example of a vertically integrated firm is Maple Leaf Foods, a major Canadian producer of fresh and processed meats whose best-selling brands include Maple Leaf and Schneiders. Maple Leaf Foods participates in hog and poultry production, with company-owned hog and poultry farms; it has its own meat-processing and rendering facilities; it packages its products and distributes them from company-owned distribution centers; and it conducts marketing, sales, and customer service activities for its wholesale and retail buyers but does not otherwise participate in the final stage of the meat-processing vertical chain—the retailing stage.

A vertical integration strategy can expand the firm's range of activities *backward* into sources of supply and/or *forward* toward end users. When Tiffany & Co., a manufacturer and retailer of fine jewelry, began sourcing, cutting, and polishing its own diamonds, it integrated backward along the diamond supply chain. Mining giant De Beers Group and Canadian miner Aber Diamond integrated forward when they entered the diamond retailing business.

A firm can pursue vertical integration by starting its own operations in other stages of the vertical activity chain or by acquiring a company already performing the activities it wants to bring in-house. Vertical integration strategies can aim at *full integration* (participating in all stages of the vertical chain) or *partial integration* (building positions in selected stages of the vertical chain). Firms can also engage in *tapered integration* strategies, which involve a mix of in-house and outsourced activity in any given stage of the vertical chain. Oil companies, for instance, supply their refineries with oil from their own wells as well as with oil that they purchase from other producers—they engage in tapered backward integration. Coach, Inc., the maker of Coach handbags and accessories, engages in tapered forward integration since it operates full-price and factory outlet stores but also sells its products through third-party department store outlets.

The Advantages of a Vertical Integration Strategy

Under the right conditions, a vertical integration strategy can add materially to a company's technological capabilities, strengthen the firm's competitive position, and boost its profitability.[17] But it is important to keep in mind that vertical integration has no real payoff strategy-wise or profit-wise unless the extra investment can be justified by compensating improvements in company costs, differentiation, or competitive strength.

Integrating Backward to Achieve Greater Competitiveness   It is harder than one might think to generate cost savings or improve profitability by integrating backward

● LO 6-4

Explain the advantages and disadvantages of extending the company's scope of operations via vertical integration.

CORE CONCEPT

A vertically integrated firm is one that performs value chain activities along more than one stage of an industry's value chain system.

CORE CONCEPT

Backward integration involves entry into activities previously performed by suppliers or other enterprises positioned along earlier stages of the industry value chain system; forward integration involves entry into value chain system activities closer to the end user.

into activities such as the manufacture of parts and components (which could otherwise be purchased from suppliers with specialized expertise in making the parts and components). For **backward integration** to be a cost-saving and profitable strategy, a company must be able to (1) achieve the same scale economies as outside suppliers and (2) match or beat suppliers' production efficiency with no drop-off in quality. Neither outcome is easily achieved. To begin with, a company's in-house requirements are often too small to reach the optimum size for low-cost operation. For instance, if it takes a minimum production volume of 1 million units to achieve scale economies and a company's in-house requirements are just 250,000 units, then it falls far short of being able to match the costs of outside suppliers (which may readily find buyers for 1 million or more units). Furthermore, matching the production efficiency of suppliers is fraught with problems when suppliers have considerable production experience, when the technology they employ has elements that are hard to master, and/or when substantial R&D expertise is required to develop next-version components or keep pace with advancing technology in components production.

That said, occasions still arise when a company can gain or extend a competitive advantage by performing a broader range of industry value chain activities internally rather than having such activities performed by outside suppliers. There are several ways that backward vertical integration can contribute to a cost-based competitive advantage. When there are few suppliers and when the item being supplied is a major component, vertical integration can lower costs by limiting supplier power. Vertical integration can also lower costs by facilitating the coordination of production flows and avoiding bottlenecks and delays that disrupt production schedules. Furthermore, when a company has proprietary know-how that it wants to keep from rivals, then in-house performance of value-adding activities related to this know-how is beneficial even if such activities could otherwise be performed by outsiders.

Apple decided to integrate backward into producing its own chips for iPhones, chiefly because chips are a major cost component, suppliers have bargaining power, and in-house production would help coordinate design tasks and protect Apple's proprietary iPhone technology. International Paper Company backward integrates into pulp mills that it sets up near its paper mills and reaps the benefits of coordinated production flows, energy savings, and transportation economies. It does this, in part, because outside suppliers are generally unwilling to make a site-specific investment for a buyer.

Backward vertical integration can support a differentiation-based competitive advantage when performing activities internally contributes to a better-quality product or service offering, improves the caliber of customer service, or in other ways enhances the performance of the final product. On occasion, integrating into more stages along the industry value chain system can add to a company's differentiation capabilities by allowing it to strengthen its core competencies, better master key skills or strategy-critical technologies, or add features that deliver greater customer value. Spanish clothing maker Inditex has backward integrated into fabric making, as well as garment design and manufacture, for its successful Zara brand. By tightly controlling the process and postponing dyeing until later stages, Zara can respond quickly to changes in fashion trends and supply its customers with the hottest items. Amazon and Netflix backward integrated by establishing Amazon Studios and Netflix Originals to produce high-quality original content for their streaming services.

Integrating Forward to Enhance Competitiveness   Like backward integration, **forward integration** can enhance competitiveness and contribute to competitive advantage on the cost side as well as the differentiation (or value) side. On the cost side, forward integration can lower costs by increasing efficiency and reducing or eliminating the bargaining power of companies that had wielded such power further along the value system chain. It can allow manufacturers to gain better access to end users, improve market visibility, and enhance brand name awareness. For example, Harley-Davidson's and Ducati's company-owned retail stores are essentially little museums, filled with iconography, that provide an environment conducive to selling not only motorcycles and gear but also memorabilia, clothing, and other items featuring the brand. Insurance companies and brokerages like Allstate and Edward Jones have the ability to make consumers' interactions with local agents and office personnel a differentiating feature by focusing on building relationships.

In many industries, independent sales agents, wholesalers, and retailers handle competing brands of the same product and have no allegiance to any one company's brand—they tend to push whatever offers the biggest profits. To avoid dependence on distributors and dealers with divided loyalties, Goodyear has integrated forward into company-owned and franchised retail tire stores. Consumer-goods companies like Coach, Under Armour, Pepperidge Farm, Bath & Body Works, Nike, Tommy Hilfiger, and Ann Taylor have integrated forward into retailing and operate their own branded stores in factory outlet malls, enabling them to move overstocked items, slow-selling items, and seconds.

Some producers have opted to integrate forward by selling directly to customers at the company's website. Indochino in custom men's suits, Warby Parker in eyewear, and Everlane in sustainable apparel are examples. Bypassing regular wholesale and retail channels in favor of direct sales and Internet retailing can have appeal if it reinforces the brand and enhances consumer satisfaction or if it lowers distribution costs, produces a relative cost advantage over certain rivals, and results in lower selling prices to end users. In addition, sellers are compelled to include the Internet as a retail channel when a sufficiently large number of buyers in an industry prefer to make purchases online. However, a company that is vigorously pursuing online sales to consumers at the same time that it is also heavily promoting sales to consumers through its network of wholesalers and retailers is *competing directly against its distribution allies.* Such actions constitute *channel conflict* and create a tricky route to negotiate. A company that is actively trying to expand online sales to consumers is signaling a weak strategic commitment to its dealers *and* a willingness to cannibalize dealers' sales and growth potential. The likely result is angry dealers and loss of dealer goodwill. Quite possibly, a company may stand to lose more sales by offending its dealers than it gains from its own online sales effort. Consequently, in industries where the strong support and goodwill of dealer networks is essential, companies may conclude that it is important to avoid channel conflict and that *their websites should be designed to partner with dealers rather than compete against them.*

The Disadvantages of a Vertical Integration Strategy

Vertical integration has some substantial drawbacks beyond the potential for channel conflict.[18] The most serious drawbacks to vertical integration include the following concerns:

- Vertical integration raises a firm's capital investment in the industry, thereby *increasing business risk* (what if industry growth and profitability unexpectedly go sour?).
- Vertically integrated companies are often *slow to adopt technological advances or more efficient production methods* when they are saddled with older technology or facilities. A company that obtains parts and components from outside suppliers can

always shop the market for the newest, best, and cheapest parts, whereas a vertically integrated firm with older plants and technology may choose to continue making suboptimal parts rather than face the high costs of writing off undepreciated assets.

- Vertical integration can result in *less flexibility in accommodating shifting buyer preferences.* It is one thing to eliminate use of a component made by a supplier and another to stop using a component being made in-house (which can mean laying off employees and writing off the associated investment in equipment and facilities). Integrating forward or backward locks a firm into relying on its own in-house activities and sources of supply. Most of the world's automakers, despite their manufacturing expertise, have concluded that purchasing a majority of their parts and components from best-in-class suppliers results in greater design flexibility, higher quality, and lower costs than producing parts or components in-house.

- Vertical integration *may not enable a company to realize economies of scale* if its production levels are below the minimum efficient scale. Small companies in particular are likely to suffer a cost disadvantage by producing in-house.

- Vertical integration poses all kinds of *capacity-matching problems.* In motor vehicle manufacturing, for example, the most efficient scale of operation for making axles is different from the most economic volume for radiators, and different yet again for both engines and transmissions. Building the capacity to produce just the right number of axles, radiators, engines, and transmissions in-house—and doing so at the lowest unit costs for each—poses significant challenges and operating complications.

- Integration forward or backward typically *calls for developing new types of resources and capabilities.* Parts and components manufacturing, assembly operations, wholesale distribution and retailing, and direct sales via the Internet represent different kinds of businesses, operating in different types of industries, with different key success factors. Many manufacturers learn the hard way that company-owned wholesale and retail networks require skills that they lack, fit poorly with what they do best, and detract from their overall profit performance. Similarly, a company that tries to produce many components in-house is likely to find itself very hard-pressed to keep up with technological advances and cutting-edge production practices for each component used in making its product.

In today's world of close working relationships with suppliers and efficient supply chain management systems, relatively few companies can make a strong economic case for integrating backward into the business of suppliers. The best materials and components suppliers stay abreast of advancing technology and best practices and are adept in making good quality items, delivering them on time, and keeping their costs and prices as low as possible.

Weighing the Pros and Cons of Vertical Integration

All in all, therefore, a strategy of vertical integration can have both strengths and weaknesses. The tip of the scales depends on (1) whether vertical integration can enhance the performance of strategy-critical activities in ways that lower cost, build expertise, protect proprietary know-how, or increase differentiation; (2) what impact vertical integration will have on investment costs, flexibility, and response times; (3) what administrative costs will be incurred by coordinating operations across more vertical chain activities; and (4) how difficult it will be for the company to acquire the set of skills and capabilities needed to operate in another stage of the vertical chain. *Vertical integration strategies have merit according to which capabilities and value-adding activities*

Unlike many vehicle manufacturers, Tesla embraces vertical integration from component manufacturing all the way through vehicle sales and servicing. The majority of the company's $11.8 billion in 2017 revenue came from electric vehicle sales and leasing, with the remainder coming from servicing those vehicles and selling residential battery packs and solar energy systems.

At its core an electric vehicle manufacturer, Tesla uses both backward and forward vertical integration to achieve multiple strategic goals. In order to drive innovation in a critical part of its supply chain, Tesla has invested in a "gigafactory" that manufacturers the batteries that are essential for a long-lasting electric vehicle. According to Tesla's former VP of Production, in-house manufacturing of key components and new parts that require frequent updates has enabled the company to learn quickly and launch new versions faster. Moreover, having closer relationships between engineering and manufacturing gives Tesla greater control over product design. Tesla uses forward vertical integration to improve the customer experience by owning the distribution and servicing of the vehicles it builds. Their network of dealerships allows Tesla to sell directly to consumers and handle maintenance needs without relying on third parties that sometimes have competing priorities.

Beyond vertically integrating the manufacture and distribution of their electric vehicles, Tesla uses the strategy to build the ecosystem that is necessary to support further adoption of their vehicles. As many consumers perceive electric cars to have limited range and long charging times that prevent long-distance travel, Tesla is building a network of Supercharger stations to overcome this pain point. By investing in this development themselves, Tesla does not need to wait for another company to deliver the critical infrastructure

Hadrian/Shutterstock

that drivers demand before they switch from traditional gasoline-powered cars. Similarly, Tesla sells solar power generation and storage products that make it easier for customers to make the switch to transportation powered by sustainable energy.

While Tesla's mission to accelerate the world's transition to sustainable energy has required large investments throughout the value chain, this strategy has not been without challenges. Unlike batteries, seats are of limited strategic importance, yet Tesla decided to manufacture their Model 3 seats in house. While there is no indication that the seats were the source of major production delays in 2017, diverting resources to develop new manufacturing capabilities could have added to the problem. Although Tesla's vertical integration strategy is not without downsides, it has enabled the firm to quickly roll out innovative new products and launch the network that is required for widespread vehicle adoption. Investors have rewarded Tesla for this bold strategy by lifting its valuation to $80 billion by the start of 2020, higher than the other major American automakers.

Note: Developed with Edward J. Silberman.

Sources: Tesla 2017 Annual Report; G. Reichow, "Tesla's Secret Second Floor," *Wired,* October 18,2017, **https://www.wired.com/story/teslas-secret-second-floor/**; A. Sage, "Tesla's Seat Strategy Goes Against the Grain. . . For Now," *Reuters,* October 26, 2017, **https://www.reuters.com/article/us-tesla-seats/teslas-seat-strategy-goes-against-the-grain-for-now-idUSKBN1CV0DS**; Yahoo Finance.

truly need to be performed in-house and which can be performed better or cheaper by outsiders. Absent solid benefits, integrating forward or backward is not likely to be an attractive strategy option.

Electric automobile maker Tesla, Inc. has made vertical integration a central part of its strategy, as described in Illustration Capsule 6.4.

OUTSOURCING STRATEGIES: NARROWING THE SCOPE OF OPERATIONS

● ● ● ●

● LO 6-5

Recognize the conditions that favor farming out certain value chain activities to outside parties.

CORE CONCEPT

Outsourcing involves contracting out certain value chain activities that are normally performed in-house to outside vendors.

In contrast to vertical integration strategies, outsourcing strategies narrow the scope of a business's operations, in terms of what activities are performed internally. **Outsourcing** involves contracting out certain value chain activities that are normally performed in-house to outside vendors.[19] Many PC makers, for example, have shifted from assembling units in-house to outsourcing the entire assembly process to manufacturing specialists, which can operate more efficiently due to their greater scale, experience, and bargaining power over components makers. Nearly all name-brand apparel firms have in-house capability to design, market, and distribute their products but they outsource all fabric manufacture and garment-making activities. Starbucks finds purchasing coffee beans from independent growers far more advantageous than having its own coffee-growing operation, with locations scattered across most of the world's coffee-growing regions.

Outsourcing certain value chain activities makes strategic sense whenever

- *An activity can be performed better or more cheaply by outside specialists.* A company should generally *not* perform any value chain activity internally that can be performed more efficiently or effectively by outsiders—the chief exception occurs when a particular activity is strategically crucial and internal control over that activity is deemed essential. Dolce & Gabbana, for example, outsources the manufacture of its brand of sunglasses to Luxottica—a company considered to be the world's best sunglass manufacturing company, known for its Oakley, Oliver Peoples, and Ray-Ban brands. Colgate-Palmolive, for instance, has reduced its information technology operational costs by more than 10 percent annually through an outsourcing agreement with IBM.

- *The activity is not crucial to the firm's ability to achieve sustainable competitive advantage.* Outsourcing of support activities such as maintenance services, data processing, data storage, fringe-benefit management, and website operations has become commonplace. Many smaller companies, for example, find it advantages to outsource HR activities such as benefit administration, training, recruiting, hiring and payroll to specialists, such as XcelHR, Insperity, Paychex, and Aon Hewitt.

- *The outsourcing improves organizational flexibility and speeds time to market.* Outsourcing gives a company the flexibility to switch suppliers in the event that its present supplier falls behind competing suppliers. Moreover, seeking out new suppliers with the needed capabilities already in place is frequently quicker, easier, less risky, and cheaper than hurriedly retooling internal operations to replace obsolete capabilities or trying to install and master new technologies.

- *It reduces the company's risk exposure to changing technology and buyer preferences.* When a company outsources certain parts, components, and services, its suppliers must bear the burden of incorporating state-of-the-art technologies and/or undertaking redesigns and upgrades to accommodate a company's plans to introduce next-generation products. If what a supplier provides falls out of favor with buyers, or is rendered unnecessary by technological change, it is the supplier's business that suffers rather than the company's.

- *It allows a company to concentrate on its core business, leverage its key resources, and do even better what it already does best.* A company is better able to enhance its own capabilities when it concentrates its full resources and energies on performing only those activities. United Colors of Benetton and Sisley, for example, outsource the production of handbags and other leather goods while devoting their energies to the clothing lines for which they are known. Apple outsources production of its iPod, iPhone, and iPad models to Chinese contract manufacturer Foxconn and concentrates in-house on design, marketing, and innovation. Hewlett-Packard and IBM have sold some of their manufacturing plants to outsiders and contracted to repurchase the output instead from the new owners.

The Risk of Outsourcing Value Chain Activities

The biggest danger of outsourcing is that a company will farm out the wrong types of activities and thereby hollow out its own capabilities.[20] For example, in recent years companies eager to reduce operating costs have opted to outsource such strategically important activities as product development, engineering design, and sophisticated manufacturing tasks—the very capabilities that underpin a company's ability to lead sustained product innovation. While these companies have apparently been able to lower their operating costs by outsourcing these functions to outsiders, *their ability to lead the development of innovative new products is weakened because so many of the cutting-edge ideas and technologies for next-generation products come from outsiders.*

> A company must guard against outsourcing activities that hollow out the resources and capabilities that it needs to be a master of its own destiny.

Another risk of outsourcing comes from the lack of direct control. It may be difficult to monitor, control, and coordinate the activities of outside parties via contracts and arm's-length transactions alone. Unanticipated problems may arise that cause delays or cost overruns and become hard to resolve amicably. Moreover, contract-based outsourcing can be problematic because outside parties lack incentives to make investments specific to the needs of the outsourcing company's internal value chain.

Companies like Cisco Systems are alert to these dangers. Cisco guards against loss of control and protects its manufacturing expertise by designing the production methods that its contract manufacturers must use. Cisco keeps the source code for its designs proprietary, thereby controlling the initiation of all improvements and safeguarding its innovations from imitation. Further, Cisco has developed online systems to monitor the factory operations of contract manufacturers around the clock so that it knows immediately when problems arise and can decide whether to get involved.

STRATEGIC ALLIANCES AND PARTNERSHIPS

● ● ● ●

● LO 6-6

Understand how to capture the benefits and minimize the drawbacks of strategic alliances and partnerships.

Strategic alliances and cooperative partnerships provide one way to gain some of the benefits offered by vertical integration, outsourcing, and horizontal mergers and acquisitions while minimizing the associated problems. Companies frequently engage in cooperative strategies as an alternative to vertical integration or horizontal mergers and acquisitions. Increasingly, companies are also employing strategic alliances and partnerships to extend their scope of operations via international expansion and diversification strategies, as we describe in Chapters 7 and 8. Strategic alliances and cooperative arrangements are now a common means of narrowing a company's scope of operations as well, serving as a useful way to manage outsourcing (in lieu of traditional, purely price-oriented contracts).

For example, oil and gas companies engage in considerable vertical integration—but Shell Oil Company and Pemex (Mexico's state-owned petroleum company) have found that joint ownership of their Deer Park Refinery in Texas lowers their investment costs and risks in comparison to going it alone. The colossal failure of the Daimler–Chrysler merger formed an expensive lesson for Daimler AG about what can go wrong with horizontal mergers and acquisitions; the Renault–Nissan–Mitsubishi Alliance has proved more successful in developing the capabilities for the manufacture of plug-in electric vehicles and introducing the Nissan Leaf.

Many companies employ strategic alliances to manage the problems that might otherwise occur with outsourcing—Cisco's system of alliances guards against loss of control, protects its proprietary manufacturing expertise, and enables the company to monitor closely the assembly operations of its partners while devoting its energy to designing new generations of the switches, routers, and other Internet-related equipment for which it is known.

> **CORE** CONCEPT
>
> A **strategic alliance** is a formal agreement between two or more separate companies in which they agree to work cooperatively toward some common objective.

A **strategic alliance** is a formal agreement between two or more separate companies in which they agree to work collaboratively toward some strategically relevant objective. Typically, they involve shared financial responsibility, joint contribution of resources and capabilities, shared risk, shared control, and mutual dependence. They may be characterized by cooperative marketing, sales, or distribution; joint production; design collaboration; or projects to jointly develop new technologies or products. They can vary in terms of their duration and the extent of the collaboration; some are intended as long-term arrangements, involving an extensive set of cooperative activities, while others are designed to accomplish more limited, short-term objectives.

Collaborative arrangements may entail a contractual agreement, but they commonly stop short of formal ownership ties between the partners (although sometimes an alliance member will secure minority ownership of another member).

> **CORE** CONCEPT
>
> A **joint venture** is a partnership involving the establishment of an independent corporate entity that the partners own and control jointly, sharing in its revenues and expenses.

A special type of strategic alliance involving ownership ties is the **joint venture.** A joint venture entails forming a *new corporate entity that is jointly owned* by two or more companies that agree to share in the revenues, expenses, and control of the newly formed entity. Since joint ventures involve setting up a mutually owned business, they tend to be more durable but also riskier than other arrangements. In other types of strategic alliances, the collaboration between the partners involves a much less rigid structure in which the partners retain their independence from one another. If a strategic alliance is not working out, a partner can choose to simply walk away or reduce its commitment to collaborating at any time.

An alliance becomes "strategic," as opposed to just a convenient business arrangement, when it serves any of the following purposes:[21]

1. It facilitates achievement of an important business objective (like lowering costs or delivering more value to customers in the form of better quality, added features, and greater durability).
2. It helps build, strengthen, or sustain a core competence or competitive advantage.
3. It helps remedy an important resource deficiency or competitive weakness.
4. It helps defend against a competitive threat, or mitigates a significant risk to a company's business.
5. It increases bargaining power over suppliers or buyers.
6. It helps open up important new market opportunities.
7. It speeds the development of new technologies and/or product innovations.

Strategic cooperation is a much-favored approach in industries where new technological developments are occurring at a furious pace along many different paths and where advances in one technology spill over to affect others (often blurring industry boundaries). Whenever industries are experiencing high-velocity technological advances in many areas simultaneously, firms find it virtually essential to have cooperative relationships with other enterprises to stay on the leading edge of technology, even in their own area of specialization. In industries like these, alliances are all about fast cycles of learning, gaining quick access to the latest round of technological know-how, and developing dynamic capabilities. In bringing together firms with different skills and knowledge bases, alliances open up learning opportunities that help partner firms better leverage their own resources and capabilities.[22]

In 2017, Daimler entered into an agreement with automotive supplier Robert Bosch GmbH to develop self-driving taxis that customers can hail with a smartphone app; the objective is to make this a reality in urban areas by the beginning of the next decade.

Microsoft has been partnering with a variety of companies to advance technology in the healthcare industry. Its 2017 alliance with PAREXEL, a clinical research organization, aims to use their combined capabilities to accelerate drug development and bring new therapies to patients sooner. In 2018, it joined forces with immuno-sequencing company Adaptive Biotechnologies to find ways to detect cancers and other diseases earlier using Microsoft's artificial intelligence capabilities.

> Companies that have formed a host of alliances need to manage their alliances like a portfolio.

Because of the varied benefits of strategic alliances, many large corporations have become involved in 30 to 50 alliances, and a number have formed hundreds of alliances. Hoffmann-La Roche, a multinational healthcare company, has set up Roche Partnering to manage their more than 190 alliances. Companies that have formed a host of alliances need to manage their alliances like a portfolio—terminating those that no longer serve a useful purpose or that have produced meager results, forming promising new alliances, and restructuring existing alliances to correct performance problems and/or redirect the collaborative effort.

> The best alliances are highly selective, focusing on particular value chain activities and on obtaining a specific competitive benefit. They enable a firm to build on its strengths and to learn.

Capturing the Benefits of Strategic Alliances

The extent to which companies benefit from entering into alliances and partnerships seems to be a function of six factors:[23]

1. *Picking a good partner.* A good partner must bring complementary strengths to the relationship. To the extent that alliance members have nonoverlapping strengths, there is greater potential for synergy and less potential for coordination problems and conflict. In addition, a good partner needs to share the company's vision about the overall purpose of the alliance and to have specific goals that either match or complement those of the company. Strong partnerships also depend on good chemistry among key personnel and compatible views about how the alliance should be structured and managed.

2. *Being sensitive to cultural differences.* Cultural differences among companies can make it difficult for their personnel to work together effectively. Cultural differences can be problematic among companies from the same country, but when the partners have different national origins, the problems are often magnified. Unless there is respect among all the parties for cultural differences, including those stemming from different local cultures and local business practices, productive working relationships are unlikely to emerge.

3. *Recognizing that the alliance must benefit both sides.* Information must be shared as well as gained, and the relationship must remain forthright and trustful. If either partner plays games with information or tries to take advantage of the other, the resulting friction can quickly erode the value of further collaboration. Open, trustworthy behavior on both sides is essential for fruitful collaboration.

4. *Ensuring that both parties live up to their commitments.* Both parties have to deliver on their commitments for the alliance to produce the intended benefits. The division of work has to be perceived as fairly apportioned, and the caliber of the benefits received on both sides has to be perceived as adequate.

5. *Structuring the decision-making process so that actions can be taken swiftly when needed.* In many instances, the fast pace of technological and competitive changes dictates an equally fast decision-making process. If the parties get bogged down in discussions or in gaining internal approval from higher-ups, the alliance can turn into an anchor of delay and inaction.

6. *Managing the learning process and then adjusting the alliance agreement over time to fit new circumstances.* One of the keys to long-lasting success is adapting the nature and structure of the alliance to be responsive to shifting market conditions, emerging technologies, and changing customer requirements. Wise allies are quick to recognize the merit of an evolving collaborative arrangement, where adjustments are made to accommodate changing conditions and to overcome whatever problems arise in establishing an effective working relationship.

Most alliances that aim at sharing technology or providing market access turn out to be temporary, lasting only a few years. This is not necessarily an indicator of failure, however. Strategic alliances can be terminated after a few years simply because they have fulfilled their purpose; indeed, many alliances are intended to be of limited duration, set up to accomplish specific short-term objectives. Longer-lasting collaborative arrangements, however, may provide even greater strategic benefits. Alliances are more likely to be long-lasting when (1) they involve collaboration with partners that do not compete directly, such as suppliers or distribution allies; (2) a trusting relationship has been established; and (3) both parties conclude that continued collaboration is in their mutual interest, perhaps because new opportunities for learning are emerging.

The Drawbacks of Strategic Alliances and Their Relative Advantages

While strategic alliances provide a way of obtaining the benefits of vertical integration, mergers and acquisitions, and outsourcing, they also suffer from some of the same drawbacks. Anticipated gains may fail to materialize due to an overly optimistic view of the potential or a poor fit in terms of the combination of resources and capabilities. When outsourcing is conducted via alliances, there is no less risk of becoming dependent on other companies for essential expertise and capabilities—indeed, this may be the Achilles' heel of such alliances. Moreover, there are additional pitfalls to collaborative arrangements. The greatest danger is that a partner will gain access to a company's proprietary knowledge base, technologies, or trade secrets, enabling the partner to match the company's core strengths and costing the company its hard-won competitive advantage. This risk is greatest when the alliance is among industry rivals or when the alliance is for the purpose of collaborative R&D, since this type of partnership requires an extensive exchange of closely held information.

The question for managers is when to engage in a strategic alliance and when to choose an alternative means of meeting their objectives. The answer to this question depends on the relative advantages of each method and the circumstances under which each type of organizational arrangement is favored.

The principal advantages of strategic alliances over vertical integration or horizontal mergers and acquisitions are threefold:

1. They lower investment costs and risks for each partner by facilitating resource pooling and risk sharing. This can be particularly important when investment needs and uncertainty are high, such as when a dominant technology standard has not yet emerged.

2. They are more flexible organizational forms and allow for a more adaptive response to changing conditions. Flexibility is essential when environmental conditions or technologies are changing rapidly. Moreover, strategic alliances under such circumstances may enable the development of each partner's dynamic capabilities.

3. They are more rapidly deployed—a critical factor when speed is of the essence. Speed is of the essence when there is a winner-take-all type of competitive situation, such as the race for a dominant technological design or a race down a steep experience curve, where there is a large first-mover advantage.

The key advantages of using strategic alliances rather than arm's-length transactions to manage outsourcing are (1) the increased ability to exercise control over the partners' activities and (2) a greater willingness for the partners to make relationship-specific investments. Arm's-length transactions discourage such investments since they imply less commitment and do not build trust.

On the other hand, there are circumstances when other organizational mechanisms are preferable to alliances and partnering. Mergers and acquisitions are especially suited for situations in which strategic alliances or partnerships do not go far enough in providing a company with access to needed resources and capabilities. Ownership ties are more permanent than partnership ties, allowing the operations of the merger or acquisition participants to be tightly integrated and creating more in-house control and autonomy. Other organizational mechanisms are also preferable to alliances when there is limited property rights protection for valuable know-how and when companies fear being taken advantage of by opportunistic partners.

While it is important for managers to understand when strategic alliances and partnerships are most likely (and least likely) to prove useful, it is also important to know how to manage them.

How to Make Strategic Alliances Work

A surprisingly large number of alliances never live up to expectations. Even though the number of strategic alliances increases by about 25 percent annually, about 60 to 70 percent of alliances continue to fail each year.[24] The success of an alliance depends on how well the partners work together, their capacity to respond and adapt to changing internal and external conditions, and their willingness to renegotiate the bargain if circumstances so warrant. A successful alliance requires real in-the-trenches collaboration, not merely an arm's-length exchange of ideas. Unless partners place a high value on the contribution each brings to the alliance and the cooperative arrangement results in valuable win–win outcomes, it is doomed to fail.

While the track record for strategic alliances is poor on average, many companies have learned how to manage strategic alliances successfully and routinely defy this average. Samsung Group, which includes Samsung Electronics, successfully manages an ecosystem of over 1,300 partnerships that enable productive activities from global procurement to local marketing to collaborative R&D. Companies that have greater success in managing their strategic alliances and partnerships often credit the following factors:

*   *They create a system for managing their alliances.* Companies need to manage their alliances in a systematic fashion, just as they manage other functions. This means

setting up a process for managing the different aspects of alliance management from partner selection to alliance termination procedures. To ensure that the system is followed on a routine basis by all company managers, many companies create a set of explicit procedures, process templates, manuals, or the like.

- *They build relationships with their partners and establish trust.* Establishing strong interpersonal relationships is a critical factor in making strategic alliances work since such relationships facilitate opening up channels of communication, coordinating activity, aligning interests, and building trust.

- *They protect themselves from the threat of opportunism by setting up safeguards.* There are a number of means for preventing a company from being taken advantage of by an untrustworthy partner or unwittingly losing control over key assets. Contractual safeguards, including noncompete clauses, can provide other forms of protection.

- *They make commitments to their partners and see that their partners do the same.* When partners make credible commitments to a joint enterprise, they have stronger incentives for making it work and are less likely to "free-ride" on the efforts of other partners. Because of this, equity-based alliances tend to be more successful than nonequity alliances.[25]

- *They make learning a routine part of the management process.* There are always opportunities for learning from a partner, but organizational learning does not take place automatically. Whatever learning occurs cannot add to a company's knowledge base unless the learning is incorporated systematically into the company's routines and practices.

Finally, managers should realize that alliance management is an organizational capability, much like any other. It develops over time, out of effort, experience, and learning. For this reason, it is wise to begin slowly, with simple alliances designed to meet limited, short-term objectives. Short-term partnerships that are successful often become the basis for much more extensive collaborative arrangements. Even when strategic alliances are set up with the hope that they will become long-term engagements, they have a better chance of succeeding if they are phased in so that the partners can learn how they can work together most fruitfully.

KEY POINTS

1. Once a company has settled on which of the five generic competitive strategies to employ, attention turns to how strategic choices regarding (1) competitive actions, (2) timing of those actions, and (3) scope of operations can complement its competitive approach and maximize the power of its overall strategy.

2. Strategic offensives should, as a general rule, be grounded in a company's strategic assets and employ a company's strengths to attack rivals in the competitive areas where they are weakest.

3. Companies have a number of offensive strategy options for improving their market positions: using a cost-based advantage to attack competitors on the basis of price or value, leapfrogging competitors with next-generation technologies, pursuing continuous product innovation, adopting and improving the best ideas of others, using hit-and-run tactics to steal sales away from unsuspecting rivals, and launching preemptive strikes. A blue-ocean type of offensive strategy seeks to gain a dramatic new competitive advantage by inventing a new industry or distinctive market

segment that renders existing competitors largely irrelevant and allows a company to create and capture altogether new demand in the absence of direct competitors.

4. The purposes of defensive strategies are to lower the risk of being attacked, weaken the impact of any attack that occurs, and influence challengers to aim their efforts at other rivals. Defensive strategies to protect a company's position usually take one of two forms: (1) actions to block challengers or (2) actions to signal the likelihood of strong retaliation.

5. The timing of strategic moves also has relevance in the quest for competitive advantage. Company managers are obligated to carefully consider the advantages or disadvantages that attach to being a first mover versus a fast follower versus a late mover.

6. Decisions concerning the scope of a company's operations—which activities a firm will perform internally and which it will not—can also affect the strength of a company's market position. The *scope of the firm* refers to the range of its activities, the breadth of its product and service offerings, the extent of its geographic market presence, and its mix of businesses. Companies can expand their scope horizontally (more broadly within their focal market) or vertically (up or down the industry value chain system that starts with raw-material production and ends with sales and service to the end consumer). Horizontal mergers and acquisitions (combinations of market rivals) provide a means for a company to expand its horizontal scope. Vertical integration expands a firm's vertical scope.

7. Horizontal mergers and acquisitions typically have any of five objectives: lowering costs, expanding geographic coverage, adding product categories, gaining new technologies or other resources and capabilities, and preparing for the convergence of industries.

8. Vertical integration, forward or backward, makes most strategic sense if it strengthens a company's position via either cost reduction or creation of a differentiation-based advantage. Otherwise, the drawbacks of vertical integration (increased investment, greater business risk, increased vulnerability to technological changes, less flexibility in making product changes, and the potential for channel conflict) are likely to outweigh any advantages.

9. Outsourcing involves contracting out pieces of the value chain formerly performed in-house to outside vendors, thereby narrowing the scope of the firm. Outsourcing can enhance a company's competitiveness whenever (1) an activity can be performed better or more cheaply by outside specialists; (2) the activity is not crucial to the firm's ability to achieve sustainable competitive advantage; (3) the outsourcing improves organizational flexibility, speeds decision making, and cuts cycle time; (4) it reduces the company's risk exposure; and (5) it permits a company to concentrate on its core business and focus on what it does best.

10. Strategic alliances and cooperative partnerships provide one way to gain some of the benefits offered by vertical integration, outsourcing, and horizontal mergers and acquisitions while minimizing the associated problems. They serve as an alternative to vertical integration and mergers and acquisitions, and as a supplement to outsourcing, allowing more control relative to outsourcing via arm's-length transactions.

11. Companies that manage their alliances well generally (1) create a system for managing their alliances, (2) build relationships with their partners and establish trust, (3) protect themselves from the threat of opportunism by setting up safeguards, (4) make commitments to their partners and see that their partners do the same, and (5) make learning a routine part of the management process.

ASSURANCE OF LEARNING EXERCISES

LO 6-1, LO 6-2,
LO 6-3

1. Live Nation Entertainment operates music venues, provides management services to music artists, and promotes more than 35,000 shows and 100 festivals in 40 countries annually. The company acquired House of Blues, merged with Ticketmaster, and acquired concert and festival promoters in the United States, Australia, and Great Britain. How has the company used horizontal mergers and acquisitions to strengthen its competitive position? Are these moves primarily offensive or defensive? Has either Live Nation or Ticketmaster achieved any type of advantage based on the timing of its strategic moves?

LO 6-4

2. Tesla, Inc. has rapidly become a stand-out among American car companies. Illustration Capsule 6.4 describes how Tesla has made vertical integration a central part of its strategy. What value chain segments has Tesla chosen to enter and perform internally? How has vertical integration and integration of its ecosystem aided the organization in building competitive advantage? Has vertical integration strengthened its market position? Explain why or why not.

LO 6-5

3. Perform an Internet search to identify at least two companies in different industries that have entered into outsourcing agreements with firms with specialized services. In addition, describe what value chain activities the companies have chosen to outsource. Do any of these outsourcing agreements seem likely to threaten any of the companies' competitive capabilities?

LO 6-6

4. Using your university library's business research resources, find two examples of how companies have relied on strategic alliances or joint ventures to substitute for horizontal or vertical integration.

EXERCISES FOR SIMULATION PARTICIPANTS

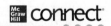

LO 6-1, LO 6-2

1. Has your company relied more on offensive or defensive strategies to achieve your rank in the industry? What options for being a first mover does your company have? Do any of these first-mover options hold competitive advantage potential?

LO 6-3

2. What would be an advantage of a horizontal merger within the industry?

LO 6-4

3. What are the pros and cons of vertical integration in the industry?

LO 6-5

4. What do you see as pros and cons of outsourcing in the business simulation?

ENDNOTES

[1] George Stalk, Jr., and Rob Lachenauer, "Hardball: Five Killer Strategies for Trouncing the Competition," *Harvard Business Review* 82, no. 4 (April 2004); Richard D'Aveni, "The Empire Strikes Back: Counterrevolutionary Strategies for Industry Leaders," *Harvard Business Review* 80, no. 11 (November 2002); David J. Bryce and Jeffrey H. Dyer, "Strategies to Crack Well-Guarded Markets," *Harvard Business Review* 85, no. 5 (May 2007).

[2] George Stalk, "Playing Hardball: Why Strategy Still Matters," *Ivey Business Journal* 69, no.2 (November–December 2004), pp. 1–2; W. J. Ferrier, K. G. Smith, and C. M. Grimm, "The Role of Competitive Action in Market Share Erosion and Industry Dethronement: A Study of Industry Leaders and Challengers," *Academy of Management Journal* 42, no. 4 (August 1999), pp. 372–388.

[3] David B. Yoffie and Mary Kwak, "Mastering Balance: How to Meet and Beat a Stronger Opponent," *California Management Review* 44, no. 2 (Winter 2002), pp. 8–24.
[4] Ian C. MacMillan, Alexander B. van Putten, and Rita Gunther McGrath, "Global Gamesmanship," *Harvard Business Review* 81, no. 5 (May 2003); Ashkay R. Rao, Mark E. Bergen, and Scott Davis, "How to Fight a Price War," *Harvard Business Review* 78, no. 2 (March–April 2000).

[5] D. B. Yoffie and M. A. Cusumano, "Judo Strategy–the Competitive Dynamics of Internet Time," *Harvard Business Review* 77, no. 1 (January–February 1999), pp. 70–81.

[6] Ming-Jer Chen and Donald C. Hambrick, "Speed, Stealth, and Selective Attack: How Small Firms Differ from Large Firms in Competitive Behavior," *Academy of Management Journal* 38, no. 2 (April 1995), pp. 453–482; William E. Rothschild, "Surprise and the Competitive Advantage," *Journal of Business Strategy* 4, no. 3 (Winter 1984), pp. 10–18.

[7] Ian MacMillan, "Preemptive Strategies," *Journal of Business Strategy* 14, no. 2 (Fall 1983), pp. 16–26.

[8] Ian C. MacMillan, "How Long Can You Sustain a Competitive Advantage?" in Liam Fahey (ed.), *The Strategic Planning Management Reader* (Englewood Cliffs, NJ: Prentice Hall, 1989), pp. 23–24.

[9] Kevin P. Coyne and John Horn, "Predicting Your Competitor's Reactions," *Harvard Business Review* 87, no. 4 (April 2009), pp. 90–97.

[10] Philip Kotler, *Marketing Management,* 5th ed. (Englewood Cliffs, NJ: Prentice Hall, 1984).

[11] W. Chan Kim and Renée Mauborgne, "Blue Ocean Strategy," *Harvard Business Review* 82, no. 10 (October 2004), pp. 76–84.

[12] Jeffrey G. Covin, Dennis P. Slevin, and Michael B. Heeley, "Pioneers and Followers: Competitive Tactics, Environment, and Growth," *Journal of Business Venturing* 15, no. 2 (March 1999), pp. 175–210; Christopher A. Bartlett and Sumantra Ghoshal, "Going Global: Lessons from Late-Movers," *Harvard Business Review* 78, no. 2 (March-April 2000), pp. 132–145.

[13] Costas Markides and Paul A. Geroski, "Racing to Be 2nd: Conquering the Industries of the Future," *Business Strategy Review* 15, no. 4 (Winter 2004), pp. 25–31.

[14] Fernando Suarez and Gianvito Lanzolla, "The Half-Truth of First-Mover Advantage," *Harvard Business Review* 83, no. 4 (April 2005), pp. 121–127.

[15] Joseph L. Bower, "Not All M&As Are Alike–and That Matters," *Harvard Business Review* 79, no. 3 (March 2001); O. Chatain and P. Zemsky, "The Horizontal Scope of the Firm: Organizational Tradeoffs vs. Buyer-Supplier Relationships," *Management Science* 53, no. 4 (April 2007), pp. 550–565.

[16] Jeffrey H. Dyer, Prashant Kale, and Harbir Singh, "When to Ally and When to Acquire," *Harvard Business Review* 82, no. 4 (July–August 2004), pp. 109–110.

[17] John Stuckey and David White, "When and When Not to Vertically Integrate," *Sloan Management Review* (Spring 1993), pp. 71–83.

[18] Thomas Osegowitsch and Anoop Madhok, "Vertical Integration Is Dead, or Is It?" *Business Horizons* 46, no. 2 (March–April 2003), pp. 25–35.

[19] Ronan McIvor, "What Is the Right Outsourcing Strategy for Your Process?" *European Management Journal* 26, no. 1 (February 2008), pp. 24–34.

[20] Gary P. Pisano and Willy C. Shih, "Restoring American Competitiveness," *Harvard Business Review* 87, no. 7-8 (July–August 2009), pp. 114–125; Jérôme Barthélemy, "The Seven Deadly Sins of Outsourcing," *Academy of Management Executive* 17, no. 2 (May 2003), pp. 87–100.

[21] Jason Wakeam, "The Five Factors of a Strategic Alliance," *Ivey Business Journal* 68, no. 3 (May–June 2003), pp. 1–4.

[22] A. Inkpen, "Learning, Knowledge Acquisition, and Strategic Alliances," *European Management Journal* 16, no. 2 (April 1998), pp. 223–229.

[23] *Advertising Age,* May 24, 2010, p. 14.

[24] Patricia Anslinger and Justin Jenk, "Creating Successful Alliances," *Journal of Business Strategy* 25, no. 2 (2004), pp. 18–23; Rosabeth Moss Kanter, "Collaborative Advantage: The Art of the Alliance," *Harvard Business Review* 72, no. 4 (July–August 1994), pp. 96-108; Gary Hamel, Yves L. Doz, and C. K. Prahalad, "Collaborate with Your Competitors–and Win," *Harvard Business Review* 67, no. 1 (January–February 1989), pp. 133–139.

[25] Y. G. Pan and D. K. Tse, "The Hierarchical Model of Market Entry Modes," *Journal of International Business Studies* 31, no. 4 (2000), pp. 535–554.

chapter 7

Strategies for Competing in International Markets

Learning Objectives

After reading this chapter, you should be able to:

LO 7-1 Identify the primary reasons companies choose to compete in international markets.

LO 7-2 Understand how and why differing market conditions across countries influence a company's strategy choices in international markets.

LO 7-3 Identify the differences among the five primary modes of entry into foreign markets

LO 7-4 Identify the three main strategic approaches for competing internationally.

LO 7-5 Explain how companies are able to use international operations to improve overall competitiveness.

LO 7-6 Identify the unique characteristics of competing in developing-country markets.

Fanatic Studio/Getty Images

Our key words now are globalization, new products and businesses, and speed.

Tsutomu Kanai—*Former chair and president of Hitachi*

You have no choice but to operate in a world shaped by globalization and the information revolution. There are two options: Adapt or die.

Andy Grove—*Former chair and CEO of Intel*

What counts in global competition is the right strategy.

Heinrich von Pierer—*Former CEO of Siemens AG*

Any company that aspires to industry leadership in the 21st century must think in terms of global, not domestic, market leadership. The world economy is globalizing at an accelerating pace as ambitious, growth-minded companies race to build stronger competitive positions in the markets of more and more countries, as countries previously closed to foreign companies open up their markets, and as information technology shrinks the importance of geographic distance. The forces of globalization are changing the competitive landscape in many industries, offering companies attractive new opportunities and at the same time introducing new competitive threats. Companies in industries where these forces are greatest are therefore under considerable pressure to come up with a strategy for competing successfully in international markets.

This chapter focuses on strategy options for expanding beyond domestic boundaries and competing in the markets of either a few or a great many countries. In the process of exploring these options, we introduce such concepts as the Porter diamond of national competitive advantage; and discuss the specific market circumstances that support the adoption of multidomestic, transnational, and global strategies. The chapter also includes sections on cross-country differences in cultural, demographic, and market conditions; strategy options for entering foreign markets; the importance of locating value chain operations in the most advantageous countries; and the special circumstances of competing in developing markets such as those in China, India, Brazil, Russia, and eastern Europe.

WHY COMPANIES DECIDE TO ENTER FOREIGN MARKETS

● **LO 7-1**

Identify the primary reasons companies choose to compete in international markets.

A company may opt to expand outside its domestic market for any of five major reasons:

1. *To gain access to new customers.* Expanding into foreign markets offers potential for increased revenues, profits, and long-term growth; it becomes an especially attractive option when a company encounters dwindling growth opportunities in its home market. Companies often expand internationally to extend the life cycle of their products, as Honda has done with its classic 50-cc motorcycle, the Honda Cub (which is still selling well in developing markets, more than 60 years after it was first introduced in Japan). A larger target market also offers companies the opportunity to earn a return on large investments more rapidly. This can be particularly important in R&D-intensive industries, where development is fast-paced or competitors imitate innovations rapidly.

2. *To achieve lower costs through economies of scale, experience, and increased purchasing power.* Many companies are driven to sell in more than one country because domestic sales volume alone is not large enough to capture fully economies of scale in product development, manufacturing, or marketing. Similarly, firms expand internationally to increase the rate at which they accumulate experience and move down the learning curve. International expansion can also lower a company's input costs through greater pooled purchasing power. The relatively small size of country markets in Europe and limited domestic volume explains why companies like Michelin, BMW, and Nestlé long ago began selling their products all across Europe and then moved into markets in North America and Latin America.

3. *To gain access to low-cost inputs of production.* Companies in industries based on natural resources (e.g., oil and gas, minerals, rubber, and lumber) often find it necessary to operate in the international arena since raw-material supplies are located in different parts of the world and can be accessed more cost-effectively at the source. Other companies enter foreign markets to access low-cost human resources; this is particularly true of industries in which labor costs make up a high proportion of total production costs.

4. *To further exploit its core competencies.* A company may be able to extend a market-leading position in its domestic market into a position of regional or global market leadership by leveraging its core competencies further. H&M Group is capitalizing on its considerable expertise in fashion retailing to expand its reach internationally. By 2020, it had more than 5000 retail stores operating in 74 countries, and was continuing to expand its global reach. Companies can often leverage their resources internationally by replicating a successful business model, using it as a basic blueprint for international operations, as Starbucks and McDonald's have done.[1]

5. *To gain access to resources and capabilities located in foreign markets.* An increasingly important motive for entering foreign markets is to acquire resources and capabilities that may be unavailable in a company's home market. Companies often make acquisitions abroad or enter into cross-border alliances to gain access to capabilities that complement their own or to learn from their partners.[2] In other cases, companies choose to establish operations in other countries to utilize local distribution networks, gain local managerial or marketing expertise, or acquire specialized technical knowledge.

In addition, companies that are the suppliers of other companies often expand internationally when their major customers do so, to meet their customers' needs abroad and retain their position as a key supply chain partner. For example, when motor vehicle companies have opened new plants in foreign locations, big automotive parts suppliers have frequently opened new facilities nearby to permit timely delivery of their parts and components to the plant. Similarly, Newell-Rubbermaid, one of Walmart's biggest suppliers of household products, has followed Walmart into foreign markets.

WHY COMPETING ACROSS NATIONAL BORDERS MAKES STRATEGY MAKING MORE COMPLEX

Crafting a strategy to compete in one or more countries of the world is inherently more complex for five reasons. First, different countries have different home-country advantages in different industries; competing effectively requires an understanding of these differences. Second, there are location-based advantages to conducting particular value chain activities in different parts of the world. Third, different political and economic conditions make the general business climate more favorable in some countries than in others. Fourth, companies face risk due to adverse shifts in currency exchange rates when operating in foreign markets. And fifth, differences in buyer tastes and preferences present a challenge for companies concerning customizing versus standardizing their products and services.

> ● **LO 7-2**
>
> Understand how and why differing market conditions across countries influence a company's strategy choices in international markets.

Home-Country Industry Advantages and the Diamond Model

Certain countries are known for their strengths in particular industries. For example, Chile has competitive strengths in industries such as copper, fruit, fish products, paper and pulp, chemicals, and wine. Japan is known for competitive strength in consumer electronics, automobiles, semiconductors, steel products, and specialty steel. Where industries are more likely to develop competitive strength depends on a set of factors that describe the nature of each country's business environment and vary from country to country. Because strong industries are made up of strong firms, the strategies of firms that expand internationally are usually grounded in one or more of these factors. The four major factors are summarized in a framework developed by Michael Porter and known as the *Diamond of National Competitive Advantage* (see Figure 7.1).[3]

Demand Conditions   The demand conditions in an industry's home market include the relative size of the market, its growth potential, and the nature of domestic buyers' needs and wants. Differing population sizes, income levels, and other demographic factors give rise to considerable differences in market size and growth rates from country to country. Industry sectors that are larger and more important in their home market tend to attract more resources and grow faster than others. For example, owing to widely differing population demographics and income levels, there is a far bigger market for luxury automobiles in the United States and Germany than in Argentina, India, Mexico, and China. At the same time, in developing markets like India, China, Brazil, and Malaysia, market growth potential is far higher than it is in the more mature economies of Britain, Denmark, Canada, and Japan. The potential for market growth

FIGURE 7.1   The Diamond of National Competitive Advantage

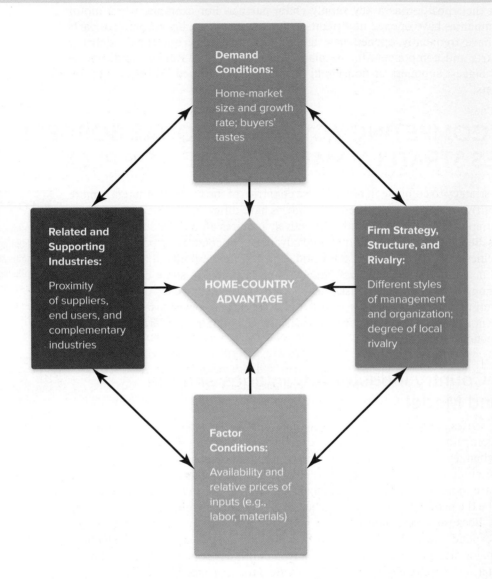

Source: Adapted from Michael E. Porter, "The Competitive Advantage of Nations," *Harvard Business Review,* March–April 1990, pp. 73–93.

in automobiles is explosive in China, where 2017 sales of new vehicles amounted to 28.9 million, surpassing U.S. sales of 17.2 million and making China the world's largest market for the eighth year in a row.[4] Demanding domestic buyers for an industry's products spur greater innovativeness and improvements in quality. Such conditions foster the development of stronger industries, with firms that are capable of translating a home-market advantage into a competitive advantage in the international arena.

Factor Conditions   Factor conditions describe the availability, quality, and cost of raw materials and other inputs (called *factors of production*) that firms in an industry require for producing their products and services. The relevant factors of production vary from industry to industry but can include different types of labor, technical or managerial knowledge, land, financial capital, and natural resources. Elements of a country's infrastructure may be included as well, such as its transportation, communication, and banking systems. For instance, in India there are efficient, well-developed national channels for distributing groceries, personal care items, and other packaged products to the country's 13 million retailers, (as of 2020) whereas in China distribution is primarily local and there is a limited national network for distributing most products. Competitively strong industries and firms develop where relevant factor conditions are favorable.

Related and Supporting Industries   Robust industries often develop in locales where there is a cluster of related industries, including others within the same value chain system (e.g., suppliers of components and equipment, distributors) and the makers of complementary products or those that are technologically related. The sports car makers Ferrari and Maserati, for example, are located in an area of Italy known as the "engine technological district," which includes other firms involved in racing, such as Ducati Motorcycles, along with hundreds of small suppliers. The advantage to firms that develop as part of a related-industry cluster comes from the close collaboration with key suppliers and the greater knowledge sharing throughout the cluster, resulting in greater efficiency and innovativeness.

Firm Strategy, Structure, and Rivalry   Different country environments foster the development of different styles of management, organization, and strategy. For example, strategic alliances are a more common strategy for firms from Asian or Latin American countries, which emphasize trust and cooperation in their organizations, than for firms from North America, where individualism is more influential. In addition, countries vary in terms of the competitive rivalry of their industries. Fierce rivalry in home markets tends to hone domestic firms' competitive capabilities and ready them for competing internationally.

> The Diamond Framework can be used to
> 1. predict from which countries foreign entrants are most likely to come
> 2. decide which foreign markets to enter first
> 3. choose the best country location for different value chain activities

For an industry in a particular country to become competitively strong, all four factors must be favorable for that industry. When they are, the industry is likely to contain firms that are capable of competing successfully in the international arena. Thus the diamond framework can be used to reveal the answers to several questions that are important for competing on an international basis. First, it can help predict *where foreign entrants into an industry are most likely to come from.* This can help managers prepare to cope with new foreign competitors, since the framework also reveals something about the basis of the new rivals' strengths. Second, it can reveal the countries in which foreign rivals are likely to be weakest and thus can help managers decide *which foreign markets to enter first.* And third, because it focuses on the attributes of a country's business environment that allow firms to flourish, it reveals something about the advantages of conducting particular business activities in that country. Thus the diamond framework is an aid to deciding *where to locate different value chain activities most beneficially*—a topic that we address next.

Opportunities for Location-Based Advantages

Increasingly, companies are locating different value chain activities in different parts of the world to exploit location-based advantages that vary from country to country. This is particularly evident with respect to the location of manufacturing activities. Differences in wage rates, worker productivity, energy costs, and the like create sizable variations in manufacturing costs from country to country. By locating its plants in certain countries, firms in some industries can reap major manufacturing cost advantages because of lower input costs (especially labor), relaxed government regulations, the proximity of suppliers and technologically related industries, or unique natural resources. In such cases, the low-cost countries become principal production sites, with most of the output being exported to markets in other parts of the world. Companies that build production facilities in low-cost countries (or that source their products from contract manufacturers in these countries) gain a competitive advantage over rivals with plants in countries where costs are higher. The competitive role of low manufacturing costs is most evident in low-wage countries like China, India, Pakistan, Cambodia, Vietnam, Mexico, Brazil, Guatemala, the Philippines, and several countries in Africa and eastern Europe that have become production havens for manufactured goods with high labor content (especially textiles and apparel). Hourly compensation for manufacturing workers in 2016 averaged about $3.27 in India, $2.06 in the Philippines, $3.60 in China, $3.91 in Mexico, $9.82 in Taiwan, $8.60 in Hungary, $7.98 in Brazil, $10.96 in Portugal, $22.98 in South Korea, $23.67 in New Zealand, $26.46 in Japan, $30.08 in Canada, $39.03 in the United States, $43.18 in Germany, and $60.36 in Switzerland.[5] China emerged as the manufacturing capital of the world in large part because of its low wages—virtually all of the world's major manufacturing companies now have facilities in China.

For other types of value chain activities, input quality or availability are more important considerations. Tiffany & Co. entered the mining industry in Canada to access diamonds that could be certified as "conflict free" and not associated with either the funding of African wars or unethical mining conditions. Many U.S. companies locate call centers in countries such as India and Ireland, where English is spoken and the workforce is well educated. Other companies locate R&D activities in countries where there are prestigious research institutions and well-trained scientists and engineers. Likewise, concerns about short delivery times and low shipping costs make some countries better locations than others for establishing distribution centers.

The Impact of Government Policies and Economic Conditions in Host Countries

Cross-country variations in government policies and economic conditions affect both the opportunities available to a foreign entrant and the risks of operating within the host country. The governments of some countries are eager to attract foreign investments, and thus they go all out to create a business climate that outsiders will view as favorable. Governments eager to spur economic growth, create more jobs, and raise living standards for their citizens usually enact policies aimed at stimulating business innovation and capital investment; Ireland is a good example. They may provide such incentives as reduced taxes, low-cost loans, site location and site development assistance, and government-sponsored training for workers to encourage companies to construct production and distribution facilities. When new business-related issues or developments arise, "pro-business" governments make a practice of seeking advice and counsel from business leaders. When tougher business-related regulations are deemed appropriate, they endeavor to make the transition to more costly and stringent regulations somewhat business-friendly rather than adversarial.

On the other hand, governments sometimes enact policies that, from a business perspective, make locating facilities within a country's borders less attractive. For example, the nature of a company's operations may make it particularly costly to achieve compliance with a country's environmental regulations. Some governments provide subsidies and low-interest loans to domestic companies to enable them to better compete against foreign companies. To discourage foreign imports, governments may enact deliberately burdensome procedures and requirements regarding customs inspection for foreign goods and may impose tariffs or quotas on imports. Additionally, they may specify that a certain percentage of the parts and components used in manufacturing a product be obtained from local suppliers, require prior approval of capital spending projects, limit withdrawal of funds from the country, and require partial ownership of foreign company operations by local companies or investors. There are times when a government may place restrictions on exports to ensure adequate local supplies and regulate the prices of imported and locally produced goods. Such government actions make a country's business climate less attractive and in some cases may be sufficiently onerous as to discourage a company from locating facilities in that country or even selling its products there.

A country's business climate is also a function of the political and economic risks associated with operating within its borders. **Political risks** have to do with the instability of weak governments, growing possibilities that a country's citizenry will revolt against dictatorial government leaders, the likelihood of new onerous legislation or regulations on foreign-owned businesses, and the potential for future elections to produce corrupt or tyrannical government leaders. In industries that a government deems critical to the national welfare, there is sometimes a risk that the government will nationalize the industry and expropriate the assets of foreign companies. In 2012, for example, Argentina nationalized the country's top oil producer, YPF, which was owned by Spanish oil major Repsol. In 2015, they nationalized all of the Argentine railway network, some of which had been in private hands. Other political risks include the loss of investments due to war or political unrest, regulatory changes that create operating uncertainties, security risks due to terrorism, and corruption. **Economic risks** have to do with instability of a country's economy and monetary system—whether inflation rates might skyrocket or whether uncontrolled deficit spending on the part of government or risky bank lending practices could lead to a breakdown of the country's monetary system and prolonged economic distress. In some countries, the threat of piracy and lack of protection for intellectual property are also sources of economic risk. Another is fluctuations in the value of different currencies—a factor that we discuss in more detail next.

> **CORE CONCEPT**
>
> **Political risks** stem from instability or weakness in national governments and hostility to foreign business. **Economic risks** stem from instability in a country's monetary system, economic and regulatory policies, and the lack of property rights protections.

The Risks of Adverse Exchange Rate Shifts

When companies produce and market their products and services in many different countries, they are subject to the impacts of sometimes favorable and sometimes unfavorable changes in currency exchange rates. The rates of exchange between different currencies can vary by as much as 20 to 40 percent annually, with the changes occurring sometimes gradually and sometimes swiftly. *Sizable shifts in exchange rates pose significant risks for two reasons:*

1. They are hard to predict because of the variety of factors involved and the uncertainties surrounding when and by how much these factors will change.
2. They create uncertainty regarding which countries represent the low-cost manufacturing locations and which rivals have the upper hand in the marketplace.

To illustrate the economic and competitive risks associated with fluctuating exchange rates, consider the case of a U.S. company that has located manufacturing facilities in Brazil (where the currency is *reals*—pronounced "ray-alls") and that exports most of the Brazilian-made goods to markets in the European Union (where the currency is euros). To keep the numbers simple, assume that the exchange rate is 4 Brazilian reals for 1 euro and that the product being made in Brazil has a manufacturing cost of 4 Brazilian reals (or 1 euro). Now suppose that the exchange rate shifts from 4 reals per euro to 5 reals per euro (meaning that the real has declined in value and that the euro is stronger). Making the product in Brazil is now more cost-competitive because a Brazilian good costing 4 reals to produce has fallen to only 0.8 euro at the new exchange rate (4 reals divided by 5 reals per euro = 0.8 euro). This clearly puts the producer of the Brazilian-made good *in a better position to compete* against the European makers of the same good. On the other hand, should the value of the Brazilian real grow stronger in relation to the euro—resulting in an exchange rate of 3 reals to 1 euro—the same Brazilian-made good formerly costing 4 reals (or 1 euro) to produce now has a cost of 1.33 euros (4 reals divided by 3 reals per euro = 1.33 euros), putting the producer of the Brazilian-made good in a weaker competitive position vis-à-vis the European producers. Plainly, the attraction of manufacturing a good in Brazil and selling it in Europe is far greater when the euro is strong (an exchange rate of 1 euro for 5 Brazilian reals) than when the euro is weak and exchanges for only 3 Brazilian reals.

But there is one more piece to the story. When the exchange rate changes from 4 reals per euro to 5 reals per euro, not only is the cost-competitiveness of the Brazilian manufacturer stronger relative to European manufacturers of the same item but the Brazilian-made good that formerly cost 1 euro and now costs only 0.8 euro can also be sold to consumers in the European Union for a lower euro price than before. In other words, the combination of a stronger euro and a weaker real acts to *lower the price of Brazilian-made goods* in all the countries that are members of the European Union, which is likely to *spur sales of the Brazilian-made good in Europe and boost Brazilian exports to Europe.* Conversely, should the exchange rate shift from 4 reals per euro to 3 reals per euro—which makes the Brazilian manufacturer less cost-competitive with European manufacturers of the same item—the Brazilian-made good that formerly cost 1 euro and now costs 1.33 euros will sell for a higher price in euros than before, thus weakening the demand of European consumers for Brazilian-made goods and acting to reduce Brazilian exports to Europe. Brazilian exporters are likely to experience (1) rising demand for their goods in Europe whenever the Brazilian real grows weaker relative to the euro and (2) falling demand for their goods in Europe whenever the real grows stronger relative to the euro. Consequently, from the standpoint of a company with Brazilian manufacturing plants, *a weaker Brazilian real is a favorable exchange rate shift* and *a stronger Brazilian real is an unfavorable exchange rate shift.*

It follows from the previous discussion that shifting exchange rates have a big impact on the ability of domestic manufacturers to compete with foreign rivals. For example, U.S.-based manufacturers locked in a fierce competitive battle with low-cost foreign imports benefit from a *weaker* U.S. dollar. There are several reasons why this is so:

- Declines in the value of the U.S. dollar against foreign currencies raise the U.S. dollar costs of goods manufactured by foreign rivals at plants located in the countries whose currencies have grown stronger relative to the U.S. dollar. A *weaker* dollar acts to reduce or eliminate whatever cost advantage foreign manufacturers may have had over U.S. manufacturers (and helps protect the manufacturing jobs of U.S. workers).

- A *weaker* dollar makes foreign-made goods more expensive in dollar terms to U.S. consumers—this curtails U.S. buyer demand for foreign-made goods, stimulates greater demand on the part of U.S. consumers for U.S.-made goods, and reduces U.S. imports of foreign-made goods.

- A *weaker* U.S. dollar enables the U.S.-made goods to be sold at lower prices to consumers in countries whose currencies have grown stronger relative to the U.S. dollar—such lower prices boost foreign buyer demand for the now relatively cheaper U.S.-made goods, thereby stimulating exports of U.S.-made goods to foreign countries and creating more jobs in U.S.-based manufacturing plants.
- A *weaker* dollar has the effect of increasing the dollar value of profits a company earns in foreign-country markets where the local currency is stronger relative to the dollar. For example, if a U.S.-based manufacturer earns a profit of €10 million on its sales in Europe, those €10 million convert to a larger number of dollars when the dollar grows weaker against the euro.

> Fluctuating exchange rates pose significant economic risks to a company's competitiveness in foreign markets. Exporters are disadvantaged when the currency of the country where goods are being manufactured grows stronger relative to the currency of the importing country.

A weaker U.S. dollar is therefore an economically favorable exchange rate shift for manufacturing plants based in the United States. A decline in the value of the U.S. dollar strengthens the cost-competitiveness of U.S.-based manufacturing plants and boosts buyer demand for U.S.-made goods. When the value of the U.S. dollar is expected to remain weak for some time to come, foreign companies have an incentive to build manufacturing facilities in the United States to make goods for U.S. consumers rather than export the same goods to the United States from foreign plants where production costs in dollar terms have been driven up by the decline in the value of the dollar. Conversely, a *stronger* U.S. dollar is an *unfavorable exchange rate shift* for U.S.-based manufacturing plants because it makes such plants less cost-competitive with foreign plants and weakens foreign demand for U.S.-made goods. A strong dollar also weakens the incentive of foreign companies to locate manufacturing facilities in the United States to make goods for U.S. consumers. The same reasoning applies to companies that have plants in countries in the European Union where euros are the local currency. A weak euro versus other currencies enhances the cost-competitiveness of companies manufacturing goods in Europe vis-à-vis foreign rivals with plants in countries whose currencies have grown stronger relative to the euro; a strong euro versus other currencies weakens the cost-competitiveness of companies with plants in the European Union.

> Domestic companies facing competitive pressure from lower-cost imports benefit when their government's currency grows *weaker* in relation to the currencies of the countries where the lower-cost imports are being made.

Cross-Country Differences in Demographic, Cultural, and Market Conditions

Buyer tastes for a particular product or service sometimes differ substantially from country to country. In France, consumers prefer top-loading washing machines, whereas in most other European countries consumers prefer front-loading machines. People in Hong Kong prefer compact appliances, but in Taiwan large appliances are more popular. Ice cream flavors like matcha, black sesame, and red beans have more appeal to East Asian customers than they have for customers in the United States and in Europe. Sometimes, product designs suitable in one country are inappropriate in another because of differing local standards—for example, in the United States electrical devices run on 110-volt electric systems, but in some European countries the standard is a 240-volt electric system, necessitating the use of different electrical designs and components. Cultural influences can also affect consumer demand for a product. For instance, in South Korea many parents are reluctant to purchase PCs even when they can afford them because of concerns that their children will be distracted from their schoolwork by surfing the Web, playing PC-based video games, and becoming Internet "addicts."[6]

Consequently, companies operating in an international marketplace have to wrestle with *whether and how much to customize their offerings in each country market to match local buyers' tastes and preferences or whether to pursue a strategy of offering a mostly standardized product worldwide.* While making products that are closely matched to local tastes makes them more appealing to local buyers, customizing a company's products country by country may raise production and distribution costs due to the greater variety of designs and components, shorter production runs, and the complications of added inventory handling and distribution logistics. Greater standardization of a global company's product offering, on the other hand, can lead to scale economies and learning-curve effects, thus reducing per-unit production costs and contributing to the achievement of a low-cost advantage. *The tension between the market pressures to localize a company's product offerings country by country and the competitive pressures to lower costs is one of the big strategic issues that participants in foreign markets have to resolve.*

STRATEGIC OPTIONS FOR ENTERING INTERNATIONAL MARKETS

LO 7-3

Identify the differences among the five primary modes of entry into foreign markets.

Once a company decides to expand beyond its domestic borders, it must consider the question of how to enter foreign markets. There are five primary *modes of entry* to choose among:

1. Maintain a home-country production base and *export* goods to foreign markets.
2. *License* foreign firms to produce and distribute the company's products abroad.
3. Employ a *franchising* strategy in foreign markets.
4. Establish a *subsidiary* in a foreign market via acquisition or internal development.
5. Rely on *strategic alliances* or joint ventures with foreign companies.

Which mode of entry to employ depends on a variety of factors, including the nature of the firm's strategic objectives, the firm's position in terms of whether it has the full range of resources and capabilities needed to operate abroad, country-specific factors such as trade barriers, and the transaction costs involved (the costs of contracting with a partner and monitoring its compliance with the terms of the contract, for example). The options vary considerably regarding the level of investment required and the associated risks—but higher levels of investment and risk generally provide the firm with the benefits of greater ownership and control.

Export Strategies

Using domestic plants as a production base for exporting goods to foreign markets is an excellent initial strategy for pursuing international sales. It is a conservative way to test the international waters. The amount of capital needed to begin exporting is often minimal; existing production capacity may well be sufficient to make goods for export. With an export-based entry strategy, a manufacturer can limit its involvement in foreign markets by contracting with foreign wholesalers experienced in importing to handle the entire distribution and marketing function in their countries or regions of the world. If it is more advantageous to maintain control over these functions, however, a manufacturer can establish its own distribution and sales organizations in some or all of the target foreign markets. Either way, a home-based production and export strategy helps the firm minimize its direct investments in foreign countries. Such strategies are commonly favored by Chinese, Korean, and Italian companies—products are designed and manufactured at home and then distributed through local channels in the importing countries. The primary functions performed abroad relate chiefly to establishing a network of distributors and perhaps conducting sales promotion and brand-awareness activities.

Whether an export strategy can be pursued successfully over the long run depends on the relative cost-competitiveness of the home-country production base. In some industries, firms gain additional scale economies and learning-curve benefits from centralizing production in plants whose output capability exceeds demand in any one country market; exporting enables a firm to capture such economies. However, an export strategy is vulnerable when (1) manufacturing costs in the home country are substantially higher than in foreign countries where rivals have plants, (2) the costs of shipping the product to distant foreign markets are relatively high, (3) adverse shifts occur in currency exchange rates, and (4) importing countries impose tariffs or erect other trade barriers. Unless an exporter can keep its production and shipping costs competitive with rivals' costs, secure adequate local distribution and marketing support of its products, and effectively hedge against unfavorable changes in currency exchange rates, its success will be limited.

Licensing Strategies

Licensing as an entry strategy makes sense when a firm with valuable technical know-how, an appealing brand, or a unique patented product has neither the internal organizational capability nor the resources to enter foreign markets. Licensing also has the advantage of avoiding the risks of committing resources to country markets that are unfamiliar, politically volatile, economically unstable, or otherwise risky. By licensing the technology, trademark, or production rights to foreign-based firms, a company can generate income from royalties while shifting the costs and risks of entering foreign markets to the licensee. One downside of the licensing alternative is that the partner who bears the risk is also likely to be the biggest beneficiary from any upside gain. Disney learned this lesson when it relied on licensing agreements to open its first foreign theme park, Tokyo Disneyland. When the venture proved wildly successful, it was its licensing partner, the Oriental Land Company, and not Disney who reaped the windfall. Another disadvantage of licensing is the risk of providing valuable technological know-how to foreign companies and thereby losing some degree of control over its use; monitoring licensees and safeguarding the company's proprietary know-how can prove quite difficult in some circumstances. But if the royalty potential is considerable and the companies to which the licenses are being granted are trustworthy and reputable, then licensing can be a very attractive option. Many software and pharmaceutical companies use licensing strategies to participate in foreign markets.

Franchising Strategies

While licensing works well for manufacturers and owners of proprietary technology, franchising is often better suited to the international expansion efforts of service and retailing enterprises. McDonald's, Yum! Brands (the parent of Pizza Hut, KFC, Taco Bell, and WingStreet), the UPS Store, Roto-Rooter, 7-Eleven, and Hilton Hotels have all used franchising to build a presence in foreign markets. Franchising has many of the same advantages as licensing. The franchisee bears most of the costs and risks of establishing foreign locations; a franchisor has to expend only the resources to recruit, train, support, and monitor franchisees. The big problem a franchisor faces is maintaining quality control; foreign franchisees do not always exhibit strong commitment to consistency and standardization, especially when the local culture does not stress the same kinds of quality concerns. A question that can arise is whether to allow foreign franchisees to make modifications in the franchisor's product offering so as to better satisfy the tastes and expectations of local buyers. Should McDonald's give franchisees in each nation some leeway in what products they put on their menus? Should franchised KFC units in China be permitted to substitute spices that appeal to Chinese consumers? Or should the same menu offerings be rigorously and unvaryingly required of all franchisees worldwide?

Foreign Subsidiary Strategies

> **CORE** CONCEPT
>
> A **greenfield venture** (or internal startup) is a subsidiary business that is established by setting up the entire operation from the ground up.

Very often companies electing to compete internationally prefer to have direct control over all aspects of operating in a foreign market. Companies that want to participate in direct performance of all essential value chain activities typically establish a wholly owned subsidiary, either by acquiring a local company or by establishing its own new operating organization from the ground up. A subsidiary business that is established internally from scratch is called an *internal startup* or a **greenfield venture.**

Acquiring a local business is the quicker of the two options; it may be the least risky and most cost-efficient means of hurdling such entry barriers as gaining access to local distribution channels, building supplier relationships, and establishing working relationships with government officials and other key constituencies. Buying an ongoing operation allows the acquirer to move directly to the task of transferring resources and personnel to the newly acquired business, redirecting and integrating the activities of the acquired business into its own operation, putting its own strategy into place, and accelerating efforts to build a strong market position.

One thing an acquisition-minded firm must consider is whether to pay a premium price for a successful local company or to buy a struggling competitor at a bargain price. If the buying firm has little knowledge of the local market but ample capital, it is often better off purchasing a capable, strongly positioned firm. However, when the acquirer sees promising ways to transform a weak firm into a strong one and has the resources and managerial know-how to do so, a struggling company can be the better long-term investment.

Entering a new foreign country via a greenfield venture makes sense when a company already operates in a number of countries, has experience in establishing new subsidiaries and overseeing their operations, and has a sufficiently large pool of resources and capabilities to rapidly equip a new subsidiary with the personnel and what it needs otherwise to compete successfully and profitably. Four more conditions combine to make a greenfield venture strategy appealing:

- When creating an internal startup is cheaper than making an acquisition.
- When adding new production capacity will not adversely impact the supply-demand balance in the local market.
- When a startup subsidiary has the ability to gain good distribution access (perhaps because of the company's recognized brand name).
- When a startup subsidiary will have the size, cost structure, and capabilities to compete head-to-head against local rivals.

Greenfield ventures in foreign markets can also pose problems, just as other entry strategies do. They represent a costly capital investment, subject to a high level of risk. They require numerous other company resources as well, diverting them from other uses. They do not work well in countries without strong, well-functioning markets and institutions that protect the rights of foreign investors and provide other legal protections. Moreover, an important disadvantage of greenfield ventures relative to other means of international expansion is that they are the slowest entry route—particularly if the objective is to achieve a sizable market share. On the other hand, successful greenfield ventures may offer higher returns to compensate for their high risk and slower path.

Collaborative strategies involving alliances or joint ventures with foreign partners are a popular way for companies to edge their way into the markets of foreign countries.

Alliance and Joint Venture Strategies

Strategic alliances, joint ventures, and other cooperative agreements with foreign companies are a widely used means of entering foreign markets.[7] A company can benefit immensely from a foreign partner's familiarity with local government regulations, its knowledge of the buying habits and product preferences of consumers, its distribution-channel relationships, and so on.[8] Both Japanese and American companies are actively forming alliances with European companies to better compete in the 28-nation European Union (and the five countries that are candidates to become EU members). Many U.S. and European companies are allying with Asian companies in their efforts to enter markets in China, India, Thailand, Indonesia, and other Asian countries.

Another reason for cross-border alliances is to capture economies of scale in production and/or marketing. By joining forces in producing components, assembling models, and marketing their products, companies can realize cost savings not achievable with their own small volumes. A third reason to employ a collaborative strategy is to share distribution facilities and dealer networks, thus mutually strengthening each partner's access to buyers. A fourth benefit of a collaborative strategy is the learning and added expertise that comes from performing joint research, sharing technological know-how, studying one another's manufacturing methods, and understanding how to tailor sales and marketing approaches to fit local cultures and traditions. A fifth benefit is that cross-border allies can direct their competitive energies more toward mutual rivals and less toward one another; teaming up may help them close the gap on leading companies. And, finally, alliances can be a particularly useful way for companies across the world to gain agreement on important technical standards—they have been used to arrive at standards for assorted PC devices, Internet-related technologies, high-definition televisions, and mobile phones.

Cross-border alliances enable a growth-minded company to widen its geographic coverage and strengthen its competitiveness in foreign markets; at the same time, they offer flexibility and allow a company to retain some degree of autonomy and operating control.

Cross-border alliances are an attractive means of gaining the aforementioned types of benefits (as compared to merging with or acquiring foreign-based companies) because they allow a company to preserve its independence (which is not the case with a merger) and avoid using scarce financial resources to fund acquisitions. Furthermore, an alliance offers the flexibility to readily disengage once its purpose has been served or if the benefits prove elusive, whereas mergers and acquisitions are more permanent arrangements.[9]

Alliances may also be used to pave the way for an intended merger; they offer a way to test the value and viability of a cooperative arrangement with a foreign partner before making a more permanent commitment. Illustration Capsule 7.1 shows how Walgreens pursued this strategy with Alliance Boots in order to facilitate its expansion abroad.

Walgreens Boots Alliance, Inc.: Entering Foreign Markets via Alliance Followed by Merger

Walgreens pharmacy began in 1901 as a single store on the South Side of Chicago and grew to become the largest chain of pharmacy retailers in America. Walgreens was an early pioneer of the "self-service" pharmacy and found success by moving quickly to build a vast domestic network of stores after the Second World War. This growth-focused strategy served Walgreens well up until the beginning of the 21st century, by which time it had nearly saturated the U.S. market. By 2014, 75 percent of Americans lived within five miles of a Walgreens. The company was also facing threats to its core business model. Walgreens relies heavily on pharmacy sales, which generally are paid for by someone other than the patient, usually the government or an insurance company. As the government and insurers started to make a more sustained effort to cut costs, Walgreens's core profit center was at risk. To mitigate these threats, Walgreens looked to enter foreign markets.

Walgreens found an ideal international partner in Alliance Boots. Based in the UK, Alliance Boots had a global footprint with 3,300 stores across 10 countries. A partnership with Alliance Boots had several strategic advantages, allowing Walgreens to gain swift entry into foreign markets as well as complementary assets and expertise. First, it gave Walgreens access to new markets beyond the saturated United States for its retail pharmacies. Second, it provided Walgreens with a new revenue stream in wholesale drugs. Alliance Boots held a vast European distribution network for wholesale drug sales; Walgreens could leverage that network and expertise to build a similar model in the United States. Finally, a merger with Alliance Boots would strengthen Walgreens's existing business by increasing the company's market position and therefore bargaining power

Jonathan Weiss/Shutterstock

with drug companies. In light of these advantages, Walgreens moved quickly to partner with and later acquire Alliance Boots and merged both companies in 2014 to become Walgreens Boots Alliance. Walgreens Boots Alliance, Inc. is now one of the world's largest drug purchasers, able to negotiate from a strong position with drug companies and other suppliers to realize economies of scale in its current businesses.

The market has thus far responded favorably to the merger. Walgreens Boots Alliance's stock has more than doubled in value since the first news of the partnership in 2012. However, the company is still struggling to integrate and faces new risks such as currency fluctuation in its new combined position. Yet as the pharmaceutical industry continues to consolidate, Walgreens is in an undoubtedly stronger position to continue to grow in the future thanks to its strategic international acquisition.

Note: Developed with Katherine Coster.

Sources: Company 10-K Form, 2015, investor.walgreensbootsalliance.com/secfiling.cfm?filingID=1140361-15-38791&CIK=1618921; L. Capron and W. Mitchell, "When to Change a Winning Strategy," *Harvard Business Review,* July 25, 2012, hbr.org/2012/07/when-to-change-a-winning-strat; T. Martin and R. Dezember, "Walgreen Spends $6.7 Billion on Alliance Boots Stake," *The Wall Street Journal,* June 20, 2012.

The Risks of Strategic Alliances with Foreign Partners Alliances and joint ventures with foreign partners have their pitfalls, however. Sometimes a local partner's knowledge and expertise turns out to be less valuable than expected (because its knowledge is rendered obsolete by fast-changing market conditions or because its operating practices are archaic). Cross-border allies typically must overcome language and cultural barriers and figure out how to deal with diverse (or conflicting) operating practices. The transaction costs of working out a mutually agreeable arrangement and monitoring partner compliance with the terms of the arrangement can be high. The communication, trust building, and coordination costs are not trivial in terms of management time.[10] Often, partners soon discover they have conflicting objectives and strategies, deep differences of opinion about how to proceed, or important differences in corporate values and ethical standards. Tensions build, working relationships cool, and the hoped-for benefits never materialize.[11] It is not unusual for there to be little personal chemistry among some of the key people on whom the success or failure of the alliance depends—the rapport such personnel need to work well together may never emerge. And even if allies are able to develop productive personal relationships, they can still have trouble reaching mutually agreeable ways to deal with key issues or launching new initiatives fast enough to stay abreast of rapid advances in technology or shifting market conditions.

One worrisome problem with alliances or joint ventures is that a firm may risk losing some of its competitive advantage if an alliance partner is given full access to its proprietary technological expertise or other competitively valuable capabilities. There is a natural tendency for allies to struggle to collaborate effectively in competitively sensitive areas, thus spawning suspicions on both sides about forthright exchanges of information and expertise. It requires many meetings of many people working in good faith over a period of time to iron out what is to be shared, what is to remain proprietary, and how the cooperative arrangements will work.

Even if the alliance proves to be a win–win proposition for both parties, there is the danger of becoming overly dependent on foreign partners for essential expertise and competitive capabilities. Companies aiming for global market leadership need to develop their own resources and capabilities in order to be masters of their destiny. Frequently, experienced international companies operating in 50 or more countries across the world find less need for entering into cross-border alliances than do companies in the early stages of globalizing their operations.[12] Companies with global operations make it a point to develop senior managers who understand how "the system" works in different countries, plus they can avail themselves of local managerial talent and know-how by simply hiring experienced local managers and thereby detouring the hazards of collaborative alliances with local companies. One of the lessons about cross-border partnerships is that they are more effective in helping a company establish a beachhead of new opportunity in world markets than they are in enabling a company to achieve and sustain global market leadership.

INTERNATIONAL STRATEGY: THE THREE MAIN APPROACHES

Broadly speaking, a firm's **international strategy** is simply its strategy for competing in two or more countries simultaneously. Typically, a company will start to compete internationally by entering one or perhaps a select few foreign markets—selling its products or services in countries where there is a ready market for them. But as it expands further internationally, it will have to confront head-on two conflicting pressures: the demand for responsiveness to local needs versus the prospect of efficiency gains from offering a standardized product globally. Deciding on the competitive approach to best address these competing pressures is perhaps the foremost strategic issue that must be addressed when a company is operating in two or more foreign markets.[13] Figure 7.2 shows a company's three options for resolving this issue: choosing a *multidomestic, global,* or *transnational* strategy.

LO 7-4

Identify the three main strategic approaches for competing internationally.

CORE CONCEPT

An **international strategy** is a strategy for competing in two or more countries simultaneously.

FIGURE 7.2 Three Approaches for Competing Internationally

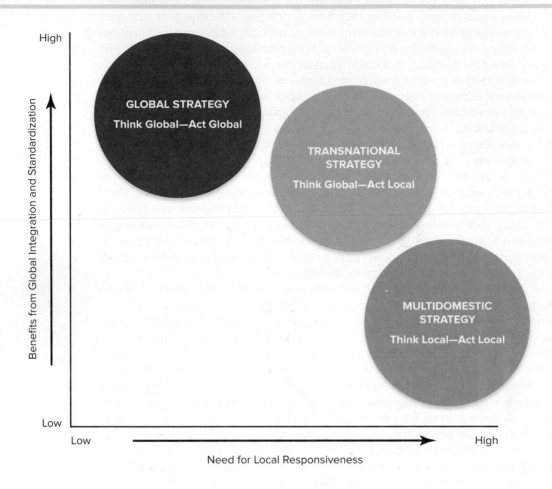

Multidomestic Strategies—a "Think-Local, Act-Local" Approach

A **multidomestic strategy** is one in which a company varies its product offering and competitive approach from country to country in an effort to meet differing buyer needs and to address divergent local-market conditions. It involves having plants produce different product versions for different local markets and adapting marketing and distribution to fit local customs, cultures, regulations, and market requirements. In the food products industry, it is common for companies to vary the ingredients in their products and sell the localized versions under local brand names to cater to country-specific tastes and eating preferences. Government requirements for gasoline additives that help reduce carbon monoxide, smog, and other emissions are almost never the same from country to country. BP utilizes localized strategies in its gasoline and service station business segment because of these cross-country formulation differences and because of customer familiarity with local brand names. For example, the company markets gasoline in the United States under its BP and Arco brands, but markets gasoline in Germany, Belgium, Poland, Hungary, and the Czech Republic under the Aral brand. Castrol, a BP-owned specialist in oil lubricants, produces over 3,000 different formulas of lubricants to meet the requirements of different climates, vehicle types and uses, and equipment applications that characterize different country markets.

In essence, a multidomestic strategy represents a **think-local, act-local** approach to international strategy. A think-local, act-local approach to strategy making is most appropriate when the need for local responsiveness is high due to significant cross-country differences in demographic, cultural, and market conditions and when the potential for efficiency gains from standardization is limited, as depicted in Figure 7.2. A think-local, act-local approach is possible only when decision making is decentralized, giving local managers considerable latitude for crafting and executing strategies for the country markets they are responsible for. Giving local managers decision-making authority allows them to address specific market needs and respond swiftly to local changes in demand. It also enables them to focus their competitive efforts, stake out attractive market positions vis-à-vis local competitors, react to rivals' moves in a timely fashion, and target new opportunities as they emerge.[14]

Despite their obvious benefits, think-local, act-local strategies have three big drawbacks:

1. They hinder transfer of a company's capabilities, knowledge, and other resources across country boundaries, since the company's efforts are not integrated or coordinated across country boundaries. This can make the company less innovative overall.

2. They raise production and distribution costs due to the greater variety of designs and components, shorter production runs for each product version, and complications of added inventory handling and distribution logistics.

3. They are not conducive to building a single, worldwide competitive advantage. When a company's competitive approach and product offering vary from country to country, the nature and size of any resulting competitive edge also tends to vary. At the most, multidomestic strategies are capable of producing a group of local competitive advantages of varying types and degrees of strength.

Global Strategies—a "Think-Global, Act-Global" Approach

A **global strategy** contrasts sharply with a multidomestic strategy in that it takes a standardized, globally integrated approach to producing, packaging, selling, and delivering the company's products and services worldwide. Companies employing a global strategy sell the same products under the same brand names everywhere, utilize much the same distribution channels in all countries, and compete on the basis of the same capabilities and marketing approaches worldwide. Although the company's strategy or product offering may be adapted in minor ways to accommodate specific situations in a few host countries, the company's fundamental competitive approach (low cost, differentiation, best cost, or focused) remains very much intact worldwide and local managers stick close to the global strategy.

A **think-global, act-global** approach prompts company managers to integrate and coordinate the company's strategic moves worldwide and to expand into most, if not all, nations where there is significant buyer demand. It puts considerable strategic emphasis on building a *global* brand name and aggressively pursuing opportunities to transfer ideas, new products, and capabilities from one country to another. Global strategies are characterized by relatively centralized value chain activities, such as production and distribution. While there may be more than one manufacturing plant and distribution center to minimize transportation costs, for example, they tend to be few

CORE CONCEPT

A **global strategy** is one in which a company employs the same basic competitive approach in all countries where it operates, sells standardized products globally, strives to build global brands, and coordinates its actions worldwide with strong headquarters control. It represents a **think-global, act-global** approach.

in number. Achieving the efficiency potential of a global strategy requires that resources and best practices be shared, value chain activities be integrated, and capabilities be transferred from one location to another as they are developed. These objectives are best facilitated through centralized decision making and strong headquarters control.

Because a global strategy cannot accommodate varying local needs, it is an appropriate strategic choice when there are pronounced efficiency benefits from standardization and when buyer needs are relatively homogeneous across countries and regions. A globally standardized and integrated approach is especially beneficial when high volumes significantly lower costs due to economies of scale or added experience (moving the company further down a learning curve). It can also be advantageous if it allows the firm to replicate a successful business model on a global basis efficiently or engage in higher levels of R&D by spreading the fixed costs and risks over a higher-volume output. It is a fitting response to industry conditions marked by global competition.

Consumer electronics companies such as Apple, Nokia, and Motorola Mobility tend to employ global strategies. The development of universal standards in technology is one factor supporting the use of global strategies. So is the rise of global accounting and financial reporting standards. Whenever country-to-country differences are small enough to be accommodated within the framework of a global strategy, a global strategy is preferable because a company can more readily unify its operations and focus on establishing a brand image and reputation that are uniform from country to country. Moreover, with a global strategy a company is better able to focus its full resources on securing a sustainable low-cost or differentiation-based competitive advantage over both domestic rivals and global rivals.

There are, however, several drawbacks to global strategies: (1) They do not enable firms to address local needs as precisely as locally based rivals can; (2) they are less responsive to changes in local market conditions, in the form of either new opportunities or competitive threats; (3) they raise transportation costs and may involve higher tariffs; and (4) they involve higher coordination costs due to the more complex task of managing a globally integrated enterprise.

Transnational Strategies—a "Think-Global, Act-Local" Approach

A **transnational strategy** (sometimes called *glocalization*) incorporates elements of both a globalized and a localized approach to strategy making. This type of middle-ground strategy is called for when there are relatively high needs for local responsiveness as well as appreciable benefits to be realized from standardization, as Figure 7.2 suggests. A transnational strategy encourages a company to use a **think-global, act-local** approach to balance these competing objectives.

Often, companies implement a transnational strategy with mass-customization techniques that enable them to address local preferences in an efficient, semi-standardized manner. McDonald's, KFC, and Starbucks have discovered ways to customize their menu offerings in various countries without compromising costs, product quality, and operating effectiveness. Unilever is responsive to local market needs regarding its consumer products, while realizing global economies of scale in certain functions. Otis Elevator found that a transnational strategy delivers better results than a global strategy when it is competing in countries like China, where local needs are highly differentiated. By switching from its customary single-brand approach to a multibrand strategy aimed at serving different segments of the market, Otis was able to double its market share in China and increased its revenues sixfold over a nine-year period.[15]

As a rule, most companies that operate internationally endeavor to employ as global a strategy as customer needs and market conditions permit. Electronic Arts (EA) has two major design studios—one in Vancouver, British Columbia, and one in Los Angeles—and smaller design studios in locations including San Francisco, Orlando, London, and Tokyo. This dispersion of design studios helps EA design games that are specific to different cultures—for example, the London studio took the lead in designing the popular FIFA Soccer game to suit European tastes and to replicate the stadiums, signage, and team rosters; the U.S. studio took the lead in designing games involving NFL football, NBA basketball, and NASCAR racing.

A transnational strategy is far more conducive than other strategies to transferring and leveraging subsidiary skills and capabilities. But, like other approaches to competing internationally, transnational strategies also have significant drawbacks:

1. They are the most difficult of all international strategies to implement due to the added complexity of varying the elements of the strategy to situational conditions.

2. They place large demands on the organization due to the need to pursue conflicting objectives simultaneously.

3. Implementing the strategy is likely to be a costly and time-consuming enterprise, with an uncertain outcome.

Illustration Capsule 7.2 explains how Four Seasons Hotels has been able to compete successfully on the basis of a transnational strategy.

Table 7.1 provides a summary of the pluses and minuses of the three approaches to competing internationally.

TABLE 7.1 Advantages and Disadvantages of Multidomestic, Global, and Transnational Strategies

	Advantages	Disadvantages
Multidomestic (think local, act local)	• Can meet the specific needs of each market more precisely • Can respond more swiftly to localized changes in demand • Can target reactions to the moves of local rivals • Can respond more quickly to local opportunities and threats	• Hinders resource and capability sharing or cross-market transfers • Has higher production and distribution costs • Is not conducive to a worldwide competitive advantage
Global (think global, act global)	• Has lower costs due to scale and scope economies • Can lead to greater efficiencies due to the ability to transfer best practices across markets • Increases innovation from knowledge sharing and capability transfer • Offers the benefit of a global brand and reputation	• Cannot address local needs precisely • Is less responsive to changes in local market conditions • Involves higher transportation costs and tariffs • Has higher coordination and integration costs
Transnational (think global, act local)	• Offers the benefits of both local responsiveness and global integration • Enables the transfer and sharing of resources and capabilities across borders • Provides the benefits of flexible coordination	• Is more complex and harder to implement • Entails conflicting goals, which may be difficult to reconcile and require trade-offs • Involves more costly and time-consuming implementation

Four Seasons Hotels: Local Character, Global Service

Four Seasons Hotels is a Toronto, Canada-based manager of luxury hotel properties. With more than 100 properties located in many of the world's most popular tourist destinations and business centers, Four Seasons commands a following of many of the world's most discerning travelers. In contrast to its key competitor, Ritz-Carlton, which strives to create one uniform experience globally, Four Seasons Hotels has gained market share by deftly combining local architectural and cultural experiences with globally consistent luxury service.

When moving into a new market, Four Seasons always seeks out a local capital partner. The understanding of local custom and business relationships this financier brings is critical to the process of developing a new Four Seasons hotel. Four Seasons also insists on hiring a local architect and design consultant for each property, as opposed to using architects or designers it's worked with in other locations. While this can be a challenge, particularly in emerging markets, Four Seasons has found it is worth it in the long run to have a truly local team.

The specific layout and programming of each hotel is also unique. For instance, when Four Seasons opened its hotel in Mumbai, India, it prioritized space for large banquet halls to target the Indian wedding market. In India, weddings often draw guests numbering in the thousands. When moving into the Middle East, Four Seasons designed its hotels with separate prayer rooms for men and women. In Bali, where destination weddings are common, the hotel employs a "weather shaman" who, for some guests, provides reassurance that the weather will cooperate for their special day. In all cases, the objective is to provide a truly local experience.

When staffing its hotels, Four Seasons seeks to strike a fine balance between employing locals who have

Chris Lawrence/Alamy Stock Photo

an innate understanding of the local culture alongside expatriate staff or "culture carriers" who understand the DNA of Four Seasons. It also uses global systems to track customer preferences and employs globally consistent service standards. Four Seasons claims that its guests experience the same high level of service globally but that no two experiences are the same.

While it is much more expensive and time-consuming to design unique architectural and programming experiences, doing so is a strategic trade-off Four Seasons has made to achieve the local experience demanded by its high-level clientele. Likewise, it has recognized that maintaining globally consistent operation processes and service standards is important too. Four Seasons has struck the right balance between thinking globally and acting locally—the marker of a truly transnational strategy. As a result, the company has been rewarded with an international reputation for superior service and a leading market share in the luxury hospitality segment.

Note: Developed with Brian R. McKenzie.

Sources: Four Seasons annual report and corporate website; interview with Scott Woroch, executive vice president of development, Four Seasons Hotels, February 22, 2014.

INTERNATIONAL OPERATIONS AND THE QUEST FOR COMPETITIVE ADVANTAGE

There are three important ways in which a firm can gain competitive advantage (or offset domestic disadvantages) by expanding outside its domestic market. First, it can use location to lower costs or achieve greater product differentiation. Second, it can transfer competitively valuable resources and capabilities from one country to another or share them across international borders to extend its competitive advantages. And third, it can benefit from cross-border coordination opportunities that are not open to domestic-only competitors.

● **LO 7-5**

Explain how companies are able to use international operations to improve overall competitiveness.

Using Location to Build Competitive Advantage

To use location to build competitive advantage, a company must consider two issues: (1) whether or not to concentrate some of the activities it performs in only a few select countries of those in which they operate and if so (2) in which countries to locate particular activities.

> Companies that compete internationally can pursue competitive advantage in world markets by locating their value chain activities in whatever nations prove most advantageous.

When to Concentrate Activities in a Few Locations   It is advantageous for a company to concentrate its activities in a limited number of locations when

- *The costs of manufacturing or other activities are significantly lower in some geographic locations than in others.* For example, much of the world's athletic footwear is manufactured in Asia (China, Vietnam, and Indonesia) because of low labor costs; much of the production of circuit boards for PCs is located in Taiwan because of both low costs and the high-caliber technical skills of the Taiwanese labor force.

- *Significant scale economies exist in production or distribution.* The presence of significant economies of scale in components production or final assembly means that a company can gain major cost savings from operating a few super-efficient plants as opposed to a host of small plants scattered across the world. Makers of digital cameras and LED TVs located in Japan, South Korea, and Taiwan have used their scale economies to establish a low-cost advantage in this way. Achieving low-cost leadership status often requires a company to have the largest worldwide manufacturing share (as distinct from brand share or market share), with production centralized in one or a few giant plants. Some companies even use such plants to manufacture units sold under the brand names of rivals to further boost production-related scale economies. Likewise, a company may be able to reduce its distribution costs by establishing large-scale distribution centers to serve major geographic regions of the world market (e.g., North America, Latin America, Europe and the Middle East, and the Asia-Pacific region).

- *Sizable learning and experience benefits are associated with performing an activity.* In some industries, learning-curve effects can allow a manufacturer to lower unit costs, boost quality, or master a new technology *more quickly* by concentrating production in a few locations. The key to riding down the learning curve is to concentrate production in a few locations to increase the cumulative volume at a plant (and thus the experience of the plant's workforce) as rapidly as possible.

- *Certain locations have superior resources, allow better coordination of related activities, or offer other valuable advantages.* Companies often locate a research unit or a sophisticated production facility in a particular country to take advantage of its pool of technically trained personnel. Adidas located its first robotic "speedfactory" in Germany to benefit from its superior technological resources and to allow greater oversight from the company's headquarters (which are in Germany). Where just-in-time inventory practices yield big cost savings and/or where an assembly firm has long-term partnering arrangements with its key suppliers, parts manufacturing plants may be clustered around final-assembly plants. A customer service center or sales office may be opened in a particular country to help cultivate strong relationships with pivotal customers located nearby. Airbus established a major assembly site for their commercial aircraft in Alabama since the United States is a major market.

When to Disperse Activities across Many Locations   In some instances, dispersing activities across locations is more advantageous than concentrating them. Buyer-related activities—such as distribution, marketing, and after-sale service—usually must take place close to buyers. This makes it necessary to physically locate the capability to perform such activities in every country or region where a firm has major customers. For example, firms that make mining and oil-drilling equipment maintain operations in many locations around the world to support customers' needs for speedy equipment repair and technical assistance. Large public accounting firms have offices in numerous countries to serve the foreign operations of their international corporate clients. Dispersing activities to many locations is also competitively important when high transportation costs, diseconomies of large size, and trade barriers make it too expensive to operate from a central location. Many companies distribute their products from multiple locations to shorten delivery times to customers. In addition, dispersing activities helps hedge against the risks of fluctuating exchange rates, supply interruptions (due to strikes, natural disasters, or transportation delays), and adverse political developments. Such risks are usually greater when activities are concentrated in a single location.

Even though global firms have strong reason to disperse buyer-related activities to many international locations, such activities as materials procurement, parts manufacture, finished-goods assembly, technology research, and new product development can frequently be decoupled from buyer locations and performed wherever advantage lies. Components can be made in Mexico; technology research done in Frankfurt; new products developed and tested in Phoenix; and assembly plants located in Spain, Brazil, Taiwan, or South Carolina, for example. Capital can be raised wherever it is available on the best terms.

Sharing and Transferring Resources and Capabilities across Borders to Build Competitive Advantage

When a company has competitively valuable resources and capabilities, it may be able to leverage them further by expanding internationally. If its resources retain their value in foreign contexts, then entering new foreign markets can extend the company's resource-based competitive advantage over a broader domain. For example, companies like Tiffany, Cartier, and Rolex have utilized their powerful brand names to extend their differentiation-based competitive advantages into markets far beyond their home-country origins. In each of these cases, the luxury brand name represents a valuable competitive asset that can readily be *shared* by all of the company's international stores, enabling them to attract buyers and gain a higher degree of market penetration over a wider geographic area than would otherwise be possible.

Another way for a company to extend its competitive advantage internationally is to *transfer* technological know-how or other important resources and capabilities from its operations in one country to its operations in other countries. For instance, if a company discovers ways to assemble a product faster and more cost-effectively at one plant, then that know-how can be transferred to its assembly plants in other countries. Whirlpool's efforts to link its product R&D and manufacturing operations in North America, Latin America, Europe, and Asia allowed it to accelerate the discovery of innovative appliance features, coordinate the introduction of these features in the appliance products marketed in different countries, and create a cost-efficient worldwide supply chain. Whirlpool's conscious efforts to integrate and coordinate its various operations around the world have helped it achieve operational excellence and speed product innovations to market. Walmart is expanding its international operations with a strategy that involves transferring its considerable resource capabilities in distribution and discount retailing to its retail units in 28 foreign countries.

Cross-border sharing or transferring resources and capabilities provides a cost-effective way for a company to leverage its core competencies more fully and extend its competitive advantages into a wider array of geographic markets. The cost of sharing or transferring already developed resources and capabilities across country borders is low in comparison to the time and considerable expense it takes to create them. Moreover, deploying them abroad spreads the fixed development costs over a greater volume of unit sales, thus contributing to low unit costs and a potential cost-based competitive advantage in recently entered geographic markets. Even if the shared or transferred resources or capabilities have to be adapted to local-market conditions, this can usually be done at low additional cost.

Consider the case of Walt Disney's theme parks as an example. The success of the theme parks in the United States derives in part from core resources such as the Disney brand name and characters like Mickey Mouse that have universal appeal and worldwide recognition. These resources can be freely shared with new theme parks as Disney expands internationally. Disney can also replicate its theme parks in new countries cost-effectively since it has already borne the costs of developing its core resources, park attractions, basic park design, and operating capabilities. The cost of replicating its theme parks abroad is relatively low, even if the parks need to be adapted to a variety of local country conditions. Thus, in establishing Disney parks in Tokyo, Paris, Hong Kong, and Shanghai, Disney has been able to leverage the differentiation advantage conferred by resources such as the Disney name and the park attractions. And by moving into new foreign markets, it has augmented its competitive advantage further through the efficiency gains that come from cross-border resource sharing and low-cost capability transfer and business model replication.

Sharing and transferring resources and capabilities across country borders may also contribute to the development of broader or deeper competencies and capabilities—helping a company achieve *dominating depth* in some competitively valuable area. For example, the reputation for quality that Honda established worldwide began in motorcycles but enabled the company to command a position in both automobiles and outdoor power equipment in multiple-country markets. A one-country customer base is often too small to support the resource buildup needed to achieve such depth; this is particularly true in a developing or protected market, where competitively powerful resources are not required. By deploying capabilities across a larger international domain, a company can gain the experience needed to upgrade them to a higher performance standard. And by facing a more challenging set of international competitors, a company may be spurred to develop a stronger set of competitive capabilities. Moreover, by entering international markets, firms may be able to augment their capability set by learning from international rivals, cooperative partners, or acquisition targets.

However, cross-border resource sharing and transfers of capabilities are not guaranteed recipes for competitive success. For example, whether a resource or capability can confer a competitive advantage abroad depends on the conditions of rivalry in each particular market. If the rivals in a foreign-country market have superior resources and capabilities, then an entering firm may find itself at a competitive disadvantage even if it has a resource-based advantage domestically and can transfer the resources at low cost. In addition, since lifestyles and buying habits differ internationally, resources and capabilities that are valuable in one country may not have value in another. Sometimes a popular or well-regarded brand in one country turns out to have little competitive clout against local brands in other countries.

Benefiting from Cross-Border Coordination

Companies that compete on an international basis have another source of competitive advantage relative to their purely domestic rivals: They are able to benefit from coordinating activities across different countries' domains.[16] For example, an international manufacturer can shift production from a plant in one country to a plant in another to take advantage of exchange rate fluctuations, to cope with components shortages, or to profit from changing wage rates or energy costs. Production schedules can be coordinated worldwide; shipments can be diverted from one distribution center to another if sales rise unexpectedly in one place and fall in another. By coordinating their activities, international companies may also be able to enhance their leverage with host-country governments or respond adaptively to changes in tariffs and quotas. Efficiencies can also be achieved by shifting workloads from where they are unusually heavy to locations where personnel are underutilized.

CROSS-BORDER STRATEGIC MOVES

While international competitors can employ any of the offensive and defensive moves discussed in Chapter 6, there are two types of strategic moves that are particularly suited for companies competing internationally. The first is an offensive move that an international competitor is uniquely positioned to make, due to the fact that it may have a strong or protected market position in more than one country. The second type of move is a type of defensive action involving multiple markets.

Waging a Strategic Offensive

CORE CONCEPT

Cross-market subsidization—supporting competitive offensives in one market with resources and profits diverted from operations in another market—can be a powerful competitive weapon.

One advantage to being an international competitor is the possibility of having more than one significant and possibly protected source of profits. This may provide the company with the financial strength to engage in strategic offensives in selected country markets. The added financial capability afforded by multiple profit sources gives an international competitor the financial strength to wage an offensive campaign against a domestic competitor whose only source of profit is its home market. The international company has the flexibility of lowballing its prices or launching high-cost marketing campaigns in the domestic company's home market and grabbing market share at the domestic company's expense. Razor-thin margins or even losses in these markets can be subsidized with the healthy profits earned in its markets abroad—a practice called **cross-market subsidization.**

The international company can adjust the depth of its price cutting to move in and capture market share quickly, or it can shave prices slightly to make gradual market inroads (perhaps over a decade or more) so as not to threaten domestic firms precipitously and trigger protectionist government actions. If the domestic company retaliates with matching price cuts or increased marketing expenses, it thereby exposes its entire revenue stream and profit base to erosion; its profits can be squeezed substantially and its competitive strength sapped, even if it is the domestic market leader.

When taken to the extreme, cut-rate pricing attacks by international competitors may draw charges of unfair "dumping." A company is said to be *dumping* when it sells its goods in foreign markets at prices that are (1) well below the prices at which it normally sells them in its home market or (2) well below its full costs per unit. Almost all governments can be expected to retaliate against perceived dumping practices by imposing special tariffs on goods being imported from the countries of the guilty companies. Indeed, as the trade among nations has mushroomed over the past 10 years, most governments have joined the World Trade Organization (WTO), which promotes fair trade practices among nations and actively polices dumping. Companies deemed guilty of dumping frequently come under pressure from their own government to cease and desist, especially if the tariffs adversely affect innocent companies based in the same country or if the advent of special tariffs raises the specter of an international trade war.

> A company is said to be *dumping* when it sells its goods in foreign markets at prices that are
> 1. well below the prices at which it normally sells them in its home market or
> 2. well below its full costs per unit.

Defending against International Rivals

Cross-border tactics involving multiple country markets can also be used as a means of defending against the strategic moves of rivals with multiple profitable markets of their own. If a company finds itself under competitive attack by an international rival in one country market, one way to respond is to conduct a counterattack against the rival in one of its key markets in a different country—preferably where the rival is least protected and has the most to lose. This is a possible option when rivals compete against one another in much the same markets around the world and engage in *multimarket competition.*

For companies with at least one major market, having a presence in a rival's key markets can be enough to deter the rival from making aggressive attacks. The reason for this is that the combination of market presence in the rival's key markets and a highly profitable market elsewhere can send a signal to the rival that the company could quickly ramp up production (funded by the profit center) to mount a competitive counterattack if the rival attacks one of the company's key markets.

When international rivals compete against one another in multiple-country markets, this type of deterrence effect can restrain them from taking aggressive action against one another, due to the fear of a retaliatory response that might escalate the battle into a cross-border competitive war. **Mutual restraint** of this sort tends to stabilize the competitive position of multimarket rivals against one another. And while it may prevent each firm from making any major market share gains at the expense of its rival, it also protects against costly competitive battles that would be likely to erode the profitability of both companies without any compensating gain.

> *Multimarket competition* refers to a situation where rivals compete against one another in many of the same markets.

> **CORE** CONCEPT
>
> When the same companies compete against one another in multiple geographic markets, the threat of cross-border counterattacks may be enough to encourage **mutual restraint** among international rivals.

STRATEGIES FOR COMPETING IN THE MARKETS OF DEVELOPING COUNTRIES

● ● ● ●

Companies racing for global leadership have to consider competing in developing-economy markets like China, India, Brazil, Indonesia, Thailand, Poland, Mexico, and Russia—countries where the business risks are considerable but where the opportunities for growth are huge, especially as their economies develop and living standards climb toward levels in the industrialized world.[17] In today's world, a company that aspires to international market leadership (or to sustained rapid growth) cannot ignore the market opportunities or the base of technical and managerial talent such countries offer. For example, in 2018, China was the world's second-largest economy (behind the United States), based on the purchasing power of its population of over 1.4 billion people. China's growth in demand for consumer goods has made it the fifth largest market for luxury goods, with sales greater than those in developed markets such as Germany, Spain, and the United Kingdom. Thus, no company that aspires to global market leadership can afford to ignore the strategic importance of establishing competitive market positions in the so-called BRIC countries (Brazil, Russia, India, and China), as well as in other parts of the Asia-Pacific region, Latin America, and eastern Europe.

Tailoring products to fit market conditions in developing countries, however, often involves more than making minor product changes and becoming more familiar with local cultures. McDonald's has had to offer vegetable burgers in parts of Asia and to rethink its prices, which are often high by local standards and affordable only by the well-to-do. Kellogg has struggled to introduce its cereals successfully because consumers in many less developed countries do not eat cereal for breakfast. Single-serving packages of detergents, shampoos, pickles, cough syrup, and cooking oils are very popular in India because they allow buyers to conserve cash by purchasing only what they need immediately. Thus, many companies find that trying to employ a strategy akin to that used in the markets of developed countries is hazardous.[18] Experimenting with some, perhaps many, local twists is usually necessary to find a strategy combination that works.

Strategy Options for Competing in Developing-Country Markets

There are several options for tailoring a company's strategy to fit the sometimes unusual or challenging circumstances presented in developing-country markets:

- *Prepare to compete on the basis of low price.* Consumers in developing markets are often highly focused on price, which can give low-cost local competitors the edge unless a company can find ways to attract buyers with bargain prices as well as better products. For example, in order to enter the market for laundry detergents in India, Unilever had to develop a low-cost detergent (named Wheel), construct new low-cost production facilities, package the detergent in single-use amounts so that it could be sold at a very low unit price, distribute the product to local merchants by handcarts, and craft an economical marketing campaign that included painted signs on buildings and demonstrations near stores. The new brand quickly captured $100 million in sales and by 2014 was the top detergent brand in India-based dollar sales. Unilever replicated the strategy in India with low-priced packets of shampoos and deodorants and in South America with a detergent brand-named Ala.

- *Modify aspects of the company's business model to accommodate the unique local circumstances of developing countries.* For instance, Honeywell had sold industrial products and services for more than 100 years outside the United States and Europe using a foreign subsidiary model that focused international activities on sales only. When Honeywell entered China, it discovered that industrial customers in that country considered how many key jobs foreign companies created in China, in addition to the quality and price of the product or service when making purchasing decisions. Honeywell added about 150 engineers, strategists, and marketers in China to demonstrate its commitment to bolstering the Chinese economy. Honeywell replicated its "East for East" strategy when it entered the market for industrial products and services in India. Within 10 years of Honeywell establishing operations in China and three years of expanding into India, the two emerging markets accounted for 30 percent of the firm's worldwide growth.

- *Try to change the local market to better match the way the company does business elsewhere.* An international company often has enough market clout to drive major changes in the way a local country market operates. When Japan's Suzuki entered India, it triggered a quality revolution among Indian auto parts manufacturers. Local component suppliers teamed up with Suzuki's vendors in Japan and worked with Japanese experts to produce higher-quality products. Over the next two decades, Indian companies became proficient in making top-notch components for vehicles, won more prizes for quality than companies in any country other than Japan, and broke into the global market as suppliers to many automakers in Asia and other parts of the world. Mahindra and Mahindra, one of India's premier automobile manufacturers, has been recognized by a number of organizations for its product quality. Among its most noteworthy awards was its number-one ranking by J.D. Power Asia Pacific for new-vehicle overall quality.

- *Stay away from developing markets where it is impractical or uneconomical to modify the company's business model to accommodate local circumstances.* Home Depot expanded successfully into Mexico, but it has avoided entry into other developing countries because its value proposition of good quality, low prices, and attentive customer service relies on (1) good highways and logistical systems to minimize store inventory costs, (2) employee stock ownership to help motivate store personnel to provide good customer service, and (3) high labor costs for housing construction and home repairs that encourage homeowners to engage in do-it-yourself projects. Relying on these factors in North American markets has worked spectacularly for Home Depot, but the company found that it could not count on these factors in China, from which it withdrew in 2012.

Company experiences in entering developing markets like Brazil, Russia, India, and China indicate that profitability seldom comes quickly or easily. Building a market for the company's products can often turn into a long-term process that involves reeducation of consumers, sizable investments in advertising to alter tastes and buying habits, and upgrades of the local infrastructure (transportation systems, distribution channels, etc.). In such cases, a company must be patient, work within the system to improve the infrastructure, and lay the foundation for generating sizable revenues and profits once conditions are ripe for market takeoff.

> Profitability in developing markets rarely comes quickly or easily—new entrants have to adapt their business models to local conditions, which may not always be possible.

DEFENDING AGAINST GLOBAL GIANTS: STRATEGIES FOR LOCAL COMPANIES IN DEVELOPING COUNTRIES

If opportunity-seeking, resource-rich international companies are looking to enter developing-country markets, what strategy options can local companies use to survive? As it turns out, the prospects for local companies facing global giants are by no means grim. Studies of local companies in developing markets have disclosed five strategies that have proved themselves in defending against globally competitive companies[19]:

1. *Develop business models that exploit shortcomings in local distribution networks or infrastructure.* In many instances, the extensive collection of resources possessed by the global giants is of little help in building a presence in developing markets. The lack of well-established local wholesaler and distributor networks, telecommunication systems, consumer banking, or media necessary for advertising makes it difficult for large internationals to migrate business models proved in developed markets to emerging markets. Emerging markets sometimes favor local companies whose managers are familiar with the local language and culture and are skilled in selecting large numbers of conscientious employees to carry out labor-intensive tasks. Shanda, a Chinese producer of massively multiplayer online role-playing games (MMORPGs), overcame China's lack of an established credit card network by selling prepaid access cards through local merchants. The company's focus on online games also protects it from shortcomings in China's software piracy laws. An India-based electronics company carved out a market niche for itself by developing an all-in-one business machine, designed especially for India's millions of small shopkeepers, that tolerates the country's frequent power outages.

2. *Utilize keen understanding of local customer needs and preferences to create customized products or services.* When developing-country markets are largely made up of customers with strong local needs, a good strategy option is to concentrate on customers who prefer a local touch and to accept the loss of the customers attracted to global brands.[20] A local company may be able to astutely exploit its local orientation—its familiarity with local preferences, its expertise in traditional products, its long-standing customer relationships. A small Middle Eastern cell phone manufacturer competes successfully against industry giants Samsung, Apple, Nokia, and Motorola by selling a model designed especially for Muslims—it is loaded with the Koran, alerts people at prayer times, and is equipped with a compass that points them toward Mecca. Shenzhen-based Tencent has become the leader in instant messaging in China through its unique understanding of Chinese behavior and culture.

3. *Take advantage of aspects of the local workforce with which large international companies may be unfamiliar.* Local companies that lack the technological capabilities of foreign entrants may be able to rely on their better understanding of the local labor force to offset any disadvantage. Focus Media is China's largest outdoor advertising firm and has relied on low-cost labor to update its more than 170,000 LCD displays and billboards in over 90 cities in a low-tech manner, while international companies operating in China use electronically networked screens that

allow messages to be changed remotely. Focus uses an army of employees who ride to each display by bicycle to change advertisements with programming contained on a USB flash drive or DVD. Indian information technology firms such as Infosys Technologies and Satyam Computer Services have been able to keep their personnel costs lower than those of international competitors EDS and Accenture because of their familiarity with local labor markets. While the large internationals have focused recruiting efforts in urban centers like Bangalore and Delhi, driving up engineering and computer science salaries in such cities, local companies have shifted recruiting efforts to second-tier cities that are unfamiliar to foreign firms.

4. *Use acquisition and rapid-growth strategies to better defend against expansion-minded internationals.* With the growth potential of developing markets such as China, Indonesia, and Brazil obvious to the world, local companies must attempt to develop scale and upgrade their competitive capabilities as quickly as possible to defend against the stronger international's arsenal of resources. Most successful companies in developing markets have pursued mergers and acquisitions at a rapid-fire pace to build first a nationwide and then an international presence. Hindalco, India's largest aluminum producer, has followed just such a path to achieve its ambitions for global dominance. By acquiring companies in India first, it gained enough experience and confidence to eventually acquire much larger foreign companies with world-class capabilities.[21] When China began to liberalize its foreign trade policies, Lenovo (the Chinese PC maker) realized that its long-held position of market dominance in China could not withstand the onslaught of new international entrants such as Dell and HP. Its acquisition of IBM's PC business allowed Lenovo to gain rapid access to IBM's globally recognized PC brand, its R&D capability, and its existing distribution in developed countries. This has allowed Lenovo not only to hold its own against the incursion of global giants into its home market but also to expand into new markets around the world.[22]

5. *Transfer company expertise to cross-border markets and initiate actions to contend on an international level.* When a company from a developing country has resources and capabilities suitable for competing in other country markets, launching initiatives to transfer its expertise to foreign markets becomes a viable strategic option. Televisa, Mexico's largest media company, used its expertise in Spanish culture and linguistics to become the world's most prolific producer of Spanish-language soap operas. By continuing to upgrade its capabilities and learn from its experience in foreign markets, a company can sometimes transform itself into one capable of competing on a worldwide basis, as an emerging global giant. Sundaram Fasteners of India began its foray into foreign markets as a supplier of radiator caps to General Motors—an opportunity it pursued when GM first decided to outsource the production of this part. As a participant in GM's supplier network, the company learned about emerging technical standards, built its capabilities, and became one of the first Indian companies to achieve QS 9000 quality certification. With the expertise it gained and its recognition for meeting quality standards, Sundaram was then able to pursue opportunities to supply automotive parts in Japan and Europe.

Illustration Capsule 7.3 discusses the strategy behind the success of WeChat (China's most popular messenger app), in keeping out international social media rivals.

WeChat's Strategy for Defending against International Social Media Giants in China

WeChat, a Chinese social media and messenger app similar to Whatsapp, allows users to chat, post photos, shop online, and share information as well as music. It has continued to add new features, such as WeChat Games and WePay, which allow users to send money electronically, much like Venmo. The company now serves more than a billion active users, a testament to the success of its strategy.

WeChat has also had incredible success keeping out international rivals. Due to censorship and regulations in China, Chinese social media companies have an inherent advantage over foreign competitors. However, this is not why WeChat has become an indispensable part of Chinese life.

WeChat has been able to surpass international rivals because, by better understanding Chinese customer needs, it can anticipate their desires. WeChat added features that allow users to check traffic cameras during rush hour, purchase tickets to movies, and book doctor appointments all on the app. Booking appointments with doctors is a feature that is wildly popular with the Chinese customer base due to common scheduling difficulties. Essentially, WeChat created its own distribution network for sought after information and goods in busy Chinese cities.

WeChat also has an understanding of local customs that international rivals can't match. In order to promote WePay, WeChat created a Chinese New Year lottery-like promotion in which users could win virtual "red envelopes" on the app. Red envelopes of money are traditionally given on Chinese New Year as presents. WePay was able to grow users from 30 to 100 million in the month following the

BigTunaOnline/Shutterstock

promotion due to the popularity of the New Year's feature. By 2020, many of WeChat's over one billion active users were also using WePay. WeChat continues to allow users to send red envelopes and has continued New Year's promotions in subsequent years with success. Even Chinese companies have been bested by WeChat. Rival founder of Alibaba, Jack Ma, admitted the promotion put WeChat ahead of his company, saying it was a "pearl harbor attack" on his company. Chinese tech experts noted that the promotion was Ma's nightmare because it pushed WeChat to the forefront of Chinese person-to-person payments.

WeChat's strategy of continually developing new features also keeps the competition at bay. As China's "App for Everything," it now permeates all walks of life in China in a way that will likely continue to keep foreign competitors out.

Note: Developed with Meaghan I. Haugh.

Sources: Guilford, Gwynn. "WeChat's Little Red Envelopes Are Brilliant Marketing for Mobile Payments." *Quartz,* January 29, 2014; Pasternack, Alex. "How Social Cash Made WeChat the App for Everything," *Fast Company,* January 3, 2017; "WeChat's World," *The Economist,* August 6, 2016; Stanciu, Tudor. "Why WeChat City Services Is a Game-Changing Move for Smartphone Adoption," *TechCrunch,* April 24, 2015.

KEY POINTS

1. Competing in international markets allows a company to (1) gain access to new customers; (2) achieve lower costs through greater economies of scale, learning, and increased purchasing power; (3) gain access to low-cost inputs of production; (4) further exploit its core competencies; and (5) gain access to resources and capabilities located outside the company's domestic market.

2. Strategy making is more complex for five reasons: (1) Different countries have *home-country advantages* in different industries; (2) there are location-based advantages to performing different value chain activities in different parts of the world; (3) varying political and economic risks make the business climate of some countries more favorable than others; (4) companies face the risk of adverse shifts in exchange rates when operating in foreign countries; and (5) differences in buyer tastes and preferences present a conundrum concerning the trade-off between customizing and standardizing products and services.

3. The strategies of firms that expand internationally are usually grounded in home-country advantages concerning demand conditions; factor conditions; related and supporting industries; and firm strategy, structure, and rivalry, as described by the Diamond of National Competitive Advantage framework.

4. There are five strategic options for entering foreign markets. These include maintaining a home-country production base and *exporting* goods to foreign markets, *licensing* foreign firms to produce and distribute the company's products abroad, employing a *franchising* strategy, establishing a foreign *subsidiary via an acquisition or greenfield venture,* and using *strategic alliances or other collaborative partnerships.*

5. A company must choose among three alternative approaches for competing internationally: (1) a *multidomestic strategy*—a *think-local, act-local* approach to crafting international strategy; (2) a *global strategy*—a *think-global, act-global* approach; and (3) a combination *think-global, act-local* approach, known as a *transnational strategy.* A multidomestic strategy (think local, act local) is appropriate for companies that must vary their product offerings and competitive approaches from country to country in order to accommodate different buyer preferences and market conditions. The global strategy (think global, act global) works best when there are substantial cost benefits to be gained from taking a standardized, globally integrated approach and there is little need for local responsiveness. A transnational strategy (think global, act local) is called for when there is a high need for local responsiveness as well as substantial benefits from taking a globally integrated approach. In this approach, a company strives to employ the same basic competitive strategy in all markets but still customizes its product offering and some aspect of its operations to fit local market circumstances.

6. There are three general ways in which a firm can gain competitive advantage (or offset domestic disadvantages) in international markets. One way involves locating various value chain activities among nations in a manner that lowers costs or achieves greater product differentiation. A second way draws on an international competitor's ability to extend its competitive advantage by cost-effectively sharing, replicating, or transferring its most valuable resources and capabilities across borders. A third looks for benefits from cross-border coordination that are unavailable to domestic-only competitors.

7. Two types of strategic moves are particularly suited for companies competing internationally. The first involves waging strategic offenses in international markets through *cross-subsidization*—a practice of supporting competitive offensives in one

market with resources and profits diverted from operations in another market. The second is a defensive move used to encourage *mutual restraint* among competitors when there is international *multimarket competition* by signaling that each company has the financial capability for mounting a strong counterattack if threatened. For companies with at least one highly profitable or well defended market, having a presence in a rival's key markets can be enough to deter the rival from making aggressive attacks.

8. Companies racing for global leadership have to consider competing in developing markets like the BRIC countries—Brazil, Russia, India, and China—where the business risks are considerable but the opportunities for growth are huge. To succeed in these markets, companies often have to (1) compete on the basis of low price, (2) modify aspects of the company's business model to accommodate local circumstances, and/or (3) try to change the local market to better match the way the company does business elsewhere. Profitability is unlikely to come quickly or easily in developing markets, typically because of the investments needed to alter buying habits and tastes, the increased political and economic risk, and/or the need for infrastructure upgrades. And there may be times when a company should simply stay away from certain developing markets until conditions for entry are better suited to its business model and strategy.

9. Local companies in developing-country markets can seek to compete against large international companies by (1) developing business models that exploit shortcomings in local distribution networks or infrastructure, (2) utilizing a superior understanding of local customer needs and preferences or local relationships, (3) taking advantage of competitively important qualities of the local workforce with which large international companies may be unfamiliar, (4) using acquisition strategies and rapid-growth strategies to better defend against expansion-minded international companies, or (5) transferring company expertise to cross-border markets and initiating actions to compete on an international level.

ASSURANCE OF LEARNING EXERCISES

LO 7-1, LO 7-3

1. L'Oréal markets over 500 brands of products in all sectors of the beauty business in 140 countries. The company's international strategy involves manufacturing these products in 43 plants located around the world. L'Oréal's international strategy is discussed in its operations section of the company's website (www .loreal.com/careers/who-you-can-be/operations) and in its press releases, annual reports, and presentations. Why has the company chosen to pursue a foreign subsidiary strategy? Are there strategic advantages to global sourcing and production in the cosmetics, fragrances, and hair care products industry relative to an export strategy?

McGraw Hill connect

LO 7-1, LO 7-3

2. Alliances, joint ventures, and mergers with foreign companies are widely used as a means of entering foreign markets. Such arrangements have many purposes, including learning about unfamiliar environments, and the opportunity to access the complementary resources and capabilities of a foreign partner. Illustration Capsule 7.1 provides an example of how Walgreens used a strategy of entering foreign markets via alliance, followed by a merger with the same entity. What was this entry strategy designed to achieve, and why would this make sense for a company like Walgreens?

3. Assume you are in charge of developing the strategy for an international company selling products in some 50 different countries around the world. One of the issues you face is whether to employ a multidomestic strategy, a global strategy, or a transnational strategy.

LO 7-2, LO 7-4

    a. If your company's product is mobile phones, which of these strategies do you think it would make better strategic sense to employ? Why?

    b. If your company's product is dry soup mixes and canned soups, would a multidomestic strategy seem to be more advisable than a global strategy or a transnational strategy? Why or why not?

    c. If your company's product is large home appliances such as washing machines, ranges, ovens, and refrigerators, would it seem to make more sense to pursue a multidomestic strategy, a global strategy, or a transnational strategy? Why?

4. Using your university library's business research resources and Internet sources, identify and discuss three key strategies that General Motors is using to compete in China.

LO 7-5, LO 7-6

EXERCISES FOR SIMULATION PARTICIPANTS

The following questions are for simulation participants whose companies operate in an international market arena. If your company competes only in a single country, then skip the questions in this section.

1. To what extent, if any, have you and your co-managers adapted your company's strategy to take shifting exchange rates into account? In other words, have you undertaken any actions to try to minimize the impact of adverse shifts in exchange rates?

LO 7-2

2. To what extent, if any, have you and your co-managers adapted your company's strategy to take geographic differences in import tariffs or import duties into account?

LO 7-2

3. What are the attributes of each of the following approaches to competing in international markets?

- Multidomestic or think-local, act-local approach.
- Global or think-global, act-global approach.
- Transnational or think-global, act-local approach.

Explain your answer and indicate two or three chief elements of your company's strategy for competing in two or more different geographic regions.

ENDNOTES

[1] Sidney G. Winter and Gabriel Szulanski, "Getting It Right the Second Time," *Harvard Business Review* 80, no. 1 (January 2002), pp. 62–69.
[2] P. Dussauge, B. Garrette, and W. Mitchell, "Learning from Competing Partners: Outcomes and Durations of Scale and Link Alliances in Europe, North America and Asia," *Strategic Management Journal* 21, no. 2 (February

2000), pp. 99–126; K. W. Glaister and P. J. Buckley, "Strategic Motives for International Alliance Formation," *Journal of Management Studies* 33, no. 3 (May 1996), pp. 301–332.
[3] Michael E. Porter, "The Competitive Advantage of Nations," *Harvard Business Review*, March–April 1990, pp. 73–93.
[4] Tom Mitchell and Avantika Chilkoti, "China Car Sales Accelerate Away from US and Brazil

in 2013," *Financial Times*, January 9, 2014, www.ft.com/cms/s/0/8c649078-78f8-11e3-b381-00144feabdc0.html#axzz2rpEqjkZO.
[5] U.S. Department of Labor, Bureau of Labor Statistics, "International Comparisons of Hourly Compensation Costs in Manufacturing 2012," August 9, 2013. (The numbers for India and China are estimates.)

⁶ Sangwon Yoon, "South Korea Targets Internet Addicts; 2 Million Hooked," *Valley News,* April 25, 2010, p. C2.

⁷ Joel Bleeke and David Ernst, "The Way to Win in Cross-Border Alliances," *Harvard Business Review* 69, no. 6 (November–December 1991), pp. 127–133; Gary Hamel, Yves L. Doz, and C. K. Prahalad, "Collaborate with Your Competitors— and Win," *Harvard Business Review* 67, no. 1 (January–February 1989), pp. 134–135.

⁸ K. W. Glaister and P. J. Buckley, "Strategic Motives for International Alliance Formation," *Journal of Management Studies* 33, no. 3 (May 1996), pp. 301–332.

⁹ Jeffrey H. Dyer, Prashant Kale, and Harbir Singh, "When to Ally and When to Acquire," *Harvard Business Review* 82, no. 7–8 (July–August 2004).

¹⁰ Yves Doz and Gary Hamel, *Alliance Advantage: The Art of Creating Value through Partnering* (Harvard Business School Press, 1998); Rosabeth Moss Kanter, "Collaborative Advantage: The Art of the Alliance," *Harvard Business Review* 72, no. 4 (July–August 1994), pp. 96–108.

¹¹ Jeremy Main, "Making Global Alliances Work," *Fortune,* December 19, 1990, p. 125.

¹² C. K. Prahalad and Kenneth Lieberthal, "The End of Corporate Imperialism," *Harvard Business Review* 81, no. 8 (August 2003), pp. 109–117.

¹³ Pankaj Ghemawat, "Managing Differences: The Central Challenge of Global Strategy," *Harvard Business Review* 85, no. 3 (March 2007).

¹⁴ C. A. Bartlett and S. Ghoshal, *Managing across Borders: The Transnational Solution,* 2nd ed. (Boston: Harvard Business School Press, 1998).

¹⁵ Lynn S. Paine, "The China Rules," *Harvard Business Review* 88, no. 6 (June 2010), pp. 103–108.

¹⁶ C. K. Prahalad and Yves L. Doz, *The Multinational Mission: Balancing Local Demands and Global Vision* (New York: Free Press, 1987).

¹⁷ David J. Arnold and John A. Quelch, "New Strategies in Emerging Markets," *Sloan Management Review* 40, no. 1 (Fall 1998), pp. 7–20.

¹⁸ Tarun Khanna, Krishna G. Palepu, and Jayant Sinha, "Strategies That Fit Emerging Markets," *Harvard Business Review* 83, no. 6 (June 2005), p. 63; Arindam K. Bhattacharya and David C. Michael, "How Local Companies Keep Multinationals at Bay," *Harvard Business Review* 86, no. 3 (March 2008), pp. 94–95.

¹⁹ Tarun Khanna and Krishna G. Palepu, "Emerging Giants: Building World-Class Companies in Developing Countries," *Harvard Business Review* 84, no. 10 (October 2006), pp. 60–69.

²⁰ Niroj Dawar and Tony Frost, "Competing with Giants: Survival Strategies for Local Companies in Emerging Markets," *Harvard Business Review* 77, no. 1 (January–February 1999), p. 122; Guitz Ger, "Localizing in the Global Village: Local Firms Competing in Global Markets," *California Management Review* 41, no. 4 (Summer 1999), pp. 64–84.

²¹ N. Kumar, "How Emerging Giants Are Rewriting the Rules of M&A," *Harvard Business Review,* May 2009, pp. 115–121.

²² H. Rui and G. Yip, "Foreign Acquisitions by Chinese Firms: A Strategic Intent Perspective," *Journal of World Business* 43 (2008), pp. 213–226.

chapter 8

Corporate Strategy

Diversification and the Multibusiness Company

Learning Objectives

After reading this chapter, you should be able to:

LO 8-1 Explain when and how business diversification can enhance shareholder value.

LO 8-2 Describe how related diversification strategies can produce cross-business strategic fit capable of delivering competitive advantage.

LO 8-3 Identify the merits and risks of unrelated diversification strategies.

LO 8-4 Use the analytic tools for evaluating a company's diversification strategy.

LO 8-5 Understand the four main corporate strategy options a diversified company can employ to improve company performance.

Richard Schneider/Getty Images

I suppose my formula might be: dream, diversify, and never miss an angle.

Walt Disney—*Founder of the Walt Disney Company*

Make winners out of every business in your company. Don't carry losers.

Jack Welch—*Legendary CEO of General Electric*

Fit between a parent and its businesses is a two-edged sword: A good fit can create value; a bad one can destroy it.

Andrew Campbell, Michael Goold, and Marcus Alexander—*Academics, authors, and consultants*

This chapter moves up one level in the strategy-making hierarchy, from strategy making in a single-business enterprise to strategy making in a diversified, multibusiness enterprise. Because a diversified company is a collection of individual businesses, the strategy-making task is more complicated. In a one-business company, managers have to come up with a plan for competing successfully in only a single industry environment—the result is what Chapter 2 labeled as *business strategy* (or *business-level strategy*). But in a diversified company, the strategy-making challenge involves assessing multiple industry environments and developing a *set of business strategies,* one for each industry arena in which the diversified company operates. And top executives at a diversified company must still go one step further and devise a companywide (or *corporate*) strategy for improving the performance of the company's overall business lineup and for making a rational whole out of its diversified collection of individual businesses.

In the first part of this chapter, we describe what crafting a diversification strategy entails, when and why diversification makes good strategic sense, the various approaches to diversifying a company's business lineup, and the pros and cons of related versus unrelated diversification strategies. The second part of the chapter looks at how to evaluate the attractiveness of a diversified company's business lineup, how to decide whether it has a good diversification strategy, and the strategic options for improving a diversified company's future performance.

WHAT DOES CRAFTING A DIVERSIFICATION STRATEGY ENTAIL?

The task of crafting a diversified company's overall *corporate strategy* falls squarely in the lap of top-level executives and involves three distinct facets:

1. *Picking new industries to enter and deciding on the means of entry.* Pursuing a diversification strategy requires that management decide which new industries to enter and then, for each new industry, whether to enter by starting a new business from the ground up, by acquiring a company already in the target industry, or by forming a joint venture or strategic alliance with another company. The choice of industries depends upon on the strategic rationale (or justification) for diversifying and the type of diversification being pursued—important issues that we discuss more fully in sections to follow.

2. *Pursuing opportunities to leverage cross-business value chain relationships, where there is strategic fit, into competitive advantage.* The task here is to determine whether there are opportunities to strengthen a diversified company's businesses by such means as transferring competitively valuable resources and capabilities from one business to another, combining the related value chain activities of different businesses to achieve lower costs, sharing resources, such as the use of a powerful and well-respected brand name or an R&D facility, across multiple businesses, and encouraging knowledge sharing and collaborative activity among the businesses.

3. *Initiating actions to boost the combined performance of the corporation's collection of businesses.* Strategic options for improving the corporation's overall performance include (1) sticking closely with the existing business lineup and pursuing opportunities presented by these businesses, (2) broadening the scope of diversification by entering additional industries, (3) retrenching to a narrower scope of diversification by divesting either poorly performing businesses or those that no longer fit into management's long-range plans, and (4) broadly restructuring the entire company by divesting some businesses, acquiring others, and reorganizing, to put a whole new face on the company's business lineup.

The demanding and time-consuming nature of these three tasks explains why corporate executives generally refrain from becoming immersed in the details of crafting and executing business-level strategies. Rather, the normal procedure is to delegate lead responsibility for business strategy to the heads of each business, giving them the latitude to develop strategies suited to the particular industry environment in which their business operates and holding them accountable for producing good financial and strategic results.

WHEN TO CONSIDER DIVERSIFYING

As long as a company has plentiful opportunities for profitable growth in its present industry, there is no urgency to pursue diversification. But growth opportunities are often limited in mature industries and markets where buyer demand is flat or declining. In addition, changing industry conditions—new technologies, inroads being made by substitute products, fast-shifting buyer preferences, or intensifying competition— can undermine a company's ability to deliver ongoing gains in revenues and profits.

Consider, for example, what mobile phone companies and marketers of Voice over Internet Protocol (VoIP) have done to the revenues of long-distance providers such as AT&T, British Telecommunications, and NTT in Japan. Thus, diversifying into new industries always merits strong consideration whenever a single-business company encounters diminishing market opportunities and stagnating sales in its principal business.

The decision to diversify presents wide-ranging possibilities. A company can diversify into closely related businesses or into totally unrelated businesses. It can diversify its present revenue and earnings base to a small or major extent. It can move into one or two large new businesses or a greater number of small ones. It can achieve diversification by acquiring an existing company, starting up a new business from scratch, or forming a joint venture with one or more companies to enter new businesses. In every case, however, the decision to diversify must start with a strong economic justification for doing so.

BUILDING SHAREHOLDER VALUE: THE ULTIMATE JUSTIFICATION FOR DIVERSIFYING

Diversification must do more for a company than simply spread its business risk across various industries. In principle, diversification cannot be considered wise or justifiable unless it results in *added long-term economic value for shareholders*—value that shareholders cannot capture on their own by purchasing stock in companies in different industries or investing in mutual funds to spread their investments across several industries. A move to diversify into a new business stands little chance of building shareholder value without passing the following three **Tests of Corporate Advantage**[1]:

• LO 8-1

Explain when and how business diversification can enhance shareholder value.

1. *The industry attractiveness test.* The industry to be entered through diversification must be structurally attractive (in terms of the five forces), have resource requirements that match those of the parent company, and offer good prospects for growth, profitability, and return on investment.

2. *The cost of entry test.* The cost of entering the target industry must not be so high as to exceed the potential for good profitability. A catch-22 can prevail here, however. The more attractive an industry's prospects are for growth and good long-term profitability, the more expensive it can be to enter. Entry barriers for startup companies are likely to be high in attractive industries—if barriers were low, a rush of new entrants would soon erode the potential for high profitability. And buying a well-positioned company in an appealing industry often entails a high acquisition cost that makes passing the cost of entry test less likely. Since the owners of a successful and growing company usually demand a price that reflects their business's profit prospects, it's easy for such an acquisition to fail the cost of entry test.

3. *The better-off test.* Diversifying into a new business must offer potential for the company's existing businesses and the new business to perform better together under a single corporate umbrella than they would perform operating as independent, stand-alone businesses—an effect known as **synergy**. For example, let's say that company A diversifies by purchasing company B in another industry. If A and B's consolidated profits in the years to come prove no greater than what each could have earned on its own, then A's diversification won't provide

CORE CONCEPT

To add shareholder value, a move to diversify into a new business must pass the three **Tests of Corporate Advantage:**
1. The industry attractiveness test
2. The cost of entry test
3. The better-off test

CORE CONCEPT

Creating added value for shareholders via diversification requires building a multibusiness company in which the whole is greater than the sum of its parts; such 1 + 1 = 3 effects are called **synergy.**

its shareholders with any added value. Company A's shareholders could have achieved the same $1 + 1 = 2$ result by merely purchasing stock in company B. Diversification does not result in added long-term value for shareholders unless it produces a $1 + 1 = 3$ effect, whereby the businesses *perform better together as part of the same firm than they could have performed as independent companies.*

Diversification moves must satisfy all three tests to grow shareholder value over the long term. Diversification moves that can pass only one or two tests are suspect.

APPROACHES TO DIVERSIFYING THE BUSINESS LINEUP

The means of entering new businesses can take any of three forms: acquisition, internal startup, or joint ventures with other companies.

Diversifying by Acquisition of an Existing Business

Acquisition is a popular means of diversifying into another industry. Not only is it quicker than trying to launch a new operation, but it also offers an effective way to hurdle such entry barriers as acquiring technological know-how, establishing supplier relationships, achieving scale economies, building brand awareness, and securing adequate distribution. Acquisitions are also commonly employed to access resources and capabilities that are complementary to those of the acquiring firm and that cannot be developed readily internally. Buying an ongoing operation allows the acquirer to move directly to the task of building a strong market position in the target industry rather than getting bogged down in trying to develop the knowledge, experience, scale of operation, and market reputation necessary for a startup entrant to become an effective competitor.

> **CORE CONCEPT**
>
> An **acquisition premium,** or control premium, is the amount by which the price offered exceeds the pre-acquisition market value or stock price of the target company.

However, acquiring an existing business can prove quite expensive. The costs of acquiring another business include not only the acquisition price but also the costs of performing the due diligence to ascertain the worth of the other company, the costs of negotiating the purchase transaction, and the costs of integrating the business into the diversified company's portfolio. If the company to be acquired is a successful company, the acquisition price will include a hefty *premium* over the preacquisition value of the company for the right to control the company. For example, the $1.2 billion that luxury fashion company Michael Kors paid to acquire luxury accessories brand Jimmy Choo included a 36.5 percent premium over Jimmy Choo's share price before being put up for sale. Premiums are paid in order to convince the shareholders and managers of the target company that it is in their financial interests to approve the deal. The average premium paid by U.S. companies over the last 15 years was more often in the 20 to 25 percent range.

While acquisitions offer an enticing means for entering a new business, many fail to deliver on their promise.[2] Realizing the potential gains from an acquisition requires a successful integration of the acquired company into the culture, systems, and structure of the acquiring firm. This can be a costly and time-consuming operation. Acquisitions can also fail to deliver long-term shareholder value if the acquirer overestimates the potential gains and pays a premium in excess of the realized gains. High integration costs and excessive price premiums are two reasons that an acquisition might fail the cost of entry test. Firms with significant experience in making acquisitions are better able to avoid these types of problems.[3]

Entering a New Line of Business through Internal Development

Achieving diversification through *internal development* involves starting a new business subsidiary from scratch. Internal development has become an increasingly important way for companies to diversify and is often referred to as **corporate venturing** or *new venture development*. Although building a new business from the ground up is generally a time-consuming and uncertain process, it avoids the pitfalls associated with entry via acquisition and may allow the firm to realize greater profits in the end. It may offer a viable means of entering a new or emerging industry where there are no good acquisition candidates.

Entering a new business via internal development, however, poses some significant hurdles. An internal new venture not only has to overcome industry entry barriers but also must invest in new production capacity, develop sources of supply, hire and train employees, build channels of distribution, grow a customer base, and so on, unless the new business is quite similar to the company's existing business. The risks associated with internal startups can be substantial, and the likelihood of failure is often high. Moreover, the culture, structures, and organizational systems of some companies may impede innovation and make it difficult for corporate entrepreneurship to flourish.

Generally, internal development of a new business has appeal only when (1) the parent company already has in-house most of the resources and capabilities it needs to piece together a new business and compete effectively; (2) there is ample time to launch the business; (3) the internal cost of entry is lower than the cost of entry via acquisition; (4) adding new production capacity will not adversely impact the supply-demand balance in the industry; and (5) incumbent firms are likely to be slow or ineffective in responding to a new entrant's efforts to crack the market.

Using Joint Ventures to Achieve Diversification

Entering a new business via a joint venture can be useful in at least three types of situations.[4] First, a joint venture is a good vehicle for pursuing an opportunity that is too complex, uneconomical, or risky for one company to pursue alone. Second, joint ventures make sense when the opportunities in a new industry require a broader range of competencies and know-how than a company can marshal on its own. Many of the opportunities in satellite-based telecommunications, biotechnology, and network-based systems that blend hardware, software, and services call for the coordinated development of complementary innovations and the tackling of an intricate web of financial, technical, political, and regulatory factors simultaneously. In such cases, pooling the resources and competencies of two or more companies is a wiser and less risky way to proceed. Third, companies sometimes use joint ventures to diversify into a new industry when the diversification move entails having operations in a foreign country. However, as discussed in Chapters 6 and 7, partnering with another company can have significant drawbacks due to the potential for conflicting objectives, disagreements over how to best operate the venture, culture clashes, and so on. Joint ventures are generally the least durable of the entry options, usually lasting only until the partners decide to go their own ways.

Choosing a Mode of Entry

The choice of how best to enter a new business—whether through internal development, acquisition, or joint venture—depends on the answers to four important questions:

- Does the company have all of the resources and capabilities it requires to enter the business through internal development, or is it lacking some critical resources?
- Are there entry barriers to overcome?
- Is speed an important factor in the firm's chances for successful entry?
- Which is the least costly mode of entry, given the company's objectives?

The Question of Critical Resources and Capabilities   If a firm has all the resources it needs to start up a new business or will be able to easily purchase or lease any missing resources, it may choose to enter the business via internal development. However, if missing critical resources cannot be easily purchased or leased, a firm wishing to enter a new business must obtain these missing resources through either acquisition or joint venture. Bank of America acquired Merrill Lynch to obtain critical investment banking resources and capabilities that it lacked. The acquisition of these additional capabilities complemented Bank of America's strengths in corporate banking and opened up new business opportunities for the company. Firms often acquire other companies as a way to enter foreign markets where they lack local marketing knowledge, distribution capabilities, and relationships with local suppliers or customers. McDonald's acquisition of Burghy, Italy's only national hamburger chain, offers an example.[5] If there are no good acquisition opportunities or if the firm wants to avoid the high cost of acquiring and integrating another firm, it may choose to enter via joint venture. This type of entry mode has the added advantage of spreading the risk of entering a new business, an advantage that is particularly attractive when uncertainty is high. De Beers's joint venture with the luxury goods company LVMH provided De Beers not only with the complementary marketing capabilities it needed to enter the diamond retailing business but also with a partner to share the risk.

The Question of Entry Barriers   The second question to ask is whether entry barriers would prevent a new entrant from gaining a foothold and succeeding in the industry. If entry barriers are low and the industry is populated by small firms, internal development may be the preferred mode of entry. If entry barriers are high, the company may still be able to enter with ease if it has the requisite resources and capabilities for overcoming high barriers. For example, entry barriers due to reputational advantages may be surmounted by a diversified company with a widely known and trusted corporate name. But if the entry barriers cannot be overcome readily, then the only feasible entry route may be through acquisition of a well-established company. While entry barriers may also be overcome with a strong complementary joint venture, this mode is the more uncertain choice due to the lack of industry experience.

The Question of Speed   Speed is another determining factor in deciding how to go about entering a new business. Acquisition is a favored mode of entry when speed is of the essence, as is the case in rapidly changing industries where fast movers can secure long-term positioning advantages. Speed is important in industries where early movers gain experience-based advantages that grow ever larger over time as they move down the learning curve. It is also important in technology-based industries where there is a race to establish an industry standard or leading technological platform. But, in other cases, it can be better to enter a market after the uncertainties about technology or consumer preferences have been resolved and learn from the missteps of early entrants. In these cases, when it is more advantageous to be a second-mover, joint venture or internal development may be preferred.

The Question of Comparative Cost   The question of which mode of entry is most cost-effective is a critical one, given the need for a diversification strategy to pass the cost of entry test. Acquisition can be a high-cost mode of entry due to the need to pay a premium over the share price of the target company. When the premium is high, the price of the deal will exceed the worth of the acquired company as a stand-alone business by a substantial amount. Whether it is worth it to pay that high a price will depend on how much extra value will be created by the new combination of companies in the form of synergies. Moreover, the true cost of an acquisition must include the **transaction costs** of identifying and evaluating potential targets, negotiating a price, and completing other aspects of deal making. Often, companies pay hefty fees to investment banking firms, lawyers, and others to advise them and assist with the deal-making process. Finally, the true cost must take into account the costs of integrating the acquired company into the parent company's portfolio of businesses.

Joint ventures may provide a way to conserve on such entry costs. But even here, there are organizational coordination costs and transaction costs that must be considered, including settling on the terms of the arrangement. If the partnership doesn't proceed smoothly and is not founded on trust, these costs may be significant.

> **CORE CONCEPT**
>
> **Transaction costs** are the costs of completing a business agreement or deal, over and above the price of the deal. They can include the costs of searching for an attractive target, the costs of evaluating its worth, bargaining costs, and the costs of completing the transaction.

CHOOSING THE DIVERSIFICATION PATH: RELATED VERSUS UNRELATED BUSINESSES

Once a company decides to diversify, it faces the choice of whether to diversify into **related businesses, unrelated businesses,** or some mix of both. Businesses are said to be *related* when their value chains exhibit competitively important cross-business commonalities. By this we mean that there is a close correspondence between the businesses in terms of *how they perform* key value chain activities and *the resources and capabilities each needs* to perform those activities. The big appeal of related diversification is the opportunity to build shareholder value by leveraging these cross-business commonalities into competitive advantages for the individual businesses, thus allowing the company as a whole to perform better than just the sum of its businesses. Businesses are said to be *unrelated* when the resource requirements and key value chain activities are so dissimilar that no competitively important cross-business commonalities exist.

> **CORE CONCEPT**
>
> **Related businesses** possess competitively valuable cross-business value chain and resource commonalities; **unrelated businesses** have dissimilar value chains and resource requirements, with no competitively important cross-business commonalities at the value chain level.

The next two sections explore the ins and outs of related and unrelated diversification.

DIVERSIFICATION INTO RELATED BUSINESSES

A related diversification strategy involves building the company around businesses where there is good *strategic fit across corresponding value chain activities.* **Strategic fit** exists whenever one or more activities constituting the value chains of different businesses are sufficiently similar to present opportunities for cross-business sharing or

● **LO 8-2**

Describe how related diversification strategies can produce cross-business strategic fit capable of delivering competitive advantage.

CORE CONCEPT

Strategic fit exists whenever one or more activities constituting the value chains of different businesses are sufficiently similar to present opportunities for cross-business sharing or transferring of the resources and capabilities that enable these activities.

CORE CONCEPT

Related diversification involves sharing or transferring *specialized* resources and capabilities. **Specialized resources and capabilities** have very specific applications and their use is limited to a restricted range of industry and business types, in contrast to **general resources and capabilities,** which can be widely applied and can be deployed across a broad range of industry and business types.

transferring of the resources and capabilities that enable these activities.[6] That is to say, it implies the existence of competitively important cross-business commonalities. Prime examples of such opportunities include:

- *Transferring specialized expertise, technological know-how, or other competitively valuable strategic assets from one business's value chain to another's.* Google's ability to transfer software developers and other information technology specialists from other business applications to the development of its Android mobile operating system and Chrome operating system for PCs aided considerably in the success of these new internal ventures.

  - *Sharing costs between businesses by combining their related value chain activities into a single operation.* For instance, it is often feasible to manufacture the products of different businesses in a single plant, use the same warehouses for shipping and distribution, or have a single sales force for the products of different businesses if they are marketed to the same types of customers.

  - *Exploiting the common use of a well-known brand name.* For example, Yamaha's name in motorcycles gave the company instant credibility and recognition in entering the personal-watercraft business, allowing it to achieve a significant market share without spending large sums on advertising to establish a brand identity for the WaveRunner. Likewise, Apple's reputation for producing easy-to-operate computers was a competitive asset that facilitated the company's diversification into digital music players, smartphones, and connected watches.

- *Sharing other resources (besides brands) that support corresponding value chain activities across businesses.* When Disney acquired Marvel Comics, management saw to it that Marvel's iconic characters, such as Spiderman, Iron Man, and the Black Widow, were shared with many of the other Disney businesses, including its theme parks, retail stores, motion picture division, and video game business. (Disney's characters, starting with Mickey Mouse, have always been among the most valuable of its resources.) Automobile companies like Ford share resources such as their relationships with suppliers and dealer networks across their lines of business.

- *Engaging in cross-business collaboration and knowledge sharing to create new competitively valuable resources and capabilities.* Businesses performing closely related value chain activities may seize opportunities to join forces, share knowledge and talents, and collaborate to create altogether new capabilities (such as virtually defect-free assembly methods or increased ability to speed new products to market) that will be mutually beneficial in improving their competitiveness and business performance.

Related diversification is based on value chain matchups with respect to *key* value chain activities—those that play a central role in each business's strategy and that link to its industry's key success factors. Such matchups facilitate the sharing or transfer of the resources and capabilities that enable the performance of these activities and underlie each business's quest for competitive advantage. By facilitating the sharing or transferring of such important competitive assets, related diversification can elevate each business's prospects for competitive success.

The resources and capabilities that are leveraged in related diversification are **specialized resources and capabilities.** By this we mean that they have very *specific* applications; their use is restricted to a limited range of business contexts in which these applications are competitively relevant. Because they are adapted for particular applications, specialized resources and capabilities must be utilized by particular types of businesses operating in specific kinds of industries to have value; they have limited utility outside this designated range of industry and business applications. This is in contrast to **general resources and capabilities** (such as general management capabilities, human resource management capabilities, and general accounting services), which can be applied usefully across a wide range of industry and business types.

L'Oréal is the world's largest beauty products company, with almost $30 billion in revenues and a successful strategy of related diversification built on leveraging a highly specialized set of resources and capabilities. These include 18 dermatologic and cosmetic research centers, R&D capabilities and scientific knowledge concerning skin and hair care, patents and secret formulas for hair and skin care products, and robotic applications developed specifically for testing the safety of hair and skin care products. These resources and capabilities are highly valuable for businesses focused on products for human skin and hair—they are *specialized* to such applications, and, in consequence, they are of little or no value beyond this restricted range of applications. To leverage these resources in a way that maximizes their potential value, L'Oréal has diversified into cosmetics, hair care products, skin care products, and fragrances (but not food, transportation, industrial services, or any application area far from the narrow domain in which its specialized resources are competitively relevant). L'Oréal's businesses are related to one another on the basis of its value-generating specialized resources and capabilities and the cross-business linkages among the value chain activities that they enable.

Corning's most competitively valuable resources and capabilities are specialized to applications concerning fiber optics and specialty glass and ceramics. Over the course of its 165-year history, it has developed an unmatched understanding of fundamental glass science and related technologies in the field of optics. Its capabilities now span a variety of sophisticated technologies and include expertise in domains such as custom glass composition, specialty glass melting and forming, precision optics, high-end transmissive coatings, and optomechanical materials. Corning has leveraged these specialized capabilities into a position of global leadership in five related market segments: display technologies based on glass substrates; environmental technologies using ceramic substrates and filters; optical communications, providing optical fiber, cable and connectivity solutions; life sciences supporting research and drug discovery; and specialty materials employing advanced optics and specialty glass solutions. The market segments into which Corning has diversified are all related by their reliance on Corning's specialized capability set and by the many value chain activities that they have in common as a result.

General Mills has diversified into a closely related set of food businesses on the basis of its capabilities in the realm of "kitchen chemistry" and food production technologies. Its four U.S. retail divisions—meals and baking, cereal, snacks, and yogurt—include brands such as Old El Paso, Cascadian Farm Lucky Charms and General Mills brand cereals, Nature Valley, Annie's Organic, Pillsbury and Betty Crocker, and Yoplait yogurt. Earlier it had diversified into restaurant businesses on the mistaken notion that all food businesses were related. By exiting these businesses in the mid-1990s, the company was able to improve its overall profitability and strengthen its position in its remaining businesses. The lesson from its experience—and a takeaway for the managers of any diversified company—is that *it is not product relatedness that defines a well-crafted related diversification strategy.* Rather, *the businesses must be related in terms of their key value chain activities and the specialized resources and capabilities that enable these activities.*[7] An example is Citizen Watch Company, whose products appear to be different (watches, machine tools, and flat panel displays) but are related in terms of their common reliance on miniaturization know-how and advanced precision technologies.

While companies pursuing related diversification strategies may also have opportunities to share or transfer their *general* resources and capabilities (e.g., information systems; human resource management practices; accounting and tax services; budgeting, planning, and financial reporting systems; expertise in legal and regulatory affairs; and fringe-benefit management systems), *the most competitively valuable opportunities for resource sharing or transfer always come from leveraging their specialized resources and capabilities.* The reason for this is that specialized resources and capabilities drive the key value-creating activities that both connect the businesses (at points along their value chains where there is strategic fit) and link to the key success factors in the markets where they are competitively relevant. Figure 8.1 illustrates the range of opportunities to share and/or transfer specialized resources and capabilities among the value chain activities of related businesses. It is important to recognize that *even though general resources and capabilities may be also shared by multiple business units, such resource sharing alone cannot form the backbone of a strategy keyed to related diversification.* Illustration Capsule 8.1 provides examples of a few successful firms with related diversification strategies.

Identifying Cross-Business Strategic Fit along the Value Chain

Cross-business strategic fit can exist anywhere along the value chain—in R&D and technology activities, in supply chain activities and relationships with suppliers, in manufacturing, in sales and marketing, in distribution activities, or in customer service activities.[8]

FIGURE 8.1   Related Businesses Provide Opportunities to Benefit from Competitively Valuable Strategic Fit

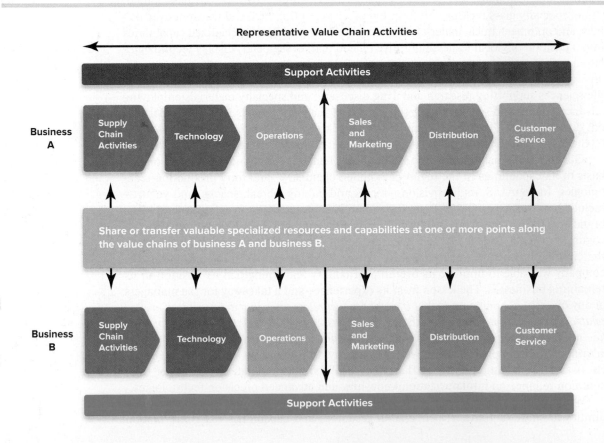

Examples of Companies Pursuing a Related Diversification Strategy

INDITEX

Inditex began as a small family business making women's clothing, but it has since evolved into one of the world's largest and most successful fashion retailers. The company is not just a retailer, however—it is involved with all aspects of producing fashion: design, manufacture, distribution, and retail. Its growth has been driven by acquisition as well as by internal growth and development. By 2020, Inditex included eight distinct brands or lines of business: Zara, Zara Home, Pull&Bear, Massimo Dutti, Berksha (which includes the BSK and Man brands), Stradivarius, Oysho (women's lingerie, beachwear, and sport), and Uterqüe (accessories, leatherwear).

NEWS CORP

News Corp was created in 2013 when News Corporation was split into two independent companies: 21st Century Fox and News Corp. This move allowed News Corp to focus on the newspaper and publishing businesses, while 21st Century Fox retained the other parts of News Corporation (mainly television and film). News Corp characterizes itself today as a mass media company. The companies in its network include The New York Post, Harper Collins Publishers, News Corp Australia, News UK, News America Marketing, Storyful (a social media newswire), Dow Jones and Move (a provider of real estate information). News Corp Australia actually includes a broad portfolio of national, metropolitan, regional, and community newspapers; while News UK has similar breadth. Despite the general disruption in the newspaper industry due to Internet-related developments, News Corp recently announced record-setting subscriber performances at Dow Jones and the Wall Street Journal—two of their most important holdings.

KIMBERLY-CLARK CORPORATION

Kimberly-Clark is a Texas based multinational in the personal care industry, producing mostly paper-based consumer products. Its products include iconic brands such as Kleenex, Huggies, Pull-Ups, Cottonelle, Scott, Viva, Kotex, and Depend. The company has organized its products into five related lines of business: Adult Care, Baby and Child Care, Family Care, Feminine Care, and K-C Professional. Its products are recognized and trusted around the world—distributed across more than 175 countries. With its sharp focus on the consumer and financial discipline,

(top): Shutterstock/lentamart; (middle): Edith38/Shutterstock; (bottom): Neilson Barnard/Staff/Getty Images

Kimberly-Clark has managed to sustain its record of solid performance and growth even during recessionary periods, since the types of products it offers are always in demand. Its outlook for 2020 and beyond continues to look rosy.

Sources: Company websites, Wikipedia; https://www.businesswire.com/news/home/20200207005506/en/News-Corp-Announces-Record-Setting-Subscriber-Performances-Dow; https://finance.yahoo.com/news/kimberly-clarks-impressive-momentum-continue-130001056.html, accessed February 10, 2020.

Strategic Fit in Supply Chain Activities   Businesses with strategic fit with respect to their supply chain activities can perform better together because of the potential for transferring skills in procuring materials, sharing resources and capabilities in logistics, collaborating with common supply chain partners, and/or increasing leverage with shippers in securing volume discounts on incoming parts and components. Dell's strategic partnerships with leading suppliers of microprocessors, circuit boards, disk drives, memory chips, flat-panel displays, wireless capabilities, long-life batteries, and other PC-related components have been an important element of the company's strategy to diversify into servers, data storage devices, networking components, plasma TVs, and printers—products that include many components common to PCs and that can be sourced from the same strategic partners that provide Dell with PC components.

Strategic Fit in R&D and Technology Activities   Businesses with strategic fit in R&D or technology development perform better together than apart because of potential cost savings in R&D, shorter times in getting new products to market, and more innovative products or processes. Moreover, technological advances in one business can lead to increased sales for both. Technological innovations have been the driver behind the efforts of cable TV companies to diversify into high-speed Internet access (via the use of cable modems) and, further, to explore providing local and long-distance telephone service to residential and commercial customers either through a single wire or by means of Voice over Internet Protocol (VoIP) technology. These diversification efforts have resulted in companies such as DISH Network and Comcast (through its XFINITY subsidiary) offering TV, Internet, and phone bundles.

Manufacturing-Related Strategic Fit   Cross-business strategic fit in manufacturing-related activities can be exploited when a diversifier's expertise in quality control and cost-efficient production methods can be transferred to another business. When Emerson Electric diversified into the chain-saw business, it transferred its expertise in low-cost manufacture to its newly acquired Beaird-Poulan business division. The transfer drove Beaird-Poulan's new strategy—to be the low-cost provider of chainsaw products—and fundamentally changed the way Beaird-Poulan chain saws were designed and manufactured. Another benefit of production-related value chain commonalities is the ability to consolidate production into a smaller number of plants and significantly reduce overall production costs. When snowmobile maker Bombardier diversified into motorcycles, it was able to set up motorcycle assembly lines in the manufacturing facility where it was assembling snowmobiles. When Smucker's acquired Procter & Gamble's Jif peanut butter business, it was able to combine the manufacture of the two brands of peanut butter products while gaining greater leverage with vendors in purchasing its peanut supplies.

Strategic Fit in Sales and Marketing Activities   Various cost-saving opportunities spring from diversifying into businesses with closely related sales and marketing activities. When the products are sold directly to the same customers, sales costs can often be reduced by using a single sales force instead of having two different salespeople call on the same customer. The products of related businesses can be promoted at the same website and included in the same media ads and sales brochures. There may be opportunities to reduce costs by consolidating order processing and billing and by using common promotional tie-ins. When global power toolmaker Black & Decker acquired Vector Products, it was able to use its own global sales force to sell the newly acquired

Vector power inverters, vehicle battery chargers, and rechargeable spotlights because the types of customers that carried its power tools (discounters like Kmart, home centers, and hardware stores) also stocked the types of products produced by Vector.

A second category of benefits arises when different businesses use similar sales and marketing approaches. In such cases, there may be competitively valuable opportunities to transfer selling, merchandising, advertising, and product differentiation skills from one business to another. Procter & Gamble's product lineup includes Pampers diapers, Olay beauty products, Tide laundry detergent, Crest toothpaste, Charmin toilet tissue, Gillette razors and blades, Vicks cough and cold products Oral-B toothbrushes, and Head & Shoulders shampoo. All of these have different competitors and different supply chain and production requirements, but they all move through the same wholesale distribution systems, are sold in common retail settings to the same shoppers, and require the same marketing and merchandising skills.

Distribution-Related Strategic Fit   Businesses with closely related distribution activities can perform better together than apart because of potential cost savings in sharing the same distribution facilities or using many of the same wholesale distributors and retail dealers. When Conair Corporation acquired Allegro Manufacturing's travel bag and travel accessory business, it was able to consolidate its own distribution centers for hair dryers and curling irons with those of Allegro, thereby generating cost savings for both businesses. Likewise, since Conair products and Allegro's neck rests, ear plugs, luggage tags, and toiletry kits were sold by the same types of retailers (discount stores, supermarket chains, and drugstore chains), Conair was able to convince many of the retailers not carrying Allegro products to take on the line.

Strategic Fit in Customer Service Activities   Strategic fit with respect to customer service activities can enable cost savings or differentiation advantages, just as it does along other points of the value chain. For example, cost savings may come from consolidating after-sale service and repair organizations for the products of closely related businesses into a single operation. Likewise, different businesses can often use the same customer service infrastructure. For instance, an electric utility that diversifies into natural gas, water, appliance repair services, and home security services can use the same customer data network, the same call centers and local offices, the same billing and accounting systems, and the same customer service infrastructure to support all of its products and services. Through the transfer of best practices in customer service across a set of related businesses or through the sharing of resources such as proprietary information about customer preferences, a multibusiness company can also create a differentiation advantage through higher-quality customer service.

Strategic Fit, Economies of Scope, and Competitive Advantage

Strategic fit in the value chain activities of a diversified corporation's different businesses opens up opportunities for **economies of scope**—a concept distinct from *economies of scale*. Economies of *scale* are cost savings that accrue directly from a larger-sized operation—for example, unit costs may be lower in a large plant than in a small plant. In contrast, economies of scope are cost savings that flow from operating in multiple businesses (a larger *scope* of

> **CORE CONCEPT**
>
> **Economies of scope** are cost reductions that flow from operating in multiple businesses (a larger scope of operation). This is in contrast to economies of scale, which accrue from a larger-sized operation.

operation). *They stem directly from strategic fit along the value chains of related businesses,* which in turn enables the businesses to share resources or to transfer them from business to business at low cost. Significant scope economies are open only to firms engaged in related diversification, since they are the result of related businesses performing R&D together, transferring managers from one business to another, using common manufacturing or distribution facilities, sharing a common sales force or dealer network, using the same established brand name, and the like. *The greater the cross-business economies associated with resource sharing and transfer, the greater the potential for a related diversification strategy to give the individual businesses of a multibusiness enterprise a cost advantage over rivals.*

From Strategic Fit to Competitive Advantage, Added Profitability, and Gains in Shareholder Value The cost advantage from economies of scope is due to the fact that resource sharing allows a multibusiness firm to spread resource costs across its businesses and to avoid the expense of having to acquire and maintain duplicate sets of resources—one for each business. But related diversified companies can benefit from strategic fit in other ways as well.

Sharing or transferring valuable specialized assets among the company's businesses can help each business perform its value chain activities more proficiently. This translates into competitive advantage for the businesses in one or two basic ways: (1) The businesses can contribute to greater efficiency and lower costs relative to their competitors, and/or (2) they can provide a basis for differentiation so that customers are willing to pay relatively more for the businesses' goods and services. In either or both of these ways, a firm with a well-executed related diversification strategy can boost the chances of its businesses attaining a competitive advantage.

> Diversifying into related businesses where competitively valuable strategic-fit benefits can be captured puts a company's businesses in position to perform better financially as part of the company than they could have performed as independent enterprises, thus providing a clear avenue for increasing shareholder value and satisfying the better-off test.

The greater the relatedness among a diversified company's businesses, the bigger a company's window for converting strategic fit into competitive advantage. The strategic and business logic is compelling: Capturing the benefits of strategic fit along the value chains of its related businesses gives a diversified company a clear path to achieving competitive advantage over undiversified competitors and competitors whose own diversification efforts don't offer equivalent strategic-fit benefits.[9] Such competitive advantage potential provides a company with a dependable basis for earning profits and a return on investment that exceeds what the company's businesses could earn as stand-alone enterprises. Converting the competitive advantage potential into greater profitability is what fuels $1 + 1 = 3$ gains in shareholder value—the necessary outcome for satisfying the *better-off test* and proving the business merit of a company's diversification effort.

There are five things to bear in mind here:

1. Capturing cross-business strategic-fit benefits via a strategy of related diversification builds shareholder value in ways that shareholders cannot undertake by simply owning a portfolio of stocks of companies in different industries.

2. The capture of cross-business strategic-fit benefits is possible only via a strategy of related diversification.

3. The greater the relatedness among a diversified company's businesses, the bigger the company's window for converting strategic fit into competitive advantage for its businesses.

4. The benefits of cross-business strategic fit come from the transferring or sharing of competitively valuable resources and capabilities among the businesses—resources

The Kraft–Heinz Merger: Pursuing the Benefits of Cross-Business Strategic Fit

The $62.6 billion merger between Kraft and Heinz that was finalized in the summer of 2015 created the third largest food and beverage company in North America and the fifth largest in the world. It was a merger predicated on the idea that the strategic fit between these two companies was such that they could create more value as a combined enterprise than they could as two separate companies. As a combined enterprise, Kraft Heinz would be able to exploit its cross-business value chain activities and resource similarities to more efficiently produce, distribute, and sell profitable processed food products.

Kraft and Heinz products share many of the same raw materials (milk, sugar, salt, wheat, etc.), which allows the new company to leverage its increased bargaining power as a larger business to get better deals with suppliers, using strategic fit in supply chain activities to achieve lower input costs and greater inbound efficiencies. Moreover, because both of these brands specialized in prepackaged foods, there is ample manufacturing-related strategic fit in production processes and packaging technologies that allow the new company to trim and streamline manufacturing operations.

Their distribution-related strategic fit will allow for the complete integration of distribution channels and transportation networks, resulting in greater outbound efficiencies and a reduction in travel time for products moving from factories to stores. The Kraft Heinz Company is currently looking to leverage Heinz's global platform to expand Kraft's products internationally. By utilizing Heinz's already highly developed global distribution network and brand familiarity (key specialized resources), Kraft can more easily expand into the global

Hayden Stirling/Shutterstock

market of prepackaged and processed food. Because these two brands are sold at similar types of retail stores (supermarket chains, wholesale retailers, and local grocery stores), they are now able to claim even more shelf space with the increased bargaining power of the combined company.

Strategic fit in sales and marketing activities will allow the company to develop coordinated and more effective advertising campaigns. Toward this aim, the Kraft Heinz Company is moving to consolidate its marketing capabilities under one marketing firm. Also, by combining R&D teams, the Kraft Heinz Company could come out with innovative products that may appeal more to the growing number of on-the-go and health-conscious buyers in the market. Many of these potential and predicted synergies for the Kraft Heinz Company have yet to be realized, since merger integration activities always take time.

Note: Developed with Maria Hart.

Sources: www.forbes.com/sites/paulmartyn/2015/03/31/heinz-and-kraft-merger-makes-supply-management-sense/; fortune.com/2015/03/25/kraft-mess-how-heinz-deal-helps/; www.nytimes.com/2015/03/26/business/dealbook/kraft-and-heinz-to-merge.html?_r=2; company websites (accessed December 3, 2015).

and capabilities that are *specialized* to certain applications and have value only in specific types of industries and businesses.

5. The benefits of cross-business strategic fit are not automatically realized when a company diversifies into related businesses; *the benefits materialize only after management has successfully pursued internal actions to capture them.*

Illustration Capsule 8.2 describes the merger of Kraft Foods Group, Inc. with the H. J. Heinz Holding Corporation, in pursuit of the strategic-fit benefits of a related diversification strategy.

DIVERSIFICATION INTO UNRELATED BUSINESSES

● ● ● ●

● **LO 8-3**

Identify the merits and risks of unrelated diversification strategies.

A willingness to diversify into any business in any industry is unlikely to result in successful unrelated diversification. The key to success even for unrelated diversification is to create economic value for shareholders.

Achieving cross-business strategic fit is not a motivation for unrelated diversification. Companies that pursue a strategy of unrelated diversification often exhibit a willingness to diversify into *any business in any industry* where senior managers see an opportunity to realize consistently good financial results. Such companies are frequently labeled *conglomerates* because their business interests range broadly across diverse industries. Companies engaged in unrelated diversification nearly always enter new businesses by acquiring an established company rather than by forming a startup subsidiary within their own corporate structures or participating in joint ventures.

With a strategy of unrelated diversification, an acquisition is deemed to have potential if it passes the industry-attractiveness and cost of entry tests and if it has good prospects for attractive financial performance. Thus, with an unrelated diversification strategy, company managers spend much time and effort screening acquisition candidates and evaluating the pros and cons of keeping or divesting existing businesses, using such criteria as

- Whether the business can meet corporate targets for profitability and return on investment.
- Whether the business is in an industry with attractive growth potential.
- Whether the business is big enough to contribute *significantly* to the parent firm's bottom line.

But the key to successful unrelated diversification is to go beyond these considerations and *ensure that the strategy passes the better-off test as well.* This test requires more than just growth in revenues; it requires *growth in profits*—beyond what could be achieved by a mutual fund or a holding company that owns shares of the businesses without adding any value. Unless the combination of businesses is more profitable together under the corporate umbrella than they are apart as independent businesses, *the strategy cannot create economic value for shareholders.* And unless it does so, there is *no real justification for unrelated diversification,* since top executives have a fiduciary responsibility to maximize long-term shareholder value for the company's owners (its shareholders). Illustration Capsule 8.3 provides some examples of successful companies with unrelated diversification.

Building Shareholder Value via Unrelated Diversification

Given the absence of cross-business strategic fit with which to create competitive advantages, building shareholder value via unrelated diversification ultimately hinges on the ability of the parent company to improve its businesses (and make the combination *better off*) via other means. Critical to this endeavor is the role that the parent company plays as a *corporate parent.*[10] To the extent that a company has strong *parenting capabilities*—capabilities that involve nurturing, guiding, grooming, and governing constituent businesses—a corporate parent can propel its businesses forward and help them gain ground over their market rivals. Corporate parents also contribute to the competitiveness of their unrelated businesses by sharing or transferring *general resources and capabilities* across the businesses—competitive assets that have utility in *any type* of industry and that can be leveraged across a wide range of business types as a result. Examples of the kinds of general resources that a corporate parent leverages in unrelated diversification include the corporation's reputation, credit rating, and

Examples of Companies Pursuing an Unrelated Diversification Strategy

TATA

The Tata group is a global enterprise with total revenues exceeding $115 billion in 2020. It is organized into 11 "verticals," which are essentially industry domains. The verticals include Information Technology, Steel, Automotive, Consumer and Retail, Infrastructure, Financial Services, Aerospace and Defense, Tourism and Travel, Telecom and Media, and Trading and Investments. Within these 11 verticals are 30 or more independently managed companies. The most well-known of these include: Tata Motors, Tata Steel, Tata Chemicals, Titan (jewelry and eyewear), Tata Power, Tata Communications, Tata Consumer Products, Tata Capital, Tata Consultancy Services, and Indian Hotels.

BERKSHIRE HATHAWAY

Berkshire Hathaway is an American conglomerate with a long and successful history, often attributed to the sage investment and acquisition strategy of its Chairman and CEO, Warren Buffet. Its holdings include an insurance group, an energy group, a financial products group, and a diverse group covering manufacturing, service, and retailing. Companies that are wholly owned by Berkshire Hathaway include GEICO, Dairy Queen, Duracell, Fruit of the Loom, Burlington Northern Sante Fe Railway, and Helzberg Diamonds. It owns a significant share of a number of other companies, including Bank of America, Southwest Airlines, Kraft Heinz, American Express, and Coca Cola.

YAMAHA CORPORATION

The Yamaha Corporation no longer includes Yamaha Motor Co. (the motorcycle, snowmobile, boat, and motorized product maker), although it is still a major shareholder. But even without Yamaha Motor, the Yamaha Corporation still produces a wide array of products. It is the world's largest producer of all types of musical instruments, along

(top): The India Today Group/Contributor/Getty Images; (middle): Ranta Images/ Shutterstock; (bottom): Gwenael_LE_VOT/Getty Images

with arguably related audio equipment and communication devices. But, in addition, it is involved in the production of industrial robots, home appliances, sporting goods, industrial machinery and components, specialty metals, golf products, resorts, and semiconductors.

Sources: Company websites, Wikipedia, accessed February 14, 2020.

access to financial markets; governance mechanisms; management training programs; a corporate ethics program; a central data and communications center; shared administrative resources such as public relations and legal services; and common systems for functions such as budgeting, financial reporting, and quality control.

The Benefits of Astute Corporate Parenting   One of the most important ways that corporate parents contribute to the success of their businesses is by offering high-level oversight and guidance.[11] The top executives of a large diversified corporation have among them many years of accumulated experience in a variety of business settings and can often contribute expert problem-solving skills, creative strategy suggestions, and first-rate advice and guidance on how to improve competitiveness and financial performance to the heads of the company's various business subsidiaries. This is especially true in the case of newly acquired, smaller businesses. Particularly astute high-level guidance from corporate executives can help the subsidiaries perform better than they would otherwise be able to do through the efforts of the business unit heads alone. The outstanding leadership of Royal Little, the founder of Textron, was a major reason that the company became an exemplar of the unrelated diversification strategy while he was CEO. Little's bold moves transformed the company from its origins as a small textile manufacturer into a global powerhouse known for its Bell helicopters, Cessna aircraft, and a host of other strong brands in a wide array of industries. Norm Wesley, a former CEO of the conglomerate Fortune Brands, is similarly credited with driving the sharp rise in the company's stock price while he was at the helm. Under his leadership, Fortune Brands became the $7 billion maker of products ranging from spirits (e.g., Jim Beam bourbon and rye, Gilbey's gin and vodka, Courvoisier cognac) to golf products (e.g., Titleist golf balls and clubs, FootJoy golf shoes and apparel, Scotty Cameron putters) to hardware (e.g., Moen faucets, American Lock security devices). (Fortune Brands has since been converted into two separate entities, Beam Inc. and Fortune Brands Home & Security.)

Corporate parents can also create added value for their businesses by providing them with other types of general resources that lower the operating costs of the individual businesses or that enhance their operating effectiveness. The administrative resources located at a company's corporate headquarters are a prime example. They typically include legal services, accounting expertise and tax services, and other elements of the administrative infrastructure, such as risk management capabilities, information technology resources, and public relations capabilities. Providing individual businesses with general support resources such as these creates value by *lowering companywide overhead costs,* since each business would otherwise have to duplicate the centralized activities.

Corporate brands that do not connote any specific type of product are another type of general corporate resource that can be shared among unrelated businesses. General Electric, for example, successfully applied its GE brand to such unrelated products and businesses as medical products and health care (GE Healthcare), jet engines (GE Aviation), and power and water technologies (GE Power and Water). Corporate brands that are applied in this fashion are sometimes called **umbrella brands.** Utilizing a well-known corporate name (GE) in a diversified company's individual businesses has the potential not only to lower costs (by spreading the fixed cost of developing and maintaining the brand over many businesses) but also to enhance each business's customer value proposition by linking its products to a name that consumers trust. In similar fashion, a corporation's reputation for well-crafted products, for product reliability, or for trustworthiness can lead to greater customer willingness to purchase the products of a wider range of a diversified company's businesses. Incentive systems, financial control systems, and a company's culture are other types of general corporate resources that may prove useful in enhancing the daily operations of a diverse set of businesses. The parenting activities of corporate executives may also include recruiting and hiring talented managers to run individual businesses.

We discuss two other commonly employed ways for corporate parents to add value to their unrelated businesses next.

Judicious Cross-Business Allocation of Financial Resources   By reallocating surplus cash flows from some businesses to fund the capital requirements of other businesses—in essence, having the company serve as an *internal capital market*—corporate parents may also be able to create value. Such actions can be particularly important in times when credit is unusually tight (such as in the wake of the worldwide banking crisis that began in 2008) or in economies with less well developed capital markets. Under these conditions, with strong financial resources a corporate parent can add value by shifting funds from business units generating excess cash (more than they need to fund their own operating requirements and new capital investment opportunities) to other, cash-short businesses with appealing growth prospects. A parent company's ability to function as its own internal capital market enhances overall corporate performance and increases shareholder value to the extent that (1) its top managers have better access to information about investment opportunities internal to the firm than do external financiers or (2) it can provide funds that would otherwise be unavailable due to poor financial market conditions.

Acquiring and Restructuring Undervalued Companies   Another way for parent companies to add value to unrelated businesses is by acquiring weakly performing companies at a bargain price and then *restructuring* their operations in ways that produce sometimes dramatic increases in profitability. **Restructuring** refers to overhauling and streamlining the operations of a business—combining plants with excess capacity, selling off underutilized assets, reducing unnecessary expenses, revamping its product offerings, consolidating administrative functions to reduce overhead costs, and otherwise improving the operating efficiency and profitability of a company. Restructuring generally involves transferring seasoned managers to the newly acquired business, either to replace the top layers of management or to step in temporarily until the business is returned to profitability or is well on its way to becoming a major market contender.

Restructuring is often undertaken when a diversified company acquires a new business that is performing well below levels that the corporate parent believes are achievable. Diversified companies that have proven *turnaround capabilities* in rejuvenating weakly performing companies can often apply these capabilities in a relatively wide range of unrelated industries. Newell Brands (whose diverse product line includes Rubbermaid food storage, Sharpie pens, Graco strollers and car seats, Goody hair accessories, Calphalon cookware, and Yankee Candle—all businesses with different value chain activities) developed such a strong set of turnaround capabilities that the company was said to "Newellize" the businesses it acquired.

Successful unrelated diversification strategies based on restructuring require the parent company to have considerable expertise in identifying underperforming target companies and in negotiating attractive acquisition prices so that each acquisition passes the cost of entry test. The capabilities in this regard of Lord James Hanson and Lord Gordon White, who headed up the storied British conglomerate Hanson Trust, played a large part in Hanson Trust's impressive record of profitability.

The Path to Greater Shareholder Value through Unrelated Diversification

For a strategy of unrelated diversification to produce companywide financial results above and beyond what the businesses could generate operating as standalone entities, corporate executives must do three things to pass the three Tests of Corporate Advantage:

1. Diversify into industries where the businesses can produce consistently good earnings and returns on investment (to satisfy the industry-attractiveness test).
2. Negotiate favorable acquisition prices (to satisfy the cost of entry test).
3. Do a superior job of corporate parenting via high-level managerial oversight and resource sharing, financial resource allocation and portfolio management, and/or the restructuring of underperforming businesses (to satisfy the better-off test).

> **CORE CONCEPT**
>
> A diversified company has a **parenting advantage** when it is more able than other companies to boost the combined performance of its individual businesses through high-level guidance, general oversight, and other corporate-level contributions.

The best corporate parents understand the nature and value of the kinds of resources at their command and know how to leverage them effectively across their businesses. Those that are able to create more value in their businesses than other diversified companies have what is called a **parenting advantage.** When a corporation has a parenting advantage, its top executives have the best chance of being able to craft and execute an unrelated diversification strategy that can satisfy all three Tests of Corporate Advantage and truly enhance long-term economic shareholder value.

The Drawbacks of Unrelated Diversification

Unrelated diversification strategies have two important negatives that undercut the pluses: very demanding managerial requirements and limited competitive advantage potential.

Demanding Managerial Requirements   Successfully managing a set of fundamentally different businesses operating in fundamentally different industry and competitive environments is a challenging and exceptionally difficult proposition.[12] Consider, for example, that corporations like General Electric, ITT, Mitsubishi, and Bharti Enterprises have dozens of business subsidiaries making hundreds and sometimes thousands of products. While headquarters executives can glean information about an industry from third-party sources, ask lots of questions when making occasional visits to the operations of the different businesses, and do their best to learn about the company's different businesses, they still remain heavily dependent on briefings from business unit heads and on "managing by the numbers"—that is, keeping a close track on the financial and operating results of each subsidiary. Managing by the numbers works well enough when business conditions are normal and the heads of the various business units are capable of consistently meeting their numbers. But problems arise if things start to go awry in a business and corporate management has to get deeply involved in the problems of a business it does not know much about. Because every business tends to encounter rough sledding at some juncture, unrelated diversification is thus a somewhat risky strategy from a managerial perspective.[13] Just one or two unforeseen problems or big strategic mistakes—which are much more likely without close corporate oversight—can cause a precipitous drop in corporate earnings and crash the parent company's stock price.

Hence, competently overseeing a set of widely diverse businesses can turn out to be much harder than it sounds. In practice, comparatively few companies have proved that they have top-management capabilities that are up to the task. There are far more companies whose corporate executives have failed at delivering consistently good financial results with an unrelated diversification strategy than there are companies with corporate executives who have been successful.[14] Unless a company truly has a parenting advantage, the odds are that the result of unrelated diversification will be $1 + 1 = 2$ or even less.

Limited Competitive Advantage Potential   The second big negative is that *unrelated diversification offers only a limited potential for competitive advantage beyond what each individual business can generate on its own.* Unlike a related diversification strategy, unrelated diversification provides no cross-business strategic-fit benefits that allow each business to perform its key value chain activities in a more efficient and effective manner. A cash-rich corporate parent pursuing unrelated diversification can provide its subsidiaries with much-needed capital, may achieve economies of scope in activities relying on general corporate resources, may extend an umbrella brand and may even offer some managerial know-how to help resolve problems in particular business units, but otherwise it has little to add in the way of enhancing the competitive strength of its individual business units. In comparison to the highly specialized resources that facilitate related diversification, the general resources that support unrelated diversification tend to be relatively low value, for the simple reason that they are more common. Unless they are of exceptionally high quality (such as GE's world-renowned general management capabilities and umbrella brand or Newell Rubbermaid's turnaround capabilities), resources and capabilities that are general in nature are less likely to provide a significant source of competitive advantage for the businesses of diversified companies. Without the competitive advantage potential of strategic fit in competitively important value chain activities, consolidated performance of an unrelated group of businesses may not be very much more than the sum of what the individual business units could achieve if they were independent, in most circumstances.

> Relying solely on leveraging general resources and the expertise of corporate executives to wisely manage a set of unrelated businesses is a much weaker foundation for enhancing shareholder value than is a strategy of related diversification.

Misguided Reasons for Pursuing Unrelated Diversification

Companies sometimes pursue unrelated diversification for reasons that are entirely misguided. These include the following:

- *Risk reduction.* Spreading the company's investments over a set of diverse industries to spread risk cannot create long-term shareholder value since the company's shareholders can more flexibly (and more efficiently) reduce their exposure to risk by investing in a diversified portfolio of stocks and bonds.

- *Growth.* While unrelated diversification may enable a company to achieve rapid or continuous growth, firms that pursue growth for growth's sake are unlikely to maximize shareholder value. Only *profitable growth*—the kind that comes from creating added value for shareholders—can justify a strategy of unrelated diversification.

- *Stabilization.* Managers sometimes pursue broad diversification in the hope that market downtrends in some of the company's businesses will be partially offset by cyclical upswings in its other businesses, thus producing somewhat less earnings volatility. In actual practice, however, there's no convincing evidence that the consolidated profits of firms with unrelated diversification strategies are more stable or less subject to reversal in periods of recession and economic stress than the profits of firms with related diversification strategies.

- *Managerial motives.* Unrelated diversification can provide benefits to managers such as higher compensation (which tends to increase with firm size and degree of diversification) and reduced their unemployment risk. Pursuing diversification for these reasons will likely reduce shareholder value and violate managers' fiduciary responsibilities.

Because unrelated diversification strategies *at their best* have only a limited potential for creating long-term economic value for shareholders, it is essential that managers not compound this problem by taking a misguided approach toward unrelated diversification, in pursuit of objectives that are more likely to destroy shareholder value than create it.

> Only profitable growth—the kind that comes from creating added value for shareholders—can justify a strategy of unrelated diversification.

COMBINATION RELATED–UNRELATED DIVERSIFICATION STRATEGIES

There's nothing to preclude a company from diversifying into both related and unrelated businesses. Indeed, in actual practice the business makeup of diversified companies varies considerably. Some diversified companies are really *dominant-business enterprises*—one major "core" business accounts for 50 to 80 percent of total revenues and a collection of small related or unrelated businesses accounts for the remainder. Some diversified companies are *narrowly diversified* around a few (two to five) related or unrelated businesses. Others are *broadly diversified* around a wide-ranging collection of related businesses, unrelated businesses, or a mixture of both. A number of multibusiness enterprises have diversified into unrelated areas but have a collection of related businesses within each area—thus giving them a business portfolio consisting of *several unrelated groups of related businesses*. There's ample room for companies to customize their diversification strategies to incorporate elements of both related and unrelated diversification, as may suit their own competitive asset profile and strategic vision. *Combination related–unrelated diversification strategies have particular appeal for companies with a mix of valuable competitive assets, covering the spectrum from general to specialized resources and capabilities.*

Figure 8.2 shows the range of alternatives for companies pursuing diversification.

EVALUATING THE STRATEGY OF A DIVERSIFIED COMPANY

> ● **LO 8-4**
>
> Use the analytic tools for evaluating a company's diversification strategy.

Strategic analysis of diversified companies builds on the concepts and methods used for single-business companies. But there are some additional aspects to consider and a couple of new analytic tools to master. The procedure for evaluating the pluses and minuses of a diversified company's strategy and deciding what actions to take to improve the company's performance involves six steps:

1. Assessing the attractiveness of the industries the company has diversified into, both individually and as a group.
2. Assessing the competitive strength of the company's business units and drawing a nine-cell matrix to simultaneously portray industry attractiveness and business unit competitive strength.

FIGURE 8.2   Three Strategy Options for Pursuing Diversification

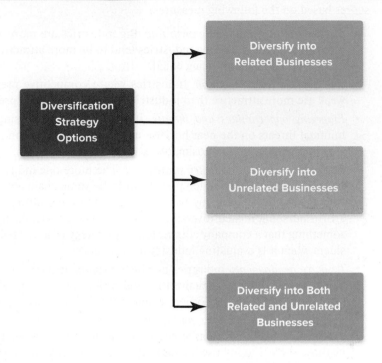

3. Evaluating the extent of cross-business strategic fit along the value chains of the company's various business units.
4. Checking whether the firm's resources fit the requirements of its present business lineup.
5. Ranking the performance prospects of the businesses from best to worst and determining what the corporate parent's priorities should be in allocating resources to its various businesses.
6. Crafting new strategic moves to improve overall corporate performance.

The core concepts and analytic techniques underlying each of these steps merit further discussion.

Step 1: Evaluating Industry Attractiveness

A principal consideration in evaluating the caliber of a diversified company's strategy is the attractiveness of the industries in which it has business operations. Several questions arise:

1. Does each industry the company has diversified into represent a good market for the company to be in—does it pass the industry-attractiveness test?
2. Which of the company's industries are most attractive, and which are least attractive?
3. How appealing is the whole group of industries in which the company has invested?

The more attractive the industries (both individually and as a group) that a diversified company is in, the better its prospects for good long-term performance.

Calculating Industry-Attractiveness Scores   A simple and reliable analytic tool for gauging industry attractiveness involves calculating quantitative industry-attractiveness scores based on the following measures:

- *Market size and projected growth rate.* Big industries are more attractive than small industries, and fast-growing industries tend to be more attractive than slow-growing industries, other things being equal.
- *The intensity of competition.* Industries where competitive pressures are relatively weak are more attractive than industries where competitive pressures are strong.
- *Emerging opportunities and threats.* Industries with promising opportunities and minimal threats on the near horizon are more attractive than industries with modest opportunities and imposing threats.
- *The presence of cross-industry strategic fit.* The more one industry's value chain and resource requirements match up well with the value chain activities of other industries in which the company has operations, the more attractive the industry is to a firm pursuing related diversification. However, cross-industry strategic fit is not something that a company committed to a strategy of unrelated diversification considers when it is evaluating industry attractiveness.
- *Resource requirements.* Industries in which resource requirements are within the company's reach are more attractive than industries in which capital and other resource requirements could strain corporate financial resources and organizational capabilities.
- *Social, political, regulatory, and environmental factors.* Industries that have significant problems in such areas as consumer health, safety, or environmental pollution or those subject to intense regulation are less attractive than industries that do not have such problems.
- *Industry profitability.* Industries with healthy profit margins and high rates of return on investment are generally more attractive than industries with historically low or unstable profits.

Each attractiveness measure is then assigned a weight reflecting its relative importance in determining an industry's attractiveness, since not all attractiveness measures are equally important. The intensity of competition in an industry should nearly always carry a high weight (say, 0.20 to 0.30). Strategic-fit considerations should be assigned a high weight in the case of companies with related diversification strategies; but for companies with an unrelated diversification strategy, strategic fit with other industries may be dropped from the list of attractiveness measures altogether. The importance weights must add up to 1.

Finally, each industry is rated on each of the chosen industry-attractiveness measures, using a rating scale of 1 to 10 (where a *high* rating signifies *high* attractiveness, and a *low* rating signifies *low* attractiveness). *Keep in mind here that the more intensely competitive an industry is, the lower the attractiveness rating for that industry.* Likewise, the more the resource requirements associated with being in a particular industry are beyond the parent company's reach, the lower the attractiveness rating. On the other hand, the presence of good cross-industry strategic fit should be given a very high attractiveness rating, since there is good potential for competitive advantage and added shareholder value. Weighted attractiveness scores are then calculated by multiplying the industry's rating on each measure by the corresponding weight. For example, a rating of 8 times a weight of 0.25 gives a weighted attractiveness score of 2. The sum of the weighted scores for all the attractiveness measures provides an overall industry-attractiveness score. This procedure is illustrated in Table 8.1.

TABLE 8.1   Calculating Weighted Industry-Attractiveness Scores

Industry-Attractiveness Measure	Importance Weight	Industry-Attractiveness Assessments					
		Industry A		Industry B		Industry C	
		Attractiveness Rating*	Weighted Score	Attractiveness Rating*	Weighted Score	Attractiveness Rating*	Weighted Score
Market size and projected growth rate	0.10	8	0.80	3	0.30	5	0.50
Intensity of competition	0.25	8	2.00	2	0.50	5	1.25
Emerging opportunities and threats	0.10	6	0.60	5	0.50	4	0.40
Cross-industry strategic fit	0.30	8	2.40	2	0.60	3	0.90
Resource requirements	0.10	5	0.50	5	0.50	4	0.40
Social, political, regulatory, and environmental factors	0.05	8	0.40	3	0.15	7	1.05
Industry profitability	0.10	5	0.50	4	0.40	6	0.60
Sum of importance weights	**1.00**						
Weighted overall industry-attractiveness scores			**7.20**		**2.95**		**5.10**

*Rating scale: 1 = very unattractive to company; 10 = very attractive to company.

Interpreting the Industry-Attractiveness Scores   Industries with a score much below 5 probably do not pass the attractiveness test. If a company's industry-attractiveness scores are all above 5, it is probably fair to conclude that the group of industries the company operates in is attractive as a whole. But the group of industries takes on a decidedly lower degree of attractiveness as the number of industries with scores below 5 increases, especially if industries with low scores account for a sizable fraction of the company's revenues.

For a diversified company to be a strong performer, a substantial portion of its revenues and profits must come from business units with relatively high attractiveness scores. It is particularly important that a diversified company's principal businesses be in industries with a good outlook for growth and above-average profitability. Having a big fraction of the company's revenues and profits come from industries with slow growth, low profitability, intense competition, or other troubling conditions tends to drag overall company performance down. Business units in the least attractive industries are potential candidates for divestiture, unless they are positioned strongly enough to overcome the unattractive aspects of their industry environments or they are a strategically important component of the company's business makeup.

Step 2: Evaluating Business Unit Competitive Strength

The second step in evaluating a diversified company is to appraise the competitive strength of each business unit in its respective industry. Doing an appraisal of each business unit's strength and competitive position in its industry not only reveals its chances for success in its industry but also provides a basis for ranking the units from competitively strongest to competitively weakest and sizing up the competitive strength of all the business units as a group.

Calculating Competitive-Strength Scores for Each Business Unit   Quantitative measures of each business unit's competitive strength can be calculated using a procedure similar to that for measuring industry attractiveness. The following factors are used in quantifying the competitive strengths of a diversified company's business subsidiaries:

- *Relative market share.* A business unit's *relative market share* is defined as the ratio of its market share to the market share held by the largest rival firm in the industry, with market share measured in unit volume, not dollars. For instance, if business A has a market-leading share of 40 percent and its largest rival has 30 percent, A's relative market share is 1.33. (Note that only business units that are market share leaders in their respective industries can have relative market shares greater than 1.) If business B has a 15 percent market share and B's largest rival has 30 percent, B's relative market share is 0.5. *The further below 1 a business unit's relative market share is, the weaker its competitive strength and market position vis-à-vis rivals.*

- *Costs relative to competitors' costs.* Business units that have low costs relative to those of key competitors tend to be more strongly positioned in their industries than business units struggling to maintain cost parity with major rivals. The only time a business unit's competitive strength may not be undermined by having higher costs than rivals is when it has incurred the higher costs to strongly differentiate its product offering and its customers are willing to pay premium prices for the differentiating features.

- *Ability to match or beat rivals on key product attributes.* A company's competitiveness depends in part on being able to satisfy buyer expectations with regard to features, product performance, reliability, service, and other important attributes.

- *Brand image and reputation.* A widely known and respected brand name is a valuable competitive asset in most industries.

- *Other competitively valuable resources and capabilities.* Valuable resources and capabilities, including those accessed through collaborative partnerships, enhance a company's ability to compete successfully and perhaps contend for industry leadership.

- *Ability to benefit from strategic fit with other business units.* Strategic fit with other businesses within the company enhances a business unit's competitive strength and may provide a competitive edge.
- *Ability to exercise bargaining leverage with key suppliers or customers.* Having bargaining leverage signals competitive strength and can be a source of competitive advantage.
- *Profitability relative to competitors.* Above-average profitability on a consistent basis is a signal of competitive advantage, whereas consistently below-average profitability usually denotes competitive disadvantage.

After settling on a set of competitive-strength measures that are well matched to the circumstances of the various business units, the company needs to assign weights indicating each measure's importance. As in the assignment of weights to industry-attractiveness measures, the importance weights must add up to 1. Each business unit is then rated on each of the chosen strength measures, using a rating scale of 1 to 10 (where a *high* rating signifies competitive *strength,* and a *low* rating signifies competitive *weakness*). In the event that the available information is too limited to confidently assign a rating value to a business unit on a particular strength measure, it is usually best to use a score of 5—this avoids biasing the overall score either up or down. Weighted strength ratings are calculated by multiplying the business unit's rating on each strength measure by the assigned weight. For example, a strength score of 6 times a weight of 0.15 gives a weighted strength rating of 0.90. The sum of the weighted ratings across all the strength measures provides a quantitative measure of a business unit's overall competitive strength. Table 8.2 provides sample calculations of competitive-strength ratings for three businesses.

Interpreting the Competitive-Strength Scores   Business units with competitive-strength ratings above 6.7 (on a scale of 1 to 10) are strong market contenders in their industries. Businesses with ratings in the 3.3-to-6.7 range have moderate competitive strength vis-à-vis rivals. Businesses with ratings below 3.3 have a competitively weak standing in the marketplace. If a diversified company's business units all have competitive-strength scores above 5, it is fair to conclude that its business units are all fairly strong market contenders in their respective industries. But as the number of business units with scores below 5 increases, there's reason to question whether the company can perform well with so many businesses in relatively weak competitive positions. This concern takes on even more importance when business units with low scores account for a sizable fraction of the company's revenues.

Using a Nine-Cell Matrix to Simultaneously Portray Industry Attractiveness and Competitive Strength   The industry-attractiveness and business-strength scores can be used to portray the strategic positions of each business in a diversified company. Industry attractiveness is plotted on the vertical axis and competitive strength on the horizontal axis. A nine-cell grid emerges from dividing the vertical axis into three regions (high, medium, and low attractiveness) and the horizontal axis into three regions (strong, average, and weak competitive strength). As shown in Figure 8.3, scores of 6.7 or greater on a rating scale of 1 to 10 denote high industry attractiveness, scores of 3.3 to 6.7 denote medium attractiveness, and scores below 3.3 signal low attractiveness. Likewise, high competitive strength is defined as scores greater than 6.7, average strength as scores of 3.3 to 6.7, and low strength as scores below 3.3. *Each business unit*

TABLE 8.2　Calculating Weighted Competitive-Strength Scores for a Diversified Company's Business Units

Competitive-Strength Measures	Importance Weight	Business A in Industry A		Business B in Industry B		Business C in Industry C	
		Strength Rating*	Weighted Score	Strength Rating*	Weighted Score	Strength Rating*	Weighted Score
Relative market share	0.15	10	1.50	2	0.30	6	0.90
Costs relative to competitors' costs	0.20	7	1.40	4	0.80	5	1.00
Ability to match or beat rivals on key product attributes	0.05	9	0.45	5	0.25	8	0.40
Ability to benefit from strategic fit with sister businesses	0.20	8	1.60	4	0.80	8	0.80
Bargaining leverage with suppliers/customers	0.05	9	0.45	2	0.10	6	0.30
Brand image and reputation	0.10	9	0.90	4	0.40	7	0.70
Other valuable resources/ capabilities	0.15	7	1.05	2	0.30	5	0.75
Profitability relative to competitors	0.10	5	0.50	2	0.20	4	0.40
Sum of importance weights	**1.00**						
Weighted overall competitive strength scores			**7.85**		**3.15**		**5.25**

Rating scale: 1 = very weak; 10 = very strong.

is plotted on the nine-cell matrix according to its overall attractiveness score and strength score, and then it is shown as a "bubble." The size of each bubble is scaled to the percentage of revenues the business generates relative to total corporate revenues. The bubbles in Figure 8.3 were located on the grid using the three industry-attractiveness scores from Table 8.1 and the strength scores for the three business units in Table 8.2.

The locations of the business units on the attractiveness–strength matrix provide valuable guidance in deploying corporate resources. Businesses positioned in the three cells in the upper left portion of the attractiveness–strength matrix (like business A) have both favorable industry attractiveness and competitive strength.

Next in priority come businesses positioned in the three diagonal cells stretching from the lower left to the upper right (like business C). Such businesses usually merit intermediate priority in the parent's resource allocation ranking. However, some

FIGURE 8.3   A Nine-Cell Industry-Attractiveness–Competitive-Strength Matrix

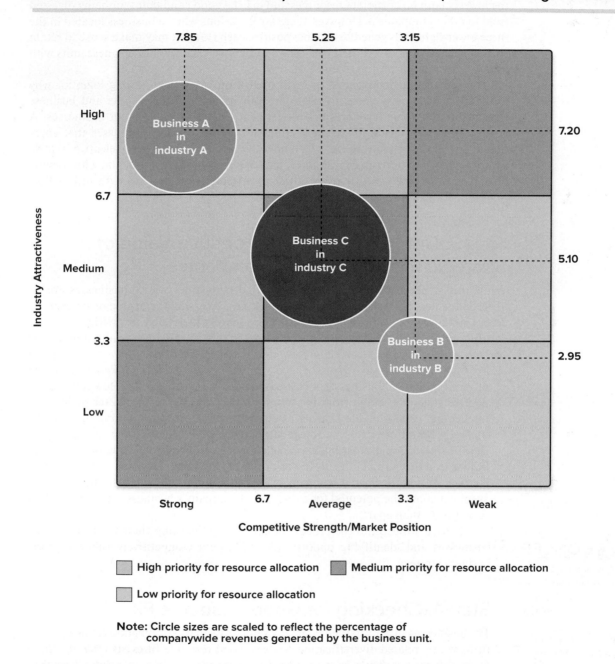

Note: Circle sizes are scaled to reflect the percentage of companywide revenues generated by the business unit.

businesses in the medium-priority diagonal cells may have brighter or dimmer prospects than others. For example, a small business in the upper right cell of the matrix, despite being in a highly attractive industry, may occupy too weak a competitive position in its industry to justify the investment and resources needed to turn it into a strong market contender.

Businesses in the three cells in the lower right corner of the matrix (like business B) have comparatively low industry attractiveness and minimal competitive strength, making them weak performers with little potential for improvement. At best, they have the lowest claim on corporate resources and may be good candidates for being divested (sold to other companies). However, there are occasions when a business located in the three lower-right cells generates sizable positive cash flows. It may make sense to retain such businesses and divert their cash flows to finance expansion of business units with greater potential for profit growth.

The nine-cell attractiveness–strength matrix provides clear, strong logic for why a diversified company needs to consider both industry attractiveness and business strength in allocating resources and investment capital to its different businesses. A good case can be made for concentrating resources in those businesses that enjoy higher degrees of attractiveness and competitive strength, being very selective in making investments in businesses with intermediate positions on the grid, and withdrawing resources from businesses that are lower in attractiveness and strength unless they offer exceptional profit or cash flow potential.

Step 3: Determining the Competitive Value of Strategic Fit in Diversified Companies

While this step can be bypassed for diversified companies whose businesses are all unrelated (since, by design, strategic fit is lacking), assessing the degree of strategic fit across a company's businesses is central to evaluating its related diversification strategy. But more than just checking for the presence of strategic fit is required here. *The real question is how much competitive value can be generated from whatever strategic fit exists.* Are the cost savings associated with economies of scope likely to give one or more individual businesses a cost-based advantage over rivals? How much competitive value will come from the cross-business transfer of skills, technology, or intellectual capital or the sharing of competitive assets? Can leveraging a potent umbrella brand or corporate image strengthen the businesses and increase sales significantly? Could cross-business collaboration to create new competitive capabilities lead to significant gains in performance? Without significant cross-business strategic fit and dedicated company efforts to capture the benefits, one has to be skeptical about the potential for a diversified company's businesses to perform better together than apart.

Figure 8.4 illustrates the process of comparing the value chains of a company's businesses and identifying opportunities to exploit competitively valuable cross-business strategic fit.

Step 4: Checking for Good Resource Fit

The businesses in a diversified company's lineup need to exhibit good **resource fit.** In firms with a related diversification strategy, good resource fit exists *when the firm's businesses have well-matched specialized resource requirements at points along their value chains* that are critical for the businesses' market success. Matching resource requirements are important in related diversification because they facilitate resource sharing and low-cost resource transfer. In companies pursuing unrelated diversification, resource fit exists when the company has solid *parenting capabilities or resources of a general nature that it can share or transfer to its component businesses.* Firms pursuing related diversification and firms with combination related–unrelated diversification strategies can also benefit from leveraging corporate parenting capabilities

> The greater the value of cross-business strategic fit in enhancing the performance of a diversified company's businesses, the more competitively powerful is the company's related diversification strategy.

CORE CONCEPT

A company pursuing related diversification exhibits **resource fit** when its businesses have matching specialized resource requirements along their value chains; a company pursuing unrelated diversification has resource fit when the parent company has adequate corporate resources (parenting and general resources) to support its businesses' needs and add value.

and other general resources. Another dimension of resource fit that concerns all types of multibusiness firms is whether they have resources sufficient to support their group of businesses without being spread too thin.

Financial Resource Fit   The most important dimension of financial resource fit concerns whether a diversified company can generate the internal cash flows sufficient to fund the capital requirements of its businesses, pay its dividends, meet its debt obligations, and otherwise remain financially healthy. (Financial resources, including the firm's ability to borrow or otherwise raise funds, are a type of general resource.) While additional capital can usually be raised in financial markets, it is important for a diversified firm to have a healthy **internal capital market** that can support the financial requirements of its business lineup. The greater the extent to which a diversified company is able to fund investment in its businesses through internally generated cash flows rather than from equity issues or borrowing, the more powerful its financial resource fit and the less dependent the firm is on external financial resources. This can provide a competitive advantage over single business rivals when credit market conditions are tight, as they have been in the United States and abroad in recent years.

> **CORE CONCEPT**
>
> A strong **internal capital market** allows a diversified company to add value by shifting capital from business units generating free cash flow to those needing additional capital to expand and realize their growth potential.

FIGURE 8.4   Identifying the Competitive Advantage Potential of Cross-Business Strategic Fit

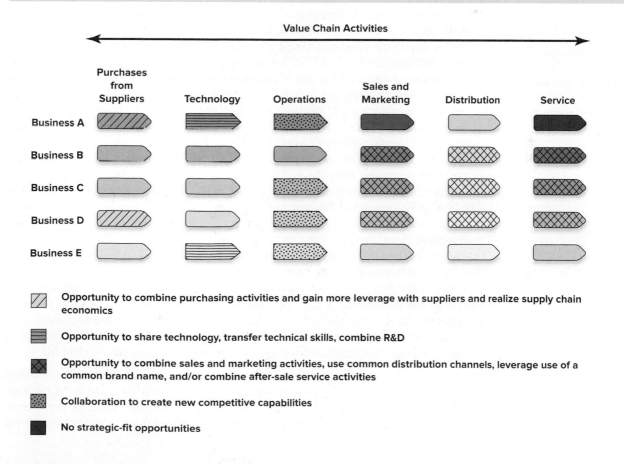

Opportunity to combine purchasing activities and gain more leverage with suppliers and realize supply chain economics

Opportunity to share technology, transfer technical skills, combine R&D

Opportunity to combine sales and marketing activities, use common distribution channels, leverage use of a common brand name, and/or combine after-sale service activities

Collaboration to create new competitive capabilities

No strategic-fit opportunities

A **portfolio approach** to ensuring financial fit among a firm's businesses is based on the fact that different businesses have different cash flow and investment characteristics. For example, business units in rapidly growing industries are often **cash hogs**—so labeled because the cash flows they are able to generate from internal operations aren't big enough to fund their operations and capital requirements for growth. To keep pace with rising buyer demand, rapid-growth businesses frequently need sizable annual capital investments—for new facilities and equipment, for new product development or technology improvements, and for additional working capital to support inventory expansion and a larger base of operations. Because a cash hog's financial resources must be provided by the corporate parent, corporate managers have to decide whether it makes good financial and strategic sense to keep pouring new money into a cash hog business.

In contrast, business units with leading market positions in mature industries may be **cash cows** in the sense that they generate substantial cash surpluses over what is needed to adequately fund their operations. Market leaders in slow-growth industries often generate sizable positive cash flows *over and above what is needed for growth and reinvestment* because their industry-leading positions tend to generate attractive earnings and because the slow-growth nature of their industry often entails relatively modest annual investment requirements. Cash cows, although not attractive from a growth standpoint, are valuable businesses from a financial resource perspective. The surplus cash flows they generate can be used to pay corporate dividends, finance acquisitions, and provide funds for investing in the company's promising cash hogs. It makes good financial and strategic sense for diversified companies to keep cash cows in a healthy condition, fortifying and defending their market position so as to preserve their cash-generating capability and have an ongoing source of financial resources to deploy elsewhere. General Electric considers its advanced materials, equipment services, and appliance and lighting businesses to be cash cow businesses.

Viewing a diversified group of businesses as a collection of cash flows and cash requirements (present and future flows) can be helpful in understanding what the financial ramifications of diversification are and why having businesses with good financial resource fit can be important. For instance, *a diversified company's businesses exhibit good financial resource fit when the excess cash generated by its cash cow businesses is sufficient to fund the investment requirements of promising cash hog businesses.* Ideally, investing in promising cash hog businesses over time results in growing the hogs into self-supporting *star businesses* that have strong or market-leading competitive positions in attractive, high-growth markets and high levels of profitability. Star businesses are often the cash cows of the future. When the markets of star businesses begin to mature and their growth slows, their competitive strength should produce self-generated cash flows that are more than sufficient to cover their investment needs. The "success sequence" is thus cash hog to young star (but perhaps still a cash hog) to self-supporting star to cash cow. While the practice of viewing a diversified company in terms of cash cows and cash hogs has declined in popularity, it illustrates one approach to analyzing financial resource fit and allocating financial resources across a portfolio of different businesses.

Aside from cash flow considerations, there are two other factors to consider in assessing whether a diversified company's businesses exhibit good financial fit:

- *Do any of the company's individual businesses present financial challenges with respect to contributing adequately to achieving companywide performance targets?* A business exhibits poor financial fit if it soaks up a disproportionate share of the company's financial resources, while making subpar or insignificant contributions to the bottom line. Too many underperforming businesses reduce the company's overall performance and ultimately limit growth in shareholder value.

- *Does the corporation have adequate financial strength to fund its different businesses and maintain a healthy credit rating?* A diversified company's strategy fails the resource-fit test when the resource needs of its portfolio unduly stretch the company's financial health and threaten to impair its credit rating. Many of the world's largest banks, including Royal Bank of Scotland, Citigroup, and HSBC, recently found themselves so undercapitalized and financially overextended that they were forced to sell off some of their business assets to meet regulatory requirements and restore public confidence in their solvency.

Nonfinancial Resource Fit   Just as a diversified company must have adequate financial resources to support its various individual businesses, it must also have a big enough and deep enough pool of managerial, administrative, and other parenting capabilities to support all of its different businesses. The following two questions help reveal whether a diversified company has sufficient nonfinancial resources:

- *Does the parent company have (or can it develop) the specific resources and capabilities needed to be successful in each of its businesses?* Sometimes the resources a company has accumulated in its core business prove to be a poor match with the competitive capabilities needed to succeed in the businesses into which it has diversified. For instance, BTR, a multibusiness company in Great Britain, discovered that the company's resources and managerial skills were quite well suited for parenting its industrial manufacturing businesses but not for parenting its distribution businesses (National Tyre Services and Texas-based Summers Group). As a result, BTR decided to divest its distribution businesses and focus exclusively on diversifying around small industrial manufacturing. For companies pursuing related diversification strategies, a mismatch between the company's competitive assets and the key success factors of an industry can be serious enough to warrant divesting businesses in that industry or not acquiring a new business. In contrast, when a company's resources and capabilities are a good match with the key success factors of industries it is not presently in, it makes sense to take a hard look at acquiring companies in these industries and expanding the company's business lineup.

- *Are the parent company's resources being stretched too thinly by the resource requirements of one or more of its businesses?* A diversified company must guard against overtaxing its resources and capabilities, a condition that can arise when (1) it goes on an acquisition spree and management is called on to assimilate and oversee many new businesses very quickly or (2) it lacks sufficient resource depth to do a creditable job of transferring skills and competencies from one of its businesses to another. The broader the diversification, the greater the concern about whether corporate executives are overburdened by the demands of competently parenting so many different businesses. Plus, the more a company's diversification strategy is tied to transferring know-how or technologies from existing businesses to newly acquired businesses, the more time and money that has to be put into developing a deep-enough resource pool to supply these businesses with the resources and capabilities they need to be successful.[15] Otherwise, its resource pool ends up being spread too thinly across many businesses, and the opportunity for achieving $1 + 1 = 3$ outcomes slips through the cracks.

Step 5: Ranking Business Units and Assigning a Priority for Resource Allocation

Once a diversified company's strategy has been evaluated from the perspective of industry attractiveness, competitive strength, strategic fit, and resource fit, the next step is to use this information to rank the performance prospects of the businesses from best to worst. Such ranking helps top-level executives assign each business a priority for resource support and capital investment.

The locations of the different businesses in the nine-cell industry-attractiveness–competitive-strength matrix provide a solid basis for identifying high-opportunity businesses and low-opportunity businesses. Normally, competitively strong businesses in attractive industries have significantly better performance prospects than competitively weak businesses in unattractive industries. Also, the revenue and earnings outlook for businesses in fast-growing industries is normally better than for businesses in slow-growing industries. As a rule, *business subsidiaries with the brightest profit and growth prospects, attractive positions in the nine-cell matrix, and solid strategic and resource fit should receive top priority for allocation of corporate resources.* However, in ranking the prospects of the different businesses from best to worst, it is usually wise to also take into account each business's past performance in regard to sales growth, profit growth, contribution to company earnings, return on capital invested in the business, and cash flow from operations. While past performance is not always a reliable predictor of future performance, it does signal whether a business is already performing well or has problems to overcome.

Allocating Financial Resources   Figure 8.5 shows the chief strategic and financial options for allocating a diversified company's financial resources. Divesting businesses

FIGURE 8.5   The Chief Strategic and Financial Options for Allocating a Diversified Company's Financial Resources

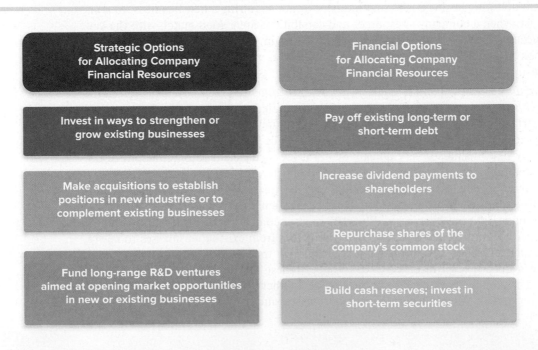

Strategic Options for Allocating Company Financial Resources

- Invest in ways to strengthen or grow existing businesses
- Make acquisitions to establish positions in new industries or to complement existing businesses
- Fund long-range R&D ventures aimed at opening market opportunities in new or existing businesses

Financial Options for Allocating Company Financial Resources

- Pay off existing long-term or short-term debt
- Increase dividend payments to shareholders
- Repurchase shares of the company's common stock
- Build cash reserves; invest in short-term securities

with the weakest future prospects and businesses that lack adequate strategic fit and/ or resource fit is one of the best ways of generating additional funds for redeployment to businesses with better opportunities and better strategic and resource fit. Free cash flows from cash cow businesses also add to the pool of funds that can be usefully redeployed. *Ideally,* a diversified company will have sufficient financial resources to strengthen or grow its existing businesses, make any new acquisitions that are desirable, fund other promising business opportunities, pay off existing debt, and periodically increase dividend payments to shareholders and/or repurchase shares of stock. But, as a practical matter, a company's financial resources are limited. Thus, to make the best use of the available funds, top executives must steer resources to those businesses with the best prospects and either divest or allocate minimal resources to businesses with marginal prospects—this is why ranking the performance prospects of the various businesses from best to worst is so crucial. *Strategic* uses of corporate financial resources should usually take precedence over strictly financial considerations (see Figure 8.5) unless there is a compelling reason to strengthen the firm's balance sheet or better reward shareholders.

Step 6: Crafting New Strategic Moves to Improve Overall Corporate Performance

● **LO 8-5**

Understand the four main corporate strategy options a diversified company can employ to improve company performance.

The conclusions flowing from the five preceding analytic steps set the agenda for crafting strategic moves to improve a diversified company's overall performance. The strategic options boil down to four broad categories of actions (see Figure 8.6):

1. Sticking closely with the existing business lineup and pursuing the opportunities these businesses present.
2. Broadening the company's business scope by making new acquisitions in new industries.
3. Divesting certain businesses and retrenching to a narrower base of business operations.
4. Restructuring the company's business lineup and putting a whole new face on the company's business makeup.

Sticking Closely with the Present Business Lineup The option of sticking with the current business lineup makes sense when the company's existing businesses offer attractive growth opportunities and can be counted on to create economic value for shareholders. As long as the company's set of existing businesses have good prospects and are in alignment with the company's diversification strategy, then major changes in the company's business mix are unnecessary. Corporate executives can concentrate their attention on getting the best performance from each of the businesses, steering corporate resources into the areas of greatest potential and profitability. The specifics of "what to do" to wring better performance from the present business lineup have to be dictated by each business's circumstances and the preceding analysis of the corporate parent's diversification strategy.

Broadening a Diversified Company's Business Base Diversified companies sometimes find it desirable to build positions in new industries, whether related or unrelated. Several motivating factors are in play. One is sluggish growth that makes the potential revenue and profit boost of a newly acquired business look attractive. A second is the potential for transferring resources and capabilities to other related or complementary businesses.

FIGURE 8.6   A Company's Four Main Strategic Alternatives after It Diversifies

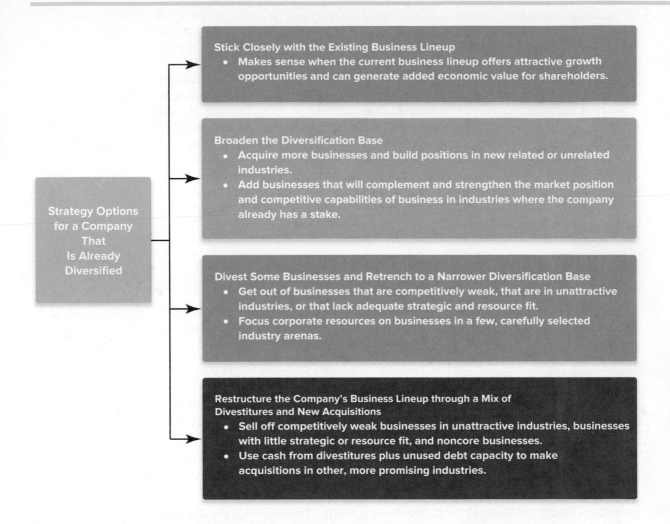

A third is rapidly changing conditions in one or more of a company's core businesses, brought on by technological, legislative, or demographic changes. For instance, the passage of legislation in the United States allowing banks, insurance companies, and stock brokerages to enter each other's businesses spurred a raft of acquisitions and mergers to create full-service financial enterprises capable of meeting the multiple financial needs of customers. A fourth, and very important, motivating factor for adding new businesses is to complement and strengthen the market position and competitive capabilities of one or more of the company's present businesses. Procter & Gamble's acquisition of Gillette strengthened and extended P&G's reach into personal care and household products—Gillette's businesses included Oral-B toothbrushes, Gillette razors and razor blades, Duracell batteries, Braun shavers, small appliances (coffeemakers, mixers, hair dryers, and electric toothbrushes), and toiletries. Johnson & Johnson has used acquisitions to diversify far beyond its well-known Band-Aid and baby care businesses and become a major player in pharmaceuticals, medical devices, and medical diagnostics.

Another important avenue for expanding the scope of a diversified company is to grow by extending the operations of existing businesses into additional country markets, as discussed in Chapter 7. Expanding a company's geographic scope may offer an exceptional competitive advantage potential by facilitating the full capture of economies of scale and learning- and experience-curve effects. In some businesses, the volume of sales needed to realize full economies of scale and/or benefit fully from experience-curve effects exceeds the volume that can be achieved by operating within the boundaries of just one or several country markets, especially small ones.

Retrenching to a Narrower Diversification Base   A number of diversified firms have had difficulty managing a diverse group of businesses and have elected to exit some of them. Selling a business outright to another company is far and away the most frequently used option for divesting a business. In 2017, Samsung Electronics sold its printing business to HP, Inc. in order better focus on its core smartphone, television, and memory chip businesses. But sometimes a business selected for divestiture has ample resources and capabilities to compete successfully on its own. In such cases, a corporate parent may elect to *spin off* the unwanted business as a financially and managerially independent company, either by selling shares to the public via an initial public offering or by distributing shares in the new company to shareholders of the corporate parent. eBay spun off PayPal in 2015 at a valuation of $45 billion—a value 30 times more than what eBay paid for the company in a 2002 acquisition. In 2018, pesticide maker FMC Corp. spun off its lithium business to boost profitability by focusing on its core business.

Retrenching to a narrower diversification base is usually undertaken when top management concludes that its diversification has ranged too far afield and that the company can improve long-term performance by concentrating on a smaller number of businesses. But there are other important reasons for divesting one or more of a company's present businesses. Sometimes divesting a business has to be considered because market conditions in a once-attractive industry have badly deteriorated. A business can become a prime candidate for divestiture because it lacks adequate strategic or resource fit, because it is a cash hog with questionable long-term potential, or because remedying its competitive weaknesses is too expensive relative to the likely gains in profitability. Sometimes a company acquires businesses that, down the road, just do not work out as expected even though management has tried its best. Subpar performance by some business units is bound to occur, thereby raising questions of whether to divest them or keep them and attempt a turnaround. Other business units, despite adequate financial performance, may not mesh as well with the rest of the firm as was originally thought. For instance, PepsiCo divested its group of fast-food restaurant businesses (Kentucky Fried Chicken, Pizza Hut, and Taco Bell) to focus on its core soft-drink and snack-food businesses, where their specialized resources and capabilities could add more value.

On occasion, a diversification move that seems sensible from a strategic-fit standpoint turns out to be a poor *cultural fit.*[16] When several pharmaceutical companies diversified into cosmetics and perfume, they discovered their personnel had little respect for the "frivolous" nature of such products compared to the far nobler task of developing miracle drugs to cure the ill. The absence of shared values and cultural compatibility between the medical research and chemical-compounding expertise of the pharmaceutical companies and the fashion and marketing orientation of the cosmetics business was the undoing of what otherwise was diversification into businesses

> A **spin-off** is an independent company created when a corporate parent divests a business either by selling shares to the public via an initial public offering or by distributing shares in the new company to shareholders of the corporate parent.

Diversified companies need to divest low-performing businesses or businesses that don't fit in order to concentrate on expanding existing businesses and entering new ones where opportunities are more promising.

CORE CONCEPT

Companywide restructuring *(corporate restructuring)* involves making major changes in a diversified company by divesting some businesses and/or acquiring others, so as to put a whole new face on the company's business lineup.

with technology-sharing potential, product development fit, and some overlap in distribution channels.

A useful guide to determine whether or when to divest a business subsidiary is to ask, "If we were not in this business today, would we want to get into it now?" When the answer is no or probably not, divestiture should be considered. Another signal that a business should be divested occurs when it is worth more to another company than to the present parent; in such cases, shareholders would be well served if the company sells the business and collects a premium price from the buyer for whom the business is a valuable fit.

Restructuring a Diversified Company's Business Lineup Restructuring a diversified company on a companywide basis *(corporate restructuring)* involves divesting some businesses and/or acquiring others, so as to put a whole new face on the company's business lineup.[17] Performing radical surgery on a company's business lineup is appealing when its financial performance is being squeezed or eroded by

- A serious mismatch between the company's resources and capabilities and the type of diversification that it has pursued.
- Too many businesses in slow-growth, declining, low-margin, or otherwise unattractive industries.
- Too many competitively weak businesses.
- The emergence of new technologies that threaten the survival of one or more important businesses.
- Ongoing declines in the market shares of one or more major business units that are falling prey to more market-savvy competitors.
- An excessive debt burden with interest costs that eat deeply into profitability.
- Ill-chosen acquisitions that haven't lived up to expectations.

On occasion, corporate restructuring can be prompted by special circumstances—such as when a firm has a unique opportunity to make an acquisition so big and important that it has to sell several existing business units to finance the new acquisition or when a company needs to sell off some businesses in order to raise the cash for entering a potentially big industry with wave-of-the-future technologies or products. As businesses are divested, corporate restructuring generally involves aligning the remaining business units into groups with the best strategic fit and then redeploying the cash flows from the divested businesses to either pay down debt or make new acquisitions to strengthen the parent company's business position in the industries it has chosen to emphasize.

Over the past decade, corporate restructuring has become a popular strategy at many diversified companies, especially those that had diversified broadly into many different industries and lines of business. Google is a prime example, having acquired over 200 businesses of varying types within the past 20 years. This rapid expansion led to a corporate restructuring in 2015 that created a new holding company called Alphabet, Inc. into which businesses other than Internet services were moved, each to be managed by its own CEO. Google remained the umbrella company for its core Internet service businesses, such as YouTube, Waze, the Android mobile operating system, and Google Search. Ultimately, Google was also folded into Alphabet and became its largest subsidiary. This restructuring allowed Google

Restructuring Strategically at VF Corporation

Over its 120 year history, VF Corporation has become one of the world's largest apparel, footwear, and accessories companies through an aggressive acquisition strategy. Brands that they have acquired include North Face, Timberland, Wrangler, Lee, Jan Sport, Nautica, Eagle Creek, Smart Wool, and Altra Footwear. In recent years, however, the company's top managers began to notice that different segments of their business had diverging management requirements, due to differing distribution channels, customer needs, and growth patterns. The solution was to restructure the company, which was characterized as very much a strategic move, since there was an absence of good strategic fit among these two different types of businesses.

In 2019, the company split itself into two separate organizations, moving VF's Jeanswear organization into an independent, publicly traded company (a type of move known as a *spin-off*). The new company was named Kontoor Brands, Inc., and included the Wrangler, Lee, and Rock & Republic brands, along with the VF Outlet business. VF Corporation, also known as VFC, would retain the more dynamic, faster-moving active-lifestyle brands. The split was hoped to enable the faster growing segments retained within VFC to pursue opportunities that

Soundaholic studio/Shutterstock

are less relevant to the concerns of the more staid sister business of Kontoor. It would also enable the brands within VFC to respond in a more nimble way to the rapid changes that tend to characterize the world of fashion. While there are always risks and uncertainties that come along with spin-offs, such as the risk of disruption of the businesses, and the temporary diversion of management resources, the full year 2019 revenue was up by 13 percent, and the prospects going forward looked rosy.

Sources: Company website; https://www.thestreet.com/investing/stocks/v-f-corp-ceo-why-we-just-made-one-of-the-biggest-decisions-in-our-company-history-14681383, accessed February 4, 2020.

to slim down a bit and focus more on its core businesses, while allowing the more unrelated companies greater independence under Alphabet. The restructuring has purportedly accomplished much of its aims, reaching $1 trillion market value by January 2020. Other seemingly successful restructuring efforts include Disney's reorganization into four business units to help it capitalize on growth opportunities, Hulu's steps to streamline while accommodating further growth, and the Wall Street Journal's efforts to shift toward a more digital strategy.

Illustration Capsule 8.4 discusses how VF Corporation, maker of North Face and other popular "lifestyle" apparel brands, has used a restructuring strategy to rationalize its management of different types of companies.

KEY POINTS

1. The purpose of diversification is to build shareholder value. Diversification builds shareholder value only when a diversified group of businesses can perform better under the auspices of a single corporate parent than they would as independent, standalone businesses. The goal is to achieve not just a $1 + 1 = 2$ result but rather to realize important $1 + 1 = 3$ performance benefits—an effect known as *synergy*. For a move to diversify into a new business to have a reasonable prospect of adding shareholder value, it must be capable of passing the three Tests of Corporate Advantage: the industry attractiveness test, the cost-of-entry test, and the better-off test.

2. Entry into new businesses can take any of three forms: acquisition, internal startup, or joint venture. The choice of which is best depends on the firm's resources and capabilities, the industry's entry barriers, the importance of speed, and relative costs.

3. There are two fundamental approaches to diversification—into related businesses and into unrelated businesses. The rationale for *related* diversification is to benefit from *strategic fit:* diversify into businesses with commonalities across their respective value chains, and then capitalize on the strategic fit by sharing or transferring the resources and capabilities across matching value chain activities to gain competitive advantages.

4. *Unrelated* diversification strategies surrender the competitive advantage potential of strategic fit at the value chain level in return for the potential that can be realized from superior corporate parenting or the sharing and transfer of general resources and capabilities. An outstanding corporate parent can benefit its businesses through (1) providing high-level oversight and making available other corporate resources, (2) allocating financial resources across the business portfolio (under certain circumstances), and (3) restructuring underperforming acquisitions.

5. Related diversification provides a stronger foundation for creating shareholder value than does unrelated diversification, since the *specialized resources and capabilities* that are leveraged in related diversification tend to be more valuable competitive assets than the *general resources and capabilities* underlying unrelated diversification, which in most cases are relatively common and easier to imitate.

6. Analyzing how good a company's diversification strategy is consists of a six-step process:

   Step 1: *Evaluate the long-term attractiveness of the industries into which the firm has diversified.* Determining industry attractiveness involves developing a list of industry-attractiveness measures, each of which might have a different importance weight.

   Step 2: *Evaluate the relative competitive strength of each of the company's business units.* The purpose of rating the competitive strength of each business is to gain a clear understanding of which businesses are strong contenders in their industries, which are weak contenders, and what the underlying reasons are for their strength or weakness. The conclusions about industry attractiveness can be joined with the conclusions about competitive strength by drawing a nine-cell industry-attractiveness–competitive-strength matrix that helps identify the prospects of each business and the level of priority each business should be given in allocating corporate resources and investment capital.

   Step 3: *Check for the competitive value of cross-business strategic fit.* A business is more attractive strategically when it has value chain relationships with the other business units that offer the potential to (1) combine operations to realize economies of scope, (2) transfer technology, skills, know-how, or other resource capabilities from one business to another, (3) leverage the use of a trusted brand name or other resources that enhance differentiation, (4) share other competitively valuable resources among the company's businesses, and (5) build new resources and competitive capabilities via cross-business collaboration. Cross-business strategic fit represents a significant avenue for producing competitive advantage beyond what any one business can achieve on its own.

Step 4: *Check whether the firm's resources fit the resource requirements of its present business lineup.* In firms with a related diversification strategy, resource fit exists when the firm's businesses have matching resource requirements at points along their value chains that are critical for the businesses' market success. In companies pursuing unrelated diversification, resource fit exists when the company has solid parenting capabilities or resources of a general nature that it can share or transfer to its component businesses. When there is financial resource fit among the businesses of any type of diversified company, the company can generate internal cash flows sufficient to fund the capital requirements of its businesses, pay its dividends, meet its debt obligations, and otherwise remain financially healthy.

Step 5: *Rank the performance prospects of the businesses from best to worst, and determine what the corporate parent's priority should be in allocating resources to its various businesses.* The most important considerations in judging business unit performance are sales growth, profit growth, contribution to company earnings, and the return on capital invested in the business. Normally, strong business units in attractive industries should head the list for corporate resource support.

Step 6: *Craft new strategic moves to improve overall corporate performance.* This step draws on the results of the preceding steps as the basis for selecting one of four different strategic paths for improving a diversified company's performance: (1) Stick closely with the existing business lineup and pursue opportunities presented by these businesses, (2) broaden the scope of diversification by entering additional industries, (3) retrench to a narrower scope of diversification by divesting poorly performing businesses, or (4) broadly restructure the business lineup with multiple divestitures and/or acquisitions.

ASSURANCE OF LEARNING EXERCISES

LO 8-1, LO 8-2, LO 8-3, LO 8-4

1. See if you can identify the value chain relationships that make the businesses of the following companies related in competitively relevant ways. In particular, you should consider whether there are cross-business opportunities for (1) transferring skills and technology, (2) combining related value chain activities to achieve economies of scope, and/or (3) leveraging the use of a well-respected brand name or other resources that enhance differentiation.

Bloomin' Brands
- Outback Steakhouse
- Carrabba's Italian Grill
- Bonefish Grill (market-fresh fine seafood)
- Fleming's Prime Steakhouse & Wine Bar

L'Oréal
- Maybelline, Lancôme, Helena Rubinstein, essie, Kiehl's and Shu Uemura cosmetics
- L'Oréal and Soft Sheen/Carson hair care products

- Redken, Matrix, L'Oréal Professional, and Kerastase Paris professional hair care and skin care products
- Ralph Lauren and Giorgio Armani fragrances
- Biotherm skin care products
- La Roche–Posay and Vichy Laboratories dermo-cosmetics

Johnson & Johnson

- Baby products (powder, shampoo, oil, lotion)
- Band-Aids and other first-aid products
- Women's health and personal care products (Stayfree, Carefree, Sure & Natural)
- Neutrogena, and Aveeno skin care products
- Nonprescription drugs (Tylenol, Motrin, Pepcid AC, Mylanta, Monistat)
- Prescription drugs
- Prosthetic and other medical devices
- Surgical and hospital products
- Acuvue contact lenses

LO 8-1, LO 8-2, LO 8-3, LO 8-4

2. Peruse the business group listings for 3M Company shown as follows and listed at its website. How would you characterize the company's corporate strategy—related diversification, unrelated diversification, or a combination related–unrelated diversification strategy? Explain your answer.

- Consumer products—for the home and office including Post-it® and Scotch®
- Electronics and Energy—technology solutions for customers in electronics and energy markets
- Health Care—products for health care professionals
- Industrial—abrasives, adhesives, specialty materials and filtration systems
- Safety and Graphics—safety and security products; graphic solutions

Mc Graw Hill connect

LO 8-1, LO 8-2, LO 8-3, LO 8-4, LO 8-5

3. ITT is a technology-oriented engineering and manufacturing company with the following business divisions and products:

- Industrial Process Division—industrial pumps, valves, and monitoring and control systems; aftermarket services for the chemical, oil and gas, mining, pulp and paper, power, and biopharmaceutical markets
- Motion Technologies Division—durable brake pads, shock absorbers, and damping technologies for the automotive and rail markets
- Interconnect Solutions—connectors and fittings for the production of automobiles, aircraft, railcars and locomotives, oil field equipment, medical equipment, and industrial equipment
- Control Technologies—energy absorption and vibration dampening equipment, transducers and regulators, and motion controls used in the production of robotics, medical equipment, automobiles, subsea equipment, industrial equipment, aircraft, and military vehicles

Based on the previous listing, would you say that ITT's business lineup reflects a strategy of related diversification, unrelated diversification, or a combination of related and unrelated diversification? What benefits are generated from any strategic fit existing between ITT's businesses? Also, what types of companies should ITT consider acquiring that might improve shareholder value? Justify your answer.

EXERCISES FOR SIMULATION PARTICIPANTS

1. In the event that your company has the opportunity to diversify into other products or businesses of your choosing, what would be the advantages of opting to pursue related diversification, unrelated diversification, or a combination of both? Explain why.

   LO 8-1, LO 8-2, LO 8-3

2. What strategic-fit benefits might be captured by transferring resources and competitive capabilities to newly acquired related businesses.

3. If your company opted to pursue a strategy of related diversification, what industries or product categories could it diversify into that would allow it to achieve economies of scope? Name at least two or three such industries or product categories, and indicate the specific kinds of cost savings that might accrue from entry into each.

   LO 8-1, LO 8-2

4. If your company opted to pursue a strategy of unrelated diversification, what industries or product categories could it diversify into that would allow it to capitalize on using its present brand name and corporate image to good advantage in the newly entered businesses or product categories? Name at least two or three such industries or product categories, and indicate the *specific benefits* that might be captured by transferring your company's umbrella brand name to each.

   LO 8-1, LO 8-3

ENDNOTES

[1] Michael E. Porter, "From Competitive Advantage to Corporate Strategy," *Harvard Business Review* 45, no. 3 (May–June 1987), pp. 46–49.

[2] A. Shleifer and R. Vishny, "Takeovers in the 60s and the 80s—Evidence and Implications," *Strategic Management Journal* 12 (Winter 1991), pp. 51–59; T. Brush, "Predicted Change in Operational Synergy and Post-Acquisition Performance of Acquired Businesses," *Strategic Management Journal* 17, no. 1 (1996), pp. 1–24; J. P. Walsh, "Top Management Turnover Following Mergers and Acquisitions," *Strategic Management Journal* 9, no. 2 (1988), pp. 173–183; A. Cannella and D. Hambrick, "Effects of Executive Departures on the Performance of Acquired Firms," *Strategic Management Journal* 14 (Summer 1993), pp. 137–152; R. Roll, "The Hubris Hypothesis of Corporate Takeovers," *Journal of Business* 59, no. 2 (1986), pp. 197–216; P. Haspeslagh and D. Jemison, *Managing Acquisitions* (New York: Free Press, 1991).

[3] M.L.A. Hayward, "When Do Firms Learn from Their Acquisition Experience? Evidence from 1990–1995," *Strategic Management Journal* 23, no. 1 (2002), pp. 21–29; G. Ahuja and R. Katila, "Technological Acquisitions and the Innovation Performance of Acquiring Firms: A Longitudinal Study," *Strategic Management Journal* 22, no. 3 (2001), pp. 197–220; H. Barkema and F. Vermeulen, "International Expansion through Start-Up or Acquisition: A Learning Perspective," *Academy of Management Journal* 41, no. 1 (1998), pp. 7–26.

[4] Yves L. Doz and Gary Hamel, *Alliance Advantage: The Art of Creating Value through Partnering* (Boston: Harvard Business School Press, 1998), chaps. 1 and 2.

[5] J. Glover, "The Guardian," March 23, 1996, www.mcspotlight.org/media/press/guardpizza_23mar96.html.

[6] Michael E. Porter, *Competitive Advantage* (New York: Free Press, 1985), pp. 318–319, 337–353; Porter, "From Competitive Advantage to Corporate Strategy," pp. 53–57; Constantinos C. Markides and Peter J. Williamson, "Corporate Diversification and Organization Structure: A Resource-Based View," *Academy of Management Journal* 39, no. 2 (April 1996), pp. 340–367.

[7] David J. Collis and Cynthia A. Montgomery, "Creating Corporate Advantage," *Harvard Business Review* 76, no. 3 (May–June 1998), pp. 72–80; Markides and Williamson, "Corporate Diversification and Organization Structure."

[8] Jeanne M. Liedtka, "Collaboration across Lines of Business for Competitive Advantage," *Academy of Management Executive* 10, no. 2 (May 1996), pp. 20–34.

[9] Kathleen M. Eisenhardt and D. Charles Galunic, "Coevolving: At Last, a Way to Make Synergies Work," *Harvard Business Review* 78, no. 1 (January–February 2000), pp. 91–101; Constantinos C. Markides and Peter J. Williamson, "Related Diversification, Core Competences and Corporate Performance," *Strategic Management Journal* 15 (Summer 1994), pp. 149–165.

[10] A. Campbell, M. Goold, and M. Alexander, "Corporate Strategy: The Quest for Parenting Advantage," *Harvard Business Review* 73, no. 2 (March–April 1995), pp. 120–132.

[11] Cynthia A. Montgomery and B. Wernerfelt, "Diversification, Ricardian Rents, and Tobin-Q," *RAND Journal of Economics* 19, no. 4 (1988), pp. 623–632.

[12] Patricia L. Anslinger and Thomas E. Copeland, "Growth through Acquisitions: A Fresh Look," *Harvard Business Review* 74, no. 1 (January–February 1996), pp. 126–135.

[13] M. Lubatkin and S. Chatterjee, "Extending Modern Portfolio Theory," *Academy of Management Journal* 37, no.1 (February 1994), pp. 109–136.

[14] Lawrence G. Franko, "The Death of Diversification? The Focusing of the World's Industrial Firms, 1980–2000," *Business Horizons* 47, no. 4 (July–August 2004), pp. 41–50.

[15] David J. Collis and Cynthia A. Montgomery, "Competing on Resources: Strategy in the 90s," *Harvard Business Review* 73, no. 4 (July–August 1995), pp. 118–128.

[16] Peter F. Drucker, *Management: Tasks, Responsibilities, Practices* (New York: Harper & Row, 1974), p. 709.

[17] Lee Dranikoff, Tim Koller, and Anton Schneider, "Divestiture: Strategy's Missing Link," *Harvard Business Review* 80, no. 5 (May 2002), pp. 74–83.

chapter 9

Ethics, Corporate Social Responsibility, Environmental Sustainability, and Strategy

Learning Objectives

After reading this chapter, you should be able to:

LO 9-1 Understand why the standards of ethical behavior in business are no different from ethical standards in general.

LO 9-2 Recognize conditions that give rise to unethical business strategies and behavior.

LO 9-3 Identify the costs of business ethics failures.

LO 9-4 Understand the concepts of corporate social responsibility and environmental sustainability and how companies balance these duties with economic responsibilities to shareholders.

Richard Schneider/Getty Images

A well-run business must have high and consistent standards of ethics.

Richard Branson—*Founder of Virgin Atlantic Airlines and Virgin Group*

When sustainability is viewed as being a matter of survival for your business, I believe you can create massive change.

Cameron Sinclair—*Head of social innovation at Airbnb*

Clearly, in capitalistic or market economies, a company has a responsibility to make a profit and grow the business. Managers of public companies have a fiduciary duty to operate the enterprise in a manner that creates value for the company's shareholders—a legal obligation. Just as clearly, a company and its personnel are duty-bound to obey the law otherwise and comply with governmental regulations. But does a company also have a duty to go beyond legal requirements and hold all company personnel responsible for conforming to high ethical standards? Does it have an obligation to contribute to the betterment of society, independent of the needs and preferences of the customers it serves? Should a company display a social conscience by devoting a portion of its resources to bettering society? Should its strategic initiatives be screened for possible negative effects on future generations of the world's population?

This chapter focuses on whether a company, in the course of trying to craft and execute a strategy that delivers value to both customers and shareholders, also has a duty to (1) act in an ethical manner; (2) be a committed corporate citizen and allocate some of its resources to improving the well-being of employees, the communities in which it operates, and society as a whole; and (3) adopt business practices that conserve natural resources, protect the interests of future generations, and preserve the well-being of the planet.

WHAT DO WE MEAN BY *BUSINESS ETHICS?*

Ethics concerns principles of right or wrong conduct. **Business ethics** is the application of ethical principles and standards to the actions and decisions of business organizations and the conduct of their personnel.[1] *Ethical principles in business are not materially different from ethical principles in general.* Why? Because business actions have to be judged in the context of society's standards of right and wrong, not with respect to a special set of ethical standards applicable only to business situations. If dishonesty is considered unethical and immoral, then dishonest behavior in business—whether it relates to customers, suppliers, employees, shareholders, competitors, or government—qualifies as equally unethical and immoral. If being ethical entails not deliberately harming others, then businesses are ethically obliged to recall a defective or unsafe product swiftly, regardless of the cost. If society deems bribery unethical, then it is unethical for company personnel to make payoffs to government officials to win government contracts or bestow favors to customers to win or retain their business. In short, ethical behavior in business situations requires adhering to generally accepted norms about right or wrong conduct. As a consequence, company managers have an obligation—indeed, a duty—to observe ethical norms when crafting and executing strategy.

● **LO 9-1**

Understand why the standards of ethical behavior in business are no different from ethical standards in general.

WHERE DO ETHICAL STANDARDS COME FROM—ARE THEY UNIVERSAL OR DEPENDENT ON LOCAL NORMS?

Notions of right and wrong, fair and unfair, moral and immoral are present in all societies and cultures. But there are three distinct schools of thought about the extent to which ethical standards travel across cultures and whether multinational companies can apply the same set of ethical standards in any and all locations where they operate.

The School of Ethical Universalism

According to the school of **ethical universalism,** the most fundamental conceptions of right and wrong are *universal* and transcend culture, society, and religion.[2] For instance, being truthful (not lying and not being deliberately deceitful) strikes a chord of what's right in the peoples of all nations. Likewise, demonstrating integrity of character, not cheating or harming people, and treating others with decency are concepts that resonate with people of virtually all cultures and religions.

Common moral agreement about right and wrong actions and behaviors across multiple cultures and countries gives rise to universal ethical standards that apply to members of all societies, all companies, and all businesspeople. These universal ethical principles set forth the traits and behaviors that are considered virtuous and that a good person is supposed to believe in and to display. Thus, adherents of the school of ethical universalism maintain that it is entirely appropriate to expect all members of society (including all personnel of all companies worldwide) to conform to these universal ethical standards.[3] For example, people in most societies would concur that it is unethical for companies to knowingly expose workers to toxic chemicals and hazardous materials or to sell products known to be unsafe or harmful to the users.

The strength of ethical universalism is that it draws on the collective views of multiple societies and cultures to put some clear boundaries on what constitutes ethical and unethical business behavior, regardless of the country or culture in which a company's personnel are conducting activities. This means that with respect to basic moral standards that do not vary significantly according to local cultural beliefs, traditions, or religious convictions, a multinational company can develop a code of ethics that it applies more or less evenly across its worldwide operations. It can avoid the slippery slope that comes from having different ethical standards for different company personnel depending on where in the world they are working.

The School of Ethical Relativism

While undoubtedly there are some universal moral prescriptions (like being truthful and trustworthy), there are also observable variations from one society to another as to what constitutes ethical or unethical behavior. Indeed, differing religious beliefs, social customs, traditions, core values, and behavioral norms frequently give rise to different standards about what is fair or unfair, moral or immoral, and ethically right or wrong. For instance, European and American managers often establish standards of business conduct that protect human rights such as freedom of movement and residence, freedom of speech and political opinion, and the right to privacy. In China, where societal commitment to basic human rights is weak, human rights considerations play a small role in determining what is ethically right or wrong in conducting business activities. In Japan, managers believe that showing respect for the collective good of society is a more important ethical consideration. In Muslim countries, managers typically apply ethical standards compatible with the teachings of Muhammad. Consequently, the school of **ethical relativism** holds that a "one-size-fits-all" template for judging the ethical appropriateness of business actions and the behaviors of company personnel is totally inappropriate. Rather, the underlying thesis of ethical relativism is that whether certain actions or behaviors are ethically right or wrong depends on the ethical norms of the country or culture in which they take place. For businesses, this implies that when there are cross-country or cross-cultural differences in ethical standards, it is appropriate for *local ethical standards to take precedence over what the ethical standards may be in a company's home market.*[4] In a world of ethical relativism, there are few absolutes when it comes to business ethics, and thus few ethical absolutes for consistently judging the ethical correctness of a company's conduct in various countries and markets.

This need to contour local ethical standards to fit local customs, local notions of fair and proper individual treatment, and local business practices gives rise to multiple sets of ethical standards. It also poses some challenging ethical dilemmas. Consider the following two examples.

The Use of Underage Labor
In industrialized nations, the use of underage workers is considered taboo. Social activists are adamant that child labor is unethical and that companies should neither employ children under the age of 18 as full-time employees nor source any products from foreign suppliers that employ underage workers. Many countries have passed legislation forbidding the use of underage labor or, at a minimum, regulating the employment of people under the age of 18. However, in Eretria, Uzbekistan, Myanmar, Somalia, Zimbabwe, Afghanistan, Sudan, North Korea, Yemen, and more than 50 other countries, it is customary to view children as potential, even necessary, workers. In other countries, like China, India, Russia, and Brazil, child

> **CORE CONCEPT**
>
> The school of **ethical relativism** holds that differing religious beliefs, customs, and behavioral norms across countries and cultures give rise to *differing of standards concerning what is ethically right or wrong.* These differing standards mean that whether business-related actions are right or wrong depends on the prevailing local ethical standards.

> Under ethical relativism, there can be no one-size-fits-all set of authentic ethical norms against which to gauge the conduct of company personnel.

labor laws are often poorly enforced.[5] As of 2016, the International Labor Organization estimated that there were about 152 million child laborers age 5 to 17 and that some 73 million of them were engaged in hazardous work.[6]

While exposing children to hazardous work and long work hours is unquestionably deplorable, the fact remains that poverty-stricken families in many poor countries cannot subsist without the work efforts of young family members; sending their children to school instead of having them work is not a realistic option. If such children are not permitted to work (especially those in the 12-to-17 age group)—due to pressures imposed by activist groups in industrialized nations—they may be forced to go out on the streets begging or to seek work in parts of the "underground" economy such as drug trafficking and prostitution.[7] So, if all businesses in countries where employing underage workers is common succumb to the pressures to stop employing underage labor, then have they served the best interests of the underage workers, their families, and society in general? In recognition of this issue, organizations opposing child labor are targeting certain forms of child labor such as enslaved child labor and hazardous work. IKEA is an example of a company that has worked hard to prevent any form of child labor by its suppliers. Its practices go well beyond standards and safeguards to include measures designed to address the underlying social problems of the communities in which their suppliers operate.

The Payment of Bribes and Kickbacks   A particularly thorny area facing multinational companies is the degree of cross–country variability in paying bribes.[8] In many countries in eastern Europe, Africa, Latin America, and Asia, it is customary to pay bribes to government officials in order to win a government contract, obtain a license or permit, or facilitate an administrative ruling.[9] In some developing nations, it is difficult for any company, foreign or domestic, to move goods through customs without paying off low-level officials. Senior managers in China and Russia often use their power to obtain kickbacks when they purchase materials or other products for their companies.[10] Likewise, in many countries it is normal to make payments to prospective customers in order to win or retain their business. Some people stretch to justify the payment of bribes and kickbacks on grounds that bribing government officials to get goods through customs or giving kickbacks to customers to retain their business or win new orders is simply a payment for services rendered, in the same way that people tip for service at restaurants.[11] But while this is a clever rationalization, it rests on moral quicksand.

Companies that forbid the payment of bribes and kickbacks in their codes of ethical conduct and that are serious about enforcing this prohibition face a particularly vexing problem in countries where bribery and kickback payments are an entrenched local custom. Complying with the company's code of ethical conduct in these countries is very often tantamount to losing business to competitors that have no such scruples—an outcome that penalizes ethical companies and ethical company personnel (who may suffer lost sales commissions or bonuses). On the other hand, the payment of bribes or kickbacks not only undercuts the company's code of ethics but also risks breaking the law. The Foreign Corrupt Practices Act (FCPA) prohibits U.S. companies from paying bribes to government officials, political parties, political candidates, or others in all countries where they do business. The Organization for Economic Cooperation and Development (OECD) has antibribery standards that criminalize the bribery of foreign public officials in international business transactions—all 35 OECD member countries and seven nonmember countries have adopted these standards.

Despite laws forbidding bribery to secure sales and contracts, the practice persists. As of January 2017, 443 individuals and 158 entities were sanctioned under criminal proceedings for foreign bribery by the OECD. At least 125 of the sanctioned individuals were sentenced to prison. In 2017, in the midst of a national opioid drug crisis, the executive chairman of Insys Therapeutics was arrested for bribing doctors to overpre-scribe the company's opioid products. In the same year, oil services giant Halliburton agreed to pay $29.2 million to settle charges brought against it by the Security and Exchange Commission's Foreign Corrupt Practices Act Enforcement Division; one of their executives had to pay a $75,000 penalty. The global snack company Cadbury Limited/Mondelez International had to pay a $13 million penalty for violations that included illicit payments to get approvals for a new chocolate factory in India. Other well-known companies caught up in recent bribery cases include JPMorgan; pharma-ceutical companies GlaxoSmithKline, Novartis, and AstraZeneca; casino company Las Vegas Sands; and aircraft manufacturer Embraer.

Why Ethical Relativism Is Problematic for Multinational Companies   Relying on the principle of ethical relativism to determine what is right or wrong poses major problems for multinational companies trying to decide which ethical standards to enforce companywide. It is a slippery slope indeed to resolve conflicting ethical stan-dards for operating in different countries without any kind of higher-order moral com-pass. Consider, for example, the ethical inconsistency of a multinational company that, in the name of ethical relativism, declares it impermissible to engage in kickbacks unless such payments are customary and generally overlooked by legal authorities. It is likewise problematic for a multinational company to declare it ethically acceptable to use underage labor at its plants in those countries where child labor is allowed but ethically inappropriate to employ underage labor at its plants elsewhere. If a country's culture is accepting of environmental degradation or practices that expose workers to dangerous con-ditions (toxic chemicals or bodily harm), should a multinational company lower its ethical bar in that country but rule the very same actions to be ethically wrong in other countries?

> Codes of conduct based on ethical relativism can be *ethically problematic* for multinational companies by creating a maze of conflict-ing ethical standards.

Business leaders who rely on the principle of ethical relativism to justify conflicting ethical standards for operating in different countries have little moral basis for estab-lishing or enforcing ethical standards companywide. Rather, when a company's ethical standards vary from country to country, the clear message being sent to employees is that the company has no ethical standards or convictions of its own and prefers to let its standards of ethical right and wrong be governed by the customs and practices of the countries in which it operates. Applying multiple sets of ethical standards without some kind of higher-order moral compass is scarcely a basis for holding company person-nel to high standards of ethical behavior. And it can lead to prosecutions of both companies and individuals alike when there are conflicting sets of laws.

Ethics and Integrative Social Contracts Theory

Integrative social contracts theory provides a middle position between the opposing views of ethical universalism and ethical relativism.[12] According to this theory, the ethical standards a company should try to uphold are governed by both (1) a limited number of universal ethical principles that are widely recognized as putting legiti-mate ethical boundaries on behaviors in *all* situations and (2) the circumstances of local cultures, traditions, and values that further prescribe what constitutes ethi-cally permissible behavior. The universal ethical principles are based on the collec-tive views of multiple cultures and societies and combine to form a "social contract" that all individuals, groups, organizations, and businesses in all situations have a duty to observe. *Within the boundaries of this social contract,* local cultures or groups can specify what *other* actions may or may not be ethically permissible. While this

> **CORE** CONCEPT
>
> According to **integrated social contracts theory**, universal ethical principles based on the collective views of multiple societies form a "social contract" that all individuals and organiza-tions have a duty to observe in all situations. *Within the boundaries of this social contract,* local cultures or groups can specify what *additional* actions may or may not be ethically permissible.

system leaves some "moral free space" for the people in a particular country (or local culture, or profession, or even a company) to make specific interpretations of what other actions may or may not be permissible, *universal ethical norms always take precedence.* Thus, local ethical standards can be *more* stringent than the universal ethical standards but *never less so.* For example, both the legal and medical professions have standards regarding what kinds of advertising are ethically permissible that extend beyond the universal norm that advertising not be false or misleading.

The strength of integrated social contracts theory is that it accommodates the best parts of ethical universalism and ethical relativism. Moreover, integrative social contracts theory offers managers in multinational companies clear guidance in resolving cross-country ethical differences: Those parts of the company's code of ethics that involve universal ethical norms must be enforced worldwide, but within these boundaries there is room for ethical diversity and the opportunity for host-country cultures to exert *some* influence over the moral and ethical standards of business units operating in that country.

A good example of the application of integrative social contracts theory to business involves the payment of bribes and kickbacks. Yes, bribes and kickbacks are common in some countries. But the fact that bribery flourishes in a country does not mean it is an authentic or legitimate ethical norm. Virtually all of the world's major religions (e.g., Buddhism, Christianity, Confucianism, Hinduism, Islam, Judaism, Sikhism, and Taoism) and all moral schools of thought condemn bribery and corruption. Therefore, a multinational company might reasonably conclude that there is a universal ethical principle to be observed here—one of refusing to condone bribery and kickbacks on the part of company personnel no matter what the local custom is and no matter what the sales consequences are.

> According to integrated social contracts theory, adherence to universal or "first-order" ethical norms should always take precedence over local or "second-order" norms.

> In instances involving *universally applicable* ethical norms (like paying bribes), there can be *no compromise* on what is ethically permissible and what is not.

HOW AND WHY ETHICAL STANDARDS IMPACT THE TASKS OF CRAFTING AND EXECUTING STRATEGY

Many companies have acknowledged their ethical obligations in official codes of ethical conduct. In the United States, for example, the Sarbanes-Oxley Act, passed in 2002, requires that companies whose stock is publicly traded have a code of ethics or else explain in writing to the SEC why they do not. But the senior executives of ethically principled companies understand that there's a big difference between having a code of ethics because it is mandated and having ethical standards that truly provide guidance for a company's strategy and business conduct.[13] They know that *the litmus test of whether a company's code of ethics is cosmetic is the extent to which it is embraced in crafting strategy and in operating the business day to day.* Executives committed to high standards make a point of considering three sets of questions whenever a new strategic initiative or policy or operating practice is under review:

- Is what we are proposing to do fully compliant with our code of ethical conduct? Are there any areas of ambiguity that may be of concern?
- Is there any aspect of the strategy (or policy or operating practice) that gives the appearance of being ethically questionable?
- Is there anything in the proposed action that customers, employees, suppliers, stockholders, competitors, community activists, regulators, or the media might consider ethically objectionable?

Unless questions of this nature are posed—either in open discussion or by force of habit in the minds of company managers—there's a risk that strategic initiatives and/or the way daily operations are conducted will become disconnected from the company's code of ethics. If a company's executives believe strongly in living up to the company's ethical standards, they will unhesitatingly reject strategic initiatives and operating approaches that don't measure up. However, in companies with a cosmetic approach to ethics, any linkage of the professed standards to its strategy and operating practices stems mainly from a desire to avoid the risk of embarrassment and possible disciplinary action for approving actions that are later deemed unethical and perhaps illegal.

While most company managers are careful to ensure that a company's strategy is within the bounds of what is *legal,* evidence indicates they are not always so careful to ensure that all elements of their strategies and operating activities are within the bounds of what is considered *ethical.* In recent years, there have been revelations of ethical misconduct on the part of managers at such companies as Samsung, Kobe Steel, credit rating firm Equifax, United Airlines, several leading investment banking firms, and a host of mortgage lenders. Sexual harassment allegations plagued many companies in 2017, including film company Weinstein Company LLC and entertainment giant 21st Century Fox. The consequences of crafting strategies that cannot pass the test of moral scrutiny are manifested in sizable fines, devastating public relations hits, sharp drops in stock prices that cost shareholders billions of dollars, criminal indictments, and convictions of company executives. The fallout from all these scandals has resulted in heightened management attention to legal and ethical considerations in crafting strategy.

● **LO 9-2**

Recognize conditions that give rise to unethical business strategies and behavior.

DRIVERS OF UNETHICAL BUSINESS STRATEGIES AND BEHAVIOR

Apart from the "business of business is business, not ethics" kind of thinking apparent in recent high-profile business scandals, three other main drivers of unethical business behavior also stand out[14]:

- Faulty oversight, enabling the unscrupulous pursuit of personal gain and self-interest.
- Heavy pressures on company managers to meet or beat short-term performance targets.
- A company culture that puts profitability and business performance ahead of ethical behavior.

Faulty Oversight, Enabling the Unscrupulous Pursuit of Personal Gain and Self-Interest   People who are obsessed with wealth accumulation, power, status, and their own self-interest often push aside ethical principles in their quest for personal gain. Driven by greed and ambition, they exhibit few qualms in skirting the rules or doing whatever is necessary to achieve their goals. A general disregard for business ethics can prompt all kinds of unethical strategic maneuvers and behaviors at companies. The numerous scandals that have tarnished the reputation of ridesharing company Uber and forced the resignation of its CEO is a case in point, as described in Illustration Capsule 9.1.

Responsible corporate governance and oversight by the company's corporate board is necessary to guard against self-dealing and the manipulation of information to

Ethical Violations at Uber and their Consequences

The peer-to-peer ridesharing company Uber has been credited with transforming the transportation industry, upending the taxi market, and changing the way consumers travel from place to place. But its lack of attention to ethics has resulted in numerous scandals, a tarnished reputation, a loss of market share to rival companies, and the ouster of its co-founder Travis Kalanick from his position as the company's CEO. The ethical lapses for which Uber has been criticized include the following:

- **Sexual harassment and a toxic workplace culture.** In June 2017, Uber fired over 20 employees as a result of an investigation that uncovered widespread sexual harassment that had been going on for years at the company. Female employees who had reported incidents of sexual harassment were subjected to retaliation by their managers, and reports of the incidents to senior executives resulted in inaction.

- **Price gouging during crises.** During emergency situations such as Hurricane Sandy and the 2017 London Bridge attack, Uber added high surcharges to the cost of their services. This drew much censure, particularly since its competitors offered free or reduced cost rides during those same times.

- **Data breaches and violations of user privacy.** Since 2014, the names, email addresses, and license information of over 700,000 drivers and the personal information of over 65 million users have been disclosed as a result of data breaches. Moreover, in 2016 the company paid a hacker $100,000 in ransom to prevent the dissemination of personal driver and user data that had been breached, but it failed to publicly disclose the situation for over six months.

- **Inadequate attention to consumer safety.** Substandard vetting practices at Uber came to light after one of its drivers was arrested as the primary suspect in a mass shooting in Kalamazoo, Michigan, and after a series of reports alleging sexual assault and misconduct by its drivers. Uber's concern for safety was further questioned

TY Lim/Shutterstock

when a pedestrian was tragically struck and killed by one of its self-driving vehicles in 2018.

- **Unfair competitive practices.** When nascent competitor Gett launched in New York City, Uber employees ordered and cancelled hundreds of rides to waste driver's time and then offered the drivers cash to drop Gett and join Uber. Uber has been accused of employing similar practices against Lyft.

The ethical violations at Uber have not been without economic consequence. They contributed to a significant market share loss to Lyft, Uber's closest competitor in the United States. In January 2017, when Uber was thought to have gouged its prices during protests against legislation banning immigrants from specific countries, its market share dropped 5 percentage points in a week. While Uber's ethical dilemmas are not the sole contributor to Lyft's increase in market share and expansion rate, the negative perceptions of Uber's brand from its unethical actions has afforded its competitors significant opportunities for brand and market share growth. And without a real change in Uber's culture and corporate governance practices, there is a strong likelihood that ethical scandals involving Uber will continue to surface.

Note: Developed with Alen A. Amini.

Sources: https://www.recode.net/2017/8/31/16227670/uber-lyft-market-share-deleteuber-decline-users; https://www.inc.com/associated-press/lyft-thrives-while-rival-uber-tries-to-stabilize-regain-control-2017.html; https://www.entrepreneur.com/article/300789.

disguise such actions by a company's managers. **Self-dealing** occurs when managers take advantage of their position to further their own private interests rather than those of the firm. As discussed in Chapter 2, the duty of the corporate board (and its compensation and audit committees in particular) is to guard against such actions. A strong, independent board is necessary to have proper oversight of the company's financial practices and to hold top managers accountable for their actions.

> **CORE CONCEPT**
>
> **Self-dealing** occurs when managers take advantage of their position to further their own private interests rather than those of the firm.

A particularly egregious example of the lack of proper oversight is the scandal over mortgage lending and banking practices that resulted in a crisis for the U.S. residential real estate market and heartrending consequences for many home buyers. This scandal stemmed from consciously unethical strategies at many banks and mortgage companies to boost the fees they earned on home mortgages by deliberately lowering lending standards to approve so-called subprime loans for home buyers whose incomes were insufficient to make their monthly mortgage payments. Once these lenders earned their fees on these loans, they repackaged the loans to hide their true nature and auctioned them off to unsuspecting investors, who later suffered huge losses when the high-risk borrowers began to default on their loan payments. (Government authorities later forced some of the firms that auctioned off these packaged loans to repurchase them at the auction price and bear the losses themselves.) A lawsuit by the attorneys general of 49 states charging widespread and systematic fraud ultimately resulted in a $26 billion settlement by the five largest U.S. banks (Bank of America, Citigroup, JPMorgan Chase, Wells Fargo, and Ally Financial). Included in the settlement were new rules designed to increase oversight and reform policies and practices among the mortgage companies. The settlement includes what are believed to be a set of robust monitoring and enforcement mechanisms that should help prevent such abuses in the future.[15]

Heavy Pressures on Company Managers to Meet Short-Term Performance Targets When key personnel find themselves scrambling to meet the quarterly and annual sales and profit expectations of investors and financial analysts, they often feel enormous pressure to *do whatever it takes* to protect their reputation for delivering good results. Executives at high-performing companies know that investors will see the slightest sign of a slowdown in earnings growth as a red flag and drive down the company's stock price. In addition, slowing growth or declining profits could lead to a downgrade of the company's credit rating if it has used lots of debt to finance its growth. The pressure to "never miss a quarter"—to not upset the expectations of analysts, investors, and creditors—prompts nearsighted managers to engage in short-term maneuvers to make the numbers, regardless of whether these moves are really in the best long-term interests of the company. Sometimes the pressure induces company personnel to continue to stretch the rules until the limits of ethical conduct are overlooked.[16] Once ethical boundaries are crossed in efforts to "meet or beat their numbers," the threshold for making more extreme ethical compromises becomes lower.

To meet its demanding profit target, Wells Fargo put such pressure on its employees to hit sales quotas that many employees responded by fraudulently opening customer accounts. In 2017, after the practices came to light, the bank was forced to return $2.6 million to customers and pay $186 million in fines to the government. Wells Fargo's reputation took a big hit, its stock price plummeted, and its CEO lost his job.

Company executives often feel pressured to hit financial performance targets because their compensation depends heavily on the company's performance. Over the last two decades, it has become fashionable for boards of directors to grant lavish bonuses, stock option awards, and other compensation benefits to executives for meeting specified performance targets. So outlandishly large were these rewards that executives had strong personal incentives to bend the rules and engage in behaviors that allowed the targets to be met. Much of the accounting manipulation at the root of recent corporate scandals has entailed situations in which executives benefited enormously from misleading accounting or other shady activities that allowed them to hit the numbers and receive incentive awards ranging from $10 million to more than $1 billion for hedge fund managers.

The fundamental problem with **short-termism**—the tendency for managers to focus excessive attention on short-term performance objectives—is that it doesn't create value for customers or improve the firm's competitiveness in the marketplace; that is, it sacrifices the activities that are the most reliable drivers of higher profits and added shareholder value in the long run. Cutting ethical corners in the name of profits carries exceptionally high risk for shareholders—the steep stock price decline and tarnished brand image that accompany the discovery of scurrilous behavior leave shareholders with a company worth much less than before—and the rebuilding task can be arduous, taking both considerable time and resources.

CORE CONCEPT

Short-termism is the tendency for managers to focus excessively on short-term performance objectives at the expense of longer-term strategic objectives. It has negative implications for the likelihood of ethical lapses as well as company performance in the longer run.

A Company Culture That Puts Profitability and Business Performance Ahead of Ethical Behavior

When a company's culture spawns an ethically corrupt or amoral work climate, people have a company-approved license to ignore "what's right" and engage in any behavior or strategy they think they can get away with. Such cultural norms as "Everyone else does it" and "It is okay to bend the rules to get the job done" permeate the work environment. At such companies, ethically immoral people are certain to play down observance of ethical strategic actions and business conduct. Moreover, cultural pressures to utilize unethical means if circumstances become challenging can prompt otherwise honorable people to behave unethically. A perfect example of a company culture gone awry on ethics is Enron, a now-defunct but infamous company found guilty of one of the most sprawling business frauds in U.S. history.[17]

Enron's leaders pressured company personnel to be innovative and aggressive in figuring out how to grow current earnings—*regardless of the methods.* Enron's annual "rank and yank" performance evaluation process, in which the lowest-ranking 15 to 20 percent of employees were let go, made it abundantly clear that bottom-line results were what mattered most. The name of the game at Enron became devising clever ways to boost revenues and earnings, even if this sometimes meant operating outside established policies (and legal limits). In fact, outside-the-lines behavior was celebrated if it generated profitable new business.

A high-performance–high-rewards climate came to pervade the Enron culture, as the best workers (determined by who produced the best bottom-line results) received impressively large incentives and bonuses. On Car Day at Enron, an array of luxury sports cars arrived for presentation to the most successful employees. Understandably, employees wanted to be seen as part of Enron's star team and partake in the benefits granted to Enron's best and brightest employees. The high monetary rewards, the ambitious and hard-driving people whom the company hired and promoted, and the competitive, results-oriented culture combined to give Enron a reputation not only for trampling competitors but also for internal ruthlessness. The company's win-at-all-costs mindset nurtured a culture that gradually and then more rapidly fostered the erosion of ethical standards, eventually making a mockery of the company's stated values of integrity and respect. When it became evident that Enron was a house of cards propped up by deceitful accounting and myriad unsavory practices, the company imploded in a matter of weeks—one of the biggest bankruptcies of all time, costing investors $64 billion in losses.

In contrast, when high ethical principles are deeply ingrained in the corporate culture of a company, culture can function as a powerful mechanism for communicating ethical behavioral norms and gaining employee buy-in to the company's moral standards, business principles, and corporate values. In such cases, the ethical principles embraced in the company's code of ethics and/or in its statement of corporate values are seen as integral to the company's identity, self-image, and ways of operating. The message that ethics matters—and matters a lot—resounds loudly and clearly throughout the organization and in its strategy and decisions.

WHY SHOULD COMPANY STRATEGIES BE ETHICAL? ● ● ● ●

There are two reasons why a company's strategy should be ethical: (1) because a strategy that is unethical is morally wrong and reflects badly on the character of the company and its personnel, and (2) because an ethical strategy can be good business and serve the self-interest of shareholders.

The Moral Case for an Ethical Strategy

Managers do not dispassionately assess what strategic course to steer—how strongly committed they are to observing ethical principles and standards definitely comes into play in making strategic choices. Ethical strategy making is generally the product of managers who are of strong moral character (i.e., who are trustworthy, have integrity, and truly care about conducting the company's business honorably). Managers with high ethical principles are usually advocates of a corporate code of ethics and strong ethics compliance, and they are genuinely committed to upholding corporate values and ethical business principles. They demonstrate their commitment by displaying the company's stated values and living up to its business principles and ethical standards. They understand the difference between merely adopting value statements and codes of ethics and ensuring that they are followed strictly in a company's actual strategy and business conduct. As a consequence, ethically strong managers consciously opt for strategic actions that can pass the strictest moral scrutiny—they display no tolerance for strategies with ethically controversial components.

● **LO 9-3**

Identify the costs of business ethics failures.

The Business Case for Ethical Strategies

In addition to the moral reasons for adopting ethical strategies, there may be solid business reasons. Pursuing unethical strategies and tolerating unethical conduct not only damages a company's reputation but also may result in a wide-ranging set of other costly consequences. Figure 9.1 shows the kinds of costs a company can incur when unethical behavior on its part is discovered, the wrongdoings of company personnel are headlined in the media, and it is forced to make amends for its behavior. The more egregious are a company's ethical violations, the higher the costs and the bigger the damage to its reputation (and to the reputations of the company personnel involved). In high-profile instances, the costs of ethical misconduct can easily run into the hundreds of millions and even billions of dollars, especially if they provoke widespread public outrage and many people were harmed. The penalties levied on executives caught in wrongdoing can skyrocket as well, as the 150-year prison term sentence of infamous financier and Ponzi scheme perpetrator Bernie Madoff illustrates.

The fallout of a company's ethical misconduct goes well beyond the costs of making amends for the misdeeds. Customers shun companies caught up in highly publicized

FIGURE 9.1   The Costs Companies Incur When Ethical Wrongdoing Is Discovered

Visible Costs	Internal Administrative Costs	Intangible or Less Visible Costs
• Government fines and penalties • Civil penalties arising from class-action lawsuits and other litigation aimed at punishing the company for its offense and the harm done to others • The costs to shareholders in the form of a lower stock price (and possibly lower dividends)	• Legal and investigative costs incurred by the company • The costs of providing remedial education and ethics training to company personnel • The costs of taking corrective actions • Administrative costs associated with ensuring future compliance	• Customer defections • Loss of reputation • Lost employee morale and higher degrees of employee cynicism • Higher employee turnover • Higher recruiting costs and difficulty in attracting talented employees • Adverse effects on employee productivity • The costs of complying with often harsher government regulations

Source: Adapted from Terry Thomas, John R. Schermerhorn, and John W. Dienhart, "Strategic Leadership of Ethical Behavior," *Academy of Management Executive* 18, no. 2 (May 2004), p. 58.

ethical scandals. Rehabilitating a company's shattered reputation is time-consuming and costly. Companies with tarnished reputations have difficulty in recruiting and retaining talented employees. Most ethically upstanding people are repulsed by a work environment where unethical behavior is condoned; they don't want to get entrapped in a compromising situation, nor do they want their personal reputations tarnished by the actions of an unsavory employer. Creditors are unnerved by the unethical actions of a borrower because of the potential business fallout and subsequent higher risk of default on loans.

> Shareholders suffer major damage when a company's unethical behavior is discovered. Making amends for unethical business conduct is costly, and it takes years to rehabilitate a tarnished company reputation.

All told, a company's unethical behavior can do considerable damage to shareholders in the form of lost revenues, higher costs, lower profits, lower stock prices, and a diminished business reputation. To a significant degree, therefore, ethical strategies and ethical conduct are *good business.* Most companies understand the value of operating in a manner that wins the approval of suppliers, employees, investors, and society at large. Most businesspeople recognize the risks and adverse fallout attached to the discovery of unethical behavior. Hence, companies have an incentive to employ strategies that can pass the test of being ethical. Even if a company's managers are not personally committed to high ethical standards, they have good reason to operate within ethical bounds, if only to (1) avoid the risk of embarrassment, scandal, disciplinary action, fines, and possible jail time for unethical conduct on their part; and (2) escape being held accountable for lax enforcement of ethical standards and unethical behavior by personnel under their supervision. Illustration Capsule 9.2 discusses PepsiCo's commitment to high ethical standards and their approach to putting their ethical principles into practice.

PepsiCo is one of the world's leading food and beverage companies with over $65 billion in net revenue, coming from iconic brands such as Lays and Ruffles potato chips, Quaker Oatmeal, Tropicana juice, Mountain Dew, and Diet Pepsi. The company is also known for its dedication to ethical business practices, having ranked consistently as among the World's Most Ethical Companies by business ethics think tank *Ethicsphere* ever since the award program was initiated. PepsiCo's Global Code of Conduct plays a pivotal role in ensuring that PepsiCo's employees, managers, and directors around the world are complying with the company's high ethical standards. It provides specific guidance concerning how to make decisions, how to treat others, and how to conduct business globally, organized around four key operating principles: (1) respect in the workplace, (2) integrity in the marketplace, (3) ethics in business activities, and (4) responsibility to shareholders. Essentially, the Code of Conduct lays out a set of behavioral norms that has come to define the company's culture.

Even with a strong ethical culture, implementing a code of conduct across a global organization of over 263,000 employees is challenging. To assist, PepsiCo set up a Global Compliance & Ethics Department with primary responsibility for promoting, monitoring, and enforcing the code. Employees at all levels are required to participate in annual Code of Conduct training, through online courses as well as in-person, manager-led workshops. Compliance training also takes place in a more targeted fashion, based on role and geography, concerning such issues as bribery. Other types of communications throughout the year, such as internal newsletter articles and messaging from the leadership, reinforce the annual training.

monticello/Shutterstock

Employees are encouraged to seek guidance when faced with an ethical dilemma. They are also encouraged to raise concerns and are obligated to report any Code violations. A variety of channels have been set up for them to do this, including a hotline operated by an independent third party. All reports of suspected violations are reviewed in accordance with company policies designed to foster consistency of the investigative process and corrective actions (which may include termination of employment). PepsiCo has also established an annual peer-nominated Ethical Leadership Award designed to recognize instances of exceptional ethical conduct by employees.

The leadership at PepsiCo believes that their commitment to ethical principles has helped the company in attracting and retaining the best people. Indeed, PepsiCo has been listed as among the Top Attractors of talent globally. In addition, the company has regularly been listed as among the World's Most Respected Companies (Barron) and the World's Most Admired Companies (Fortune).

Sources: Company website; https://ethisphere.com/pepsico-performance-purpose/ .

STRATEGY, CORPORATE SOCIAL RESPONSIBILITY, AND ENVIRONMENTAL SUSTAINABILITY
●●●●

The idea that businesses have an obligation to foster social betterment, a much-debated topic over the past 50 years, took root in the 19th century when progressive companies in the aftermath of the industrial revolution began to provide workers with housing and other amenities. The notion that corporate executives should balance the interests of all stakeholders—shareholders, employees, customers, suppliers, the communities in

CORE CONCEPT

Corporate social responsibility (CSR) refers to a company's *duty* to operate in an honorable manner, provide good working conditions for employees, encourage workforce diversity, be a good steward of the environment, and actively work to better the quality of life in the local communities where it operates and in society at large.

which they operate, and society at large—began to blossom in the 1960s. Some years later, a group of chief executives of America's 200 largest corporations, calling themselves the Business Roundtable, came out in strong support of the concept of **corporate social responsibility (CSR):**

> Balancing the shareholder's expectations of maximum return against other priorities is one of the fundamental problems confronting corporate management. The shareholder must receive a good return but the legitimate concerns of other constituencies (customers, employees, communities, suppliers and society at large) also must have the appropriate attention. . . . [Leading managers] believe that by giving enlightened consideration to balancing the legitimate claims of all its constituents, a corporation will best serve the interest of its shareholders.

Today, corporate social responsibility is a concept that resonates in western Europe, the United States, Canada, and such developing nations as Brazil and India.

The Concepts of Corporate Social Responsibility and Good Corporate Citizenship

The essence of socially responsible business behavior is that a company should balance strategic actions to benefit shareholders against the *duty* to be a good corporate citizen. The underlying thesis is that company managers should display a *social conscience* in operating the business and specifically take into account how management decisions and company actions affect the well-being of employees, local communities, the environment, and society at large.[18] Acting in a socially responsible manner thus encompasses more than just participating in community service projects and donating money to charities and other worthy causes. Demonstrating social responsibility also entails undertaking actions that earn trust and respect from all stakeholders—operating in an honorable and ethical manner, striving to make the company a great place to work, demonstrating genuine respect for the environment, and trying to make a difference in bettering society. As depicted in Figure 9.2, corporate responsibility programs commonly include the following elements:

- *Striving to employ an ethical strategy and observe ethical principles in operating the business.* A sincere commitment to observing ethical principles is a necessary component of a CSR strategy simply because unethical conduct is incompatible with the concept of good corporate citizenship and socially responsible business behavior.

- *Making charitable contributions, supporting community service endeavors, engaging in broader philanthropic initiatives, and reaching out to make a difference in the lives of the disadvantaged.* Some companies fulfill their philanthropic obligations by spreading their efforts over a multitude of charitable and community activities—for instance, Cisco, LinkedIn, IBM, and Google support a broad variety of community, art, and social welfare programs. Others prefer to focus their energies more narrowly. McDonald's concentrates on sponsoring the Ronald McDonald House program (which provides a home away from home for the families of seriously ill children receiving treatment at nearby hospitals). Genentech and many pharmaceutical companies run prescription assistance programs to provide expensive medications at little or no cost to needy patients. Companies frequently reinforce their philanthropic efforts by encouraging employees to support charitable causes and participate in community affairs, often through programs that match employee contributions.

- *Taking actions to protect the environment and, in particular, to minimize or eliminate any adverse impact on the environment stemming from the company's own business activities.*

FIGURE 9.2   The Five Components of a Corporate Social Responsibility Strategy

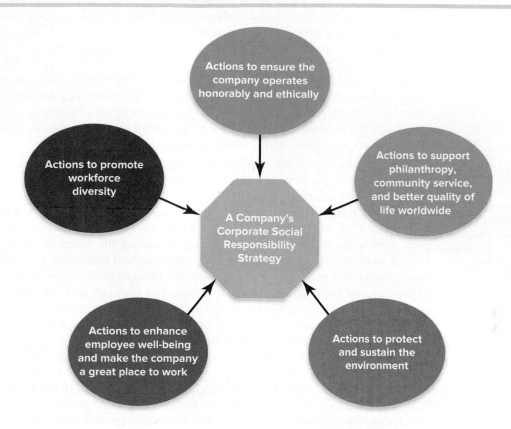

Source: Adapted from material in Ronald Paul Hill, Debra Stephens, and Iain Smith, "Corporate Social Responsibility: An Examination of Individual Firm Behavior," *Business and Society Review* 108, no. 3 (September 2003), p. 348.

Corporate social responsibility as it applies to environmental protection entails actively striving to be a good steward of the environment. This means using the best available science and technology to reduce environmentally harmful aspects of the company's operations *below the levels required by prevailing environmental regulations.* It also means putting time and money into improving the environment in ways that extend beyond a company's own industry boundaries—such as participating in recycling projects, adopting energy conservation practices, and supporting efforts to clean up local water supplies. Häagen-Dazs, a maker of all-natural ice creams, started a social media campaign to raise awareness about the dangers associated with the decreasing honeybee population; it donates a portion of its profits to research on this issue. The Walt Disney Company has created strict environmental targets for themselves and created the "Green Standard" to inspire employees to reduce their environmental impact.

• *Creating a work environment that enhances the quality of life for employees.* Numerous companies exert extra effort to enhance the quality of life for their employees at work and at home. This can include onsite day care, flexible work schedules, workplace exercise facilities, special leaves for employees to care for sick family members, work-at-home opportunities, career development programs and education opportunities, showcase plants and offices, special safety programs, and the like.

- *Building a diverse workforce with respect to gender, race, national origin, and other aspects that different people bring to the workplace.* Most large companies in the United States have established workforce diversity programs, and some go the extra mile to ensure that their workplaces are attractive to ethnic minorities and inclusive of all groups and perspectives. At some companies, the diversity initiative extends to suppliers—sourcing items from small businesses owned by women or members of ethnic minorities, for example. The pursuit of workforce diversity can also be good business. At Coca-Cola, where strategic success depends on getting people all over the world to become loyal consumers of the company's beverages, efforts to build a public persona of inclusiveness for people of all races, religions, nationalities, interests, and talents have considerable strategic value.

The particular combination of socially responsible endeavors a company elects to pursue defines its **corporate social responsibility (CSR) strategy.** The specific components emphasized in a CSR strategy vary from company to company and are typically linked to a company's core values. Few companies have managed to integrate CSR as fully and seamlessly throughout their organization as Burt's Bees; there a special committee is dedicated to leading the organization to attain its CSR goals with respect to three primary areas: natural well-being, humanitarian responsibility, and environmental sustainability. General Mills also centers its CSR strategy around three themes: nourishing lives (via healthier and easier-to-prepare foods), nourishing communities (via charitable donations to community causes and volunteerism for community service projects), and nourishing the environment (via efforts to conserve natural resources, reduce energy and water usage, promote recycling, and otherwise support environmental sustainability).[19] Starbucks's CSR strategy includes four main elements (ethical sourcing, community service, environmental stewardship, and farmer support), all of which have touch points with the way that the company procures its coffee—a key aspect of its product differentiation strategy. Some companies use other terms, such as *corporate citizenship, corporate responsibility,* or *sustainable responsible business (SRB)* to characterize their CSR initiatives. Illustration Capsule 9.3 describes Warby Parker's approach to corporate social responsibility—an approach that ensures that social responsibility is reflected in all of the company's actions and endeavors.

Although there is wide variation in how companies devise and implement a CSR strategy, communities of companies concerned with corporate social responsibility (such as CSR Europe) have emerged to help companies share best CSR practices. Moreover, a number of reporting standards have been developed, including ISO 26000—a new internationally recognized standard for social responsibility set by the International Standards Organization (ISO).[20] Companies that exhibit a strong commitment to corporate social responsibility are often recognized by being included on lists such as *Corporate Responsibility* magazine's "100 Best Corporate Citizens" or *Corporate Knights* magazine's "Global 100 Most Sustainable Corporations."

Corporate Social Responsibility and the Triple Bottom Line   CSR initiatives undertaken by companies are frequently directed at improving the company's *triple bottom line (TBL)*—a reference to three types of performance metrics: *economic, social,* and *environmental.* The goal is for a company to succeed simultaneously in all three dimensions, as illustrated in Figure 9.3.[21] The three dimensions of performance are often referred to in terms of the "three pillars" of "people, planet, and profit." The term *people* refers to the various social initiatives that make up CSR strategies, such as corporate giving, community involvement, and company efforts to improve the lives of its internal

Warby Parker: Combining Corporate Social Responsibility with Affordable Fashion

Since its founding in 2010, Warby Parker has succeeded in selling over one million pairs of high-fashion glasses at a discounted price of $95—roughly 80 percent below the average $500 price tag on a comparable pair of eyeglasses from another producer. With more than 70 stores in the United States, the company has built a brand recognized universally as one of the strongest in the world; it consistently posts a net promoter score (a measure of how likely someone would be to recommend the product) of close to 90—higher than companies like Zappos and Apple.

Under its Buy a Pair, Give a Pair program, nearly more than five million pairs of glasses have been distributed to needy people in more than 50 countries. Warby Parker also supports partners, like Vision Spring, enabling them to provide basic eye exams and teach community members how to manufacture and sell glasses at very low prices, thereby providing vocational training and improving the standard of living in these communities. The average impact on a recipient of a pair of donated glasses was a 20 percent increase in personal income and a 35 percent increase in productivity.

Efforts to be a responsible company expand beyond Warby Parker's international partnerships. The company voluntarily evaluates itself against benchmarks in the fields of "environment," "workers," "customers," "community," and "governance," demonstrating a nearly unparalleled dedication to outcomes outside of profit. The company is widely seen as an employer of choice and regularly attracts top talent for all roles across the organization. It holds to an extremely high environmental standard, running an entirely carbon neutral operation.

While socially impactful actions matter at Warby Parker, the company is mindful of the critical role of its suppliers as well. Both founders spent countless hours coordinating partnerships with dedicated suppliers to ensure quality, invested deeply in building a lean

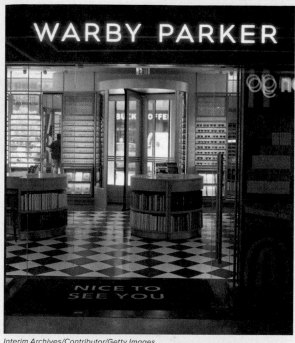

Interim Archives/Contributor/Getty Images

manufacturing operation to minimize cost, and sought to build an organization that would keep buyers happy. The net effect is a very economically healthy company—they post around $3,000 in sales per square foot, second only to Apple stores—with financial stability to pursue responsibilities outside of customer satisfaction.

The strong fundamentals put in place by the firm's founders blend responsibility into its DNA and attach each piece of commercial success to positive outcomes in the world. The company was recently recognized as number one on *Fast Company*'s "Most Innovative Companies" list and continues to build loyal followers—both of its products and its CSR efforts—as it expands.

Note: Developed with Jeremy P. Reich.

Sources: Warby Parker and "B Corp" websites; Max Chafkin, "Warby Parker Sees the Future of Retail," *Fast Company,* February 17, 2015 (accessed February 22, 2016); Jenni Avins, "Warby Parker Proves Customers Don't Have to Care about Your Social Mission," *Quartz,* December 29, 2014 (accessed February 14, 2016).

and external stakeholders. *Planet* refers to a firm's ecological impact and environmental practices. The term *profit* has a broader meaning with respect to the triple bottom line than it does otherwise. It encompasses not only the profit a firm earns for its shareholders but also the economic impact that the company has on society more generally, in terms of the overall value that it creates and the overall costs that it imposes on society. For example, Procter & Gamble's Swiffer cleaning system, one of the company's

FIGURE 9.3   The Triple Bottom Line: Excelling on Three Measures of Company
Performance

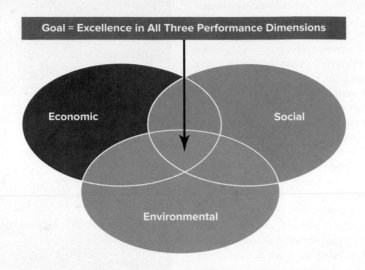

Source: Developed with help from Amy E. Florentino.

best-selling products, not only offers an earth-friendly design but also outperforms less
ecologically friendly alternatives in terms of its broader economic impact: It reduces
demands on municipal water sources, saves electricity that would be needed to heat
mop water, and doesn't add to the amount of detergent making its way into waterways
and waste treatment facilities. Nike sees itself as bringing people, planet, and profits
into balance by producing innovative new products in a more sustainable way, recognizing that sustainability is key to its future profitability. TOMS shoes, which donates a
pair of shoes to a child in need in over 50 different countries for every pair purchased,
has also built its strategy around maintaining a well-balanced triple bottom line.

Many companies now make a point of citing the beneficial outcomes of their CSR
strategies in press releases and issue special reports for consumers and investors to
review. Southwest Airlines makes reporting an important part of its commitment to corporate responsibility; the company posts its annual Southwest Airlines One Report on
its website that describes its initiatives and accomplishments with respect to each of the
three pillars of triple bottom line performance—people, planet, profit. Triple-bottom-line
reporting is emerging as an increasingly important way for companies to make the results
of their CSR strategies apparent to stakeholders and for stakeholders to hold companies
accountable for their impact on society. The use of standard reporting frameworks and
metrics, such as those developed by the Global Reporting Initiative, promotes greater
transparency and facilitates benchmarking CSR efforts across firms and industries.

Investment firms have created mutual funds consisting of companies that are excelling on the basis of the triple bottom line in order to attract funds from environmentally and socially aware investors. The Dow Jones Sustainability World Index is made
up of the top 10 percent of the 2,500 companies listed in the Dow Jones World Index in
terms of economic performance, environmental performance, and social performance.
Companies are evaluated in these three performance areas, using indicators such as corporate governance, climate change mitigation, and labor practices. Table 9.1 shows a sampling of the companies selected for the Dow Jones Sustainability World Index in 2013.

TABLE 9.1 A Selection of Companies Recognized for Their Triple-Bottom-Line Performance in 2013

Name	Market Sector	Country
Peugeot SA	Automobiles & Components	France
Westpac Banking Group	Banks	Australia
CNH Industrial NV	Capital Goods	Great Britain
SGS SA	Commercial & Professional Services	Switzerland
LG Electronics Inc.	Consumer Durables & Apparel	South Korea
InterContinental Hotels Group	Consumer Services	Great Britain
UBS Group AB	Diversified Financials	Switzerland
Thai Oil PCL	Energy	Thailand
METRO AG	Food & Staples Retailing	Germany
Coca-Cola HBC AG	Food, Beverage & Tobacco	Switzerland
Abbott Laboratories	Health Care Equipment & Services	United States
Henkel AG & Co. KGaA	Household & Personal Products	Germany
Allianz SE	Insurance	Germany
Grupo Argos SA	Materials	Colombia
Pearson PLC	Media	Great Britain
Roche Holding AG	Pharmaceuticals, Biotechnology & Life Sciences	Switzerland
Mirvac Group	Real Estate	Australia
Industria de Diseno Textil SA	Retailing	Spain
Advanced Semiconductor Engineering Inc.	Semiconductors & Semiconductor Equipment	Taiwan
Amadeus IT Group SA	Software & Services	Spain
Konica Minolta Inc.	Technology Hardware & Equipment	Japan
Koninklijke KPN NV	Telecommunication Services	Netherlands
Royal Mail PLC	Transportation	Great Britain
Red Electric Corp SA	Utilities	Spain

Source: Adapted from RobecoSAM AG, **www.sustainability-indices.com/review/industry-group-leaders-2017.jsp** (accessed March 4, 2018).

What Do We Mean by *Sustainability* and *Sustainable Business Practices?*

The term *sustainability* is used in a variety of ways. In many firms, it is synonymous with corporate social responsibility; it is seen by some as a term that is gradually replacing *CSR* in the business lexicon. Indeed, sustainability reporting and TBL reporting are often one and the same, as illustrated by the Dow Jones Sustainability World Index, which tracks the same three types of performance measures that constitute the triple bottom line.

More often, however, the term takes on a more focused meaning, concerned with the relationship of a company to its *environment* and its use of *natural resources,* including land, water, air, plants, animals, minerals, fossil fuels, and biodiversity. It is widely recognized that the world's natural resources are finite and are being consumed and degraded at rates that threaten their capacity for renewal. Since corporations are the biggest users of natural resources, managing and maintaining these resources is critical for the long-term economic interests of corporations.

For some companies, this issue has direct and obvious implications for the continued viability of their business model and strategy. Pacific Gas and Electric has begun measuring the full carbon footprint of its supply chain to become not only a "greener" company but a more efficient energy producer.[22] Beverage companies such as Coca-Cola and PepsiCo are having to rethink their business models because of the prospect of future worldwide water shortages. For other companies, the connection is less direct, but all companies are part of a business ecosystem whose economic health depends on the availability of natural resources. In response, most major companies have begun to change *how* they do business, emphasizing the use of **sustainable business practices,** defined as those capable of meeting the needs of the present without compromising the ability to meet the needs of the future. Many have also begun to incorporate a consideration of environmental sustainability into their strategy-making activities.

Environmental sustainability strategies entail deliberate and concerted actions to operate businesses in a manner that protects natural resources and ecological support systems, guards against outcomes that will ultimately endanger the planet, and is therefore sustainable for centuries.[23] One aspect of environmental sustainability is keeping use of the Earth's natural resources within levels that can be replenished via the use of sustainable business practices. In the case of some resources (like crude oil, freshwater, and edible fish from the oceans), scientists say that use levels either are already unsustainable or will be soon, given the world's growing population and propensity to consume additional resources as incomes and living standards rise. Another aspect of sustainability concerns containing the adverse effects of greenhouse gases and other forms of air pollution to reduce their impact on undesirable climate and atmospheric changes. Other aspects of sustainability include greater reliance on sustainable energy sources; greater use of recyclable materials; the use of sustainable methods of growing foods (to reduce topsoil depletion and the use of pesticides, herbicides, fertilizers, and other chemicals that may be harmful to human health or ecological systems); habitat protection; environmentally sound waste management practices; and increased attempts to decouple environmental degradation and economic growth (according to scientists, economic growth has historically been accompanied by declines in the well-being of the environment).

Unilever, a diversified producer of processed foods, personal care, and home cleaning products, is among the many committed corporations pursuing sustainable business practices. The company tracks 11 sustainable agricultural indicators in its processed-foods business and has launched a variety of programs to improve the environmental performance of its suppliers. Examples of such programs include special low-rate financing for tomato suppliers choosing to switch to water-conserving irrigation systems and training programs in India that have allowed contract cucumber growers to reduce pesticide use by 90 percent while improving yields by 78 percent. Unilever has also

CORE CONCEPT

Sustainable business practices are those that meet the needs of the present without compromising the ability to meet the needs of the future.

CORE CONCEPT

A company's **environmental sustainability strategy** consists of its deliberate actions to protect the environment, provide for the longevity of natural resources, maintain ecological support systems for future generations, and guard against ultimate endangerment of the planet.

reengineered many internal processes to improve the company's overall performance on sustainability measures. For example, the company has reduced water usage in the production of their products by 37 percent since 2008 through the implementation of sustainability initiatives. Unilever has also redesigned packaging for many of its products to conserve natural resources and reduce the volume of consumer waste. The company's Suave shampoo bottles were reshaped to save almost 150 tons of plastic resin per year, which is the equivalent of 15 million fewer empty bottles making it to landfills annually. As the producer of Lipton Tea, Unilever is the world's largest purchaser of tea leaves; the company committed to sourcing all of its tea from Rainforest Alliance Certified farms, due to its comprehensive triple-bottom-line approach toward sustainable farm management. Illustration Capsule 9.4 sheds more light on Unilever's focus on sustainability.

Crafting Corporate Social Responsibility and Sustainability Strategies

While CSR and environmental sustainability strategies take many forms, those that both provide valuable social benefits *and* fulfill customer needs in a superior fashion may also contribute to a company's competitive advantage.[24] For example, while carbon emissions may be a generic social concern for financial institutions such as Wells Fargo, Ford's sustainability strategy for reducing carbon emissions has produced both competitive advantage and environmental benefits. Its Ford Fusion hybrid is among the least polluting automobiles The Ford Explorer plug-in hybrid SUV launched in Europe in 2019 provides 7-passenger seating capacity and has a 40-kilometer zero-emission city driving range. The development of hybrid models like the Fusion and the Explorer have helped Ford gain the loyalty of fuel-conscious buyers and given the company a new green image. Keurig Green Mountain (now part of Keurig Dr. Pepper) is committed to caring for the environment while also improving the livelihoods in coffee-growing communities. Their focus is on three primary solutions: (1) helping farmer improve their farming techniques; (2) addressing local water scarcity and planning for climate change; and (3) strengthening farmers' organizations. Its consumers are aware of these efforts and purchase Green Mountain coffee, in part, to encourage such practices.

CSR strategies and environmental sustainability strategies are more likely to contribute to a company's competitive advantage if they are linked to a company's competitively important resources and capabilities or value chain activities. Thus, it is common for companies engaged in natural resource extraction, electric power production, forestry and paper products manufacture, motor vehicles production, and chemical production to place more emphasis on addressing environmental concerns than, say, software and electronics firms or apparel manufacturers. Companies whose business success is heavily dependent on maintaining high employee morale or attracting and retaining the best and brightest employees are somewhat more prone to stress the well-being of their employees and foster a positive, high-energy workplace environment that elicits the dedication and enthusiastic commitment of employees, thus putting real meaning behind the claim "Our people are our greatest asset." EY, the third largest global accounting firm, has been on Fortune's list of 100 Best Companies to Work for every year for the last 20 years. It has long been known for respecting differences, fostering individuality, and promoting inclusiveness so that its more than 245,000 employees in over 150 countries can feel valued, engaged, and empowered in developing creative ways to serve the firm's clients.

At Whole Foods Market, a $16 billion supermarket chain specializing in organic and natural foods, its environmental sustainability strategy is evident in almost every

> CSR strategies and environmental sustainability strategies that both provide valuable social benefits *and* fulfill customer needs in a superior fashion can lead to competitive advantage. Corporate social agendas that address only social issues may help boost a company's reputation for corporate citizenship but are unlikely to improve its competitive strength in the marketplace.

Unilever's Focus on Sustainability

With over 53.7 billion euros in revenue in 2017, Unilever is one of the world's largest companies. The global consumer goods giant has products that are used by over 2 billion people on any given day. It manufactures iconic global brands like Dove, Axe, Hellman's, Heartbrand, and many others. What it is also known for, however, is its commitment to sustainability, leading GlobeScan's Global Sustainability Survey for sustainable companies with a score 2.5 times higher than its closest competitor.

Unilever implemented its sustainability plan in as transparent and explicit way as possible, evidenced by the Unilever Sustainable Living Plan (USLP). The USLP was released in 2010 by CEO Paul Polman, stating that the company's goal was to double the size of the business while halving its environmental footprint by 2020. Importantly, the USLP has remained a guiding force for the company, which dedicates significant resources and time to pursuing its sustainability goals. The plan is updated each year with targets and goals, as well as an annual progress report.

According to Polman, Unilever's focus on sustainability isn't just charity, but is really an act of self-interest. The company's most recent annual report states "growth and sustainability are not in conflict. In fact, in our experience, sustainability drives growth." Polman insists that this is the modern-day way to maximize profits, and that doing so is simply rational business thinking.

To help implement this plan, Unilever has instituted a corporate accountability plan. Each year, Unilever benchmarks its progress against three leading indices: the UN Global Compact, the Global Reporting Initiative's Index, and the UN Millennium Development Goals. In its annual sustainability report, the company details its progress

GeoPic/Alamy Stock Photo

toward its many sustainability goals. By 2018, Unilever had helped more than 601 million people to improve their health and hygiene habits and had enabled over 716,000 small farmers to improve their agricultural practices and/or their incomes.

Unilever has also created new business practices to reach even more ambitious targets. Unilever set up a central corporate team dedicated to spreading best sustainability practices from one factory or business unit to the rest of the company, a major change from the siloed manner in which the company previously operated. Moreover, the company set up a "small actions, big differences" fund to invest in innovative ideas that help the company achieve its sustainability goal. To reduce emissions from the overall footprint of its products and extend its sustainability efforts to its entire supply chain, it has worked with its suppliers to source sustainable agricultural products, improving from 14 percent sustainable in 2010 to 56 percent in 2017.

Note: Developed with Byron G. Peyster.

Sources: www.globescan.com/component/edocman/?view=document&id=179&Itemid=591; www.fastcocreate.com/3051498/behind-the-brand/why-unilever-is-betting-big-on-sustainability; www.economist.com/news/business/21611103-second-time-its-120-year-history—unilever-trying-redefine-what-it-means-be; *company website (accessed March 13, 2016).*

segment of its company value chain and is a big part of its differentiation strategy. The company's procurement policies encourage stores to purchase fresh fruits and vegetables from local farmers and screen processed-food items for more than 400 common ingredients that the company considers unhealthy or environmentally unsound. Spoiled food items are sent to regional composting centers rather than landfills, and all cleaning products used in its stores are biodegradable. The company also has created the Animal Compassion Foundation to develop natural and humane ways of raising farm animals and has converted all of its vehicles to run on biofuels.

Not all companies choose to link their corporate environmental or social agendas to their value chain, their business model, or their industry. For example, the Clorox Company Foundation supports programs that serve youth, focusing its giving on non-profit civic organizations, schools, and colleges. However, unless a company's social responsibility initiatives become part of the way it operates its business every day, the initiatives are unlikely to catch fire and be fully effective. As an executive at Royal Dutch/Shell put it, corporate social responsibility "is not a cosmetic; it must be rooted in our values. It must make a difference to the way we do business."[25] The same is true for environmental sustainability initiatives.

The Moral Case for Corporate Social Responsibility and Environmentally Sustainable Business Practices

The moral case for why businesses should act in a manner that benefits all of the company's stakeholders—not just shareholders—boils down to "It's the right thing to do." Ordinary decency, civic-mindedness, and contributions to society's well-being should be expected of any business.[26] In today's social and political climate, most business leaders can be expected to acknowledge that socially responsible actions are important and that businesses have a duty to be good corporate citizens. But there is a complementary school of thought that business operates on the basis of an implied social contract with the members of society. According to this contract, society grants a business the right to conduct its business affairs and agrees not to unreasonably restrain its pursuit of a fair profit for the goods or services it sells. In return for this "license to operate," a business is obligated to act as a responsible citizen, do its fair share to promote the general welfare, and avoid doing any harm. Such a view clearly puts a moral burden on a company to operate honorably, provide good working conditions to employees, be a good environmental steward, and display good corporate citizenship.

> Every action a company takes can be interpreted as a statement of what it stands for.

The Business Case for Corporate Social Responsibility and Environmentally Sustainable Business Practices

Whatever the moral arguments for socially responsible business behavior and environmentally sustainable business practices, there are definitely good business reasons why companies should be public-spirited and devote time and resources to social responsibility initiatives, environmental sustainability, and good corporate citizenship:

- *Such actions can lead to increased buyer patronage.* A strong visible social responsibility or environmental sustainability strategy gives a company an edge in appealing to consumers who prefer to do business with companies that are good corporate citizens. Ben & Jerry's, Whole Foods Market, Stonyfield Farm, TOMS, Keurig Green Mountain, and Patagonia have definitely expanded their customer bases because of their visible and well-publicized activities as socially conscious companies. More and more companies are also recognizing the cash register payoff of social responsibility strategies that reach out to people of all cultures and demographics (women, retirees, and ethnic groups).

- *A strong commitment to socially responsible behavior reduces the risk of reputation-damaging incidents.* Companies that place little importance on operating in a socially responsible manner are more prone to scandal and embarrassment. Consumer, environmental, and human rights activist groups are quick to criticize businesses whose behavior they consider to be out of line, and they are adept at getting their message into the media and onto the Internet. Pressure groups can generate widespread adverse publicity, promote boycotts, and influence like-minded or sympathetic buyers to avoid an offender's products.

> The higher the public profile of a company or its brand, the greater the scrutiny of its activities and the higher the potential for it to become a target for pressure group action.

Research has shown that product boycott announcements are associated with a decline in a company's stock price.[27] When a major oil company suffered damage to its reputation on environmental and social grounds, the CEO repeatedly said that the most negative impact the company suffered—and the one that made him fear for the future of the company—was that bright young graduates were no longer attracted to working for the company. For many years, Nike received stinging criticism for not policing sweatshop conditions in the Asian factories that produced Nike footwear, a situation that caused Nike cofounder and chair Phil Knight to observe that "Nike has become synonymous with slave wages, forced overtime, and arbitrary abuse."[28] In response, Nike began an extensive effort to monitor conditions in the 800 factories of the contract manufacturers that produced Nike shoes. As Knight said, "Good shoes come from good factories and good factories have good labor relations." Nonetheless, Nike has continually been plagued by complaints from human rights activists that its monitoring procedures are flawed and that it is not doing enough to correct the plight of factory workers. As this suggests, a damaged reputation is not easily repaired.

- *Socially responsible actions and sustainable business practices can lower costs and enhance employee recruiting and workforce retention.* Companies with deservedly good reputations for social responsibility and sustainable business practices are better able to attract and retain employees, compared to companies with tarnished reputations. Some employees just feel better about working for a company committed to improving society. This can contribute to lower turnover and better worker productivity. Other direct and indirect economic benefits include lower costs for staff recruitment and training. For example, Starbucks is said to enjoy much lower rates of employee turnover because of its full-benefits package for both full-time and part-time employees, management efforts to make Starbucks a great place to work, and the company's socially responsible practices. Sustainable business practices are often concomitant with greater operational efficiencies. For example, when a U.S. manufacturer of recycled paper, taking eco-efficiency to heart, discovered how to increase its fiber recovery rate, it saved the equivalent of 20,000 tons of waste paper—a factor that helped the company become the industry's lowest-cost producer. By helping two-thirds of its employees to stop smoking and by investing in a number of wellness programs for employees, Johnson & Johnson saved $250 million on its health care costs over a 10-year period.[29]

- *Opportunities for revenue enhancement may also come from CSR and environmental sustainability strategies.* The drive for sustainability and social responsibility can spur innovative efforts that in turn lead to new products and opportunities for revenue enhancement. Electric cars such as the Chevy Bolt and the Nissan Leaf are one example. In many cases, the revenue opportunities are tied to a company's core products. PepsiCo and Coca-Cola, for example, have expanded into the juice business to offer a healthier alternative to their carbonated beverages. General Electric has created a profitable new business in wind turbines. In other cases, revenue enhancement opportunities come from innovative ways to reduce waste and use the by-products of a company's production. Tyson Foods now produces jet fuel for B-52 bombers from the vast amount of animal waste resulting from its meat product business. Staples has become one of the largest nonutility corporate producers of renewable energy in the United States due to its installation of solar power panels in all of its outlets (and the sale of what it does not consume in renewable energy credit markets).

- *Well-conceived CSR strategies and sustainable business practices are in the best long-term interest of shareholders.* When CSR and sustainability strategies increase buyer patronage, offer revenue-enhancing opportunities, lower costs, increase productivity, and reduce the risk of reputation-damaging incidents, they contribute to the economic value created by a company and improve its profitability. A two-year study of leading companies found that improving environmental compliance and developing environmentally friendly products can enhance earnings per share, profitability, and the likelihood of winning contracts. The stock prices of companies that rate high on social and environmental performance criteria have been found to perform 35 to 45 percent better than the average of the 2,500 companies that constitute the Dow Jones Global Index.[30] A review of 135 studies indicated there is a positive, but small, correlation between good corporate behavior and good financial performance; only two percent of the studies showed that dedicating corporate resources to social responsibility harmed the interests of shareholders.[31] Furthermore, socially responsible business behavior helps avoid or preempt legal and regulatory actions that could prove costly and otherwise burdensome. In some cases, it is possible to craft corporate social responsibility strategies that contribute to competitive advantage and, at the same time, deliver greater value to society. For instance, Walmart, by working with its suppliers to reduce the use of packaging materials and revamping the routes of its delivery trucks to cut out 100 million miles of travel, saved $200 million in costs (which enhanced its cost-competitiveness vis-à-vis rivals) and lowered carbon emissions.[32] Thus, a social responsibility strategy that packs some punch and is more than rhetorical flourish can produce outcomes that are in the best interest of shareholders.

In sum, companies that take social responsibility and environmental sustainability seriously can improve their business reputations and operational efficiency while also reducing their risk exposure and encouraging loyalty and innovation. Overall, companies that take special pains to protect the environment (beyond what is required by law), are active in community affairs, and are generous supporters of charitable causes and projects that benefit society are more likely to be seen as good investments and as good companies to work for or do business with. Shareholders are likely to view the business case for social responsibility as a strong one, particularly when it results in the creation of more customer value, greater productivity, lower operating costs, and lower business risk—all of which should increase firm profitability and enhance shareholder value even as the company's actions address broader stakeholder interests.

Companies are, of course, sometimes rewarded for bad behavior—a company that is able to shift environmental and other social costs associated with its activities onto society as a whole can reap large short-term profits. The major cigarette producers for many years were able to earn greatly inflated profits by shifting the health-related costs of smoking onto others and escaping any

> Socially responsible strategies that create value for customers and lower costs can improve company profits and shareholder value at the same time that they address other stakeholder interests.

> There's little hard evidence indicating shareholders are disadvantaged in any meaningful way by a company's actions to be socially responsible.

responsibility for the harm their products caused to consumers and the general public. Only recently have they been facing the prospect of having to pay high punitive damages for their actions. Unfortunately, the cigarette makers are not alone in trying to evade paying for the social harms of their operations for as long as they can. Calling a halt to such actions usually hinges on (1) the effectiveness of activist social groups in publicizing the adverse consequences of a company's social irresponsibility and marshaling public opinion for something to be done, (2) the enactment of legislation or regulations to correct the inequity, and (3) decisions on the part of socially conscious buyers to take their business elsewhere.

KEY POINTS

1. Ethics concerns standards of right and wrong. Business ethics concerns the application of ethical principles to the actions and decisions of business organizations and the conduct of their personnel. Ethical principles in business are not materially different from ethical principles in general.

2. There are three schools of thought about ethical standards for companies with international operations:
    - According to the *school of ethical universalism,* common understandings across multiple cultures and countries about what constitutes right and wrong behaviors give rise to universal ethical standards that apply to members of all societies, all companies, and all businesspeople.
    - According to the *school of ethical relativism,* different societal cultures and customs have divergent values and standards of right and wrong. Thus, what is ethical or unethical must be judged in the light of local customs and social mores and can vary from one culture or nation to another.
    - According to the *integrated social contracts theory,* universal ethical principles based on the collective views of multiple cultures and societies combine to form a "social contract" that all individuals in all situations have a duty to observe. Within the boundaries of this social contract, local cultures or groups can specify what additional actions are not ethically permissible. However, universal norms always take precedence over local ethical norms.

3. Apart from the "business of business is business, not ethics" kind of thinking, three other factors contribute to unethical business behavior: (1) faulty oversight that enables the unscrupulous pursuit of personal gain, (2) heavy pressures on company managers to meet or beat short-term earnings targets, and (3) a company culture that puts profitability and good business performance ahead of ethical behavior. In contrast, culture can function as a powerful mechanism for promoting ethical business conduct when high ethical principles are deeply ingrained in the corporate culture of a company.

4. Business ethics failures can result in three types of costs: (1) visible costs, such as fines, penalties, and lower stock prices; (2) internal administrative costs, such as legal costs and costs of taking corrective action; and (3) intangible costs or less visible costs, such as customer defections and damage to the company's reputation.

5. The term *corporate social responsibility* concerns a company's *duty* to operate in an honorable manner, provide good working conditions for employees, encourage workforce diversity, be a good steward of the environment, and support philanthropic endeavors in local communities where it operates and in society at large.

The particular combination of socially responsible endeavors a company elects to pursue defines its corporate social responsibility (CSR) strategy.

6. The triple bottom line refers to company performance in three realms: economic, social, and environmental, often referred to as profit, people, and planet. Increasingly, companies are reporting their performance with respect to all three performance dimensions.

7. *Sustainability* is a term that is used in various ways, but most often it concerns a firm's relationship to the environment and its use of natural resources. Sustainable business practices are those capable of meeting the needs of the present without compromising the world's ability to meet future needs. A company's environmental sustainability strategy consists of its deliberate actions to protect the environment, provide for the longevity of natural resources, maintain ecological support systems for future generations, and guard against ultimate endangerment of the planet.

8. CSR strategies and environmental sustainability strategies that both provide valuable social benefits *and* fulfill customer needs in a superior fashion can lead to competitive advantage.

9. The moral case for corporate social responsibility and environmental sustainability boils down to a simple concept: It's the right thing to do. There are also solid reasons why CSR and environmental sustainability strategies may be good business—they can be conducive to greater buyer patronage, reduce the risk of reputation-damaging incidents, provide opportunities for revenue enhancement, and lower costs. Well-crafted CSR and environmental sustainability strategies are in the best long-term interest of shareholders, for the reasons just mentioned and because they can avoid or preempt costly legal or regulatory actions.

ASSURANCE OF LEARNING EXERCISES

1. Widely known as an ethical company, Dell recently committed itself to becoming a more environmentally sustainable business. After reviewing the About Dell section of its website (www.dell.com/learn/us/en/uscorp1/about-dell), prepare a list of eight specific policies and programs that help the company achieve its vision of driving social and environmental change while still remaining innovative and profitable. **LO 9-1, LO 9-4**

2. Prepare a one- to two-page analysis of a recent ethics scandal using your university library's resources. Your report should (1) discuss the conditions that gave rise to unethical business strategies and behavior and (2) provide an overview of the costs to the company resulting from the company's business ethics failure. **LO 9-2, LO 9-3**

3. Based on information provided in Illustration Capsule 9.3, explain how Warby Parker's CSR strategy has contributed to its success in the marketplace. How are the company's various stakeholder groups affected by its commitment to social responsibility? How would you evaluate its triple-bottom-line performance? **connect** **LO 9-4**

4. The British outdoor clothing company Páramo was a Guardian Sustainable Business Award winner in 2016. (Guardian stopped giving the award afterward.) The company's fabric technology and use of chemicals is discussed at https://www.theguardian.com/sustainable-business/2016/may/27/outdoor-clothing-paramo-toxic-pfc-greenpeace-fabric-technology. Describe how Páramo's business practices allowed it to become recognized for its bold moves. How do these initiatives help build competitive advantage? **connect** **LO 9-4**

EXERCISES FOR SIMULATION PARTICIPANTS

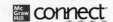

LO 9-1   1.   What factors build the business case for operating your company in an ethical manner?

LO 9-4   2.   In what ways, if any, is your company exercising corporate social responsibility? What are the elements of your company's CSR strategy? Are there any changes to this strategy that you would suggest?

LO 9-3, LO 9-4   3.   If some shareholders complained that you and your co-managers have been spending too little or too much on corporate social responsibility, what would you tell them?

LO 9-4   4.   Is your company striving to conduct its business in an environmentally sustainable manner? What specific *additional* actions could your company take that would make an even greater contribution to environmental sustainability?

LO 9-4   5.   In what ways do a company's environmental sustainability strategy in the best long-term interest of shareholders? Does it contribute to your company's competitive advantage or profitability?

ENDNOTES

[1] James E. Post, Anne T. Lawrence, and James Weber, *Business and Society: Corporate Strategy, Public Policy, Ethics,* 10th ed. (New York: McGraw-Hill, 2002).

[2] Mark S. Schwartz, "Universal Moral Values for Corporate Codes of Ethics," *Journal of Business Ethics* 59, no. 1 (June 2005), pp. 27–44.

[3] Mark S. Schwartz, "A Code of Ethics for Corporate Codes of Ethics," *Journal of Business Ethics* 41, no. 1–2 (November–December 2002), pp. 27–43.

[4] T. L. Beauchamp and N. E. Bowie, *Ethical Theory and Business* (Upper Saddle River, NJ: Prentice-Hall, 2001).

[5] www.cnn.com/2013/10/15/world/child-labor-index-2014/ (accessed February 6, 2014).

[6] U.S. Department of Labor, "The Department of Labor's 2013 Findings on the Worst Forms of Child Labor," www.dol.gov/ilab/programs/ocft/PDF/2012OCFTreport.pdf.

[7] W. M. Greenfield, "In the Name of Corporate Social Responsibility," *Business Horizons* 47, no. 1 (January–February 2004), p. 22.

[8] Rajib Sanyal, "Determinants of Bribery in International Business: The Cultural and Economic Factors," *Journal of Business Ethics* 59, no. 1 (June 2005), pp. 139–145.

[9] Transparency International, *Global Corruption Report,* www.globalcorruptionreport.org.

[10] Roger Chen and Chia-Pei Chen, "Chinese Professional Managers and the Issue of Ethical Behavior," *Ivey Business Journal* 69, no. 5 (May–June 2005), p. 1.

[11] Antonio Argandoa, "Corruption and Companies: The Use of Facilitating Payments," *Journal of Business Ethics* 60, no. 3 (September 2005), pp. 251–264.

[12] Thomas Donaldson and Thomas W. Dunfee, "Towards a Unified Conception of Business Ethics: Integrative Social Contracts Theory," *Academy of Management Review* 19, no. 2 (April 1994), pp. 252–284; Andrew Spicer, Thomas W. Dunfee, and Wendy J. Bailey, "Does National Context Matter in Ethical Decision Making? An Empirical Test of Integrative Social Contracts Theory," *Academy of Management Journal* 47, no. 4 (August 2004), p. 610.

[13] Lynn Paine, Rohit Deshpandé, Joshua D. Margolis, and Kim Eric Bettcher, "Up to Code: Does Your Company's Conduct Meet World-Class Standards?" *Harvard Business Review* 83, no. 12 (December 2005), pp. 122–133.

[14] John F. Veiga, Timothy D. Golden, and Kathleen Dechant, "Why Managers Bend Company Rules," *Academy of Management Executive* 18, no. 2 (May 2004).

[15] Lorin Berlin and Emily Peck, "National Mortgage Settlement: States, Big Banks Reach $25 Billion Deal," *Huff Post Business,* February 9, 2012, www.huffingtonpost.com/2012/02/09/-national-mortgage-settlement_n_1265292.html (accessed February 15, 2012).

[16] Ronald R. Sims and Johannes Brinkmann, "Enron Ethics (Or: Culture Matters More than Codes)," *Journal of Business Ethics* 45, no. 3 (July 2003), pp. 244–246.

[17] Kurt Eichenwald, *Conspiracy of Fools: A True Story* (New York: Broadway Books, 2005).

[18] Timothy M. Devinney, "Is the Socially Responsible Corporation a Myth? The Good, the Bad, and the Ugly of Corporate Social Responsibility," *Academy of Management Perspectives* 23, no. 2 (May 2009), pp. 44–56.

[19] Information posted at www.generalmills.com (accessed March 13, 2013).

[20] Adrian Henriques, "ISO 26000: A New Standard for Human Rights?" *Institute for Human Rights and Business,* March 23, 2010, www.institutehrb.org/blogs/guest/iso_26000_a_new_standard_for_human_rights.html?gclid=CJih7NjN2aICFVs65QodrVOdyQ (accessed July 7, 2010).

[21] Gerald I. J. M. Zetsloot and Marcel N. A. van Marrewijk, "From Quality to Sustainability," *Journal of Business Ethics* 55 (2004), pp. 79–82.

[22] Tilde Herrera, "PG&E Claims Industry First with Supply Chain Footprint Project," **GreenBiz.com,** June 30, 2010, www.greenbiz.com/news/2010/06/30/-pge—claims-industry-first-supply-chain-carbon-footprint-project.

[23] J. G. Speth, *The Bridge at the End of the World: Capitalism, the Environment, and Crossing from Crisis to Sustainability* (New Haven, CT: Yale University Press, 2008).

[24] Michael E. Porter and Mark R. Kramer, "Strategy & Society: The Link between Competitive Advantage and Corporate Social Responsibility," *Harvard Business Review* 84, no. 12 (December 2006), pp. 78–92.

[25] N. Craig Smith, "Corporate Responsibility: Whether and How," *California Management Review* 45, no. 4 (Summer 2003), p. 63.

[26] Jeb Brugmann and C. K. Prahalad, "Cocreating Business's New Social Compact," *Harvard Business Review* 85, no. 2 (February 2007), pp. 80–90.

[27] Wallace N. Davidson, Abuzar El-Jelly, and Dan L. Worrell, "Influencing Managers to Change Unpopular Corporate Behavior through Boycotts and Divestitures: A Stock Market Test," *Business and Society* 34, no. 2 (1995), pp. 171–196.

[28] Tom McCawley, "Racing to Improve Its Reputation: Nike Has Fought to Shed Its Image as an Exploiter of Third-World Labor Yet It Is Still a Target of Activists," *Financial Times,* December 2000, p. 14.

[29] Michael E. Porter and Mark Kramer, "Creating Shared Value," *Harvard Business Review* 89, no. 1–2 (January–February 2011).

[30] James C. Collins and Jerry I. Porras, *Built to Last: Successful Habits of Visionary Companies,* 3rd ed. (London: HarperBusiness, 2002).

[31] Joshua D. Margolis and Hillary A. Elfenbein, "Doing Well by Doing Good: Don't Count on It," *Harvard Business Review* 86, no. 1 (January 2008), pp. 19–20; Lee E. Preston, Douglas P. O'Bannon, Ronald M. Roman, Sefa Hayibor, and Bradley R. Agle, "The Relationship between Social and Financial Performance: Repainting a Portrait," *Business and Society* 38, no. 1 (March 1999), pp. 109–125.

[32] Leonard L. Berry, Ann M. Mirobito, and William B. Baun, "What's the Hard Return on Employee Wellness Programs?" *Harvard Business Review* 88, no. 12 (December 2010), p. 105.

chapter 10

Building an Organization Capable of Good Strategy Execution

People, Capabilities, and Structure

Learning Objectives

After reading this chapter, you should be able to:

LO 10-1 Understand what managers must do to execute strategy successfully.

LO 10-2 Understand why hiring, training, and retaining the right people constitute a key component of the strategy execution process.

LO 10-3 Recognize that good strategy execution requires continuously building and upgrading the organization's resources and capabilities.

LO 10-4 Identify and establish a strategy-supportive organizational structure and organize the work effort.

LO 10-5 Comprehend the pros and cons of centralized and decentralized decision making in implementing the chosen strategy.

Richard *Schneider/Getty Images*

Strategies most often fail because they aren't executed well.

Larry Bossidy and Ram Charan
Former CEO of Honeywell; Author and Consultant

I try to motivate people and align our individual incentives with organizational incentives. And then let people do their best.

John D. Liu—*CEO, Essex Equity Management*

People are not your most important asset. The right people are.

Jim Collins—*Professor and author*

Once managers have decided on a strategy, the emphasis turns to converting it into actions and good results. Putting the strategy into place and getting the organization to execute it will call for different sets of managerial skills rather than crafting strategy. Whereas crafting strategy is largely an analysis-driven activity focused on market conditions and the company's resources and capabilities, executing strategy is primarily operations-driven, revolving around the management of people, resources, business processes, and organizational structure. Successful strategy execution depends on doing a good job of working with and through others; building and strengthening competitive capabilities; creating an appropriate organizational structure; allocating resources; instituting strategy-supportive policies, processes, and systems; and instilling a discipline of getting things done. Executing strategy is an action-oriented task that tests a manager's ability to direct organizational change, achieve improvements in day-to-day operations, create and nurture a culture that supports good strategy execution, and meet or beat performance targets.

Experienced managers are well aware that it is much easier to develop a sound strategic plan than it is to execute the plan and achieve targeted outcomes. A study of 400 CEOs in the United States, Europe, and Asia found that executional excellence was the number-one challenge facing their companies.[1] According to one executive, "It's been rather easy for us to decide where we wanted to go. The hard part is to get the organization to act on the new priorities."[2] It takes adept managerial leadership to convincingly communicate the reasons for a new strategy and overcome pockets of doubt, secure the commitment of key personnel, build consensus for how to implement the strategy, and move forward to get all the pieces into place and deliver results. *Just because senior managers announce a new strategy doesn't mean that organization members will embrace it and move forward enthusiastically to implement it.* Company personnel must understand—in their heads and hearts—why a new strategic direction is necessary and where the new strategy is taking them.[3] Instituting change is, of course, easier when the problems with the old strategy have become obvious and/or the company has spiraled into a financial crisis.

But the challenge of successfully implementing new strategic initiatives goes well beyond managerial adeptness in overcoming resistance to change. What really make executing strategy a tougher, more time-consuming management challenge than crafting strategy are the wide array of managerial activities that must be attended to, the many ways to put new strategic initiatives in place and keep things moving, and the number of bedeviling issues that always crop up and have to be resolved. It takes first-rate "managerial smarts" to zero in on what exactly needs to be done and how to get good results in a timely manner. Excellent people-management skills and perseverance are needed to get a variety of initiatives underway and to integrate the efforts of many different work groups into a smoothly functioning whole. Depending on how much consensus building and organizational change is involved, the process of implementing strategy changes can take several months to several years. And executing the strategy with *real proficiency* takes even longer.

Like crafting strategy, *executing strategy is a job for a company's whole management team—not just a few senior managers.* While the chief executive officer and the heads of major units (business divisions, functional departments, and key operating units) are ultimately responsible for seeing that strategy is executed successfully, the process typically affects every part of the firm—all value chain activities and all work groups. Top-level managers must rely on the active support of middle and lower managers to institute whatever new operating practices are needed in the various operating units to achieve proficient strategy execution. Middle- and lower-level managers must ensure that frontline employees perform strategy-critical value chain activities proficiently enough to allow companywide performance targets to be met. Consequently, *all company personnel are actively involved in the strategy execution process in one way or another.*

A FRAMEWORK FOR EXECUTING STRATEGY

CORE CONCEPT

Good strategy execution requires a *team effort.* All managers have strategy-executing responsibility in their areas of authority, and all employees are active participants in the strategy execution process.

The managerial approach to executing a strategy always has to be customized to fit the particulars of a company's situation. Making minor changes in an existing strategy differs from implementing radical strategy changes. The techniques for successfully executing a low-cost leader strategy are different from those for executing a high-end differentiation strategy. Implementing a new strategy for a struggling company in the midst of a financial crisis is a different job from improving strategy execution in a company that is doing relatively well. Moreover, some managers are more adept than others at using particular approaches to achieving certain kinds of organizational changes. Hence, there's no definitive managerial recipe for successful strategy execution that cuts across all company situations and strategies or that works for all managers. Rather, the specific actions required to execute a strategy—the "to-do list" that constitutes management's action agenda—always represent management's judgment about how best to proceed in light of prevailing circumstances.

● **LO 10-1**

Understand what managers must do to execute strategy successfully.

The Principal Components of the Strategy Execution Process

Despite the need to tailor a company's strategy-executing approaches to the situation at hand, certain managerial bases must be covered no matter what the circumstances. These include 10 basic managerial tasks (see Figure 10.1):

1. Staffing the organization with managers and employees capable of executing the strategy well.

2. Developing the resources and organizational capabilities required for successful strategy execution.

3. Creating a strategy-supportive organizational structure.

4. Allocating sufficient resources (budgetary and otherwise) to the strategy execution effort.

5. Instituting policies and procedures that facilitate strategy execution.

6. Adopting business management processes that drive continuous improvement in how value chain activities are performed.

7. Installing information and operating systems that support strategy implementation activities.

8. Tying rewards directly to the achievement of performance objectives.

9. Fostering a corporate culture that promotes good strategy execution.

10. Exercising the leadership needed to propel strategy execution forward.

> When strategies fail, it is often because of poor execution. Strategy execution is therefore a critical managerial endeavor.

How well managers perform these 10 tasks has a decisive impact on whether the outcome of the strategy execution effort is a spectacular success, a colossal failure, or something in between.

In devising an action agenda for executing strategy, managers should start by conducting *a probing assessment of what the organization must do differently to carry out the strategy successfully.* Each manager needs to ask the question "What needs to be done in my area of responsibility to implement our part of the company's strategy, and what should I do to get these things accomplished in a timely fashion?" It is then incumbent on every manager to determine *precisely how to make the necessary internal changes.* Strong managers have a knack for diagnosing what their organizations need to do to execute the chosen strategy well and figuring out how to get these things done efficiently. They are masters in promoting results-oriented behaviors on the part of company personnel and following through on making the right things happen to achieve the target outcomes.[4]

> The two best signs of good strategy execution are whether a company is meeting its performance targets and whether it has attained real proficiency in performing strategy-critical value chain activities.

When strategies fail, it is often because of poor execution. Strategy execution is therefore a critical managerial endeavor. The two best signs of good strategy execution are whether a company is meeting its performance targets and whether it is performing value chain activities in a manner that is conducive to companywide operating excellence. In big organizations with geographically scattered operating units, senior executives' action agenda mostly involves communicating the case for change, building consensus for how to proceed, installing strong managers to move the process forward in key organizational units, directing resources to the right places, establishing deadlines and measures of progress, rewarding those who achieve implementation milestones, and personally leading the strategic change process. Thus, the bigger the organization, the more that successful strategy execution depends on the cooperation and implementation skills of operating managers who can promote needed changes at the lowest organizational levels and deliver results. In small organizations, top managers can deal directly with frontline managers and employees, personally orchestrating the action steps and implementation sequence, observing firsthand how implementation is progressing, and deciding how hard and how fast to push the process along. Whether the organization is large or small and whether strategy implementation involves sweeping or minor changes, effective leadership requires a keen grasp of what to do and how to do it in light of the organization's circumstances. Then it remains for company personnel in strategy-critical areas to step up to the plate and produce the desired results.

What's Covered in Chapters 10, 11, and 12   In the remainder of this chapter and in the next two chapters, we discuss what is involved in performing the 10 key managerial tasks that shape the process of executing strategy. This chapter explores the first three of these tasks (highlighted in blue in Figure 10.1): (1) staffing the organization with people

FIGURE 10.1   The 10 Basic Tasks of the Strategy Execution Process

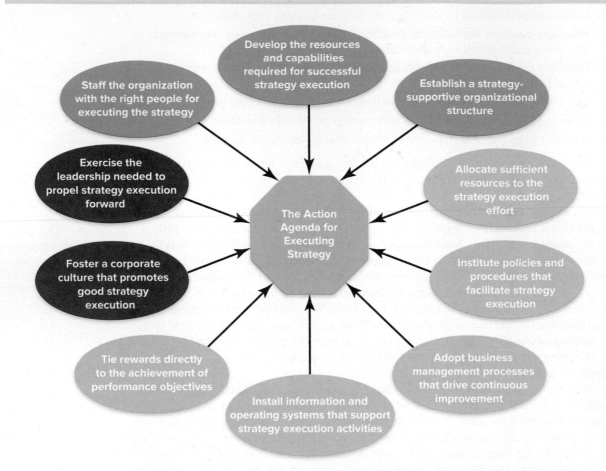

capable of executing the strategy well, (2) developing the resources and organizational capabilities needed for successful strategy execution, and (3) creating an organizational structure supportive of the strategy execution process. Chapter 11 concerns the tasks of allocating resources (budgetary and otherwise), instituting strategy-facilitating policies and procedures, employing business process management tools installing operating and information systems, and tying rewards to the achievement of good results (highlighted in green in Figure 10.1). Chapter 12 deals with the two remaining tasks: instilling a corporate culture conducive to good strategy execution, and exercising the leadership needed to drive the execution process forward (highlighted in purple).

BUILDING AN ORGANIZATION CAPABLE OF GOOD STRATEGY EXECUTION: THREE KEY ACTIONS

Proficient strategy execution depends foremost on having in place an organization capable of the tasks demanded of it. Building an execution-capable organization is thus always a top priority. As shown in Figure 10.2, three types of organization-building actions are paramount:

1. *Staffing the organization*—putting together a strong management team, and recruiting and retaining employees with the needed experience, technical skills, and intellectual capital.
2. *Acquiring, developing, and strengthening the resources and capabilities required for good strategy execution*—accumulating the required resources, developing proficiencies in performing strategy-critical value chain activities, and updating the company's capabilities to match changing market conditions and customer expectations.
3. *Structuring the organization and work effort*—organizing value chain activities and business processes, establishing lines of authority and reporting relationships, and deciding how much decision-making authority to delegate to lower-level managers and frontline employees.

Implementing a strategy depends critically on ensuring that strategy-supportive resources and Organizational capabilities are in place, ready to be deployed. These include the skills, talents, experience, and knowledge of the company's human resources (managerial and otherwise)—see Figure 10.2. Proficient strategy execution

FIGURE 10.2 **Building an Organization Capable of Proficient Strategy Execution: Three Key Actions**

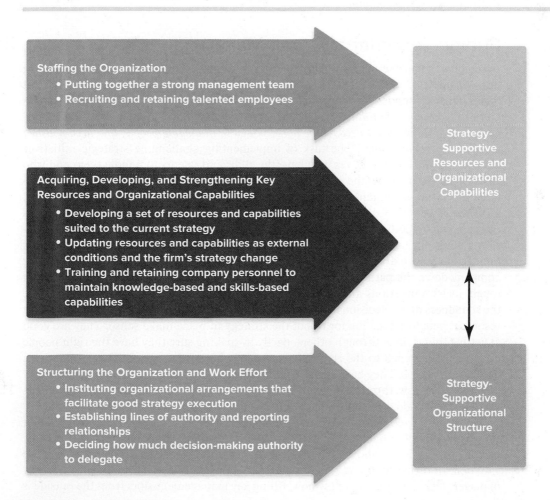

depends heavily on competent personnel of all types, but because of the many managerial tasks involved and the role of leadership in strategy execution, assembling a strong management team is especially important.

If the strategy being implemented is a new strategy, the company may need to add to its resource and capability mix in other respects as well. But renewing, upgrading, and revising the organization's resources and capabilities is a part of the strategy execution process even if the strategy is fundamentally the same, since strategic assets depreciate and conditions are always changing. Thus, augmenting and strengthening the firm's core competencies and seeing that they are suited to the current strategy are also top priorities.

Structuring the organization and work effort is another critical aspect of building an organization capable of good strategy execution. An organization structure that is well matched to the strategy can help facilitate its implementation; one that is not well suited can lead to higher bureaucratic costs and communication or coordination breakdowns.

STAFFING THE ORGANIZATION

LO 10-2

Understand why hiring, training, and retaining the right people constitute a key component of the strategy execution process.

No company can hope to perform the activities required for successful strategy execution without attracting and retaining talented managers and employees with suitable skills and *intellectual capital*.

Putting Together a Strong Management Team

Assembling a capable management team is a cornerstone of the organization-building task.[5] While different strategies and company circumstances often call for different mixes of backgrounds, experiences, management styles, and know-how, *the most important consideration is to fill key managerial slots with smart people who are clear thinkers, good at figuring out what needs to be done, skilled in managing people, and accomplished in delivering good results.*[6] The task of implementing challenging strategic initiatives must be assigned to executives who have the skills and talents to handle them and who can be counted on to get the job done well. Without a capable, results-oriented management team, the implementation process is likely to be hampered by missed deadlines, misdirected or wasteful efforts, and managerial ineptness. Weak executives are serious impediments to getting optimal results—the caliber of work done under their supervision suffers.[7] In contrast, managers with strong strategy implementation capabilities understand how to drive organizational change, and know how to motivate and lead the company down the path for first-rate strategy execution. They have a talent for asking tough, incisive questions and know enough about the details of the business to ensure the soundness of the decisions of the people around them—they can discern whether the resources people are asking for to put the strategy in place make sense. They are good at getting things done through others, partly by making sure they have the right people under them, assigned to the right jobs and partly because they know how to motivate and inspire people. They have strong social skills and high emotional intelligence. They consistently follow through on issues, monitor progress carefully, make adjustments when needed, and keep important details from slipping through the cracks.

Sometimes a company's existing management team is up to the task. At other times it may need to be strengthened by promoting qualified people from within or by bringing in outsiders whose experiences, talents, and leadership styles better suit the situation. In turnaround and rapid-growth situations, and in instances when company managers lack the requisite know-how, filling key management slots from the outside is

a standard organization-building approach. In all situations, it is important to identify and replace managers who are incapable, for whatever reason, of making the
required changes in a timely and cost-effective manner. For a management team to
be truly effective at strategy execution, it must be composed of managers who recognize that organizational changes are needed and who are both capable and ready
to get on with the process.

> Putting together a talented management team with the right mix of experiences, skills, and abilities to get things done is one of the first steps to take in launching the strategy-executing process.

The overriding aim in building a management team should be to assemble a *critical mass* of talented managers who can function as agents of change and spearhead
excellent strategy execution. Every manager's success is enhanced (or limited) by
the quality of his or her managerial colleagues and the degree to which they freely
exchange ideas, debate ways to make operating improvements, and join forces to tackle
issues and solve problems. When a first-rate manager enjoys the help and support of
other first-rate managers, it's possible to create a managerial whole that is greater than
the sum of individual efforts—talented managers who work well together as a team can
produce organizational results that are dramatically better than what one or two star
managers acting individually can achieve.[8]

Illustration Capsule 10.1 describes Deloitte's highly effective approach to developing employee talent and a top-caliber management team.

Recruiting, Training, and Retaining Capable Employees

Assembling a capable management team is not enough. Staffing the organization
with the right kinds of people must extend to all kinds of company personnel for
value chain activities to be performed competently. *The caliber of an organization's
people is always an essential ingredient of successful strategy execution.* Companies
like Mercedes-Benz, Alphabet, SAS, Boston Consulting Group, Edward Jones,
Quicken Loans, Genentech, Intuit, Salesforce.com, and Goldman Sachs make a
concerted effort to recruit the best and brightest people they can find and then
retain them with excellent compensation packages, opportunities for rapid advance-
ment and professional growth, and interesting assignments. Having a pool of "A
players" with strong skill sets and lots of brainpower is essential to their business.

> In many industries, adding to a company's talent base and building intellectual capital are more important to good strategy execution than are additional invest-ments in capital projects.

Facebook makes a point of hiring the very brightest and most talented programmers it can find and motivating them with both good monetary incentives and the
challenge of working on cutting-edge technology projects. McKinsey & Company, one
of the world's premier management consulting firms, recruits only cream-of-the-crop
MBAs at the nation's top-10 business schools; such talent is essential to McKinsey's
strategy of performing high-level consulting for the world's top corporations. The leading global accounting firms screen candidates not only on the basis of their accounting expertise but also on whether they possess the people skills needed to relate well
with clients and colleagues. Zappos goes to considerable lengths to hire people who
can have fun and be fun on the job; it has done away with traditional job postings and
instead asks prospective hires to join a social network called Zappos Insiders where
they will interact with current employees and have opportunities to demonstrate their
passion for joining the company. Zappos is so selective about finding people who fit
their culture that only about 1.5 percent of the people who apply are offered jobs.

In high-tech companies, the challenge is to staff work groups with gifted, imaginative, and energetic people who can bring life to new ideas quickly and inject into
the organization what one Dell executive calls "hum."[9] The saying "People are our
most important asset" may seem trite, but it fits high-technology companies precisely.
Besides checking closely for functional and technical skills, Dell tests applicants for

Management Development at Deloitte Touche Tohmatsu Limited

Kent *Johansson/Shutterstock*

Hiring, retaining, and cultivating talent are critical activities at Deloitte, the world's largest professional services firm. By offering robust learning and development programs, Deloitte has been able to create a strong talent pipeline to the firm's partnership. Deloitte's emphasis on learning and development, across all stages of the employee life cycle, has led to recognitions such as being ranked number-one on *Chief Executives*'s list of "Best Private Companies for Leaders" and being listed among *Fortune*'s "100 Best Companies to Work For." The following programs contribute to Deloitte's successful execution of its talent strategy:

- *Clear path to partnership.* During the initial recruiting phase and then throughout an employee's tenure at the firm, Deloitte lays out a clear career path. The path indicates the expected timeline for promotion to each of the firm's hierarchy levels, along with the competencies and experience required. Deloitte's transparency on career paths, coupled with its in-depth performance management process, helps employees clearly understand their performance. This serves as a motivational tool for top performers, often leading to career acceleration.

- *Formal training programs.* Like other leading organizations, Deloitte has a program to ensure that recent college graduates are equipped with the necessary training and tools for succeeding on the job. Yet Deloitte's commitment to formal training is evident at all levels within the organization. Each time an employee is promoted, he or she attends "milestone" school, a weeklong simulation that replicates true business situations employees would face as they transition to new stages of career development. In addition, Deloitte institutes mandatory training hours for all of its employees to ensure that individuals continue to further their professional development.

- *Special programs for high performers.* Deloitte also offers fellowships and programs to help employees acquire new skills and enhance their leadership development. For example, the Global Fellows program helps top performers work with senior leaders in the organization to focus on the realities of delivering client service across borders. Deloitte has also established the Emerging Leaders Development program, which utilizes skill building, 360-degree feedback, and one-on-one executive coaching to help top-performing managers and senior managers prepare for partnership.

- *Sponsorship, not mentorship.* To train the next generation of leaders, Deloitte has implemented formal mentorship programs to provide leadership development support. Deloitte, however, uses the term *sponsorship* to describe this initiative. A sponsor is tasked with taking a vested interest in an individual and advocating on his or her behalf. Sponsors help rising leaders navigate the firm, develop new competencies, expand their network, and hone the skills needed to accelerate their career.

Note: Developed with Heather Levy.

Sources: Company websites; www.accountingweb.com/article/leadership-development-community-service-integral-deloitte-university/220845 (accessed February 2014).

their tolerance of ambiguity and change, their capacity to work in teams, and their ability to learn on the fly. Companies like LinkedIn, Credit Suisse, IDEO, Amazon.com, Google, and Cisco Systems have broken new ground in recruiting, hiring, cultivating, developing, and retaining talented employees—almost all of whom are in their 20s and 30s. Cisco goes after the top 10 percent, raiding other companies and endeavoring to retain key people at the companies it acquires. Cisco executives believe that a cadre of star engineers, programmers, managers, salespeople, and support personnel is the backbone of the company's efforts to execute its strategy and remain the world's leading provider of Internet infrastructure products and technology.

In recognition of the importance of a talented and energetic workforce, companies have instituted a number of practices aimed at staffing jobs with the best people they can find:

1. Spending considerable effort on screening and evaluating job applicants—selecting only those with suitable skill sets, energy, initiative, judgment, aptitude for learning, and personality traits that mesh well with the company's work environment and culture.

2. Providing employees with training programs that continue throughout their careers.

3. Offering promising employees challenging, interesting, and skill-stretching assignments.

4. Rotating people through jobs that span functional and geographic boundaries. Providing people with opportunities to gain experience in a variety of international settings is increasingly considered an essential part of career development in multinational companies.

5. Making the work environment stimulating and engaging so that employees will consider the company a great place to work.

6. Encouraging employees to challenge existing ways of doing things, to be creative in proposing better ways of operating, and to push their ideas for new products or businesses. Progressive companies work hard at creating an environment in which employees are made to feel that their views and suggestions count.

7. Striving to retain talented, high-performing employees via promotions, salary increases, performance bonuses, stock options and equity ownership, benefit packages including health insurance and retirement packages, and other perks, such as flexible work hours and onsite day care.

8. Coaching average performers to improve their skills and capabilities, while weeding out underperformers.

> The best companies make a point of recruiting and retaining talented employees—the objective is to make the company's entire workforce (managers and rank-and-file employees) a genuine competitive asset.

DEVELOPING AND BUILDING CRITICAL RESOURCES AND ORGANIZATIONAL CAPABILITIES

High among the organization-building priorities in the strategy execution process is the need to build and strengthen the company's portfolio of resources and capabilities with which to perform strategy-critical value chain activities. As explained in Chapter 4, a company's chances of gaining a sustainable advantage over its market rivals depends on the caliber of its resource portfolio. In the course of crafting strategy, managers may well have well have identified the strategy-critical resources and capabilities it needs. But getting the strategy execution process underway requires acquiring or developing these resources and capabilities, putting them into place, upgrading them as needed, and then modifying them as market conditions evolve.

If the strategy being implemented has important new elements, company managers may have to acquire new resources, significantly broaden or deepen certain capabilities, or even add entirely new competencies in order to put the strategic initiatives in place and execute them proficiently. But even when a company's strategy has not changed materially, good strategy execution still involves continually upgrading the firm's resources and capabilities to keep them in top form and perform value chain activities ever more proficiently.

> **LO 10-3**
> Recognize that good strategy execution requires continuously building and upgrading the organization's resources and capabilities.

Three Approaches to Building and Strengthening Organizational Capabilities

Building the right kinds of organizational capabilities and keeping them finely honed is a time-consuming, managerially challenging exercise. While some assistance can be gotten from discovering how best-in-industry or best-in-world companies perform a particular activity, trying to replicate and then improve on the capabilities of other companies is easier said than done—for the same reasons that one is unlikely to ever become a world-class halfpipe snowboarder just by studying legendary Olympic gold medalist Shaun White.

With deliberate effort, well-orchestrated organizational actions, and continued practice, however, it is possible for a firm to become proficient at capability building despite the difficulty. Indeed, by making capability-building activities a *routine* part of their strategy execution endeavors, some firms are able to develop *dynamic capabilities* that assist them in managing resource and capability change, as discussed in Chapter 4. The most common approaches to capability building include (1) developing and strengthening capabilities internally, (2) acquiring capabilities through mergers and acquisitions, and (3) developing new organizational capabilities via collaborative partnerships.

Developing Organizational Capabilities Internally Internal efforts to create or upgrade organizational capabilities is an evolutionary process that entails a series of deliberate and well-orchestrated steps as organizations search for solutions to their problems. The process is a complex one, since capabilities are the product of *bundles of skills and know-how that are integrated into organizational routines* and *deployed within activity systems* through the combined efforts of teams that are often cross-functional in nature, spanning a variety of departments and locations. For instance, the capability of speeding new products to market involves the *collaborative efforts* of personnel in R&D, engineering and design, purchasing, production, marketing, and distribution. Similarly, the capability to provide superior customer service is a team effort among people in customer call centers (where orders are taken and inquiries are answered), shipping and delivery, billing and accounts receivable, and after-sale support. The process of building an organizational capability begins when managers set an objective of developing a particular capability and organize activity around that objective.[10]

Because the process is incremental, the first step is to develop the *ability* to do something, however imperfectly or inefficiently. This entails selecting people with the requisite skills and experience, enabling them to upgrade their abilities as needed, and then molding the efforts of individuals into a joint effort to create an organizational ability. At this stage, progress can be fitful since it depends on experimenting, actively searching for alternative solutions, and learning through trial and error.[11]

As experience grows and company personnel learn how to perform the activities consistently well and at an acceptable cost, the ability *evolves* into a tried-and-true competence. Getting to this point requires a *continual investment* of resources and *systematic efforts* to improve processes and solve problems creatively as they arise. Improvements in the functioning of an organizational capability come from task repetition and the resulting *learning by doing* of individuals and teams. But the process can be accelerated by making learning a more deliberate endeavor and providing the incentives that will motivate company personnel to achieve the desired ends.[12] This can be critical to successful strategy execution when market conditions are changing rapidly.

It is generally much easier and less time-consuming to update and remodel a company's existing capabilities as external conditions and company strategy change than it is to create them from scratch. Maintaining organizational capabilities in top form may simply require exercising them continually and fine-tuning them as necessary. Similarly, augmenting a capability may require less effort if it involves the recombination of well-established company capabilities and draws on existing company resources. For example, Williams-Sonoma first developed the capability to expand sales beyond its brick-and-mortar location in 1970, when it launched a catalog that was sent to customers throughout the United States. The company extended its mail-order business with the acquisitions of Hold Everything, a garden products catalog, and Pottery Barn, and entered online retailing in 2000 when it launched e-commerce sites for Pottery Barn and Williams-Sonoma. The ongoing renewal of these capabilities has allowed Williams-Sonoma to generate revenues of more than $5.6 billion in 2019 and become one of the largest online retailers in the United States. Toyota, en route to overtaking General Motors as the global leader in motor vehicles, aggressively upgraded its capabilities in fuel-efficient hybrid engine technology and constantly fine-tuned its famed Toyota Production System to enhance its already proficient capabilities in manufacturing top-quality vehicles at relatively low costs.

Managerial actions to develop competitive capabilities generally take one of two forms: either strengthening the company's base of skills, knowledge, and experience or coordinating and integrating the efforts of the various work groups and departments. Actions of the first sort can be undertaken at all managerial levels, but actions of the second sort are best orchestrated by senior managers who not only appreciate the strategy-executing significance of strong capabilities but also have the clout to enforce the necessary cooperation and coordination among individuals, groups, and departments.[13]

Acquiring Capabilities through Mergers and Acquisitions   Sometimes the best way for a company to upgrade its portfolio of capabilities is by acquiring (or merging with) another company with attractive resources and capabilities.[14] An acquisition aimed at building a stronger portfolio of resources and capabilities can be every bit as valuable as an acquisition aimed at adding new products or services to the company's lineup of offerings. The advantage of this mode of acquiring new capabilities is primarily one of speed, since developing new capabilities internally can, at best, take many years of effort and, at worst, come to naught. Capabilities-motivated acquisitions are essential (1) when the company does not have the ability to create the needed capability internally (perhaps because it is too far afield from its existing capabilities) and (2) when industry conditions, technology, or competitors are moving at such a rapid clip that time is of the essence.

At the same time, acquiring capabilities in this way is not without difficulty. Capabilities involve tacit knowledge and complex routines that cannot be transferred readily from one organizational unit to another. This may limit the extent to which the new capability can be utilized. For example, Facebook acquired Oculus VR, a company that makes virtual reality headsets, to add capabilities that might enhance the social media experience. Transferring and integrating these capabilities to other parts of the Facebook organization may prove easier said than done, however, as many technology acquisitions fail to yield the hoped-for benefits. Integrating the capabilities of two companies is particularly problematic when there are underlying incompatibilities in their supporting systems or processes. Moreover, since internal fit is important, there is always the risk that under new management the acquired capabilities may not be as productive as they had been. In a worst-case scenario, the acquisition process may end up damaging or destroying the very capabilities that were the object of the acquisition in the first place.

Accessing Capabilities through Collaborative Partnerships   A third way of obtaining valuable resources and capabilities is to form collaborative partnerships with suppliers, competitors, or other companies having the cutting-edge expertise. There are three basic ways to pursue this course of action:

1. *Outsource the function in which the company's capabilities are deficient to a key supplier or another provider.* Whether this is a wise move depends on whether developing the capabilities internally are key to the company's long-term success. But if this is not the case, then outsourcing may be a good choice especially for firms that are too small and resource-constrained to execute all the parts of their strategy internally.

2. *Collaborate with a firm that has complementary resources and capabilities in a joint venture, strategic alliance, or other type of partnership established for the purpose of achieving a shared strategic objective.* This requires launching initiatives to identify the most attractive potential partners and to establish collaborative working relationships. Since the success of the venture will depend on how well the partners work together, potential partners should be selected as much for their management style, culture, and goals as for their resources and capabilities. In the past 15 years, close collaboration with suppliers to achieve mutually beneficial outcomes has become a common approach to building supply chain capabilities.

3. *Engage in a collaborative partnership for the purpose of learning how the partner does things, internalizing its methods and thereby acquiring its capabilities.* This may be a viable method when each partner has something to learn from the other and can achieve an outcome *beneficial to both partners.* For example, firms sometimes enter into collaborative marketing arrangements whereby each partner is granted access to the other's dealer network for the purpose of expanding sales in geographic areas where the firms lack dealers. But if the intended gains are only one-sided, the arrangement more likely involves an abuse of trust. In consequence, it not only puts the cooperative venture at risk but also encourages the firm's partner to treat the firm similarly or refuse further dealings with the firm.

Collaborative arrangements tend to be less risky when the partnership involves companies from different industries. In racing to develop motor vehicles with self-driving capability, most all vehicle manufacturers are supplementing their own internal efforts with collaborative partnerships with one or more of the growing number of hardware and software firms operating in the driverless vehicle space. These include those developing self-driving software (Alphabet's Waymo, Aurora Innovation, Tesla, Oxbotica, Zoox), makers of the two competing radar systems to spot road obstacles and read traffic signs and signals (RADAR, LiDAR), computing platforms (Nvidia, Qualcomm, Intel), and driverless car technology systems (Mobileye, Bosch, Aptiv).

Nike entered into a strategic partnership with Swiss company Bluesign Technologies for the purpose of making two innovative Bluesign tools available to the hundreds of textile manufacturers supplying the contract factories making Nike products. The tools enable the textile manufacturers to access more than 30,000 materials produced with chemicals that have undergone rigorous assessment for safe use in apparel products. In these types of cases, working together to achieve a capability-related outcome can be beneficial to all the partners.

The Strategic Role of Employee Training

Training and retraining are important when a company shifts to a strategy requiring different skills, competitive capabilities, and operating methods. Training is also strategically important in organizational efforts to build skill-based competencies. And it is a key activity in businesses where technical know-how is changing so rapidly that a company loses its ability to compete unless its employees have cutting-edge knowledge and expertise. Successful strategy implementation requires that the training function is both adequately funded and effective. If better execution of the chosen strategy calls for new skills, deeper technological capability, or the building and deploying of new capabilities, training efforts need to be placed near the top of the action agenda.

The strategic importance of training has not gone unnoticed. Over 4,000 companies around the world have established internal "universities" to lead the training effort, facilitate continuous organizational learning, and upgrade their company's knowledge resources. General Electric has long been known for the excellence of its management training program at Crotonville, outside of New York City. McDonald's maintains a 130,000-square-foot training facility that they call Hamburger University.

Many companies conduct orientation sessions for new employees, fund an assortment of competence-building training programs, and reimburse employees for tuition and other expenses associated with obtaining additional college education, attending professional development courses, and earning professional certification of one kind or another. A number of companies offer online training courses that are available to employees around the clock. Increasingly, companies are expecting employees at all levels are expected to take an active role in their own professional development and assume responsibility for keeping their skills up to date and in sync with the company's needs.

Strategy Execution Capabilities and Competitive Advantage

As firms get better at executing their strategies, they develop capabilities in the domain of strategy execution much as they build other organizational capabilities. Superior strategy execution capabilities allow companies to get the most from their other organizational resources and competitive capabilities. In this way they contribute to the success of a firm's business model. But excellence in strategy execution can also be a more direct source of competitive advantage, since more efficient and effective strategy execution can lower costs and permit firms to deliver more value to customers. Superior strategy execution capabilities may also enable a company to react more quickly to market changes and beat other firms to the market with new products and services. This can allow a company to profit from a period of uncontested market dominance. See Illustration Capsule 10.2 for an example of Zara's route to competitive advantage.

Because strategy execution capabilities are socially complex capabilities that develop with experience over long periods of time, they are hard to imitate. And there is no substitute for good strategy execution. (Recall the tests of resource advantage from Chapter 4.) As such, they may be as important a source of sustained competitive advantage as the core competencies that drive a firm's strategy. Indeed, they may be a far more important avenue for securing a competitive edge over rivals in situations where it is relatively easy for rivals to copy promising strategies. In such cases, the only way for firms to achieve lasting competitive advantage is to *out-execute* their competitors.

> Superior strategy execution capabilities are the only source of sustainable competitive advantage when strategies are easy for rivals to copy.

monticello/Shutterstock

Zara, a major division of Inditex Group, is a leading "fast fashion" retailer. As soon as designs are seen in high-end fashion houses such as Prada, Zara's design team sets to work altering the clothing designs so that it can produce high fashion at mass-retailing prices. Zara's strategy is clever, but by no means unique. The company's competitive advantage is in strategy execution. Every step of Zara's value chain execution is geared toward putting fashionable clothes in stores quickly, realizing high turnover, and strategically driving traffic.

The first key lever is a quick production process. Zara's design team uses inspiration from high fashion and nearly real-time feedback from stores to create up-to-the-minute pieces. Manufacturing largely occurs in factories close to headquarters in Spain, northern Africa, and Turkey, all areas considered to have a high cost of labor. Placing the factories strategically close allows for more flexibility and greater responsiveness to market needs, thereby outweighing the additional labor costs. The entire production process, from design to arrival at stores, takes only two weeks, while other retailers take six months. Whereas traditional retailers commit up to 80 percent of their lines by the start of the season, Zara commits only 50 to 60 percent, meaning that up to half of the merchandise to hit stores is designed and manufactured during the season. Zara purposefully manufactures in small lot sizes to avoid discounting later on and also to encourage impulse shopping, as a particular item could be gone in a few days. From start to finish, Zara has engineered its production process to maximize turnover and turnaround time, creating a true advantage in this step of strategy execution.

Zara also excels at driving traffic to stores. First, the small lot sizes and frequent shipments (up to twice a week per store) drive customers to visit often and purchase quickly. Zara shoppers average 17 visits per year, versus four to five for The Gap. On average, items stay in a Zara store only 11 days. Second, Zara spends no money on advertising, but it occupies some of the most expensive retail space in town, always near the high-fashion houses it imitates. Proximity reinforces the high-fashion association, while the busy street drives significant foot traffic. Overall, Zara has managed to create competitive advantage in every level of strategy execution by tightly aligning design, production, advertising, and real estate with the overall strategy of fast fashion: extremely fast and extremely flexible.

Note: Developed with Sara Paccamonti.

Sources: Suzy Hansen, "How Zara Grew into the World's Largest Fashion Retailer," *The New York Times,* November 9, 2012, www.nytimes.com/2012/11/11/magazine/how-zara-grew-into-the-worlds-largest-fashion-retailer.html?pagewanted=all (accessed February 5, 2014); Seth Stevenson, "Polka Dots Are In? Polka Dots It Is!" *Slate,* June 21, 2012, www.slate.com/articles/arts/operations/2012/06/zara_s_fast_fashion_how_the_company_gets_new_styles_to_stores_so_quickly.html (accessed February 5, 2014).

MATCHING ORGANIZATIONAL STRUCTURE TO THE STRATEGY

While there are few hard-and-fast rules for organizing the work effort to support good strategy execution, there is one: A firm's organizational structure should be *matched* to the particular requirements of implementing the firm's strategy. Every company's strategy is grounded in its own set of organizational capabilities and value chain activities. Moreover, every firm's organizational chart is partly a product of its particular situation, reflecting prior organizational patterns, varying internal circumstances, and executive judgments about how to best structure reporting relationships. Thus, the determinants of the fine details of each firm's organizational structure are unique. But some considerations in organizing the work effort are common to all companies. These are summarized in Figure 10.3 and discussed in the following sections.

● **LO 10-4**

Identify and establish a strategy-supportive organizational structure and organize the work effort.

Deciding Which Value Chain Activities to Perform Internally and Which to Outsource

Aside from the fact that an outsider, because of its expertise and specialized know-how, may be able to perform certain value chain activities better or cheaper than a company can perform them internally (as discussed in Chapter 6), outsourcing can also sometimes contribute to better strategy execution. Outsourcing the performance of selected activities to outside vendors enables a company to heighten its strategic focus and *concentrate its full energies on performing those value chain activities that are at the core of its strategy, where it can create unique value.* For example, 83 percent of the top 10 pharmaceutical companies outsource tactical roles such as clinical data management and trial monitoring; they are much less likely to outsource more strategic functions, such as new product planning. Broadcom, (now part of semiconductor maker Avago Technologies) outsources the manufacture of its chips, thus freeing company personnel to focus their full energies on R&D, new chip design, and marketing. Nike concentrates on design, marketing, and distribution to retailers, while outsourcing virtually all production of its shoes and sporting apparel. Interestingly,

A company's organizational structure should be matched to the particular requirements of implementing the firm's strategy.

FIGURE 10.3   Structuring the Work Effort to Promote Successful Strategy Execution

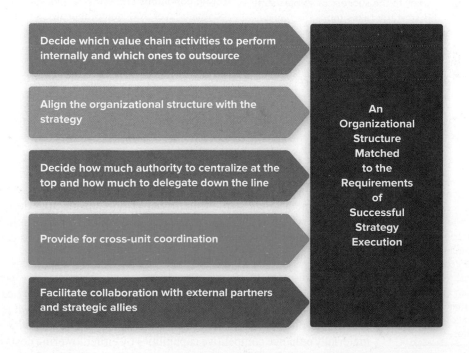

Which Value Chain Activities Does Apple Outsource and Why?

DAVID CHANG/EPA-EFE/Shutterstock

Innovation and design are core competencies for Apple and the drivers behind the creation of winning products such as the iPod, iPhone, and iPad. In consequence, all activities directly related to new product development and product design are performed internally. For example, Apple's Industrial Design Group is responsible for creating the look and feel of all Apple products—from the MacBook Air to the iPhone, and beyond to future products.

Producing a continuing stream of great new products and product versions is key to the success of Apple's strategy. But executing this strategy takes more than innovation and design capabilities. Manufacturing flexibility and speed are imperative in the production of Apple products to ensure that the latest ideas are reflected in the products and that the company meets the high demand for its products—especially around launch.

For these capabilities, Apple turns to outsourcing, as do the majority of its competitors in the consumer electronics space. Apple outsources the manufacturing of products like its iPhone to Asia, where contract manufacturing organizations (CMOs) create value through their vast scale, high flexibility, and low cost. Perhaps no company better epitomizes the Asian CMO value proposition than Foxconn, a company that assembles not only for Apple but for Hewlett-Packard, Motorola, Amazon.com, and Samsung as well. Foxconn's scale is incredible, with 1.3 million people on its payroll as of 2017. Such scale offers companies a significant degree of flexibility, as Foxconn has the ability to hire 3,000 employees on practically a moment's notice. Apple, more so than its competitors, is able to capture CMO value creation by leveraging its immense sales volume and strong cash position to receive preferred treatment. While outsourcing has allowed Apple to reap the benefits of lower cost and more flexible manufacturing, the lack of direct control has proven to be a challenge. Working conditions at Foxconn were so bad at one point that Foxconn installed suicide prevention nets below its windows. Apple responded by tightening its supplier standards and increasing its efforts at monitoring conditions and enforcing its standards. Apple now conducts over 700 comprehensive site audits each year to ensure compliance.

Note: Developed with Margaret W. Macauley.

Sources: Company website; Charles Duhigg and Keith Bradsher, "How the U.S. Lost Out on iPhone Work," *The New York Times,* January 21, 2012, www.nytimes.com/2012/01/22/business/apple-america-and-a-squeezed-middle-class.html?pagewanted=all&_r=0 (accessed March 5, 2012).

Wisely choosing which activities to perform internally and which to outsource can lead to several strategy-executing advantages—lower costs, heightened strategic focus, less internal bureaucracy, speedier decision making, and a better arsenal of organizational capabilities.

e-commerce powerhouse Alibaba got its start by outsourcing web development (a key function) to a U.S. firm; but this was due to the fact that China lacked sufficient development talent at the time. Illustration Capsule 10.3 describes Apple's decisions about which activities to outsource and which to perform in-house.

Such heightened focus on performing strategy-critical activities can yield three important execution-related benefits:

- *The company improves its chances for outclassing rivals in the performance of strategy-critical activities and turning a competence into a distinctive competence.* At the very least, the heightened focus on performing a select few value chain activities should promote more effective performance of those activities. This could materially enhance competitive capabilities by either lowering costs or improving product or service quality. Businesses that get a lot of inquiries from customers or that have to provide 24/7 technical support to users of their products around the world often find that it is considerably less expensive to outsource these functions to specialists (often located in foreign countries where skilled personnel are readily available and worker compensation costs are much lower) than to operate their own call centers. Many businesses also outsource IT functions such as desktop support, disaster recovery, help desk, and data center operations, which often results in cost savings due to the economies of scale available to service providers.

- *The streamlining of internal operations that flows from outsourcing often acts to decrease internal bureaucracies, flatten the organizational structure, speed internal decision making, and shorten the time it takes to respond to changing market conditions.* In consumer electronics, where advancing technology drives new product innovation, organizing the work effort in a manner that expedites getting next-generation products to market ahead of rivals is a critical competitive capability. The world's motor vehicle manufacturers have found that they can shorten the cycle time for new models by outsourcing the production of many parts and components to independent suppliers. They then work closely with the suppliers to swiftly incorporate new technology and to better integrate individual parts and components to form engine cooling systems, transmission systems, electrical systems, and so on.

- *Partnerships with outside vendors can add to a company's arsenal of capabilities and contribute to better strategy execution.* Outsourcing activities to vendors with first-rate capabilities can enable a firm to concentrate on strengthening its own complementary capabilities internally; the result will be a more powerful package of organizational capabilities that the firm can draw upon to deliver more value to customers and attain competitive success. Soft-drink and beer manufacturers cultivate their relationships with their bottlers and distributors to strengthen access to local markets and build loyalty, support, and commitment for corporate marketing programs, without which their own sales and growth would be weakened. Similarly, fast-food enterprises like Wendy's and Burger King find it essential to work hand in hand with franchisees on outlet cleanliness, consistency of product quality, in-store ambience, courtesy and friendliness of store personnel, and other aspects of store operations. Unless franchisees continuously deliver sufficient customer satisfaction to attract repeat business, a fast-food chain's reputation, sales, and competitive standing will quickly suffer. Companies like Boeing, Dell, and Apple have learned that their central R&D groups cannot begin to match the innovative capabilities of a well-managed network of supply chain partners.

However, as emphasized in Chapter 6, a company must guard against going overboard on outsourcing and becoming overly dependent on outside suppliers. A company cannot be the master of its own destiny unless it maintains expertise and resource depth in performing those value chain activities that underpin its long-term competitive success.[15]

Aligning the Firm's Organizational Structure with Its Strategy

The design of the firm's **organizational structure** is a critical aspect of the strategy execution process. The organizational structure comprises the formal and informal arrangement of tasks, responsibilities, and lines of authority and communication by which the firm is administered.[16] It specifies the linkages among parts of the

CORE CONCEPT

A firm's **organizational structure** comprises the formal and informal arrangement of tasks, responsibilities, lines of authority, and reporting relationships by which the firm is administered.

organization, the reporting relationships, the direction of information flows, and the decision-making processes. It is a key factor in strategy implementation since it exerts a strong influence on how well managers can coordinate and control the complex set of activities involved.[17]

A well-designed organizational structure is one in which the various parts (e.g., decision-making rights, communication patterns) are aligned with one another and also matched to the requirements of the strategy. With the right structure in place, managers can orchestrate the various aspects of the implementation process with an even hand and a light touch. Without a supportive structure, strategy execution is more likely to become bogged down by administrative confusion, political maneuvering, and bureaucratic waste.

Good organizational design may even contribute to the firm's ability to create value for customers and realize a profit. By enabling lower bureaucratic costs and facilitating operational efficiency, it can lower a firm's operating costs. By facilitating the coordination of activities within the firm, it can improve the capability-building process, leading to greater differentiation and/or lower costs. Moreover, by improving the speed with which information is communicated and activities are coordinated, it can enable the firm to beat rivals to the market and profit from a period of unrivaled advantage.

Making Strategy-Critical Activities the Main Building Blocks of the Organizational Structure
In any business, some activities in the value chain are always more critical to successful strategy execution than others. For instance, ski apparel companies like Sport Obermeyer, Arc'teryx, and Spyder must be good at styling and design, low-cost manufacturing, distribution (convincing an attractively large number of dealers to stock and promote the company's brand), and marketing and advertising (building a brand image that generates buzz among ski enthusiasts). For brokerage firms like Charles Schwab Corporation and TD Ameritrade, the strategy-critical activities are fast access to information, accurate order execution, efficient record keeping and transaction processing, and full-featured customer service. With respect to such core value chain activities, it is important for management to build its organizational structure around proficient performance of these activities, making them the centerpieces or main building blocks in the enterprise's organizational structure.

The rationale is compelling: If activities crucial to strategic success are to have the resources, decision-making influence, and organizational impact they need, they must be centerpieces in the enterprise's organizational scheme. Making them the focus of structuring efforts will also facilitate their coordination and promote good internal fit—an essential attribute of a winning strategy, as summarized in Chapter 1 and elaborated in Chapter 4. To the extent that implementing a new strategy entails new or altered key activities or capabilities, different organizational arrangements may be required.

Matching Type of Organizational Structure to Strategy Execution Requirements
Organizational structures can be classified into a limited number of standard types. Which type makes the most sense for a given firm depends largely on the firm's size and business makeup, but not so much on the specifics of its strategy. As firms grow and their needs for structure evolve, their structural form is likely to evolve from one type to another. The four basic types are the *simple structure,* the *functional structure,* the *multidivisional structure,* and the *matrix structure,* as described next.

1. Simple Structure   A **simple structure** is one in which a central executive (often the owner-manager) handles all major decisions and oversees the operations of the organization with the help of a small staff.[18] Simple structures are also known as *line-and-staff structures,* since a central administrative staff supervises line employees who conduct the operations of the firm, or *flat structures,* since there are few levels of hierarchy. The simple structure is characterized by limited task specialization; few rules; informal relationships; minimal use of training, planning, and liaison devices; and a lack of sophisticated support systems. It has all the advantages of simplicity, including low administrative costs, ease of coordination, flexibility, quick decision making, adaptability, and responsiveness to change. Its informality and lack of rules may foster creativity and heightened individual responsibility.

> **CORE CONCEPT**
>
> A **simple structure** consists of a central executive (often the owner-manager) who handles all major decisions and oversees all operations with the help of a small staff. Simple structures are also called *line-and-staff structures* or *flat structures.*

Simple organizational structures are typically employed by small firms and entrepreneurial startups. The simple structure is the most common type of organizational structure since small firms are the most prevalent type of business. As an organization grows, however, this structural form becomes inadequate to the demands that come with size and complexity. In response, growing firms tend to alter their organizational structure from a simple structure to a *functional structure.*

2. Functional Structure   A **functional structure** is one that is organized along functional lines, where a function represents a major component of the firm's value chain, such as R&D, engineering and design, manufacturing, sales and marketing, logistics, and customer service. Each functional unit is supervised by functional line managers who report to the chief executive officer and a corporate staff. This arrangement allows functional managers to focus on their area of responsibility, leaving it to the CEO and headquarters to provide direction and ensure that the activities of the functional managers are coordinated and integrated. Functional structures are also known as *departmental structures,* since the functional units are commonly called departments, and *unitary structures* or *U-forms,* since a single unit is responsible for each function.

> **CORE CONCEPT**
>
> A **functional structure** is organized into functional departments, with departmental managers who report to the CEO and small corporate staff. Functional structures are also called *departmental structures* and *unitary structures* or *U-forms.*

In large organizations, functional structures lighten the load on top management, in comparison to simple structures, and enable more efficient use of managerial resources. Their primary advantage, however, is greater *task specialization,* which promotes learning, enables the realization of scale economies, and offers productivity advantages not otherwise available. Their chief disadvantage is that the departmental boundaries can inhibit the flow of information and limit the opportunities for cross-functional cooperation and coordination.

> The primary advantage of a functional structure is greater task specialization, which promotes learning, enables the realization of scale economies, and offers productivity advantages not otherwise available.

It is generally agreed that a functional structure is the best organizational arrangement when a company is in just one particular business (irrespective of which of the five generic competitive strategies it opts to pursue). For instance, a technical instruments manufacturer may be organized around research and development, engineering, supply chain management, assembly, quality control, marketing, and technical services. A discount retailer, such as Dollar General or Family Dollar, may organize around such functional units as purchasing, warehousing, distribution logistics, store operations, advertising, merchandising and promotion, and customer service. Functional structures can also be appropriate for firms with high-volume production, products that are closely related, and a limited degree of vertical integration. For example, General Motors now manages all of its brands (Cadillac, GMC, Chevrolet, Buick, etc.) under a common functional structure designed to promote technical transfer and capture economies of scale.

As firms continue to grow, they often become more diversified and complex, placing a greater burden on top management. At some point, the centralized control that characterizes the functional structure becomes a liability, and the advantages of functional specialization begin to break down. To resolve these problems and address a growing need for coordination across functions, firms generally turn to the *multidivisional structure.*

CORE CONCEPT

A **multidivisional structure** is a decentralized structure consisting of a set of operating divisions organized along business, product, customer group, or geographic lines and a central corporate headquarters that allocates resources, provides support functions, and monitors divisional activities. Multidivisional structures are also called *divisional structures* or *M-forms.*

3. Multidivisional Structure   A **multidivisional structure** is a decentralized structure consisting of a set of operating divisions organized along market, customer, product, or geographic lines, along with a central corporate headquarters, which monitors divisional activities, allocates resources, performs assorted support functions, and exercises overall control. Since each division is essentially a business (often called a *single business unit* or *SBU*), the divisions typically operate as independent profit centers (i.e., with profit and loss responsibility) and are organized internally along functional lines. Division managers oversee day-to-day operations and the development of business-level strategy, while corporate executives attend to overall performance and corporate strategy, the elements of which were described in Chapter 8. Multidivisional structures are also called *divisional structures* or *M-forms,* in contrast with U-form (functional) structures.

Multidivisional structures are common among companies pursuing some form of diversification strategy or international strategy, with operations in a number of businesses or countries. When the strategy is one of unrelated diversification, as in a conglomerate, the divisions generally represent businesses in separate industries. When the strategy is based on related diversification, the divisions may be organized according to industries, customer groups, product lines, geographic regions, or technologies. In this arrangement, the decision about where to draw the divisional lines depends foremost on the nature of the relatedness and the strategy-critical building blocks, in terms of which businesses have key value chain activities in common. For example, a company selling closely related products to business customers as well as two types of end consumers—online buyers and in-store buyers—may organize its divisions according to customer groups since the value chains involved in serving the three groups differ. Another company may organize by product line due to commonalities in product development and production within each product line. Multidivisional structures are also common among vertically integrated firms. There the major building blocks are often divisional units performing one or more of the major processing steps along the value chain (e.g., raw-material production, components manufacture, assembly, wholesale distribution, retail store operations).

Multidivisional structures offer significant advantages over functional structures in terms of facilitating the management of a complex and diverse set of operations.[19] Putting business-level strategy in the hands of division managers while leaving corporate strategy to top executives reduces the potential for information overload and improves the quality of decision making in each domain. This also minimizes the costs of coordinating division-wide activities while enhancing top management's ability to control a diverse and complex operation. Moreover, multidivisional structures can help align individual incentives with the goals of the corporation and spur productivity by encouraging competition for resources among the different divisions.

But a multidivisional structure can also present some problems to a company pursuing related diversification, because having independent business units—each running its own business in its own way—inhibits cross-business collaboration and the capture of cross-business synergies, which are critical for the success of a related diversification strategy, as Chapter 8 explains. To solve this type of problem, firms turn to more complex structures, such as the matrix structure.

4. Matrix Structure   A **matrix structure** is a combination structure in which the organization is organized along two or more dimensions at once (e.g., business, geographic area, value chain function) for the purpose of enhancing cross-unit communication, collaboration, and coordination. In essence, it overlays one type of structure onto another type. Matrix structures are managed through multiple reporting relationships, so a middle manager may report to several bosses. For instance, in a matrix structure based on product line, region, and function, a sales manager for plastic containers in Georgia might report to the manager of the plastics division, the head of the southeast sales region, and the head of marketing.

Matrix organizational structures have evolved from the complex, over-formalized structures that were popular in the late 20th century but often produced inefficient, unwieldy bureaucracies. The modern incarnation of the matrix structure is generally a more flexible arrangement, with a single primary reporting relationship that can be overlaid with a *temporary* secondary reporting relationship as need arises. For example, a software company that is organized into functional departments (software design, quality control, customer relations) may assign employees from those departments to different projects on a temporary basis, so an employee reports to a project manager as well as to his or her primary boss (the functional department head) for the duration of a project.

Matrix structures are also called *composite structures* or *combination structures.* They are often used for project-based, process-based, or team-based management. Such approaches are common in businesses involving projects of limited duration, such as consulting, architecture, and engineering services. The type of close cross-unit collaboration that a flexible matrix structure supports is also needed to build competitive capabilities in strategically important activities, such as speeding new products to market, that involve employees scattered across several organizational units.[20] Capabilities-based matrix structures that combine process departments (like new product development) with more traditional functional departments provide a solution.

An advantage of matrix structures is that they facilitate the sharing of plant and equipment, specialized knowledge, and other key resources. Thus, they lower costs by enabling the realization of economies of scope. They also have the advantage of flexibility in form and may allow for better oversight since supervision is provided from more than one perspective. A disadvantage is that they add another layer of management, thereby increasing bureaucratic costs and possibly decreasing response time to new situations.[21] In addition, there is a potential for confusion among employees due to dual reporting relationships and divided loyalties. While there is some controversy over the utility of matrix structures, the modern approach to matrix structures does much to minimize their disadvantages.[22]

Determining How Much Authority to Delegate

Under any organizational structure, there is room for considerable variation in how much authority top-level executives retain and how much is delegated to down-the-line managers and employees. In executing strategy and conducting daily operations, companies must decide how much authority to delegate to the managers of each organizational unit—especially the heads of divisions, functional departments, plants, and other operating units—and how much decision-making latitude to give individual employees in performing their jobs. The two extremes are to *centralize decision making* at the top or to *decentralize decision making* by giving managers and employees at all levels considerable decision-making latitude in their areas of responsibility. As shown in Table 10.1, the two approaches are based on sharply different underlying principles and beliefs, with each having its pros and cons.

TABLE 10.1   Advantages and Disadvantages of Centralized versus Decentralized Decision Making

Centralized Organizational Structures	Decentralized Organizational Structures
Basic tenets	**Basic tenets**
• Decisions on most matters of importance should be in the hands of top-level managers who have the experience, expertise, and judgment to decide what is the best course of action. • Lower-level personnel have neither the knowledge, time, nor inclination to properly manage the tasks they are performing. • Strong control from the top is a more effective means for coordinating company actions.	• Decision-making authority should be put in the hands of the people closest to, and most familiar with, the situation. • Those with decision-making authority should be trained to exercise good judgment. • A company that draws on the combined intellectual capital of all its employees can outperform a command-and-control company.
Chief advantages	**Chief advantages**
• Fixes accountability through tight control from the top. • Eliminates potential for conflicting goals and actions on the part of lower-level managers. • Facilitates quick decision making and strong leadership under crisis situations.	• Encourages company employees to exercise initiative and act responsibly. • Promotes greater motivation and involvement in the business on the part of more company personnel. • Spurs new ideas and creative thinking. • Allows for fast response to market change. • Entails fewer layers of management.
Primary disadvantages	**Primary disadvantages**
• Lengthens response times by those closest to the market conditions because they must seek approval for their actions. • Does not encourage responsibility among lower-level managers and rank-and-file employees. • Discourages lower-level managers and rank-and-file employees from exercising any initiative.	• May result in higher-level managers being unaware of actions taken by empowered personnel under their supervision. • Can lead to inconsistent or conflicting approaches by different managers and employees. • Can impair cross-unit collaboration.

Centralized Decision Making: Pros and Cons   In a highly centralized organizational structure, *top executives retain authority for most strategic and operating decisions* and keep a tight rein on business unit heads, department heads, and the managers of key operating units. Comparatively little discretionary authority is granted to frontline supervisors and rank-and-file employees. The command-and-control paradigm of centralized decision making is based on the underlying assumptions that frontline personnel have neither the time nor the inclination to direct and properly control the work they are performing and that they lack the knowledge and judgment to make wise decisions about how best to do it—hence the need for prescribed policies and procedures for a wide range of activities, close supervision, and tight control by top executives. The thesis underlying centralized structures is that strict enforcement of detailed procedures backed by rigorous managerial oversight is the most reliable way to keep the daily execution of strategy on track.

One advantage of a centralized structure, with tight control by the manager in charge, is that it is easy to know who is accountable when things do not go well. This structure can also reduce the potential for conflicting decisions and actions among lower-level managers who may have differing perspectives and ideas about how to tackle certain tasks or resolve particular issues. For example, a manager in charge of an engineering department may be more interested in pursuing a new technology than is a marketing manager who doubts that customers will value the technology as highly. Another advantage of a command-and-control structure is that it can facilitate strong leadership from the top in a crisis situation that affects the organization as a whole and can enable a more uniform and swift response.

But there are some serious disadvantages as well. Hierarchical command-and-control structures do not encourage responsibility and initiative on the part of lower-level managers and employees. They can make a large organization with a complex structure sluggish in responding to changing market conditions because of the time it takes for the review-and-approval process to run up all the layers of the management bureaucracy. Furthermore, to work well, centralized decision making requires top-level managers to gather and process whatever information is relevant to the decision. When the relevant knowledge resides at lower organizational levels (or is technical, detailed, or hard to express in words), it is difficult and time-consuming to get all the facts in front of a high-level executive located far from the scene of the action—full understanding of the situation cannot be readily copied from one mind to another. Hence, centralized decision making is often impractical—the larger the company and the more scattered its operations, the more that decision-making authority must be delegated to managers closer to the scene of the action.

Decentralized Decision Making: Pros and Cons

In a highly decentralized organization, *decision-making authority is pushed down to the lowest organizational level capable of making timely, informed, competent decisions.* The objective is to put adequate decision-making authority in the hands of the people closest to and most familiar with the situation and train them to weigh all the factors and exercise good judgment. At Starbucks, for example, employees are encouraged to exercise initiative in promoting customer satisfaction—there's the oft-repeated story of a store employee who, when the computerized cash register system went offline, offered free coffee to waiting customers, thereby avoiding customer displeasure and damage to Starbucks's reputation.[23]

> The ultimate goal of decentralized decision making is to put authority in the hands of those persons closest to and most knowledgeable about the situation.

The case for empowering down-the-line managers and employees to make decisions related to daily operations and strategy execution is based on the belief that a company that draws on the combined intellectual capital of all its employees can outperform a command-and-control company.[24] The challenge in a decentralized system is maintaining adequate control. With decentralized decision making, top management maintains control by placing limits on the authority granted to company personnel, installing companywide strategic control systems, holding people accountable for their decisions, instituting compensation incentives that reward people for doing their jobs well, and creating a corporate culture where there's strong peer pressure on individuals to act responsibly.[25]

Decentralized organizational structures have much to recommend them. Delegating authority to subordinate managers and rank-and-file employees encourages them to take responsibility and exercise initiative. It shortens organizational response times to market changes and spurs new ideas, creative thinking, innovation, and greater involvement on the part of all company personnel. At TJX Companies Inc., parent company of T.J.Maxx, Marshalls, and five other fashion and home decor retail store chains, buyers are encouraged to be intelligent risk takers in deciding what items to purchase for TJX stores—there's the story of a buyer for a seasonal product category who cut her own budget to have dollars allocated to other categories where sales were expected to be stronger. In worker-empowered structures, jobs can be defined more broadly, several tasks can be integrated into a single job, and people can direct their own work. Fewer managers are needed because deciding how to do things becomes part of each person's or team's job. Further, today's online communication systems and smartphones make it easy and relatively inexpensive for people at all organizational levels to have direct access to data, other employees, managers, suppliers, and customers. They can access information quickly (via the Internet or company network), readily check with superiors or whomever else as needed, and take responsible action. Typically, there are genuine gains in morale and productivity when people are provided with the tools and information they need to operate in a self-directed way.

But decentralization also has some disadvantages. Top managers lose an element of control over what goes on and may thus be unaware of actions being taken by personnel under their supervision. Such lack of control can be problematic in the event that empowered employees make decisions that conflict with those of others or that serve their unit's interests at the expense of other parts of the company. Moreover, because decentralization gives organizational units the authority to act independently, there is risk of too little collaboration and coordination between different units.

Many companies have concluded that the advantages of decentralization outweigh the disadvantages. Over the past several decades, there's been a decided shift from centralized, hierarchical structures to flatter, more decentralized structures that stress employee empowerment. This shift reflects a strong and growing consensus that authoritarian, hierarchical organizational structures are not well suited to implementing and executing strategies in an era when extensive information and instant communication are the norm and when a big fraction of the organization's most valuable assets consists of intellectual capital that resides in its employees' capabilities.

> Efforts to decentralize decision making and give company personnel some leeway in conducting operations must be tempered with the need to maintain adequate control and cross-unit coordination.

Capturing Cross-Business Strategic Fit in a Decentralized Structure

Diversified companies striving to capture the benefits of synergy between separate businesses must beware of giving business unit heads full rein to operate independently. Cross-business strategic fit typically must be captured either by enforcing close cross-business collaboration or by centralizing the performance of functions requiring close coordination at the corporate level.[26] For example, if businesses with overlapping process and product technologies have their own independent R&D departments—each pursuing its own priorities, projects, and strategic agendas—it's hard for the corporate parent to prevent duplication of effort, capture either economies of scale or economies of scope, or encourage more collaborative R&D efforts. Where cross-business strategic fit with respect to R&D is important, one solution is to centralize the R&D function and have a coordinated corporate R&D effort that serves the interests of both the individual businesses and the company as a whole. Likewise, centralizing the related activities of separate businesses makes sense when there are opportunities to share a common sales force, use common distribution channels, rely on a common field service organization, use common e-commerce systems, and so on. Another structural solution to realizing the benefits of strategic fit is to create business groups consisting of those business units with common strategic-fit opportunities.

Providing for Internal Cross-Unit Coordination

Close cross-unit collaboration is usually needed to build capabilities in such strategically important activities as speeding new products to market and providing superior customer service. This is because these activities involve collaboration among the efforts of company personnel who work in different departments or organizational units (and perhaps the employees of outside strategic partners or specialty vendors). For example, being first-to-market with new products involves coordinating the efforts of personnel in R&D (to develop a stream of new products with appealing attributes), design and engineering (to prepare a cost-efficient design and set of specifications), purchasing (to obtain the needed parts and components), manufacturing (to carry out all the production activities), and sales and marketing (to secure orders, arrange for introductory advertising and the distribution of product information, and get the products on retailers' shelves). Achieving the simple strategic objective of filling customer orders accurately and promptly involves personnel from sales (to win the order); finance (to check credit terms or approve special financing); production (to produce the goods and replenish warehouse inventories as needed); and warehousing and shipping (to verify whether the items are in stock, pick the order from the warehouse, package it for shipping, and choose the best carrier to deliver the goods).

To achieve tight coordination when pieces of execution-critical tasks are performed in multiple organizational units, company executives typically emphasize the necessity of cross-unit teamwork and cooperation and the importance of frequent back-and-forth communication among key people in the various related organizational units to resolve problems, avoid delays, and keep things moving along. The executives supervising the units performing parts of the execution-critical task typically make it clear that the relevant department heads and key personnel are all *expected to work closely together and coordinate their actions.* There are meetings to discuss schedules and set deadlines, often ending with the verbal commitments of everyone involved to stick close to the agreed-upon schedule, coordinate their activities, and meet the established deadlines. Gaining such commitments is almost always imperative, along with ensuring that everyone lives up to their commitments.

Normally, the supervising executives follow up, check on progress, and, in many cases, visit the different units to personally determine how well things are going and solicit the views of numerous people about what problems exist and what they think should be done to resolve them. They seldom hesitate to intervene to make corrective adjustments and to reiterate their expectations of teamwork, close communication, effective collaboration, and cooperation to resolve issues, avoid delays, and achieve the needed degree of cross-unit coordination. Such executive interventions, together with added executive pressure on the managers of units where close collaboration and coordinated action is lacking, may suffice. If it does, then all is well and good. But if such efforts fail, execution suffers and it becomes the responsibility of executives to determine the causes and take corrective action.

In many instances, the chief cause of ineffective cross-unit coordination in building capabilities rests with departmental-level managers and other key operating personnel who, for assorted reasons, don't or won't spend the time and effort needed to partner with other organizational units in the capability-building process. But it also has to be recognized that top-executive urging that departmental managers and their staff *voluntarily* place high priority on coordinating their respective activities *poses significant challenges* in achieving effective cross-unit coordination. This is especially true in decentralized organizational structures where department heads are delegated a high degree of decision-making authority in running their respective units and, thus, have a natural tendency to place a lower priority on cooperating closely with other organizational units than on ensuring that the activities under their direct supervision are done well. The weakness of heavily depending on the largely voluntary efforts of personnel for the development of critical cross-unit capabilities has prompted many companies to supplement such efforts by forming cross-functional committees, project management teams, and centralized project management offices to forge better cross-unit working relationships and improve coordination across multiple organizational units. While these arrangements have proved helpful in a number of organizations, more effective solutions involve creating incentive compensation systems where the payouts are tied to effective group performance of cross-unit tasks.

Facilitating Collaboration with External Partners and Strategic Allies

> Getting managers of execution-critical activities to live up to their commitments to coordinate closely with sister organizational unit is a *key* factor in achieving good internal cross-unit coordination.

Organizational mechanisms—whether formal or informal—are also required to ensure effective working relationships with each major outside constituency involved in strategy execution. Strategic alliances, outsourcing arrangements, joint ventures, and cooperative partnerships can contribute little of value without active management of the relationship. Unless top management sees that constructive organizational bridge building with external partners occurs and that productive working relationships emerge, the potential value of cooperative relationships is lost and the company's power to execute its strategy is weakened. For example, if close working relationships with suppliers are crucial, then supply chain management must enter into considerations of how to create an effective organizational structure. If distributor, dealer, or franchisee relationships are important, then someone must be assigned the task of nurturing the relationships with such forward-channel allies.

Building organizational bridges with external partners and strategic allies can be accomplished by appointing "relationship managers" with responsibility for making particular strategic partnerships generate the intended benefits. Relationship managers have many roles and functions: getting the right people together, promoting good rapport, facilitating the flow of information, nurturing interpersonal communication and cooperation, and ensuring effective coordination.[27] Multiple cross-organization ties have to be established and kept open to ensure proper communication and coordination. There has to be enough information sharing to make the relationship work and periodic frank discussions of conflicts, trouble spots, and changing situations.

> A **network structure** is a configuration composed of a number of independent organizations engaged in some common undertaking, with one firm typically taking on a more central role.

Organizing and managing a network structure provides a mechanism for encouraging more effective collaboration and cooperation among external partners. A **network structure** is the arrangement linking a number of independent organizations involved in some common undertaking. A well-managed network structure typically includes one firm in a more central role, with the responsibility of ensuring that the right partners are included and the activities across the network are coordinated. The high-end Italian motorcycle company Ducati operates in this manner, assembling its motorcycles from parts obtained from a handpicked integrated network of parts suppliers.

Further Perspectives on Structuring the Work Effort

All organizational designs have their strategy-related strengths and weaknesses. To do a good job of matching structure to strategy, strategy implementers first have to pick a basic organizational design and modify it as needed to fit the company's particular business lineup. They must then (1) supplement the design with appropriate coordinating mechanisms (cross-functional task forces, special project teams, self-contained work teams, etc.) and (2) institute whatever networking and communications arrangements are necessary to support effective execution of the firm's strategy. Some companies may avoid setting up "ideal" organizational arrangements because they do not want to disturb existing reporting relationships or because they need to accommodate other situational idiosyncrasies, yet they must still work toward the goal of building a competitively capable organization.

What can be said unequivocally is that building a capable organization entails a process of consciously knitting together the efforts of individuals and groups. Organizational capabilities emerge from establishing and nurturing cooperative working relationships among people and groups to perform activities in a more efficient, value-creating fashion. While an appropriate organizational structure can facilitate this, organization building is a task in which senior management must be deeply involved. Indeed, effectively managing both internal organizational processes and external collaboration to create and develop competitively valuable organizational capabilities remains a top challenge for senior executives in today's companies.

KEY POINTS

1. Executing strategy is an action-oriented, operations-driven activity revolving around the management of people, business processes, and organizational structure. In devising an action agenda for executing strategy, managers should start by conducting a probing assessment of what the organization must do to carry out the strategy successfully. They should then consider precisely *how* to go about this.

2. Good strategy execution requires a *team effort*. All managers have strategy-executing responsibility in their areas of authority, and all employees are active participants in the strategy execution process.

3. Ten managerial tasks are part of every company effort to execute strategy: (1) staffing the organization with the right people, (2) developing and augmenting the necessary resources and organizational capabilities, (3) creating a supportive organizational structure, (4) allocating sufficient resources (budgetary and otherwise), (5) instituting supportive policies and procedures, (6) adopting processes for continuous improvement, (7) installing systems that enable proficient company operations, (8) tying incentives to the achievement of desired targets, (9) instilling the right corporate culture, and (10) exercising the leadership needed to propel strategy execution forward.

4. The two best signs of good strategy execution are that a company is meeting or beating its performance targets and is performing value chain activities in a manner that is conducive to companywide operating excellence. *Shortfalls in performance signal weak strategy, weak execution, or both.*

5. Building an organization capable of good strategy execution entails three types of actions: (1) *staffing the organization*—assembling a talented management team and recruiting and retaining employees with the needed experience, technical skills, and intellectual capital; (2) *acquiring, developing, and strengthening strategy-supportive resources and capabilities*—accumulating the required resources, developing proficiencies in performing strategy-critical value chain activities, and updating the company's capabilities to match changing market conditions and customer expectations; and (3) *structuring the organization and work effort*—instituting organizational arrangements that facilitate good strategy execution, deciding how much decision-making authority to delegate, facilitating cross-unit coordination, and managing external relationships.

6. Building competitive capabilities is a time-consuming, managerially challenging exercise that can be approached in three ways: (1) developing capabilities internally, (2) acquiring capabilities through mergers and acquisitions, and (3) accessing capabilities via collaborative partnerships.

7. In building capabilities internally, the first step is to develop the *ability* to do something, through experimenting, actively searching for alternative solutions, and learning by trial and error. As experience grows and company personnel learn how to perform the activities consistently well and at an acceptable cost, the ability evolves into a tried-and-true capability. The process can be accelerated by making learning a more deliberate endeavor and providing the incentives that will motivate company personnel to achieve the desired ends.

8. As firms get better at executing their strategies, they develop capabilities in the domain of strategy execution. Superior strategy execution capabilities allow companies to get the most from their resources and capabilities. But excellence in strategy execution can also be a more direct source of competitive advantage, since more efficient and effective strategy execution can lower costs and permit firms to deliver more value to customers. Because they are socially complex capabilities, superior strategy execution capabilities are hard to imitate and have no good substitutes. As such, they can be an important source of *sustainable* competitive advantage. Anytime rivals can readily duplicate successful strategies, making it impossible to *out-strategize* rivals, the chief way to achieve lasting competitive advantage is to *out-execute* them.

9. Structuring the organization and organizing the work effort in a strategy-supportive fashion has five aspects: (1) deciding which value chain activities to perform internally and which ones to outsource; (2) aligning the firm's organizational structure with its strategy; (3) deciding how much authority to centralize at the top and how much to delegate to down-the-line managers and employees; (4) providing for the internal cross-unit coordination needed to build and strengthen capabilities; and (5) facilitating the necessary collaboration and coordination with external partners and strategic allies.

10. To align the firm's organizational structure with its strategy, it is important to make strategy-critical activities the main building blocks. There are four basic types of organizational structures: the simple structure, the functional structure, the multidivisional structure, and the matrix structure. Which is most appropriate depends on the firm's size, complexity, and strategy.

ASSURANCE OF LEARNING EXERCISES

LO 10-1

1. The heart of Zara's strategy in the apparel industry is to outcompete rivals by putting fashionable clothes in stores quickly and maximizing the frequency of customer visits. Illustration Capsule 10.2 discusses the capabilities that the company has developed in the execution of its strategy. How do its capabilities lead to a quick production process and new apparel introductions? How do these capabilities encourage customers to visit its stores every few weeks? Does the execution of the company's site selection capability also contribute to its competitive advantage? Explain.

LO 10-2

2. Search online to read about Jeff Bezos's management of his new executives. Specifically, explore **Amazon.com's** "S-Team" meetings (**management.fortune .cnn.com/2012/11/16/jeff-bezos-amazon/**). Why does Bezos begin meetings of

senior executives with 30 minutes of silent reading? How does this focus the group? Why does Bezos insist new ideas must be written and presented in memo form? How does this reflect the founder's insistence on clear, concise, and innovative thinking in his company? And does this exercise work as a de facto crash course for new Amazon executives? Explain why this small but crucial management strategy reflects Bezos's overriding goal of cohesive and clear idea presentation.

3. Review Facebook's Careers page (**www.Facebook.com/careers/**). The page emphasizes Facebook's core values and explains how potential employees could fit that mold. Bold and decisive thinking and a commitment to transparency and social connectivity drive the page and the company as a whole. Then research Facebook's internal management training programs, called "employee boot camps," using a search engine like Google or Bing. How do these programs integrate the traits and stated goals on the Careers page into specific and tangible construction of employee capabilities? Boot camps are open to all Facebook employees, not just engineers. How does this internal training prepare Facebook employees of all types to "move fast and break things"?   **LO 10-2, 10-3**

4. Review Valve Corporation's company handbook online: **www.valvesoftware.com/company/Valve_Handbook_LowRes.pdf.** Specifically, focus on Valve's corporate structure. Valve has hundreds of employees but no managers or bosses at all. Valve's gaming success hinges on innovative and completely original experiences like Portal and Half-Life. Does it seem that Valve's corporate structure uniquely promotes this type of gaming innovation? Why or why not? How would you characterize Valve's organizational structure? Is it completely unique, or could it be characterized as a multidivisional, matrix, or functional structure? Explain your answer.   **LO 10-4**

5. Johnson & Johnson, a multinational health care company responsible for manufacturing medical, pharmaceutical, and consumer goods, has been a leader in promoting a decentralized management structure. Perform an Internet search to gain some background information on the company's products, value chain activities, and leadership. How does Johnson & Johnson exemplify (or not exemplify) a decentralized management strategy? Describe the advantages and disadvantages of a decentralized system of management in the case of Johnson & Johnson. Why was it established in the first place? Has it been an effective means of decision making for the company?   **LO 10-5**

EXERCISES FOR SIMULATION PARTICIPANTS

1. How would you describe the organization of your company's top-management team? Is some decision making decentralized and delegated to individual managers? If so, explain how the decentralization works. Or are decisions made more by consensus, with all co-managers having input? What do you see as the advantages and disadvantages of the decision-making approach your company is employing?   **LO 10-5**

2. What specific actions have you and your co-managers taken to develop core competencies or competitive capabilities that can contribute to good strategy execution and potential competitive advantage? If no actions have been taken, explain your rationale for doing nothing.   **LO 10-3**

3. What value chain activities are most crucial to good execution of your company's strategy? Does your company have the ability to outsource any value chain activities? If so, have you and your co-managers opted to engage in outsourcing? Why or why not?   **LO 10-1**

ENDNOTES

[1] Donald Sull, Rebecca Homkes, and Charles Sull, "Why Strategy Execution Unravels—and What to Do About It," *Harvard Business Review* 93, no. 3 (March 2015), p. 60.

[2] Steven W. Floyd and Bill Wooldridge, "Managing Strategic Consensus: The Foundation of Effective Implementation," *Academy of Management Executive* 6, no. 4 (November 1992), p. 27.

[3] Jack Welch with Suzy Welch, *Winning* (New York: HarperBusiness, 2005).

[4] Larry Bossidy and Ram Charan, *Execution: The Discipline of Getting Things Done* (New York: Crown Business, 2002).

[5] Christopher A. Bartlett and Sumantra Ghoshal, "Building Competitive Advantage through People," *MIT Sloan Management Review* 43, no. 2 (Winter 2002), pp. 34–41.

[6] Justin Menkes, "Hiring for Smarts," *Harvard Business Review* 83, no. 11 (November 2005), pp. 100–109; Justin Menkes, *Executive Intelligence* (New York: HarperCollins, 2005).

[7] Menkes, *Executive Intelligence,* pp. 68, 76.

[8] Jim Collins, *Good to Great* (New York: HarperBusiness, 2001).

[9] John Byrne, "The Search for the Young and Gifted," *Businessweek,* October 4, 1999, p. 108.

[10] C. Helfat and M. Peteraf, "The Dynamic Resource-Based View: Capability Lifecycles," *Strategic Management Journal* 24, no. 10 (October 2003), pp. 997–1010.

[11] G. Dosi, R. Nelson, and S. Winter (eds.), *The Nature and Dynamics of Organizational Capabilities* (Oxford, England: Oxford University Press, 2001).

[12] S. Winter, "The Satisficing Principle in Capability Learning," *Strategic Management Journal* 21, no. 10–11 (October–November 2000), pp. 981–996; M. Zollo and S. Winter, "Deliberate Learning and the Evolution of Dynamic Capabilities," *Organization Science* 13, no. 3 (May–June 2002), pp. 339–351.

[13] Robert H. Hayes, Gary P. Pisano, and David M. Upton, *Strategic Operations: Competing through Capabilities* (New York: Free Press, 1996); Jonas Ridderstrale, "Cashing In on Corporate Competencies," *Business Strategy Review* 14, no. 1 (Spring 2003), pp. 27–38; Danny Miller, Russell Eisenstat, and Nathaniel Foote, "Strategy from the Inside Out: Building Capability-Creating Organizations," *California Management Review* 44, no. 3 (Spring 2002), pp. 37–55.

[14] S. Karim and W. Mitchell, "Path-Dependent and Path-Breaking Change: Reconfiguring Business Resources Following Acquisitions in the US Medical Sector, 1978–1995," *Strategic Management Journal* 21, no. 10–11 (October–November 2000), pp. 1061–1082; L. Capron, P. Dussauge, and W. Mitchell, "Resource Redeployment Following Horizontal Acquisitions in Europe and North America, 1988–1992," *Strategic Management Journal* 19, no. 7 (July 1998), pp. 631–662.

[15] Gary P. Pisano and Willy C. Shih, "Restoring American Competitiveness," *Harvard Business Review* 87, no. 7–8 (July–August 2009), pp. 114–125.

[16] A. Chandler, *Strategy and Structure* (Cambridge, MA: MIT Press, 1962).

[17] E. Olsen, S. Slater, and G. Hult, "The Importance of Structure and Process to Strategy Implementation," *Business Horizons* 48, no. 1 (2005), pp. 47–54; H. Barkema, J. Baum, and E. Mannix, "Management Challenges in a New Time," *Academy of Management Journal* 45, no. 5 (October 2002), pp. 916–930.

[18] H. Mintzberg, *The Structuring of Organizations* (Englewood Cliffs, NJ: Prentice Hall, 1979); C. Levicki, *The Interactive Strategy Workout,* 2nd ed. (London: Prentice Hall, 1999).

[19] O. Williamson, *Market and Hierarchies* (New York: Free Press, 1975); R. M. Burton and B. Obel, "A Computer Simulation Test of the M-Form Hypothesis," *Administrative Science Quarterly* 25 (1980), pp. 457–476.

[20] J. Baum and S. Wally, "Strategic Decision Speed and Firm Performance," *Strategic Management Journal* 24 (2003), pp. 1107–1129.

[21] C. Bartlett and S. Ghoshal, "Matrix Management: Not a Structure, a Frame of Mind," *Harvard Business Review,* July–August 1990, pp. 138–145.

[22] M. Goold and A. Campbell, "Structured Networks: Towards the Well Designed Matrix," *Long Range Planning* 36, no. 5 (2003), pp. 427–439.

[23] Iain Somerville and John Edward Mroz, "New Competencies for a New World," in Frances Hesselbein, Marshall Goldsmith, and Richard Beckard (eds.), *The Organization of the Future* (San Francisco: Jossey-Bass, 1997), p. 70.

[24] Stanley E. Fawcett, Gary K. Rhoads, and Phillip Burnah, "People as the Bridge to Competitiveness: Benchmarking the 'ABCs' of an Empowered Workforce," *Benchmarking: An International Journal* 11, no. 4 (2004), pp. 346–360.

[25] Robert Simons, "Control in an Age of Empowerment," *Harvard Business Review* 73 (March–April 1995), pp. 80–88.

[26] Jeanne M. Liedtka, "Collaboration across Lines of Business for Competitive Advantage," *Academy of Management Executive* 10, no. 2 (May 1996), pp. 20–34.

[27] Rosabeth Moss Kanter, "Collaborative Advantage: The Art of the Alliance," *Harvard Business Review* 72, no. 4 (July–August 1994), pp. 96–108.

chapter 11

Managing Internal Operations

Actions That Promote Good Strategy Execution

Learning Objectives

After reading this chapter, you should be able to:

LO 11-1 Explain why resource allocation should always be based on strategic priorities.

LO 11-2 Comprehend how well-designed policies and procedures can facilitate good strategy execution.

LO 11-3 Understand how process management tools drive continuous improvement in the performance of value chain activities.

LO 11-4 Recognize the role of information systems and operating systems in enabling company personnel to carry out their strategic roles proficiently.

LO 11-5 Explain how and why the use of well-designed incentives can be management's single most powerful tool for promoting adept strategy execution.

Matt Herring/Ikon Images/Media Bakery

Processes underpin business capabilities, and capabilities underpin strategy execution.

Pearl Zhu

Pay your people the least possible and you'll get the same from them.

Malcolm Forbes—late Publisher of *Forbes Magazine*

Apple is a very disciplined company, and we have great processes. But that's not what it's about. Process makes you more efficient.

Steve Jobs—*Cofounder of Apple, Inc.*

In Chapter 10, we emphasized that proficient strategy execution begins with three types of managerial actions: staffing the organization with the right people; acquiring, developing, and strengthening the firm's resources and capabilities; and structuring the organization in a manner supportive of the strategy execution effort.

In this chapter, we discuss five additional managerial actions that advance the cause of good strategy execution:

- Allocating ample resources to the strategy execution effort.

- Instituting policies and procedures that facilitate good strategy execution.
- Employing process management tools to drive continuous improvement in how value chain activities are performed.
- Installing information and operating systems that support strategy implementation activities.
- Tying rewards and incentives to the achievement of performance objectives.

ALLOCATING RESOURCES TO THE STRATEGY EXECUTION EFFORT

● ● ● ●

● LO 11-1

Explain why resource allocation should always be based on strategic priorities.

Early in the strategy implementation process, managers must determine what resources (in terms of funding, people, and so on) will be required and how they should be distributed across the company's various organizational units. This includes carefully screening requests for more people and new facilities and equipment, approving those that will contribute to the strategy execution effort, and turning down those that don't. Should internal cash flows prove insufficient to fund the planned strategic initiatives, then management must raise additional funds through borrowing or selling additional shares of stock to investors.

A company's strategic priorities must drive how capital allocations are made and the size of each unit's operating budgets.

A company's ability to marshal the resources needed to support new strategic initiatives has a major impact on the strategy execution process. Too little funding and an insufficiency of other types of resources slow progress and impede the efforts of organizational units to execute their pieces of the strategic plan competently. Too much funding of particular organizational units and value chain activities wastes organizational resources and reduces financial performance. Both of these scenarios argue for managers to become deeply involved in reviewing budget proposals and directing the proper kinds and amounts of resources to strategy-critical organizational units.

A change in strategy nearly always calls for budget reallocations and resource shifting. Previously important units with a lesser role in the new strategy may need downsizing. Units that now have a bigger strategic role may need more people, new equipment, additional facilities, and above-average increases in their operating budgets. Implementing new strategy initiatives requires managers to take an active and sometimes forceful role in shifting resources, not only to better support activities now having a higher priority but also to capture opportunities to operate more cost-effectively. This requires putting enough resources behind new strategic initiatives to fuel their success and making the tough decisions to kill projects and activities that are no longer justified.

Visible actions to reallocate operating funds and move people into new organizational units signal a determined commitment to strategic change. Such actions can catalyze the implementation process and give it credibility. Microsoft has made a practice of regularly shifting hundreds of programmers to new high-priority programming initiatives within a matter of weeks or even days. Fast-moving developments in many markets are prompting companies to abandon traditional annual budgeting and resource allocation cycles in favor of resource allocation processes supportive of more rapid adjustments in strategy. In response to rapid technological change in the communications industry, AT&T has prioritized investments and acquisitions that have allowed it to offer its enterprise customers faster, more flexible networks and provide innovative new customer services, such as its Sponsored Data plan.

Merely fine-tuning the execution of a company's existing strategy seldom requires big shifts of resources from one area to another. In contrast, new strategic initiatives generally require not only big shifts in resources but a larger allocation of resources to the effort as well. However, there are times when strategy changes or new execution initiatives need to be made without adding to total company expenses. In such circumstances, managers have to work their way through the existing budget line by line and activity by activity, looking for ways to trim costs and shift resources to activities that are higher-priority in the strategy execution effort. In the event that a company needs to make significant cost cuts during the course of launching new strategic initiatives, managers must be especially creative in finding ways to do more with less. Indeed, it is common for strategy changes and the drive for good strategy execution to be aimed at achieving considerably higher levels of operating efficiency and, at the same time, making sure the most important value chain activities are performed as effectively as possible.

INSTITUTING POLICIES AND PROCEDURES THAT FACILITATE STRATEGY EXECUTION

A company's policies and procedures can either support or hinder good strategy execution. Anytime a company moves to put new strategy elements in place or improve its strategy execution capabilities, some changes in work practices are usually needed. Managers are thus well advised to carefully consider whether existing policies and procedures fully support such changes and to revise or discard those that do not.

> ● **LO 11-2**
>
> Comprehend how well-designed policies and procedures can facilitate good strategy execution.

As shown in Figure 11.1, well-conceived policies and operating procedures facilitate strategy execution in two significant ways:

1. *By providing top-down guidance regarding how things need to be done.* Policies and procedures provide company personnel with a set of guidelines for how to perform organizational activities, conduct various aspects of operations, solve problems as they arise, and accomplish particular tasks. They clarify uncertainty about how to proceed in executing strategy and align the actions and behavior of company personnel with the requirements for good strategy execution. Moreover, they place limits on ineffective independent action. When they are well matched with the requirements of the strategy implementation plan, they channel the efforts of individuals along a path that supports the plan. When existing ways of doing things pose a barrier to strategy execution initiatives, actions and behaviors have to be changed. Under these conditions, the managerial role is to establish and enforce new policies and operating practices that are more conducive to executing the strategy appropriately. Policies are a particularly useful way to counteract tendencies for some people to resist change. People generally refrain from violating company policy or going against recommended practices and procedures without gaining clearance or having strong justification.

2. *By helping ensure consistency in how execution-critical activities are performed.* Policies and procedures serve to standardize the way that activities are performed. In essence, they represent a store of organizational or managerial knowledge about efficient and effective ways of doing things—a set of well-honed routines for running the company. This can be important for ensuring the quality and reliability of the strategy execution process. It helps align and coordinate the strategy execution efforts of individuals and groups throughout the organization—a feature that is particularly beneficial when there are geographically scattered operating units. For example, eliminating significant differences in the operating practices of different plants, sales regions, or customer service centers

> A company's policies and procedures provide a set of well-honed routines for running the company and executing the strategy.

FIGURE 11.1   How Policies and Procedures Facilitate Good Strategy Execution

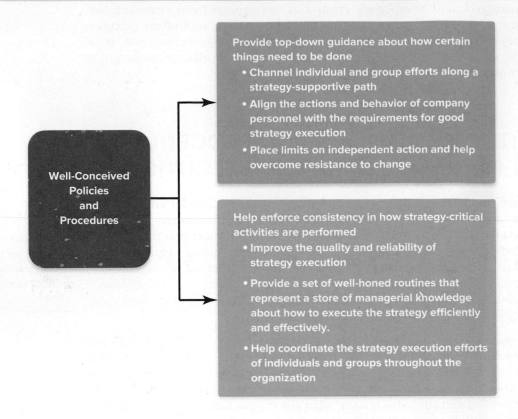

Well-Conceived Policies and Procedures

Provide top-down guidance about how certain things need to be done
- Channel individual and group efforts along a strategy-supportive path
- Align the actions and behavior of company personnel with the requirements for good strategy execution
- Place limits on independent action and help overcome resistance to change

Help enforce consistency in how strategy-critical activities are performed
- Improve the quality and reliability of strategy execution
- Provide a set of well-honed routines that represent a store of managerial knowledge about how to execute the strategy efficiently and effectively.
- Help coordinate the strategy execution efforts of individuals and groups throughout the organization

or in the individual outlets in a chain operation helps a company deliver consistent product quality and service to customers. Good strategy execution nearly always entails an ability to replicate product quality and the caliber of customer service at every location where the company does business—anything less blurs the company's image and lowers customer satisfaction.

3. *By promoting the creation of a work climate that facilitates good strategy execution.* A company's policies and procedures help set the tone of a company's work climate and contribute to a common understanding of "how we do things around here." Because abandoning old policies and procedures in favor of new ones invariably alters the internal work climate, managers can use the policy-changing process as a powerful lever for changing the corporate culture in ways that better support new strategic initiatives. The trick here, obviously, is to come up with new policies or procedures that catch the immediate attention of company personnel and prompt them to quickly shift their actions and behaviors in the desired ways.

To ensure consistency in product quality and service behavior patterns, McDonald's policy manual spells out detailed procedures that personnel in each McDonald's unit are expected to observe. For example, "Cooks must turn, never flip, hamburgers. If they haven't been purchased, Big Macs must be discarded in 10 minutes after being cooked and French fries in 7 minutes. Cashiers must make eye contact with and smile at every customer." Retail chain stores and other organizational chains (e.g., hotels, hospitals, child care centers) similarly rely on detailed policies and procedures to ensure consistency in their operations and reliable service to their customers. Video game developer Valve Corporation prides itself on a lack of rigid policies and procedures; its 37-page handbook for new employees details how things get done in such an environment—an ironic tribute to the fact that all types of companies need policies.

One of the big policy-making issues concerns what activities need to be strictly prescribed and what activities ought to allow room for independent action on the part of personnel. Few companies need thick policy manuals to prescribe exactly how daily operations are to be conducted. Too much policy can be as obstructive as wrong policy and as confusing as no policy. There is wisdom in a middle approach: *Prescribe enough policies to give organization members clear direction and to place reasonable boundaries on their actions; then empower them to act within these boundaries in pursuit of company goals.* Allowing company personnel to act with some degree of freedom is especially appropriate when individual creativity and initiative are more essential to good strategy execution than are standardization and strict conformity. Instituting policies that facilitate strategy execution can therefore mean policies more policies, fewer policies, or different policies. It can mean policies that require things be done according to a precisely defined standard or policies that give employees substantial leeway to do activities the way they think best.

> There is wisdom in a middle-ground approach: Prescribe enough policies to give organization members clear direction and to place reasonable boundaries on their actions; then empower them to act within these boundaries in pursuit of company goals.

EMPLOYING BUSINESS PROCESS MANAGEMENT TOOLS

Company managers can significantly advance the cause of competent strategy execution by using business process management tools to drive continuous improvement in how internal operations are conducted. Process management tools are used to model, control, measure, and optimize a variety of organizational activities that may span departments, functions, value chain systems, employees, customers, suppliers, and other partners in support of company goals. They also provide corrective feedback, allowing managers to change and improve company operations in an ongoing manner.

LO 11-3

Understand how process management tools drive continuous improvement in the performance of value chain activities.

Promoting Operating Excellence: Three Powerful Business Process Management Tools

Three of the most powerful management tools for promoting operating excellence and better strategy execution are business process reengineering, total quality management (TQM) programs, and Six Sigma quality control programs. Each of these merits discussion since many companies around the world use these tools to help execute strategies tied to cost reduction, defect-free manufacture, superior product quality, superior customer service, and total customer satisfaction.

Business Process Reengineering   Companies searching for ways to improve their operations have sometimes discovered that the execution of strategy-critical activities is hampered by a disconnected organizational arrangement whereby pieces of an activity are performed in several different functional departments, with no one manager or group being accountable for optimal performance of the entire activity. This can easily occur in such inherently cross-functional activities as customer service (which can involve personnel in order filling, warehousing and shipping, invoicing, accounts receivable, after-sale repair, and technical support), particularly for companies with a functional organizational structure.

To address the suboptimal performance problems that can arise from this type of situation, a company can *reengineer the work effort,* pulling the pieces of an activity out of different departments and creating a cross-functional work group or single department (often called a *process department*) to take charge of the whole process. The use of cross-functional teams has been popularized by the practice of **business process reengineering,** which involves radically redesigning and streamlining the workflow (typically enabled by cutting-edge use of online technology and information systems), with the goal of achieving quantum gains in performance of the activity.[1]

The reengineering of value chain activities has been undertaken at many companies in many industries all over the world, with excellent results being achieved at some firms.[2] Hallmark reengineered its process for developing new greeting cards, creating teams of mixed-occupation personnel (artists, writers, lithographers, merchandisers, and administrators) to work on a single holiday or greeting card theme. The reengineered process speeded development times for new lines of greeting cards by up to 24 months, reduced costs, and increased customer satisfaction.[3] In the order-processing section of General Electric's circuit breaker division, elapsed time from order receipt to delivery was cut from three weeks to three days by consolidating six production units into one, reducing a variety of former inventory and handling steps, automating the design system to replace a human custom-design process, and cutting the organizational layers between managers and workers from three to one. Productivity rose 20 percent in one year, and unit manufacturing costs dropped 30 percent. In the health care industry, business process reengineering is being used to lower health care costs and improve patient outcomes in a variety of ways. South Africa is attempting to reengineer its primary health care system, which is in need of significant reform. Similar initiatives are ongoing in India. In the United States, exemplary health care providers, such as Mayo Clinic, are using reengineering tools on a continuous basis to achieve outcomes such as fewer hospitalizations, improved patient–physician interactions, and the delivery of lower cost health care.

While business process reengineering has been criticized as an excuse for downsizing, it has nonetheless proved itself a useful tool for streamlining a company's work effort and moving closer to operational excellence. It has also inspired more technologically based approaches to integrating and streamlining business processes, such as *enterprise resource planning,* a software-based system implemented with the help of consulting companies such as SAP (the leading provider of business software).

Total Quality Management Programs   **Total quality management (TQM)** is a management approach that emphasizes continuous improvement in all phases of operations, 100 percent accuracy in performing tasks, involvement and empowerment of employees at all levels, team-based work design, benchmarking, and total customer satisfaction.[4] While TQM concentrates on producing quality goods and fully satisfying customer expectations, it achieves its biggest successes when it is extended to employee efforts in *all departments*—human resources, billing, accounting, and information systems—that may lack pressing, customer-driven incentives to improve. It involves reforming the corporate culture and shifting to a continuous-improvement business philosophy that permeates every facet of the organization.[5] TQM aims at instilling enthusiasm and commitment to doing things right from the top to the bottom of the organization. Management's job is to kindle an organizationwide search for ways to improve that involves all company personnel exercising initiative and using their ingenuity. TQM doctrine preaches that there's no such thing as "good enough" and that everyone has a responsibility to participate in continuous improvement. TQM is thus a race without a finish. Success comes from making little steps forward each day, a process that the Japanese call *kaizen*.

TQM takes a fairly long time to show significant results—very little benefit emerges within the first six months. The long-term payoff of TQM, if it comes, depends heavily on management's success in implanting a culture within which the TQM philosophy and practices can thrive. But it is a management tool that has attracted numerous users and advocates over several decades, and it can deliver good results when used properly.

Six Sigma Quality Control Programs **Six Sigma programs** offer another way to drive continuous improvement in quality and strategy execution. This approach entails the use of advanced statistical methods to identify and remove the causes of defects (errors) and undesirable variability in performing an activity or business process. When performance of an activity or process reaches "Six Sigma quality," there are *no more than 3.4 defects per million iterations* (equal to 99.9997 percent accuracy).[6]

> **CORE CONCEPT**
>
> **Six Sigma programs** utilize advanced statistical methods to improve quality by reducing defects and variability in the performance of business processes.

There are two important types of Six Sigma programs. The Six Sigma process of define, measure, analyze, improve, and control (DMAIC, pronounced "de-may-ic") is an improvement system for existing processes falling below specification and needing incremental improvement. The Six Sigma process of define, measure, analyze, design, and verify (DMADV, pronounced "de-mad-vee") is used to develop *new* processes or products at Six Sigma quality levels. DMADV is sometimes referred to as Design for Six Sigma, or DFSS. Both Six Sigma programs are overseen by personnel who have completed Six Sigma "master black belt" training, and they are executed by personnel who have earned Six Sigma "green belts" and Six Sigma "black belts." According to the Six Sigma Academy, personnel with black belts can save companies approximately $230,000 per project and can complete four to six projects a year.[7]

The statistical thinking underlying Six Sigma is based on the following three principles: (1) All work is a process, (2) all processes have variability, and (3) all processes create data that explain variability.[8] Six Sigma's DMAIC process is a particularly good vehicle for improving performance when there are *wide variations* in how well an activity is performed. For instance, airlines striving to improve the on-time performance of their flights have more to gain from actions to curtail the number of flights that are late by more than 30 minutes than from actions to reduce the number of flights that are late by less than five minutes. Six Sigma quality control programs are of particular interest for large companies, which are better able to shoulder the cost of the large investment required in employee training, organizational infrastructure, and consulting services. For example, to realize a cost savings of $4.4 billion from rolling out its Six Sigma program, GE had to invest $1.6 billion and suffer losses from the program during its first year.[9]

Since the programs were first introduced, thousands of companies and nonprofit organizations around the world have used Six Sigma to promote operating excellence. For companies at the forefront of this movement, such as Motorola, General Electric (GE), Ford, and Honeywell (Allied Signal), the cost savings as a percentage of revenue varied from 1.2 to 4.5 percent, according to data analysis conducted by iSixSigma (an organization that provides free articles, tools, and resources concerning Six Sigma). More recently, there has been a resurgence of interest in Six Sigma practices, with companies such as Siemens, Coca-Cola, Ocean Spray, GEICO, and Merrill Lynch turning to Six Sigma as a vehicle to improve their bottom lines. In the first five years of its adoption, Six Sigma at Bank of America helped the bank reap about $2 billion in revenue gains and cost savings; the bank holds an annual "Best of Six Sigma Expo" to celebrate the teams and the projects with the greatest contribution to the company's bottom line. GE, one of the most successful companies implementing Six Sigma training and pursuing Six Sigma perfection across the company's entire operations, estimated benefits of some $10 billion during the first five years of implementation—its Lighting division, for example, cut invoice defects and disputes by 98 percent.[10]

Six Sigma has also been used to improve processes in health care. Froedtert Hospital in Milwaukee, Wisconsin, used Six Sigma to improve the accuracy of administering the proper drug doses to patients. DMAIC analysis of the three-stage process by which prescriptions were written by doctors, filled by the hospital pharmacy, and then administered to patients by nurses revealed that most mistakes came from misreading the doctors' handwriting. The hospital implemented a program requiring doctors to enter the prescription on the hospital's computers, which slashed the number of errors dramatically. In recent years, Pfizer embarked on 85 Six Sigma projects to streamline its R&D process and lower the cost of delivering medicines to patients in its pharmaceutical sciences division.

Illustration Capsule 11.1 describes Charleston Area Medical Center's use of Six Sigma as a health care provider coping with the current challenges facing this industry.

Despite its potential benefits, Six Sigma is not without its problems. There is evidence, for example, that Six Sigma techniques can stifle innovation and creativity. The essence of Six Sigma is to reduce variability in processes, but creative processes, by nature, include quite a bit of variability. In many instances, breakthrough innovations occur only after thousands of ideas have been abandoned and promising ideas have gone through multiple iterations and extensive prototyping. Alphabet Executive Chairman of the Board Eric Schmidt has declared that applying Six Sigma measurement and control principles to creative activities at Google would choke off innovation altogether.[11]

CORE CONCEPT

Ambidextrous organizations are adept at employing continuous improvement in operating processes while allowing R&D and other areas engaged in development of new ideas freer rein.

A blended approach to Six Sigma implementation that is gaining in popularity pursues incremental improvements in operating efficiency, while R&D and other processes that allow the company to develop new ways of offering value to customers are given freer rein. Managers of these **ambidextrous organizations** are adept at employing continuous improvement in operating processes but allowing R&D to operate under a set of rules that allows for exploration and the development of breakthrough innovations. However, the two distinctly different approaches to managing employees must be carried out by tightly integrated senior managers to ensure that the separate and diversely oriented units operate with a common purpose. Ciba Vision, now part of eye care multinational Alcon, dramatically reduced operating expenses through the use of continuous-improvement programs, while simultaneously and harmoniously developing a new series of contact lens products that have allowed its revenues to increase by 300 percent over a 10-year period.[12] An enterprise that systematically and wisely applies Six Sigma methods to its value chain, activity by activity, can make major strides in improving the proficiency with which its strategy is executed without sacrificing innovation. As is the case with TQM, obtaining managerial commitment, establishing a quality culture, and fully involving employees are all of critical importance to the successful implementation of Six Sigma quality programs.[13]

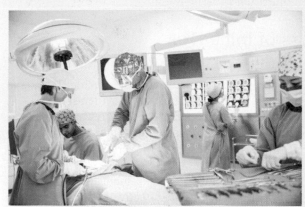

Caiaimage/Robert Daly/Getty Images

Established in 1972, Charleston Area Medical Center (CAMC) is West Virginia's largest health care provider in terms of beds, admissions, and revenues. In 2000, CAMC implemented a Six Sigma program to examine quality problems and standardize care processes. Performance improvement was important to CAMC's management for a variety of strategic reasons, including competitive positioning and cost control.

The United States has been evolving toward a pay-for-performance structure, which rewards hospitals for providing quality care. CAMC has utilized its Six Sigma program to take advantage of these changes in the health care environment. For example, to improve its performance in acute myocardial infarction (AMI), CAMC applied a Six Sigma DMAIC (define-measure-analyze-improve-control) approach. Nursing staff members were educated on AMI care processes, performance targets were posted in nursing units, and adherence to the eight Hospital Quality Alliance (HQA) indicators of quality care for AMI patients was tracked. As a result of the program, CAMC improved its compliance with HQA-recommended treatment for AMI from 50 to 95 percent. Harvard researchers identified CAMC as one of the top-performing hospitals reporting comparable data.

Controlling cost has also been an important aspect of CAMC's performance improvement initiatives due to local regulations. West Virginia is one of two states where medical services rates are set by state regulators. This forces CAMC to limit expenditures because the hospital cannot raise prices. CAMC first applied Six Sigma in an effort to control costs by managing the supply chain more effectively. The effort created a one-time $150,000 savings by working with vendors to remove outdated inventory. As a result of continuous improvement, CAMC managed to achieve supply chain management savings of $12 million in just four years.

Since CAMC introduced Six Sigma, over 100 quality improvement projects have been initiated. A key to CAMC's success has been instilling a continuous improvement mindset into the organization's culture. Dale Wood, chief quality officer at CAMC, stated: "If you have people at the top who completely support and want these changes to occur, you can still fall flat on your face. . . . You need a group of networkers who can carry change across an organization." Due to CAMC's performance improvement culture, the hospital ranks high nationally in ratings for quality of care and patient safety, as reported on the Centers for Medicare and Medicaid Services (CMS) website.

Note: Developed with Robin A. Daley.

Sources: CAMC website; Martha Hostetter, "Case Study: Improving Performance at Charleston Area Medical Center," *The Commonwealth Fund,* November–December 2007, www.commonwealthfund.org/publications/newsletters/quality-matters/2007/november-december/case-study-improving-performance-at-charleston-area-medical-center (accessed January 2016); J. C. Simmons, "Using Six Sigma to Make a Difference in Health Care Quality," *The Quality Letter,* April 2002.

The Difference between Business Process Reengineering and Continuous-Improvement Programs Like Six Sigma and TQM Whereas business process reengineering aims at *quantum gains* on the order of 30 to 50 percent or more, total quality programs like TQM and Six Sigma stress *ongoing incremental progress,* striving for inch-by-inch gains again and again in a never-ending stream. The two approaches to improved performance of value chain activities and operating excellence are not mutually exclusive; it makes sense to use them in tandem. Reengineering can be used first to produce a good basic design that yields quick,

> Business process reengineering aims at one-time quantum improvement, while continuous-improvement programs like TQM and Six Sigma aim at ongoing incremental improvements.

dramatic improvements in performing a business process. TQM or Six Sigma programs can then be used as a follow-on to reengineering and/or best-practice implementation to deliver incremental improvements over a longer period of time.

Capturing the Benefits of Initiatives to Improve Operations

The biggest beneficiaries of process improvement initiatives, reengineering, TQM, and Six Sigma are companies that view such programs not as ends in themselves but as tools for implementing company strategy more effectively. The least rewarding payoffs occur when company managers seize on the programs as novel ideas that might be worth a try. In most such instances, they result in strategy-blind efforts to simply manage better.

There's an important lesson here. Business process management tools all need to be linked to a company's strategic priorities to contribute effectively to improving the strategy's execution. Only strategy can point to which value chain activities matter and what performance targets make the most sense. Without a strategic framework, managers lack the context in which to fix things that really matter to business unit performance and competitive success.

To get the most from initiatives to execute strategy more proficiently, managers must have a clear idea of what specific outcomes really matter. Is it high on-time delivery, lower overall costs, fewer customer complaints, shorter cycle times, a higher percentage of revenues coming from recently introduced products, or something else? Benchmarking best-in-industry and best-in-world performance of targeted value chain activities provides a realistic basis for setting internal performance milestones and longer-range targets. Once initiatives to improve operations are linked to the company's strategic priorities, then comes the managerial task of building a total quality culture that is genuinely committed to achieving the performance outcomes that strategic success requires.[14]

Managers can take the following action steps to realize full value from TQM, reengineering, or Six Sigma initiatives and promote a culture of operating excellence[15]:

1. Demonstrating visible, unequivocal, and unyielding commitment to total quality and continuous improvement, including specifying measurable objectives for increasing quality and making continual progress.
2. Nudging people toward quality-supportive behaviors by
    a. Screening job applicants rigorously and hiring only those with attitudes and aptitudes that are right for quality-based performance.
    b. Providing quality training for employees.
    c. Using teams and team-building exercises to reinforce and nurture individual effort. (The creation of a quality culture is facilitated when teams become more cross-functional, multitask-oriented, and increasingly self-managed.)
    d. Recognizing and rewarding individual and team efforts to improve quality regularly and systematically.
    e. Stressing prevention (doing it right the first time), not correction (instituting ways to undo or overcome mistakes).
3. Empowering employees so that authority for delivering great service or improving products is in the hands of those who do the job rather than their managers: *improving quality has to be seen as part of everyone's job.*

4. Using online systems to provide all relevant parties with the latest best practices, thereby speeding the diffusion and adoption of best practices throughout the organization. Online systems can also allow company personnel to exchange data and opinions about how to upgrade the prevailing best-in-company practices.

5. Emphasizing that performance can and must be improved, because competitors are not resting on their laurels and customers are always looking for something better.

In sum, initiatives to improve operations, like business process reengineering, TQM, and Six Sigma techniques all need to be seen and used as part of a bigger-picture effort to execute strategy proficiently. Used properly, all of these tools are capable of improving the proficiency with which an organization performs its value chain activities. Not only do improvements from such initiatives add up over time and strengthen organizational capabilities, but they also help build a culture of operating excellence. All this lays the groundwork for gaining a competitive advantage.[16] While it is relatively easy for rivals to also implement process management tools, it is much more difficult and time-consuming for them to instill a deeply ingrained culture of operating excellence (as occurs when such techniques are religiously employed and top management exhibits lasting commitment to operational excellence throughout the organization).

> The purpose of using business process management tools, such as business process reengineering, TQM, and Six Sigma programs is to improve the performance of strategy-critical activities and thereby enhance strategy execution.

INSTALLING INFORMATION AND OPERATING SYSTEMS

Company strategies can't be executed well without a number of internal systems for business operations. American Airlines, Delta, Ryanair, Lufthansa, and other successful airlines cannot hope to provide passenger-pleasing service without a user-friendly online reservation system, an accurate and speedy baggage-handling system, and a strict aircraft maintenance program that minimizes problems requiring at-the-gate service that delays departures. FedEx has internal communication systems that allow it to coordinate its over 100,000 vehicles in handling a daily average of 12.1 million shipments to more than 220 countries and territories. Its leading-edge flight operations systems allow a single controller to direct as many as 200 of FedEx's 659 aircraft simultaneously, overriding their flight plans should weather problems or other special circumstances arise. FedEx also has created a series of e-business tools for customers that allow them to ship and track packages online, create address books, review shipping history, generate custom reports, simplify customer billing, reduce internal warehousing and inventory management costs, purchase goods and services from suppliers, and respond to their own quickly changing customer demands. All of FedEx's systems support the company's strategy of providing businesses and individuals with a broad array of package delivery services and enhancing its competitiveness against United Parcel Service, DHL, and the U.S. Postal Service.

Amazon.com ships customer orders from a global network of some 707 technologically sophisticated order fulfillment and distribution centers. Using complex picking algorithms, computers initiate the order-picking process by sending signals to workers' wireless receivers, telling them which items to pick off the shelves in which order. Computers also generate data on mix-boxed items, chute backup times, line speed, worker productivity, and shipping weights on orders. Systems are upgraded regularly, and productivity improvements are aggressively pursued. Amazon has been experimenting with drone delivery in order to lower costs and speed package delivery;

LO 11-4

Recognize the role of information systems and operating systems in enabling company personnel to carry out their strategic roles proficiently.

more recently it has begun marketing a pilot project called "Seller Flex" as part of its effort to develop its own delivery service.

Otis Elevator, the world's largest manufacturer of elevators, with more than 2.6 million elevators and escalators installed worldwide, has a 24/7 remote electronic monitoring system that can detect when an elevator or escalator installed on a customer's site has any of 325 problems. If the monitoring system detects a problem, it analyzes and diagnoses the cause and location, then makes the service call to an Otis mechanic at the nearest location, and helps the mechanic (who is equipped with a web-enabled cell phone) identify the component causing the problem. The company's maintenance system helps keep outage times under three hours—the elevators are often back in service before people even realize there was a problem. All trouble-call data are relayed to design and manufacturing personnel, allowing them to quickly alter design specifications or manufacturing procedures when needed to correct recurring problems. All customers have online access to performance data on each of their Otis elevators and escalators.

Well-conceived state-of-the-art operating systems not only enable better strategy execution but also strengthen organizational capabilities—enough at times to provide a competitive edge over rivals. For example, a company with a differentiation strategy based on superior quality has added capability if it has systems for training personnel in quality techniques, tracking product quality at each production step, and ensuring that all goods shipped meet quality standards. If these quality control systems are better than those employed by rivals, they provide the company with a competitive advantage. Similarly, a company striving to be a low-cost provider is competitively stronger if it has an unrivaled benchmarking system that identifies opportunities to implement best-in-the-world practices and drive costs out of the business faster than rivals. Fast-growing companies get an important assist from having capabilities in place to recruit and train new employees in large numbers and from investing in infrastructure that gives them the capability to handle rapid growth as it occurs, rather than having to scramble to catch up to customer demand.

Instituting Adequate Information Systems, Performance Tracking, and Controls

Accurate and timely information about daily operations is essential if managers are to gauge how well the strategy execution process is proceeding. Companies everywhere are capitalizing on today's technology to install real-time data-generating capability. Most retail companies now have automated online systems that generate daily sales reports for each store and maintain up-to-the-minute inventory and sales records on each item. Manufacturing plants typically generate daily production reports and track labor productivity on every shift. Transportation companies have elaborate information systems to provide real-time arrival information for buses and trains that is automatically sent to digital message signs and platform audio address systems.

Siemens Healthcare, one of the largest suppliers to the health care industry, uses a cloud-based business activity monitoring (BAM) system to continuously monitor and improve the company's processes across more than 190 countries. Customer satisfaction is one of Siemens's most important business objectives, so the reliability of its order management and services is crucial. Caesars Entertainment, owner of casinos and hotels, uses a sophisticated customer relationship database that records detailed information about its customers' gambling habits. When a member of Caesars's Total Rewards program calls to make a reservation, the representative can review previous spending, including average bet size, to offer an upgrade or complimentary stay at

Caesars Palace or one of the company's other properties. At Uber, the popular ride-sharing service, there are systems for locating vehicles near a customer and real-time demand monitoring to price fares during high-demand periods.

Information systems need to cover five broad areas: (1) customer data, (2) operations data, (3) employee data, (4) supplier and/or strategic partner data, and (5) financial performance data. All key strategic performance indicators must be tracked and reported in real time whenever possible. Real-time information systems permit company managers to stay on top of implementation initiatives and daily operations and to intervene if things seem to be drifting off course. Tracking key performance indicators, gathering information from operating personnel, quickly identifying and diagnosing problems, and taking corrective actions are all integral pieces of the process of managing strategy execution and overseeing operations.

Statistical information gives managers a feel for the numbers, briefings and meetings provide a feel for the latest developments and emerging issues, and personal contacts add a feel for the people dimension. All are good barometers of how well things are going and what operating aspects need management attention. Managers must identify problem areas and deviations from plans before they can take action to get the organization back on course by either improving the approaches to strategy execution or fine-tuning the strategy. Jeff Bezos, Amazon.com's CEO, is an ardent proponent of managing by the numbers. As he puts it, "Math-based decisions always trump opinion and judgment. The trouble with most corporations is that they make judgment-based decisions when data-based decisions could be made."[17]

> Having state-of-the-art operating systems, information systems, and real-time data is integral to superior strategy execution and operating excellence.

Monitoring Employee Performance   Information systems also provide managers with a means for monitoring the performance of empowered workers to see that they are acting within the specified limits.[18] Leaving empowered employees to their own devices in meeting performance standards without appropriate checks and balances can expose an organization to excessive risk.[19] Instances abound of employees' decisions or behavior going awry, sometimes costing a company huge sums or producing lawsuits and reputation-damaging publicity.

Scrutinizing daily and weekly operating statistics is one of the ways in which managers can monitor the results that flow from the actions of subordinates without resorting to constant over-the-shoulder supervision; if the operating results look good, then it is reasonable to assume that empowerment is working. But close monitoring of operating performance is only one of the control tools at management's disposal. Another valuable lever of control in companies that rely on empowered employees, especially in those that use self-managed work groups or other such teams, is peer-based control. Because peer evaluation is such a powerful control device, companies organized into teams can remove some layers of the management hierarchy and rely on strong peer pressure to keep team members operating between the white lines. This is especially true when a company has the information systems capability to monitor team performance daily or in real time.

USING REWARDS AND INCENTIVES TO PROMOTE BETTER STRATEGY EXECUTION

It is essential that company personnel be enthusiastically committed to executing strategy successfully and achieving performance targets. Enlisting such commitment typically requires use of an assortment of motivational techniques and rewards.

Indeed, *an effectively designed incentive and reward structure is the single most powerful tool management has for mobilizing employee commitment to successful strategy execution.* But incentives and rewards do more than just strengthen the resolve of company personnel to succeed—they also focus employees' attention on the accomplishment of specific strategy execution objectives. Not only do they spur the efforts of individuals to achieve those aims, but they also help coordinate the activities of individuals throughout the organization by aligning their personal motives with the goals of the organization. In this manner, reward systems serve as an indirect type of control mechanism that conserves on the more costly control mechanism of supervisory oversight.

To win employees' sustained, energetic commitment to the strategy execution process, management must be resourceful in designing and using motivational incentives—*both monetary and nonmonetary.* The more a manager understands what motivates subordinates and the more he or she relies on motivational incentives as a tool for achieving the targeted strategic and financial results, the greater will be employees' commitment to good day-in, day-out strategy execution and the achievement of performance targets.[20]

Incentives and Motivational Practices That Facilitate Good Strategy Execution

Financial incentives generally head the list of motivating tools for gaining wholehearted employee commitment to good strategy execution and focusing attention on strategic priorities. Generous financial rewards always catch employees' attention and produce *high-powered incentives* for individuals to exert their best efforts. A company's package of monetary rewards typically includes some combination of base-pay increases, performance bonuses, profit-sharing plans, stock awards, company contributions to employee 401(k) or retirement plans, and piecework incentives (in the case of production workers). But most successful companies and managers also make extensive use of nonmonetary incentives. Some of the most important nonmonetary approaches companies can use to enhance employee motivation include the following[21]:

- *Providing attractive perks and fringe benefits.* The various options include coverage of health insurance premiums, wellness programs, college tuition reimbursement, generous paid vacation time, onsite child care, onsite fitness centers and massage services, opportunities for getaways at company-owned recreational facilities, personal concierge services, subsidized cafeterias and free lunches, casual dress every day, personal travel services, paid sabbaticals, maternity and paternity leaves, paid leaves to care for ill family members, telecommuting, compressed workweeks (four 10-hour days instead of five 8-hour days), flextime (variable work schedules that accommodate individual needs), college scholarships for children, and relocation services.

- *Giving awards and public recognition to high performers and showcasing company successes.* Many companies hold award ceremonies to honor top-performing individuals, teams, and organizational units and to celebrate important company milestones and achievements. Others make a special point of recognizing the outstanding accomplishments of individuals, teams, and organizational units at informal company gatherings or in the company newsletter. Such actions foster a positive *esprit de corps* within the organization and may also act to spur healthy competition among units and teams within the company.

- *Relying on promotion from within whenever possible.* This practice helps bind workers to their employer, and employers to their workers. Moreover, it provides strong incentives for good performance. Promoting from within also helps ensure that people in positions of responsibility have knowledge specific to the business, technology, and operations they are managing.

- *Inviting and acting on ideas and suggestions from employees.* Many companies find that their best ideas for nuts-and-bolts operating improvements come from the suggestions of employees. Moreover, research indicates that giving decision-making power to down-the-line employees increases their motivation and satisfaction as well as their productivity. The use of self-managed teams has much the same effect.

- *Creating a work atmosphere in which there is genuine caring and mutual respect among workers and between management and employees.* A "family" work environment where people are on a first-name basis and there is strong camaraderie promotes teamwork and cross-unit collaboration.

- *Stating the strategic vision in inspirational terms that make employees feel they are a part of something worthwhile in a larger social sense.* There's strong motivating power associated with giving people a chance to be part of something exciting and personally satisfying. Jobs with a noble purpose tend to inspire employees to give their all. As described in Chapter 9, this not only increases productivity but reduces turnover and lowers costs for staff recruitment and training as well.

- *Sharing information with employees about financial performance, strategy, operational measures, market conditions, and competitors' actions.* Broad disclosure and prompt communication send the message that managers trust their workers and regard them as valued partners in the enterprise. Keeping employees in the dark denies them information useful to performing their jobs, prevents them from being intellectually engaged, saps their motivation, and detracts from performance.

- *Providing an appealing working environment.* An appealing workplace environment can have decidedly positive effects on employee morale and productivity. Providing a comfortable work environment, designed with ergonomics in mind, is particularly important when workers are expected to spend long hours at work. But some companies go beyond the mundane to design exceptionally attractive work settings. The workspaces and surrounding parklands of Apple's new multibillion dollar campus headquarters were designed to inspire Apple's people, foster innovative collaboration, while also benefiting the environment. Employees have access to a 100,000 square foot fitness center, two miles of walking and running paths, an orchard, meadow, and pond as well as community bicycles, electric golf carts, and commuter shuttles for getting around. Facebook and defense contractor Oshkosh Corporation also have dramatic headquarters projects underway.

For a specific example of the motivational tactics employed by one of the best companies to work for in America, see Illustration Capsule 11.2 on the supermarket chain Wegmans.

Striking the Right Balance between Rewards and Punishment

While most approaches to motivation, compensation, and people management accentuate the positive, companies also make it clear that lackadaisical or indifferent effort and subpar performance can result in negative consequences. At General Electric,

How Wegmans Rewards and Motivates its Employees

JHVEPhoto/Shutterstock

Companies use a variety of tools and strategies designed to motivate employees and engender superior strategy execution. In this respect, Wegmans Food Markets, Inc. serves as an exemplar. With approximately 49,000 employees spread across more than 100 stores across the Northeast and Mid-Atlantic, Wegmans stands out as an organization that delivers above average results in an industry known for its low margins, low wages, and challenging employee relationships. Guided by a philosophy of *employees first,* Wegmans employs an array of programs that enables the company to attract and retain the best people.

Since the creation of its broad benefits program for full-time employees in the 1950s, Wegmans has had

a strong benefits philosophy. Today, flexible or compressed schedules are common, and policies extend to same-sex partners. Regarding financial compensation, wages are above average for the grocery retail industry, which also has an added benefit of keeping its workforce nonunionized.

In addition to the traditional elements of compensation and benefits, Wegmans invests considerably in the training and education of its employees. Known for its strength in employee development, upwards of $50 million annually is spent on employee learning. Since 1984, the company has awarded nearly $110 million in tuition assistance and over $50 million in scholarships.

Another crucial aspect of employee motivation is feeling heard. Employees see their ideas put into action through a series of programs designed to capture and implement their ideas. Wegmans deploys a series of programs, including open-door days, team huddles, focus groups, and two-way Q&As with senior management.

With the recognition that employees are critical to delivering a great customer experience, Wegmans directs a considerable amount of resources to its biggest asset, its people. Its suite of programs and benefits, along with a policy of filling at least half of its open opportunities internally, lead to one of the lowest turnover rates in its industry. They have also resulted in Wegmans placing among the top five firms on Fortune's list of *The 100 Best Companies to Work For* year after year.

Note: Developed with Sadé M. Lawrence.

Sources: Company website; Boyle, M., *The Wegmans Way,* January 24, 2005, http://archive.fortune.com/magazines/fortune/fortune_archive/2005/01/24/8234048/index.htm; "Great Place to Work," *Wegmans Food Markets, Inc.—Great Place to Work Reviews,* February 14, 2018, http://reviews.greatplacetowork.com/wegmans-food-markets-inc.

McKinsey & Company, several global public accounting firms, and other companies that look for and expect top-notch individual performance, there's an "up-or-out" policy—managers and professionals whose performance is not good enough to warrant promotion are first denied bonuses and stock awards and eventually weeded out. At most companies, senior executives and key personnel in underperforming units are pressured to raise performance to acceptable levels and keep it there or risk being replaced.

As a general rule, it is unwise to take off the pressure for good performance or play down the adverse consequences of shortfalls in performance. There is scant evidence that a no-pressure, no-adverse-consequences work environment leads to superior strategy execution or operating excellence. As the CEO of a major bank put it, "There's a deliberate policy here to create a level of anxiety. Winners usually play like they're one touchdown behind."[22] A number of companies deliberately give employees heavy work-loads and tight deadlines to test their mettle—personnel are pushed hard to achieve "stretch" objectives and are expected to put in long hours (nights and weekends if need be). High-performing organizations nearly always have a cadre of ambitious people who relish the opportunity to climb the ladder of success, love a challenge, thrive in a performance-oriented environment, and find some competition and pressure useful to satisfy their own drives for personal recognition, accomplishment, and self-satisfaction.

However, if an organization's motivational approaches and reward structure induce too much stress, internal competitiveness, job insecurity, and fear of unpleasant con-sequences, the impact on workforce morale and strategy execution can be counter-productive. Evidence shows that managerial initiatives to improve strategy execution should incorporate more positive than negative motivational elements because when cooperation is positively enlisted and rewarded, rather than coerced by orders and threats (implicit or explicit), people tend to respond with more enthusiasm, dedication, creativity, and initiative.[23]

Linking Rewards to Achieving the Right Outcomes

To create a strategy-supportive system of rewards and incentives, a company must reward people for accomplishing results, not for just dutifully performing assigned tasks. Showing up for work and performing assignments do not, by themselves, guaran-tee results. To make the work environment results-oriented, managers need to focus jobholders' attention and energy on what to *achieve* as opposed to what to *do*.[24] Employee productivity among employees at Best Buy's corporate headquarters rose by 35 percent after the company began to focus on the results of each employee's work rather than on employees' willingness to come to work early and stay late.

Ideally, every organizational unit, every manager, every team or work group, and every employee should be held accountable for achieving outcomes that con-tribute to good strategy execution and business performance. If the company's strategy is to be a low-cost leader, the incentive system must reward actions and achievements that result in lower costs. If the company has a differentiation strat-egy focused on delivering superior quality and service, the incentive system must reward such outcomes as Six Sigma defect rates, infrequent customer complaints, speedy order processing and delivery, and high levels of customer satisfaction. If a company's growth is predicated on a strategy of new product innovation, incentives should be tied to such metrics as the percentages of revenues and profits coming from newly introduced products.

> Incentives must be based on accomplishing results, not on dutifully performing assigned tasks.

Incentive compensation for top executives is typically tied to such financial mea-sures as revenue and earnings growth, stock price performance, return on investment, and creditworthiness or to strategic measures such as market share growth. However, incentives for department heads, teams, and individual workers tend to be tied to per-formance outcomes more closely related to their specific area of responsibility. For instance, in manufacturing, it makes sense to tie incentive compensation to such out-comes as unit manufacturing costs, on-time production and shipping, defect rates, the number and extent of work stoppages due to equipment breakdowns, and so on. In sales and marketing, incentives tend to be based on achieving dollar sales or unit vol-ume targets, market share, sales penetration of each target customer group, the fate of newly introduced products, the frequency of customer complaints, the number of new accounts acquired, and measures of customer satisfaction. Which performance measures to base incentive compensation on depends on the situation—the priority placed on various financial and strategic objectives, the requirements for strategic and competitive success, and the specific results needed to keep strategy execution on track.

Illustration Capsule 11.3 provides a vivid example of how one company has designed incentives linked directly to outcomes reflecting good execution.

> The first principle in designing an effective incentive compensation system is to tie rewards to performance outcomes directly linked to good strategy execution and the achievement of financial and strategic objectives.

Additional Guidelines for Designing Incentive Compensation Systems   It is not enough to link incentives to the right kinds of results—performance outcomes that signal that the company's strategy and its execution are on track. For a company's reward system to truly motivate organization members, inspire their best efforts, and sustain high levels of productivity, it is also important to observe the following additional guidelines in designing and administering the reward system:

- *Make the performance payoff a major, not minor, piece of the total compensation package.* Performance bonuses must be at least 10 to 12 percent of base salary to have much impact. Incentives that amount to 20 percent or more of total compensation are big attention-getters, likely to really drive individual or team efforts. Incentives amounting to less than five percent of total compensation have a comparatively weak motivational impact. Moreover, the payoff for high-performing individuals and teams must be meaningfully greater than the payoff for average performers, and the payoff for average performers meaningfully bigger than that for below-average performers.

- *Have incentives that extend to all managers and all workers, not just top management.* It is a gross miscalculation to expect that lower-level managers and employees will work their hardest to hit performance targets if only senior executives qualify for lucrative rewards.

- *Administer the reward system with scrupulous objectivity and fairness.* If performance standards are set unrealistically high or if individual and group performance evaluations are not accurate and well documented, dissatisfaction with the system will overcome any positive benefits.

- *Ensure that the performance targets set for each individual or team involve outcomes that the individual or team can personally affect.* The role of incentives is to enhance individual commitment and channel behavior in beneficial directions. This role is not well served when the performance measures by which company personnel are judged are outside their arena of influence.

- *Keep the time between achieving the performance target and receiving the reward as short as possible.* Nucor, a leading producer of steel products, has achieved high labor productivity by paying its workers weekly bonuses based on prior-week production levels. Annual bonus payouts work best for higher-level managers and for situations where the outcome target relates to overall company profitability.

- *Avoid rewarding effort rather than results.* While it is tempting to reward people who have tried hard, gone the extra mile, and yet fallen short of achieving performance targets because of circumstances beyond their control, it is ill advised to do so. The problem with making exceptions for unknowable, uncontrollable, or unforeseeable circumstances is that once "good excuses" start to creep into justifying rewards for subpar results, the door opens to all kinds of reasons why actual performance has failed to match targeted performance. A "no excuses" standard is more evenhanded, easier to administer, and more conducive to creating a results-oriented work climate.

Nucor Corporation: Tying Incentives Directly to Strategy Execution

The strategy at Nucor Corporation, the largest steel producers in the United States, is to be *the* low-cost producer of steel products. Because labor costs are a significant fraction of total cost in the steel business, successful implementation of Nucor's low-cost leadership strategy entails achieving lower labor costs per ton of steel than competitors' costs. Nucor management uses an incentive system to promote high worker productivity and drive labor costs per ton below those of rivals. Each plant's workforce is organized into production teams (each assigned to perform particular functions), and weekly production targets are established for each team. Base-pay scales are set at levels comparable to wages for similar manufacturing jobs in the local areas where Nucor has plants, but workers can earn a one percent bonus for each one percent that their output exceeds target levels. If a production team exceeds its weekly production target by 10 percent, team members receive a 10 percent bonus in their next paycheck; if a team exceeds its quota by 20 percent, team members earn a 20 percent bonus. Bonuses, paid every two weeks, are based on the prior two weeks' actual production levels measured against the targets.

Nucor's piece-rate incentive plan has produced impressive results. The production teams put forth exceptional effort; it is not uncommon for most teams to beat their weekly production targets by 20 to 50 percent. When added to employees' base pay, the bonuses earned by Nucor workers make Nucor's workforce among the highest paid in the U.S. steel industry. From a management perspective, the incentive system has resulted in Nucor having labor productivity levels 10 to 20 percent above the average of the unionized workforces at several of its largest rivals, which in turn has given Nucor a significant labor cost advantage over most rivals.

Westend61/Getty Images

After years of record-setting profits, Nucor struggled in the last major economic downturn, along with the manufacturers and builders who buy its steel. But while bonuses dwindled, Nucor showed remarkable loyalty to its production workers, avoiding layoffs by having employees get ahead on maintenance, perform work formerly done by contractors, and search for cost savings. Morale at the company remained high, and Nucor's CEO at the time, Daniel DiMicco, was inducted into *Industry-Week* magazine's Manufacturing Hall of Fame because of his no-layoff policies. As industry growth resumed, Nucor was in the position of having a well-trained workforce, more committed than ever to achieving the kind of productivity for which Nucor is justifiably famous. DiMicco had good reason to expect Nucor to be "first out of the box" following the crisis, and although he has since stepped aside, the company's culture of making its employees think like owners has not changed.

Sources: Company website (accessed March 2012); N. Byrnes, "Pain, but No Layoffs at Nucor," *BusinessWeek*, March 26, 2009; J. McGregor, "Nucor's CEO Is Stepping Aside, but Its Culture Likely Won't," *The Washington Post* Online, November 20, 2012 (accessed April 3, 2014).

For an organization's incentive system to work well, the details of the reward structure must be communicated and explained. Everybody needs to understand how his or her incentive compensation is calculated and how individual and group performance targets contribute to organizational performance targets. The pressure to achieve the targeted financial and strategic performance objectives and continuously improve on strategy execution should be unrelenting. People at all levels must be held accountable for carrying out their assigned parts of the strategic

> The unwavering standard for judging whether individuals, teams, and organizational units have done a good job must be whether they meet or beat performance targets that reflect good strategy execution.

plan, and they must understand that their rewards are based on the caliber of results achieved. But with the pressure to perform should come meaningful rewards. Without an attractive payoff, the system breaks down, and managers are left with the less workable options of issuing orders, trying to enforce compliance, and depending on the goodwill of employees.

KEY POINTS

1. Implementing a new or different strategy calls for managers to identify the resource requirements of each new strategic initiative and then consider whether the current pattern of resource allocation and the budgets of the various subunits are suitable.

2. Company policies and procedures facilitate strategy execution when they are designed to fit the strategy and its objectives. Anytime a company alters its strategy, managers should review existing policies and operating procedures and replace those that are out of sync. Well-conceived policies and procedures aid the task of strategy execution by (1) providing top-down guidance to company personnel regarding how things need to be done and what the limits are on independent actions; (2) enforcing consistency in the performance of strategy-critical activities, thereby improving the quality of the strategy execution effort and coordinating the efforts of company personnel, however widely dispersed; and (3) promoting the creation of a work climate conducive to good strategy execution.

3. Competent strategy execution entails visible unyielding managerial commitment to continuous improvement. Business process management tools, such as reengineering, total quality management (TQM), and Six Sigma programs are important process management tools for promoting better strategy execution.

4. Company strategies can't be implemented or executed well without well-conceived internal systems to support daily operations. Real-time information systems and control systems further aid the cause of good strategy execution. In some cases, state-of-the-art operating and information systems strengthen a company's strategy execution capabilities enough to provide a competitive edge over rivals.

5. Strategy-supportive motivational practices and reward systems are powerful management tools for gaining employee commitment and focusing their attention on the strategy execution goals. The key to creating a reward system that promotes good strategy execution is to make measures of good business performance and good strategy execution the *dominating basis* for designing incentives, evaluating individual and group efforts, and handing out rewards. While financial rewards provide high-powered incentives, nonmonetary incentives are also important. For an incentive compensation system to work well, (1) the performance payoff should be a major percentage of the compensation package, (2) the use of incentives should extend to all managers and workers, (3) the system should be administered with objectivity and fairness, (4) each individual's performance targets should involve outcomes the person can personally affect, (5) rewards should promptly follow the achievement of performance targets, and (6) rewards should be given for results and not just effort.

ASSURANCE OF LEARNING EXERCISES

1. Implementing a new or different strategy calls for new resource allocations. Using your university's library resources search for recent articles that discuss how a company has revised its pattern of resource allocation and divisional budgets to support new strategic initiatives.

   LO 11-1

2. Netflix avoids the use of formal policies and procedures to better empower its employees to maximize innovation and productivity. The company goes to great lengths to hire, reward, and tolerate only what it considers mature, "A" player employees. How does the company's selection process affect its ability to operate without formal travel and expense policies, a fixed number of vacation days for employees, or a formal employee performance evaluation system?

   LO 11-2

3. Illustration Capsule 11.1 discusses Charleston Area Medical Center's use of Six Sigma practices. List three tangible benefits provided by the program. Explain why a commitment to quality control is particularly important in the hospital industry. How can the use of a Six Sigma program help medical providers survive and thrive in the current industry climate?

   LO 11-3

4. Read some of the recent Six Sigma articles posted at **www.isixsigma.com**. Prepare a one-page report to your instructor detailing how Six Sigma is being used in two companies and what benefits the companies are reaping as a result. Further, discuss two to three criticisms of, or potential difficulties with, Six Sigma implementation.

   LO 11-3

5. Company strategies can't be executed well without a number of support systems to carry on business operations. Using your university's library resources, search for recent articles that discuss how a company has used real-time information systems and control systems to aid the cause of good strategy execution.

   LO 11-4

6. Illustration Capsule 11.2 provides a description of the motivational practices employed by Wegmans Food Markets, a supermarket chain that is routinely listed as among the top five companies to work for in the United States. Discuss how rewards and practices at Wegman's aid in the company's strategy execution efforts.

   Mc Graw Hill connect
   LO 11-5

EXERCISES FOR SIMULATION PARTICIPANTS

Mc Graw Hill connect ● ● ● ●

1. What are the ways that resource allocation contributes to good strategy execution and improved company performance.

   LO 11-1

2. What actions, if any, is your company taking to pursue continuous improvement in how it performs certain value chain activities?

   LO 11-2, LO 11-3, LO 11-4

3. Are benchmarking data available in the simulation exercise in which you are participating? If so, do you and your co-managers regularly study the benchmarking data to see how well your company is doing? Do you consider the benchmarking information provided to be valuable? Why or why not? Cite three recent instances in which your examination of the benchmarking statistics has caused you and your co-managers to take corrective actions to improve operations and boost company performance.

   LO 11-3

4. What hard evidence can you cite that indicates your company's management team is doing a *better* or *worse* job of achieving operating excellence and executing strategy than are the management teams at rival companies?

   LO 11-3

LO 11-2, LO 11-3, LO 11-4

5. Are you and your co-managers consciously trying to achieve operating excellence? Explain how you are doing this and how you will track the progress you are making.

LO 11-5

6. What are ways that incentive compensation can affect productivity gains and lower labor cost per unit?

ENDNOTES

••••

1 M. Hammer and J. Champy, *Reengineering the Corporation: A Manifesto for Business Revolution* (New York: HarperCollins, 1993).
2 James Brian Quinn, *Intelligent Enterprise* (New York: Free Press, 1992); Ann Majchrzak and Qianwei Wang, "Breaking the Functional Mind-Set in Process Organizations," *Harvard Business Review* 74, no. 5 (September–October 1996), pp. 93–99; Stephen L. Walston, Lawton R. Burns, and John R. Kimberly, "Does Reengineering Really Work? An Examination of the Context and Outcomes of Hospital Reengineering Initiatives," *Health Services Research* 34, no. 6 (February 2000), pp. 1363–1388; Allessio Ascari, Melinda Rock, and Soumitra Dutta, "Reengineering and Organizational Change: Lessons from a Comparative Analysis of Company Experiences," *European Management Journal* 13, no. 1 (March 1995), pp. 1–13; Ronald J. Burke, "Process Reengineering: Who Embraces It and Why?" *The TQM Magazine* 16, no. 2 (2004), pp. 114–119.
3 www.answers.com (accessed July 8, 2009); "Reengineering: Beyond the Buzzword," *Businessweek*, May 24, 1993, www.businessweek.com (accessed July 8, 2009).
4 M. Walton, *The Deming Management Method* (New York: Pedigree, 1986); J. Juran, *Juran on Quality by Design* (New York: Free Press, 1992); Philip Crosby, *Quality Is Free: The Act of Making Quality Certain* (New York: McGraw-Hill, 1979); S. George, *The Baldrige Quality System* (New York: Wiley, 1992); Mark J. Zbaracki, "The Rhetoric and Reality of Total Quality Management," *Administrative Science Quarterly* 43, no. 3 (September 1998), pp. 602–636.
5 Robert T. Amsden, Thomas W. Ferratt, and Davida M. Amsden, "TQM: Core Paradigm Changes," *Business Horizons* 39, no. 6 (November–December 1996), pp. 6–14.
6 Peter S. Pande and Larry Holpp, *What Is Six Sigma?* (New York: McGraw-Hill, 2002); Jiju Antony, "Some Pros and Cons of Six Sigma: An Academic Perspective," *TQM Magazine* 16, no. 4 (2004), pp. 303–306; Peter S. Pande, Robert P. Neuman, and Roland R. Cavanagh, *The Six Sigma Way: How GE, Motorola and Other Top

Companies Are Honing Their Performance* (New York: McGraw-Hill, 2000); Joseph Gordon and M. Joseph Gordon, Jr., *Six Sigma Quality for Business and Manufacture* (New York: Elsevier, 2002); Godecke Wessel and Peter Burcher, "Six Sigma for Small and Medium-Sized Enterprises," *TQM Magazine* 16, no. 4 (2004), pp. 264–272.
7 www.isixsigma.com (accessed November 4, 2002); www.villanovau.com/certificate-programs/six-sigma-training.aspx (accessed February 16, 2012).
8 Kennedy Smith, "Six Sigma for the Service Sector," *Quality Digest Magazine,* May 2003; www.qualitydigest.com (accessed September 28, 2003).
9 www.isixsigma.com/implementation/-financial-analysis/six-sigma-costs-and-savings/ (accessed February 23, 2012).
10 Pande, Neuman, and Cavanagh, *The Six Sigma Way*, pp. 5–6.
11 "A Dark Art No More," *The Economist* 385, no. 8550 (October 13, 2007), p. 10; Brian Hindo, "At 3M, a Struggle between Efficiency and Creativity," *Businessweek,* June 11, 2007, pp. 8–16.
12 Charles A. O'Reilly and Michael L. Tushman, "The Ambidextrous Organization," *Harvard Business Review* 82, no. 4 (April 2004), pp. 74–81.
13 Terry Nels Lee, Stanley E. Fawcett, and Jason Briscoe, "Benchmarking the Challenge to Quality Program Implementation," *Benchmarking: An International Journal* 9, no. 4 (2002), pp. 374–387.
14 Milan Ambroé, "Total Quality System as a Product of the Empowered Corporate Culture," *TQM Magazine* 16, no. 2 (2004), pp. 93–104; Nick A. Dayton, "The Demise of Total Quality Management," *TQM Magazine* 15, no. 6 (2003), pp. 391–396.
15 Judy D. Olian and Sara L. Rynes, "Making Total Quality Work: Aligning Organizational Processes, Performance Measures, and Stakeholders," *Human Resource Management* 30, no. 3 (Fall 1991), pp. 310–311; Paul S. Goodman and Eric D. Darr, "Exchanging Best Practices Information through Computer-Aided Systems," *Academy of Management Executive* 10, no. 2 (May 1996), p. 7.

16 Thomas C. Powell, "Total Quality Management as Competitive Advantage," *Strategic Management Journal* 16 (1995), pp. 15–37; Richard M. Hodgetts, "Quality Lessons from America's Baldrige Winners," *Business Horizons* 37, no. 4 (July–August 1994), pp. 74–79; Richard Reed, David J. Lemak, and Joseph C. Montgomery, "Beyond Process: TQM Content and Firm Performance," *Academy of Management Review* 21, no. 1 (January 1996), pp. 173–202.
17 Fred Vogelstein, "Winning the Amazon Way," *Fortune* 147, no. 10 (May 26, 2003), pp. 60–69.
18 Robert Simons, "Control in an Age of Empowerment," *Harvard Business Review* 73 (March–April 1995), pp. 80–88.
19 David C. Band and Gerald Scanlan, "Strategic Control through Core Competencies," *Long Range Planning* 28, no. 2 (April 1995), pp. 102–114.
20 Stanley E. Fawcett, Gary K. Rhoads, and Phillip Burnah, "People as the Bridge to Competitiveness: Benchmarking the 'ABCs' of an Empowered Workforce," *Benchmarking: An International Journal* 11, no. 4 (2004), pp. 346–360.
21 Jeffrey Pfeffer and John F. Veiga, "Putting People First for Organizational Success," *Academy of Management Executive* 13, no. 2 (May 1999), pp. 37–45; Linda K. Stroh and Paula M. Caliguiri, "Increasing Global Competitiveness through Effective People Management," *Journal of World Business* 33, no. 1 (Spring 1998), pp. 1–16; articles in *Fortune* on the 100 best companies to work for (various issues).
22 As quoted in John P. Kotter and James L. Heskett, *Corporate Culture and Performance* (New York: Free Press, 1992), p. 91.
23 Clayton M. Christensen, Matt Marx, and Howard Stevenson, "The Tools of Cooperation and Change," *Harvard Business Review* 84, no. 10 (October 2006), pp. 73–80.
24 Steven Kerr, "On the Folly of Rewarding A While Hoping for B," *Academy of Management Executive* 9, no. 1 (February 1995), pp. 7–14; Doran Twer, "Linking Pay to Business Objectives," *Journal of Business Strategy* 15, no. 4 (July–August 1994), pp. 15–18.

chapter 12

Corporate Culture and Leadership

Keys to Good Strategy Execution

Fanatic Studio/Alamy Stock Photo

Learning Objectives

After reading this chapter, you should be able to:

LO 12-1 Understand the key features of a company's corporate culture and the role of a company's core values and ethical standards in building corporate culture.

LO 12-2 Explain how and why a company's culture can aid the drive for proficient strategy execution.

LO 12-3 Identify the kinds of actions management can take to change a problem corporate culture.

LO 12-4 Recognize what constitutes effective managerial leadership in achieving superior strategy execution.

I came to see, in my time at IBM, that culture isn't just one aspect of the game, it is the game.

Louis Gerstner—*Former Chairman and CEO of IBM*

As we look ahead into the next century, leaders will be those who empower others.

Bill Gates—*Cofounder and former CEO and chair of Microsoft*

A genuine leader is not a searcher for consensus but a molder of consensus.

Martin Luther King, Jr.—*Civil Rights Leader*

In the previous two chapters, we examined eight of the managerial tasks that drive good strategy execution: staffing the organization, acquiring the needed resources and capabilities, designing the organizational structure, allocating resources, establishing policies and procedures, employing process management tools, installing operating systems, and providing the right incentives. In this chapter, we explore the two remaining managerial tasks that contribute to good strategy execution: creating a supportive corporate culture and leading the strategy execution process.

INSTILLING A CORPORATE CULTURE CONDUCIVE TO GOOD STRATEGY EXECUTION

CORE CONCEPT

Corporate culture refers to the shared values, ingrained attitudes, core beliefs, and company traditions that determine norms of behavior, accepted work practices, and styles of operating.

● **LO 12-1**

Understand the key features of a company's corporate culture and the role of a company's core values and ethical standards in building corporate culture.

Every company has its own unique **corporate culture**—the shared values, ingrained attitudes, and company traditions that determine norms of behavior, accepted work practices, and styles of operating.[1] The character of a company's culture is a product of the core values and beliefs that executives espouse, the standards of what is ethically acceptable and what is not, the "chemistry" and the "personality" that permeate the work environment, the company's traditions, and the stories that get told over and over to illustrate and reinforce the company's values, business practices, and traditions. In a very real sense, the culture is the company's automatic, self-replicating "operating system" that defines "how we do things around here."[2] It can be thought of as the company's psyche or *organizational DNA*.[3] A company's culture is important because it influences the organization's actions and approaches to conducting business. As such, it plays an important role in strategy execution and may have an appreciable effect on business performance as well.

Corporate cultures vary widely. For instance, the bedrock of Walmart's culture is zealous pursuit of low costs and frugal operating practices, a strong work ethic, ritualistic headquarters meetings to exchange ideas and review problems, and company executives' commitment to visiting stores, listening to customers, and soliciting suggestions from employees. The culture at Apple is customer-centered, secretive, and highly protective of company-developed technology. Apple employees share a common goal of making the best products for the consumer; the aim is to make the customer feel delight, surprise, and connection to each Apple device. The company expects creative thinking and inspired solutions from everyone—as the company puts it, "We're perfectionists. Idealists. Inventors. Forever tinkering with products and processes, always on the lookout for better." According to a former employee, "Apple is one of those companies where people work on an almost religious level of commitment." To spur innovation and creativity, the company fosters extensive collaboration and cross-pollination among different work groups. But it does so in a manner that demands secrecy—employees are expected not to reveal anything relevant about what new project they are working on, not to employees outside their immediate work group and especially not to family members or other outsiders; it is common for different employees working on the same project to be assigned different project code names. The different pieces of a new product launch often come together like a puzzle at the last minute.[4] W. L. Gore & Associates, best known for GORE-TEX, credits its unique culture for allowing the company to pursue multiple end-market applications simultaneously, enabling rapid growth from a niche business into a diversified multinational company. The company's culture is team-based and designed to foster personal initiative, with no traditional organizational charts, no chains of command, no predetermined channels of communication. The culture encourages multidiscipline teams to organize around opportunities, and in the process, leaders emerge. At Nordstrom, the corporate culture is centered on delivering exceptional service to customers, where the company's motto is "Respond to unreasonable customer requests," and each out-of-the-ordinary request is seen as an opportunity for a "heroic" act by an employee that can further the company's reputation for unparalleled customer service. Nordstrom makes a point of promoting employees noted for their heroic acts and dedication to outstanding service.

Identifying the Key Features of a Company's Corporate Culture

A company's corporate culture is mirrored in the character or "personality" of its work environment—the features that describe how the company goes about its business and the workplace behaviors that are held in high esteem. Some of these features are readily apparent, and others operate quite subtly. The chief things to look for include:

- The values, business principles, and ethical standards that management preaches and *practices*—these are the key to a company's culture, but actions speak much louder than words here.
- The company's approach to people management and the official policies, procedures, and operating practices that provide guidelines for the behavior of company personnel.
- The atmosphere and spirit that pervades the work climate—whether the workplace is competitive or cooperative, innovative or resistant to change, collegial or politicized, all business or fun-loving, and the like.
- How managers and employees interact and relate to one another—whether there is heavy or weak reliance on collaboration and teamwork, whether communications among employees are free-flowing or restrictive and infrequent, whether employees are empowered to exercise their initiative or whether actions are directed mostly by higher authority, whether co-workers spend little or lots of time together outside the workplace, and so on.
- The strength of peer pressure to do things in particular ways and conform to expected norms.
- The actions and behaviors that management explicitly encourages and rewards and those that are frowned upon.
- The company's revered traditions and oft-repeated stories about "heroic acts" and "how we do things around here."
- The manner in which the company deals with external stakeholders—whether it treats suppliers as business partners or prefers hard-nosed, arm's-length business arrangements and whether its commitment to corporate citizenship and environmental sustainability is strong and genuine.

The values, beliefs, and practices that undergird a company's culture can come from anywhere in the organizational hierarchy. Typically, key elements of the culture originate with a founder or certain strong leaders who articulated them as a set of business principles, company policies, operating approaches, and ways of dealing with employees, customers, vendors, shareholders, and local communities where the company has operations. They also stem from exemplary actions on the part of company personnel and evolving consensus about "how we ought to do things around here."[5] Over time, these cultural underpinnings take root, come to be accepted by company managers and employees alike, and become ingrained in the way the company conducts its business.

> A company's culture is grounded in and shaped by its core values and ethical standards.

The Role of Core Values and Ethics   The foundation of a company's corporate culture nearly always resides in its dedication to certain core values and the bar it sets for ethical behavior. The culture-shaping significance of core values and ethical behaviors accounts for why so many companies have developed a formal value statement and a code of ethics. Many executives want the work climate at their companies to mirror certain values and ethical standards, partly because of personal

> A company's value statement and code of ethics communicate expectations of how employees should conduct themselves in the workplace.

FIGURE 12.1   The Two Culture-Building Roles of a Company's Core Values and Ethical Standards

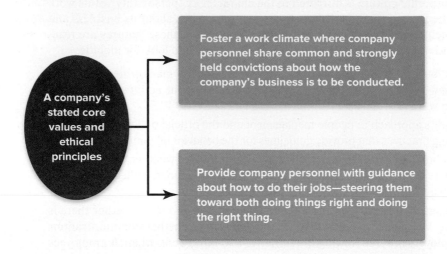

convictions but mainly because they are convinced that adherence to such principles will promote better strategy execution, make the company a better performer, and positively impact its reputation.[6] Not incidentally, strongly ingrained values and ethical standards reduce the likelihood of lapses in ethical behavior that mar a company's public image and put its financial performance and market standing at risk.

As depicted in Figure 12.1, a company's stated core values and ethical principles have two roles in the culture-building process. First, they can foster a work climate in which company personnel share strongly held convictions about how the company's business is to be conducted. Second, they provide company personnel with guidance about the manner in which they are to do their jobs—which behaviors and ways of doing things are approved (and expected) and which are out-of-bounds. These value-based and ethics-based cultural norms serve as yardsticks for gauging the appropriateness of particular actions, decisions, and behaviors, thus helping steer company personnel toward both doing things right and doing the right thing.

Embedding Behavioral Norms in the Organization and Perpetuating the Culture

Once values and ethical standards have been formally adopted, they must be institutionalized in the company's policies and practices and embedded in the conduct of company personnel. This can be advanced in a number of different ways.[7] Tradition-steeped companies with a rich folklore rely heavily on word-of-mouth indoctrination and the power of tradition to instill values and enforce ethical conduct. But most companies employ a variety of techniques, drawing on some or all of the following:

1. Screening applicants and hiring those who will mesh well with the culture.
2. Incorporating discussions of the company's culture and behavioral norms into orientation programs for new employees and training courses for managers and employees.
3. Having senior executives frequently reiterate the importance and role of company values and ethical principles at company events and in internal communications to employees.

4. Expecting managers at all levels to be cultural role models and exhibit the advocated cultural norms in their own behavior.

5. Making the display of cultural norms a factor in evaluating each person's job performance, granting compensation increases, and offering promotions.

6. Stressing that line managers all the way down to first-level supervisors give ongoing attention to explaining the desired cultural traits and behaviors in their areas and clarifying why they are important.

7. Encouraging company personnel to exert strong peer pressure on co-workers to conform to expected cultural norms.

8. Holding periodic ceremonies to honor people who excel in displaying the company values and ethical principles.

To deeply ingrain the stated core values and high ethical standards, companies must turn them into *strictly enforced cultural norms.* They must make it unequivocally clear that living up to the company's values and ethical standards has to be "a way of life" at the company and that there will be little toleration for errant behavior.

The Role of Stories   Frequently, a significant part of a company's culture is captured in the stories that get told over and over again to illustrate to newcomers the importance of certain values and the depth of commitment that various company personnel have displayed. One of the folktales at Zappos, known for its outstanding customer service, is about a customer who ordered shoes for her ill mother from Zappos, hoping the shoes would remedy her mother's foot pain and numbness. When the shoes didn't work, the mother called the company to ask how to return them and explain why she was returning them. Two days later, she received a large bouquet of flowers from the company, along with well wishes and a customer upgrade giving her free expedited service on all future orders. Specialty food market Trader Joe's is similarly known for its culture of going beyond the call of duty for its customers. When a World War II veteran was snowed in without any food for meals, his daughter called several supermarkets to see if they offered grocery delivery. Although Trader Joe's technically doesn't offer delivery, it graciously helped the veteran, even recommending items for his low-sodium diet. When the store delivered the groceries, the veteran wasn't charged for either the groceries or the delivery. Stories of employees at Ritz Carlton going the extra mile for customers both showcase and reinforce its customer-centric culture. Recently, a family arrived at a Ritz-Carlton only to find that the specialized eggs and milk they had brought along for their son had spoiled. (The child suffered from food allergies.) When the products could not be found locally, the hotel's staff had the products flown in from Singapore, approximately 1,050 miles away!

Forces That Cause a Company's Culture to Evolve   Despite the role of time-honored stories and long-standing traditions in perpetuating a company's culture, cultures are far from static—just like strategy and organizational structure, they evolve. New challenges in the marketplace, revolutionary technologies, and shifting internal conditions—especially an internal crisis, a change in company direction, or top-executive turnover—tend to breed new ways of doing things and, in turn, drive cultural evolution. An incoming CEO who decides to shake up the existing business and take it in new directions often triggers a cultural shift, perhaps one of major proportions. Likewise, diversification into new businesses, expansion into foreign countries, rapid growth that brings an influx of new employees, and the merger with or acquisition of another company can all precipitate significant cultural change.

The Presence of Company Subcultures   Although it is common to speak about corporate culture in the singular, it is not unusual for companies to have multiple cultures (or subcultures). Values, beliefs, and practices within a company sometimes vary significantly by department, geographic location, division, or business unit. Subcultures can exist because a company has recently acquired other companies. Global and multinational companies tend to be at least partly multicultural because cross-country organization units have different operating histories and work climates, as well as members who speak different languages, have grown up under different social customs and traditions, and have different sets of values and beliefs. The problem with subcultures is that they can clash, or at least not mesh well, particularly if they embrace conflicting business philosophies or operating approaches, if key executives employ different approaches to people management, or if important differences between a company's culture and those of recently acquired companies have not yet been ironed out. On a number of occasions, companies have decided to pass on acquiring particular companies because of culture conflicts they believed would be hard to resolve.

Nonetheless, the existence of subcultures does not preclude important areas of commonality and compatibility. Company managements are quite alert to the importance of cultural compatibility in making acquisitions and the need to integrate the cultures of newly acquired companies. Indeed, cultural due diligence is often as important as financial due diligence in deciding whether to go forward on an acquisition or merger. Also, in today's globalizing world, multinational companies are learning how to make strategy-critical cultural traits travel across country boundaries and create a workably uniform culture worldwide. AES, a sustainable energy company with more than 10,000 employees and operations on four continents, has found that people in most countries readily embrace the five core values that underlie its culture—putting safety first, acting with integrity, remaining nimble, having fun through work, and striving for excellence. Moreover, AES tries to define and practice its cultural values the same way in all of its locations while still being sensitive to differences that exist among various peoples and groups around the world. Top managers at AES have expressed the view that people across the globe are more similar than different and that the company's culture is as meaningful in Brazil, Vietnam, or Kazakhstan as in the United States.

Strong versus Weak Cultures

Company cultures vary widely in strength and influence. Some are strongly embedded and have a big influence on a company's operating practices and the behavior of company personnel. Others are weakly ingrained and have little effect on behaviors and how company activities are conducted.

Strong-Culture Companies   The hallmark of a **strong-culture company** is the dominating presence of certain deeply rooted values, business principles, and behavioral norms that "regulate" the conduct of company personnel and determine the climate of the workplace.[8] In strong-culture companies, senior managers make a point of explaining and reiterating why these values, principles, norms, and operating approaches need to govern how the company conducts its business and how they ultimately lead to better business performance. Furthermore, they make a conscious effort to display these values, principles, and behavioral norms in their own actions—*they walk the talk*. An unequivocal expectation that company personnel will act and behave in accordance with the adopted values and ways of doing business leads to two important outcomes: (1) Over time, the professed values come to be widely shared by rank-and-file employees—people who dislike the culture tend to leave—and (2) individuals encounter strong peer pressure from co-workers to observe the culturally approved norms and behaviors. Hence, a strongly implanted corporate culture ends up having a powerful influence on behavior because so many company personnel are accepting of the company's culturally approved traditions and because this acceptance is reinforced by both management expectations and co-worker peer pressure to conform to cultural norms.

Strong cultures emerge only after a period of deliberate and rather intensive culture building that generally takes years (sometimes decades). Two factors contribute to the development of strong cultures: (1) a founder or strong leader who established core values, principles, and practices that are viewed as having contributed to the success of the company; and (2) a sincere, long-standing company commitment to operating the business according to these established traditions and values. Continuity of leadership, low workforce turnover, geographic concentration, and considerable organizational success all contribute to the emergence and sustainability of a strong culture.[9]

In strong-culture companies, values and behavioral norms are so ingrained that they can endure leadership changes at the top—although their strength can erode over time if new CEOs cease to nurture them or move aggressively to institute cultural adjustments. The cultural norms in a strong-culture company typically do not change much as strategy evolves, either because the culture constrains the choice of new strategies or because the dominant traits of the culture are somewhat strategy-neutral and compatible with evolving versions of the company's strategy. As a consequence, *strongly implanted cultures provide a huge assist in executing strategy* because company managers can use the traditions, beliefs, values, common bonds, or behavioral norms as levers to mobilize commitment to executing the chosen strategy.

Weak-Culture Companies   In direct contrast to strong-culture companies, weak-culture companies lack widely shared and strongly held values, principles, and behavioral norms. As a result, they also lack cultural mechanisms for aligning, constraining, and regulating the actions, decisions, and behaviors of company personnel. In the absence of any long-standing top management commitment to particular values, beliefs, operating practices, and behavioral norms, individuals encounter little pressure to do things in particular ways. Such a dearth of companywide cultural influences and revered traditions produces a work climate where there is no strong employee allegiance to what the company stands for or to operating the business in well-defined ways. While individual employees may well have some bonds of identification with and loyalty toward their department, their colleagues, their union, or their immediate boss, there's neither passion about the company nor emotional commitment to what it is trying to accomplish—a condition that often results in many employees' viewing their company as just a place to work and their job as just a way to make a living.

As a consequence, *weak cultures provide little or no assistance in executing strategy* because there are no traditions, beliefs, values, common bonds, or behavioral norms that management can use as levers to mobilize commitment to executing the chosen strategy. Without a work climate that channels organizational energy in the direction of good strategy execution, managers are left with the options of either using compensation incentives and other motivational devices to mobilize employee commitment, supervising and monitoring employee actions more closely, or trying to establish cultural roots that will in time start to nurture the strategy execution process.

Why Corporate Cultures Matter to the Strategy Execution Process

Even if a company has a strong culture, the culture and work climate may or may not be compatible with what is needed for effective implementation of the chosen strategy. When a company's present culture promotes attitudes, behaviors, and ways of doing things that are *in sync with the chosen strategy and conducive to first-rate strategy execution,* the culture functions as a valuable ally in the strategy execution process. For example, a corporate culture characterized by frugality and thrift prompts employee actions to identify cost-saving opportunities—the very behavior needed for successful execution of a low-cost leadership strategy. A culture that celebrates taking initiative, exhibiting creativity, taking risks, and embracing change is conducive to successful execution of product innovation and technological leadership strategies.[10]

A culture that is grounded in actions, behaviors, and work practices that are conducive to good strategy implementation supports the strategy execution effort in three ways:

1. *A culture that is well matched to the chosen strategy and the requirements of the strategy execution effort focuses the attention of employees on what is most important to this effort.* Moreover, it directs their behavior and serves as a guide to their decision making. In this manner, it can align the efforts and decisions of employees throughout the firm and minimize the need for direct supervision.

2. *Culture-induced peer pressure further induces company personnel to do things in a manner that aids the cause of good strategy execution.* The stronger the culture (the more widely shared and deeply held the values), the more effective peer pressure is in shaping and supporting the strategy execution effort. Research has shown that strong group norms can shape employee behavior even more powerfully than can financial incentives.

3. *A company culture that is consistent with the requirements for good strategy execution can energize employees, deepen their commitment to execute the strategy flawlessly, and enhance worker productivity in the process.* When a company's culture is grounded in many of the needed strategy-executing behaviors, employees feel genuinely better about their jobs, the company they work for, and the merits of what the company is trying to accomplish. Greater employee buy-in for what the company is trying to accomplish boosts motivation and marshals organizational energy behind the drive for good strategy execution. An energized workforce enhances the chances of achieving execution-critical performance targets and good strategy execution.

In sharp contrast, when a culture is in conflict with the chosen strategy or what is required to execute the company's strategy well, the culture becomes a stumbling block.[11] Some of the very behaviors needed to execute the strategy successfully run contrary to the attitudes, behaviors, and operating practices embedded in the prevailing culture. Such a clash poses a real dilemma for company personnel. Should they be loyal to the culture and company traditions (to which they are likely to be emotionally attached) and

thus resist or be indifferent to actions that will promote better strategy execution—a choice that will certainly weaken the drive for good strategy execution? Alternatively, should they go along with management's strategy execution effort and engage in actions that run counter to the culture—a choice that will likely impair morale and lead to a less-than-enthusiastic commitment to good strategy execution? Neither choice leads to desirable outcomes. Culture-bred resistance to the actions and behaviors needed for good strategy execution, particularly if strong and widespread, poses a formidable hurdle that must be cleared for a strategy's execution to be successful.

The consequences of having—or not having—an execution-supportive corporate culture says something important about the task of managing the strategy execution process: *Closely aligning corporate culture with the requirements for proficient strategy execution merits the full attention of senior executives.* The culture-building objective is to create a work climate and style of operating that mobilize the energy of company personnel squarely behind efforts to execute strategy competently. The more deeply management can embed execution-supportive ways of doing things, the more management can rely on the culture to automatically steer company personnel toward behaviors and work practices that aid good strategy execution and veer from doing things that impede it. Moreover, culturally astute managers understand that nourishing the right cultural environment not only adds power to their push for proficient strategy execution but also promotes strong employee identification with, and commitment to, the company's vision, performance targets, and strategy.

> It is in management's best interest to dedicate considerable effort to establishing a corporate culture that encourages behaviors and work practices conducive to good strategy execution.

Healthy Cultures That Aid Good Strategy Execution

A strong culture, provided it fits the chosen strategy and embraces execution-supportive attitudes, behaviors, and work practices, is definitely a healthy culture. Two other types of cultures exist that tend to be healthy and largely supportive of good strategy execution: high-performance cultures and adaptive cultures.

High-Performance Cultures   Some companies have so-called high-performance cultures where the standout traits are a "can-do" spirit, pride in doing things right, no-excuses accountability, and a pervasive results-oriented work climate in which people go all out to meet or beat stretch objectives.[12] In high-performance cultures, there's a strong sense of involvement on the part of company personnel and emphasis on individual initiative and effort. Performance expectations are clearly delineated for the company as a whole, for each organizational unit, and for each individual. Issues and problems are promptly addressed; there's a razor-sharp focus on what needs to be done. The clear and unyielding expectation is that all company personnel, from senior executives to frontline employees, will display high-performance behaviors and a passion for making the company successful. Such a culture—permeated by a spirit of achievement and constructive pressure to achieve good results—is a valuable contributor to good strategy execution and operating excellence.[13]

Epic Systems, a company well-known by healthcare providers for the excellence of their record-keeping software, attributes much of its success to their strong, high-performance culture. By emphasizing the importance of the company's "Ten Commandments" and guiding principles, Epic has created a work climate in which employees have an overarching standard that helps guide and coordinate their actions. Epic fosters this high-performance culture from the get-go. They target top tier universities to hire entry-level talent, focusing on skills rather than personality. A rigorous training and orientation program indoctrinates each new employee. This culture positively affects Epic's strategy execution because employees are focused on the most important actions, there is peer pressure to contribute to Epic's success, and employees are genuinely excited to be involved. Epic's faith in its ability to acculturate new team members and remain true to its core values has helped sustain its status as a premier provider of healthcare IT systems over many years.

The challenge in creating a high-performance culture is to inspire high loyalty and dedication on the part of employees, such that they are energized to put forth their very best efforts. Managers have to take pains to reinforce constructive behavior, reward top performers, and purge habits and behaviors that stand in the way of high productivity

PUMA's High-Performance Culture

nexusby/Shutterstock

As the third largest sportswear manufacturer in the world, PUMA is racing to catch up with its competitors, Nike and Adidas. Its mission, encapsulated in the phrase "Forever Faster", speaks to its drive to out-innovate and out-pace its formidable rivals. But the more consequential driver of PUMA's speed and agility is its high performance culture.

In 2020, PUMA won Glassdoor's award for the Best Place to Work in Germany, where the company is headquartered. To inspire and energize employees at the headquarters, PUMA offers a fast-paced, fun work environment, centered on a sporting lifestyle. Employees are encouraged to enjoy the company's organic canteen, state-of-the-art gym, nature running trails, soccer fields, and basketball courts. This not only helps workers to form strong bonds with one another but it provides a kind of test lab for the company's latest innovations and designs.

As a multinational company, with nearly 15,000 employees and three international hubs outside of Germany (Hong Kong; Somerville, MA; Ho Chi Minh City, Vietnam), PUMA's challenge has been to ensure that this culture spans the entire reach of the company and unites the parts. This requires much more than ensuring that every hub has a sports driven campus like the one in Germany. It begins with hiring practices to attract and retain those people whose values, drive, and passion for sports match those of others in the company. Accordingly, PUMA is a youthful company, with the average age of its employees hovering just above 30. New employees are exposed to the company culture through learning videos and literature that support their working with "Speed and Spirit" from day one. Rookies are matched with a veteran to show them the ropes and facilitate their becoming acculturated quickly. Talent management and training at PUMA (including International Leadership Programs) contribute similarly to the company's high-performance culture. High potential and high performance individuals are identified and promoted regardless of level and across functions in the belief that successful teams and led by successful leaders.

In their annual survey of employees across many companies, Glassdoor reports that PUMA's employees rave about the speed and spirit ethos that they experience at PUMA. From its flexible hours, generous benefits, personal development opportunities, on-site recreational facilities, team-spiritedness, and commitment to work-life balance, PUMA demonstrates that it puts its people first. For that is ultimately the only sure foundation of a high-performance culture.

Sources: Glassdoor.com/employers/blog/puma-2020, by Amy Elissa Jackson, December 11, 2019; Company website, accessed 4/1/20.

and good results. They must work at knowing the strengths and weaknesses of their subordinates to better match talent with task and enable people to make meaningful contributions by doing what they do best. They have to stress learning from mistakes and must put an unrelenting emphasis on moving forward and making good progress—in effect, there has to be a disciplined, performance-focused approach to managing the organization. Illustration Capsule 12.1 describes the attention that Puma gives toward maintaining its high-performance culture.

Adaptive Cultures   The hallmark of adaptive corporate cultures is willingness on the part of organization members to accept change and take on the challenge of introducing and executing new strategies. Company personnel share a feeling of confidence that the organization can deal with whatever threats and opportunities arise; they are receptive to risk taking, experimentation, innovation, and changing strategies and practices. The work climate is supportive of managers and employees who propose or initiate useful change. Internal entrepreneurship (often called *intrapreneurship*) on the part of individuals and groups is encouraged and rewarded. Senior executives seek out, support, and promote individuals who exercise initiative, spot opportunities for improvement, and display the skills to implement them. Managers openly evaluate ideas and suggestions, fund initiatives to develop new or better products, and take prudent risks to pursue emerging market opportunities. As in high-performance cultures, the company exhibits a proactive approach to identifying issues, evaluating the implications and options, and moving ahead quickly with workable solutions. Strategies and traditional operating practices are modified as needed to adjust to, or take advantage of, changes in the business environment.

> As a company's strategy evolves, an adaptive culture is a definite ally in the strategy-implementing, strategy-executing process as compared to cultures that are resistant to change.

But why is change so willingly embraced in an adaptive culture? Why are organization members not fearful of how change will affect them? Why does an adaptive culture not break down from the force of ongoing changes in strategy, operating practices, and behavioral norms? The answers lie in two distinctive and dominant traits of an adaptive culture: (1) Changes in operating practices and behaviors must *not* compromise core values and long-standing business principles (since they are at the root of the culture); and (2) changes that are instituted must satisfy the legitimate interests of key constituencies— customers, employees, shareholders, suppliers, and the communities where the company operates. In other words, what sustains an adaptive culture is that organization members perceive the changes that management is trying to institute as *legitimate,* in keeping with the core values, and in the overall best interests of stakeholders.[14] Not surprisingly, company personnel are usually more receptive to change when their employment security is not threatened and when they view new duties or job assignments as part of the process of adapting to new conditions. Should workforce downsizing be necessary, it is important that layoffs be handled humanely and employee departures be made as painless as possible.

Technology companies, software companies, and Internet-based companies are good illustrations of organizations with adaptive cultures. Such companies thrive on change— driving it, leading it, and capitalizing on it. Companies like Amazon, Google, Apple, Facebook, Adobe, Groupon, Intel, and Yelp cultivate the capability to act and react rapidly. They are avid practitioners of entrepreneurship and innovation, with a demonstrated willingness to take bold risks to create altogether new products, new businesses, and new industries. To create and nurture a culture that can adapt rapidly to shifting business conditions, they make a point of staffing their organizations with people who are flexible, who rise to the challenge of change, and who have an aptitude for adapting well to new circumstances. Wayfair, the largest online retailer of home furnishings in the United States, attributes its rapid growth to an entrepreneurial and collaborative culture that encourages employee innovation. They hire individuals who are willing to solve problems creatively and develop new initiatives, and empower them to take measured risks.

In fast-changing business environments, a corporate culture that is receptive to altering organizational practices and behaviors is a virtual necessity. However, adaptive cultures work to the advantage of all companies, not just those in rapid-change environments. Every company operates in a market and business climate that is changing to one degree or another and that, in turn, requires internal operating responses and new behaviors on the part of organization members.

Unhealthy Cultures That Impede Good Strategy Execution

The distinctive characteristic of an unhealthy corporate culture is the presence of counterproductive cultural traits that adversely impact the work climate and company performance. Five particularly unhealthy cultural traits are hostility to change, heavily politicized decision making, insular thinking, unethical and greed-driven behaviors, and the presence of incompatible, clashing subcultures.

Change-Resistant Cultures   Change-resistant cultures—where fear of change and skepticism about the importance of new developments are the norm—place a premium on not making mistakes, prompting managers to lean toward safe, conservative options intended to maintain the status quo, protect their power base, and guard their immediate interests. When such companies encounter business environments with accelerating change, going slow on altering traditional ways of doing things can be a serious liability. Under these conditions, change-resistant cultures encourage a number of unhealthy behaviors—avoiding risks, not capitalizing on emerging opportunities, taking a lax approach to both product innovation and continuous improvement in performing value chain activities, and responding more slowly than is warranted to market change. In change-resistant cultures, proposals to do things differently face an uphill battle and people who champion them may be seen as something of a nuisance or a troublemaker. Instead, a lot of energy goes into justifying what the company is presently doing, with little discussion of what it should consider doing differently—there is strong aversion to bold action. Executives who don't value managers or employees with initiative and new ideas put a damper on product innovation, experimentation, and efforts to improve.

Hostility to change is most often found in companies with stodgy bureaucracies that have enjoyed considerable market success in years past and that are wedded to the "We have done it this way for years" syndrome. Sears, and Eastman Kodak are classic examples of companies whose change-resistant bureaucracies have damaged their market standings and financial performance; clinging to what made them successful, they were reluctant to alter operating practices and modify their business approaches when signals of market change first sounded. As strategies of "hold-the-course" won out over bold innovation, they lost market share to rivals that quickly moved to institute changes more in tune with evolving market conditions and buyer preferences. In consequence, both of these companies ultimately ended up in bankruptcy court.

Politicized Cultures   What makes a politicized internal environment so unhealthy is that political infighting consumes a great deal of organizational energy, often with the result that what's best for the company takes a backseat to political maneuvering. In companies where internal politics pervades the work climate, empire-building managers pursue their own agendas and operate the work units under their supervision as autonomous "fiefdoms." The positions they take on issues are usually aimed at protecting or expanding their own turf. Collaboration with other organizational units is viewed with suspicion, and cross-unit cooperation occurs grudgingly. The support or opposition of politically influential executives and/or coalitions among departments with vested interests in a particular outcome tends to shape what actions the company takes. All this political maneuvering takes away from efforts to execute strategy with real proficiency and frustrates company personnel who are less political and more inclined to do what is in the company's best interests.

Insular, Inwardly Focused Cultures   Sometimes a company reigns as an industry leader or enjoys great market success for so long that its personnel start to believe they have all the answers or can develop them on their own. There is a strong tendency to neglect what customers are saying and how their needs and expectations are changing. Such confidence in the correctness of how the company does things and an unflinching belief in its competitive superiority breed arrogance, prompting company personnel to discount the merits of what outsiders are doing and to see little payoff from studying best-in-class performers. Insular thinking, internally driven solutions, and a must-be-invented-here mindset come to permeate the corporate culture. An inwardly focused corporate culture gives rise to managerial inbreeding and a failure to recruit people who can offer fresh thinking and outside perspectives. The big risk of insular cultural thinking is that the company can underestimate the capabilities of rival companies while overestimating its own—all of which diminishes a company's competitiveness over time.

Unethical and Greed-Driven Cultures   Companies that have little regard for ethical standards or are run by executives driven by greed and ego gratification are scandals waiting to happen. Executives exude the negatives of arrogance, ego, greed, and an "ends-justify-the-means" mentality in pursuing overambitious revenue and profitability targets.[15] Senior managers wink at unethical behavior and may cross over the line to unethical (and sometimes criminal) behavior themselves. They are prone to adopt accounting principles that make financial performance look better than it really is. Legions of companies have fallen prey to unethical behavior and greed, most notably Turing Pharmaceuticals (whose name was changed to Vyera in the wake of scandal) and Mylan, both known for their unconscionable price hikes on life-saving medications. Notorious others include Enron, BP, AIG, Countrywide Financial, and JPMorgan Chase, Deutsche Bank, and HSBC (Europe's biggest bank) with executives being indicted and/or convicted of criminal behavior.

Incompatible, Clashing Subcultures   Company subcultures are unhealthy when they embrace conflicting business philosophies, support inconsistent approaches to strategy execution, and encourage incompatible methods of people management. Clashing subcultures can prevent a company from coordinating its efforts to craft and execute strategy and can distract company personnel from the business of business. Internal jockeying among the subcultures for cultural dominance impedes teamwork among the company's various organizational units and blocks the emergence of a collaborative approach to strategy execution. Such a lack of consensus about how to proceed is likely to result in fragmented or inconsistent approaches to implementing new strategic initiatives and in limited success in executing the company's overall strategy.

Changing a Problem Culture

When a culture is unhealthy or otherwise out of sync with the actions and behaviors needed to execute the strategy successfully, the culture must be changed as rapidly as can be managed. This means eliminating any unhealthy or dysfunctional cultural traits as fast as possible and aggressively striving to ingrain new behaviors and work practices that will enable first-rate strategy execution. The more entrenched the unhealthy or mismatched aspects of a company culture, the more likely the culture will impede strategy execution and the greater the need for change.

Changing a problem culture is among the toughest management tasks because of the heavy anchor of ingrained behaviors and attitudes. It is natural for company personnel to cling to familiar practices and to be wary of change, if not hostile to new approaches concerning how things are to be done. Consequently, it takes concerted management action over a period of time to root out unwanted behaviors and replace an unsupportive culture with more effective ways of doing things. *The single most visible factor that distinguishes successful culture-change efforts from failed attempts is competent leadership at the top.* Great power is needed to force major cultural change and overcome the stubborn resistance of entrenched cultures—and great power is possessed only by the most senior executives, especially the CEO. However, while top management must lead the change effort, the tasks of marshaling support for a new culture and

● LO 12-3

Identify the kinds of actions management can take to change a problem corporate culture.

FIGURE 12.2   Changing a Problem Culture

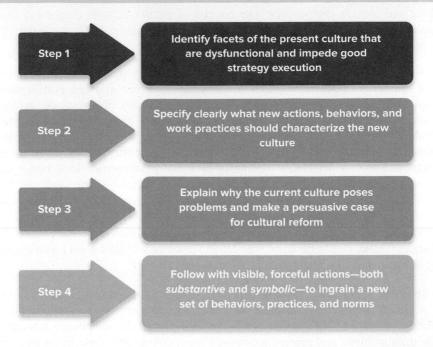

Step 1 — Identify facets of the present culture that are dysfunctional and impede good strategy execution

Step 2 — Specify clearly what new actions, behaviors, and work practices should characterize the new culture

Step 3 — Explain why the current culture poses problems and make a persuasive case for cultural reform

Step 4 — Follow with visible, forceful actions—both *substantive* and *symbolic*—to ingrain a new set of behaviors, practices, and norms

instilling the desired cultural behaviors must involve a company's whole management team. Middle managers and frontline supervisors play a key role in implementing the new work practices and operating approaches, helping win rank-and-file acceptance of and support for changes, and instilling the desired behavioral norms.

As shown in Figure 12.2, the first step in fixing a problem culture is for top management to identify those facets of the present culture that are dysfunctional and pose obstacles to executing strategic initiatives. Second, managers must clearly define the desired new behaviors and features of the culture they want to create. Third, they must convince company personnel of why the present culture poses problems and why and how new behaviors and operating approaches will improve company performance—the case for cultural reform has to be persuasive. Finally, and most important, all the talk about remodeling the present culture must be followed swiftly by visible, forceful actions to promote the desired new behaviors and work practices—actions that company personnel will interpret as a determined top-management commitment to bringing about a different work climate and new ways of operating. The actions to implant the new culture must be both substantive and symbolic.

Making a Compelling Case for Culture Change   The way for management to begin a major remodeling of the corporate culture is by selling company personnel on the need for new-style behaviors and work practices. This means making a compelling case for why the culture-remodeling efforts are in the organization's best interests and why company personnel should wholeheartedly join the effort to do things somewhat differently. This can be done by

- Explaining why and how certain behaviors and work practices in the current culture pose obstacles to good strategy execution.
- Explaining how new behaviors and work practices will be more advantageous and produce better results. Effective culture-change leaders are good at telling stories to describe the new values and desired behaviors and connect them to everyday practices.

- Citing reasons why the current strategy has to be modified, if the need for cultural change is due to a change in strategy. This includes explaining why the new strategic initiatives will bolster the company's competitiveness and performance and how a change in culture can help in executing the new strategy.

It is essential for the CEO and other top executives to talk personally to personnel all across the company about the reasons for modifying work practices and culture-related behaviors. For the culture-change effort to be successful, frontline supervisors and employee opinion leaders must be won over to the cause, which means convincing them of the merits of *practicing* and *enforcing* cultural norms at every level of the organization, from the highest to the lowest. Arguments for new ways of doing things and new work practices tend to be embraced more readily if employees understand how they will benefit company stakeholders (particularly customers, employees, and shareholders). Until a large majority of employees accept the need for a new culture and agree that different work practices and behaviors are called for, there's more work to be done in selling company personnel on the whys and wherefores of culture change. Building widespread organizational support requires taking every opportunity to repeat the message of why the new work practices, operating approaches, and behaviors are good for company stakeholders and essential for the company's future success.

Substantive Culture-Changing Actions   No culture-change effort can get very far when leaders merely talk about the need for different actions, behaviors, and work practices. Company executives must give the culture-change effort some teeth by initiating *a series of actions* that company personnel will see as unmistakably indicative of the seriousness of management's commitment to cultural change. The strongest signs that management is truly committed to instilling a new culture include

- Replacing high-profile executives and managers who are allied with the old culture and either openly or covertly oppose needed organizational and cultural changes.
- Promoting individuals who have stepped forward to spearhead the shift to a different culture and who can serve as role models for the desired cultural behavior.
- Appointing outsiders with the desired cultural attributes to influential positions—bringing in new-breed managers sends an unambiguous message that a new era is dawning.
- Screening all candidates for new positions carefully, hiring only those who appear to fit in with the new culture. For example, a company that stresses operating with integrity and fairness must hire people who themselves have integrity and place a high value on fair play. A company whose culture revolves around creativity, product innovation, and leading change must screen new hires for their ability to think outside the box, generate new ideas, and thrive in a climate of rapid change and ambiguity.
- Mandating that all company personnel attend culture-training programs to better understand the new culture-related actions and behaviors that are expected.
- Designing compensation incentives that boost the pay of teams and individuals who display the desired cultural behaviors. Company personnel are much more inclined to exhibit the desired kinds of actions and behaviors when it is in their financial best interest to do so.
- Letting word leak out that generous pay raises have been awarded to individuals who have stepped out front, led the adoption of the desired work practices, displayed the new-style behaviors, and achieved pace-setting results.
- Revising policies and procedures in ways that will help drive cultural change.

Executives must launch enough companywide culture-change actions at the outset to leave no room for doubt that management is dead serious about changing the present culture and that a cultural transformation is inevitable. Management's commitment to cultural change in the company must be made credible. The series of actions initiated by top management must command attention, get the change process off to a fast start, and be followed by unrelenting efforts to firmly establish the new work practices, desired behaviors, and style of operating as "standard."

The most important symbolic cultural-changing action that top executives can take is to *lead by example*.

Symbolic Culture-Changing Actions   There's also an important place for symbolic managerial actions to alter a problem culture and tighten the strategy–culture fit. The most important symbolic actions are those that top executives take to *lead by example*. For instance, if the organization's strategy involves a drive to become the industry's low-cost producer, senior managers must display frugality in their own actions and decisions. Examples include inexpensive decorations in the executive suite, conservative expense accounts and entertainment allowances, a lean staff in the corporate office, scrutiny of budget requests, few executive perks, and so on. At Walmart, all the executive offices are simply decorated; executives are habitually frugal in their own actions, and they are zealous in their efforts to control costs and promote greater efficiency. At Nucor, one of the world's low-cost producers of steel products, executives fly coach class and use taxis at airports rather than limousines. Top executives must be alert to the fact that company personnel will be watching their behavior to see if their actions match their rhetoric. Hence, they need to make sure their current decisions and actions will be construed as consistent with the new cultural values and norms.[16]

Another category of symbolic actions includes holding ceremonial events to single out and honor people whose actions and performance exemplify what is called for in the new culture. Such events also provide an opportunity to celebrate each culture-change success. Executives sensitive to their role in promoting strategy–culture fit make a habit of appearing at ceremonial functions to praise individuals and groups that exemplify the desired behaviors. They show up at employee training programs to stress strategic priorities, values, ethical principles, and cultural norms. Every group gathering is seen as an opportunity to repeat and ingrain values, praise good deeds, expound on the merits of the new culture, and cite instances of how the new work practices and operating approaches have produced good results. Ceremonial events can also be used to drive home the commitment to changing culture. The late Steve Jobs, visionary co-founder of Apple, once countered resistance to change by dramatizing the death of "the old" with a coffin.

The use of symbols in culture building is widespread. Numerous businesses have employee-of-the-month awards. The military has a long-standing custom of awarding ribbons and medals for exemplary actions. Mary Kay Cosmetics awards an array of prizes ceremoniously to its beauty consultants for reaching various sales plateaus, including the iconic pink Cadillac.

How Long Does It Take to Change a Problem Culture?   Planting the seeds of a new culture and helping the culture grow strong roots require a determined, sustained effort by the chief executive and other senior managers. Changing a problem culture is never a short-term exercise; it takes time for a new culture to emerge and take root. And it takes even longer for a new culture to become deeply embedded. The bigger the organization and the greater the cultural shift needed to produce an execution-supportive fit, the longer it takes. In large companies, fixing a problem culture and instilling a new set of attitudes and behaviors can take two to five years. In fact, it is usually tougher to reform an entrenched problematic culture than it is to instill a strategy-supportive culture from scratch in a brand-new organization.

Illustration Capsule 12.2 discusses the approaches used at Goldman Sachs to change a culture that was impeding its efforts to recruit the best young talent.

Driving Cultural Change at Goldman Sachs

Goldman Sachs was long considered one of the best financial services companies to work for, due to its prestige, high salaries, bonuses, and perks. Yet by 2014, Goldman was beginning to have trouble recruiting the best and brightest MBAs at top business schools. Part of this was due to the banking crisis of 2008–2009 and the scandals that continued to plague the industry year after year, tarnishing the industry's reputation. But another reason was a change in the values and aspirations of the younger generation that made banking culture far less appealing than that of consulting, technology, and start-up companies. Newly minted MBAs were no longer as willing to accept the grueling hours and unpredictable schedules that were the norm in investment banking. They wanted to derive meaning and purpose from their work and prized work/life balance over monetary gain. The tech industry was known for fun, youth-oriented, and collaborative working environments, while the excitement and promise of entrepreneurial ventures offered much appeal. Goldman found itself competing with Amazon, Google, Microsoft, and Facebook as well as with start-ups for the best young talent—and losing out.

Goldman's problem was compounded by the fact that its culture was regarded as stuffy and stodgy—qualities not likely to appeal to the young, particularly when contrasted with the hip cultures of tech and start-up companies. Further, it had always been slow-moving in terms of implementing organizational change. Recognizing the problem, the leadership at Goldman attempted to pivot sharply, asking its executives to think of Goldman as a tech company, complete with the associated values. The Chief Learning Office at Goldman Sachs was put in charge of the effort to transform its culture and began taking deliberate steps to enact changes. Buy-in was

JUSTIN LANE/EPA-EFE/Shutterstock

sought from the full C-suite—the leadership team at the very top of the firm. To foster a more familial atmosphere at work, the company began with small steps, such as setting up sports leagues and encouraging regular team happy hours. More significantly, they instituted more employee-friendly work schedules and policies, more accommodating of work-life balance. They liberalized their parental leave policies, provided greater flexibility in work schedules, and enacted protections for interns and junior bankers designed to limit their working hours. They also overhauled their performance review and promotion systems as well as their recruiting practices and policies regarding diversity. Although cultural change never comes swiftly, by 2017 results were apparent even to outside observers. That year, the career website Vault.com named Goldman Sachs as the best banking firm to work for, noting that when it came to workplace policies, Goldman led the industry.

Sources: http://www.goldmansachs.com/careers/blog/posts/goldman-sachs-vault-2017.html; http://sps.columbia.edu/news/how-goldman-sachs-drives-culture-change-in-the-financial-industry.

LEADING THE STRATEGY EXECUTION PROCESS

● ● ● ●

For an enterprise to execute its strategy in truly proficient fashion, top executives must take the lead in the strategy implementation process and personally drive the pace of progress. They have to be out in the field, seeing for themselves how well operations are going, gathering information firsthand, and gauging the progress being made. Proficient strategy execution requires company managers to be diligent and adept in spotting problems, learning what obstacles lay in the path of good execution, and then clearing the way for progress—the goal must be to produce better

● **LO 12-4**

Recognize what constitutes effective managerial leadership in achieving superior strategy execution.

results speedily and productively. There must be constructive, but unrelenting, pressure on organizational units to (1) demonstrate excellence in all dimensions of strategy execution and (2) do so on a consistent basis—ultimately, that's what will enable a well-crafted strategy to achieve the desired performance results.

The specifics of how to implement a strategy and deliver the intended results must start with understanding the requirements for good strategy execution. Afterward comes a diagnosis of the organization's preparedness to execute the strategic initiatives and decisions on how to move forward and achieve the targeted results.[17] In general, leading the drive for good strategy execution and operating excellence calls for three actions on the part of the managers in charge:

- Staying on top of what is happening and closely monitoring progress.
- Putting constructive pressure on the organization to execute the strategy well and achieve operating excellence.
- Initiating corrective actions to improve strategy execution and achieve the targeted performance results.

Staying on Top of How Well Things Are Going

To stay on top of how well the strategy execution process is going, senior executives have to tap into information from a wide range of sources. In addition to communicating regularly with key subordinates and reviewing the latest operating results, watching the competitive reactions of rival firms, and visiting with key customers and suppliers to get their perspectives, they usually visit various company facilities and talk with many

> **CORE** CONCEPT
>
> **Management by walking around (MBWA)** is one of the techniques that effective leaders use to stay informed about how well the strategy execution process is progressing.

different company personnel at many different organizational levels—a technique often labeled **management by walking around (MBWA).** Most managers attach great importance to spending time with people at company facilities, asking questions, listening to their opinions and concerns, and gathering firsthand information about how well aspects of the strategy execution process are going. Facilities tours and face-to-face contacts with operating-level employees give executives a good grasp of what progress is being made, what problems are being encountered, and whether additional resources or different approaches may be needed. Just as important, MBWA provides opportunities to give encouragement, lift spirits, focus attention on key priorities, and create some excitement—all of which generate positive energy and help boost strategy execution efforts.

Jeff Bezos, Amazon's CEO, is noted for his practice of MBWA, firing off a battery of questions when he tours facilities, and insisting that Amazon managers spend time in the trenches with their people to prevent getting disconnected from the reality of what's happening. Walmart executives have had a long-standing practice of spending two to three days every week visiting Walmart's stores and talking with store managers and employees. Sam Walton, Walmart's founder, insisted, "The key is to get out into the store and listen to what the associates have to say." Jack Welch, the highly effective former CEO of General Electric, not only made it a priority to personally visit GE operations and talk with major customers but also routinely spent time exchanging information and ideas with GE managers from all over the world who were attending classes at the company's leadership development center near GE's headquarters.

Many manufacturing executives make a point of strolling the factory floor to talk with workers and meeting regularly with union officials. Some managers operate out of open cubicles in big spaces filled with open cubicles for other personnel so that they can interact easily and frequently with co-workers. Managers at some companies host weekly get-togethers (often on Friday afternoons) to create a regular opportunity for information to flow freely between down-the-line employees and executives.

Mobilizing the Effort for Excellence in Strategy Execution

Part of the leadership task in mobilizing organizational energy behind the drive for good strategy execution entails nurturing a results-oriented work climate, where performance standards are high and a spirit of achievement is pervasive. Successfully leading the effort is typically characterized by such leadership actions and managerial practices as

- *Treating employees as valued partners.* Some companies symbolize the value of individual employees and the importance of their contributions by referring to them as cast members (Disney), crew members (McDonald's), job owners (Graniterock), partners (Starbucks), or associates (Walmart, LensCrafters, W. L. Gore, Edward Jones, Publix Supermarkets, and Marriott International). Very often, there is a strong company commitment to training each employee thoroughly, offering attractive compensation and benefits, emphasizing promotion from within and promising career opportunities, providing a high degree of job security, and otherwise making employees feel well treated and valued.

- *Fostering an esprit de corps that energizes organization members.* The task here is to skillfully use people-management practices calculated to build morale, foster pride in working for the company, promote teamwork and collaborative group effort, win the emotional commitment of individuals and organizational units to what the company is trying to accomplish, and inspire company personnel to do their best in achieving good results.[18]

- *Using empowerment to help create a fully engaged workforce.* Top executives—and, to some degree, the enterprise's entire management team—must seek to engage the full organization in the strategy execution effort. A fully engaged workforce, where individuals bring their best to work every day, is necessary to produce great results.[19] So is having a group of dedicated managers committed to making a difference in their organization. The two best things top-level executives can do to create a fully engaged organization are (1) delegate authority to middle and lower-level managers to get the strategy execution process moving and (2) empower rank-and-file employees to act on their own initiative. Operating excellence requires that everybody contribute ideas, exercise initiative and creativity in performing his or her work, and have a desire to do things in the best possible manner.

- *Nurturing a results-oriented work climate and clearly communicating an expectation that company personnel are to give their best in achieving performance targets.* Managers must make it abundantly clear that they expect all company personnel to put forth every effort to meet performance targets. But executives cannot expect directives to "try harder" to produce the desired outcomes in the absence of a results-oriented work climate. Nor can they expect innovative improvements in operations if they do no more than exhort people to "be creative." Rather, they must foster a strong culture with high performance standards and where innovative ideas and experimentation with new ways of doing things can blossom and thrive.

- *Using the tools of benchmarking, best practices, business process reengineering, TQM, and Six Sigma to focus attention on continuous improvement.* These are proven approaches to getting better operating results and facilitating better strategy execution.
- *Using the full range of motivational techniques and compensation incentives to inspire company personnel and reward high performance.* Individuals and groups should be strongly encouraged to brainstorm, let their imaginations fly in all directions, and come up with proposals for improving the way that things are done. This means giving company personnel enough autonomy to stand out, excel, and contribute. And it means that the rewards for successful champions of new ideas and operating improvements should be large and visible. It is particularly important that people who champion an unsuccessful idea are not punished or sidelined but, rather, encouraged to try again. Finding great ideas requires taking risks and recognizing that many ideas won't pan out.
- *Celebrating individual, group, and company successes.* Top management should miss no opportunity to express respect for individual employees and appreciation of extraordinary individual and group effort.[20] Companies like Google, Mary Kay, Tupperware, and McDonald's actively seek out reasons and opportunities to give pins, ribbons, buttons, badges, and medals for good showings by average performers—the idea being to express appreciation and give a motivational boost to people who stand out in doing ordinary jobs. At Kimpton Hotels and Restaurants, employees who create special moments for guests are rewarded with "Kimpton Moment" tokens that can be redeemed for paid days off, gift certificates to restaurants, flat-screen TVs, and other prizes. Cisco Systems and 3M Corporation make a point of ceremoniously honoring individuals who believe so strongly in their ideas that they take it on themselves to hurdle the bureaucracy, maneuver their projects through the system, and turn them into improved services, new products, or even new businesses.

While leadership efforts to instill a results-oriented, high-performance culture usually accentuate the positive, negative consequences for poor performance must be in play as well. Managers whose units consistently perform poorly must be replaced. Low-performing employees must be weeded out or at least employed in ways better suited to their aptitudes. Average performers should be candidly counseled that they have limited career potential unless they show more progress in the form of additional effort, better skills, and improved ability to execute the strategy well and deliver good results.

Leading the Process of Making Corrective Adjustments

There comes a time at every company when managers have to fine-tune or overhaul the approaches to strategy execution since no action plan for executing strategy can foresee all the problems that will arise. Clearly, when a company's strategy execution effort is not delivering good results, it is the leader's responsibility to step forward and initiate corrective actions, although sometimes it must be recognized that unsatisfactory performance may be due as much or more to flawed strategy as to weak strategy execution.[21]

Success in making corrective adjustments hinges on (1) a thorough analysis of the situation, (2) the exercise of good business judgment in deciding what actions to take, and (3) good implementation of the corrective actions that are initiated. Successful managers are skilled in getting an organization back on track rather quickly. They (and their staffs) are good at discerning what adjustments to make and in bringing them to a successful conclusion. Managers who struggle to show measurable progress in implementing corrective actions in a timely fashion are candidates for being replaced.

The *process* of making corrective adjustments in strategy execution varies according to the situation. In a crisis, taking remedial action quickly is of the essence. But it still takes time to review the situation, examine the available data, identify and evaluate options (crunching whatever numbers may be appropriate to determine which options are likely to generate the best outcomes), and decide what to do. When the situation allows managers to proceed more deliberately in deciding when to make changes and what changes to make, most managers seem to prefer a process of incrementally solidifying commitment to a particular course of action.[22] The process that managers go through in deciding on corrective adjustments is essentially the same for both proactive and reactive changes: They sense needs, gather information, broaden and deepen their understanding of the situation, develop options and explore their pros and cons, put forth action proposals, strive for a consensus, and finally formally adopt an agreed-on course of action. The time frame for deciding what corrective changes to initiate can be a few hours, a few days, a few weeks, or even a few months if the situation is particularly complicated.

The challenges of making the right corrective adjustments and leading a successful strategy execution effort are, without question, substantial.[23] There's no generic, by-the-books procedure to follow. Because each instance of executing strategy occurs under different organizational circumstances, the managerial agenda for executing strategy always needs to be situation-specific. But the job is definitely doable. Although there is no prescriptive answer to the question of exactly what to do, any of several courses of action may produce good results. As we said at the beginning of Chapter 10, executing strategy is an action-oriented task that challenges a manager's ability to lead and direct organizational change, create or reinvent business processes, manage and motivate people, and achieve performance targets. If you now better understand what the challenges are, what tasks are involved, what tools can be used to aid the managerial process of executing strategy, and why the action agenda for implementing and executing strategy sweeps across so many aspects of managerial work, then the discussions in Chapters 10, 11, and 12 have been a success.

A FINAL WORD ON LEADING THE PROCESS OF CRAFTING AND EXECUTING STRATEGY

In practice, it is hard to separate leading the process of executing strategy from leading the other pieces of the strategy process. As we emphasized in Chapter 2, the job of crafting and executing strategy consists of five interrelated and linked stages, with much looping and recycling to fine-tune and adjust the strategic vision, objectives, strategy, and implementation approaches to fit one another and to fit changing circumstances. The process is continuous, and the conceptually separate acts of crafting and executing strategy blur together in real-world situations. *The best tests of good strategic leadership are whether the company has a good strategy (given its internal and external situation), whether the strategy is being competently executed, and whether the enterprise is meeting or beating its performance targets.* If these three conditions exist, then there is every reason to conclude that the company has good strategic leadership and is a well-managed enterprise.

KEY POINTS

1. Corporate culture is the character of a company's internal work climate—the shared values, ingrained attitudes, core beliefs and company traditions that determine norms of behavior, accepted work practices, and styles of operating. A company's culture is important because it influences the organization's actions, its approaches to conducting business, and ultimately its performance in the marketplace. It can be thought of as the company's organizational DNA.

2. The key features of a company's culture include the company's values and ethical standards, its approach to people management, its work atmosphere and company spirit, how its personnel interact, the strength of peer pressure to conform to norms, the behaviors awarded through incentives (both financial and symbolic), the traditions and oft-repeated "myths," and its manner of dealing with stakeholders.

3. A company's culture is grounded in and shaped by its core values and ethical standards. Core values and ethical principles serve two roles in the culture-building process: (1) They foster a work climate in which employees share common and strongly held convictions about how company business is to be conducted; and (2) they provide company personnel with guidance about the manner in which they are to do their jobs—which behaviors and ways of doing things are approved (and expected) and which are out-of-bounds. They serve as yardsticks for gauging the appropriateness of particular actions, decisions, and behaviors.

4. Company cultures vary widely in strength and influence. Some cultures are *strong* and have a big impact on a company's practices and behavioral norms. Others are *weak* and have comparatively little influence on company operations.

5. Strong company cultures can have either positive or negative effects on strategy execution. When they are in sync with the chosen strategy and well matched to the behavioral requirements of the company's strategy implementation plan, they can be a powerful aid to strategy execution. A culture that is grounded in the types of actions and behaviors that are conducive to good strategy execution assists the effort in three ways:

   • By focusing employee attention on the actions that are most important in the strategy execution effort.

   • By inducing peer pressure for employees to contribute to the success of the strategy execution effort.

   • By energizing employees, deepening their commitment to the strategy execution effort, and increasing the productivity of their efforts

   It is thus in management's best interest to dedicate considerable effort to establishing a strongly implanted corporate culture that encourages behaviors and work practices conducive to good strategy execution.

6. Strong corporate cultures that are conducive to good strategy execution are healthy cultures. So are high-performance cultures and adaptive cultures. The latter are particularly important in dynamic environments. Strong cultures can also be unhealthy. The five types of unhealthy cultures are those that are (1) change-resistant, (2) heavily politicized, (3) insular and inwardly focused, (4) ethically unprincipled and infused with greed, and (5) composed of incompatible, clashing subcultures. All five impede good strategy execution.

7. Changing a company's culture, especially a strong one with traits that don't fit a new strategy's requirements, is a tough and often time-consuming challenge. Changing a culture requires competent leadership at the top. It requires making a compelling case for cultural change and employing both symbolic actions and substantive actions that unmistakably indicate serious and credible commitment on the part of top management. The more that culture-driven actions and behaviors fit what's needed for good strategy execution, the less managers must depend on policies, rules, procedures, and supervision to enforce what people should and should not do.

8. Leading the drive for good strategy execution and operating excellence calls for three actions on the part of the manager in charge:

   • Staying on top of what is happening and closely monitoring progress. This is often accomplished through management by walking around (MBWA).

   • Mobilizing the effort for excellence in strategy execution by putting constructive pressure on the organization to execute the strategy well.

   • Initiating corrective actions to improve strategy execution and achieve the targeted performance results.

ASSURANCE OF LEARNING EXERCISES

1. Salesforce.com earned the top spot on Fortune's list of the Best Companies to Work for in 2018, having been on the list for over 10 years. Use your university library's resources to see what their company culture and values might have to do with this. What are the key features of its culture? Do features of Salesforce.com's culture influence the company's ethical practices? If so, how?

   LO 12-1

2. Based on what you learned about Salesforce.com from answering the previous question, how do you think the company's culture affects its ability to execute strategy and operate with excellence?

   LO 12-2

3. Illustration Capsule 12.2 discusses culture change at Goldman Sachs. How had its organizational culture become an obstacle to its effectiveness? What substantive culture-changing actions were undertaken at Goldman Sachs? What evidence suggests that the culture change has been effective at Goldman Sachs?

   LO 12-1, LO 12-2

4. If you were an executive at a company that had a pervasive yet problematic culture, what steps would you take to change it? Using Google Scholar or your university library's access to EBSCO, LexisNexis, or other databases, search for recent articles in business publications on "culture change." What role did the executives play in the culture change? How does this differ from what you would have done to change the culture?

   LO 12-3

5. Leading the strategy execution process involves staying on top of the situation and monitoring progress, putting constructive pressure on the organization to achieve operating excellence, and initiating corrective actions to improve the execution effort. Using your university library's resources discuss a recent example of how a company's managers have demonstrated the kind of effective internal leadership needed for superior strategy execution.

   LO 12-4

EXERCISES FOR SIMULATION PARTICIPANTS

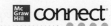

LO 12-1, LO 12-2 **1.** If you were making a speech to company personnel, what would you tell employees about the kind of corporate culture you would like to have at your company? What specific cultural traits would you like your company to exhibit? Explain.

LO 12-2 **2.** What core values would you want to ingrain in your company's culture? Why?

LO 12-3, LO 12-4 **3.** Following each decision round, do you and your co-managers make corrective adjustments in either your company's strategy or the way the strategy is being executed? List at least three such adjustments you made in the most recent decision round. What hard evidence (in the form of results relating to your company's performance in the most recent year) can you cite that indicates that the various corrective adjustments you made either succeeded at improving or failed to improve your company's performance?

LO 12-4 **4.** What would happen to your company's performance if you and your co-managers stick with the status quo and fail to make any corrective adjustments after each decision round?

ENDNOTES

[1] Jennifer A. Chatham and Sandra E. Cha, "Leading by Leveraging Culture," *California Management Review* 45, no. 4 (Summer 2003), pp. 20–34; Edgar Shein, *Organizational Culture and Leadership: A Dynamic View* (San Francisco, CA: Jossey-Bass, 1992).
[2] T. E. Deal and A. A. Kennedy, *Corporate Cultures: The Rites and Rituals of Corporate Life* (Harmondsworth, UK: Penguin, 1982).
[3] Joanne Reid and Victoria Hubbell, "Creating a Performance Culture," *Ivey Business Journal* 69, no. 4 (March–April 2005), p. 1.
[4] Ibid.
[5] John P. Kotter and James L. Heskett, *Corporate Culture and Performance* (New York: Free Press, 1992), p. 7. See also Robert Goffee and Gareth Jones, *The Character of a Corporation* (New York: HarperCollins, 1998).
[6] Joseph L. Badaracco, *Defining Moments: When Managers Must Choose between Right and Wrong* (Boston: Harvard Business School Press, 1997); Joe Badaracco and Allen P. Webb, "Business Ethics: A View from the Trenches," *California Management Review* 37, no. 2 (Winter 1995), pp. 8–28; Patrick E. Murphy, "Corporate Ethics Statements: Current Status and Future Prospects," *Journal of Business Ethics* 14 (1995), pp. 727–740; Lynn Sharp Paine, "Managing for Organizational Integrity," *Harvard Business Review* 72, no. 2 (March–April 1994), pp. 106–117.
[7] Emily F. Carasco and Jang B. Singh, "The Content and Focus of the Codes of Ethics of the World's Largest Transnational Corporations," *Business and Society Review* 108, no. 1 (January 2003), pp. 71–94; Patrick E. Murphy, "Corporate Ethics Statements: Current Status and Future Prospects," *Journal of Business Ethics* 14 (1995), pp. 727–740; John Humble, David Jackson, and Alan Thomson, "The Strategic Power of Corporate Values," *Long Range Planning* 27, no. 6 (December 1994),

pp. 28–42; Mark S. Schwartz, "A Code of Ethics for Corporate Codes of Ethics," *Journal of Business Ethics* 41, no. 1–2 (November–December 2002), pp. 27-43.
[8] Terrence E. Deal and Allen A. Kennedy, *Corporate Cultures* (Reading, MA: Addison-Wesley, 1982); Terrence E. Deal and Allen A. Kennedy, *The New Corporate Cultures: Revitalizing the Workplace after Downsizing, Mergers, and Reengineering* (Cambridge, MA: Perseus, 1999).
[9] Vijay Sathe, *Culture and Related Corporate Realities* (Homewood, IL: Irwin, 1985).
[10] Avan R. Jassawalla and Hemant C. Sashittal, "Cultures That Support Product-Innovation Processes," *Academy of Management Executive* 16, no. 3 (August 2002), pp. 42–54.
[11] Kotter and Heskett, *Corporate Culture and Performance*, p. 5.
[12] Reid and Hubbell, "Creating a Performance Culture," pp. 1–5.
[13] Jay B. Barney and Delwyn N. Clark, *Resource-Based Theory: Creating and Sustaining Competitive Advantage* (New York: Oxford University Press, 2007), chap. 4.
[14] Rosabeth Moss Kanter, "Transforming Giants," *Harvard Business Review* 86, no. 1 (January 2008), pp. 43–52.
[15] Kurt Eichenwald, *Conspiracy of Fools: A True Story* (New York: Broadway Books, 2005).
[16] Judy D. Olian and Sara L. Rynes, "Making Total Quality Work: Aligning Organizational Processes, Performance Measures, and Stakeholders," *Human Resource Management* 30, no. 3 (Fall 1991), p. 324.
[17] Larry Bossidy and Ram Charan, *Confronting Reality: Doing What Matters to Get Things Right* (New York: Crown Business, 2004); Larry Bossidy and Ram Charan, *Execution: The Discipline of Getting Things Done* (New York: Crown Business, 2002); John P. Kotter, "Leading Change: Why Transformation Efforts Fail," *Harvard Business Review* 73,

no. 2 (March–April 1995), pp. 59–67; Thomas M. Hout and John C. Carter, "Getting It Done: New Roles for Senior Executives," *Harvard Business Review* 73, no. 6 (November–December 1995), pp. 133–145; Sumantra Ghoshal and Christopher A. Bartlett, "Changing the Role of Top Management: Beyond Structure to Processes," *Harvard Business Review* 73, no. 1 (January–February 1995), pp. 86–96.
[18] For a more in-depth discussion of the leader's role in creating a results-oriented culture that nurtures success, see Benjamin Schneider, Sarah K. Gunnarson, and Kathryn Niles-Jolly, "Creating the Climate and Culture of Success," *Organizational Dynamics,* Summer 1994, pp. 17–29.
[19] Michael T. Kanazawa and Robert H. Miles, *Big Ideas to Big Results* (Upper Saddle River, NJ: FT Press, 2008).
[20] Jeffrey Pfeffer, "Producing Sustainable Competitive Advantage through the Effective Management of People," *Academy of Management Executive* 9, no.1 (February 1995), pp. 55–69.
[21] Cynthia A. Montgomery, "Putting Leadership Back into Strategy," *Harvard Business Review* 86, no. 1 (January 2008), pp. 54–60.
[22] James Brian Quinn, *Strategies for Change: Logical Incrementalism* (Homewood, IL: Irwin, 1980).
[23] Daniel Goleman, "What Makes a Leader," *Harvard Business Review* 76, no. 6 (November–December 1998), pp. 92–102; Ronald A. Heifetz and Donald L. Laurie, "The Work of Leadership," *Harvard Business Review* 75, no. 1 (January–February 1997), pp. 124–134; Charles M. Farkas and Suzy Wetlaufer, "The Ways Chief Executive Officers Lead," *Harvard Business Review* 74, no. 3 (May–June 1996), pp. 110–122; Michael E. Porter, Jay W. Lorsch, and Nitin Nohria, "Seven Surprises for New CEOs," *Harvard Business Review* 82, no. 10 (October 2004), pp. 62–72.

Company Index

Name Index

Subject Index